The King and The Kingdom
A Devotional Commentary on the Gospel of Matthew

M J Flower

The St Giles Commentary Series

Grosvenor House
Publishing Limited

This book is published by
Grosvenor House Publishing Ltd
Link House
140 The Broadway, Tolworth, Surrey, KT6 7HT.
www.grosvenorhousepublishing.co.uk

A CIP record for this book
is available from the British Library

ISBN 978-1-80381-519-0

Dedicated to
George Edward Flower
1927–2014
Husband, Mentor, Friend

CONTENTS

About the Author

M J Flower, BA (Hons); MPhil, raised a family before reading Theology and Philosophy of Religion at the University of Exeter, where she also completed a research thesis on the social theory of John Millbank. She jointly established the Institute for Christian Studies in Exeter, and worked extensively with the South West Training Ministry for the Diocese of Exeter, training and supporting Readers and non-ordained ministers. She spent many years as a Churchwarden at St Leonard's Church in Exeter, and sat on the Deanery Synod as a lay member. She has spent more years than she would like to count leading and contributing to Bible Study and Home Groups and continues this work while happily retired in Buckinghamshire, living close to a very wide circle of friends and three generations of her family.

Preface

Inspiration for attempting an overview of Matthew's gospel came originally from a Bible study group member who had been going to church from childhood without connecting in any observable way with the Bible's relevance to 'normal' life. I think we all learned a lot from her, and her insightful questions. There is an account in Acts chapter 8 of the encounter of Philip the evangelist with the Ethiopian eunuch whose study of Isaiah 53 was hampered by his reading of a scroll of which he had no understanding. Philip was able to enlighten him, and his question to the eunuch, 'Do you understand what you are reading?' provoked the answer from the eunuch, 'How can I, unless someone guides me?'

This answer also provoked a desire to enable the undertaking of a reading of at least part of the Bible by a non-academic reader, but who was also an earnest seeker after truth, which would seek to be less dry and inaccessible, and above all, relevant.

For those of us who have had the privilege of reading this wonderful book all our lives, claiming its promises, looking to it for daily guidance, and comfort, such a deprivation for one such person at least (for of course there are many others) seems insupportable. This commentary on Matthew's gospel is an attempt to clarify the text with such background details as are necessary, to make the book come alive, this treasure which we hold in our hands and which we believe to be the Word of God.

All such attempts are, of course, completely useless unless God the Holy Spirit interprets the word to our hearts. So we come to Him, asking that He will open the eyes of the understanding of all of us, however long we may have been on this journey, that we may behold wondrous things out of His law (Psalm 119:18).

And to Him be the glory!

Matthew's text is a gospel. *The gospel is good news!* May those who read it know and understand that this good news is for them, that God is not slack concerning His promise, but is longsuffering towards us, not willing that any should perish, but that all may come to eternal life (2 Peter 3:9). Matthew's concern is with the King and His Kingdom and with all who will take Him at His word, come to Him and receive from Him the gracious invitation to enter His Kingdom.

The English translation of the Bible used throughout this work has been the Revised Standard version (R.S.V.) of the Bible or the New Revised Standard Version (N.R.S.V.), with an occasional foray into the New International Version (N.I.V.) or the King James (K.J.V.) or Authorized Version (A.V.) where the English translation from the Hebrew or Greek appeared to be the more apposite to the topic discussed.

The R.S.V. was the translation recommended at the beginning of academic training as being a more accurate translation of the Bible, an opinion which it would take a scholar in these languages to dispute and which would be beyond the capabilities of the present author. Many other translations are available for those requiring a more contemporary use of language. We are privileged indeed to hold such a Book in our hands, whichever version we use, and neglect it at our peril.

There is much repetition in this text of various passages from the Bible, especially those of the New Testament; for example, Philippians 2:1-11; Ephesians 4:32. Reputable and sometimes outstanding teachers are assured that repetition of an idea or concept, in different words or different contexts, is a recognized feature of good teaching. The student may have been unaware at a first perusal of the significance of what they have read or studied, but may achieve a belated understanding after a period of repeated consideration. Other students may of course have understood the significance of what has been taught immediately; but even then it can be helpful to think about the message, the facts made clear. Such a message may then become inspirational, changing the way he or she thinks, perhaps even changing behaviour.

When repetition in this volume becomes turgid, like wading through treacle, the current advice would be to persevere. There may be something important in what has just been read, or not previously understood, which our faithful Lord wants to impart to His precious children, to their blessing, and His glory.

Introduction

There is an ancient tradition that Mathew was the first gospel to be written. Many of the early church fathers were united in the belief that this was so; that it was written by the tax collector Matthew, and that it was originally written in Hebrew (Aramaic). This belief rests mainly on the statement made by Papias in cA.D.135, and quoted by Eusebius that 'Matthew however, compiled the *logia,* the sayings of Jesus, in the Hebrew language, and each one interpreted them as he was able'. But Papias himself in his writings discussed Mark before Matthew, giving rise to the alternative claim that Mark had the priority. Mark is usually placed as having been written in A.D.65, which causes us to assume that Matthew was written after A.D.65, but possibly before the terrible events which took place in A.D.70 under Titus and Vespasian as spoken of by Jesus in Matthew 24.

The place of origin of Matthew's Gospel is thought to be either Palestine or Syria. The Gospel Indicates an intimate knowledge of Jewish customs, Jewish dress and piety and may suggest a Palestinian environment as being the situation most clearly appropriate for Matthew's encouragement of Jewish Christians. On the other hand, there is some suggestion that several Gentile features are also apparent such as the healing of the Canaanite woman in Chapter 15:21-28, strongly identifying the understanding that the gospel is for everyone, Jews and Gentiles alike. This is most strongly emphasised in the last words of Jesus to his disciples after His resurrection *'Go and make disciples of all nations'* (Matthew 28:20). We conclude that what Jesus has in mind is not a Jewish Christianity or a Gentile Christianity but a universal church, and Himself as Son of Man, and Lord of the Church.

The other alternative is to place the writing of the gospel in Syria. Matthew as a former civil servant is likely to feel at home in either environment. The church in Syria also contained both Jews and Gentiles, and together with Ephesus and Rome, Antioch in Syria was one of the great post apostolic churches. There is external evidence in the writings of Ignatius, Bishop of Antioch, who died on his way to Rome before he could be martyred in *c*107 A.D. which shows early familiarity with Matthew's Gospel. But the early Christian communities, either in Antioch or elsewhere were a mixture of Jews and Gentiles, and still needed to hear the story of Jesus, whether they were about to experience some of the events described in Matthew 24, or had already done so.

The Christian churches to whom Matthew is writing are still minority groups, living in the shadow of local Jewish communities (see Graham Stanton: *A Gospel for a New People: Studies in Matthew*, page 3). Mathew is writing with a distinctive purpose and emphasis in view, to set out in broad but precise Christological and apocalyptic terms who Jesus is and what was His destiny as He waited on God His Father, always obedient to His will. And how His destiny was fulfilled through His passion, death and resurrection, and will yet be fulfilled in greater measure again when He comes in glory as King. And that not only will Christ be manifested as King, but those who have entered His Kingdom through repentance and faith will also be with Him, where He is.

This is the gospel; dimly perceived in the prophecies of the Old Testament by the prophets of old but totally and gloriously made manifest in Christ.

Matthew is writing a Gospel, not a letter, whenever and wherever he is writing, to men and women, to challenge them, to help them to understand the gospel of the kingdom; how to enter it; how to enjoy its many blessings and sometimes its adversities, and to have an understanding of its future fulfilment when Jesus takes His power and reigns.

Matthew's use of the Old Testament.
The formula quotations

Matthew is not a theologian. His skills are those of a pastor and gifted communicator rather than those of a theologian.

Matthew's distinctive emphasis is to stress that the events which take place in his gospel are seen as a fulfilment of the scriptures as a whole, that the declaration of the prophets of the Old Testament have been fulfilled in the life of Jesus and are therefore of God's attestation because He spoke through the prophets. Matthew is making an essentially Christological commentary. *Jesus acts in accordance with scripture, and within God's will, and simultaneously, the scripture is fulfilled.*

There are 10 formula quotations from scripture in this gospel: Matthew 1:21, 2:16, 2:5-6, 4:14-16; 8:17, 12:17-21, 13:35, 21:4-5, 26:23-24, 27:9-10. Scriptural undergirding is given to many geographical places mentioned which makes them *historical* prophetic as well as *geographical* prophetic.

In Matthew 2:17-18, Matthew links the story of the infant Jesus with the Exodus and Exile experiences of Israel. 'Then was fulfilled what was spoken by the prophet Jeremiah; a voice was heard in Ramah, wailing and loud lamentation; Rachel weeping for her children and refused to be consoled because they were no more'. Just as the machinations of the opponents of God's people were thwarted by God of old, so too will Herod fail to overturn God's purpose in sending His Son.

In Matthew 2:23 Jesus is called Nazarene – Jesus is seen as the 'nezer' or branch, or 'nazir', the *Holy One of God*. 'That what was spoken by the prophets might be fulfilled, He shall be called a Nazarene'.

Two other formula quotations, Matthew 8:17 'this was to fulfil what was spoken by the prophet Isaiah, "He took our infirmities and bore our diseases"' (Isaiah 53:4); and Matthew 13:35 'this was to fulfil what was spoken by the prophet, "I will open my mouth in parables, I will utter what has been hidden from the foundation of the world"' (Psalm 78:2), stress the healing activity and parabolic teaching of Jesus as confirmation of the status of the Lord Jesus as the Messianic King, the incarnated, foreordained, Son of God.

In Matthew 5:5 and Matthew 11:29 (Psalm 37:11 and Jeremiah 6:16) and perhaps especially in Matthew 21:4-5, Jesus' triumphal entry into Jerusalem, Jesus is portrayed as the humble

One, the One who is meek and lowly of heart, and in Matthew 21:4-5, 'This took place to fulfil what was spoken by the prophet saying, 'Tell the daughter of Zion, "Behold, your King is coming to you, humble and mounted on an ass, and on a colt, the foal of an ass"' (Isaiah 62:11, Zechariah 9:9). Jesus is the humble king.

In summary, Matthew has 10 Old Testament passages, fulfilment quotations, in his gospel. They all comment on the story of Jesus and its deeper significance by stressing that the main features of His life and ministry are a fulfilment of the prophecies of scripture. The scriptures of Matthew's historical period were of course the Hebrew Bible (the Old Testament) and the Septuagint (LXX) the Greek version translated from the Hebrew by 70 scholars in 270 B.C.

Each time a prophecy about Jesus was fulfilled, it consolidated His right to reign, and so Matthew's message is this is the King, by genealogy, by birth, by worship, by the hatred of jealousy against Him, and by the fulfilment of prophecy. Jesus was born a King, for which cause He came into the world (John 18:37). His message was 'the kingdom of heaven is at hand' (Matthew 4:17), the kingdom which He had come to establish in the hearts of men and women, unseen but powerful in changing their lives; the kingdom where He is King. And to proclaim the coming fulfilment of the kingdom when He should return to this world for which He had given His life in sacrifice. He is coming, and every eye shall see Him and those who pierced Him, and all the tribes of the earth shall mourn because of Him (Revelation 1:7). Even so, come Lord Jesus (Revelation 1:8).

Matthew, the author of the gospel.
Matthew 9:9 and 10:3

As Jesus passed on from there, He saw a man called Matthew sitting at the tax office, and He said to him 'Follow Me'. And he arose and followed Him (Matthew 9:9).

And He called to Him his twelve disciples... and Mathew the tax collector (Matthew 10:3).

A gospel is not a biography, or simply the life-story of Jesus, but a foundation document specially devised for the early Christian church for their encouragement and guidance, and to prepare them for His coming again. This was the project upon which Matthew was engaged.

From Matthew 9:9 and 10:3, we learn that Matthew was one of Jesus' disciples; called to follow Him while he was seated at the receipt of custom, that is, of taxes, for he was a tax collector. Throughout his gospel, Matthew includes the tax collectors with the sinners who came to Jesus, for he recognized himself as one of those despised people, and recognized too what had been the tremendous privilege given to him to become a follower of Jesus. Tax collectors were despised by everybody because they worked for the governors of the Roman Occupation. They were collaborators. Disciples of Jesus were also often despised, but they were always aware that Jesus was with them even after His death and resurrection, and they had His peace in their hearts. They knew Jesus as 'Immanuel, God with us' (Matthew 1:23).

Mark's gospel records the call of Matthew, naming him as *Levi the son of Alphaeus* (Mark 2:13,14). Luke also records the call of Matthew as Levi (Luke 5:27-32). All three synoptic gospels describe a great feast subsequent to Matthew's call, but Luke is more specific stating that it was Levi/Matthew who made Jesus a great feast in his house.

We note a discrepancy in the name of this disciple. As Levi, did he come from the Levitical priesthood, those who occupied a special place in the worship of God? And therefore was it even more shameful that he had become a Roman civil servant? As an educated Jew, he would have been familiar with the Hebrew Bible, the Old Testament, and with its Greek translation the Septuagint (LXX).

Matthew was with the other disciples in the upper room on the Day of Pentecost and with them was filled with the Holy Spirit. Perhaps it was that experience which helped him to write his gospel. It is very possible that Matthew was tri-lingual. There are Aramaic, Hebrew and Greek elements in his gospel. As a civil servant, he would have been accustomed to taking notes and jotting down information in all these languages in a cosmopolitan society.

The possible date of composition of the gospel is thought to be A.D.80-90 but more certainly after A.D.65 when Mark was written, for it becomes evident as the two gospels are compared that they share some of the same source material.

Matthew Chapter 1

Matthew 1:1-25. The genealogy of Jesus; and the visit of the angel to Joseph

The book of the genealogy of Jesus Christ, the son of David, the son of Abraham (Matthew 1:1).

Matthew begins his gospel with the genealogy of Jesus, immediately describing Jesus as Jesus Christ, Jesus the Messiah, Jesus the Anointed One of God. He then goes on to describe him as the Son of David, the Son of Abraham (Matthew 1:1). So, right from the beginning, Matthew is positioning his gospel within the whole covenantal relationship which God had with His people and eventually with all those who will enter into that New Covenant through the incarnation of His Son, both Jew and Gentile, and His subsequent death and resurrection.

Matthew 1:6. Christ as the Son of David

Jesus was born into a Davidic family through Joseph who was descended from David. Luke also tells us that Joseph was of the Davidic line (Luke 2:5). Mary's marriage to Joseph includes her also in that line. This is important because it emphasises the Messiahship of the baby that is to be born. In verse 18, we read, 'the birth of *Jesus the Messiah* took place in this way' (R.S.V.).

God did something new through His covenant with David. He promised a Son, the Son, the Anointed one, the Messiah, He who would come, the King who would sit on His throne forever, ruling over and caring for His people (2 Samuel 7:11; Psalm 89:3,20,34; Psalm 78:70). Throughout the writings of the prophets from Isaiah through to Malachi, there is a longing to see the Davidic covenant fulfilled, for the Messiah to come. How poignant are the words of

Andrew to his brother Simon Peter in John 1:41, 'We have found the Messiah!' as he brought him to Jesus; the one for whom the whole of the Jewish nation had been waiting.

The angel's announcement to Joseph as the son of David (verse 20) calls attention to Jesus' Davidic status and above all to His deity, for the angel was emphatic that that which was conceived in Mary was of the Holy Spirit (verse 20). The conveying of the message to Joseph through an angel emphasises divine intervention in the conception of this child; and the Lord's purpose in giving to Joseph the naming of the baby underscores the adoption of Jesus by Joseph as his legal guardian. Joseph must bring Jesus into David's line so that Jesus may become, or may be seen to be, the Messianic King; and he must also care for Mary (Matthew 1:23) and the Child (Matthew 2:13,21). Joseph was a hard working artisan, a carpenter (Matthew 13:55; Mark 6:3), *and* an obedient servant of God.

The covenant on Mt. Sinai with Moses was a national covenant. Those with Abraham and David were personal in their origin, yet through their faithfulness, became part of the whole purpose of God in His desire to bring 'many sons to glory' (Hebrews 2:10), sons like His own beloved Son.

Matthew 1:1. Christ as the Son of Abraham

Abraham was another obedient servant of God. 'By faith Abraham obeyed when he was called to go out... and he went out not knowing where he was to go' (Hebrews 11:8).

Abraham's covenantal relationship with God involved not only his personal faith and justification, so that God, on that level of faith, could enter into that precious covenant with him; but also his destiny as the father of many nations through the birth of a son to him in his old age. 'Abraham believed God and it was accounted to him for righteousness'; for justification, the righteousness of God was awarded to him on the grounds of his faith, his faith that what God had promised He was able also to perform (Genesis 15:6; Romans 4:1-5, Galatians 3:6).

This covenant involved the nations which would be descended from him. What God longed for was not only the one nation, the nation of Israel that was to come into being. This nation was a chosen people, chosen by God to be 'a people that has its God so near to it as the Lord our God is to us, whenever we call upon Him' (Deuteronomy 4:7).

God wanted a people near to Himself, chosen by Him to be a people of His own possession, because He loved them and wanted to pour out His steadfast love upon them (Deuteronomy 7:6-9). God did indeed long for such a people, but also, God wanted 'all the families of the earth to be blessed (Genesis 12.3).

He longed for a people who by faith would enter into that relationship with Him, such a relationship that He had with faithful Abraham, whom He designated 'the father of many nations' (Genesis 17:5), but who actually had only one beloved son whom by faith he offered up to God when God tested him, although God had said, 'Through Isaac shall your descendants be named' (Genesis 21:12; Hebrews 11:18).

The level of trust in God displayed by Abraham foreshadowed the level of trust in God as displayed by Jesus in the Garden of Gethsemane when He prayed, 'Not my will, but yours, be done.' Abraham was also saying to God, 'not my will but yours be done', as he began to offer up Isaac on the altar in obedience to God's command, for God had tested Abraham by commanding him to offer up his son to God as a sacrifice. Isaac was prevented from becoming a sacrifice when God provided for Himself a lamb (Genesis 22:9-14), but Abraham had passed the test of perfect obedience to God no matter what the cost, and in spite of his previous understanding of the will of God.

But God's Son did become the sacrifice. He became the sacrificial Lamb of God who was born and died so that He could take away the sin of the world (John 1:29). And within His genealogy was the example of a man who fully trusted God.

There were many in the time of Jesus who gloried in their ancient paternity as children of Abraham. But to be a descendent of Abraham involved rather more than that, as Jesus reminded them, 'If you really were Abraham's children, you would do what

Abraham did' (John 8:39) enter into a relationship with God by faith and be obedient to Him. Abraham obeyed God (Hebrews 11:8; Genesis 12:4) and was given not just the reward of intimacy with God, though that in itself was a precious gift (Genesis 13:11), but a son, Isaac.

Why then was Jesus announced as a 'son of Abraham' by Matthew? This was of course genealogically true. But an even greater significance of the concept rests with God's ultimate intention of having a people for Himself who would enter into a relationship with Him *through faith* and whose obedience to Him would result in untold blessings being showered upon them. *This ultimate purpose could only be fulfilled in Jesus.*

The people of Israel had erred and strayed from God's ways like lost sheep. They had followed too much the devices and desires of their own hearts. They had offended against His holy laws, they had left undone those things that they ought to have done, they had done those things that they ought not to have done, and there was no health in them; to misquote the Book of Common Prayer. But Jesus had come, the fulfilment of the promise to Abraham, the descendent of Abraham who was Christ (Galatians 4:16).

The covenantal relationship with God is still open. God is still at work, gathering a people to Himself, and not just the Jewish people, but Gentile people, as evidenced in the inclusion in Matthew's genealogy of Rahab and Ruth (verse 5), both Gentile women.

Matthew is certain, completely assured that the group of people with whom he worships and has fellowship, which contemporary documents suggest is Antioch in Syria, is part of God's amazing plan of redemption, part of the fulfilment of God's promises to David and Abraham, one of the families of the earth that would be blessed by him (Genesis 12:2).

Jesus is all that God wanted His Son to be, utterly dependent on Him, bringing into being a people who rested completely on their covenantal relationship with Him, the *new* covenant of promise which rested on grace, the unmerited favour of God, and that what He had promised He was also able to perform (Romans 4: 16, 21).

Matthew Chapter 2

Matthew 2:1-23. The visit of the Magi

Now when Jesus was born in Bethlehem of Judea in the days of Herod the King, there came wise men from the east to Jerusalem (Matthew 2:1).

Jesus was born in Bethlehem of Judea, a town a few miles south of Jerusalem, in the city of David, David's birthplace in the days of Herod the King. Herod was born in 73 B.C. and died in 4 B.C. Therefore Jesus was born on or before 4 B.C. and possibly as early as 6 B.C. Herod was named King of Judea by the Roman Senate in 40 B.C. after having been the governor of Galilee since 47 B.C. He was not a Jew but an Idumean (Idumea was formerly known as Edom, a territory south of Judea).

Herod began the construction of the Temple in Jerusalem in 20 B.C. in an attempt to conciliate the Jewish people who resented an Idumean ruling over them. John records in his gospel that at the time of the ministry of Jesus, it had been 46 years in building (John 2:20). But Herod was not averse to welcoming to his court 'magi', sorcerers or magicians who often had great powers, like Simon in Acts 8:9 and Elymas in Acts 13:6.

These men, however, whom Herod now welcomed, were called by Matthew 'wise men from the East'. They were probably astrologers from the east of Jordan, that is, from Babylonia, Egypt, or Arabia. The theory that they were kings may have arisen from Old Testament verses like Psalm 72:11, Isaiah 49:7, and especially Isaiah 60:1-6, 'Nations shall come to your light and kings to the brightness of your rising'. Because there were triple gifts, there were assumed to be three of them. The late 6th century A.D. produced a document known as the Armenian Infancy Gospel that named the royal Magi as Melchior, Balthazar and Caspar. There is a discrepancy between the biblical text and popular piety, because In the Middle Ages, when most people were illiterate, the presentation of the birth of Christ in the mystery plays conflated the accounts of His birth in Luke's gospel and Matthew's gospel. It was often described as 'The play of the three kings', because the Magi became figures with whom believers identified, and especially with the parenetic or teaching element, and the distribution of gifts.

Like the inclusion of Rahab and Ruth in the genealogy, Matthew includes the Magi who were Gentiles, in his record of the incarnation.

Matthew 2:1, 2. Worshipping the King

Wise men from the east came to Jerusalem, saying, 'Where is He that is born King of the Jews? For we have seen His star in the east and have come to worship Him' (Matthew 2:1, 2).

All that the star indicated to the Magi was that a great person, a king, had been born, and that they wanted to come and worship Him. They did not know the scriptures as the chief priests and scribes did. Had they done so, they would not have needed to ask the way to Bethlehem. Their question to the chief priests and the scribes, 'Where is He that is born King of the Jews?' brought the answer from the chief priests and the scribes, 'In Bethlehem of Judea, for so it is written by the prophets, And you, O Bethlehem in the land of Judah, are by no means least among the rulers of Judah; for from you shall come a ruler who will govern My people Israel' (Micah 5:2). The desire of the Magi was to worship the new-born King. This question of finding Jesus so that they could worship Him 'troubled Herod' (verse 3), but not nearly as much as the implication that this child could be the longed for Christ.

Though this chapter is full of major themes governing the life and significance of the Lord Jesus, how can we help but ponder the place that the theme of worship has within it. In the desire of the Magi to worship him (2:2); the hypocritical statement of Herod who says he wants to worship the child, the new king, while at the same time already planning how to destroy Him, possibly hoping for that outcome even with the connivance of the Magi; and the genuine worship of the Magi as they fall down and worship Him; Matthew is here again directing the readers of the gospel to Jesus as the Christ, the Messiah, the King, the Son of David (1:1) the Son of God (2:15), Immanuel, God with us (1:23)], the One whom we worship as our Lord and our God, our loving and beloved Lord Jesus.

It has been suggested (by H. Foster) that the gifts which were given by the Magi to Jesus were the sovereign provision to Mary and Joseph of His heavenly Father, becoming a vital source of income as His parents became refugees.

Worshipping Jesus is a repeated and important theme in Matthew's gospel. There is worship by supplicants to Him: in 8:2 the leper; in 9:18 the ruler Jairus (Mark 5:21, Luke 8:40); in 15:25 the Canaanite woman. At 18:26 there is the parabolic account of the king and his servant and in 20:20 the worship of Him by the mother of the sons of Zebedee.

There is also the worship of Him by His disciples in 14:33 after His walking on the sea; in 28:9 after his resurrection; and in 28:17 on the Galilean mountain before His last commission to them.

Matthew is emphasising that right from the beginning, and throughout the life of Jesus, worship was due to Him. He was the King of the kingdom of heaven, which He had come to establish. We conclude that from the beginning, worship is an essential feature of coming into the presence of Jesus and very important to Matthew.

After the Magi returned to their own country came the flight into Egypt of the little family. Verses 13-15 make clear what is essential. God's hand and God's plan stand over the destiny of Jesus and it is His guidance that saves the child. How vulnerable a small child is! How wonderful that God entrusts His Son, to an ordinary working man, a carpenter, for protection, but a man who is faithful and obedient and has been so ever since the angel's visit in 1:20, through necessarily before that, for God had seen the way of life of this man, and chosen him to be a guardian to His Son (Matthew 13:55, Mark 6:3).

The number of innocent children murdered at Herod's command, (verses 16-18), shows the greatness of the danger which the child Jesus avoided by being taken by Mary and Joseph to Egypt. Even this terrible infanticide is predicted by the prophet Jeremiah (31:15). 'A voice was heard in Ramah, wailing and loud lamentation, Rachel wailing for her children. She refused to be consoled because they were no more'. God knew in advance that His Son's life would be in danger, yet still allowed Him to be incarnated because of the great love He had for humanity. God so loved the world that He gave His only begotten Son whom He loved. And He knows when mothers weep for their children.

Herod cannot be a true king of the Jews if he allows Israel's children to be killed because of Jesus. Herod is not only a wicked tyrant, he is a fearful man because he actually fears that this is indeed the case, that Jesus is indeed the Messianic king that should come.

After the death of King Herod, the family return from Egypt to the land of the people to whom Jesus is sent, to Nazareth in Galilee. With the death of Herod, Joseph was again obedient to the command of the angel and took the young child and His mother to return to Israel, but not to Judea where Archelaus now reigned, but into Galilee. Josephus the historian recounts in his 'Antiquities' that though Herod had bequeathed the title 'King' to Archelaus, together with the territories of Judea, Samaria and Idumea, Caesar Augustus withheld the title, fearing that Archelaus would not prove worthy of it, which was indeed the case, and in fact, Archelaus was banished after having ruled from 4 B.C. to 6 A.D. Archelaus was a wicked tyrant, like his father, and another illegitimate rival in kingship with Jesus, with whom the Jewish leaders throughout Matthew's gospel would cooperate in plotting the death of Jesus, the true King of the Jews.

Joseph, Mary and Jesus travel westward to Galilee, to a city called Nazareth, that what was spoken of by the prophets should be fulfilled. 'He shall be called a Nazarene' (Matthew 2:23).

But where does this quotation come from? The plural 'the prophets' indicates that we are to look for the substance of more than one Old Testament passage. 'Nazareth' as a location does not appear in the Old Testament, so we are justified in looking for a connection between the place name and an Old Testament messianic title. Nazarene has written within it, in Hebrew, n z r = nazir = holy one, or nezer = a branch (Hebrew of course has no vowels).

In Matthew 2:23, Jesus is called Ναζωραῖος, a Nazarene. Isaiah's prediction is of a 'branch' or 'shoot' from the root of Jesse (Isaiah 11:1). David's father, Jesse, provides a starting point for the understanding of this title for Jesus; Isaiah 4:2 speaks of 'the Branch' of the Lord as beautiful and glorious and the Saviour from sin for His people. More enlightening still is Jeremiah 23:5, 'behold, the days are coming says the Lord when I will raise up for David a righteous Branch and He shall reign as king. And this is the Name by which He will be called, 'the Lord our Righteousness'. This theme is repeated in Jeremiah 33:15. In Zechariah 6:12, the man whose name is 'the Branch' is crowned, building a temple and forming a peaceful alliance between the throne and the priesthood.

The righteousness and servanthood of the Messianic Branch in those famous Servant Song chapters of Isaiah, 42, 49, 50, 52/53, give an emphasis to Matthew's Christology as does the sprouting like a shoot out of the stump of David's dynasty of Isaiah 53:2. Jesus is the righteous Branch, the Holy One, the One who fulfils all the types and figures of the Old Testament; the Lord Jesus Christ. In addition to all His other titles in these first two chapters of Matthew's gospel, we have the title of the Righteous Servant, intimated especially in Isaiah 52/53; the Servant who has borne our griefs and carried our sorrows was the one who 'grew up before Him as a tender plant and as a root out of dry ground' (Isaiah 53:2), the Lamb who was led to the slaughter (verse 7) and upon whom the Lord has laid the iniquity of us all (verse 6). All of the prophets do indeed speak of Him and Matthew is included in the long line of those who saw in this Child and in the divinely human Man all the precious promises of God fulfilled.

Matthew 2:1-23. Summary of the infancy narrative

The scriptural quotations in chapter 2 appear primarily to give geographical undergirding to Matthew's design of making a Christological point: Jesus is the Son of God whose life is grounded in geography as well as history.

Jesus is born in Bethlehem (2:1). He flees with His family to Egypt (2:18), Ramah is the tragic place of mourning for those mothers whose children had died because Herod was fearful that the child who had been born was truly the Messiah, and Nazareth so that Jesus could be called a Nazarene (2:23), totally dedicated to God.

In 2:17-18, Matthew links the story of Jesus to the Exodus and Exile experiences of Israel, and in 2:23, Jesus is called Ναζωραίος. Jesus is seen as the 'nezer' or 'branch' and 'nazir' the Holy One of God. Because in this instance, Matthew has not given us a more exact biblical reference, we are permitted to see an allusion to Isaiah 11:1. 'There shall come forth a stump from the root of Jesse and a Branch 'nezer' shall grow out of its roots.

These two chapters form a prologue to Matthew's gospel, as John 1:1-16 forms a prologue to John's. It contains all the themes and all the titles of Jesus which He later fulfils and that Matthew finds fulfilled in the life of Jesus.

But especially precious were the words of the angel to Joseph. 'Thou shalt call His name Jesus, for He shall save His people from their sins' (1:21). There is no other Name under heaven given among men by which we must be saved (Acts 4:12).

Matthew Chapter 3

Matthew 3:1-17. John the Baptist

'In those days came John the Baptist, preaching in the wilderness of Judea, 'Repent, for the kingdom of heaven is at hand' (verse 1).

How John must have waited and watched over the period of 30 years, until God's timing was right, and John could now say 'Repent, for the Kingdom of heaven is at hand!'

As the cousin of Jesus, the son of Elizabeth and Zechariah, Elizabeth and Mary being cousins (Luke 1:36 A.V.), John had been aware that there was something special about Jesus. He had known that the promised King was here, though at that time he may have wondered how His kingship was going to be recognized, as He grew up in His earthly father's house. But John waited for God to say 'Now!' Now is God's time. Now is the time for repentance, because this Kingdom of Heaven, the kingdom of God, is like no other. It is a kingdom of redeemed sinners, those who have truly repented from their sin and turned to God and have received His salvation, their redemption. Now is the time for Jesus, the one whose name means 'Saviour from sin' (Matthew 1:21) to begin His ministry, for God to reveal His Son to the world, so that those who repent and turn to Him in faith might have everlasting life. John declares, 'The kingdom of heaven is at hand!'

But there may have been some who responded to John's ministry of preaching, and baptising those who came to him, without realising quite what repentance involved. There may have been some who thought it was the right thing to do because others were doing it. There are such people, even today, who perhaps would regard themselves as Christians, and perhaps need loving and praying into the kingdom; for they bear the name but not the unaccountably precious relationship with God that true repentance brings. They may be baptised with water; some may even claim to be baptised in the Holy Spirit, but the Lord knows those who are His (2 Timothy 2:19).

John the Baptist knew this and this is why in his preaching he used the example of the threshing floor, when the winnowing fork lifts the grain high into the air, and the heavy grains of wheat fall to the ground, while the wind carries the chaff, the husks, away. It becomes evident to John which are the 'wheat', the true believers, and which are the 'tares', those who have not received forgiveness for their sin for they have not repented. John says that God will cleanse His threshing floor and separate the wheat from the tares and gather the wheat into His granary, but the chaff, that which is worthless, He will burn with unquenchable fire (verses 11, 12). John's message could not have been more clear.

There were also those whom John recognized as Pharisees and Sadducees who came to the River Jordan, not with the intention of being baptised but exhibiting a tendency to believe themselves exempt from the need to repent because of their strict adherence to the Mosaic Law. These people considered themselves to be righteous because of their religious observance, and did not recognise the need to come to God in penitence and faith.

And then Someone came to be baptised who had no need of repentance, for He had never sinned, never gone against the will of His heavenly Father. Jesus came from Galilee to the Jordan to John to be baptised by him. John would have prevented him, saying 'I need to be baptised by you, and do you come to me?' But Jesus answered him 'Let it be so now; for thus it is fitting for us to fulfil all righteousness'. Then he consented (verses 13-15).

Perhaps Jesus allowed John to baptise Him, not because He needed to repent, for He was without sin (Hebrews 4:14), but because He wanted to validate John's ministry. But He has another reason too. His first recorded words in Matthew's gospel are 'Thus it becomes us to fulfil all righteousness' (verse 15).

Righteousness is total obedience to the will of God, and this is what the Pharisees and the Sadducees failed to understand. Jesus wanted them and these other people gathered at the Jordan, to understand the reality of what righteousness truly consisted. From the beginning of His ministry at His baptism, until His agony in the Garden of Gethsemane, Jesus only wanted to do His Father's will (John 4:34). This is righteousness, having a right relationship with God, and it is gifted to us by God through faith in the atoning work of Christ.

As the author of Hebrews reminds his readers in 10:7, quoting from Psalm 40:7, 8, Jesus' sole motivation throughout His life was, 'Lo, I come to do Thy will, O God'; and by His obedience to His Father's will to replace the old covenant with the new. At the conclusion of His ministry, Jesus would go to the cross to implement this new covenant, a covenant between God and men and women based on the efficacy of the precious blood poured out on the cross for them, giving them the gift of righteousness, and a peace which they had never had before.

This was a gift that the Pharisees could not earn, however hard they tried to fulfil the ceremonial and moral law laid out for them in their scriptures. This was the will of God for them, in response to the will of Jesus, in obedience to His Father's will. But it only comes through penitence and faith.

From Romans 6:3 we learn that baptism in water symbolises death, and those who are baptised are baptised into the death of Jesus, so that just as He was raised from the dead by the glory of the Father, they too might walk in newness of life.

By allowing John to baptise Him in the River Jordan, Jesus was showing forth His own death, projecting in advance of His own death, the death He would die, and the resurrection life He would live, making a declaration that He was also preparing the way for others to be dead to sin but alive to God through Him, (Romans 6:11) symbolised through baptism. Baptism was later taken up in the community of believers as a public witness that the person being baptised had already received new life in Christ. They were witnessing to their death in the waters of baptism, which were symbolically the waters of death. The baptised one was in effect declaring that he or she had died and risen again; receiving new life in Christ.

How precious then, to see the Dove alight upon the living Lord Jesus who would die, but who would rise again from the dead, and to hear the voice of the Father from heaven, 'This is my Beloved Son, with whom I am well pleased.' John's prophetic call, his call as the prophet prefigured in Isaiah 40:3; 'the voice of one crying in the wilderness, Prepare the way of the Lord, make straight in the desert a highway for our God', *was* being confirmed to John firstly by a manifestation of the Trinity, and secondly by confirming the Messiahship of Jesus.

It is noteworthy that the Levites were called to the service of the Lord from the age of 30 (Numbers 4:3), an indication that Jesus' ministry, by beginning at the age of 30, also involved that of priesthood, as we are reminded in Hebrews. Jesus is our High Priest, the One who is seated at the throne of the majesty in heaven, the One who intercedes for those who draw near to Him because He holds His priesthood permanently, for ever (Hebrews 8:1; Hebrews 7:25). He is indeed our prophet, priest and king. Jesus had now reached that age prescribed by God when He could assume His priestly ministry; God's perfect time.

Matthew begins chapter three with 'In those days'. God's estimation of time is perfect, and not necessarily ours, but in those days, John came (Matthew 3:1). It is a reminder that God's timing is always perfect. John's preaching begins the proclamation of the gospel of the kingdom, a theme repeated throughout Matthew's gospel.

Although from the first verse, John is designated 'the Baptist', his first activity is necessarily preaching, for until people respond to his call to repentance, there is obviously no need for the baptism which John offers.

Matthew says of John, 'This is he' (verse 3), the one prophesied in Isaiah 40:3 and Malachi 3:3, the one for whom Israel has been waiting, the forerunner of the Messiah. Sometimes, when in a 'wilderness' situation, as John was, we may be given an extra insight into the purposes of God for our lives and sometimes even the lives of others, as John was for

14

Jesus. John's message to these people gathered at the Jordan was 'Prepare the way of the Lord'. This was the insight which came to him from the Lord, as he waited in the wilderness to prepare the way of the Lord, for His coming, and to 'make His paths straight' through repentance. 'Repent for the kingdom of heaven is at hand!' says John, for this preparation requires repentance before an encounter with Jesus.

The people of Jerusalem and all Judea went out to John to be baptised of him in the River Jordan, confessing their sins (verses 5, 6). These people lived closest to the Temple in Jerusalem, the heart and seat of their religious faith, and yet they were going out to be baptised by an itinerant preacher? Their hearts and minds must have been hungry; for the truth of God's word, for His presence in their lives, for the conquest of the sin they so often felt guilty about, for being aware of how far short they came in their worship of God, in spite of all their biblical understanding. All of these reasons perhaps, and even a few more.

So, what motivated the Pharisees and the Sadducees to come to the River Jordan?

In the first place, conversant though they were with the Old Testament scriptures, they did not recognise the eschatological time, the fulfilment time, of verse one, 'In those days'. We too need to take account of eschatological time as we wait and watch for Christ's second coming, for the fulfilment of His promise, '*I will come again* and take you to Myself, that where I am, there you may be also' (John 14:3).

In the second place, while the crowds had mostly come out of sincerity, the Jewish leaders came out of pride (verse 9). 'We have Abraham as our father' was part of John's accusation against them; possibly they felt they did not need to listen to this strange man, but it would give them an amusing or interesting hour or so, and of course, as the nation's religious leaders, it was their obligation to investigate whatever was going on in the religious world. There may also have been an impetus towards sincerity, as shepherds might investigate whatever it was that could be damaging to the flock. But John compares them to snakes running away from the fires burning behind them, warning them of judgement to come.

So, the question arises, when they came to the Jordan, knowing that they came to God, what were they relying on? Their own perceived righteousness? Or their need for forgiveness? Or their need of a Saviour, Jesus, who had come to save them from their sins? (Matthew 1:21). Looking up, they may now see an open heaven, opened for them and for us at Jesus' baptism; a door that is opened and they and we may go in.

When the heavens were opened above Jesus, the Spirit of God descended in the form of a Dove, and the voice of the Father declared, 'This is my beloved Son, with whom I am well pleased' (verse 17). So, all three Persons of the Trinity are at work, not only at Jesus' baptism, but in our lives too, if we will let Him. Matthew remembered this event as he recorded the words of Jesus when He was about to ascend into heaven after His resurrection. Jesus says to His disciples, 'make disciples of all nations, baptising them in the name of the Father and of the Son and of the Holy Spirit and lo, I am with you always' (Matthew 28:19).

The voice from heaven was a declaration from God as to who this Man was. He was the Son of God. It was also directed at John and the crowd, for the validation of John's ministry, and the importance of the ritual in which they had so recently taken part. Not just the Twelve, but many who later became disciples of Jesus may have started their journey of faith in the River Jordan.

At about this time, there was a religious sect living in the wilderness of Judea, known as the Essenes. This sect practised baptism, but it was as a repeated ritual experience dealing with ceremonial or ritual uncleanness. John's baptism differed, in that for the repentant sinner, it was a unique, one-off occasion. It depended on repentance, recognised as more than a change of mind but as a turning or re-turning to the God of Israel, and to the covenant between God and His people. Repentance is the radical conversion to God of those who have broken faith with Him and seek to be restored.

To this demand for repentance, John adds the apocalyptic announcement, 'The Kingdom of Heaven is at hand.' The manifestation of Divine sovereignty and authority has drawn near, challenging men and women with the ineluctable necessity of responding by repentance and conversion.

No wonder Matthew equates John the Baptist with the prophet predicted in Isaiah 43. He bore the outward signs of a prophet, with regard to his clothes, and his food, (Malachi 4:5; Zechariah 13:4), but maybe Matthew was thinking specifically in terms of Malachi 4:5. 'I will send you Elijah the prophet,' the prophet who lived so close to God that he asked God to sit in judgement on His people that they might repent of their idolatry, by withholding rain; and for three and a half years there was no rain (James 5:17).

Elijah also challenged the prophets of the god Baal to an experiment whereby everyone would know for themselves that the God who answered by fire, the God of Israel, was the only true God (1 Kings 18:24). The people listening to Jesus would know that Elijah was a man so used by God that he did not even die, but was taken up to heaven in a chariot of fire (2 Kings 2:11).

This assumption that John was in the same relationship to God that Elijah had been, was echoed by and endorsed and validated by Jesus Himself in Matthew 11:14. John's declaration that the people needed to repent for the kingdom of God was at hand, positions his baptism within Jewish expectations of the coming Messiah, before whose coming there would be a forerunner like Elijah in the person of John the Baptist. Within the new kingdom, the coming of the King will not only inaugurate His kingdom with repentance and confession of one's sins as they go through the waters of baptism, but will imminently lead to baptism in the Holy Spirit and Fire, (verse 11), the same divine fire which fell upon the altar as Elijah prayed (1 Kings 18:36,37). Elijah's declaration was, 'The God who answers by fire, let Him be God!'

John sees the gospel of the kingdom not as an ethical gospel, but as a life changing metanoia experience. Μετανοία, repentance, is placed by Matthew at the very beginning of the gospel of the Kingdom of Heaven; there is no other way in. Βασίλειο των ουρανών, the Kingdom of Heaven, is that to which we orientate our lives as believers. With the coming ministry of Jesus, Matthew sees the Kingdom of Heaven, the reign of God coming down into everyday living, because as we have seen in Matthew chapters 1 and 2, Jesus is the promised King of the kingdom.

Daniel saw something of this (Daniel 4:17, 25; 5:21). He says 'The Most High rules in the kingdom of men' or human kind, and of course God does. He rules over all his creation, as proclaimed in many of the Psalms. But Matthew and John see something more pertinent and personal to the individual man or woman, the invisible, immanent, all-encompassing kingdom of heaven. The way for all to this kingdom is open, but the door to it is repentance, and only those who truly repent and believe may enter in.

This is a major theme in Matthew's gospel. When we reach the sermon on the mount we discover that Jesus' first sermon is not a reinterpretation of the Mosaic law or the ten commandments, but a description of the new life now lived by those who have entered the Kingdom of Heaven through repentance towards God and faith in our Lord Jesus Christ (Acts 20:21). This is John the Baptist's theme of preparation for the wonderful new experience that Jesus offers, of a relationship with Him through repentance and faith, a theme that is continued throughout Matthew's gospel (Matthew 4:1-11).

Matthew Chapter 4

Matthew 4:1-11. The temptation of Jesus in the wilderness

Then Jesus was led up by the Spirit into the wilderness to be tempted by the devil. And He fasted forty days and forty nights, and afterwards He was hungry.

Structurally, this pericope or self-contained section of the gospel, is a clear example of a traditional narrative framework. There is an introduction followed by a three-part narrative and a conclusion. Both introduction and conclusion closely resemble those in Mark's gospel, suggesting that both Matthew and Mark may have had access to the same or similar source material. It would be good to know that the early church had contact, connections, and fellowship with each other, even across national and geographical boundaries.

It is always interesting to note how Matthew introduces a pericope. The words he uses nearly always have something significant to show us. In Matthew 4:1 we note that the Holy Spirit *leads* Jesus into the wilderness. Mark's word is 'drove', εκβαλλει, a word of urgency, thrusting Jesus into this essential wilderness experience as though it were necessary for Him to be tempted. We seek reverently to understand why.

In the final few verses of chapter 3, we read that at His baptism, the Holy Spirit descended upon Jesus in the form of a Dove and that the voice of the Father came from heaven, 'This is my beloved Son, with whom I am well pleased'. After this wilderness experience, the Holy Spirit led Jesus on a journey through the following years just as urgently in Matthew as in Mark, from the wilderness, through many different and varied experiences, and eventually to the Cross. Throughout the progressive revelation of this gospel, He is also leading us on a journey into an understanding of who Jesus is. Jesus is an earthly human being, the Son of Man. He is also the Son of God. Entering into an appreciation of who He is requires a lifetime, followed by an eternity, to comprehend. But we can start with what is revealed to us in this gospel.

Two of the temptations emphasise His divinity, and for the third, it would be inappropriate, because the devil is unlikely to say, 'If you are the Son of God, worship the devil.'

The temptations of Jesus have often been seen at an earthly level, as temptations that affect all human beings, temptations equivalent with human experience – gluttony, vainglory, greed – or viewed psychologically – materialism, thrill seeking, power in the world. But there is also and more importantly a Messianic element to the temptations of Jesus. The tempter says 'If you are the Son of God, command that these stones become bread' (verse 3) and later 'if you are the son of God, cast yourself down from thence' (verse 6).

Matthew 3:1-4. The first temptation

And the tempter came to Him and said, 'If you are the Son of God, command these stones to become loaves of bread'. But Jesus answered and said, 'It is written "Man shall not live by bread alone but by every word that proceeds from the mouth of God."

The first temptation occurs after a period of fasting for Jesus of 40 days and 40 nights. And afterwards He was hungry. Forty days and forty nights ago, Jesus had been baptised by John in the River Jordan, declaring to John, 'Thus it becomes us to fulfil all righteousness.' Previously, we understood righteousness as being utter and complete obedience to the will of God, the gift He gives us as we are justified and made righteous through faith in Him. The opposite of obedience is rebellion, idolatry which places ourselves, or someone, or something, in the place of God. Jesus was righteous. He lived His life in total obedience to, and dependence on, God His Father. Nothing else took its place. Obviously, that was what the tempter wanted to challenge, the total reliance of Jesus on His heavenly Father.

After the tremendous experience of having the heavens opened, and the voice of the heavenly Father saying, 'This is my beloved Son in whom I am well pleased,' Jesus wanted to go away by Himself, the Spirit willingly leading Him into the wilderness. As many have found, fasting, abstaining from food for a season, not for health or cosmetic reasons, but from a desire to come closer to God, can be a precious time of communion with Him. One of the effects of spiritual fasting is an enhanced sensitivity to the presence of God. But there can be a price to pay.

Here was Jesus right at the outset of his ministry. Would the tempter do nothing to try and stop Him? First, he challenges His Sonship, 'If you are the Son God,' followed by an attempt to prevent His utter and complete dependence on His Father, to prevent that closeness with His Father which he had been enjoying for 40 days and 40 nights. 'Stop this fasting, if you are the Son of God, command these stones that they become bread.'

Jesus was hungry, the temptation was real. Later on in His ministry, He made five loaves and two fish feed 5,000 people. Surely, He could have performed this miracle for Himself? But there was something more important to Him than satisfying His hunger; legitimate though that would be. He was obedient to the will and word of God. He quotes a verse to the devil from Deuteronomy 8:3, 'Man shall not live by bread alone but by every word that proceeds from the mouth of God.' He answers the accusation of, 'If you are the Son of God,' with the answer of complete dependence on the word of God, 'every word that proceeds from the mouth of God'. He is satisfied completely, not by physical food, but by complete dependence on His Father.

21

Matthew 4:5-7. The second temptation

Then the devil took Him to the holy city, and set Him on the pinnacle of the temple, and said to Him, 'If you are the Son of God, throw yourself down, for it is written, "He will give His angels charge over you, and on their hands they will bear you up, lest you strike your foot against a stone."

The devil had not finished yet. From the wilderness of the first temptation, the devil took Jesus to the Holy City, to the pinnacle of the Temple, to tempt Him again. As Luther famously pointed out long ago, the devil can quote scripture too. This time, it was Psalm 91:11, 12, which forms the basis of the temptation. It is as if the devil is saying, 'If you are the Son of God, and if you are relying on the word of God, what about putting yourself in God's hands completely by jumping off this building?' The significance of this location was that it was a special building, the place of God's presence with His people. The tempter was implying, surely you can trust God to hold you up and prevent you from falling? Especially from falling from the place of His presence? You would only be putting your trust in the word of your Father.

Jesus answered the devil with another verse from scripture, 'You shall not put the Lord your God to the test' (Deuteronomy 6:16) or in other translations, 'You shall not tempt the Lord your God.' How is it possible to tempt the Lord God? To put Him to the test?

Jesus is referring to an episode in the wilderness wanderings of the children of Israel in the time of Moses, when Deuteronomy tells us that the people needed water but had no confidence that God could provide it. Moses struck the Rock with his rod and water came out of it so that the people could drink. In Deuteronomy 9:22, Moses recalling the incident describes it as a time of rebellion against God, when the people did not believe Him or obey His voice. Psalm 78: 19-20, describes the people as testing the Lord in their hearts, saying, 'Can God provide a table in the wilderness? Can He give water? Can He also give bread?'

22

So perhaps we may be able to say that to tempt the Lord is to deny His faithful, loving provision for us, not to believe Him and His many promises, and not to obey Him, the altogether reliable and trustworthy One. He is absolutely and utterly reliable, unlike the devil, even whose quotation from Psalm 91 is not accurate, because the Psalm speaks not of throwing oneself from a height, but of stumbling over a stone on the ground. So, the devil not only quotes scripture, but misquotes it for his own advantage.

Matthew 4:8-11. The third temptation

Again the devil took Him to a very high mountain and showed Him all the kingdoms of the world and the glory of them, and he said to Him, "All this will I give you if you will fall down and worship me." Then Jesus said, "Begone Satan! For it is written, you shall worship the Lord your God, and Him only shall you serve."

The tempter tries again in the third temptation. The devil shows Him all the Kingdoms of the world and the glory of them (verse 8) and assures Him that if He worships the devil, all would be His. What a temptation that would be! For Jesus not to have to go the way of death which He had already intimated at His baptism, He was prepared to do. Especially not to go the way of the cross, but to have authority over the kingdoms of the world on a different basis.

Luke tells us that this was no empty promise, that this authority had been given to the devil, or so he claimed, and that he had the right to give it to whom he willed (Luke 4:6). Jesus, however, perceived that the temptation was not to authority or power but to worship. How could He place the worship of the devil in place of the worship of God, His Father; with whom He had such a precious relationship; which meant more to Him than anything the devil could offer; even if obedience to His Father's will involved the way of the cross? His Father's will provided redemption for a people lost in sin and darkness (verse 16) and He was the Redeemer, the Saviour, sent by God.

23

Jesus' understanding of His Sonship of God is the foundation of His life as the incarnate Son of God. The renunciation of power by the earthly Jesus points ahead to the authority of the Risen Lord in Matthew 28:16. Also on a mountain, the Lord Jesus is able to say, 'All authority on heaven and earth is given to Me,' together with that precious promise, 'Lo, I am with you always, even to the end of the age' (Matthew 28:20).

However, it was necessary for the Son of God to be tempted on two grounds. *Firstly* because He was human. He had human appetites like hunger, the first temptation. He had an human instinct for self-preservation and would not have wanted to fall from the pinnacle of the Temple as in the second temptation. But *secondly,* it was important that He was tempted like we are, yet without sin so that He could help those who are tempted (Hebrews 4:15). He may have been tempted to take the easy way out in both the first and second temptations, but especially in the third, which challenged His destiny as Lord over all the nations of the world.

The third temptation was a challenge to Jesus' Sonship and deity as Son of God, rather than a challenge to His humanity as Son of Man, a precious title which He often used later in His ministry. On this occasion, the devil does not tempt Jesus to doubt His Sonship which was pronounced over Him by His Father at His baptism, but to suggest that He could use His Sonship In self-serving ways, ways which would eventually draw Him out of the way of obedience into disobedience and deflect Him from what He had come to do, which was to travel the path of obedience which led to the Cross.

The conflict in this third temptation was between His humanity and His deity; and ultimately His ability to redeem humanity. Only as the spotless Lamb of God could He go to the Cross and there pour out His life, taking the sin of the world upon Himself so that men and women could become the righteousness of God in Him. John the apostle was given this insight in his account of the ministry of John the Baptist in chapter 1 of his gospel. John says, referring to Jesus, 'Behold the Lamb of God who takes away the sin of the world' (John 1:29) In

Hebrews we read, 'we have a High Priest who has been tempted as we are, yet without sin (Hebrews 4:15).

God was using the devil to do His will. He was allowing Jesus to be tempted so that it could be established beyond question that Jesus was human as well as divine, Son of Man as well as Son of God. Both natures are in Him, and when He ascended back to His Father after His resurrection, He took his human nature with Him. Again in Hebrews we read 'He Himself partook of the same nature... like His brethren in every respect. Because He Himself has suffered, being tempted, He is able also to help those who are tempted' (Hebrews 2:14, 17, 18). Those dear tokens of His Passion, still His dazzling Body bears, cause of endless exaltation to his ransomed worshippers. With what rapture, with what rapture, gaze we on those glorious scars (Charles Wesley, 1758). He has taken our humanity, the marks of His suffering, on His head and hands and feet and side, into heaven with Him.

Jesus was tempted along the lines of who He is. We are also tempted, not along the same lines because we are so very different from Him. He was tempted as the Beloved Son of God. We too have become children of God through the death and resurrection of Jesus, through His atoning death on the cross, and our temptations are real. But 1 Corinthians 10:13 assures us that God is faithful and we will not be tempted above that we are able to bear, for with the temptation He will also make a way of escape, that we may be able to bear it. And Hebrews makes the emphatic declaration that we have a Saviour in heaven who intercedes for us (Hebrews 7:25).

When we pray, 'Our Father, lead us not into temptation', we are making an affirmation. We want to do His will. We do not want to be disobedient or rebellious. We want to trust Him fully. But sometimes other things get in the way. Perhaps a crisis of faith comes. Do we follow Jesus or do we go our own way? A decision has to be made. We pray 'Lord, show us the way we should go'. We do not want to be self-interested but the temptation is great. Jesus knows and understands, because He knows what it is to be tempted.

Temptation is part of discipleship, part of learning what it is to have entered into the realm of obedience, the kingdom of heaven. That is why the temptation of the Lord Jesus in the wilderness precedes the sermon on the mount and the principles of the kingdom in Matthew's gospel. The prayer 'Thy kingdom come' governs the whole of the Lord's Prayer, the kingdom which is 'now' and 'not yet', which will be fully realised at the Parousia, the second coming of Jesus to the earth, towards which everything in heaven and earth is moving. With reverential awe, we recognize that we are part of God's plan, part of the resolution of all things of which Paul writes in Romans 8:18-23, when the creation is set free from its bondage, and we enjoy the glorious liberty of the children of God. There is now and always will be, a 'remnant' such as Isaiah saw (Isaiah 10:20, 21), those who will follow the Lamb wherever He goes (Revelation 4:4). We are grateful to be able to stand on the shoulders of those who have passed this way before us, and to pray, 'Thy kingdom come'.

In Matthew's gospel, the next significant mountain is where He sits with His disciples to teach them about this life of dependence on the Father, which is the privilege of all those who have entered the Kingdom of Heaven through repentance, the repentance He announced in verse 17. The temptation for Jesus was ultimately between His humanity and His deity. Our temptations focus on whether we are prepared to go the way that in His great love He has chosen for us, or whether we choose to go our own way.

Matthew 4:12-17. Jesus begins His ministry

Now when He heard that John had been arrested, He withdrew into Galilee; and leaving Nazareth, He went and dwelt in Capernaum by the sea, in the territory of Zebulun and Naphtali, that what was spoken by the prophet Isaiah might be fulfilled. "The land of Zebulun and the land of Naphtali toward the sea, across the Jordan, Galilee of the Gentiles. The people who walked in darkness have seen a great light, and for those who sat in darkness and the shadow of death, the light has dawned" (Matthew 4: 12-14; Isaiah 9:1-2).

After this temptation experience, Jesus must have been physically exhausted. The Father knows when the battle has been long and hard, and He sent His angels to minister to Jesus. Would this have included food? How much rather would He have had food sent from heaven than bread which had formerly been stone! But this detail is not recorded for us either in Matthew, Mark or Luke.

On top of this temptation experience, Jesus heard that John had been arrested, this cousin of His who had been so important to Him. Matthew uses the word *'anchoreo'* – Jesus *'withdrew'* into Galilee. The Greek word Matthew uses here is one which later described the group of people in the Middle Ages like Julian of Norwich who were known as 'anchorites', those who had 'withdrawn' from the world to give themselves wholly up to God.

Jesus needed to withdraw from time to time, to spend time alone with His Father. Now He was grieving, for He had heard that John had been arrested, His friend and cousin, who was also a prophet and whose rejection and arrest could well be an indication to Jesus that His ministry could follow the same pattern. John had *prepared* 'the way of the Lord' (Matthew 3:3). Now Jesus *knew* that it was the beginning of His ministry.

Jesus leaves Nazareth and goes to live in Capernaum by the sea (Matthew 4:1). In the days before the Hellenization of the region and the subsequent Roman occupation, Capernaum had been in the area allotted by Joshua to the tribes of Zebulun and Naphtali after the death of Moses (Joshua 19:10,32. 1400-1200 B.C). Matthew's desire to place the ministry of Jesus in its prophetic and above all Messianic setting causes him to quote verses from Isaiah 9:2, 'Zebulun and the land of Naphtali – in the land beyond the Jordan, Galilee of the nations. The people who walked in darkness have seen a great light.' When the tribes were blessed by Moses before his death, Zebulun was blessed with joy, and Naphtali with being satisfied (Deuteronomy 33:18, 23).

In that region of Galilee, it was absolutely true, the people who walked in darkness *were* seeing a great light. Indeed, never before had such a light shined anywhere in the world since God had said, 'Let there be light.' Those who lived in Galilee were a mixture of Jews and Gentiles. This northern part of Israel had been colonised by non-Jews at the time of the Assyrian invasion under Tiglath-Pileser and again under Antiochus Epiphanes at the time of the Maccabees, and of course they were now under Roman occupation. Jesus' beginning of His ministry was not only to Israel, but also to Galilee of the Gentiles (verse 15). His was to be a worldwide evangelization movement. And His beginning statement was, 'Repent, for the Kingdom of Heaven is at hand' (Matthew 4:17). In a previous study, we understood that the Kingdom of Heaven is totally represented by the King, and that the way into the Kingdom can only be by repentance, a turning away from all else that would hold us, a turning back into repentance towards God and faith towards our Lord Jesus Christ (Acts 20:21).

Matthew 4:18-22. The call of Simon Peter, Andrew, James and John

As Jesus walked by the Sea of Galilee, He saw two brothers, Simon Peter and Andrew his brother, casting a net into the sea, for they were fishermen (Matthew 4: 18).

Because we believe that Jesus never did anything without purpose, it encourages us to speculate whether this may have been an additional reason for Jesus to leave Nazareth and go to Capernaum, a small town by the sea, where He found not only Peter and Andrew, but also James and John. These four would become the inner circle of His disciples.

'*Immediately*' (verse 20) is a term more usually associated with Mark's gospel. Here it is used of all four men as they respond to the call of Jesus to become 'fishers of men.' Immediately Peter and Andrew left their nets and followed Him, (verse 20) Immediately James and John left the boat and their father and followed Him (verse 22).

Simon is a Semitic or Hebrew name, and Peter a Greek name. Even in this representative disciple, Jesus is already calling attention to the breadth of His ministry, for His redemptive power was extended to both Gentiles and Jews.

The discipleship of these men differed greatly from the contemporary disciples of the rabbis and from the disciples of ancient prophets like Elisha who were self-selecting, and mostly lived the life of a sedentary student in the hope and expectation of one day becoming a rabbi or teacher like their master. The disciples of Jesus were called to be fishers of men, to be actively engaged in seeking out others who would follow the way of discipleship. The mention of leaving their father Zebedee by James and John indicated that this was going to be a costly way of life, both for the individual and his family. Luke and Matthew tell us that Simon Peter was married (Luke 4:3; Matthew 8:14), though we have no similar information about the others. Peter, Andrew, James and John left all to follow Jesus. Surely their families too shared in the blessing which their loved ones enjoyed, but there was a downside too.

Jesus' ministry now takes on a familiar pattern. He is *teaching* in the Jewish synagogues, *preaching* the gospel of the kingdom, and *healing* all who came to Him. And great crowds followed Him. Matthew especially mentions those of the crowds who came from Syria. Since Syria may speak of the provenance of the gospel, from where it could have been written by Matthew, it is understandable that Matthew should include it. But the crowds also came from Decapolis and Jerusalem and Judea and even beyond Jordan, possibly including some at least who had been baptised in the River Jordan under John's ministry.

These people began as part of a crowd, but many of them had now become disciples. They had come to listen to Jesus and had turned from their previous way of life and now the only course they wanted to pursue was to follow Him. Jesus understood that they needed His encouragement, His help in understanding the consequences of their decision to become His disciples, and for their better understanding. He took upon Himself the position familiarly used by the rabbis. Seeing the crowds, He went up on the mountain, and when He sat down His disciples came to Him. And He opened His mouth and taught them' (Matthew 5:1, 2).

The light had truly come into the world (John 1:5; 3:19), and many acknowledged Him, and sat down on the mountainside with hunger in their hearts to listen to Him. It is a sad fact that some loved darkness rather than light, and still do. But there is now and will always be a 'remnant' such as Isaiah saw, (Isaiah 10:20, 21); those who will follow the Lamb wherever He goes (Revelation 4:4). Already we have acknowledged our gratitude to those who have gone before and to pray 'Thy kingdom come'; to know futuristically that the kingdom of God is at hand, and will come. But is not the kingdom here already? For is He not the King? This is what Jesus is about to explain to them. He is the Son of God and King of the whole world, but as He will reveal later (Matthew 13:33), the Kingdom of God is like the leaven hidden in three measures of meal. It is at work, men and women are coming into the kingdom all the time. In the hearts of people across the world, the Kingdom of God is a reality. They acknowledge the Lord Jesus as King over their lives. They submit to Him, are obedient to Him. But His kingdom is largely hidden, unobserved by people who subscribe to another, materialistic world, careless of the claims of God upon their lives, darkened in their understanding.

But the day will come when the King will shine in all His glory. His Kingdom is an everlasting Kingdom. His kingdom is on its way. It will come. For this we pray in well-grounded hope, 'Thy kingdom come'; in expectation of the manifestation of the glory of God at the coming of the Lord Jesus, and also for an increasing acknowledgement of His reign in our lives.

Matthew Chapter 5

Matthew 5:1-11. The Sermon on the Mount; the Beatitudes

Seeing the crowds, He went up on the mountain, and when He sat down, His disciples came to Him. And He opened His mouth and taught them saying, Blessed are the poor in spirit for theirs is the kingdom of God (Matthew 5:1-3).

To understand the Sermon on the Mount is firstly to recognise who is giving this sermon, this teaching. The Sermon on the Mount is Jesus' Sermon. In Matthew 3:17, at His baptism, Jesus is proclaimed to be the Son of God, declared to be so by His Father. In this sermon Jesus the Son of God is speaking. He is setting out in foundational terms, the outworking of the kingdom in practical day-to-day living; the commitment made by those who have seen and understood that the Kingdom of God is at hand and have repented, in compliance with His word to them 'Repent, for the kingdom of heaven is at hand' (Matthew 4:17).

Through that repentance they have entered the Kingdom. Both Mark and Matthew tell us of an occasion when Jesus had compassion on the crowd, because they were like sheep without a shepherd (Mark 6:34; Matthew 9:36). Here in Matthew, the shepherd is speaking, with compassion, *to a crowd of His disciples.* Something wonderful, stupendous has happened to them. They have come under a new kingship, the kingship of Jesus and they have become different people, free to allow God to work in their lives.

Even though we are only in chapter 5 of Matthew's gospel, we have seen how important it was for the Lord Jesus to withdraw sometimes, in order to spend time with His Father. This privilege, He assures the disciples and the crowd, can be theirs also, and so the central teaching of the Sermon is on prayer, those now enjoying the Kingdom realising that prayer, far from being ritualistic or ceremonial, can now become for them an expression of such a relationship with God as enables them to call Him Father.

Jesus has proclaimed that the Kingdom of Heaven is at hand (Matthew 4:17). Peter and Andrew, James and John have responded to His call to follow Him. Great crowds have also followed Him, many of them, we may speculate, have also heard John the Baptist's teaching and perhaps have repented and been baptised under John's ministry. Now Matthew tells us that they have heard Jesus teaching and preaching and seen His healing power (Matthew 4:23). It is time for Jesus to move on to the next stage of His ministry.

'And seeing the crowds, Jesus went up into the mountain. And when He was set, His disciples came to Him. And He opened his mouth and taught them' (Matthew 5:1).

What a mixed group of people they were! Jesus looking upon them saw some who were mourning, those who were meek, some who were hungry and thirsty for righteousness, the merciful, the pure in heart, the peacemakers and some whom He knew would be persecuted for righteousness' sake. Jesus had a word of comfort, a word of encouragement, for each of them. In their desire to follow Jesus they had become the salt of the earth, the light of the world. They were blessed indeed, meaning that they were under the divine approval, and though this did not by any means guarantee them an easy life, they had grounds for rejoicing which others did not have, the knowledge that they were entering into a life which had an eternal purpose, not only in the present, the joy of the now, but in the future, the fuller manifestation of the kingdom of heaven.

The sermon on the mount is the expression of what it means, *in practical terms,* to live in the pure uninterrupted experience of the will of God, not just as it was expressed in the Law and the Prophets, though that was the revelation of who God was to His people Israel, but in the fuller life which Jesus gives to all His followers.

What are described as the Beatitudes are not a series of commandments, but a series of promises to those who have become disciples of Jesus, whether or not they belong to the Twelve. Those who walked in faith under the Old Covenant, which God had entered into with his people on Mount Sinai had also experienced the promises of God. For example, 'you *shall* remember the Sabbath day to keep it holy and enjoy the rest of God on that day'. That was a promise to them. You shall not covet, for you will have no need, being plentifully supplied by the loving provision of God. His name will be so precious to you that you will love to hear it in praise and worship and thanksgiving and will not find it in your heart to use it lightly or carelessly. You will honour your parents, for you know that your loving heavenly Father has chosen your way in life especially so that through all its difficulties and problems you might learn to love Him and trust Him more. There will be no need to kill anyone, or commit adultery or speak falsehoods, or steal, for you know that that would displease your heavenly Father, and you only want to please Him. As each of the ten commandments was a promise so too are the nine beatitudes. We owe a debt of gratitude to Matthew for preserving for us the *verbus ipsissimus,* the genuine life affirming words of the Lord Jesus.

Regarded simply as a new set of ethics, which many theologians and scholars undoubtedly do, is unhelpful, because if the sermon on the mount is taken simply as a new set of commandments, it becomes obvious that to prioritise behaviour and practice, before inculcating the will to obedience to a loving heavenly Father, together with the possibility of taking the sermon as a serious engagement towards the goal of perfection, has become a complete impossibility. *Regarded as a new law it is utterly unfulfillable, a law which nobody can keep.*

Only as it is seen in conjunction with Jesus' own proclamation and desire to communicate the truth of life in the Kingdom to the crowd and to His disciples; His proclamation that this is a life lived by and in the grace of the Heavenly Father and in living daily relationship with Him, (which is reinforced throughout Chapter 6); only through the lived expression of its central prayer to Our Father and His, what we know as the Lord's prayer; can we truly become perfect even as our Father in Heaven is perfect (Matthew 5:48), a perfectionism based not on our own efforts, but on the will and desire of our heavenly Father to bring us there, and our own response to Him in love.

The nation of Israel could not keep the Old Covenant. They could not obey the law. 'Who shall ascend into your holy place?' they cried, 'You have given us an impossible task, Lord' (Psalm 15:1). Can it therefore be at all possibly credible that Jesus would have come to give His followers, both those in the crowd and His intimate disciples, yet another set of ethical demands, even more stringent than the last. 'You have heard it said to the men of old... but I say unto you.' The complete unrealizability of obedience to the Sermon on the Mount if it is taken as pure ethics is complete discouragement. How can we be perfect even as our Father in heaven is perfect?

Matthew has given us one of his famous clues in recording for us the proclamation of the Lord Jesus in Matthew 4:17. The clue is repentance. 'Repent!' Jesus says. 'Repent for the Kingdom of Heaven is at hand'. This is the only entry requirement into the kingdom of heaven. Later He encouraged his disciples as He quoted from Zechariah. 'Behold, your *King* comes to you, meek and lowly, riding upon an ass and upon a colt, the foal of an ass' (Matthew 21:5), the gentle King in His kingdom. And in Matthew 11, 'For I am meek and lowly of heart and you shall find rest to your souls, for my yoke is easy and my burden is light' (Matthew 11:28, 29). They needed to know that Jesus is not only the Son of God, but also the meek and lowly Good Shepherd who looks after them as His sheep, and also the Lamb, the innocent, guileless 'Lamb of God, who takes away the sin of the world', including their sin (John 1:29, Isaiah 53:7). Jesus was a Lamb led to the slaughter, a sacrifice for sin on behalf of those who could not keep the law. And the promised Saviour from sin who is also the kindest and most understanding Teacher, and Shepherd of His beloved flock, ever.

Jesus warned the crowds and the disciples in Matthew 23:4 about the scribes and Pharisees who bind heavy burdens, hard to bear, and lay them on men's shoulders. The Judaizers of Paul's day tried to do the same (Galatians 3:1-5).

There have always been such. How liberating and enlightening are Jesus' words recorded in John's gospel.' Abide in Me and I in you, so shall you bring forth much fruit, for without Me you can do nothing' (John 15:5). How comforting it is to know that without Him we can do nothing, and then all the glory goes to Him. And His declaration in John 8:32, 'You will know the truth and the truth will set you free!' Paul reminds us that the righteousness of God has been manifested *apart* from the law, the righteousness of God *through faith* in Jesus Christ (Romans 3:21). There is only one law for Christians, the law of the Spirit of life in Christ Jesus which has set us *free* from the law of sin and death, so that we are no longer under condemnation (Romans 8:1).

It appears that the sermon on the mount, given and expounded by the Lord Jesus, had a different and deeper purpose, and for that it is important to look more carefully and closely at the text.

Matthew 5:3-12. Jesus gives the Beatitudes to those who follow Him

Seeing the crowds, He went up on the mountain, and when He sat down, His disciples came to Him. And He opened His mouth and taught them saying... (Matthew 5:1-2).

The Beatitudes are the *first* part of the *first* sermon or discourse given by the Lord Jesus as recorded by Matthew. They are therefore of fundamental, foundational importance.

The people were used to the Rabbis in the rabbinical schools sitting down, opening the mouth and teaching and by this action, Jesus was proclaiming Himself as a Rabbi or Teacher such as they had known before; but never a teacher like this. Traditionally, He is like the others, as is suggested by the traditional phrase 'He opened His mouth and taught them, saying', but there was an authenticity, and authority about His teaching which astonished them (Matthew 7:28).

He was not only a teacher, He was the Messiah, the promised Messiah, the One who should come, the One for whom Israel had been waiting. He was also a Prophet, for He was speaking not only to their *'sitz im leben'*, their situation in life, but to the disciples, and all disciples for all time. The mountain had become a place of revelation; who Jesus is, and how we know Him. When He opens His mouth, we hear nothing less than the word of God. This Teacher was providing foundational principles not only for His immediate hearers, but for those who would also follow Him in the future. They too will come into the blessedness, the joy and the purpose of His teaching. Now we consider the encouragement He has for His present hearers.

Earlier, we speculated on the constituents of the crowd and their relationship to Jesus. Now we turn to the first section of teaching, which appears to be almost complete in itself but which also provides an introduction to what He expands on afterwards, the meaning of discipleship. Matthew says, 'great crowds followed Him' (Matthew 4:22). The use of the word 'followed' always suggests discipleship; and indicates that His teaching was not confined to Peter and Andrew, James and John, the first to follow Him; it also had implications for those of the crowd too, those who had followed Him from the shores of the Sea of Galilee to the Mountain to hear His word, beginning to learn the happiness of sourcing their lives in the presence and activity of Jesus.

Jesus begins with the word 'blessed'. Blessed means to be congratulated, but with more emphasis on divine approval than human happiness, and indicates a complete reversal of their former experience, which for them is now framed by their new status of having their share in the kingdom of heaven.' For theirs is the kingdom of heaven' (verse 3).

Within this framework Jesus announces the blessings of those who have entered the kingdom, who are living in the blessing of relationship of children to their heavenly Father, while proclaiming the promised glorious *future* which begins in the *now* of His ministry; the now and not yet; the gospel of the kingdom which Jesus had substantiated and confirmed not only by His teaching but by His healing of every disease and every infirmity among the people before He came to the mountain (Matthew 4:23).

The gospel of the kingdom is the theme of His ministry throughout the gospel of Matthew. The sermon on the mount is for people who, having entered into a relationship with God through faith in Jesus, consider that relationship to be the most important and precious aspect of their lives. Whatever draws them closer to Him is paramount; whatever disturbs that closeness is anathema.

The First Beatitude

Blessed are the poor in spirit, for theirs is the kingdom of heaven (verse 3).

In Luke's comparable sermon which took place on the plain rather than on the mountain, Luke uses the second person plural as Jesus addresses the disciples. 'Blessed are *you* poor, for *yours* is the kingdom of God (Luke 6:20). In Matthew's sermon, Jesus' teaching is still addressed directly to the suffering but blessed ones, but in less personal terms. 'Blessed are the poor in spirit, for *theirs* is the kingdom of heaven' (Matthew 5:3), in the third person plural. In Matthew's gospel, Jesus is stating a principle, not addressing an individual, but the principle applies to all, and for all time. This reflects the didactic nature of Jesus' sermon in Matthew and the conclusion that it was intended not only for His immediate hearers but for those who would follow Him in the future. They too have come into the blessedness, the happiness of sourcing all their lives in the life of Jesus.

The poor in spirit are those of every generation of believers whose confidence is in God Alone, and their complete obedience to Him and His will are the only rule in their lives. The very first beatitude implies this. 'Blessed are the poor in spirit, for theirs is the kingdom of heaven' (Matthew 5:3). This is Kingdom living. *They are empty before God*. Paul expressed it in 2 Corinthians 6:10, 'as having nothing and yet possessing all things'. Heaven is living with Him. Hell is separation from Him and the peace which He provides.

Meister Eckhart (Dominican mystic, 1260-1327) spoke of triple poverty. The one who is poor in spirit: does not *want* anything, not even to fulfil God's will; does not *know* anything, not even about the work of God in him; does not *have* anything, not even room in himself in which God is to work.

Thus, the initial Beatitude paves the way for those which follow. The gift to *all* disciples is the gift of life in the Kingdom of Heaven expressed in different ways – for those who mourn, for those who are meek, for those who hunger and thirst after righteousness, the pure in heart, the merciful, the peacemakers, the persecuted. All depends on the attitude which declares that though I am nothing, He is everything I lack.

Jesus has unfolded before them the gospel, the good news of the Kingdom. How could the Lord Jesus give them anything but good news? Even His warning about persecution in the 9th Beatitude cannot take that away from them; even knowing that there is a cost involved; for them, and eventually for Him too.

The Second Beatitude

Blessed are they that mourn, for they shall be comforted (verse 4).

People mourn for all sorts of reasons. It may be that they are mourning over their sin, as many theologians have taught (Bede, Origen (Luz). Or they may have had a personal loss, the loss of loved ones, or livelihood or home. Or these disciples on the mountain side may have been mourning over the present state of their nation under Roman occupation. Whatever the reason for mourning, one thing is sure. They have the blessing of being comforted, Παρακαλέω, the root of the same word used of the Holy Spirit in John's gospel; the Comforter of the Authorized Version. The point of the Beatitude is not the mourning, but the way in which the mourning leads to the comfort of the Holy Spirit, for that is His ministry. They shall be comforted!

The Third Beatitude

Blessed are the meek, for they shall inherit the earth (verse 5).

Some expositors have subsumed the concept of meekness under that of the poor in spirit, but there is an alternative way of looking at meekness as a state of being in its own right. To be meek is to be submissive, like a handmaid waiting upon her mistress, a servant upon his master (Psalm 123:2). Their whole life is to do the will of another. They have no will, no life of their own. They are slaves – sometimes literally. They live in humble obedience.

The comparison with the Lord Jesus is not hard to seek. In John's gospel, Jesus says, 'I do always those things which please the Father' (John 8:29). In Matthew, Mark and Luke, in the Garden of Gethsemane, He says, 'Let this cup pass from Me, nevertheless, not my will but Thine be done' (Matt 26:39, Mark 14:36, Luke 22:43). Philippians 2 gives us a glimpse of what it cost Him, the Son of God, to leave heaven's glory and His equality with God, as He emptied Himself, taking the form of a servant and becoming obedient unto death, even death on a cross. Meekness for Him was not a soft option. So, what do the meek receive as their blessing? They inherit the earth.

At first this sounds disappointing until we look again at the life of Jesus as a servant/slave. The promise of the earth includes the earth and especially includes the people upon it. It is on earth that the will of God will be done, referred to in the prayer that Jesus later taught His disciples, 'Thy will be done on earth as it is in heaven' (Matthew 6:10). The earth is the place of the operation of the Holy Spirit as through His convicting activity men and women are brought into fellowship with God.

Those with a servant spirit, the meek, are not seeking earthly power and influence. They know that the time will come when every knee in heaven and upon earth will bow to the Lord

Jesus (Philippians 2:9) and every tongue will confess that He is Lord, to the glory of God the Father. Their reward as a consequence of their disciple-inspired living, is to be a part of this; rejoicing that through their testimony, others have come to know Jesus too. They are in the world, but not of it, completely trusting their lives to God, living in complete dependence upon Him and ready at all times to submit their will to His.

The Fourth Beatitude

Blessed are those who hunger and thirst for righteousness, for they shall be filled / satisfied (AV/RSV) (verse 6).

Hunger and thirst are primitive appetites. Without them, or the satisfaction of them, we could not live. For those who through repentance have entered the Kingdom of Heaven, the hunger and thirst for righteousness has become of paramount importance. Righteousness means being in right relation to Jesus, sharing His life, in complete obedience to Him. This is what these disciples crave. For them it has become a primary urge, a holy obsession.

Jesus later speaks of Himself as living water in John 4:10 and as the bread of life in John 6:35. These disciples will not have heard Him speak in those terms, but they know exactly what is meant by them. Without that relationship with Him, and the intimacy of it, they are completely unsatisfied; they are dead. They are hungry for Him and the life of righteousness which is His gift to them. The promise is that no cloud shall come between them and their Lord as they continue to hunger and thirst after righteousness, and their relationship with Him. *They will be satisfied!*

The Fifth Beatitude

Blessed are the merciful, for they shall obtain mercy (verse 7).

To be merciful is to be like God Himself. The Hebrew word 'hesed' in the Old Testament is sometimes translated *loving kindness*, or *mercy*, or *steadfast love*, and is a feature of the Covenant which the Lord made with the children of Israel on Mt Sinai.

In Deuteronomy 7, we read, 'The Lord loves you... He is a faithful God who keeps covenant and steadfast love, mercy (hesed) with those who love Him and keep His commandments' (Deuteronomy 7:8). He is a loving, faithful and merciful God. And in Luke's gospel 6:36, we read, 'Be merciful even as your Father in heaven is merciful.' This theme is taken up in Matthew 5:45, which describes the Father as sending His sun on the evil and the good, and His rain on the just and the unjust.

Without God's mercy, where would any of us be? Ephesians tells us that it was God who was rich in mercy, out of the great love wherewith He loved us, even when we were dead in our trespasses and sins, who has made us alive together with Christ (Ephesians 2:4). Our mercifulness cannot possibly hope to compete with God's, but to be merciful is to show something of God's character to the world around us, His character of unfailing, unchanging love. *Not* to be merciful is to ignore another's needs. *To be merciful* is to see where the need is, to put oneself in the place of another, and to seek to meet that need.

We may tend to link mercy with justice as in the trial of 'The Merchant of Venice', 'the quality of mercy is not strained, it droppeth as the gentle rain of heaven upon the place beneath', and of course in our own judicial system at least, there is an attempt to temper justice with mercy, but it has a much wider application. Charitable work, charitable giving, stems from mercy; voluntary care of the infirm and elderly – we can think of many examples and thank God for them all.

Yet they may not fully express what Jesus meant by the merciful, being as it is complete self-abnegation on behalf of another, just as God denied Himself in sending Jesus, giving His only begotten Son to be the mediator of a New Covenant, (Hebrews 9:15) allowing Him to give Himself to death on a Cross for us; as He did, in complete unanimity with his Father. He had complete confidence in His Father's will, giving up His life that we might live. 'Having loved His own who were in the world, He loved them to the uttermost' (John 13:1). Those who are merciful have entered into that life, having discovered the mercy of God to them. This is their blessing. *Jesus promises mercy to His merciful disciples.*

The Sixth Beatitude

Blessed are the pure in heart, for they shall see God (verse 8).

The scribes and Pharisees had a kind of virtual, ceremonial purity. But their purity was of an outward piety which Jesus afterwards castigates in chapter 6. Of what use are alms and prayers before the public? The pure in heart enter into a place where they can be alone with their heavenly Father. They do not seek the reward of praise from men and women. They want only to be alone with Him in that quiet place. The purity of their heart lies in this one desire. They allow nothing else to distract them, they have a pure, an undivided heart.

Does this mean therefore, that to withdraw from the world into a realm of private piety is an acceptable way of life for a disciple? For some it may be, but for others surely not, for in that private place they have seen God, not with the seeing eye, but with the eye of the spirit. There is a future total and overwhelming vision of God of which the psalmist speaks (Psalms 17:15) which will one day be theirs, but they have a foretaste of what that experience will be like. Revelation speaks of a time when the Lamb's servants shall worship Him and they shall see His face (Revelation 22:3-4). As the song has it: And I shall see Him face to face, And tell the story, saved by grace.

When the pure in heart leave the sanctuary, they take with them something of Jesus, something of the Father. This enters into all their relationships with others, for they see something of the image of God in them. They bring His fragrance with them. Purity of heart means that they think God's thoughts after Him and say what God would have them say to those around them, to their blessing.

The heart, in Jewish usage, is not indicative of some organ or part of the body, but rather a centre within the human person where human wanting, thinking and feeling take place. It is true, as Paul explains in 1 Corinthians 13:16 that now we see in a mirror darkly, but we do see. This sight, though partial, is the blessing given to the pure in heart. The fulfilment of the promise that we shall see God if we are pure in heart, will come. But we are grateful that meanwhile, He has allowed us to see even as much as we do of the amazing reality of who He is. Blessed are the pure in heart, *for they shall see God.*

The Seventh Beatitude

Blessed are the peacemakers, for they shall be called sons of God (verse 9).

Peacemakers are those who stand in the breach. Sometimes they stand between people in disagreement with each other; sometimes the opposition is against them personally. Peace-making is making peace with others, and making peace between others. In attempting to mediate, they also attempt to lead others to the one God, and the one mediator between God and men, the Man Christ Jesus (1 Timothy 2:5).

These disciples are blessed by knowing that they belong to God. They are His sons, (a generic term including daughters!). They may call Him Father. And even more importantly, it is God who is calling them His sons. As Paul writes in Romans 8:15, they have received the spirit of sonship whereby we cry Abba! Father! This understanding of sonship with God opens up a completely new perspective for these disciples. They recognise that peace with God comes only through repentance and faith. On these two principles peace-making becomes their mission in life, to bring the peace of God which He gives, to those in sore need of it, and to assure them that relationship with God through Jesus will bring peace not only to them, but to all their family and friends. Jesus has forgiven them, now they forgive one another. Their message is: 'Be kind to one another, tender-hearted, forgiving one another, even as God for Christ's sake has forgiven you' (Ephesians 4:32).

How precious is peace after the storm! How precious those who come to us, bringing the peace of God with them! They bear all the characteristics of God. *They shall be called sons of God.* The calling of God is on their lives.

The Eighth and Ninth Beatitudes

Blessed are those who are persecuted for righteousness sake; for theirs is the Kingdom of Heaven (verse 10).

All peoples from many nations, all down the ages, have been persecuted. We can think of many examples in our own day.

The persecution of believers is different. The people of Israel had been through times of foreign occupation, through exile, through invasion by world powers. But Jesus is not speaking about those, although throughout the Old Testament, there are those who stood firm in their faith against malignant opposition. The eleventh chapter of Hebrews enumerates many of them.

Jesus is speaking about these present (contemporary) disciples who are undergoing persecution for righteousness sake, the present experience of those who confess Christ. Though so recently entered into a relationship with Him through repentance and faith, persecution for them may have already begun. They were being faithful to what they had already received of the grace of God to them. But Jesus is speaking not only to them, but to those who should come after them, for there have always been Christians who were and are persecuted for their faith.

The promise of the Kingdom of Heaven takes on a different note in this beatitude. Amplified as it is in what has been regarded as the *ninth beatitude,* it predicts the full consummation involved in following Christ, of being reviled, being falsely accused, being persecuted. But *also,* the joy, the gladness when Jesus comes into His ultimate kingdom, the kingdom which is *yet to come.* Nevertheless, it *will* be theirs, for theirs is *already* the Kingdom of Heaven.

The *first four* beatitudes have emphasised the intimate relationship of Jesus to His disciples, or perhaps even more significantly, their relationship to Him. They are, by definition, *learners*. It is what discipleship means. They have entered into the Kingdom of Heaven through repentance and faith and are now learning from their great Teacher how to live the kingdom life. The *latter four* beatitudes are still principles for the discipleship of the disciples, but describe how they relate to the world and the people around them.

The ninth and final beatitude, as an extension of the eighth, indicates the cost of discipleship.

There is a Taizé song, 'Jesus, remember me when you come into your Kingdom.' They are the words of the repentant thief who was crucified at the same time as Jesus (Luke 23:42). They also reflect the desire of James and John as they come to recognise more fully who this wonderful, special person is who has called them into fellowship with Him (Matthew 20:20). But Jesus never forgets those who trust in Him (Isaiah 49:14-15). And He has a place for them all in His kingdom.

While we can enjoy His loving presence with us here and now, a new time is coming. It will be at the marriage supper of the Lamb when the Bride has made herself ready (Revelation 19:7), when there is a great multitude that no man can number, from every nation, from all tribes and peoples and tongues, standing before the throne of God and before the Lamb, worshipping God (Revelation 7:9). This is the future fulfilment of the coming Kingdom of God when Jesus is on the throne, with His bride, that is, all those who love Him, and who love each other, before Him. To be part of that great assembly is the reward for those who are persecuted for righteousness sake, *theirs is the Kingdom of Heaven*. The kingdom of heaven is henceforth to be their true home, both now and in the future.

Yet even as we consider this beatitude, we recognize that there are in a sense degrees of persecution. Because the believer has not been beheaded, or thrown to the lions, or burnt at the stake, or in many and other ways suffered for his faith, does not mean that his being persecuted in less dramatic ways does not entitle him to this great reward. We do not all suffer for our faith as Paul did, and who can determine whether what some go through is trivial or serious? Yet there is a place for us too.

Many Christians throughout the world are today suffering for their faith. We do not know how we would react if that persecution came to us. But we believe that we would be given grace and strength, and forgiveness for our persecutors, even as they.

The genocide of the Armenian Christians in 1915, the sufferings of Christians in China, the individual sufferings of people like Terry Waite and Corrie ten Boom, to name but a very few, all lead us to believe that the word is true that says, 'In all their affliction He was afflicted, and the angel of His presence saved them' (Isaiah 63:9).

There is always a cost in following Jesus. Perhaps the persecution had already begun in Matthew's community in Syria, adding a further dimension to his recording of the words of Jesus. Jesus knew it would get progressively worse, so that some would turn away from Him, as they did in John chapter 6. Jesus says to his disciples, 'Would you also go away?' to which we have Peter's poignant reply, 'Lord, to whom should we go? *You* have the words of eternal life. And we have believed and have come to know, that you are the Holy One of God' (John 6:66).

This becomes even more poignant as we consider the reaction of the crowd at the trial and crucifixion of Jesus when they cry 'Away with Him! Crucify Him!' (John 19:15). But there is always a remnant, a core of believers who are prepared to suffer all for His dear name's sake. Sometimes they come from unexpected places, like Nicodemus and Joseph of Arimathea, members of the Sanhedrin at the time of Jesus. These have been written about, but there must have been so many others, their lives hidden with Christ in God.

Suffering is part of the human condition, 'from life's first breath to latest cry'. Persecution is different. It is the intentional mind-set that wishes to do harm, especially to those who are known to follow Christ. Jesus has a word for both! Come unto Me, all ye that labour and are heavy laden and I will give you rest. Take my yoke upon you and learn of Me, for I am meek and lowly of heart and you shall find rest to your souls. For my yoke is easy and my burden is light' (Matthew 11:28).

Paul, who knew a good deal about persecution in his own life wrote to the Philippians, 'It has been granted to you – *it is a gift to you'* – not only to believe in Christ, but also to suffer for His sake (Philippians 1:29, AV & RSV), and in 2 Corinthians 4:17, 'This light affliction, which is but for a moment, worketh for us a far more exceeding and eternal weight of glory, while we look not at the things which are seen but the things which are not seen, for the things which are seen are temporal, but the things which are not seen are eternal.' That is pretty inclusive and conclusive.

Matthew 5:13. The salt of the earth

You are the salt of the earth, but if the salt has lost its savour, its taste, how shall its saltiness be restored? It is no longer good for anything but to be thrown out and trodden under foot by men (Matthew 5:13).

Matthew's gospel is the gospel of the Kingdom – the good news of the Kingdom. How could the Lord Jesus give us anything but good news? The sermon on the mount does not presuppose the gospel but *is* the gospel. The teaching of Jesus makes concrete and very substantial the way of living the gospel, which is the way of living under the blessing of divine approval. The attitudes and actions of those who are learning, as disciples, this way of living, become proclamation and praise, proclamation as the salt of the earth, 'as they see your good works', and praise as 'they glorify your Father who is in heaven' (verse 16). They are truly letting their light shine before men (verse 16).

Those who are the salt of the earth go *beyond* the merely ethical into a fuller fulfilment of the law and prophets, a deeper entering into the life of Jesus through relationship to Him and

His Father and obedience to His will. Through the outworking of His will in their lives, the learners, the disciples, proclaim what is God's will for the whole world; for the people around them who have not yet entered the Kingdom. *They are the light of the world. They are the salt of the earth.*

Salt cannot help being salt. It is salty, it gives flavour to food and is used to preserve food for when food is scarce. That is all it does. It cannot do anything else. Yet without it neither humans or animals can live. But salt may be contaminated with gypsum or some other substance for commercial reasons. How then can its saltiness be restored? It is good for nothing but to be thrown out onto the street with the other refuse.

Jesus could not have said, for example, 'You are the sugar of the earth.' Salt has a distinctive and necessary function and is irreplaceable and chemically cannot lose its quality. It only loses its saltiness when *mixed* with something else. There is no room for mixture, for compromise, for believers. Jesus is emphatic. '*You* are the salt of the earth.' He is referring to all believers, but He may especially have had the persecuted in mind as He has just said they are blessed. Those who are the salt of the earth are salt not for themselves, but for the 'seasoning' of others or to prevent 'degeneration' or 'decomposition' setting in. To fulfil this function, they need to be wholly and entirely given up to it, to allow for no distraction or compromise to 'contaminate' them. *To be 'salt for Jesus' is their whole life.*

Matthew 5:14-16. The light of the world

You are the light of the world. A city set on a hill cannot be hid. Nor do men light a lamp and put it under a bushel, but on a lampstand, and it gives light to all in the house (Matthew 5:14).

The disciples of Jesus are the light of the world. The preferred site for a city to be built is on a hill so that it is easy to fortify, as was Jerusalem. Those who are the light of the world are like this, easily identified and known to all.

No sane householder would light a lamp and then hide it under a pot for storing bread. The whole purpose of the light is that it should give light to all in the house. Without light, we are in darkness, we cannot see. Those who are the light of the world bring enlightenment into the darkness surrounding them. They point the way to Jesus, who said, 'I am the Light of the world' (John 8:12). They help us to see Jesus. They are in such close communion with Him that the Light which He is, is *reflected* from them, and this light draws others into that relationship so that the Father is glorified. They are the light of the world.

Matthew 5:17-20. The law and the prophets

Think not that I have come to abolish the law and the prophets, I have come not to abolish them but to fulfil them. For truly I say to you, till heaven and earth pass away, not an iota nor a jot will pass away from the law until all is accomplished. Whoever then relaxes one of the least of these commandments and teaches men so, shall be called least in the kingdom, but he who does them and teaches them shall be called great in the kingdom of heaven. For I tell you, unless your righteousness exceeds that of the scribes and Pharisees, you will never enter the kingdom of heaven (Matthew 5:17-20).

These verses describe the outworking of the righteousness given to these disciples who have entered the Kingdom, in their daily living. They begin to give the reasons for the antithetical statements which follow in verses 21-48.

Jesus says that the righteousness of the scribes and Pharisees is not righteous enough! For they regard the law and the prophets as rules to be obeyed, not as inspiration for obedience. They are concerned with the letter of the law and not with the character of God behind it, that is, the law as the revelation of who God is, and how the lives of those who believe in Him reflect His character.

God is holy. He is the One who has set His love upon men and women because He wants them to be holy too. 'Be holy for

I am holy', He tells the children of Israel through Moses in Leviticus 11:44, because He wants them to share His life, a life clean and free from any defilement of body or soul. And He has summarised the life of holiness in the ten commandments. This is why Jesus says He has not come to abolish or destroy the law and the prophets in verse 17. How could He, when by doing so, He would impugn the character of God? And all God's purpose for His people?

Revelation In the scriptures is progressive, not partial. We cannot add anything to the character of God, nor can we take anything away from Him, not a jot, the smallest letter in the Greek alphabet (iota, Greek) nor a tittle, (little pen stroke on a letter, Hebrew). Revelation about Him cannot be partial. But we can learn more about Him as it is revealed to us in Jesus. This is why anyone who lessens or relaxes the commandments of God is *least* in the Kingdom of Heaven, because in effect, he or she is attempting to diminish the character of God. But anyone who follows and teaches the commandments of God will be called great in the Kingdom of Heaven because he or she will be extolling and magnifying and rejoicing in the God whose character is thus displayed (verse 19).

In verse 18, Jesus says, '*Truly*, I say unto you, not one jot or tittle will pass away from the law till all is accomplished. 'Truly' is a translation of the word 'Amen' and is one of the names of Jesus in the book of Revelation (Revelation 3:14). It means 'the divine faithfulness'. It is saying that this is so and cannot be otherwise. It has overtones of Isaiah 65:16 where God is spoken of as the God of truth and 1 Corinthians 10:13, where it is emphasised that 'God is faithful'.

When Jesus uses this word, He is putting the divine stamp on what He is saying. He is stating that He is God, for when He is saying, 'Amen, amen, *I* say to you', He is actually aligning Himself with the God who is faithful, the God of truth. Surely that is not too heavy an emphasis to place on the expression He uses. We know that He is God, but perhaps at this stage of the revelation to the disciples of who He is, these new disciples may not have recognised that in Him. It is certain that the scribes and Pharisees saw in Him only an opposition to the validity of the law, and therefore of their own way of living. No wonder that they conspired to kill Him.

Righteousness for the Jews, according to the Hebrew scriptures, consisted in first seeing who God is and then being obedient to Him and His will in all things. It was having a right relationship with God. Abraham was given this revelation at the very beginning. The Lord appeared to Abraham, and said to him, 'I am God almighty. Walk before Me and be perfect' (Genesis 17:1). The scribes and Pharisees of Jesus's day are starting from the wrong end. They are attempting, perhaps struggling, to do His will, to obey the law, but without the comprehension of who He is. So, they end up worshipping the law rather than the Giver of the law, which is of course idolatry.

Jesus is the fulfilment of the law because He is Jesus, the Messiah, the perfect, holy, blameless one, who is able in complete truth to say, 'I do always those things which please Him' (John 8:29). He was the one who should come, the one for whom the Jews had been waiting down the centuries, but whom the Pharisees and scribes did not recognise when He came. Because He went to the Cross as a perfect, sinless sacrifice for sin, He is able to endue those who believe in Him and enter into His life with *His* righteousness. When Jesus hung on the Cross it was the end of the Old covenant and the institution of the New.

These difficult verses at the beginning of the main part of the sermon, the preamble as it were, are foundationally important to Matthew, describing as they do the relation of the Mosaic law to the new law, the law of love, as expounded by Jesus when He came as the anointed One, the Messiah. The law of love, which paradoxically is not a new law, but the former one fully realised in Jesus, is being reinterpreted by Him as He goes about His healing ministry, and preaching the gospel of the kingdom. This is why it sometimes appears throughout the gospel of Matthew that He is breaking the law, as when He heals on the Sabbath day. Because He is Jesus, we learn not only from what He teaches, but from what He does.

Paul rightly interprets the law this way, 'Love is the fulfilling of the law' (Romans 13:5) *because God is love* (1 John 4:8). His whole character may be thus summed up. Heaven and earth will one day pass away (verse 15). Only God will never pass away for He is God and He is eternal and He is love, and only that which speaks of Him will remain. The dual love commandment, to love God and to love one's neighbour, completely summarises all that Jesus is teaching in this sermon. He who loves his neighbour has fulfilled the law (Romans 13:8).

When Jesus says that He came not to abolish, but to fulfil the law, He is not advocating that the law should be done away with. How is that possible when it speaks so wonderfully of the character of His Father? But He is saying that there is a *continuity* between the Old Covenant and the New, or the Old Testament and the New. Jesus is the bridge between them because in Him all that is intended in the purposes of God for His people and which could never have been accomplished through the old dispensation because of the waywardness of His people, was fulfilled in Jesus. Only through Jesus could the purpose of God to all humanity be fulfilled.

At the time of writing his gospel, the Jewish Christians in Matthew's community had experienced a painful break with the synagogue and all that it stood for in terms of Jewish traditions and way of life. They were also situated outside Israel, in Syria. Matthew's repetition and recall of the words of Jesus and the sense of continuity which they demonstrated must have been of inestimable comfort to them, as they found access to all their history and culture, through Jesus, to God the Father. At the same time, Gentile Christians could also appropriate the Old Testament scriptures, especially the Prophetic writings, to themselves as they began to understand the nature of their heavenly Father through Matthew's gospel.

There is a difference of course between moral law and ceremonial law. The moral law, as we have seen, displays the character of God. The ceremonial law, with its symbolism and the significance of its many rituals was also designed to exhibit the character of God; to make it easier for His people to understand *visually* how privileged they were to have God in their midst, and to have a way to approach Him. But Jesus is saying through the following antithetical statements that there is an even more satisfying way of knowing God, even a way of becoming like Him, becoming perfect 'even as your Heavenly Father is perfect' (verse 48).

And so, we come to consider the antithetical statements of Jesus. *'You have heard that it was said...'* (thesis) *'But I say unto you...'* (antithesis) (Matthew 5:21, 28, 34, 38, 43). And what has been described as the *Golden Rule* which sums them up in 7:12, 'Whatever you wish that men would do to you, do so to them, for this is the law and the prophets'.

Matthew 5:21-48. Five antithetical statements of Jesus

Jesus said to them, 'You have heard that it was said to the men of old, "You shall not kill, and whoever kills will be liable to judgement". But I say to you that every one who is angry with his brother shall be liable to judgement; whoever insults his brother shall be liable to the council and whoever says "you fool" shall be liable to the hell of fire' (Matthew 5: 21-22).

What we know as the antithetical statements of Matthew's gospel exemplify for the disciples how the Kingdom of God becomes operative in the heart of the believer, and as we would expect, love is the answer. As Jesus says in verse 44, 'Love your enemies', and in chapter 7:12: 'Whatsoever you wish that men should do to you, do so to them'. *You have heard that it was said... but I say unto you that...*

The first statement in chapter 5:21 relies on the sixth commandment. Jesus says 'You have heard that it was said to the men of old, "You shall not kill and whoever kills shall be liable to judgement". But I say to you that everyone who is angry with his brother shall be liable to judgement'. He says because you love your brother, you will not get angry with him, you will not want to hurt him, you will seek for reconciliation.

Secondly, in chapter 5:27 Jesus refers to the seventh commandment that says you will not commit adultery. If you love your wife, you will not look at another woman, you will not be the cause of the breakup of another man's marriage.

Thirdly, in chapter 5:31, because you love your wife you will not want to divorce her, you will not be attracted to other women, nor cause her to become an adulteress.

Fourthly, in chapter 5:33, because you love God, you will not take the Name of the Lord in vain, or swear an oath, or use His name or His habitation of heaven unworthily but limit your speech to 'yes' and 'no'.

And finally, because you love those who hurt you, you will not want to see them punished unmercifully, but will do all you can to rehabilitate them even if it means giving up your coat, your cloak, or other possessions. You will love your enemy and pray for him, even as God loves enemies of His, causing His sun to rise and His rain to fall on the just and on the unjust.

'You will be perfect, even as your Father, which is in heaven, is perfect' (verse 48).

These examples pretty much cover all the familial and social relationships which a disciple is likely to have. And as it deals comprehensively with life, so it also delivers the universal stratagem by which he may live. The perfection of which Matthew speaks, following the words of Jesus, in the concluding verse of this chapter, is the perfection of love. You therefore must be perfect, as your Father in heaven is perfect (Matthew 5:48), is God's love manifested through the loving care and concern shown by His disciples in every circumstance, and to everybody regardless of their status before God.

They will not cease to be disciples, learners, when they become sons of God, 'sons of your Father who is in heaven' (Matthew 5:45). So, these statements are not exhaustive, but examples of the life now lived by the believer, and these examples indicate that this is the fruit of the life lived by faith, lives known by their fruit even as a tree is known (Matthew 7:16).

Jesus says, 'Love your neighbour, love your enemy.' Those who have some connection with you. Is our love finite? It is certainly unlike His love, or the love of the Father, who loved the world so much that He gave His only Son for our redemption. But according to His grace, His love is poured into our hearts by the Holy Spirit (Romans 5:5).

Is then the gift of His love proportional to our capacity? We cannot love the world as He loved it, or we would be God. Our responsibility is towards those whom He has by one means or another placed in our lives, for good or ill, according to His will. Love is active, not passive, not just a warm emotional feeling. God so *loved* that He *gave*, and what He gave was His only begotten Son (John 3:16). If it remains in the realm of the emotions, it is not love. Love *suffers* long and is kind (1 Corinthians 13:4). Having loved His own which were in the world, Jesus loved them to the uttermost (John 13:1), even to death on the Cross. God's love is love with a positive outcome, and sometimes, suffering love, and so will our love be if it is the love that comes from Him.

A man may lay down his life for his friends, or a husband for his wife, or a mother for her children. The love of God in us will cause us to lay down our lives for other people's friends, for other people's wives and families, not necessarily in a heroic way but as a daily task. This is where the test comes. These are our neighbours, and sometimes our enemies.

We cannot do it!

Only the Holy Spirit in us can pour out His love as we yield ourselves as channels through which he can work, and then all the glory goes to Him. Loving your family may be construed as natural love. To love your neighbour and especially to love your enemy is a different sort of love. When the Lord Jesus says, 'Be ye therefore perfect, even as your Father in heaven is perfect', He is encouraging us to love as He loves.

Luther used to say, 'In scripture, every little daisy becomes a meadow'. The word comes from 2 Kings 4:2, 'Thine handmaid hath not anything in the house.' How little equipped we are to serve our dear Lord, but He brings everything needful with Him, love, grace, patience, kindness, and to what was dead, life returns.

Matthew 5:43-48. The sixth antithesis

The sixth antithesis, Matthew 5:43-48, gives us the concluding section of chapter 5 and It concerns love for your enemy. This section sums up and is the culmination of all that has gone before in this first teaching that Jesus gave to His disciples. The transitional verse, 'therefore, be perfect even as your Father in heaven is perfect, (verse 48) is given as a conclusion at the end of the chapter, introducing a new and different aspect of the believer's life as Jesus continues His teaching in chapter 6.

As we have seen, verses 17-42 had described all the practical ways in which believers should live: towards their brothers, fellow members of the community, towards their wives, towards their own habits of speech, and towards those who would wish them harm. Now, in verse 43, having described all the different ways in which a disciple lives in the love of God, for the first time in this gospel, Jesus uses the word '*love*', a concept which had suffused all the preceding verses without making it explicit. In this sixth antithesis, Jesus says, 'You shall love your enemy, pray for him' (verse 44).

The command to love your neighbour was part of the behaviour expected of the observant Jew, as recorded in Leviticus 19:8. In Jesus' fulfilment of the law and the prophets something more is expected of His disciples. And as we have noted in the previous five antitheses, love is not just a warm emotional feeling, but concrete action, beginning with prayer for them. This becomes for 'those who persecute you' (verse 44) in the sixth antithesis.

Even at this early stage of their discipleship, there appear to be those who would not only try to discourage the believers, but actively attempt to hinder them in various ways from following Jesus; a persecution which became even more vindictive as Jesus' ministry progressed, and of course, following His death and resurrection, many were persecuted for His sake. Even today there are many Christians who are being persecuted for their faith. We may and do pray for these, some for whom we may have a name, but many others unknown to us. And now, into this sixth antithesis comes a concept, an idea, a revelation of the most amazing magnitude. 'Love your enemies, pray for your persecutors so that you may be the sons of your Father who is in heaven' (verse 44). (We recognise that 'sons' used in this way is a generic term and includes daughters).

How these words must have trembled on the lips of Jesus. It was what He had come to earth for, that His Father could have many sons like His own dear Son, and would bring many sons to glory (Hebrews 2:10; Ephesians 1:5; Romans 8:14). Jesus had not yet gone to His Cross and there poured out His blood for the forgiveness of sins, but these disciples were the first fruits, the earnest, the promise of what was to come. And His death on the Cross was retrospective as well as prospective, for it was foreordained from before the foundation of the world.

The love that we have towards an enemy exposes a very precious fact, that entering upon the Kingdom of Heaven experience has enabled us to recognise our status as sons of our Father who is in heaven because His sun and His rain, expressive of His providential love in such a climate, falls on the just and on the unjust (Matthew 5:45).

This is the first time that the appellation 'son' and even more glorious 'of your Father' has been used of human beings in this gospel. His life, the life of the Father, and His love, the love of the Father, has entered into our lives, so that we may show forth His character of love, and *we may call Him Father*, the Father who is no respecter of persons, whose love extends to all, whose sun rises and whose rain falls on the just and the unjust.

And this universal love is displayed by His sons. They don't only love those who love them – even tax collectors do as much (verse 46). They do not only greet their brethren – salutation of others is something that everyone does (verse 47). They must be perfect, even as their Father in heaven is perfect; not sinless, for only the Lord Jesus was sinless, but perfect in showing the love of Jesus, the love of the Father, to all whom He allows into our lives. This however is the conclusion. We must think about Jesus's words more closely and return to the first antithesis.

Matthew 5:22, 29, 30. The teaching of Jesus on the hell of fire.

But I say to you ... whoever says 'You fool', shall be liable to the hell of fire.

If your right eye ... or your right hand, cause you to sin, cut it off and cast it from you. It is better that you lose one of your members than that your whole body be cast into hell.

These verses as we have seen are to do with relationships. In verses 21-27, Jesus is concerned with the relationship of the believer with his brother. The commandment says 'Thou shalt not kill', but Jesus goes further. He says 'do not be angry with your brother', and especially 'do not call him a fool', for the punishment for this is so great that it could incur the judgement of 'the hell of fire' (verse 22). Your gift at the altar is worthless if you are not reconciled to your brother.

Three times in this chapter, hell is mentioned by the Lord Jesus (verses 22, 29, 30). Hell or Hades is the Greek equivalent of the Hebrew Sheol, of which the Old Testament speaks, especially in the Psalms, a place to which it was thought the souls of people went after death, the soul being that part of a person which survives death.

This place was also known as Gehenna, a reference to a place outside Jerusalem where in earlier times, human sacrifice had been offered to the god Moloch, a sacrifice made by fire. It had come to be seen as symbolic of what could happen to people after death if they did not obey the law. Jesus was using symbolism that was familiar to them, but was not an actual location beyond the earth.

In Ephesians 4:9, we read that after Jesus died, He descended into hell, perhaps indicating that whatever the place where unbelieving souls went after death, Jesus was able to go to them and give them an opportunity to rise with Him to some different place or realm. Peter also writes that Jesus was put to death in the flesh, but made alive in the spirit in which He went and preached to the spirits in prison who formerly did not obey, perhaps giving them a further opportunity for repentance (1 Peter 3:18,19). In 2 Peter 3:7, Peter is very sure that ungodly men will be punished, but leaves the mode of punishment unspecified.

We are probably not concerned so much about the destiny of really wicked people as with people whom we have known and loved, who have lived decent lives, who were warm and generous and kind but yet did not have faith. Thankfully we are not in a position to judge what may have transpired in the heart of anyone, least of all those facing death. We do know that we have a loving and merciful God, and we reject the atheist's claim that there is no God, especially that there is no God of mercy, and also reject the beliefs of those who believe that there is no part of a human being which survives death. Though they are of course entitled to their viewpoint, we read in Ephesians 2:12 that to have no belief in God is to be without God and to be without hope in the world.

The use of the word 'hell' shows the seriousness of the situation of those who turn their backs on Jesus, or who are ignorant of His claim upon their lives. There is an eschatological judgement, a time of judgement at the end of time, described in Matthew 7:21 and Matthew 25:30 and 46, where the concept though not the term hell is described as a place of punishment.

We can only re-affirm that we believe God to be a merciful Judge. Paul writes: 'We must all stand before the judgement seat of God, (Romans 14:10), and each of us must give account of himself to God (verse 12). He also writes: 'O death, where is thy sting? O grave, where is thy victory? The sting of death is sin, the strength of sin is the law' (1 Corinthians 15:55. A.V. margin). Hell has no terrors for those who know the Lord Jesus. Their responsibility is to love and pray for others, that they might have an openness of heart, and the kind of hunger only He can satisfy... this is what we pray for them, for we know that God will not lightly condemn those for whom His Son shed His precious blood.

If heaven is where we see Jesus face to face (1 Corinthians 13:12), then hell is the opposite, a place where we cannot see

Him, where we are eternally and entirely separated from Him, where we cannot talk to Him, pray to Him, receive His comforting presence and assurance of salvation. For most of us, that would be hell indeed. Hell: separation from God. Heaven: to see His face.

Matthew 5:27-34. The teaching of Jesus on adultery and divorce

You have heard that it was said, You shall not commit adultery. But I say to you, that everyone who looks at a woman lustfully has already committed adultery with her in his heart (Matthew 5: 27).

It was also said, 'whoever divorces his wife, let him give her a certificate of divorce. But I say to you, that everyone who divorces his wife, except on the grounds of unchastity, makes her an adulteress, and wherever marries a divorced woman commits adultery' (Matthew 5: 31).

Jesus describes the thesis in verse 31. He says, 'Whoever divorces his wife, let him give her a certificate of divorce' for this is what was said under the law (Deuteronomy 24:1-4). But Jesus says, 'But I say to you', this is His antithetical statement, 'I say to you, that everyone who divorces his wife except on the grounds of unchastity makes her an adulteress' (verse 32).

We find the thesis statement in Deuteronomy as repeated by Mathew difficult on two levels but still need some reassurance about the antithetical statement of Jesus. According to Deuteronomy, our first difficulty is the assumption that it is always the man who has the ability to divorce his wife, whether or not that is her desire too, which in our society is not always the case, and thus it appears to suggest that the responsibility for maintaining the marriage lies ultimately with the husband's decision. Even when the bond between them is broken beyond repair and for the wife the only acceptable solution is divorce, the wife still has no say in the matter. It is hard for us to accept the Old Testament view of divorce even though Deuteronomy is there for our guidance.

Secondly, the charge of adultery or unchastity must always lie against the woman though the man and not the woman may have been the one to commit adultery. This indicates an inequality in marriage, suggesting as it does that the adultery of a wife is more to be condemned than that of a husband; that her infidelity becomes a reasonable ground for divorce, even though her husband too may have been unfaithful. Though we do not know what form the marriage ceremony would have taken in the time when Deuteronomy was written, assuming there to have been one, it is safe to assume that there was some form of a vow or vows which were binding on both husband and wife. In ancient times, women often had no privileges, no rights, not even over their own children or their own bodies, yet were often expected to be the linchpin of the family, though of course, then as now, every family is and was different and what is true for one is not necessarily true for another.

Adultery may be a reason for divorce. It may also lead to further adultery after divorce. And Jesus says that unchastity cannot be tolerated within marriage, and further, if unchastity has occurred, then after divorce, remarriage is forbidden. This may appear draconian, until we attempt to unravel the reasons behind what Jesus is saying. We have seen from verse 21 onwards that what Jesus is aiming for in these verses is the expression of love; love for brothers, both natural brothers and brothers in the church, for enemies, for persecutors. Love expresses itself in compassion and kindness. This is the righteousness of which Jesus speaks in verses 19 and 20, for God is love.

Adultery implies covetousness and theft, and a lack of love for the persons in another marriage, covetousness perhaps leading to the theft of another man's wife, or another woman's husband. Jesus also speaks here of looking lustfully at a woman, in such a way as to have already committed adultery with her in his heart. Such is the standard of purity against adultery which Jesus expects of His followers (verse 28).

61

Unchastity, marital infidelity is the breaking of the bond between husband and wife, the bond which He created and which was His design when He instituted marriage. 'Therefore a man leaves his father and mother and cleaves to his wife and the two become one flesh. What God has joined, let no man put asunder' (Matthew 19:6). We remember that Jesus is speaking to His disciples. He is saying that this is the way for them to go; He is not making a juridical statement for the secular world.

The very fact that not to commit adultery is contained in the list of requirements to be adhered to in the Ten Commandments, proves that there always has been a tendency on the part of human beings to look further than their own marriage partners. But these disciples have entered the kingdom of heaven through faith. What may have been a temptation for them should no longer apply, for having become sons of their Father who is in heaven, they have the life of their Father, the life of the Lord Jesus within them governing their actions. They have entered a new realm, where Jesus reigns, a realm of love where love determines life, living.

The ten commandments are very precious. They are a description of the nature of God, who He is, and how we know Him. But Jesus is going back beyond the Mosaic law and the ten commandments to the creation of a man and a woman in the Garden of Eden, to that which God had intended from the beginning when He had created them. Eve came from Adam. She had been part of him. Now she was part of him in a new and different way. God joined them together. They were one (Genesis 2:24). God was creating the bedrock of family life, the foundation of society.

But Jesus is going even beyond that. In Chapter 19, verse 9, He says, 'whoever divorces his wife *except for unchastity* commits adultery'. Because marriage is so important, it is only unchastity, immorality, which can truly break the marriage bond. Under Jewish law, as we have seen, the wife, the woman, was entirely dependent upon her husband. She belonged to him. He owned her. She was his possession. We recall throughout the gospels the kindness of Jesus towards women, and His respect for them.

By declaring their unity in marriage, for God had made them one, Jesus was also declaring their equality before God.

This is why adultery is inconsistent with marriage for the believer. God has joined them, one to the other, and through adultery they are seeking to undo, to destroy what God has done. He has created a unity, an equality between men and women, an equality between *this* man and *this* woman, based on self-giving love for one another.

But Jesus recognizes that even for believers, adultery, seeking some other partner, happens. To mitigate the effect of adultery on the marriage for the woman, He allows her husband to divorce her, to remove the adultery from the marriage, thus returning them both into the unmarried status. We do not know how many divorced women there were in Palestine at the time of Jesus. Being unable to marry again, perhaps they lived as widows, or returned to their parent's home, for to be divorced was a matter of shame, whether they themselves had been guilty of adultery or not.

In Hebrews 13:4 we read, 'Let marriage be held in honour among all, and let the marriage bed be undefiled'. Marriage is honourable in all and must therefore be protected against impurity, defilement, for through impurity, marriage is destroyed. On this level, divorce becomes the instrument through which marriage is protected.

O, the grace and mercy of the Lord Jesus! He could have advocated excommunication for adultery but He did not, thus avoiding catastrophic consequences especially for the woman who was financially dependent on her husband, and above all, ensuring that repentance and reconciliation within the community remained a possibility.

There is forgiveness!

Marriage in the secular world is a different experience. Jesus is talking about marriage between believers, understood differently, *sacramentally*, for He is also present in the marriage. It is not pre-eminently a legal contract though of course it is recognized as such. Christian marriage within the Christian community should make possible the provision of pastoral care in love, and the proclamation of grace, to support the marriage, and to provide help if at any time it appears to be in danger of breaking down; and certainly *never* to excommunicate those whose marriage has ended in divorce.

On the occasion of the incident of the woman taken in adultery as recorded in John's gospel (John 8:1-11), Jesus said, 'Let him that is without sin cast the first stone at her', for stoning was the recommended punishment meted out to women taken in adultery. Jesus was making two points here. One, where was the man, for the woman could not have committed adultery by herself, and two, adultery was not unknown even among religious leaders such as the scribes and Pharisees (verse 3). Thus challenged by Jesus, they crept away one by one until Jesus and the woman were left alone. There was no condemnation from Jesus for the woman, only compassion. Jesus said to the woman 'Where are your accusers? Has no one condemned you?' She said, 'no one, Lord'. And Jesus said, 'neither do I condemn you. Go and sin no more' (John 8:10, 11).

Was Jesus reneging on His earlier teaching about adultery? No. He had compassion on the sinner, not the sin. The centre of Jesus' teaching, the very core, was the unconditional love of God for men and women. He rejected divorce and unchastity because they destroy lives, the lives of the perpetrators and very often, the lives of those closest to them. But He also rejects the indifference to the sanctity of marriage of church members. In the case of the woman of John 8 He rejected those religious Jewish people who would have condemned the woman to death. In either case, He rejects those neglecting to maintain the highest standards of married life in marital faithfulness, and yet quick to judge others.

He is the God of all grace (1 Peter 5:10). In the final analysis, however distressing divorce may be, excommunication, cutting someone off from the means of reconciliation and forgiveness would be and in some cases, has been, among some believers, much worse. Whatever has caused the breakdown of the marriage, these hurt, vulnerable believers must be welcomed back into the fold of God where they may find forgiveness and love and compassion.

Paul had this astounding revelation, that marriage reflects the relationship between Christ and the Church, that His aim is to present the church to Himself as a glorious church, without spot or blemish or any such thing, a church nourished and cherished by Him as His Bride (Ephesians 6:25-33).

This wonderful truth is portrayed in even greater magnificence at the marriage supper of the Lamb in Revelation 19:7. Ephesians 6:25 says 'Husbands, love your wives as Christ loved the church'. This is quite an expectation to put upon husbands. The passage continues in verse 28, 'Husbands should love their wives as their own bodies for no man ever hates his own flesh but nourishes and cherishes it as Christ does the church'. With such a husband, a wife would gladly be subject to her husband as to the Lord (verse 22). Indeed, being subject to one another out of reverence for Christ would become a total joy and privilege (verse 21). We are well aware that this is by no means the case in every marriage, and separation is sometimes the only answer for the protection of both the wife and children. Under the conditions advocated by Paul however, every Christian marriage would indeed reflect the marriage between Christ and the church.

Marriage takes on the character of a sacrament, as sacred, as we reflect on the words of Jesus, and on the mystery which Paul describes in Ephesians 6:32, and not to be undertaken lightly, as the Book of Common Prayer has it. We thank God again and again for His grace and forgiveness when we fail, when we come short of the ideal which He has set before us. We also thank Him for the joy and happiness and fulfilment we find within marriage and pray for those whose experience of marriage has been, and perhaps still is, a bondage from which they long to escape. Jesus' compassion extends to us all.

The basis Jesus gives for divorce is unchastity, usually regarded as adultery, and of course, unchastity does have the connotation of adultery. But unchastity can mean much more and also much less than adultery. Adultery involves another person, someone from outside the marriage. Either the husband or wife has discovered another person who appears to fulfil their needs more adequately. But there is also a tendency within the human heart, which is not just the desire for, or the wish to involve, the companionship of another person. This other relationship could apparently quite legitimately involve long hours at work, pursuing a lucrative career at the expense of time with the children, or their mother, leaving her feeling neglected. Or it could be a feeling of inadequacy which prompts the husband into belittling his wife, not only at home in front of the children, but in public too.

There are many *apparently* trivial ways in which a woman can be regarded as insignificant, worthless in her husband's eyes; which may not seem to be terribly important to others, and yet over a long period, devastatingly cruel. This sometimes occurs when the husband has high paternalistic values, regarding himself as the naturally prominent figure in this marriage on the grounds of his gender. Surely Jesus, with His knowledge of human nature must have had such cruelty in mind when He used the word 'unchastity'. And surely He would allow that such behaviour also merits divorce if or when the situation becomes unbearable.

This also encourages us, members of the same family of God, to look with compassion on those who suffer in this way, to love them and do all that we are permitted to do for them without intrusion or invasion of privacy. May the Lord teach us how to be humble servants of one another; to love one another for His dear sake.

Marital fidelity, faithfulness to each other in all circumstances and whatever the present difficulties within the family, is what Jesus desires for us all. When things become strained, as they can do sometimes, there is Jesus. He is there holding out His scarred hands in compassion and welcome, His arms to embrace. Come to Me, He says and you will find rest to your souls, for My yoke is easy and My burden is light. And if we are wise, we avail ourselves *together* of His invitation.

Matthew 5:33. The prohibition against swearing

Again you have heard that it was said to the men of old, 'You shall not swear falsely, but shall perform to the Lord what you have sworn'. But I say to you, Do not swear at all, either by heaven, for it is the throne of God, or by the earth, for it is His footstool, or by Jerusalem, for it is the city of the Great King (Matthew 5:33-34).

In Numbers we read, 'This is what the Lord has commanded. When a man vows a vow to the Lord, or swears an oath to bind himself by a pledge, he shall not break his word; he shall do according to all that proceeds out of his mouth' (Numbers 30:2). and in Deuteronomy 'When you make a vow to the Lord your God, you shall not be slack to pay it; for the Lord your God will surely require it of you, and it would be sin in you. But if you refrain from vowing, it shall be no sin in you. You shall be careful to perform what has passed your lips, for you have voluntarily vowed to the Lord your God what you have promised with your mouth' (Deuteronomy 23:21-22).

In the Old Testament, an oath was a solemn commitment to God to do or give something to Him, or for Him. The story of Jephthah's daughter is a terrible warning against vowing an oath which had appalling consequences. Jephthah, one of the judges of Israel before the people of Israel demanded a king, promised God that if he won a victory over the Ammonites, he would offer up as a sacrifice to the Lord the first thing that came to meet him when he returned home (Judges 11:31). The tragedy was that his beloved daughter came to meet him, verse 34, rather than the animal he had been expecting, but he kept his vow and sacrificed his daughter. He was being obedient to Numbers 30:3 and Deuteronomy 23:21, but surely that was not God's Intention The words we speak are very powerful. We can hurt someone with words. Deuteronomy 23 recommends that a person thinks twice before committing himself to making a vow.

People do make vows, however. Sometimes quite unconsciously, in a crisis or an emergency they will say, 'O God, if you will only get me out of this mess... this predicament... then I will...' They are looking for a quid pro quo arrangement. His ears are always open to our cry, and He will answer according to His omniscient compassion, His lovingkindness and His knowledge of what is best for us.

While Jesus is sympathetic to the Old Testament way of performing a vow, He takes it further. He say, 'Do not swear *at all*' (verse 34). This can be a problem for people serving on a jury, or for witnesses in a trial, though now provision is made for people to make a solemn affirmation which makes no reference to God or the Bible. Jews do not swear before a court.

So, what does Jesus mean by His statement 'do not swear at all'? Is there a difference between swearing a solemn oath as in Leviticus 19:11 and taking the Name of the Lord in vain as in Exodus 20:7, as opposed to the casual use of swear words used by many people today? Does Jesus forbid all three?

A person should be reliable, not given to false statements, and therefore it should not be necessary to back up one's word with an oath 'Let your yes be yes and your no, no', He says (verse 37). We do not need the support of heaven or earth or Jerusalem to suggest that our word is reliable (verse 35). He says, 'Swear not at all'. Did Jesus ever resort to swearing? Then neither should we. At the trial before Caiaphas, the High Priest, Caiaphas adjures Jesus 'by the living God' to tell him whether He is indeed the Son of God. This is to understand Caiaphas as exhorting Jesus to an oath. Jesus does not answer with an oath, but with the simple statement, 'you have said', leaving the responsibility for the statement with the High Priest without contesting its truth.

To swear by God is to bring God down into our little humanness, to desecrate and dishonour His Name, using His Nature, His Name, even though ultimately we can have only a limited conception of who He is, for He is far beyond our understanding. 'To whom, then, will you liken God, or what likeness can compare with Him? (Isaiah 40:18). Frequent swearing is an indication of the untrustworthiness of the person using it. In rabbinical Judaism, they made a 'fence around the Torah', to prevent the misuse of the Divine Name.

What Jesus is demanding is utter truthfulness. This cannot be achieved by using a formula. In fact, suspicion falls upon those who routinely use swear words formulaically. It may be an indication that the person cannot be trusted, or maybe not honest. It gives sanction to the common lie. But above all, when the name of God is invoked it is as though God Himself is reduced to a mere formula. Jesus is really pleading for a more comprehensive sanctification of the Name of God, His heavenly Father, and consequently, as a result, the abrogation of oaths. How powerless after all is the human being, who, however many oaths he uses, still cannot even change the colour of his hair by speaking to it (verse 36). So there is no point in swearing. It does not change anything.

According to William Penn the Quaker, swearing is forbidden by Christ, is detrimental to human nature because it creates two kinds of truth, and is unnecessary (*Principles of Quakerism*, W Comfort, 1909). The prohibition against swearing is one of the principles of the kingdom, the kingdom of heaven which Jesus' disciples are experiencing as they have come to repentance and faith, according to His proclamation in Matthew 4:17.

The question is, how far, if at all, are the prohibitions of the Lord Jesus intended for the kingdoms of this world, as we saw in the discussion about divorce and marriage. Jesus is moving towards perfection. 'Be ye therefore perfect, even as your Father in heaven is perfect,' He says. Such perfection, the perfection of love for one's brother, wife, enemy, and love for God the Father, is available only to those who have embraced the way of discipleship, who are enjoying their status as people of the kingdom of God, and are living in obedience to the word of God and His will, and by His grace, His perfecting grace.

There are many good, upright people, full of kindness and helpful support for others who yet would not claim, or wish to consider, entering into the kingdom of heaven through the door of repentance. Billy Graham is reported as having said, 'It is the Holy Spirit's job to convict, It is God's job to judge, it is my job to love'. We do not judge them. We love them.

Matthew 5:38-42. The teaching of Jesus on retaliation and non-violence

You have heard that it was said, 'An eye for an eye, and a tooth for a tooth' (Exodus 21:24, Leviticus 24:20, Deuteronomy 19:21). But I say unto you, αλλα υμιν λεγω. Do not resist one who is evil (who intends to do you harm). But if anyone strikes you on the right cheek, turn to him the other also. And if anyone would sue you and take your coat, let him have your cloak as well. And if anyone forces you to go with him one mile, go with him two miles. Give to him who begs from you, and do not refuse him who would borrow from you.

Jesus goes back to the law of retaliation, *lex talionis*, an eye for an eye, and a tooth for a tooth. This was in itself a good law because it limited the amount of damage you could do to someone who had damaged you. If he had knocked out one of your teeth, you could knock out one of his, but only one. So a limit was set to vengeance and hot-headed retaliation, vindictiveness and cruelty. It is justice. It means that you cannot take the law into your own hands.

At the time of Jesus, the rabbis were already limiting the use of force by legitimating the payment of money as restitution, a new interpretation of an Old Testament commandment which perhaps left neither the victim nor the perpetrator completely satisfied. Jesus is going further. He is saying, 'According to the law, you have the right of limited retaliation, but I say to you, *forgo your right.*'

All the way through this chapter, Jesus has been recommending that life in the Kingdom of Heaven is a different kind of life. Forgoing one's rights proclaims to the world around, through this lived discipleship, that it is possible to live a life which gives glory to the Father who is in heaven (verse 16).

The kingdom life is a life of love. Love means that we renounce violence and retaliation (verses 39-41). Love means giving up one's rights in order to allow the other person the advantage. But these verses are not so easy of interpretation. We are insulted, perhaps not once or twice, even if the insult does not take the form of a slap on the cheek. We are taken to court, and sued for our tunic or undergarment, which in some instances in the time of Jesus could be the only one we possess; and we offer our cloak also which also serves as a blanket to keep us warm at night. A Roman soldier, part of the occupying power, forces us to go with him to carry his baggage, which he is legally entitled to do, and even though his destination may be different from our own, we offer to go the second mile with him.

This is revolutionary behaviour. Can Jesus really mean that his disciples should behave like this? Are we being passive? A soft touch? Don't we recognise that the person who slaps us on the cheek is capable of further and more damaging aggression? That losing our cloak/blanket in the cold night is really not a good idea. That carrying the soldier's impedimenta in the heat of the day is bad enough for one mile let alone two.

All we can do is look to Jesus. Jesus commands the disciple who hurries to Him with a sword to protect Him, to put it away (Matthew 26:51-54); He said that He had the right to appeal to His Father to send Him more than twelve legions of angels to prevent His arrest, but chose to allow the chief priests and the elders of the people to seize him (Matthew 26:53-57).

Some have used these verses as an opportunity given by Jesus to participate responsibly in secular judicial power (thus obliterating the demands of Jesus in respect of the Kingdom of Heaven). Others have seen the attempt to include Jesus' words as participation in worldly authority, even in politics, but with an attempt at evangelical love for the neighbour. But it is impossible to forgo the use of force on the basis of rationality alone, as these interpretations of the text demonstrate.

This new way of righteousness opened up for us by Jesus demands renunciation of one's own rights as an expression of love, and as a way of proclaiming the kingdom. It sets the disciple free from looking ahead to the consequences. It gives him peace in his heart. Love cannot be used as a secular aid to societal survival as these expositors suggest, because it becomes our own characteristic only as it derives from God, who is outside all worldly authority and over it at the same time.

We turn again to Jesus. Philippians 2:1-11 gives us such a wonderful picture of the Lord Jesus leaving His heavenly home and coming down to earth, giving up, renouncing, all His rights as the eternal Son of God in order to make Himself of no reputation, emptying himself and taking the form of a servant, enduring death on a cross. No wonder God highly exalted Him and gave Him the Name above every Name, that at the Name of Jesus every knee should bow. This was love indeed. He did it for us, because He loved us. And this is the standard by which we 'love one another as I have loved you. Continue in My love' (John 15:12).

And this love overflows even to our enemies.

Matthew 5:43-48. The teaching of Jesus about our enemies

You have heard that it was said, 'You shall love your neighbour, but hate your enemy'. But I say to you, love your enemies and pray for them who persecute you, that you may be the sons of your Father in heaven, for He makes His sun to rise on the evil and the good, and sends rain on the just and on the unjust. For if you love those who love you, what reward have you? Do not even the tax collectors do the same? And if you salute only your brethren, what more are you doing than others? You therefore must be perfect even as your Father in Heaven is perfect.

Earlier, we thought about this last statement of Jesus. He had been speaking in a negative way. 'But I say to you, do not resist one who is evil. If anyone strikes you on the right cheek, turn the other cheek also' (verse 39).

Now His command becomes more positive and urgent. 'But I say to you, love your enemies; be perfect'. The tone is different but continues the theme of love in action. This love is where the compatibility of the commands of Jesus lies. As we have noted, life in the kingdom is a life of love, and what our heavenly Father wants for us is to enjoy a life of love such as He and His Son enjoy, in the precious communion they have with one another. Jesus says, 'I and the Father are one' (John 10:30). And He goes on to pray to His Father in John 17:23, 'I in them and You in Me, so that they may become perfectly one and that the world may know that You have sent Me and have loved them even as You love Me'.

This is Jesus' prayer to His Father for His disciples before He was taken from the Garden of Gethsemane to His death on the cross. We cannot believe that His Father would not have heard and answered that prayer, the whole import of which is that the love of the Son for the Father, and the love of the Father for the Son is graciously, wonderfully extended to those whom He has redeemed with His precious blood.

We read these verses on the knees of the spirit, knowing our own frailty, but also knowing that what He has promised He is more than able to perform (Romans 4:21.) This is a life lived in fellowship, in loving fellowship with the Father and the Son and the Holy Spirit, which reaches out to others in love; to friends, neighbours, wives and husbands, and enemies; even as God has reached out to us in His great love wherewith He loved us, even when we dead in our trespasses and sins (Ephesians 2:4).

Viewed in this context, love for our enemies becomes the most natural thing in the world for believers. Living in this fellowship, this kingdom, one with their loving heavenly Father and the Lord Jesus, there is no question of hate, only benediction, blessing, intercession for those whose lives have been affected in some way that precludes them from seeking to enter the kingdom. We pray for our friends and our enemies as Jesus taught us. He says 'pray for those who despitefully use you and persecute you, that you may be sons of your Father in heaven, for He makes His sun to rise and His rain to fall on all, indiscriminately, without respect of persons.

Is this a counsel of perfection? Yes, indeed if it is regarded as purely ethical. And few, if any, would claim to have arrived at that stage of discipleship. But God! But God who is rich in mercy has shed His love abroad in our hearts by the Holy Spirit

(Ephesians 2:4, Romans 5:5). We cannot do it, but He can and does do it in us. Gundry writes, the perfection of love brings to a climax the description of surpassing righteousness in the sixth antithesis. In all of them, Matthew has shown that Jesus carried out the tendencies of the Old Testament law to their true ends. Old Testament prohibitions of murder and adultery escalate to prohibitions of anger and lust. Old Testament prohibitions or limitations on divorce or oaths escalate to demands for marital compassion and simple truthfulness, and the guard against revenge, to love neighbours and hate enemies escalates to the requirements of meekness and love even for enemies. [Robert. H. Gundry, Wm B Eerdmans Publishing Co, 1994]

Jesus uses the word for a personal enemy in everyday life rather than the word for an enemy of the state. This is important because it indicates enemies who come against a man or woman personally, with evil intent. Luz (p 350), quotes Dietrich Bonhoeffer, a German theologian and scholar who was executed at the end of World War 2 for an assassination attempt on Hitler, as saying, 'By our enemies Jesus means those who are quite intractable and utterly unresponsive to our love'. To anticipate Matthew 7:1, the believer does not judge, but leaves the judgement to a merciful Judge who knows all things, the Father of the One who prayed, 'Father, forgive them, for they know not what they do' (Luke 23:34).

Jesus is speaking of perfection not in terms of evolution but of transformation, 'so that you may be sons of your Father who is in heaven (verse 45). As John expresses it, 'But to all who received Him, He gave the power to become children of God, even to them who believed on His Name' (John 1:12), giving believers the privilege of calling Him Father (Matthew 6:9).

This is why the imperative 'Be perfect', is so radical. It leaves no room for an either/or both/and way of life. This of course is the way Jesus lived, walked. Only one uncompromised way of life could be perfect, whole, complete; a life of complete dependence on, and utter obedience to the will of God, a renunciation of all perceived rights, a life of walking in love towards all.

Many have tried to walk His way. Such a way has sometimes been referred to as the 'imitation of Christ', and though it was the way He lived, our lives are both more and less an imitation of His. Less, because He was the spotless Lamb of God, taking upon Himself the sins of the world, something which of course we could never imitate. More because by His grace we are being conformed, transformed, transfigured, metamorphosed, into the image of God's dear Son, (Romans 8:29), a transformation of which He had no need.

By His grace, though we have the treasure of the living Christ within us, we are like worthless, fragile, earthen vessels, clay pots (2 Corinthians 4:7), but the life of love which He generates within us is genuine, real and above all, our own, as each believer becomes another ray of the same sun, another facet of the same diamond, and all together proclaim the beauty of the Lord Jesus.

Matthew 5:17-48. A summary

Do not think that I came to abolish the Law and the prophets.
I came not to destroy but to fulfil (Matthew 5:17).

Jesus has made His intention clear. This section of the sermon on the mount is surely an intentional intensification of the Torah by Jesus, such that life was never before experienced like this until He came to reveal it to us, and to make it possible for us to receive it by the convicting power of the Holy Spirit.

Throughout Hebrews chapter 11, there is a catalogue of Old Testament servants of God who had an intimate knowledge of God through faith. Hebrews tells us, these men and women of faith all died in faith, not having received the promise, God having provided some better thing for us, that they without us should not be made perfect (Hebrews 11:39). God has provided some better thing for us! How absolutely wonderful become the words of Jesus to us, as we begin to understand their import, 'Think not that I have come to abolish the law and the prophets. I came not to abolish them but to *fulfil* them (Matthew 5:17).

What a glorious fulfilment is this, that under the New Covenant, the New Testament, in the new kingdom, we frail and flawed human beings can become sons of God, living the perfect life of love even as Jesus did.

Christians are not super-achievers, merely humble vessels, through whom the light of the glorious gospel of God in the face of Jesus Christ can be seen (2 Corinthians 4:6). Nobody rejects the statement that 'your heavenly Father is perfect'. Of course He is. Perfect and complete and whole. Nothing can be added to Him or taken away from Him. There is absolutely no doubt that He is all that He is claimed to be in His word, and more, because even the greatest theologically trained mind cannot 'find out God' (Job 37:23). If they could, He would not be God.

Can such perfection be extended to humble believers? This may appear to be more doubtful, and the further along the Christian journey we travel the greater the element of doubt as to our fitness to come into the presence of a Holy God. All we can do is to trust in the word of God which invites us into His presence; that He has provided for us 'a new and living way, which He has consecrated for us, through the veil, that is to say, His flesh; the boldness to enter into the holiest by the blood of Jesus (Hebrews 10:19). And so we do, trusting in Him, and in His grace which is sufficient for us, for His strength is made perfect in our weakness (2 Corinthians 12:9).

To summarise Matthew 5:17-48, we could say that these verses are *humanly* pragmatic. Jesus uses parts of the body; eye, hand, head, hair, and clothing; tunic/coat, cloak, to emphasise His teaching. They emphasise the human part of daily living as a disciple, as a learner, and their relationships within the community; their brothers and sisters; and also those outside the community who could be in need; official representatives of the government; or people who want to do them harm.

Matthew Chapter 6

Matthew 6:1-34. The teaching of Jesus on the Mount continued

Beware of practising your piety before men, in order to be seen by them, for then you will have no reward from your Father who is in heaven (verse 1).

In chapter 6, we come to a different relationship, that of the disciple to God whom he is learning to call 'Father'. In Chapter 5:17, we had seen how Jesus came not to abolish but to fulfil the law and the prophets; and that through Him His disciples could experience, not a different law but the law filled out and overflowing with the love of God, manifested in His 'sons', Matthew 5:45 (the generic term for both sons and daughters), in their personal and public lives.

At that time, the Mosaic law was expected to be observed and relevant to both Jewish society and individuals, but Jesus says that the upholders of the law, the scribes and Pharisees were actually, in effect, the opposers of the law because their understanding of it was only ritualistically societal.

For many ordinary Jews, the law had become the religious ritual into which they as the Jewish people as a whole had been instructed, but it did not necessarily or always have for them a personal application. It was a profound regret for Jesus that their religious observation was only that. It appeared not to touch the hearts of the scribes and the Pharisees, the leaders and shepherds of God's people, or the people themselves, although no doubt there were many exceptions. They were following a code of conduct and however hard they tried, it did not grant them the righteousness they craved, for it did not bring into a personal relationship with God. This was of course not true of all the people nor of all the Pharisees. Certainly,

Nicodemus had thought deeply about his relationship with God (John 3:1,2) and we may believe that Joseph of Arimathea did too (John 19:38).

This is what the Prophets understood, that there was a need for God to become real to His people on a personal level, as individuals, even as they followed the sacrifices and legal teaching which was designed to bring them nearer to Him. This is why the Lord Jesus came to fulfil both the law and the prophets.

Prophecy stretches from a prophetic concern with daily life (see 1 Sam 9:6, 1 Kings 14:7) through the proclamation of the eternal principles of the unchanging God, to the mysterious forthtelling of the distant future, and each of these manifestations of prophecy were of inestimable value to the people of Israel, especially in times of war, or distress or exile.

But even a cursory glance at the Old Testament prophetic scriptures will uncover the theme of a necessary repentance towards God because of a turning *away* from Him, from His holiness, from His worship; and in many cases, *towards* idolatry, replacing and sometimes including the worship of Yahweh with the worship of the gods of the nations surrounding Israel. As the prophets had foretold, here, in this insignificant corner of Israel, on this mountain, Jesus, the dayspring from on high, was visiting His people to give light to those who sat in darkness and in the shadow of death, and to guide their feet into the way of peace (Luke 1:78,79). Zechariah the father of John the Baptist had prophesied this, right from the beginning of the coming of the Lord Jesus as a child, Jesus the incarnate Son of God.

The true light that enlightens every man was coming into the world... and to all who received Him, who believed in His name, He gave the power to become children of God (John 1:9,12). The word became flesh and dwelt among us! (John 1:14). How those prophets of old would have rejoiced to see His day, even as Abraham did (John 8:56). Jesus was setting His seal of authority on all that the prophets had said and done in the power of the Holy Spirit who inspired them, not only through their witness to the truth, but in many cases their torture and martyrdom 'of whom the world was not worthy' (Hebrews 11:38).

He Himself, in and of Himself, was the fulfilment of the law and the prophets. This was what He came to do 'when He came unto His own' (John 1:11). How utterly incomprehensible that His own received Him not (John 1:11) He, the precious, long foretold Messiah for whom they had been waiting, Jesus. He is the prophet foretold by Moses whom the Lord raised up (Deuteronomy 18:15). He is prophet, priest and king. In Him dwells all the fullness of the Godhead bodily, and we are complete in Him (Colossians 2:10 A.V.).

The Pharisees, we may believe, with great sincerity, were trying to follow the Torah as revealed to Moses, attempting through their minute observation of every detail of the law to achieve purity before God. But they had missed the point. Pharisee means *'separate'*, and originally, this indicated that they considered themselves to be separated to God, as representative of His chosen people.

How wonderful if that had continued to be the case! But in effect, they separated themselves from the ordinary people as being spiritually superior to them. Separation in the sense of sanctification, becoming holy, separate from all that would hinder a right relationship with God, is not 'separation *from*' people but utter separation *to* God alone, the Sanctifier. And when had the prophets of old ever separated themselves from the people? They sat among them (Ezekiel 8:1); they walked among them (Elijah, 1Kings 18:21); they laboured among them (Amos 1:1); encouraging them to return to the Lord (Hosea 6:1).

This the Pharisees had not grasped. They were indeed blind guides leading the blind (Matthew 23:16, 15:4). In Hebrew, *hearing means receiving*, acting upon what is heard. They had not really heard or received the word which said that God desires mercy and steadfast love and not sacrifice, the Kingdom of God rather than burnt offerings, a verse in Hosea's prophecy of which Jesus twice reminded them (Hosea 6:6; Matthew 9:13; 12:7).

Jesus' condemnation of them was that they shut the Kingdom of Heaven against men, for they neither entered it themselves nor allowed those who would enter, to go in (Matthew 23:13), and for that Jesus called them *'hypocrites'*, play actors, playing a role but not aware of the reality behind what they were doing. They wanted to hang on to their cosy esoteric way of life and yet came no nearer to that precious relationship with God for which many of them had been seeking.

We have noted that as members of the Sanhedrin, the ruling council of the Jews, it is possible that Nicodemus and Joseph of Arimathea were Pharisees, and there may well have been others. The teaching of Jesus for them was life-transforming, and there is always a remnant, a group of those who see things differently (Isaiah 6:13; 10: 20-21).

But it is therefore significant but not surprising that in Chapter 6, the next part of the Sermon on the Mount, the scribes and Pharisees are referred to by Jesus as hypocrites. Jesus says to His disciples, 'Beware of practising your righteousness, δικαιοσύνην, before men' (Matthew 6:1). Righteousness means being in a right relationship with God which these people patently were not. Righteousness is a very personal, private thing, between the believer and His Lord, and not to be paraded before others.

Jesus says that the righteousness of His disciples must exceed that of the scribes and Pharisees (Matthew 5:20). They must look to Him only, the author and finisher of their faith, and not to men for approval, as the Pharisees did. They must look to Him because their righteousness, their right relationship with the Father, comes through Him, by faith. This special relationship encompasses almsgiving, praying and fasting (verse 2, 5, 16), not as ritually religious practises, but as an expression of that relationship with their Lord. Jesus' disciples may practise all these important aspects of piety, almsgiving, prayer and fasting in loving response to their heavenly Father, but Jesus speaks of the futility of all these when performed purely as a religious or devotional exercise seen by others and designed to boost the religious reputation of the one who practises it.

Matthew 6:1-5. The teaching of Jesus on almsgiving

When you give alms, sound no trumpet before you as the hypocrites do in the streets and in the synagogues that they may be praised by men. Truly I say to you, they have their reward. But when you give alms, let not your right hand know what your left hand is doing.

In Jesus' inimitable way, He uses these three aspects of Pharisaic piety, almsgiving, prayer and fasting, to show His disciples another way, a way by which they may draw near to their Father who is in heaven. He begins with almsgiving. He does not say that His disciples should not practice almsgiving. Jesus said of Himself, 'Foxes have holes, and the birds of the air have nests, but the Son of Man has nowhere to lay His head' (Matthew 8:20). He knew what it was to be homeless, and the joy of being received into the home of Mary and Martha (Luke 10:38). He was grateful for the many kindnesses shown to Him and His disciples.

But such overt almsgiving as the Pharisees practised was designed to give glory to themselves, and not to God. Their righteousness was an empty show.

It is not the practice of almsgiving that the Lord Jesus denigrates, but its degradation into something which does not have the purpose and meaning for which it was originally intended by God. The word 'almsgiving' is derived from the Greek word for 'mercy'. Both Matthew and Luke record Jesus as saying 'Blessed are the merciful ', 'Be merciful, even as your Father in heaven is merciful' (Matthew 5:7; Luke 6:36) so give alms because I have given you much.

Deuteronomy says, 'For the poor will never cease to be in your land, therefore I command you saying, you shall freely open your hand to your brother, to your needy and to the poor in your land' (Deuteronomy 15:11). I, the Lord have given to you. So now you have the ability to share with others. Be merciful! Also when you *pray,* pray so that your prayer becomes communication with God and not with yourself (Luke 18:11). When you *fast,* fast from what is bodily, earthly, so that you may enter by the Spirit, into the realm of the Spirit, and may not be seen of men to fast (verse 18).

All this pious activity on the part of the Pharisees is for personal self-gratification. Jesus wants His disciples to be as unobtrusive as possible in their private and personal lives, waiting upon His Father and theirs, as they share their God-given gifts with others.

Later, there was a certain care of the poor in the synagogue, but at the time of the gospel, the distribution of the tithe or the tenth of their income was left to the individual. It has been noted that Jesus called the Pharisees hypocrites, from the Greek meaning play actors., and that an actor is someone who takes on the character of another. In the case of the hypocrites of whom Jesus speaks, they pretend mercy, they pretend benevolence while at the same time living luxuriously and extravagantly and attempting not to get too close to the 'ordinary person'.

As an example, we remember the episode of the woman who entered the home of Simon the Pharisee, wanting to anoint Jesus (Luke 7:36), and whom Simon called a sinner. And so she was by Simon's standards. Jesus said to Simon, 'Her sins which are many, are forgiven, *for she* loved *much*,' and to her He said, 'Your faith has saved you, go in peace' – peace not as a greeting only; it took on a far deeper meaning in her life. It was her love for Him expressed in her anointing of Him rather than the expensive anointing oil which really touched His heart.

So, Jesus saw that even the mercy practised by the hypocrite is never spontaneous but always premeditated. How different was the attitude of Peter and John, filled with the Spirit, going up to the Beautiful Gate of the Temple and seeing there the man lame from his birth (Acts 3:1). These disciples had learnt Jesus' lesson. Motivated by the Holy Spirit, Peter said, 'Silver and gold have I none, but such as I have I give to you. In the Name of Jesus of Nazareth, rise up and walk'. And the man rose up and went into the temple walking and leaping and praising God! This is Jesus' promise to His disciples, that in their prayer, fasting and almsgiving, they shall be motivated by the life of the Lord Jesus within them and by the Holy Spirit who actuates and inspires them, and thus draw near to their heavenly Father who loves them (Acts 3:1-8).

Matthew 6:1-15. The teaching of Jesus on prayer

And when you pray, you must not be like the hypocrites, for they love to stand and pray in the synagogues and at the street corners, that they may be seen by men. Truly I say to you, they have received their reward. But when you pray, go into your room, your closet, and shut the door, and pray to your Father who is in secret, and your Father who sees in secret will reward you (verses 5,6).

Secondly, Jesus approaches the subject of prayer. How much the Pharisees missed by using prayer as self-gratification; and by endless repetition, thinking that they would be heard for their much speaking (verse 7 A.V.); when that close intimate conversation with God, with the door closed, could be so precious. It was so precious indeed that the Lord Jesus was frequently found to be alone with His Father (Mark 1:35, Mark 6:4-6, Luke 4:42, Luke 5:16, Luke 6:12, Luke 9:18, Luke 10:21, Luke 11:1, Luke 18:1, Luke 22:39, Matthew 11:25, Matthew 14:33). These are some recorded instances. There would have been many others unrecorded.

In Luke 10, it is obvious that Jesus did not necessarily have to 'go away' to pray, for the presence of the Holy Spirit was with Him all the time. He could pray to His Father wherever He was, being always aware of the Father's closeness to Him, and He has gifted the same great privilege to His disciples, teaching them to pray 'Our Father'; to call His Father, the Father of the Lord Jesus, our Father, in constant awareness of His presence.

It is of course possible to pray in any place, in any manner or bodily position. For the Jews, prayer was usually offered in a standing position. When Solomon began to pray at the dedication of the temple (1 Kings 8) before the altar, he was standing, but at the conclusion of his prayer we find him kneeling before the altar with his hands outstretched to heaven. At what point he changed his attitude we are not permitted to know, but we can recognise that what had begun as a prayer for protection for the people of Israel and confirmation of his own position as the son of David and therefore inheritor of the Davidic covenant, had changed to worship of God and total confidence in His power and glory (1 Kings 8:22, 54). That was when he knelt.

Jesus never advocated for His disciples, a special praying position, but we find Him kneeling in the Garden of Gethsemane. In Matthew 26:39, we read, 'He fell on His face and prayed, "My Father, if it be possible, let this cup pass from Me, nevertheless not as I will but as Thou wilt!"' Mark 14:35 has similar words, while Luke records simply that He knelt down and prayed.

There are occasions in every life when absolute prostration before our heavenly Father is the only possible attitude to take. But wherever and whenever and however we pray, prayer has to be oriented solely on God. As Jesus teaches through these verses in Matthew 6, prayer used as a didactic message, or a demonstration of oratory, or in any other way, other than the pray-er's desire for God, is not prayer at all. Jesus calls such prayer *hypocrisy*.

He has a remedy for this.

Most houses built in those days had very little privacy. A flat roof top on which to sleep in the heat of summer and other rooms readily accessible to friends and neighbours was normal. But also, in most homes was a storage room, a word translated 'closet' in some English Bibles, a room scarcely bigger than a cupboard, in most homes the only room with a door that closed. Jesus suggested to His disciples, you can enter into your closet, into that room, and close your door and you can pray to your Father in secret. And He gives them a special prayer to pray. 'Our Father in heaven'.

Jesus is not here concerned with the *community* at prayer, but with the relationship of this *(new)* disciple to his heavenly

Father; the reward of knowing that he is heard, not for his much speaking, but for the desire of his heart for communication with his God. Nevertheless, the caveat remains in the prayer of the community, the church, also. It is a comment on how one should pray with others, two or three gathering together in the name of Jesus, who will grant their requests (Matthew 18:19,20) and not prayer as a demonstration of faith or as an instrument of edification.

God loves His children to talk to Him, as what earthly father would not. He loves to hear the voice of His beloved Bride, as which Bridegroom would not. 'O you who dwell in the gardens, the companions hear your voice, *let Me hear it*' (Song of Solomon 8:13).

Luke's gospel employs the emphatic *'when'* (Luke 11:2). Jesus said to them, *'When* you pray', as if prayer is the most natural thing in the world for a Christian to engage in. For the Christian, it is as easy and necessary to pray as it is to breathe. For Christians, as for Jews, the Psalms give us a superb example of David's relationship with God through his prayer. From many instances, we could choose Psalm 63: 'O God, Thou art my God; early do I seek Thee. My soul thirsts for Thee, my flesh faints for Thee, as in a dry and thirsty land where no water is'.

How sad, that with all the heritage of the Old Testament behind them, the Pharisees failed to enter into such a relationship with God. Perhaps they viewed the psalms as beautiful poetry – which they are – and failed to see the yearning of a human heart behind it.

It Is not only the Pharisee's way of prayer that Jesus warns against. In verse 7, Jesus describes the way that the Gentiles or pagans pray; with many words and much repetition with which they hoped to reach the ear of the god they worshipped, or at least reach one of the gods. They believed that knowing the name of the god and pronouncing it correctly gave them a certain power to manipulate the god.

We thank God that there is no way we can manipulate Him or twist His arm. He is absolutely sovereign. All we can do is to love Him and trust Him because we know that He knows what we need before we ask Him (Matthew 5:4,6; Matthew 7:11). How simple, and yet how profound to pray in the economy of the words of the Lord's Prayer, to our heavenly Father. Jesus covers all the bases, in warning against Pharisaical and also Gentile prayer.

Matthew 6:7-15. The Lord's Prayer

In the words of St. Augustine, 'Pray as if everything depended on God. Act as everything depended on you'. Could it be that that is the ultimate worship? To confess one's absolute dependence on God, and complete helplessness before the One who is the only One able to save us from death – not only or even physical death, but something much worse, a deadness towards God.

Jesus' death was of an entirely different nature, yet in His dependence upon God, and in His utter and complete vulnerability, was the greatest worship of all. 'Lo, I come to Thy will, O God' (Hebrews 10:8). In His death, He bore the sins of the whole world. He was made an offering for sin (Isaiah 5:10). He reconciled men and women to God (2 Corinthians 5:19), and because of it they were granted peace, a peace which the world cannot give (John 14:17), the peace of God which passes all understanding (Philippians 4:7). How precious to us therefore become those words of Jesus in the Garden of Gethsemane, 'Not as I will, but as You will'. He went that way so that we could say in compelling truth, Abba, Father (Romans 8:15).

"Our Father..." (Matthew 6:9)

In Luke's gospel, Jesus gave this prayer to His disciples in response to their request, 'Lord, teach us how to pray!' (Luke 11:1).

In Matthew's gospel, what has become so precious to us as the Lord's Prayer is part of a raft of teaching about the relationship of the disciples to God as their Father, a relationship which left no room for self-gratification or self-aggrandisement, but was intimate and very personal. The theological perspective of each gospel tradition may have differed, Matthew's gospel being concerned as always with the kingdom of heaven, into which the believer has entered through repentance and faith;

and Luke with the daily life of the believer and the supreme position of the Servant of God; but the Lord's prayer cannot be assigned to any one doctrinal view, or any one person or group of persons. It is available for all and for all time.

The prayer is known as the Lord's prayer because it is the prayer given by the Lord Jesus to His disciples. But it could just as truthfully and thankfully be called 'the prayer to the Father', for Jesus has given to His disciples the precious right and privilege which belonged to Him as the Son of God, the privilege of calling Him Father.

The Jews were not unfamiliar with this way of addressing God. There are at least six places in the Old Testament where God is so addressed (Psalm 68:5; 103:13; Isaiah 9:6; 63:16; 64:8; Jeremiah 3:4,19). But the Lord Jesus had brought to them an entirely new view of the Fatherhood of God. In Matthew 5, He had explained to them that on the basis of their loving attitude towards their enemies and those who persecuted them, they had established that they were indeed sons of their Father in heaven. They had previously taken the enormous step of repentance, and through faith had become disciples of Jesus. Now, through their transformed lives, they had become sons, they could call God their Father. For to as many as received Him, who believed on His Name, He gave the right to be called the sons of God (John 1:12).

Because the prayer was first written in Aramaic, there is some evidence that the word for Father is 'Abba' which may be translated 'Daddy'. 'Abba' as a familial way of approaching God as Father. It is also a term used by Paul when writing of believers as sons, adopted into the family of God (Galatians 4:5-7). If this is so, it adds another dimension to this prayer. We are as little children, coming to our Father. It explains the simplicity, (and yet the profundity) of this prayer, and its economy of words. It is indeed a prayer that can be prayed by children, by people of little understanding, and by the greatest academic and theologically instructed minds. We all come to God as Our Father. He is Father to us all, and we love Him, as in a happy family, children love their father.

Of course, there are some who have had such a difficult experience of being parented that the use of such terminology is at best incomprehensible, and at worst anathema, and we feel that all we can do for them is to pray that the Lord would reveal to them something of the Father-heart of God, God who loves them and cares deeply for them as for a precious child.

"Who art in Heaven..." (Matthew 6:9)

Jesus adds to 'our Father', the phrase 'who art in heaven'. This precious way of addressing God as 'our' Father does not detract from the wonderful privilege of knowing Him personally and intimately. But reminds us that we come to Him in reverential awe, that He, Almighty God who created the heavens and still dwells within them, is still and forever will be, Sovereign Lord. And yet He is willing, and in fact, dearly loves, His children to talk to Him, recognizing their utter dependence upon Him. They are trusting their lives and their loved ones to His care, while they share with Him their concerns for His world. They receive from Him the assurance of His presence, His guidance in all the decisions they must make, and the absolute conviction that He hears and will answer their prayer according to His perfect will and perfect timing. This analysis of course goes far beyond the actual wording of the Lord's prayer, but is surely implicit in it.

"Hallowed be Thy Name..." (Matthew 6:9)

Father is the name to be hallowed, the acknowledgement of His holiness, the name to be held deep in our hearts as we ponder again how greatly He loves us, the name to be reverenced as the expression of God's relationship with those who are privileged to be called into the fellowship of His Son, and thus through their honouring of God and obedience to His commands, prepare for the coming of His kingdom.

Hallowed also is His Name Yahweh, 'I am who I am', the covenant keeping God who cares for His people and whose presence goes with them. The Name of God is fathomless in its expanse, deeper than the deepest ocean, higher than the highest mountain. Hallowed be Thy Name.

"Thy Kingdom Come..." (Matthew 6:10)

This is the first petition in the Lord's prayer. It has been said (notably by Dr Sam Wells), that the petition 'Thy kingdom come', the petition for the coming of the kingdom, is the central focus of this prayer. In spite of its brevity, there is something dynamic, powerful about it, as indeed there is about the whole concept of the reign of God. We long for His kingdom to come, for the time when Jesus will be seen to be King, acknowledged to be so by the whole world. He will govern the world in peace. There will no longer be hunger or thirst, no crying or tears, for the former things will pass away.

But we have understood from Matthew 5:3,10 that there is a 'now' and 'not yet' aspect to the kingdom of God. It may be that when the believer prays this prayer, he or she is praying for a greater acknowledgment of the reign of God in their own life, as well as perhaps in the troubled world around them, the 'now'. Or they may be anticipating the eschatological purposes of God to be fulfilled, for the glorious coming again of the Son of Man, the future kingdom of God. Or perhaps they are praying for both.

Matthew nowhere in his gospel describes in minute detail the ultimate reign of God, when the kingdom is fully come, though he refers to it many times, especially in Chapter 13, and again in Chapter 24, where he records Jesus predicting what will take place before the 'coming of the Son of Man with power and great glory' (Matthew 24:30). It is evident that the coming of the kingdom was an especially important feature of the teaching of Jesus, both through His present concern with people's individual status before God, and the ultimate consummation of all things at His return in glory. Indeed, the one would have no meaning without the other.

All the other portions of this prayer are subsumed under this first petition, the strongly expressed desire on the part of

His people that His kingdom should come. 'Thy kingdom come' because where God's sovereignty is recognized, where He is King, everything else falls into place. Where He is king, His will is done, His children are fed, provided for both spiritually and materially, the forgiveness of God for men and women and of men and women for each other is the norm rather than the exception. This is the kingdom of God in action. Where at present, the kingdom operates slowly and sometimes in a hidden manner, as leaven within the dough, so the time will come when the will of God will be universally acknowledged, the reign of God outwardly, openly and joyously received.

"Thy will be done on earth, as it is done in Heaven" (Matthew 6:10)

So we pray to our Heavenly Father that His will may be done, on earth among all his created and redeemed people, even as it is done in heaven, where there is absolutely no question as to who is on the throne, reigning in glory and majesty. This is the special understanding that Jesus has of God. God who is our Father, who is rich in glory, is not only the Father of our Lord Jesus Christ, but has become the Father of all those whom God has accepted into His family.

Jesus insists to His disciples, He is your Father in heaven, and you have been given the extreme privilege of asking for, and receiving the assurance that all the details of your life can be in His will as you yield yourself to Him, your apparently insignificant human life, (though not insignificant to Him), gathered into the will of God because He is your Father, and He cares for you. How wonderful to live in the will of God, co-operating with Him in every disposition He makes for our lives.

"Give us this day our daily bread" (Matthew 6:11)

In the petition for daily bread, we do indeed feed on Him in our hearts by faith and with thanksgiving, but all the time, not only or even pre-eminently at Holy Communion. Petitioning Him for our daily bread is a recognition that we are dependent on Him even for our physical life. Bread is necessary for existence, daily. We live in a permanent state of dependence and therefore of trust in Him.

Just as God provided manna for the children of Israel in the wilderness (Exodus 16), so His children trust Him for their daily needs, living in a state of trustful dependence, in everything by prayer and supplication letting their requests be made known to God (Philippians 4:6). And He supplies their needs. And we are especially grateful that Jesus is the Bread of life, that those who come to Him shall never hunger, and those who believe in Him shall never thirst, for He is the living bread that came down out of heaven, and if anyone eats of this bread he will live forever. He said, 'I am the bread of life' (John 6:35,51).

"And forgive us our sins as we forgive those who have sinned against us..." (Matthew 6:12)

After giving His disciples the privilege of calling God their Father, and then the privilege of recognizing His holiness, and the purpose of who He is being fulfilled as His kingdom comes, Jesus knows that to enjoy His presence with them is also to be totally dependent upon Him. So they are prompted to petition Him for their daily bread.

But He also knows that they may be in need of daily forgiveness. In both the Authorized or King James Version of the Bible and the Revised Standard Version the word used is 'debt'. 'Forgive us our debts, as we also forgive our debtors'. In Aramaic the word for debt 'hoba', was often used for 'sin' or 'transgression'. This accounts for the difference in translation. In verse 12, the imperfect tense is used. Forgive us our sins as we also go on forgiving those who sin against us. Romans 13:8 demands that we owe no man anything but to love one another. There are to be no debts between brothers and sisters. Everything that would hinder our fellowship with one another is forgiven.

How the human heart longs for human forgiveness, to be rid of the sense of guilt, of sin committed, of loved ones hurt through our action, or reaction, to their attitude or behaviour. It appears sometimes to be a burden too great to be borne. But how much worse is the knowledge that we have sinned against our loving heavenly Father, and how encouraging, lifesaving indeed, is the reminder from His word, offering us release, and a new start for the relationship which has broken down between us and Him. 'I have blotted out as a thick cloud your transgressions and as a cloud your sins!' (Isaiah 44:22).

Oh! the release and the peace which this word forgiveness brings! But He goes on to say in Matthew 6:14 and 15, 'For if you forgive men their trespasses, your heavenly Father will forgive you. But if you do not forgive men their trespasses, neither will your Father forgive your trespasses'. Only if we have forgiven the wrong that was done to us can we be forgiven. We cannot otherwise know that peace of sins forgiven.

Jesus is not making it harder for us to receive forgiveness. In His divine wisdom He is stating an undeniable fact, that forgiveness is an act of love. We have prayed, 'Forgive us our sins', and God is more than willing to forgive us our sins for He loves us, and He does so on the grounds of the precious blood of His Son shed on the Cross for us, to bring us near to a Holy God. Our sin separated us from Him. We could not approach Him in our sinful state so He sent His Son to live a spotless life among us and then give up that life on the Cross as a sacrifice. There was no other good enough to pay the price of sin. He only could unlock the gate of heaven and let us in. It is God's love for us that He sent His Son into the world, not to condemn the world, but that the world through Him might be saved (John 3:17). All that is in the heart of God for us He will fulfil, because He loves us.

What then is the alternative but that we should love and forgive one another? We cannot provide redemption for them, only God can do that. But we can let them see that just as God has forgiven us in Jesus, so we can and will forgive them through Him. 'Be kind one to another, tender hearted, forgiving one another, even as God for Christ's sake, has forgiven you' (Ephesians 4:32]). It is the love commandment all over again.'

Love one another as I have loved you' (John 13:34). 'Wash one another's feet' (John 13:14).

The prayer is love in action, the love of God for us, our love for others given to us by the Holy Spirit (Romans 5:5). For those who know themselves to be in constant need of the forgiveness of a forgiving God with whom they have such a precious relationship, forgiving others becomes the norm, the only way of life that really matters. Jesus so longed for His children to have peace in their hearts, no matter what was going on all around them, not just a cosy warm feeling, but a bulwark against which nothing could hinder that relationship with Him. And He knew that lack of forgiveness for others could certainly have that unwelcome effect, the lack of peace in our hearts. As so often, Paul has put this into words for us. 'What shall separate us from the love of God? Shall tribulation or distress, or persecution, or famine or nakedness or peril or sword?' (Romans 8:35). 'I am persuaded that nothing in all creation will be able to separate us from the love of God in Christ Jesus our Lord' (Romans 8:39). And Jesus says, 'Freely you have received, freely give' (Matthew 10:8, A.V.).

"And lead us not into temptation..." (Matthew 6:13)

In addition, we are trusting that we will not be brought into the place of discipline, of testing, of temptation, where we are tested on whether we want to go our way or God's. We pray, 'lead us not into temptation', because we recognize that though we want to be obedient to Him in all things, we so often fall short. Thus, His testing of us comes as a relief, because as Hebrews reminds us, we had fathers of our own who disciplined us because they loved us. God's disciplining of us proves that we are indeed His children, and that He wants us to share His holiness with us (Hebrews 12.5-11).

Discipline, testing, is not always a comfortable experience to go through, which is why we pray 'lead us not into temptation, bring us not to the test', but we know that we are not always perfectly obedient. If we were, we would not need Him to bring us into this place But what a lot we learn from it! And how we value the wisdom and grace of those who have been there before us, those who have known the hand of God on their lives in far greater ways than we shall ever know, and who encourage us.

"But deliver us from evil..." (Matthew 6:13)

God is not limited by our limitations. They only serve to bring more glory to Him. Jesus said, 'without Me you can do nothing' (John 15:8). We know there is evil in the world and much of it is beyond our ability to deal with. We ask for protection from it because we cannot always protect ourselves or our loved ones. There is much in the world which is totally antipathetic to the Christian gospel, and a source of danger to those who would follow Jesus.

But is this the only evil from which we ask to be delivered? There is the evil of compromise, of self-absorption, of self-indulgence, of self-importance, of lack of compassion, to name but a few. This petition will also be answered by the loving care of the Father. He delivers all who put their trust in Him, not always *from* the evil, but always *in and through* the evil. Faithful, loving Father.

The Doxology

It has been the tradition since the early days of the church to treat the Lord's prayer liturgically, and complete it with a doxology. 'For Thine is the kingdom, the power and the glory, for ever and ever. Amen.' In Matthew's version of the Lord's prayer, in the Authorized King James version of the Bible, a doxology has been included. But this is not in the original manuscripts from which the translation was made. However, the early church clearly regarded it as a necessary ending to a distinctly dominical part of the gospel, and present-day Christians are happy to say with their brothers and sisters of old: For Thine is the kingdom, the power and the glory, for ever and ever, Amen.

Matthew 6:9-13. Summary of the Lord's Prayer

The Lord's prayer was in Aramaic. Jesus used the language of the people and not the Hebrew of the synagogue prayer liturgy. His prayer was not intended as a synagogue prayer but a prayer for Jews and Gentiles alike, for those who through faith could call God, Father, *and* for those who were seeking Him.

The Lord's prayer was brief and simple. In its simplicity, the Lord's prayer agrees with the simple proclamation of the gospel and the quiet, humble ministry of Jesus. Jesus was close to the people. He spoke their language, used examples from their daily lives, told stories of the kingdom of God in terms of their everyday world which they could understand. His simple language expressed the nearness of the God whom He proclaimed, and whom He himself addressed as Abba, Father, His loving Father.

The Lord's prayer is an individual prayer. Even as Jesus was dependent on His heavenly Father, so is each disciple, for daily food, for the forgiveness of his sin, for guidance and leading in the new life of discipleship. Though the prayer declares the sovereignty of God, it is not constituted along Jewish national, historic or political lines, or of any other group of people. Especially, it is not concerned with the salvation history of the people of Israel, their history with God. Jesus' concern is the present life experience of the disciple.

But the Lord's prayer is more than personal though it is also that. It becomes so much more in the realisation of kingdom activity now and in the future consummation of all things, when, as Paul puts it, all things are summed up in Christ, and His kingdom has come, for the heart of every believer longs for that Day when the Lord Jesus will come into His glorious kingdom (Ephesians 1:10).

The Lord's prayer is concerned with the will of the Father, the coming of the kingdom, His will being done on earth as it is in heaven. And amazingly, human life, your life, my life, is caught up in God's wonderful design. This Is what God had desired from the very beginning, a people near to Him, obedient to Him, in constant fellowship with Him (Deuteronomy 4:7).

We recall that the Lord's prayer is part of the sermon on the mount, the first teaching that Jesus gave His disciples according to Matthew. It is of the first importance, and it is individual. This is the graciousness of the Lord Jesus to us. But it begins with the inclusive '*our* Father'. We are members of one another. We are not alone on the path of discipleship. We have fellowship one with another (1 John 1:7), till we all come to the unity of the faith, to the measure of the stature of the fullness of Christ (Ephesians 4:13). God, our heavenly Father, is at work in all of us, to bring us there.

But this prayer is not for believers alone. Of course, only those who have truly come to faith know that for them, God has become their heavenly Father. But the prayer can help anyone who prays it to discover the loving closeness of the Father, the love of God for them, His will that brings salvation, His provision of strength, and purpose for their lives. His really is the kingdom, the power and the glory, forever. Blessed be the Name of the Lord, the Name which is above every name. Whatever we ask in His Name, He will do it (Job 1:21; Philippians 2:9; John 14:13).

Prayer is not a fatalistic stepping aside from action, but an entering into the will of God, it is the springboard into acting within the parameters which He has set, an acknowledgement of dependence upon Him, a depth of richness of life, of living. Would we live in service to God, to others? Then we would do well to consider a foundation of prayerfulness as of absolute necessity in our walk with God.

Matthew 6:16. Jesus continues to distinguish between the almsgiving, prayer and fasting of the Pharisees with that of the disciples

And when you fast, do not look dismal like the hypocrites, for they disfigure their faces that their fasting may be seen by men. Truly, I say to you, they have received their reward. But when you fast, anoint your head and wash your face, that your fasting may not be seen by men but by your Father who is in secret; and your Father who sees in secret will reward you (Matthew 6: 16, 17).

We have noted that fasting together with almsgiving and prayer, were the three most important facets of the outward piety of the scribes and Pharisees, facets which Jesus used in order to teach His disciples true almsgiving, true prayer and true fasting as ways in which they expressed their new relationship with their heavenly Father, into which they had entered through repentance and faith.

Jesus regards fasting as a normal part of discipleship. He says, 'When you fast', not 'if you fast', because He knows that there are times in a believer's life when the desire for God is so strong that abstinence from food, and from the satisfaction of all earthly appetite, has nothing to do with obedience to a command, but only with the prioritisation of what is most important. It is of course also a discipline, and this is of great value too, for we need discipline in our lives, wayward as we often are. But how precious to have a secret time with our Father! An anonymous gift, a secret time with Him that would normally have been taken up with food, a secret place where we go to hold communion with the One we love.

Jesus recommends that when His disciples fast, they should wash their face for cleansing and anoint their head for joy. Oil was poured upon the head of Aaron, the High Priest, so that he could minister before the Lord in joy (Psalm 133:2; Exodus 29:7). He was anointed with the oil of gladness, as David was when he was anointed king (Psalm 45:7). Jesus is the Christ, the Anointed One, both a priest greater than Aaron, and a King, greater than David, anointed by the Holy Spirit for the work He was to do on earth (Matthew 3:16).

Jesus is taking His disciples into that realm, the realm of being in the Father's will and being anointed by the Holy Spirit. He is the One who anoints the head of the believer with oil, so that his cup runs over (Psalm 23:5). It is a fearful thing to fall into the hands of the living God (Hebrews 10:31). It is also a joyful thing!

Fasting becomes, not a time of emptiness or sadness, but as we (perhaps metaphorically) anoint the head, we receive the oil of gladness, given by the Holy Spirit, who is symbolically represented by the oil.

Jesus said to His disciples 'These things have I spoken to you that My joy might be in you and that your joy may be full' (John 15:11). 'When Jesus had spoken these words, He went forth with His disciples across the Kidron valley, where there was a Garden, the Garden of Gethsemane' (John 18:1). Is this an impossibility of concatenation as these two diverse experiences come together, the joy of Jesus as He passes that joy on to His disciples, and the knowledge of what the immediate arrest in the Kidron valley will lead to? That which He had prayed to be released from? No, for joy did not depend on the circumstances for Him, but on the fact that He was about to accomplish His Father's will, and neither does it for believers, for their joy comes from the life of peace given to them through forgiveness, and includes joy through fasting; everything gifted to us by the Lord Jesus through the operation of the Holy Spirit.

Washing of the face, anointing the head with oil, and visits to the public baths, were recommended by the rabbis as part of daily hygiene, so, Jesus says, when you fast just act normally, doing what you do every day so that no one knows that you are fasting. It is the equivalent of entering into your closet privately for prayer, or not letting your left hand know what your right hand is doing in almsgiving; the hiddenness of the disciple's life in God, the desire of the disciple for orientation towards God alone, and not even to the desire of the provision of the blessings which He showers upon us.

While the washing and the anointing may be interpreted allegorically, that is, washing as the cleansing from sin, anointing as the experience of spiritual joy, and anointing for service, these interpretations are important because they lead to a more comprehensive understanding of what it means to be a disciple of Jesus.

But fasting is an indication of the seriousness with which one approaches God, and the seriousness with which one offers one's petitions to Him. The disciple does not need to look dismal, to disguise his face, (literal translation), or disfigure it when he approaches God, for God looks not on the outward appearance, but on the heart (1 Samuel 16:7). In chapter 6, Jesus is using the righteousness or piety of the Pharisees, which He describes as hypocritical, or play acting, to demonstrate to His disciples a more excellent way. As we have seen, He is saying that the scribes and Pharisees perform almsgiving, prayer and fasting in a way which they believe to be the way of righteousness, but in reality they do it only to receive glory from men (verses 2and 5).

He does not deny that His disciples will also do all these things, but He says, 'I say to you' (as He has said in chapter 5, verses 22, 28, 32 and 34), when you give alms, when you pray, when you fast, let it be to God alone. His disciples live a hidden life which only the heavenly Father knows about, for this life is lived in secret communion with Him. This theme is repeated in the next three sayings of Jesus concerning treasure in heaven, the lamp of the body, and the Master whom we serve.

Matthew 6:19-23. The Secret Disciple

Do not lay up for yourselves treasures on earth where moth and rust consume and where thieves break through and steal. But lay up for yourselves treasure in heaven where neither moth nor rust consume, and where thieves do not break in and steal. For where your treasure is, there will your heart be also.

In chapter 6, Jesus is using the righteousness or piety of the Pharisees which He describes as hypocritical, or play acting, to demonstrate to His new disciples a more excellent way. In His earlier teaching, Jesus is saying, 'The scribes and the Pharisees perform almsgiving, prayer and fasting in a way which they believe to be the way of righteousness. *'But I say unto you...'* He does not deny that His disciples will also do these things... 'When *you* pray; when *you* give alms; when *you* fast; but His disciples live *a hidden life* which only the Heavenly Father knows about, for this life is lived in secret communion with Him.

This theme is *repeated in the next three logia or sayings of Jesus;* treasure in heaven, the lamp of the body, and the Master whom we serve.

Mathew 6:19-21. Treasure in heaven

Jesus says, do not lay up for yourselves treasures on earth, where moth and rust corrupt, and where thieves break through and steal. But lay up for yourselves treasure in heaven, where neither moth nor rust corrupt, and where thieves do not break through and steal. For where your treasure is, there will your heart be also.

What is treasure? Something of supreme importance, in search of which many have given up everything, family, friends, even life itself, in the pursuit of it. It is a costly thing to lay up treasures on earth, but the thirst for it remains, because it implies the acquisition not only of money or goods, but of power. Those who are rich are often treated differently from those who are poor, even in law. Treasures confer status.

All three synoptic gospels tell of the incident of the rich young ruler who came to Jesus seeking eternal life (Matthew 19:16-20, Mark 10:17-22, Luke 18:18-30). Jesus looking on the young man *loved him* (Mark 10:21) and said, 'You lack one thing; go sell what you have and give to the poor *and you will have treasure in heaven,* and come, follow Me.' How unutterably sad is the conclusion of this story. He went away sorrowful, for he had great possessions. It would be wonderful to speculate that he was with the 120 disciples in the upper room devoting themselves to prayer before the coming of the Holy Spirit (Acts 1:14), or with the 3,000 at the birth of the church (Acts 2:41). The Lord Jesus may well have given him another opportunity to follow him, as He has so graciously given us.

Jesus is speaking however, in chapter 6, not only to those who already have treasures on earth, like the rich young ruler, but also to those who aspire to it. He says, *'Don't do it!'* Do not lay up for yourselves treasures on earth where moth and rust corrupt or consume or destroy (alternative translations) and where thieves break through and steal.

In the days when a person's status in life was so often observable through the clothes they wore, even having an extensive wardrobe was an indication of wealth. Jesus is saying, 'You will have no peace in your heart, wondering how best to protect your possessions'. The problem of having a beautiful wardrobe full of clothes renders them vulnerable to moths.

Or if you have many beautiful objects in your home, they are liable to get rusty if made of metal. For most people, the objects of everyday use were made of pottery, as archaeology attests.

And in Palestine, where many of the houses were made of sun-dried mud brick, a thief could dig through your house. Jesus is warning them that accumulating possessions may cause them to forget to concentrate on the things that really matter, and especially on their relationship with their heavenly Father. Possessions can be a distraction, even an addiction, and Jesus would have us free from anything that comes between us and Him.

If riches increase, set not your heart on them (Psalm 62:10), was the pre-New Testament way of looking at prosperity, prosperity that came from being blessed by God in obedience to Him. In the Old Testament., the heart is the seat of the understanding and the will. There are many Old Testament passages where God tests, knows and searches the heart (Psalms 17:3; 26:2; 44:21; 139:23; Jeremiah 17:10; see also Acts 1;24; 15:8; Roman 8:27; 1 Corinthians 4:5.)

The will and the understanding are all bound up with our desire for something more than we have, perhaps an attitude which doubts His continuing provision for us, or arrogantly wants the kind of power which the acquisition of possessions provides. It is true that God blesses us in many ways, including materially. Jesus is not here advocating poverty as a way of life, but is continuing to stress the importance of dependence on our heavenly Father; and of laying up treasure in heaven. What then is treasure in heaven?

Paul speaks of being blessed with every spiritual blessing in the heavenly places in Christ. (Ephesians 1:10). He goes on to enumerate them. In verse 4, he says that God has chosen us in Him before the foundation of the world – eternal election. In verse 5, he says that we are predestined to sonship. In verse 7, he says that we are redeemed through Christ's sacrifice. In verse 9, that we are given to know the mystery of His will, and in verse 10, to know God's plan for the fullness of time, the consummation of all things in Christ.

These are indeed treasures. But is this what Jesus means when He says, 'Lay up for yourselves treasure in heaven'? Paul's '*berakah*', blessings are gifts given to us. We can only give back to God what He has first given to us, for there is nothing in us which can possibly be of any value to Him. But Jesus is encouraging us to *assign to heaven* that which is precious to us.

As we pray for our family and friends, and any other situation which He lays on our hearts, as we entirely consecrate ourselves to God our Father, as we seek to build upon our relationship with Him in prayer and the study of His word, and to do His will in our lives, these are the offerings to lay on His shrine, and these offerings are miraculously accepted by, and pleasing to, God. We may present our bodies as a living sacrifice, holy and acceptable to God, which is our spiritual worship (Romans 12:1). We have not yet entered heaven ourselves, but surely something of what we have become through grace has already entered in, according to the word of Jesus, 'Lay up for yourselves treasure in heaven' (6:20).

Prayer is where heaven and earth meet, and worship the ultimate manifestation of it. Where our treasure, the Lord Jesus is, there will our heart be also. There may be many treasures, plural, on earth, but there is truly only one Treasure in Heaven. Where *your* treasure is, there will your heart be also (verse 21). Happy is that heart, that disciple.

One interpretation of these verses suggests that only in renunciation of possessions can the disciple demonstrate the direction of his heart towards God. But it is one thing to have wealth and another to be enslaved to wealth. Enslavement equates to idolatry. The rich person whose heart does not cling to wealth may be willing to give away his or her possessions, but there may be practical consequences. There is the necessity of providing for his or her family. In Wesley's 'Standard Sermons' (1:48) he suggests that providing for children and one's own house is a duty, a legitimate owning of property for the needs of others for whom we are responsible. But there is a limit. For Christians, the plain necessities of life are enough, not the superfluities.

Thus, verse 21, 'Where your treasure is, there will your heart be also,' is in one sense, nothing to do with money or wealth. It is more concerned with where the heart is.

Καρδία, the heart, is, the centre of the human being. Treasure makes it clear what is of greatest importance to the disciple, and where the centre of the human being is located. We worship the Lord in the beauty of holiness (Psalm 29:2 A.V.) in the garments which he has provided of forgiveness and restoration so that we may minister to Him (Exodus 39:1, Psalms 96:9) 'He is thy Lord, and worship thou Him,' (Psalm 45:11 A.V.) is the word given to the king's daughter who is all glorious within, His Bride. He is our treasure. We worship Him. And in our hearts enthrone Him.

Matthew 6:22-23. The Lamp of the Body

The eye is the lamp of the body. So, if your eye is sound, your whole body will be full of light. But if your eye is not sound, your whole body will be full of darkness. If then the light in you is darkness, how great is the darkness.

'If then the light in you is darkness, how great is the darkness' (Matthew 6:23). The 'light in you' has been interpreted as meaning the ability of a person to reason and we can appreciate that when someone, through disease or accident, is unable to reason, it appears that 'the light has gone out.' In antiquity, this was interpreted as 'vous', assimilated to English as 'nous'. But for Matthew, this inner light is better understood as referring to the human heart. This verse suggests that this inner light, this human heart, can become darkness. What the eye is to the body, enabling it to see, so without a human heart which is full of light, a human being walks in darkness.

As the eye is to the body, so is the human heart in its relationship with God. A healthy *'sound'* eye (Matthew 6:22) enables a person to walk carefully. An eye which is sick, *'not sound'* means that the person cannot see anything and is walking in darkness. With the body, so with the person. The eye of the body stands for the whole person.

We conclude that the text is metaphorical. It is not concerned primarily with the physical body, either the eyes or the heart, but with the direction of the whole person towards God. It is a further declaration of the impact on the life of the disciple as he goes on following Jesus and worshipping his heavenly Father. The light which is in him will result in sharing that light all around. But for those who do not have that light within them, how great is that darkness. Jesus says, 'Let your light so shine before men that they may see your good works and glorify your Father which is in heaven' (Matthew 5:16).

So we understand that these verses are a *reinforcement* of what Jesus has been saying to His disciples about treasure/possessions, and later about the contrast between the worship of God, and the worship of Mammon.

A friend used to say, 'What's bred in the bone comes out in the gravy.' Jesus is saying, 'What is inside you, the light of faith, will find expression in what you do with your possessions, your attitude towards others, the way you work for your employer. For a Christian, no part of his or her life is without significance, because it is always directed first and foremost towards the Lord Jesus and His kingdom. The Psalmist says, 'Behold, as the eyes of servants look to the hand of their master, and as the eyes of a maid to the hand of her mistress, so our eyes look to the Lord our God till He have mercy upon us (Psalm 123:2). The direction of the eyes indicates the direction of the heart. The lover of the Lord Jesus is continually *looking unto Jesus*, the author and finisher of our faith, who, for the joy that was set before Him, endured the cross, despising the shame, and is seated at the right hand of the throne of God (Hebrews 12:2). *Consider Him,*

Hebrews continues (Hebrews 12:3), lest you be weary and faint in your minds.

And we all, with unveiled face, beholding and reflecting the glory of the Lord, are being changed in His likeness from one degree of glory to another; for this comes from the Lord who is the Spirit (2 Corinthians 3:18).

Matthew 6:24. The Master whom we serve

No one can serve two masters, for either he will hate the one and love the other, or he will be devoted to the one and despise the other. You cannot serve God and Mammon.

This is the third of a trio of sayings of Jesus in the Sermon on the Mount which expound the principles behind the Lord's Prayer, and which prevent them from being merely theoretical, impinging as they do on every aspect of the life of the disciple.

In this saying, Jesus touches on the world of work, the master and the servant, the employer and the employed. This part of a person's life may take up many hours every day. If he or she is a slave, it is their whole life, quite a possibility in New Testament times. So the question arises; how to be conscientious in one's work and at the same time, offer up all the work to God as our ultimate Master.

The saying is not meant to distract the believer from serving his master to the best of his ability. It is a question of undivided loyalty to God. As the accumulation of possessions denies the faithfulness of God to provide; as the direction of the eye indicates the direction of the whole person towards the worship of God; so these verses have behind them a form of discipleship which in its essence relies totally on God; obedient to Him from the very centre of the believers being, the heart, καρδιά. This has become of extreme and utter importance to him or her.

What appears to be a somewhat stark contrast in translation, 'no man can serve two masters, hating the one and loving the other, being devoted to one and despising the other', is less so in its Semitic rendering, in which to hate means to be indifferent to, or unconcerned for, to be devoted means to hold firmly, to 'support'. The word '*mammon*' is derived from the Hebrew 'mn', that in which one has confidence (there are no vowels in Hebrew). It refers to money, profit, wealth, and not necessarily with any bad connotation. But you cannot serve God and mammon (verse 24).

But security, the confidence in this world is illusory. In the Old Testament the Israelites were constantly exhorted not to trust in outward things, but with single mindedness, to put their only trust in God. It is impossible to combine devotion to God with devotion to wealth (Hill, p143). You cannot serve God and Mammon (verse 26) is a step further on from one's relationship with one's employer. But essentially, they are the same, because the denominating factor is the *relationship*. Nothing, absolutely nothing, may be allowed to take the place of the worship of God and our obedience to Him. This is why Paul is able to say, 'Whatever you do, do all to the glory of God' (1 Corinthians 10:31). It is possible to work for an exacting, bullying boss, and yet to work to the glory of God; as many have had to do. Pray for your boss, for him/her, and seek to love them for Jesus' sake; never losing sight of your true boss, who is Jesus. We are servants of the Most High God. Loyalty to Him must be undivided. We cannot allow Mammon/money to master us, for we have a Master in heaven.

Our existence as disciples is at stake here, in these verses; our attitude to possessions, our attitude to the faithfulness of God. We must, above all things, long to worship Him. We cannot allow anything or any person to get in the way of that. 'He is thy Lord, and worship thou Him' (Psalms 45:11 A.V). Do we worship God or money, prosperity, possessions?

Matthew 6:19-34. Life free from worry, anxiety or fear of the future

Therefore I tell you, do not be anxious about your life, what you shall eat or what you shall drink, nor about your body, what you shall put on. Is not life more than food, and the body more than clothing? Look at the birds of the air. They neither sow nor reap nor gather into barns and yet your heavenly Father feeds them. Are you not of more value than they? And which of you by being anxious can add one cubit to his span of life?

We had noted that in His sermon, Jesus moves *from* the disciples' relationship with the world around, *to* relationship with His heavenly Father; a relationship adumbrated in Matthew 5:16, assumed in 5:45, and made totally clear in 5:48.

The transitional verse at the end of Matthew 5:48, 'Be ye therefore perfect, even as your Father in heaven is perfect,' *overarches chapter 6*. Because of the preceding verses in 5:21 onwards, Jesus is surely and steadily moving towards the description of a completely different kind of life from that which His disciples had formerly lived. This life is governed by love; love of your brother, your wife, your enemies. Love is the perfection of who God is, and love is the perfecting of what Jesus' disciples are.

So, as we come into chapter 6, we begin to understand more of what a relationship with God as our heavenly Father can mean for the disciple, a continued expression of his or her love for their heavenly Father, and His constant love and care for them.

This too is authoritative. Three times in chapter 6, Jesus says, 'Amen, I say to you' (Matthew 6:2,5,16]) thereby invoking all the faithfulness of the promises of God. These words of Jesus stand on solid ground. He would not have His disciples enter into a meaningless form of behaviour and speech, like the Pharisees, when the alternative for them was a close intimacy with their heavenly Father. And in verses 19-24, He continues, as we have seen, by describing three ways in which they could be distracted from orientating themselves wholeheartedly to undivided loyalty and worship of God, treasure in earth or heaven, the lamp of the body and the Master whom we serve.

In Matthew 6:25, He continues to speak authoritatively. 'Therefore, I tell you...' λέγω ὑμῖν (Matthew 6:25, 29). 'Do not be anxious' strikes an imperative as well as an instructive note.

These verses about birds and flowers could just as easily have been interpreted as sapiential admonition such as is found in Proverbs and Ecclesiastes, the wisdom literature of the Old Testament. So what is Jesus saying specifically here to His disciples? Matthew 6:33 gives us a clue. 'Seek ye first the Kingdom of God and His righteousness, and all these things shall be added to you'.

From an earlier study, we understood that many, if not most of those listening to Jesus' words on the mountain have heard His proclamation, 'Repent for the Kingdom of Heaven is at hand' (4:17) and have entered that kingdom through repentance and faith and are now seated as His feet on the mountain side. These are disciples who are experiencing the *present reality of the kingdom, the reign of God*, in their lives, while recognising through Jesus' teaching, that there is a fulfilment, a consummation, of the kingdom *yet to come*; what is described as the *now* and *not yet* of the kingdom.

So Jesus' words are not just words of wisdom, though of course they are that, but there is a different dimension to them. His disciples have entered into something far bigger, greater than themselves, the eschatological Kingdom of God. On this basis, of being already in the kingdom, but also waiting for its fulfilment, how can they live their lives in anxiety? If God can feed the birds of the air, can He not feed them? If He can clothe the grass of the field with flowers, of which even one exceeds in beauty the garments of the most glorious king in all their ancient history, can He not clothe them?

So we are given to understand that the Christian lives from a completely different ground of being, a substantial difference from that of the non-believer. They are children of the King! Seeking His righteousness! And the promise is that *all* these necessary things like food and clothes will be added to them (Matthew 6: 33). They do not have or need to be anxious or worried while they live close to their heavenly Father, because, 'Your heavenly Father knows that you have need of *all* these things' (Matthew 6:32.) This is the simplicity and profundity of life lived in communion with Him. Jesus is alive! and shares His life with us.'

The Sermon on the Mount is not an ethical treatise, but an invitation to a way of life for those who have become disciples and entered into the Kingdom of Heaven.

It has been suggested that these verses are an encouragement not to work, because God will supply food and clothes for His children, just as He does the birds and the flowers. But this is to miss the point of what Jesus is saying when He says *'Be not anxious'* and to deny that much anxiety can accrue to people *who are fully employed*; either as masters/employers or servants/employees. Will the business remain profitable? Will the wages I receive be enough to feed myself and my family? How long before I am made redundant? We could perhaps think of many other scenarios which could cause anxiety to an employed person, or an employer, whether a disciple or not.

But whether employed or unemployed, the disciple looks to His heavenly Father to supply him with the basic provisions of life, because 'He cares for you' (1 Peter 5:7). He *knows* (Matthew 6: 32) that you have need of *all* these things, that the life ψυχή is more than food, and the body σῶμα than raiment.

St Augustine's comment is, 'Quis nobis animus et corpus dedit, nisi Deus?' Who gave you the soul and body if not God? What He has given, He will care for, if committed to Him. God is not more concerned about human activity because it contributes to their livelihood, but is concerned because He is their Father. The non-working birds are a testimony to God's concern, His love for His children. The text says, *'Look* at the birds' (verse 26). *'Consider* the lilies' (verse 28). The Greek word translated 'consider' is κατά μάθετε, *'learn from'*. God's children are also His disciples, learning. The birds neither sow nor reap, nor gather into barns; the lilies neither toil nor spin.

In the first century human world of work, there was work traditionally done by men as sowing and reaping, and that which was traditionally done by women, as toiling and spinning. So Jesus is saying that men and women have equal opportunities to enter into discipleship, an equal right to serve and love God as their heavenly Father, in and for the service of the Kingdom of God and His righteousness. This is not just an alternative lifestyle for either men or women, but a life-changing encounter with the living God, in which anxiety, worry, concern are the very antithesis of faith in God.

Your heavenly Father knows (Matthew 6: 33). There are those outside the kingdom, Gentiles, ἔθνη, outside of the faith, who do not have this privilege of calling upon the Father. They worry about these things, food, drink, clothes. But the way of faith is open to them too, for *if they seek* the kingdom, *they will find* it (Matthew 7:7).

The whole of this section of chapter 6 stands under the reality of the Kingdom of God, that which is present, and that which is to come. Jesus says, 'Therefore, I tell you' (verses 25, 29). When you see a 'therefore', you wonder what it is there for. (Alec Motyer) It is not that these verses of the Sermon on the Mount are merely ethical, or a message of theological wisdom, but are fundamental in the life of the believer. They are part of Jesus' whole teaching going back to the Beatitudes, and are of supreme importance. When He says, 'Do not be anxious about tomorrow' (verse 34), He is taking all the burden of the future away.

Wesley says (Standard Sermons I 512), 'Live thou today. The past is nothing, as though it had never been. The future is nothing to you, it is not yours, perhaps it never will be.'

Bonhoeffer says (Letters and Papers from Prison p31), 'The narrow way, a way often hardly to be found, of living every day as if it were our last, yet in faith... living as though a splendid future lay before us' [Quoted by Luz p409].

The '*all things*' of verses 32 and 33, the 'all things which will be added to you as you seek God and His righteousness, emphasise the comforting omniscience of God. Since He knows 'all things' we do not need to worry either about the present or the future. We can reverently expect God to do the worrying for us in the face of every economic hardship or the unknowability of the future. Jesus' emphatic desire that His disciples should know the reality of the Fatherhood of God applies not only to the present provision of temporal needs, but to the period of the future which elapses before the enjoyment of the fulness of the kingdom yet to come.

He has given us the privilege of casting all our care upon Him, because He cares for us (1 Peter 5:7). We live one day at a time, trusting in our heavenly Father. Jesus is greater than our circumstances, greater than the many difficulties we face as we go through life. He will not fail us nor forsake us. God is at work in us, and we are being made perfect in love. Love for Him, and love for one another, and trust in Him. The believer renounces worldly security when that which promises security, delimits the freedom resulting from trusting his heavenly Father implicitly, no matter what the cost. Many of us are consumed with worry, but if we worry, we can't trust. Conversely though, if we truly trust, we can't worry. Jesus sets us free from ourselves; free to follow Him, free to love Him, *free*.

Matthew Chapter 7

Matthew 7:1-5. Do not judge

Judge not, that you be not judged. For with what judgement you judge you will be judged and the measure you give will be the measure you get. Why do you see the speck that is in your brother's eye but do not notice the log that is in your own eye? Or how can you say to your brother, 'Let me take the speck out of your eye', when there is a log in your own eye? You hypocrite, first take the log out of your own eye and then you will see clearly to take the speck out of your brother's eye (Matthew 7:1-5).

Chapter 5 of Matthew's gospel dealt with the relationship of the new disciple to his world, his brother, his wife, his enemies. Chapter 6 dealt with the disciple's relationship to his heavenly Father.

Now in chapter 7, we come to his relationships within the community as together they seek to live out the life of Jesus within them. The gospel was not originally written in chapters and verses, and we thank God that this division of the original text has proved so helpful to readers of the gospel through the years, a division surely inspired by the Holy Spirit.

In chapter 7, Jesus speaks of the relationship of believers in the community, which became the church, the church which He is establishing as recorded throughout Matthew's gospel, the church for which He came and was incarnated, and for which He gave His life, as Paul describes it in Acts 20:37, 'The church of God which He obtained with the blood of His own Son.'

This underlying principle indicates how serious are these verses in chapter 7, as they set out the primary guidance for the new exciting journey being entered upon by these new disciples;

as they learn of the joy and also the pitfalls of this new community, coming together as learners in discipleship, and as worshippers of God in an entirely different way from that of temple worship and synagogue learning to which they had become accustomed. So precious has this new community become to the Lord Jesus that Paul refers to it time and again as 'the body of Christ' and disciples as members of the body. Paul writes 'Now you are the body of Christ and individually members of it (1 Corinthians 12:27).

So, this is the kind of community/church which Jesus wants for His disciples. Firstly, a church where no one sits in judgement on anyone else (Matthew 7:1-5). Then a church which distinguishes between what is holy, and what will lead a disciple astray (Matthew 7:6). Then a church which is courageous in prayer as it trusts the Father more and more (Mathew 7:7-11). A church which practises the Golden Rule (Matthew 7:12). and is prepared for an uncomfortable, difficult and narrow life (Matthew7:13-14). Especially a church which is aware of the possibility that some teachers/prophets are not all they seem, but that the church can recognise them by their lack of genuineness or authenticity. They say, 'Lord, Lord,' but their lives do not display the Lordship of the Lord Jesus. Even so, it will be the Lord Himself who judges them (Matthew 7:15-23). And finally, that It is the responsibility of the church to listen to Jesus, to partner Him in the building of His church, with Him as the foundation even in, especially in, stormy or turbulent times.

The church is founded on Jesus (Matthew 7:24).

Matthew 7:1-5. Do not judge one another

Judge not, that you be not judged. For with the judgement you pronounce you will be judged, and the measure you give will be the measure you get. Why do you see the speck in your brother's eye, but do not notice the log that is in your own eye? Or how can you say to your brother, 'Let me take the speck out of your eye' when there is a log in your own eye? You hypocrite. First take the log out of your own eye, and then you will see clearly to take the speck out of your brother's eye.

How interesting and perhaps significant that Jesus should begin His section on the church community with, 'Judge not that you be not judged' (Matthew 7:1). How wonderful it would be to belong to a church where no-one sits in judgement on anyone else! A church full of love, one for the other, where one person recognises there is perhaps a splinter, a mote, a speck in another's eye, but out of love for the brother, and awareness of the log in one's own eye, refrains from judging the other.

The letter of John comes to mind with his constant repetition of love between believers reflecting the love of God for each of us. He writes, 'Beloved let us love one another for love is of God, and he who loves is born of God and knows God (I John 4:7). Out of His great love, God will correct that mote in my brother's eye, and by His grace, He will also remove the log from mine. We do not need to do His work for Him. And lo and behold, the next time you look at your brother, the mote is gone! Indeed we have a faithful God.

Three times in this section, we find the word *Brother*, αδελφός. Relationships within the church are familial. God is our heavenly Father. We are brothers and sisters in the church. It is a counsel of perfection! But in Matthew 5:48, we have noted that God who is perfect in love, is perfecting us also in love. We often need each other in order to learn something which would not be possible on an individual basis. The church is, in effect, a training ground. We never stop being disciples, learning. In the church, we are learning to live with each other in love, to respond to the impulses of the Holy Spirit, as we respond to each other. We make mistakes, we are not always kind to each other, forgiving one another (Ephesians 4:32), but we believe that the love of God has been shed abroad in our hearts by the Holy Spirit who has been given to us (Romans 5:5) and so we press on (Philippians 3:14).

This is the proclamation of the gospel to the world! As Tertullian (160-220 A.D.) is reputed to have said, 'See how these

Christians love one another!' This is the transforming power of the gospel of Christ, and the invitation is always to come to Him; to be part of this revolutionary process which the Lord Jesus has initiated.

We do not judge our brethren. We do not judge anyone. There are judges in the judicial system. Jesus is not speaking of them. In this sermon He is concentrating on His followers and their discipleship, learners in the Kingdom of Heaven.

Jesus says, 'With what judgement you judge, you shall be judged.' If a believer is judgemental, he places himself in the position of inviting judgement from others. But even more seriously, nothing shuts out a person more surely from love than a censorious and unforgiving disposition. Not only is he shutting himself off from love of the brethren, he is closing his own heart to God's forgiveness. It is not that God will not forgive him, but that his judgemental attitude precludes him from receiving forgiveness.

The hyperbole of getting rid of the log in your own eye before and in order to get rid of the speck in your brother's eye is not a ground for the legitimate judging of others, but is meant to exclude all condemnation of others, since no-one can get rid of his own shortcomings, or worse, his sin, to see clearly another's fault. This prerogative remains with the Lord Jesus, who alone can forgive the sin, and initiate the restoration, the transformation.

It remains a serious inquiry. What has caused the fault in the other person in the first place? We do not know what goes on in, or even what went on, in the hinterland of another's existence, their struggles, their troubles, the events which have caused them to be the way they are. Who are we to judge? What presumption! God alone knows and He understands, and where necessary, He will forgive.

So we open up our heart to one another in love, and hopefully, some understanding, 'Till we all come... to the measure of the stature of the fulness of Christ' (Ephesians 4:13).

The present tense of μη κρίνετε, *judge not,* carries the strength of the prohibition, 'stop judging' or 'don't even judge' and indicates a personal rather than a communal judging such as is found in Matthew 18:15-18. But surely, if this first prohibition is observed in the church, there would be no need for further discipline. In Matthew 7:1-5, this judging of one another is personal, and runs the risk of destroying the brotherhood. It is love and forgiveness which binds it together.

Matthew 7:6. That which is holy – and unholy

Do not give dogs that which is holy. And do not throw your pearls before swine lest they trample them underfoot, and turn to attack you.

At first sight, there seems to be little congruity between the judging of others, and *not* giving dogs what is holy; or not casting pearls before swine. So what does Jesus mean by this? Who are the dogs? Who are the swine? We recognise of course, that swine were anathema to the Jew (Leviticus 11:7, 22:10-16) as being unclean. Dogs also were unclean as they scavenged the streets for food, and possibly carried disease. They were rarely regarded with affection in the Middle East.

Jesus is warning against uncleanness in His followers. Among the Jews, dogs and pigs stood for Gentiles, non-Jews. Jesus' identification of the unclean, the unholy, is more radical. Holiness is that without which no man can see the Lord. (Hebrews 12:12). Holiness is αγιασμός, separation, setting apart. God has set His children apart from all uncleanness. Hebrews says, 'Strive for holiness' (Hebrews 12:14). Paul says, 'Touch not the unclean thing' (2 Corinthians 6:17) and in Leviticus, God says, 'You shall be holy for I am holy' (Leviticus 11:44).

We could interpret this with the sense of defilement of body and spirit. God is holy, utterly, utterly holy, and 'you shall be clean for I am clean', is a theme which permeates the Old Testament, His people set apart to Him, and for Him.

There is a paradox here. In Hebrews 12, holiness is something we strive for because we want to come into the presence of a Holy God. In Romans 3:22, God sees us as holy already because He has given us the holiness of Jesus which we could not earn and certainly don't deserve. He has clothed us in the righteousness of Jesus alone, faultless to stand before His throne, the righteousness of God through faith in Jesus Christ for all who believe. But we also guard that which has been committed to us, as Paul again writes to Timothy, 'O Timothy, guard that which has been entrusted to you' (1 Timothy 6:20).

Jesus says, 'You are holy, separated to God, given the gift of righteousness'. It is a gift to you based on your faith and your commitment to Him. Do not give yourself to the dogs, to that which is unclean. Those pearls which God has given you, the inspiration which comes from the Holy Spirit as you read His word, the blessings of joy, of love, of peace; the fellowship with other believers. These gifts are too precious to be thrown before that which is unclean. That which is precious to the disciple is regarded as worthless by dogs and swine and the price he pays will not only be rejection, but a trampling upon what has become so important and significant a part of his life.

So there is that which is a speck, a splinter in your brother's eye, which you do not judge, compounded with something equally or more serious, that which is unclean. You do not judge the speck, but you shy away completely from that which is unclean lest you are defied, whatever the source of the uncleanness. There is a world of difference between what is a speck and what is unclean.

Matthew 7:7-11. Courage in prayer

Ask and it will be given you. Seek and you will find. Knock and it will be opened to you. For every one who asks receives, and he who seeks will find, and to him who knocks it will be opened.

Or what man of you, if his son asks him for bread, will give him a stone? Or if he asks for a fish will give him a serpent? If you then know how to give good gifts to your children, how much more will your heavenly Father give good gifts to those who ask Him?

117

One wonders what more could be added concerning prayer than what the Lord Jesus has already made clear in Matthew 6:5-15. Is it that chapter 6 is setting out prayer as the result of intimacy between the *individual* disciple and his heavenly Father, whereas Jesus has in mind the *community* at prayer in 7:7-11? Is Jesus also emphasising the importance of *intercessory* prayer by both the individual and the community? For of course, when the community is at prayer, its prayer time is made up of many individuals, each of whom has his or her own request to be made known to God, in prayer and supplication, with thanksgiving, for themselves but also and perhaps especially, for others (Philippians 4:6).

We gain both these insights in these verses of Jesus' sermon. The church at prayer is powerful, a force to be reckoned with, praying in unity as one, identifying with the will of the Father in heaven while recognizing their relationship to Him in the family of God to be like that of earthly fathers concerned with their children. For those who are relying on Him, nothing that is good will go by them, as the old Scottish proverb has it. They will have bread and fish for their hunger, (Matthew 7:9,10) and all good gifts.

This is how Jesus is teaching the art and practice of intercession. It is like a child asking his father for food. Everyone who asks, receives, everyone who seeks finds, and to everyone who knocks it shall be opened. 'Who among you' (Matthew 7:9) would give his child a stone if he asked for bread, or a snake if he asked for a fish? Your heavenly Father is not about to give you stones and snakes, He only gives good gifts to His children. The love of God is more certain; more certain than the love of the most loving earthly father; yet earthly fathers too love their children. The earthly father looking to his heavenly Father cannot believe that his heavenly Father would in any way be less active and immediate in supplying whatever was lacking for the one for whom he prayed, in giving them good gifts (Matthew 7:11).

Again, how simple, yet how profound is this rationale for intercessory prayer; whether by individuals or by the church together in prayer. We come to God as children to our Father. We have as our example the unconditional trust of Jesus in His loving Father. That is what Jesus wants for us too.

Not every petition is granted. Jesus said to His Father, 'Let this cup pass from me 'as He prayed in the Garden of Gethsemane. We shall be eternally grateful that this cup did not pass from Him, that He went to the Cross and there gave His life a ransom for many, that we are the fruit of His suffering, but also those who rejoice in His risen life.

Not every petition is granted. God gives only 'good gifts' to His children, and out of His abundant and merciful knowledge He gives *only* what is good, and only in His own good time. And with God, nothing is impossible.

There is a *progressive intensity* in the text, asking, seeking, knocking, a presentation of the way of praying, not just a juxtaposition of verbs, but a process of beginning by asking, the perseverance and determination of seeking, the final fervent knocking at the heavenly door even while relying on the faithfulness of a faithful, loving God. May the Lord help us thus to pray.

Answer to prayer is implicit in the very presence of Christ in His church, but answered according to the special knowledge which only God has, His omniscience, and always according to His perfect will for His children. His presence makes the prayer not just a religious exercise, but a gathering together around Him as His beloved family. 'Where two or three are gathered together in My Name, *there am I* in the midst of them (Matthew 18:20) says the Lord Jesus. Later on in further teaching about the church He says, 'Lo *I am* with you *always*, even to the end of the age' (Matthew 28:20); the precious promise of Jesus, promising always to be with us until the fulfilment of the actuality of His reign, the Kingdom of God, when we shall be with Him forever.

God did not spare the suffering of His Son (Romans 8:32) but through it led Him to resurrection. Suffering of a different order, but nonetheless acute, may also be the way for us, but we may be sure that through prayer, and constant reference through faith back to God, we will see His hand at work in our lives, and in the lives of those for whom we pray. 'And the peace of God which passes all understanding will keep our hearts and minds' as we wait in His presence (Philippians 4:7).

We have an inextricable connection with our heavenly Father, both as individuals and as a church, a privilege which we do not take lightly, but which we sometimes fail to appreciate as the precious gift which it is. All prayer, including intercessory prayer, takes place within the Father-son relationship, the Father who is only capable of giving good gifts to his children (Matthew 7:11).

Prayer which does not have that essential quality is not prayer as Jesus describes it. In Luke's gospel, the 'good gift' is expressed as the Holy Spirit (Luke 11:13). 'How much more will the heavenly Father give the Holy Spirit to those who ask Him?' The gift of the Holy Spirit is essential as we wait upon Him for His prompting of our prayers, for His intervention where intervention is necessary, for His confirmation that what we have prayed is consistent with our Father's will. Luke throws a precious light on the Holy Spirit's activity.

We may feel we come to God as beggars seeking alms. God sees us as coming to our heavenly Father through faith in Christ, as His children, and under the control and direction of the Holy Spirit. *That describes how infinitely precious is the gift of prayer.* Almighty God allows us, invites us, to come to Him as children of a heavenly Father.

Matthew 7:12. The Golden Rule

So whatever you wish that men should do to you, do so to them, for this is the law and the prophets.

Having become children of our heavenly Father, the one who gives good gifts, we now want to do the same. Perhaps something in our own DNA has changed? We too want to give good gifts to those whom we love, those in our families, those with whom we share fellowship in the Christian community, those whom we meet at work or elsewhere. We want to behave towards them as our heavenly Father has behaved towards us, and the Holy Spirit will enable us by His grace.

So we do to others as we would that they should do to us. 'Whatever you wish that men would do to you, do so to them, for this is the law and the prophets' (Matthew 7:12).

By citing the law and the prophets, Jesus is reinforcing the continuity between His teaching and that of the Old Testament. The *law,* the word of the law was given by God to Moses on Mt. Sinai; the *prophets* mediated the word of God to the people of Israel down through the centuries. Sometimes they would listen, sometimes they would not, but there was always a remnant who did not follow the idolatrous practices of the nations round about. As the Lord said to the prophet Elijah (1 Kings 19:18), 'There are yet seven thousand in Israel, all the knees that have not bowed to Baal, and every mouth that has not kissed him.' (As an aside, we note that even idolatrous people loved their god sufficiently to kiss him as part of their worship).

Elijah had thought that he was the only one who was still following the Lord. But in spite of the terrible political and spiritual conditions of the time under King Ahab and Queen Jezebel there were still men and women whom the love of God constrained, who sought to live the life of sacrificial love for others, because they knew that greater was He who was with them, so much greater than those who were in the world around.

'Do to others as you would have them do to you,' relates to a further summation of our behaviour towards God and towards others. In Matthew 22:34, when one of the Pharisees' lawyers came to test Jesus as to which was the greatest commandment of all, He said, 'You shall love the Lord your God with all your heart, and with all your soul, and with all your mind. This is the great and first commandment.' And a second is like it. 'You shall love your neighbour as yourself.

On these two commandments depend all the law and the prophets' (Matthew 22:30-40). the law and the prophets which He came not to abolish but to fulfil (Matthew 5:17), for the law given to God's people through Moses is 'holy, and just and good' (Romans 7:12).

But the Holy Spirit has given to believers a new law. It is still the law of love, but it has become for the believer the law of the Spirit of life, by sending God's own Son to condemn sin; so that being controlled by sin and unable to keep the law becomes a distant memory. The law is fulfilled in us by the power of the Holy Spirit. (Romans 8:1-4) By faith we walk in newness of life (Romans 6:4). This is what we receive when we receive the Holy Spirit; a life free from bondage to sin, because for freedom Christ has set us free (Galatians 5:1) though if we sin we have an advocate with the Father, Jesus Christ the righteous (1John 2:1)

So Jesus becomes, and is, the end, the *telos*, purpose, completeness of the law 'to everyone who believes' (Romans 10:4) to the Jew first and also to the Gentile who does not have the law. Amazingly, God's law of love is also fulfilled in us. And though we are not of His original chosen people, we are included.

Throughout the sermon on the mount we have traced the theme of love, love to God, love to others. The clause, 'Whatever you wish that men should do to you, do so to them (7:12), is *consequent* upon, 'This is the law and the prophets' (7:12b). John writes, 'I am writing a new commandment which is true in Him and in you, but it is that which you have heard from the beginning, the twin commandments, love God, and love your neighbour. It is the old law which you have had from the beginning (I John 2:7). And Jesus says, Love one another as I have loved you (John 15:12). Continue in my love' (John 15:9).

Just as He is the fulfilment of the law and the prophets, just as they are fulfilled, completed in Him in every way, so that He *is* the law and the prophets, the νόμος, the word of the law, προφήτης the word of the prophet, the word of God which was from the beginning (John 1:1) so will the law be fulfilled in His disciples; that which is fulfilled by the law and the prophets completely summed up in the two commandments to love God and love one's neighbour. Jesus was the embodiment of that love. We share that love, as we share in the life of the obedient, eternal, Son of God, the word made flesh. And because of that love, we *will* do to others as we would wish them to do for us.

THE KING AND THE KINGDOM

These commandments are universal and sometimes they are very difficult. How does a prisoner in a concentration camp love her Nazi guards? Or a wife who is being abused by her husband? We can think of so many examples. We are children of the Father who makes His sun to rise and His rain to fall on the just and the unjust. The word does not say that these persons should also treat us in the same way as we feel compelled to treat them because of the love of God which fills our hearts. Perhaps there is no obligation on them to do so if they have not been the recipients of the love of God shed abroad in their hearts by the Holy Spirit, as Jesus' disciples have been (Romans 5:5). But that does not preclude His disciples from acting in that way.

St. Augustine speaks of the priority of love, 'Love God and do what you will,' because love of Him will prevent you from acting unlawfully, or sinfully. If all your thinking and acting are directed primarily to loving God, then with what peace you will live your life, pleasing Him, never doubting but that His grace is sufficient, even when the storms rage about you and your heart trembles. What a precious privilege it is to be a disciple of the Lord Jesus Christ!

Jesus has already warned against loving only those who love you in Matthew 5:46. The golden rule is comprehensive. Though the golden rule principle may be observed as the foundation of much ecclesiastical law, and even in English, French and German Enlightenment philosophy (Hobbes, 'Leviathan', Berkeley, John Stuart Mill, Voltaire, Leibniz) we may look to Jesus as being the messenger and advocate of an eternal truth, a truth acknowledged always and everywhere and by everybody ('*Semper et ubique et ab omnibus*'). Human beings can only progress communicatively. There always has to be interaction with others.

Immanuel Kant formulated his Categorical Imperative as a principle for acting, extending the golden rule beyond one's fellow human being to *all* people and making it a moral ethical injunction, 'you *must* love', *which it is impossible to fulfil*. Who among us has the moral or religious energy to fulfil the command of Jesus? It is only as we live in harmony with Him that we can become initiative, not reactive, to the needs of others, to be the first one to be loving, in obedience to His commands, to freely interpret in the light of His love, what our behaviour should be.

There is a sense in which the golden rule summarises for us the sermon on the mount. In fellowship with our heavenly Father, and as disciples of the Lord Jesus, we come to that perfectibility of love of Matthew 5:48, we come to a higher righteousness than that practised by the hypocrites, the scribes and Pharisees (Matthew 5:20), we learn and go on learning what it is like to live in the present reality of the Kingdom of God, where He reigns. We love others because He has first loved us.

This is radical. It is in agreement with God's love for the world of John 3:16, of Jesus' sacrifice on the Cross. It is possible only because of Him; who said, 'Without me, you can do nothing' (John 15:5).

Matthew 7:13-14. A church which is prepared for an uncomfortable, difficult and narrow life

Enter by the narrow gate, for the gate is wide and the way is easy that leads to destruction and those who enter by it are many. For the gate is narrow and the way is hard that leads to life and those who find it are few.

Every individual is faced by a choice at some point in their life. Two gates, two ways lie before them. Which will they choose? The easy way or the hard way? The wide gate or the narrow gate? Some choices we make affect us only temporally or materially. This choice offered by Jesus affects our eternal destiny. There is a choice that leads to life, but there is also a choice that leads to destruction. Knowing this, it is still possible with that knowledge to choose the way of destruction.

As far back as Deuteronomy 30:19 the Lord's people had been offered the choice between life and death, blessing and curse, through Moses. Again, in the time of Joshua, in the last chapter of that book, Joshua said to the people, 'Choose you this day whom you will serve' (Joshua 24:15). And the people answered, 'The Lord our God we will serve and His voice we will obey (Joshua 24: 24). But this commitment was soon broken.

This last chapter of Joshua leads into the Book of Judges where the prevailing theme is, 'Every man did what was right in his own eyes' (Judges 21:25). Israel had broken the covenant with God and we read these terrible words when we come to Samuel, regarded as the last of the Judges, 'The word of the Lord was rare in those days; there was no open vision' (1 Samuel 3:1). No word from the Lord! Did they feel that He had abandoned them because of the choices they had made to live idolatrously? But God raised up Samuel to restore the nation. Time and again, the Lord brought them back to this place of commitment. They knew to do good, but could not do it. The prophet Micah pleads with them. 'He has shown you, O man, what is good, and what does the Lord require of you, but to do justice and to love mercy and to walk humbly with your God? (Micah 6:8).

So this matter of choice would not be an unfamiliar theme to these new disciples sitting at the feet of Jesus on the mountain side. They knew their nation's history.

But Jesus is presenting the decision in another way, and with more than an individual emphasis. First, He is saying that the choice comes to every man and woman, and secondly, He is saying that the church is made up of those, who, recognizing that they are not choosing the easy option, nevertheless want to follow Jesus, to go this way even though the way may be hard. Perhaps as they sat there before the Lord Jesus, holding our His hands to them, they recalled the words of Isaiah 65:3. 'I have spread out my hands all the day to a rebellious people' (A.V) to a disobedient and gainsaying people' (LXX Romans 10:21). God holding out His hands to His people, pleading with them to return to Him, welcoming them back to Himself. There may still have been in the crowd those who had not yet decided on the narrow gate and the hard way. How could they resist the loving invitation of the Lord Jesus? The gospel is for all, but not all respond. Even by not choosing the narrow gate, the alternative becomes automatic. By choosing one, they reject the other.

It is not God's intention that any should go the way of destruction, but He never coerces anyone. He has given us free will, otherwise, how could we freely follow Him, love Him, worship Him? Without that freedom worship becomes a form only, with no substance, and in fact is no worship at all.

The narrowness of the gate means that only one person at a time can enter. It suggests an individual experience. There may be a place for mass evangelism, but even then the invitation comes to each person individually. Jesus says to everyone 'Come to Me and find salvation and life'. Later in His ministry, Jesus is recorded as saying that *He* is the door (A.V.) or the gate (N.I.V.). 'By Me if any man enter in he shall be saved' (John 10:8).

But there is a cost involved. Jesus is always straightforward with His disciples. He is warning them that if they want to go through that narrow gate, that this will not be the entry to a bed of roses, but to a thorn strewn highway. There is a way and it will be called the way of holiness (Isaiah 35:8 A.V.) and they that tread that way will have tribulation. Jesus says to His disciples, 'In the world you will have tribulation, but be of good cheer, I have overcome the world' (John 16:33).

He says to James and John, 'Can you drink of the cup that I drink of?' They say, 'Yes, Lord' (Matthew 20:22), not knowing how deep is that cup. For us it becomes the cup of blessing which we bless at the Lord's table (1 Corinthians 10:16), but for Him it was a cup of unimaginable suffering. He was a Man of sorrows and acquainted with grief (Isaiah 53:3). His heart was broken on the Cross, and He invites us to share in his sufferings. Paul speaks for many through the ages when he writes, 'That I may know Him and the power of His resurrection and may *share His sufferings*, becoming like Him in His death, that if possible I may attain the resurrection from the dead' (Philippians 3:10) and James declares, 'Count it all joy, my brethren, when you meet various trials' (James 1:2).

The way is hard. Those who have made the choice of the narrow gate and the hard way have entered upon a difficult life, but it is *LIFE*, life lived in and with the life of Jesus and in spite of everything, *abundant life* (John 10:10).

For those who have chosen the broad gate, the easy way, life can also be very difficult. They too may have many troubles, although for some there may be perceived compensations of power, or wealth. It is the end to which we look. The narrow gate believer enjoys living in the good of the life of Christ now, whatever the circumstances. The wide gate ones, also whatever their circumstances, will at the end find that the easy way led to destruction, for there is a judgement for all who leave God out of their lives. How acutely important it is, therefore, to share the gospel wherever and whenever and with whoever we can, the gospel of love and forgiveness, of peace and joy and unnumbered blessings.

As believers, we are not alone. Not only do we have the inestimable comfort of the presence of the Holy Spirit with us, we also have one another. God's purpose is not only for an individual to flourish in the Kingdom of God, though it is that, but that we should *all* come to the unity of the faith, to the measure of the stature of the fullness of Christ (Ephesians 4:13) building up the body of Christ (Ephesians 4:12). This is the end of the journey, the goal to which we are heading, the purpose of the way of which Jesus said, 'I am the way, I am the only way' (John 14:6). How purposeful are lives lived with Him always in view. How gracious of Him to give us a place in that church, that group of people who have become an innumerable host, those who are determined to follow the Lamb wherever He goes (Revelation 14:4).

When a man or a woman sees the gate through which they have chosen to go, they do not see the end of the way to which the gate leads. Perhaps if they saw the destruction at the end of the wide gate, the broad way, it might discourage them from going down that path. Similarly, the person who chooses the narrow gate and the hard way also does not see that this path can be full of tribulation, but in faith, trusting in the Lord Jesus and earnestly desiring the better thing of sitting at His feet and hearing His word, they choose life. Faith is the gate through which they come to Christ. Life is the way. This is the promise;

127

'therefore choose life, that thou and thy seed might live' (Deuteronomy 30:19).

Matthew 7:15-23. A church which is aware that some teachers and prophets are false

Beware of false prophets, who come to you in sheep's clothing, but inwardly they are ravening wolves. You will know them by their fruits (Matthew 7:15).

By demonstrating that some prophets are false, Jesus is teaching His disciples that there is an expectation that there will be true prophets in the church.

How important it is that Jesus warns against false prophets. Just as He shows the true way in Matthew 6:1-17 for His disciples to give alms, fast and pray by describing the false, hypocritical way taken by scribes and Pharisees, so here in Matthew 7:15, He uses the falseness of some so-called prophets to encourage believers that true prophetic function may be, perhaps should be, exercised by men and women in the church.

Describing these false prophets, He says, *first*, they come to you in sheep's clothing but inwardly they are ravening wolves. In this *new* community, this *new* church which Jesus is raising up, there are prophets who prey upon the gentle sheep of the church.

Jesus says later on in His ministry, 'I am the good shepherd; I give my life for the sheep' (John 10:11, 15), 'My sheep hear my voice and I know them, and they follow Me, and no one shall pluck them out of My hand (John 10:27,28).

These false prophets pretend to be sheep, they wear sheep's clothing. Sometimes, prophets in Israel wore a hairy mantle to proclaim their office (2 Kings 1:8, Zechariah 13:4) but without intention to deceive. The message is clear. False prophets lead the disciples into believing that they too are following Jesus, learning from Him. The sheep's clothing may be metaphorical, but the intention is clear. They are '*ravening*' (A.V.) which is perhaps more enlightening than 'ravenous' (R.S.V). According to the Oxford English Dictionary (Ninth Edition 1996), ravening has the sense of rapacious, grasping, extortionate, predatory, voracious, greedy; although the 'ravenous' of the R.S.V. does suggest a tendency to 'chew people up and spit them out' in the modern idiom. Whichever adjective is used, Jesus' judgement of them is very harsh, until we recognise why He judges them the way He does, especially when the result of their activity is made known (Matthew 7:19,23).

Secondly, Jesus uses the metaphor of trees. Jesus says, 'By their fruits you shall know them' (Matthew 7:16). Members of the congregation, the community, had looked up to these so-called prophets, expecting to receive from them grapes and figs, some precious word from the Lord to help them in their discipleship. Some kindly deed of compassion, or thoughtfulness, or understanding, for that is the function of a prophet, to bring someone near to God, not as a mediator, but as a channel from God to men and women, to encourage them, even when perhaps they have gone astray, to remember the loving kindness of the Lord, His open arms of love to all who are trusting Him. There are so many examples of this ministry to be found in the Old Testament.

Under the terms of Jesus' metaphor, there are prophets whom He describes as 'good trees bearing fruit' (Matthew 7:17) not only in themselves but in those to whom they have been sent by God, the fruit of a close and intimate relationship with Him. How terrible to hear the words of Jesus on the Day of Judgement about the bad trees, the false prophets, 'I never knew you, depart from Me' (Matthew 7:23). Knowing Him, walking close to Him, this is the fruit which the 'good tree' brings forth. The *'bad tree'* cannot bring forth this good fruit, rather the reverse, and so must submit to the fire of judgement (Matthew 7:19). So serious are the words of Jesus.

Whether in the Old or New Testament, there are examples of good and bad prophets. In the early church, Paul speaks of the spiritual gift of prophecy (1 Corinthians 12:10) as an inspiration of the Holy Spirit (1 Corinthians 12:11) the manifestation of the Holy Spirit for the common good (1 Corinthians 12: 7).

In 1 Corinthians 14:39, he earnestly desires the believers to prophesy, because he who prophesies edifies the church (1 Corinthians 14:4).

In Acts 19:6, the disciples spoke with tongues and prophesied after receiving the gift of the Holy Spirit. In Acts 21:9, we read of Philip's four unmarried daughters who prophesied. Also, in Acts 21:10, a Christian prophet came down from Jerusalem whose name was Agabus.

When Paul speaks in Ephesians 2:20 of the church being built upon the foundation of the apostles and prophets, he is speaking of New Testament rather than Old Testament prophets, but in both cases, it is the work of the Holy Spirit. In the Old Testament, when the Spirit rested upon them, they prophesied (Numbers 11:25), and where would we be who live under the new covenant without Old Testament prophets like Isaiah, Jeremiah, Ezekiel and Daniel, Hosea, Joel, Amos... we could go on. These prophecies are precious even to us who have the privilege of being under the New covenant, because they are the word of the Lord to us, just as they were to the first people who heard them.

Moses looked for a prophet greater than himself. He spoke messianically when he said, 'The Lord your God will raise up for you a prophet like me, from among you... him you shall heed' (Deuteronomy 18:15). Jesus confirmed that this prophecy referred to Him, by His comment when people rejected Him, 'A prophet is not without honour except in his own country' (Matthew 13:57) and yet all the people were stirred when Jesus entered Jerusalem on a donkey saying, 'This is the prophet from Nazareth' (Matthew 21:11).

But false prophets have entered the church. Paul uses Jesus' metaphor when he says, 'I know that after my departure, fierce wolves will come in among you, not sparing the flock' (Acts 20:29) and in Galatians, he speaks of 'false brethren secretly brought in' (Galatians 2:4), 'that they might bring us into bondage'. Jesus compared these false prophets who have crept into the church as trees which will be 'hewn down and cast into the fire' (Matthew 7:19). There is a terrible judgement waiting for those who have deceived the people of God, led them astray, preyed upon them. It is not because God is not merciful. He is. But because this is the way they have chosen to go, and these are the consequences.

And Jesus repeats, 'You shall know them by their fruits' (verse 20). Husks of people lying on the ground, left there by the people who preyed upon them. Jesus will judge them. He is looking for true prophets in His church who will be to them as Himself, who will bind up the broken-hearted, bring release to the captives, the opening of the prison to those who are in any kind of imprisonment of body or spirit, the recovery of sight to the blind in heart as well as physical sight; and all this under the anointing of the Holy Spirit, for that is His work (Isaiah 61:1-2, Luke 4:18).

It appears that under the anointing of the Holy Spirit, there was growing up in this new community of believers, that all person ministry of which Paul writes in 1 Corinthians chapters 12-14. The Holy Spirit did not confine Himself only to the leaders of the church. His gifts of healing, prophecy, tongues, interpretation of tongues, the gifts of wisdom, of faith, were available to all. The titles of leadership may differ – minister, elder, deacon, vicar, rector, bishop, curate, priest, but the principles of leadership remain the same.

In contemporary church life, welcomers, stewards or church wardens have a ministry in encouraging welcome and warmth in the church, opportunities to show compassion and integrity, to be as a father or mother to members of the congregation within the limits of their acceptance. But of course, it is up to all the members of the church to follow the words of Jesus – 'Love one another as I have loved you' (John 15:12) 'Continue in my love' (John 15:9). Continue, abide, remain, μένω. We do not want or need titles to stand in the way of our love for each other. Is the church democratic? No. but we trust that it will remain theocratic, ruled and governed by Christ who is head over all things to the church which is His Body, the fullness of Him who fills all in all (Ephesians 1:22).

All of this is implied by Jesus' injunction to 'beware of false prophets'. In verse 21, He comes to a most serious warning. 'Not everyone who says to me "Lord, Lord" shall enter the Kingdom of Heaven, but he who does the will of my Father which is in heaven; *on that day,* the day of judgement, many will say to me "Lord, Lord" did we not prophesy in your Name, and cast out demons in your Name, and do many mighty works in your Name?'

'Jesus says, these are the false prophets, because, firstly, they are not doing the will of the Father, and secondly, they are doing their own thing, that which brings glory to themselves. Jesus calls them evildoers (verse 23 R.S.V.) anomie, *άνομία,* lawless people, workers of iniquity (verse 23 A.V.).

But the Lord's people are not deceived for long, for they have the criterion, 'By their fruits *you shall know them'* (verse 16-20). This is personal recognition and personal rejection of them. It is the gift of *discernment,* unlike the passing of judgement in chapter 7, and an imperative. Jesus encourages His disciples to steer well clear of them, for they are lawless, disobedient to God and engaged in activities to which they have no right, for they had not entered the Kingdom of Heaven through the prescribed door of repentance, 'Repentance towards God and faith towards our Lord Jesus Christ' (Acts 20:21).

In chapter 7:22, Jesus is speaking of the judgement day when everyone will give account of himself to God (Romans 14:10). *'On that day,'* is an allusion to the Last Judgement. As they come before the throne of judgement they acknowledge the deity of Jesus by saying, 'Lord, Lord,' but it is too late. The time for repentance has passed. This is the fulfilment of the Kingdom of Heaven, when the Lord Jesus is given His rightful place, the judgement seat of Christ, when every knee shall bow to Him and every tongue confess that He is Lord, to the glory of God the Father (Philippians 2:11).

We know neither the day nor the hour, but it will surely come, and though people may implore Him, 'Lord, Lord,' He cannot recognise them as part of who He is, part of His Body, part of the church for which He laid down His life, 'That He might sanctify her... that He might present the church to Himself, a glorious church, without spot or wrinkle or any such thing) that she might be holy and without blemish before Him' (Ephesians 6:25-27), Jesus has to say to these others, 'I never knew you; depart from me you evildoers' (verse 23).

This is not a small problem. Jesus says, 'Many-πολλοὶ- will say to Me, "Lord, Lord," thus showing the seriousness of the threat posed by the false prophets; even doing miracles in the Name of Jesus (verse 22).

Prophesying, casting out demons and many mighty works (verse 22) are part of the ministry of true prophets, those whom Jesus has sent out under His own authority. Those who do not bear His stamp, incur His judgement. They are the deeds of the workers of iniquity (verse 23 A.V.) made much worse by using the Name of Jesus while not doing the will of the Father (verse 21) being disobedient to Him; and by their antinomianism, lawlessness, leading many astray. They call Him Lord and do not the things which He says (Luke 6:46) They use the word 'Lord' both in their exorcisms and miracle working and also in their confession of faith, while at the same time denying Him (Acts 19:13-17).

It is almost as though, the Lord Jesus having begun this section of His sermon by warning His disciples against false prophets has Himself progressed into an understanding of the evil they can do to valuable members of His community, and His complete rejection of them, 'Depart from Me, I never knew you!' (verse 23) is their complete separation from all that is represented by Him. We cannot imagine anything worse, anything more terrible than hearing those words from the lips of Jesus, 'Depart from me!'

Jesus has moved into the eschatological perspective of what will happen at the end of time, when He will become the judge. The paraenesis has become a prediction (verse 23).

Matthew 7:24-27. The church is founded on Jesus

'Everyone then who hears these words of mine and does them will be like a wise man who built his house upon the rock (verse

25), and the rain fell and the floods come and the winds blew and beat upon that house, but it did not fall, because it had been founded on the rock' (Matthew 7:24).

Jesus comes to the end of this sermon. Of course, there are going to be other discourses which Matthew records for us throughout his gospel, but the sermon on the mount is foundational. It lays out for these new disciples, principles for *their own living* as those newly entered the *now* Kingdom of Heaven and for their relationship with an Almighty and Everlasting God whom they can now call *Father*, as they become the new community, the ἐκκλησία the '*gathered together ones*' in prayer and worship, and brotherly love and discernment.

Jesus ends this discourse with the *parable of the two foundations.* In essence, what He is saying is, first find a rock, then build your house on it; first find Jesus, then build your life on Him. You will probably encounter all the trials and tribulations of life in the same way as those who have built their lives, not on Jesus, but on a shifting, unstable foundation, like sand, but with Jesus as your rock, you will not fail. Jesus is saying, 'Come to Me, build your life on me.' Blessed are those who have already done so, and blessed are all those who have not only *listened* to Him, but *heard* Him. In Hebrew, to *hear is to obey.* The concepts are virtually synonymous. Jesus says, 'Everyone who hears these words of mine, *my words, μου λόγος,* and does them, is like a wise man who built his house upon a rock (7:24) Jesus is claiming equivalence with the word of God; which is what the scriptures are; and therefore claiming to be God. Some of those seated around Him may have heard the voice which came from heaven at His baptism, 'This is my beloved Son,' but at this time, such a claim is but a whisper in the hearts of His disciples. They have not recognised the full implication of who He is. As His ministry progresses, they will come to accept the truth of what He is telling them, until we get to the question He asked Peter, 'Who do *you* say that I am?' And Peter answered, 'You are the Christ, the Son of the living God' (Matthew 16:16).

This is the Rock, the foundation on which the church is built (Matthew 16:18)

Jesus is also saying that building one's life on Him is a life of obedience. 'Everyone who hears these words of mine and *does* them' (verse 24). He has given them a springboard, launching them off into a life of faith, a life of waiting upon the will of their Father who is in heaven; of doing good to others; of ordering their church life in conformity with the complementary commandments of loving God, and loving one's neighbour.

But hearing is not enough. As James puts it (the brother of the Lord, not the disciple. Was he there in the crowd?), 'Be doers of the word, and not hearers only' (James 1:22). Jesus says, 'Everyone who hears these words of mine and does not do them will be like a foolish man who built his house upon the sand' (verse 26). James comments, 'A double-minded man unstable in all his ways' (James 1:8). *Μου λόγος – My words*, give an emphatic stress on Jesus' words as the standard by which His disciples live; and intensifies the stress by adding τούτος – these. 'Everyone then who hears *these* words of mine and does them' refers to all the words of the sermon. This is a warning and also a blessing, an exclusive and excluding reliance upon anything less than the foundation which is laid, which is Jesus.

Architectural, construction and topographical references in this parable are just references, and have very little significance in this parabolic sequence. But how impregnable is the church built upon that same rock, the rock that followed them in the wilderness, the rock that was Christ (1 Corinthians 10:45), the rock from which they drank (Deuteronomy 32:4, 15, 18, 20, 31). We drink from Him, we build our lives on Him, we are secure in Him. When the cloud bursts, when the river overflows, when the winds blow fiercely through the storm, we will not fall for our lives are founded upon the rock.

The parable is not a polemic of words over doing, of praxis over belief, of law over grace, for the life of Jesus which He has given to His disciples holds these complementary concepts in perfect balance. Jesus begins with πᾶς – *everyone* – the everyone who *hears* his words and *does* ποιέω them, and alternatively everyone who hears His words and does not do them. Thus, as previously in His sermon, the alternatives are made clear.

But hearing and following the word of Jesus, μου λόγος does not lead men and women into the condemnation of a law which they are unable to keep, but into 'the freedom of doing 'the will of My Father which is in heaven' (7:21), for that is always the effect of listening to Him and doing what He commands. Jesus says 'He is My Father and your Father, my God and your God (John 20:17), and we can scarcely believe the amazing truth of such a statement, but He says, 'You shall know the truth, and the truth shall make you *free* (John 8:32). A *new* commandment I give you, that you love one another (John 13:3). *It is not trying but living.*

Jesus is the standard. We will often fail, but He never fails, for He is God, and has provided for us the everlasting gift of returning to Him again in penitence and faith.

To us has been given the supreme privilege of building our lives on Jesus as the foundation Rock of the Eternal Word of God; which He is. If for some reason we were to lose all the rest of the Bible and were left only these few pages of the Sermon on the Mount, even if this was all we had of Jesus' teaching, it would be enough, enough to keep us close to Him, enough to go on trusting the Father who is in heaven.

We have no need to try to build upon our own piety, for we are only too well aware that we have none, except what God has graciously promised to give us as we trust in the sacrificial gift of His Son. We have not come into a new set of rules and regulations, but into a place of rest. Jesus said, 'Come to Me and I will give you rest' (Matthew 11:28) *not* I will give you a new set of rules and regulations for you to follow. We listen to Him, we hear Him and we obey Him. We walk with Him and enjoy the fellowship of prayer and intercession as part of His family in the conviction that our Heavenly Father *knows* (6:32). He will guide. He will supply. *We worship Him.*

Yet without the praxis, the doing as well as the hearing, the church becomes saltless and lightless. There will be a contradiction between the proclamation and its outworking in the individual lives of disciples and in the fuller life of the church gathered together. Obedience to 'those words of mine' of Jesus begins with the individual's private and personal commitment to Him, flows out to all members of the gathered community and then to the world around both openly and subversively.

Because the main driver is love. Love is a direct expression of the Kingdom of God. He who loves not knows not God, for God is love (1 John 4:7). The door into the kingdom is faith working by love, either a sudden or evolving awareness of the love of God 'for me', for the person in the crowd, in the marketplace, in the home: a light breaking in to a darkened mind, an unexpected awareness of the Numinous, the Other, after which nothing can ever be the same again. Different for everyone, different responses from everyone, and yet the same. *The reality of knowing Jesus. We love because He first loved us* (1 John 4:19).

The Sermon on the Mount concluded

And it came to pass when Jesus had ended these sayings, the people were astonished at His doctrine. For He taught them as one having authority, and not as the scribes (Matthew 7:28. A.V.).

And when Jesus finished these sayings (Matthew 7:28 R.S.V.).

Verse 28a introduces a concluding formula which Matthew uses at the end of all the five discourses in his gospel, thus drawing together all the teaching of the Lord Jesus as recorded by Matthew. This is καὶ ἐγένετο ὅτε ἐτέλεσεν ὁ Ἰησοῦς πάντας τοὺς λόγους, translated in the A.V. as, 'And it came to pass when Jesus had ended all these sayings', and in the R.S.V. as, 'And when Jesus finished these sayings'.

At the end of His five discourses (Matthew 7:28, 11:1, 13:55, 19:1, 26:1), it happened, or came about, or came to pass, that when Jesus had finished speaking or teaching all these words, several principles had been established to encourage His disciples.

This is what He has been teaching right from the beginning. In His first sermon. He has established the fundamental attitudes and behaviour of these new disciples who had recently entered the Kingdom of Heaven through repentance and faith. He has established Himself as the One who has the authority of the Word of God in Himself. In fact, we could draw the conclusion that He is God. He has made a distinction between those who are, and those who are not His disciples.' By their fruits you shall know them'. And above all, He has given His disciples the privilege of knowing God as Father. In effect, these concluding phrases of the sermon tell His disciples all that they need to know of the life of faith, a life lived in obedience to the will of their Father in heaven; a life of love for all is here. This is the authoritative, εξουσία, teaching of Jesus.

How long does it take us to read the sermon on the mount? Ten, fifteen minutes? And yet these chapters, Matthew 5, 6 and 7, must have been to these early disciples, and subsequently to us, some of the most revolutionary ideas the world had ever seen. No wonder then, that when Jesus had finished these sayings, *these τούτους these words*, the crowds όχλο of Matthew chapter 5 were astonished εξεπλήσσοντο at His teaching, and the difference between His authority and that of 'their' scribes.

The scribes were the experts in Mosaic law. They knew all the answers to any question raised. Jesus makes a distinction, an authoritative distinction between His teaching and theirs, for their teaching brought men and women into bondage, but his teaching set them free. In Luke 11:46, He says to the lawyers, 'Woe to you lawyers also! For you load men with burdens hard to bear and you yourselves do not touch the burdens with one of your fingers.' How potentially little the new disciples knew of the effect of that teaching of Jesus, as it set them free and they began to pray in the name of the Father, seeking only His will for their lives, as they laid down their lives in love for one another (John 15:12, 1 John 3:16) and for the world outside; but they were catching a glimpse of who Jesus was, and is, and His sovereignty, and His power, when He says, *'But I say unto you... I am the fulfilment of the law and the prophets... these words of mine.'* They are beginning to understand that the teaching of Jesus, and the Person He is, is fundamentally different from all that they have previously known.

Some theologians have seen in the Sermon on the Mount a new ethics for a new people. Dietrich Bonhoeffer, that dear servant of God, writes, 'Humanly speaking, there are countless possibilities for understanding and interpreting the Sermon on the Mount. Jesus knows only a single possibility. Simply to go out and obey. Not interpret or apply, but *do*, obey. Only in this way is Jesus' word heard. But again, not to speak of doing as an ideal possibility but *really* to start doing.' (From Kirchlidies Jarbuch 1963 ed. J. Beckmann, quoted in 'The Sermon on the Mount' by Georg Strecker 1988).

Though praxis is the driver of these sayings of Jesus, as Bonhoeffer claims, as an ethical treatise it is not enough. We so often fail. We recognise all too clearly the truth of what Jesus said in John 15:5, 'Without me you can do nothing!' Paul discovered the answer when he wrote to the Galatian Christians (Galatians 2:20), 'It is *no longer I, but Christ* living in me, and the life I now live, I live by faith in the Son of God who loved me and gave Himself for me.'

We receive Him into our hearts, into our lives, we know and experience the indwelling Christ, even though we may not be able to explain the experience rationally. Like Paul, we can say, '*I know whom* I have believed' (2 Timothy 1:12). This is what makes the life of faith expounded for us by the Lord Jesus in the sermon on the mount gloriously possible, as Bonhoeffer undoubtedly knew.

Matthew 5:1-7:29. Summary of the sermon on the mount

Watchman Nee, a great Chinese Christian theologian of the 20th century wrote (at least) three books: The Normal Christian Life; The Normal Christian Worker; The Normal Christian Church Life; accurately summing up the three chapters of the sermon on the mount.

In the sermon, Jesus reveals a secret, inner disobedience of the heart leading to a lack of relationship with God which can only be expelled by turning back to Him in penitence and faith. The hiding of oneself behind good deeds or piety, not only results in an obstruction of the penetrating, life changing love of God, but subverts the whole teaching of the Torah, reducing it to a system of casuistry. Repentance shatters the hard shell around the heart which prevents that relationship with God, opens up the whole person to God, enables an acknowledgement of God as Father and obedience to Him as the highest privilege life can offer. No other life can compare with this.

Blessed indeed are all those comprehensively included in the Beatitudes, a foretaste of all that is to come under the Lordship of Jesus. The blessings, the Beatitudes, are the blessings of love. *Because you are poor in spirit, utterly dependent upon me, I will bless you with the gift of the Kingdom of Heaven as your life... Because you are mourning, I will give you the gift of comfort, the gift of the Paraclete, the Holy Spirit. I will bless you with His comfort, the one who comes alongside...* We could go on. *Because I love you*, is what Jesus is saying.

This is grace. *Grace is love in action.* Jesus actively loves us and pours His grace into our lives. We repeat, *grace is love in action*, in every circumstance, in every difficulty, in every joy, there is grace, there is Jesus. Grace, the grace of the Lord Jesus, the love of God and the fellowship of the Holy Spirit. And the grace, the love and the fellowship are one because of who He is, the One who is with us all evermore.

The steadfast love of the Lord never ceases, His mercies never come to an end; They are new every morning; Great is Thy faithfulness. The Lord is my portion, says my soul. Therefore, I will hope in Him (Lamentations 3:22 R.S.V.).

Matthew Chapter 8

Matthew 8:1-4. The cleansing of a leper

When He came down from the mountain, great crowds followed Him; and behold a leper came to Him and knelt before Him, saying, 'Lord, if You will, You can make me clean'. And He stretched out His hand and touched him saying, 'I will. Be clean'. And immediately his leprosy was cleansed. And Jesus said to him, 'See that you say nothing to anyone, but go, show yourself to the priest, and offer the gift that Moses commanded, for a proof to the people (Matthew 8: 1-4).

We turn from the meaning of what Jesus *said* in His sermon, to what He *does* with people; and how He demonstrates the impact on their lives of their faith in Him. Matthew, His faithful biographer, chooses the cleansing of a leper as the first recorded individual healing in his gospel to show the compassion of Jesus and the leper's faith.

Psalm 103:7 says, 'He made known His *ways* to Moses', the ways revealed to Moses as He *spoke t*o him, 'His *acts* to the people of Israel.' Psalm 68:11 says, 'The Lord gave *the word*; great is the company of those that publish it.' Jesus has given the word, and made known *His ways* in the Sermon on the Mount. Now is the time to demonstrate *His acts*, the sequential following of the act of proclamation. This is the way He always works. The word must come first, the generating creative word of God (Genesis 1:3, Proverbs 8:22, John 1:1). 'And the word became flesh, and dwelt among us, full of grace and truth (John 1:14) and they called his Name Jesus.' And His word is followed by His acts.

In Matthew 4:23, Jesus had already healed a number of people subsequent to His proclamation of the gospel of the Kingdom. 'He went about healing every disease and infirmity among the people... they brought Him all the sick, those afflicted with various diseases and infirmity among the people, demoniacs, epileptics and paralytics, and He healed them (verse 24).

Now Matthew recalls an *individual* case. Jesus had come down from the mountain with an astonished crowd following Him; amazed, astounded at the authority of His teaching. He had preached the gospel to them, the gospel of the Kingdom of Heaven. He had taught them how to live in the recognition that there was more, so much more, to come in the fulfilment of the kingdom, and they were beginning to enjoy a foretaste of the kingdom even now as they entered into the experience of it through repentance and faith. His first blessing was to the poor in spirit 'for theirs *is* the Kingdom of Heaven' (Matthew 5:3); the kingdom of heaven *is* and *will be* theirs through the fulfilment of that promise, what has become known as the 'now' and 'not yet' of the kingdom of heaven.

He had said that He came to fulfil the law and the prophets (Matthew 5:17) He had recalibrated their response to brothers (verse 23) women (verse 28), wives (verse 31), language (verse 34), enemies (verse 39), urging that the new kingdom was a kingdom of love, love that was not just a warm emotional feeling but love in action. He had gone on to describe their relationship to God as children/sons of a loving Heavenly Father, and He had taught them the difference between judging another, and discerning what was negative and damaging to the community of believers from false prophets, false leadership (verse 15).

He had demonstrated His authority in His *teaching* in the sermon on the mount. Now, in chapters 8 and 9, He was demonstrating His authority in ten miracles which He performed before entering again in Chapter 10 on some further teaching. His miracles were also the proclamation of the kingdom, the kingdom in action, the kingdom under Jesus' authority, the authority of the King. He had come down from the mountain into the world where men and women were living; often suffering, often fearful, and vulnerable.

Over all these, and other conditions, He had authority. And it appears from Matthew's gospel that the first man to acknowledge this was a leper, an outcast from his community, living as best he could on the scraps of food left out for him by friends or family, but so far away from them that he was unable to communicate with them or they with him. They were absolutely forbidden by the Jewish law from touching him, for to do so might well give them the disease which they would then take back to their family. They could not risk it, and the law recognised that. In effect, to be a leper was a living death.

This leper must have come from a distance to fall at the feet of Jesus. The word for worshipping is used here, προσκυνάει, as he says, 'Lord, if you will, you can make me clean.' And Jesus' immediate response, 'I will, be clean' (verse 3) as He stretched out His hand and *touched him*, whom it was forbidden to touch. Touched by the hand of Jesus, how could he not be cleansed, yet Matthew tells us that it was the leprosy that was cleansed rather than the leper. What Jesus had done was to restore this man's identity to him, giving back to him the life he had lost, the family, friends and occupation he had had to renounce, and at the same time had given him a new life, a new identity as a follower, disciple of Jesus.

Worship came before the healing. The leper addresses Jesus as 'Lord' as do the disciples (Matthew 8:25, 14:28,30, 16:22, 17:4, 18:21), and the sick who come to Jesus for help (Matthew 8:2,6,8, 9:28, 15:22,25,27, 17:15, 20:30-31,33). This title is not used by outsiders, and is not simply polite speech. It endorses the 'if you will' of the leper's request, because it acknowledges the sovereign will of Jesus, who as the Lord has His authority from God. Jesus 'wills' and his authority immediately has healing power. Jesus stretches out His hand to people and immediately they come under His powerful protection, as do the disciples in 12:49.

We wonder why, in such a personal confrontation, yet surrounded by the crowds, Jesus gave the command to secrecy. Jesus had been followed by the crowds as He came down from the mountain. Here He was, on His way to Capernaum, surrounded by them. How could this former leper keep the secret?

Yet people have often complained of feeling lonely in a crowd, everybody being occupied or preoccupied with their own affairs. Perhaps it is not so difficult to see that a man coming to Jesus and kneeling before Him could, in just a few minutes, have received the blessing of cleansing for which he had come to Jesus. It could even be that recognising that this man was a leper, the crowd had temporarily drawn back from Jesus, leaving a space around Him and the leper. How did he know that Jesus could heal him? Lepers are not specifically mentioned when Jesus was healing people in Matthew 4:23. *He came in faith,* as well as fear and trembling and Jesus did not disappoint him. He never does.

Jesus was aware of a secondary effect that the cleansing of the leper could have. He had said in Matthew 5:17 that he came not to abolish the law, but to fulfil it. So He sent the man to the priest as prescribed in Leviticus 5:3, 13:1, proving that the cleansing had occurred, but also that which had been virtually impossible under Mosaic law, the cleansing of leprosy, had become gloriously possible under Jesus' healing hand. Jesus had not only said that He was the fulfilment of the law, but had *proved* it. The leper was the proof, the testimony, and his leprosy had been the means, at the outset of Jesus' healing ministry, of declaring that Jesus was indeed the long-looked-for Messiah. Dear John the Baptist in prison said to his disciples 'Ask Jesus, are you He that should come or do we look for another?' (Matthew 11:3). The cleansing of lepers was one of the manifestations of the Messiahship of the Lord Jesus (Matthew 11:5). The message given back to John was that Jesus fulfilled all the conditions of Messiahship and much more.

Matthew 8:4. The Messianic Secret

And Jesus said to him, 'See that you say nothing to any one, but go, show yourself to the priest' (verse 4).

From the beginning of Jesus' ministry, He is shown as someone completely different from all those prophets and priests who had gone before. He was Jesus, the Saviour, saving His people from their sins (Matthew 1:21). He was Immanuel, God with us (Matthew 1:23), the One whom the Holy Spirit had rested on at His baptism like a dove, while the voice of the Father in heaven declared, 'This is my beloved Son in whom I am well pleased' (Matthew 3:16,17).

And all these attributes He demonstrates again and again as He moves through His ministry. But the full significance of what He had done for the leper could not be deduced from this one isolated episode; it could not be the whole of the glorious truth of who Jesus is.

So Jesus said to him, 'Say nothing to anyone, but go, show yourself to the priest and offer the gift that Moses commanded,' the offering prescribed in Leviticus 14:2. This man who had worn torn clothes and let the hair of his head hang loose and covered his upper lip while he cried, 'Unclean! Unclean!' (Leviticus 13:45), who had dwelt alone in a habitation outside the camp, and later outside the city (Leviticus 13:46); he could say, 'He touched me.' The touch of Jesus' hand had stripped away all the ostracism, the loneliness. The authoritative word of Jesus, 'Be clean!' had made him whole.

But how significant that the fullness of the whole revelation of who Jesus was *could not be understood in its entirety* at this point in Jesus' ministry. The partial revelation to the former leper was outstandingly wonderful to him, but there was so much more to come. It would be interesting to speculate that he was one of the 120 in the upper room before the Day of Pentecost, at the very beginning of the church. Certainly, that day would come when he could proclaim to the whole world, 'I am clean! He healed me!' In some mysterious way, he had become part of the plan of salvation:

Matthew 8:5-13. The centurion

As He entered Capernaum a centurion came forward to Him, beseeching Him and saying, 'Lord, my servant is lying paralysed at home, in terrible distress.' And He said to him,

> 'I will come and heal him'. But the centurion answered him,
> 'Lord, I am not worthy to have You come under my roof, but
> only say the word and my servant will be healed'. For I am a
> man under authority, with soldiers under me, and I say to one,
> 'Go', and he goes, and to another 'Come', and he comes, and to
> my slave, Do this, and he does it' (Matthew 8:5-13).

Matthew had written (Matthew 8:2), 'And behold, a *leper* came,' προσελθών, *came near, approached*. Now, in Matthew 8:6, a *centurion* came forward, came near, approached Him, an indication that before the healing, there was an overwhelming desire on behalf of the supplicant for the blessing which only Jesus could give. Though one was a Jew and one a Gentile, He encourages both to come to Him. We too, however weak and heavy laden we are, may come to Him, and He will give us rest (Matthew 11:28), and how blessed are those who hunger and thirst for Him.

The leper was obviously Jewish, and could be commanded by Jesus to offer a sacrifice according to Jewish law. So in a sense, he represents the Jewish people who can turn to Jesus as the Messiah without compromising His relationship with Israel, for whom He has left His Father's glory in order to include them in His New Covenant. The leper is a new disciple, representative of Jewish believers who come to Christ, and receive new life from Him. How wonderful that God has not cast off His people whom He foreknew! (Romans 11:2). No-one who believes in Him will be ashamed (Isaiah 28:16, Romans 10:11), for there is no distinction between Jew and Gentile, but the same Lord is Lord of all and bestows His riches upon all who call upon Him (Romans 10:12).

This theme is given a different emphasis as we turn to the experience of the possibly Roman, certainly Gentile centurion. We have seen Jesus' authority in fulfilling the law concerning leprosy. Now His authority is shown in His pronouncement that *all people of faith*, whether Jews or Gentiles, are accepted; and *all unbelievers*, even though they may be Israelites/Jews, are rejected.

In the centurion, Jesus had found a man of faith. Jesus says to the crowd, 'I have not found such faith, not even in Israel, not even among the Jews, and many shall come from the east and the west and shall sit at table with Abraham, Isaac and Jacob in the kingdom of heaven, but others will be thrown into outer darkness' (Matthew 8:10-11). Here at the beginning of His ministry, Jesus is giving this authoritative warning which can only be described as prophetic. He speaks of those who come from the east and the west to share in the heavenly banquet prepared for them, but also of those who are 'outside' (Matthew 8:10), those who have not accepted, but rejected Him.

But just as had the prophets of old, Jesus is here offering to all, both Jews and Gentiles alike, an alternative to that dreadful prospect, and an invitation to this representative Gentile, this centurion, as well as those under the law of Moses, to sit or recline at the banquet which is to come (to recline was more usual than to sit).

Matthew, Luke and John all give quite different versions of this event, according to the particular emphasis each evangelist is placing on the ministry of Jesus, and according as each one is inspired by the Holy Spirit, the One promised by Jesus as the Remembrancer, the One who would bring to their remembrance all that Jesus said to them (John 14:26).

So in Matthew's gospel, we have the authority of Jesus as King in his Kingdom, in Luke we have an understanding of Jesus as the Son of Man, the One who is concerned for the inferior members of society, the poor, the outcast, widows and children. In Mark, we have the Lord Jesus portrayed as the suffering Servant. In John's gospel, Jesus is portrayed as the Son of God who comes to give life, and to give it more abundantly (John 10:10).

In John's version of this event, at John 4:14 Jesus had already promised the gift of the water of life to the Samaritan woman at the well, and those who believed because of her testimony; now in John 4:46 He heals the official's *son* (not the centurion and his servant), in response to faith.

Like the accounts in Luke and John (Luke 7:1-10, John 4:46-54), Matthew's narrative too focuses on the faith shown by the centurion. According to Professor I. H. Marshall (The Gospel of Luke, p 279) there were no Roman forces in Galilee before 44 A.D. and therefore it is more likely that the centurion was a centurion over the soldiery of Herod Antipas, the Tetrarch of Galilee, who were organised on Roman lines. The centurion's nationality is not stated, but he would not have been a Jew, nor is there any indication that he was a proselyte.

But he was a caring, compassionate man, concerned for his servant, a young man paralysed and in great distress (verse 6). He was willing to humble himself before the itinerant preacher from Galilee, because he was desperate for the plight of the young man and believed that only Jesus could heal him.

Though he himself was a man under authority, he recognised that the authority of Jesus was greater because He was under the delegation of a greater power. Jesus had a power and authority which he had never seen in anyone else through all his campaigning life, and the experience of maintaining law and order which he had endured as a military commander. He recognized that here was something higher, far above him. He says to Jesus, 'Simply say the word, and my servant will be healed' (verse 8) expressing the unlimited confidence he had in the word of Jesus which can heal, even from a distance. And the centurion also appreciates that as a Jew, Jesus could not enter a Gentile's premises.

The centurion's request amazes Jesus. He turns to the crowd which is still following and exclaims, 'I have not found so great faith, no, not in Israel' (verse 10) and He repeats the alternatives which He has already outlined in the Sermon on the Mount, speaking of those whose faith will enable them to come from the east and the west to join others of faith, Abraham, Isaac and Jacob, at the royal banquet, but will eclipse those who, while claiming to be children of Abraham, will be excluded because of their lack of faith in Jesus, the Messiah, the Anointed of God.

How terrible will be the pain and anguish of those left outside (verse 12). He came unto His own and His own received Him not, but to them who received Him, He gave the right, the authority, εξουσία, to become the children of God, even to those who believe on His Name, and to sit with Him in His Kingdom and at His banquet (John 1:12). The amazing gift of God.

No wonder that Jesus could say to the centurion, 'Go, be it done for you as you have believed.' And the servant was healed from that moment (verse 13).

Jesus wants to exclude no-one. He wants that everyone should repent and come to the knowledge of the truth, and at the culmination of His three-year ministry, He will demonstrate His great purpose for men and women, Jew and Gentile, by taking the burden of their sin upon Himself on the Cross, the Lamb of God who takes away the sin of the world (John 1:29). This man, the centurion, had brought joy and encouragement to the heart of Jesus, who declared, 'I have not found so great faith, no, not in Israel (verse 10).

Matthew 8:14-16. Peter's mother-in-law

And when Jesus entered Peter's house, He saw his mother-in-law sick with a fever; He touched her hand and the fever left her. And she arose and served Him. (R.S.V) ministered to Him (Matthew 8:14. A.V.).

After such an exhausting day, Jesus must have been glad of Peter's invitation to rest awhile at his home, only to find that Peter's mother-in-law was lying sick of a fever. But at the touch of Jesus, her fever left her and she was able to rise and serve Him (verse 14).

There is no record of her faith. Perhaps her illness was too severe for her to rise to faith. There is no mention of her calling Him 'Lord' as the leper (verse 2) and the centurion (verses 6 and 8) had done. Yet at His touch, she was immediately healed, demonstrating once again that it is not the faith of the person concerned which effects the miracle, but the authority of Jesus, His authoritative word. Faith brings the person near, but it is the love and compassion and authority of Jesus that demonstrates His saving and healing power. Even the faith is the gift of God, 'So that no human being might boast in the presence of God' (1 Corinthians 1:29).

This poor sick woman had nothing to bring to Jesus, yet He healed her. She had the wonderful privilege of serving Him, ministering to Jesus, and as far as the gospel of Matthew was concerned, was never heard of again! But we may be sure that she was among the many women who followed Jesus from Galilee, ministering to Him, and who then sat at the foot of the Cross where He died, until they saw Joseph of Arimathea come to the Cross, the one who had been given permission to take down His body from the Cross and place it in his own new tomb (Matthew 27:55-61). And we may be sure that she too will be among those at the marriage supper of the Lamb in Revelation 19:9.

There is a significant difference in these three recorded events in the early ministry of Jesus. In Matthew, the person who is sick is described as the centurion's *servant*. This is a translation of the Greek παῖς a child or a servant; and he could have been both, a child and a servant. In Luke, he is described as a slave, δοῦλος who is dear to the centurion. In John, the one who is ill is described as ο υιος that is, the son of Βασιλικός – translated as 'nobleman' in John 4:46 A.V and 'official' in R.S.V., the son of someone very important.

The significance of these apparent discrepancies lies in the fact that in some sense, the ill person was secondary to the message which all three gospels were emphasising, and focusing on. Jesus is the Messiah, the Son of God, and those who come to Him must believe that He is, and that He is the rewarder of them that seek Him. (Hebrews 11:6). Without faith it is impossible to please Him.

Faith was the obvious requirement in the episodes of the leper and the centurion/official/nobleman. But what about Peter's mother-in-law?

1 Samuel 16:7 observes that the Lord looks not on the outward appearance but on the heart. And there may be something else. There are times in a person's life when they feel that they are brought very low, to nothing, for example, when

suffering illness, or bereavement. They have nothing left to give, they feel empty of everything, even faith. Then they discover that the compassion of the Lord never ceases, His mercies never come to an end. Jesus takes over. He demands nothing from us that we are unable to give, only reaches out His hand and touches us, and the fever, though not always the circumstances, leaves us. How great is our God, how wonderfully kind to His children! We cannot see Him, we cannot feel Him, but we know He is near.

And she arose, and ministered to Him (verse 15).

Matthew 8:16. The healing of the many

That evening, they brought to Him many who were possessed with demons; and He cast out the spirits with a word, and healed all that were sick. This was to fulfil what was spoken by the prophet Isaiah, 'He took our infirmities and bore our diseases (Matthew 8:16, 18).

It seems that nothing could prevent the crowd from wanting to see Jesus, and Matthew describes for us the scene around the door of Peter's house. It is Mark's version of the event which states, 'At even when the sun was set' (Mark 1:32 A.V.), that is, that the sick and demon oppressed people were brought to Jesus after sunset on the sabbath day when healing (as work) became permissible.

Jesus as we know, did heal on the sabbath day in response to need, but He forbore to antagonise the upholders of the Mosaic law, the scribes and Pharisees, unnecessarily. The healing of the leper had perhaps gone unremarked, hence Jesus' request for secrecy (Matthew 8:4), and the healing of the Centurion's servant was from a distance (verse 13).

Again, Matthew emphasises that Jesus healed all that were sick, and cast out demons, *with a word* (verse 16), the word of His ultimate authority. Although Matthew was apparently determined to show Jesus acting in individual healing in this section of his gospel, he could not forbear to bring the whole of

Jesus' healing ministry under the scrutiny of its readers. Demons and spirits, regarded as the agents of illness at that time, both mental and physical, were dealt with by Jesus with a word, the fulfilment of the prophecy of Isaiah in chapter 53:4. 'He took our infirmities and bore our diseases.' Took them away, bore them away.

Throughout his gospel, as we saw in chapter 2, and will see as the fuller picture of the Lord Jesus emerges, Matthew uses Old Testament prophecy to demonstrate that He was indeed the true Messiah for whom His people had been waiting and longing. Ten times Matthew uses variations on this formula, 'This was to fulfil what was spoken by the prophet' (Matthew 1:22, 2:15,17,23, 4:14-16, 8:17, 12:18-21, 13:35, 24:15, 27:9).

There are often quotations from the Old Testament (e.g. 2:5, 3:3, 13:14, 24:15), which are not introduced by this formula. The significance is to be found in its relation to Jesus. Jesus is fulfilling before the very eyes of the people the scriptures concerning Himself. His life of obedience to the demands of the law and the prophets and yet far transcending them, because He was the only one who *could* fulfil them, corresponds to the plan of salvation instituted and now being fulfilled in Jesus as He lives, moves and acts in the will of God His Father.

These quotations keep before us those truths which are pertinent to the understanding of the gospel; who Jesus is, and how we know Him; as Immanuel (1:23); Son (2:15); Healer; (8:16), the Messiah of Israel; (12:18-21), and King; (21:5). We no longer know Him as past history. There is a historical viewpoint of course to the life of Jesus, as He lived among men and women before He went to the Cross, but the life of Jesus is eternal life, it is the life which began in eternity before time was, and will never, ever cease. This is the life which He gives to all His children. It is the life of *now*; the Kingdom is now, the King is King now, and the future is but the now fulfilled in all its fullness. All the fullness of God dwells in Him and we are complete in Him (Colossians 2:9 A.V.).

Comparing Matthew 8:17 with Isaiah 53:4 discovers some ambiguity. Matthew 8:17 notes, 'He took our infirmities and bore our diseases.' Isaiah 53:4 says, 'Surely He has borne our griefs and carried our sorrows.' It is evident that Matthew uses the Septuagint or Greek version of the Old Testament, but more importantly that In these verses Matthew is concentrating on Jesus as the Healer. He is both Healer and Saviour, and it is important that this corresponds to the plan of God predicted by the prophet. But when bereavement comes, we still know Him as the One who bears our griefs and carries our sorrows.

Isaiah's prophecy of the One who was to come, the Suffering Servant of chapters 42, 49, 50, 52-53 becomes interpretive of the life of Jesus who came with full authority; who heals with a word; the One to whom the very demons are subject. Surely, surely, as Isaiah says, 'He has borne our griefs and carried our sorrows,' and, 'Surely with his agonising stripes, we are healed' (Isaiah 53:5). The Messianic age has come.

Matthew 8:18-22. The cost of discipleship

Now when Jesus saw great crowds around Him, He gave orders to go over to the other side. And a scribe came to Him and said, 'Teacher, I will follow You wherever You go'. And Jesus said to him, 'Foxes have holes and the birds of the air have nests, but the Son of Man has nowhere to lay His head' (Matthew 8:18-22).

Another of the disciples said to Him, 'Lord, let me go first and bury my father'. But Jesus said to him, 'Follow Me and leave the dead to bury their own dead'.

This has truly been a long and exhausting day for Jesus and He is about to get into a boat with His disciples to go over to the other shore of the Sea of Galilee, when first a scribe, and then a disciple waylay Him. The scribe says to Him, 'Master, I will follow You wherever you go.' And Jesus replied, 'Foxes have holes, and the birds of the air have nests, but the Son of Man has nowhere to lay His head.' Later, another disciple says to Him, 'Lord, I will follow you, but first let me go and bury my father.' And Jesus replied, 'Follow me, and let the dead bury their dead.'

Here were two followers of Jesus. Jesus came to seek and save that which was lost. Why did He apparently make it so hard for these two to fulfil their discipleship?

Matthew 8:19 The scribe

Jesus has much to say about 'their' scribes, e.g. 7:28, the scribes who were always associated with the Pharisees. But this scribe is a disciple of Jesus, like the scribes of 13:52, and 23:34 who are trained for the Kingdom of Heaven and bring out of their treasure what is new and what is old, and like those scribes who are liable to be scourged, crucified and killed in the time of persecution. This scribe is a disciple of Jesus (verse 21), and not among those who with the Pharisees and elders constitute opposition to Jesus.

Perhaps this scribe had been among those who 'followed' (a discipleship word) Jesus to the mountain upon which He gave His sermon, or a member of the crowd which followed Jesus even to Peter's house. Now Jesus had decided to 'go over to the other side' (verse 18) of the Sea of Galilee, and the scribe seized his chance to speak to Jesus. 'Master,' he says, translated from διδάσκαλε 'teacher', 'I will follow you wherever you go' (verse 19). Did he have in mind the usual way in which the Jewish rabbis taught? A man who often had a group of students who would follow him, hanging on his every word of wisdom that they too might become wise? There were many such in Judaism, both before and after Jesus' time on earth.

This teacher was different, however. Jesus could not offer cosy chats or profound philosophy before a group of eager young men. To be His disciple involved homelessness and poverty and rejection. 'Foxes have holes and the birds of the air have nests, but the Son of Man has nowhere to lay His head.'

Perhaps the scribe recognised that discipleship under Jesus would be different, but still wanted it on his own terms, or on what he had observed of other teachers. He *is* taught by Jesus, but discipleship as taught by Him involves something quite different from what the scribe had expected. He is taught that firstly, Jesus is the Son of Man, and secondly, that even though He is the Son of Man, the Judge of the whole world, it was necessary for Him to live in absolute poverty and homelessness. Matthew 8:34 is an example. He is even expelled from the land of the Gadarenes because they could not accept His casting out of the legion of demons into their herd of unclean swine. In Mark's version of the narrative of when Jesus is in the boat, in a storm, Jesus is asleep on a pillow. In Matthew, even the pillow is missing.

Down the ages, poverty has been regarded as the ultimate in discipleship, an aspiration for really committed believers, and many have chosen that path. Evangelical missionaries, Hudson Taylor, C.T. Studd, Gladys Aylward, Mildred Cable and Francesca French, Jim Eliot, Simon Guillebaud and many of our own generation, as well as Catholic priests and nuns have given up everything to follow Jesus. But Jesus was glad to go to the home of Mary and Martha at Bethany, and was grateful to those women who ministered to Him (Matthew 27:55). He did not despise those who had homes and resources to share with others, who were able to feed the hungry and thirsty, clothe the naked, to visit those who were sick or in prison (Matthew 25:40). On the contrary, He said that those who did it for the least of His brethren, did it as for Him. Nevertheless, He did not hide from the scribe that the way of discipleship is costly.

Matthew 8:20. Jesus as Son of Man

The Son of Man has nowhere to lay His head (verse 20).

What is striking at this point is Jesus' self-referential title, Son of Man. This is the first time that Jesus uses this title in Matthew's gospel and it is combined with a reference to His homelessness in which His followers must share in order to understand Him. Matthew records Him as using the title several times in his gospel, summing up as it did the whole redemptive purpose which Jesus had had in view with His Father from before the foundation of the world (1 Peter 1:20; Ephesians 1:4).

The scribe was just being given a glimpse of all that was to come. The twelve disciples were given a fuller insight as His ministry among those whom He had come to seek and to save, was revealed to them.

Daniel (Daniel 7:13) and the apostle John (Revelation 1:13) both had a glimpse of who He was; Daniel, had a vision of One like unto the Son of Man, coming to the Ancient of Days, to His God, and being presented before Him; John had a vision of the Son of Man, clothed with a long robe and with a golden girdle round His breast. His head and His hair were white, as white as wool, white as snow; His eyes were as a flame of fire, His feet like burnished bronze, refined as in a furnace, and His voice was as the sound of many waters. From His mouth issued a sharp, two-edged sword, and His face was like the sun shining in full strength.

The day is coming and is perhaps nearer than we think when we too shall see the Son of Man coming on the clouds of heaven with power and great glory (Matthew 24:30). Perhaps we shall recognize Him from John's description of Him. Even so, come Lord Jesus (Revelation 22:20).

Using the title 'Son of Man' identifies Jesus with humanity, just as the title 'Son of God' identifies Him with deity. The Lord Jesus is both, for both aspects of who He is, function independently and yet simultaneously. The human intellect may baulk at this attempt to understand the dual nature of Jesus, but faith gladly accepts it as the whole wonderful essence of the word made flesh, God become Man, Jesus glorified and men and women justified, made righteous by the redemptive work which Jesus agreed with His Father to accomplish before the world was (Ephesians 1:4).

Time and again, He teaches His inner circle of disciples what it means for Him to be the Son of Man. Twenty-eight times in this gospel, He refers to Himself in this way; and these occurrences may be divided into three groups: those that speak of Him publicly as presently active among the people; and when speaking to His opponents (8:20, 9:6, 10:23, 11:18, 12:8, 12:32, 12:40, 13:37, 13:41); those that speak of His suffering, death and rising again, privately, to His disciples (16:13, 16:27, 16:8, 17:9, 17:12, 17:22, 18:11, 19:28, 20:18, 20:28) and those which speak of

Him as *the* coming Son of Man, the Judge, again to His disciples (24:27, 24:30, 24:37, 24:39, 24:44, 25:31, 26:2, 26:24, 26:45); a cluster of references which indicate the urgency of what He wants them to know before He goes to the Cross; the exception being His answer to the High Priest at His first trial (Matthew 26:64).

A rough scanning of the text reveals that the times Jesus uses this description or definition of Himself tend to be in clusters of His sayings. He is never addressed *by* others as 'Son of Man', unlike 'Lord', or 'Son of David' or 'Son of God'. The use of the term is not evenly distributed throughout the gospel.

It appears that though in the early chapters, Jesus is willing occasionally to use this precious title, there comes a point in His ministry, one might say a turning point, at Caesarea Philippi when He asks His disciples, 'Who do men say that the Son of Man is?' (Matthew 6:13), followed by the question in verse 15, 'Who do *you* say that I am?' And it was from that time that Jesus began to teach them about his suffering and death. Until then, He had used this title publicly about His present activity. Afterwards, He uses it only when speaking to His disciples, and especially at the time of His transfiguration when it reinforces the theme of His coming suffering (Matthew 17:1-9, 22) and later when He follows it up in the concentrated passage of 24:27-25:31, when He speaks of His coming in judgement.

What do we learn from this analysis?

These were not themes that the usual crowd which followed Him could understand, for they were not ready for them. Jesus always tempers the wind to the shorn lamb.

Were the disciples then given a special revelation? They may have remembered Daniel's reference to the Son of Man in Daniel 7:13, but even so, Son of Man, ὁ υἱὸς τοῦ ἀνθρώπου was a strange and mysterious expression, bound up with Jesus' destiny both in the immediate future and in the long-term fulfilment of His purpose in allowing himself to be aligned with humanity.

Only in Matthew 26:64 does Jesus use His beloved title when speaking once again publicly to Caiaphas the High Priest. In answer to Caiaphas, Jesus says 'Hereafter, you will see the Son of

Man seated at the right hand of power'. Jesus pronounces judgement on His judges, and the High Priest tears his garments, as he should do in view of what was to come, but not because of his charge against Jesus that Jesus had blasphemed. Jesus pronounces judgement on His judges and they do not understand, do not even notice it.

But what He is doing by using the term 'Son of Man' Is showing the difference between His opponents and His disciples. Though the understanding of the disciples is limited, they recognise that there is a mystery here. Jesus is Son of Man *and* Son of God. They know that He will die and rise again, and be exalted and will come to judge men and women, because He has told them so, yet they still go to sleep as He agonises over the will of His Father in the Garden of Gethsemane.

We cannot blame them. Even after three years of walking and talking with Jesus, there were many things hard to understand. But after His resurrection, and the outpouring of the Holy Spirit on the Day of Pentecost, they were bold in their proclamation of Jesus, the Messiah, the Christ, the Name which is above all other names, for there is no other name under heaven whereby we must be saved (Acts 4:12).

Jesus speaks of Himself as the Son of Man when He speaks of the direction He Himself is taking. He is described as a glutton and a drunkard (Matthew 11:19). He is homeless, despised, handed over to be scourged, spat upon, killed. But through it all, *He is the One who is directing the chain of events*. Of course, He had authority to heal with a word, to bid the winds and the waves to cease, to feed multitudes with a few loaves and fishes. Of course, He changed the course of history. Jesus, and not His enemies, determined the time of His death, and He will determine the time of His coming again, when we shall see Him coming on the clouds of heaven in great glory when Jesus, the Son of Man, will be revealed not just to a privileged group of people in the first century, but universally, to the whole world. It is His delight and our salvation, that He calls Himself Son of Man, the One who indwells the humanity which He has created.

To the scribe was given a significant revelation of who Jesus is. He is the Son of Man. Throughout the sermon on the mount, Jesus had used the word 'I'. 'I say unto you'. We could say He is declaring Himself to be the fulfilment of the word of God to His people, because He is the word. He is the 'I', the word of God, with all the authority and power of God behind what He was teaching His new disciples, the fulfilment of the law and the prophets. Here was a *further* revelation of who He is, and *progressively*, as we go through the gospel, there is an unveiling of Himself and His purposes for mankind.

For His great love, wherewith He loved us, He did not leave us in our trespasses and sins, but became one with us, to lift us up with Him, to raise us up and to make us sit with Him in the heavenly places (Ephesians 2:4-7). He did not create us, and then withdraw from us. His whole purpose was to bring many sons to glory (Hebrews 2:10) and therefore He had to be made like His brethren in every respect (Hebrews 2:17) partaking of the same nature (Hebrews 2:14). He is the Son of Man.

Matthew 8:21. Another disciple

Another of the disciples said to Him, 'Lord, let me go first and bury my father'. But Jesus said to him, 'Follow Me and leave the dead to bury their own dead'.

This man is described as 'another disciple' who also wanted to speak to Jesus before He got into the boat. He wanted to follow Jesus, but he also wanted to fulfil his filial duty towards his father.

In many earlier societies, and even today, the responsibility to give a father the burial due to him, lay with the son. This was one reason why sons were so important in ancient culture. So this disciple said to Jesus, 'Lord, let me first go and bury my father,' no doubt expecting that Jesus would understand and approve such a request.

How shocked he must have been at Jesus' response, 'Follow Me and leave the dead to bury their own dead.' What did Jesus mean? Obviously, He was stressing the priority of following Him above everything, even above the fulfilling of the accepted tradition of his culture, for which there were both religious and hygienic reasons in a Middle Eastern climate. One of the Ten Commandments is to honour your father and mother, and this was a sound religious reason for the disciple's request, and climatic conditions ensured that burial took place as soon after death as possible, usually on the same day.

But how do the dead bury their own dead? This appears to be such a harsh statement from Jesus that attempts have been made to mitigate it. There are others who will bury the dead, brothers, uncles. By putting the following of Jesus first, the disciples could proclaim to the world the absolute priority of following Jesus and allowing others to perform that function. Was the disciple prepared to take that opportunity of declaring that Jesus, and following Him, was the most important thing in his life? There are many people to bury the dead, but only a few who proclaim the Kingdom of God. Perhaps this was the challenge Jesus was giving him.

A second interpretation of this verse suggests that νεκρός refers to the *spiritually dead*; unbelievers. Thomas Aquinas (Lecture no.722) held that 'perfect faith is not bound by any ties to a secular duty that is mutually incumbent on people'. The disciple is not bound by any duty, however pious, if it gets in the way of discipleship. Another interpretation suggests that this harsh saying of Jesus was not intended for all disciples, but for those called to an itinerant prophetic ministry. This special calling included symbolic actions, portraying the deep divide between the Kingdom of God and the world.

Yet another view indicates that since the period of mourning after a burial was six days, it may be that the disciple who was speaking to Jesus was showing a lack of willingness to obey and follow immediately by deferring the following of Jesus for at least six days, and possibly for an indefinite period. It has also been suggested that the father had not yet died, perhaps was in reasonable health. Of course, this is mere speculation but a distinct possibility.

There are no excuses or reasons for not following Jesus when He calls. But these seemingly harsh words of Jesus give us pause for thought. Is He abnegating all that He has said about love and discipleship behaviour? None of these attempts to explain Jesus' words enlighten us as to the apparent contrast between what He has so wonderfully and astonishingly been teaching so far, and this mysterious warning seemingly at odds with it.

To try to understand, we must first acknowledge the strong emphasis on Jesus' authority in this gospel. Secondly, Jesus was saying to those who would listen, that it is always more comfortable to stay with the customs and traditions that we know, even Christian customs and traditions, than to entertain the thought of going out of our comfort zone, even our obligations, into the unknown with God. But sometimes that is the way of blessing; HIs way of blessing us.

At the wedding in Cana in Galilee, Mary said to the servants 'Whatsoever He says to you, do it' (John 2:5). It is a good and safe principle on which to build and base our lives, but not necessarily an easy one, and may even incur opprobrium from those we respect and love because they – and possibly we – do not understand, but can only trust, even if it appears wrong to others. For the disciple there must be no compromise. Whatever Jesus commands out of His love for us and for others, is His perfect and compassionate will.

Matthew 8:23-27. The stilling of the storm

And when He got into the boat, His disciples followed Him. And behold, there arose a great storm on the sea, so that the boat was being swamped by the waves. But He was asleep. And they went and woke Him saying, 'Save, Lord, we are perishing'. And He said to them, 'Why are you afraid, O men of little faith?' Then He arose, and rebuked the winds and the sea, and there was a great calm. And the men marvelled, saying, 'What manner of man is this, that even the winds and sea obey Him?'

Matthew is still retaining the two themes already set out in this chapter. First, the authority of Jesus, over disease and demons, and now over natural phenomena. And secondly, discipleship. Jesus had decided to go over to the 'other side' of the Sea of Galilee (verse 18) and had been waylaid, first by a scribe (verse 19) and secondly by 'another disciple' (verse 21). Now He got into the boat, and His disciples 'followed' Him, the use of that discipleship word again. The incident of the storm is concerned with discipleship.

Until now, Jesus regards all who have come to Him in penitence and faith as disciples, as indeed they were. Jesus is now gathering around Him '*the*' disciples, the Twelve, who were later called 'apostles', meaning 'those who were sent' (Matthew 10:2). Discipleship is for all who come to Jesus, but starting in chapter 4, He calls Peter and Andrew, James and John, not only to follow Him, but to become 'fishers of men' (Matthew 4:19). In chapter 9:9, He calls Matthew; and by chapter 10, He has the Twelve, including Judas Iscariot who also betrayed Him (Matthew 10:1-4).

The names of the disciples who were with Him in the boat are not given, but it is legitimate to suppose that they included Peter and Andrew, James and John because they had been fishermen and were well acquainted with the storms which could arise on the Sea of Galilee.

This storm however was probably unlike anything they had experienced before. It is called a great storm in the R.S.V., a great tempest in the A.V. translated from the Greek σεισμός, seismic, an earthquake. The wind and the waves symbolise the death and destruction which threaten to overwhelm not only the disciples, but the Lord, and He is asleep. With all their skill and experience, they know there is nothing they can do to avert tragedy. Their only hope is Jesus and they cry out in terror, 'Save us Lord! We are perishing!' (verse 25).

Typically, Jesus' first response was not to the storm but to the disciples, 'Why are you afraid, O you of little faith?' (verse 26). They had not learnt to rest in the divine authority of Jesus. He rebuked them for their fear, but not for their little faith.

He was saying, 'OK. On this occasion you have not fully appreciated the extent of My power and authority. But faith is something that grows with discipleship. You are learning, and next time your faith will be stronger.'

Then He arose, and rebuked the winds and the waves, and there was a great calm (verse 26). A calm of the elements and a calm in the hearts of the disciples as they marvelled saying, 'What manner of man is this?'

How often do we, as believers, when in the middle of a 'storm', forget to think about the presence and power of the Lord Jesus? Instead, fear has crept into our thinking and stifled us, suffocated us, so that we cannot act in faith. What this passage suggests to us is that what we need to do is turn to Him, trust in Him, even if we feel that our faith is small. The essence of discipleship is faith, and faith is the central theme of this text. Faith lives in the reality of who Jesus is, the risen Christ, the glorified One who has promised to support us and who never breaks His promises. Faith has come into our lives through a personal encounter with this living, Holy One. He will never let us down.

There is nothing passive about discipleship. Jesus said, 'In the world you will have tribulation, but be of good cheer, I have overcome the world' (John 16:33). His help is always there, always available. We can risk everything, because we know that the power and authority belong to Him. We do not need to be afraid.

Matthew 8:28-34. The Gadarene Demoniacs

And when He came to the other side, to the country of the Gadarenes, two demoniacs met Him, coming out of the tombs, so fierce that no man could pass that way. And behold, they cried out, 'What have you to do with us, O Son of God? Have you come here to torment us before the time? Now a herd of many swine were feeding, at some distance from them. And the demons begged Him, 'if you cast us out, send us away into the herd of swine. And He said to them, 'Go'.

The storm is stilled and Jesus comes to 'the other side'; the Gentile side of the Sea of Galilee, near a town called Gadara. The location is uncertain. Both Mark (Mark 5:1-17) and Luke (Luke 8:26-27) have 'the country of the Gergesenes'. But Jesus' intention is sure. Just as in John 4:4, where 'He must needs go through Samaria' A.V. in order to speak to a thirsty Samaritan woman, who needed the water of life which only He could give, so He intentionally comes to the country of the Gadarenes where two violent men are living in the tombs outside the city, men 'so fierce that no-one could pass that way' (verse 28); to deliver them from their bondage to demons, and to be restored to normal human life.

Jesus had dealt with the violence of the storm. Now He was about to deal with the violence which rose up in these men, this completely uncontrollable passion which was destroying them. When they saw Jesus, they cried out to Him, 'What are you doing here? Have you come in judgement upon us? We know that a time for judgement is coming, but you are the Son of God. You can and perhaps want to judge us now!' Jesus made no answer to this, understanding that it was the demons who were speaking through these men. But as they continued to plead with Him, and pointed out the herd of pigs feeding at some distance, Jesus agreed to their suggestion that that awful thing which was in them, that which was bigger than they, which was dominating their lives, should be sent away to the pigs. Jesus used one word only, 'Go'. And the demons went. The herd rushed down the steep bank into the sea and were drowned.

We hear no more about these erstwhile demoniacs from Matthew's gospel. We would love to know that they went home to their families and lived the rest of their lives thanking God for their encounter with Jesus. But we are not told, and must not over-interpret scripture.

But there are some aspects of the story which are obvious: First, the compassion of Jesus even for Gentiles. Only in a Gentile region would there be a herd of swine because it was forbidden for Jews to eat their meat (Leviticus 11:7). They were unclean animals to the Jews though an important sacrificial animal in some Hellenistic cults. Secondly, the complete authority of Jesus over evil; demonstrated by His authority over the evil which had dominated the lives of these men. 'Demoniac' suggests a personification of evil in the shape of demons.

Jesus is more than able to deal with all that will not bow to His authority. He had declared Himself in Luke 4:18 as bringing release to the captives, recovery of sight to the blind, setting at liberty those who are bound or oppressed. This incident is certainly an example of the fulfilment of that purpose for which He had come, and for which He had been anointed by the Spirit of the Lord (Luke 4:18); authority motivated by compassion, the triumph of the Kingdom of God over evil powers (Matthew 11:4) in merciful deliverance, setting men and women free.

The disciples in the boat had asked, 'What manner of man is this?' This healing of the demoniacs was, in part at least, a demonstration of the manner of man that Jesus, the Son of God, is. The demons were an extreme example of the power of evil in the life of a human being. Their being delivered was an extreme example of the more extensive, supreme power of Jesus' authority over evil and His compassion for all those for whom this had become a daily reality. The act of healing and delivering these burdened, driven demoniacs was a far greater act than the stilling of the great seismic storm over the Sea of Galilee. Where Jesus is, evil will never have the last word.

Both Mark and Luke have only one demoniac in their version of this narrative. Matthew has two. Bearing in mind that there is also an oral tradition behind the written gospel, this agrees with Matthew's emphasis on the principle that on the evidence of two or three witnesses, every word shall be established (Numbers 35:30; Deuteronomy 17:6; Deuteronomy 19:15; Matthew 18:16). Where two or three are gathered together in His Name, He is there in the midst of them (Matthew 18:20).

This incident closes the chapter which has seen an escalation from the leper, the centurion, Peter's mother-in-law, the crowds at Peter's door, the scribe and the other disciple, the storm on the sea, and now the two demoniacs. The progress is intentional. There is an appreciable sense of climax as we recognise the absolute authority of Jesus, the cost of following Him, an increasing sense of who He is, and *the time structure*, for the demoniacs intuited that there was another time coming for judgement, when all evil will be judged.

Was Jesus introducing another level of time? They asked, 'Have you come to torment us *before the time*?' Has Jesus got the *eschaton,* the last days, in mind? The 'end time' προ καιρού after the time of 'now'? (verse 29). Were they anticipating the triumph of God's Kingdom, and the vanquishing of evil through the presence of Jesus? But of course, Jesus is the King as Matthew has insisted from the earliest chapters of his gospel. And as the King, as sovereign Lord, Jesus holds within His hands both the καιρός and the χρόνος, *the kairos* and the *chronos,* the now and the not yet of time, the fixed times and seasons καιρός, within the greater continuum of time span χρόνος. New Testament Greek uses both words which are translated time, but with such a wealth of meaning between them.

Jesus said to His disciples before His ascension, 'It is not for you to know times or seasons which the Father has fixed by His own authority' (Acts 1:7); the immediate *and* the ultimate fulfilment of His purposes are in His hands, and in His hands they are safe. Time is a continuum in which times and seasons occur until there shall be time 'no more' (Revelation 10:6).

God lives in eternity (Isaiah 57:15). He is 'the high and lofty One that inhabits eternity', because He is the eternal God (Deuteronomy 33:27), and, wonderful promise, underneath are the Everlasting Arms. He is before time because time is His construct, and He allowed His Son to come into time in order to bring human beings into eternal life where they could be with Him in eternity where He dwells. The gift of God is eternal life through Jesus Christ our Lord (Romans 6:23). So simple really and yet so profound.

As creatures of time, we could not live with Him in eternity. He wanted us to live with Him, so Jesus came to put eternal life within us so that we could be with Him. The cost to Him was the Cross, the full and terrible ordeal of taking upon Himself the sin of the world, for nothing unholy or unclean could enter eternity, that glorious place where the Father dwells, but 'God so loved the world, that He gave His only begotten Son, that whosoever believes in Him should not perish but have everlasting life', the life of eternity (John 3:16). These are such precious words, to be read on the knees of the spirit. By faith we have entered upon that eternal life and 'so shall we ever be with the Lord; therefore comfort one another with these words' (1 Thessalonians 4:17,18).

When all His purposes are complete, then He will roll up time, time shall be no more, but there will be a new heaven and a new earth and a great city, the new Jerusalem (Revelation 21:10) whose gates shall not be shut at all by day and there shall be no night there (Revelation 21:25). Since day and night determine time, the conclusion is that the city is an eternal city. 'God has called us into His eternal glory by Christ Jesus' (1 Peter 5:10). 'To Him be glory and dominion for ever!' (1 Peter 5:11).

To all intents and purposes, it would appear that this expedition to Gadara had been a complete failure. The terrified swineherds had rushed into the city and 'told everything, and what had happened to the demoniacs' (verse 32). And all the city came out to meet Jesus, and when they saw Him, they begged Him to leave their country (verse 34).

They came, not to see the demoniacs, but to see Jesus. Three times in these few verses, Matthew uses the word, 'Behold' (verse 29, 32, 34). 'Behold, the demoniacs cried out' (verse 29). 'Behold, the whole herd rushed down the steep bank into the sea, and perished in the waters' (verse 32) and, 'Behold, the whole city came out to meet Jesus' (verse 34). Matthew is making a Christological point; underlining the episode itself is the underlining of Jesus' divine sonship. Behold, look. Take note of this. This is the Jesus whom we worship.

It is the Son of God who is visiting them. He is not only visiting the demoniacs, but the Gentile people of Gadara, as the demoniacs had recognised when they begged Him to leave. As Isaiah says, 'He was despised and rejected of men' (Isaiah 53:3). They may reject Him, but He will not reject them. At the end of this gospel, Jesus is saying to His disciples, 'Go therefore and make disciples of *all* nations' (Matthew 28:19) 'for *all* authority has been given to Me in heaven and upon earth,' and in Mark's gospel, 'Go ye into all the world and preach the gospel to every creature' (Mark 16:15. A.V.) not only to Jews, but to Gentiles also. Perhaps this time they will respond to Him and eventually enter into His glorious, eternal kingdom.

Matthew Chapter 9

Matthew 9:1-8. The healing of the paralytic

And getting into a boat, He crossed over and came to His own city. And behold, they brought to Him a paralytic, lying on his bed; and when Jesus saw their faith, He said to the paralytic, 'Take heart, My son; your sins are forgiven'. And behold, some of the scribes said to themselves, "This man is blaspheming". But He, knowing their thoughts, said, ''Why do you think evil in your hearts? For which is easier to say "Your sins are forgiven you", or to say "Rise up, and walk" (verses 1-5).

Generally speaking, we are more accustomed to difficult climatic conditions than we are to the sense of being overtaken by something evil which rises up in us, so we regard the stilling of the storm in 8:23-27 as more impressive of Jesus' authority than the healing of the demoniacs in 8:32-34. But both hold within them an acknowledgement of controlled power, of ability far beyond anything ever seen by a human being before or since, underlying the truth that Jesus is indeed the Son of God.

And here in chapter 9, Jesus' authority is again seen to be more than human, as He forgives the sin of the paralytic and later on raises a little girl from death.

These are not actions performed by Jesus in order to draw praise from the crowds, or simply to demonstrate how authoritative He is to His disciples, though He is that. They are concerned with the disciples learning the principles of discipleship, and even to discern through the opposition of the scribes and Pharisees, the kind and degree of discipleship which Jesus espouses. Everything which the Lord Jesus does is purposeful, with the ultimate intention of offering to men and women a life lived to the full (John 10:10), especially and essentially a life lived in fellowship with His heavenly Father, for that was the life He Himself lived. His intention was to show them that no other life is worth living. This is the life He wants to share with His disciples, beginning with His proclamation of the Kingdom of Heaven in Matthew 4:17, and culminating in the glorious coming again of the King in triumph to reign, and for His followers to be with Him forever (Matthew 24:30,31).

These expressions of Jesus' authority appear to be incremental, progressive, steps along the way in the revelation He was giving the disciples. Could He not have demonstrated His full glory to those who would oppose Him? Or even to those who would praise Him?

There is going to be a time later on in the gospel when He does so reveal Himself on the Mount of Transfiguration (Matthew 17:1-8) to a small group of His disciples. But even they did not fully understand. How much less these people who crowded around Him, some to take Him sincerely at His word, to repent and receive the eternal life which He offered them; others to wonder what He was doing and wander away; others to oppose what they regarded as blasphemy because they thought it contravened their sacred scripture, not realising that He was the fulfilment of all scripture (Matthew 5:17). And in this instance of Matthew 9:1-8, He is actually forgiving the sin of a paralysed man who had to be carried to Him on a pallet because he could not walk. For these scribes, it was the ultimate blasphemy, Jesus taking upon Himself the prerogative of God Himself, the power to forgive sins.

Jesus had crossed over the sea and come again to Capernaum, 'His own city' (Matthew 9:1). We may say, how did the friends of the paralytic know He was coming? Or at which point on the seashore He would land? Perhaps these four men who carried the man on his litter really loved him and wanted him to be healed, and were willing to wait and watch for Jesus, to see which house He entered so that they could take him to Him. When Jesus saw them, He saw *their* faith, and said to the paralysed man, 'Be of good courage my son, your sins are forgiven' (verse 2).

From Luke and Mark's account of this incident, it seems that Jesus was indeed already in the house at Capernaum (Luke 5:17-26, Mark 2:1-12). But Matthew leaves out some detail because he again centres the story on Jesus' authority, this time, His authority over sin. We do not know in what way the man had sinned, nor if it was in some way connected to his physical condition. But we do know that he had lost heart. It was not only the paralysis which Jesus healed, but a deep-down feeling of helplessness, of unworthiness, brought about by the sin. Jesus said to him, 'Take heart, be of good courage'. In some versions of the Bible, the translation of $\theta\alpha\rho\sigma\epsilon\omega$ is given as, 'Cheer up!' Jesus saw deeper than that. Jesus heals the whole person, body, soul, and spirit. When Jesus heals, He heals completely.

The scribes saw only what they wanted to see, that this man was blaspheming. 'Who can forgive sins,' they say, 'but God alone?' The penalty for blasphemy was death by stoning, for the name of God was very precious to them. Throughout their history, they had been surrounded by nations whose gods had challenged their own true God (1 Kings 18 is an example of this). And even at this point, they were under the occupation of the Romans who had a pantheon of many gods and goddesses. How could they keep their religion pure and undefiled if an upstart itinerant preacher from Galilee was going to claim that He could forgive sins, the prerogative of their God?

Jesus knew what they were thinking. 'But Jesus, knowing their thoughts' (verse 4), said to them, 'Which is easier to say, "Your sins are forgiven," or to say, "Rise up and walk"? But that you may know that the Son of Man has authority on earth to forgive sins.' He then said to the paralytic, 'Rise, take up your bed and go home.' And he rose and went home (verse 4-7), healed, restored, forgiven.

Jesus was careful to heal him on the grounds of His title of Son of Man. He said to the scribes 'That you may know that the Son of Man has power on earth to forgive sins, He said to the paralytic, "Rise, take up your bed and go home". Did the scribes understand His self-referential title *'Son of Man'*? That God had come down to earth in human form, as John wonderfully put it, 'The word was made *flesh'* (John 1:14) and dwelt among us, full of grace and truth'. Though He was the Son of God, He did not count equality with God a thing to be grasped, but emptied Himself, taking the form of a servant, being born in the likeness of men. And being found in human form, He humbled Himself, and became obedient unto death, even death on a Cross (Philippians 2:6-8). We would like to think that at least some of the scribes went away to reflect on what they had seen and heard, and also become followers of Jesus, though many opposed Him. Though His glory was veiled, it is difficult to envisage that having seen Him, and heard Him speak, they would not be drawn to Him.

Meanwhile, the formerly paralysed man had taken up his bed, and with joy in his erstwhile heavy heart, put his arms around his friends and walked off down the road towards his home.

But the crowds were afraid. They had seen something of tremendous significance, God in person, forgiving sin. They glorified God, but could not bring themselves to recognise God in Jesus, and just praised God that He had given authority to forgive sins to *men*.

Can we give absolution to each other? Jesus had taught the disciples on the mountainside to pray to their heavenly Father, asking Him, 'Forgive us our sins, as we also forgive those who sin against us' (Matthew 6:12). Jesus' forgiveness of sin is of a different order from ours. God does indeed forgive us our sin when we pray to Him as 'Our Father', but on the basis that Jesus 'bore our sins in His body on the tree' (1 Peter 2:24). We do forgive one another, but our love and forgiveness are at best finite and incomplete. We remember that our heavenly Father *alone* 'as far as the earth is from the west, so far can *He* remove our transgressions from us' (Psalms 103:12). God has forgiven us because of Jesus' sacrifice on the Cross. But He has given us the ability and the desire to forgive whatever has been done to us, because we know the glorious freedom of being children of God and we long for others to come into that place of freedom too. We open up our hearts to others as Jesus has opened up His arms of love to us. We read in Ephesians 4:32, 'Be kind one to another, tender-hearted, forgiving one another, even as God for Christ's sake has forgiven you'. We can forgive others because God has forgiven us; and He has forgiven us so much.

Matthew 9:9. The call of Matthew

As Jesus passed on from there, He saw a man called Matthew sitting at the tax office, and He said to him, 'Follow Me'. And he arose and followed Him (Matthew 9:9).

At this crucial point in the gospel, Matthew introduces his own calling to discipleship. Just as Peter and Andrew, James and John were at work, doing the job for which they had been trained, when Jesus called them, so Matthew was sitting at his desk in the tax office, for he was a tax collector. But Jesus saw a man (verse 9), not a reprehensible tax collector for, 'He Himself knew what was in man' (John 2:25). 'As Jesus passed on from there', He said to this man, "Follow me", and he arose and followed Him.'

Matthew tells us nothing of his background, but Mark calls him *'Levi, the son of Alphaeus'*, and Luke just gives him the name *'Levi'*. In Matthew 10:2, James, known as James the Less to distinguish him from James the son of Zebedee, is also described as being the son of Alphaeus, so perhaps Matthew and James were brothers, or had fathers with the same name?

The name 'Levi' suggests that he was of the tribe of Levi, in other words, a member of the tribe that was called by God to serve Him, first in the Tabernacle, and then in the Temple at Jerusalem, in all the sorts of practical ways of which such an institution has need. He was a Levite.

Had Matthew reneged on this ministry in order to become a tax gatherer? Or had he like Barnabas in Acts 4:3b given up his identity as a Levite because he saw the corruption which existed in certain areas of Temple life, and as a man educated in Hebrew, Aramaic, Greek and possibly Latin, could not tolerate the inconsistency with the Hebrew scriptures which he saw there? There is so much in the background of the New Testament which we shall never know. We do know however, that Matthew means *'gift of Yahweh'* in Aramaic (Gundry p166).

This man 'whom Jesus saw' may have worked at a customs post where he collected charges on goods going from the territory of Philip the Tetrarch to that of Herod Antipas, a customs post situated on the outskirts of Capernaum. By being involved in tax collecting in Capernaum, Matthew was in the direct service of Herod Antipas rather than the Romans. Nevertheless, tax collectors were despised because they were often in collaboration with the occupying power; they were in contact with 'unclean, iconoclastic pagans', and were often dishonest.

But Matthew's name, 'gift of Yahweh', especially if he had changed it from 'Levi', indicates that he still retained God in his life and although the former tendency to dishonesty was true of many tax collectors, it does not follow that Matthew was dishonest. Just as Jesus had known the thoughts of the scribes when He forgave the paralysed man, so too He knew what had gone on in Matthew's life. He 'saw a man' (verse 9), not a tax collector, and He said, 'Follow me'. And Matthew arose and followed Him. And became one of the Twelve.

When Jesus called Peter and Andrew, two fishermen, to be His disciples, He said to them, 'Follow Me, and I will make you fishers of men'. When He called Matthew, perhaps He had in mind that as an accountant, Matthew would take note of, and account for, the reactions of people to Jesus, and His wisdom and compassion towards them. Jesus could have said, 'Follow Me and I will help you to understand why people behave in different ways in relation to Me'. It seems that God is not dismissive of experiences and abilities which we had before, or indeed since, we were given the privilege of following Him, but uses them to enrich the gospel message.

But as a man used to dealing with money, it is surprising that Matthew was not given the task of looking after the money box. Instead, Jesus gave it to Judas Iscariot, whom John describes as a thief who used to take what was in it (John 12:6). Jesus often does things we do not understand. Truly, His ways are not our ways, nor His thoughts our thoughts.

Matthew 9:10-13. Eating with tax collectors and sinners

And as He sat at table in the house, behold many tax collectors and sinners came and sat down with Jesus and His disciples. And when the Pharisees saw this, they said to His disciples, 'Why does your teacher eat with tax collectors and sinners?' But when He heard it He said, 'Those who are well have no need of a physician, but those who are sick. Go and learn what this means, "I desire mercy and not sacrifice". For I came not to call the righteous, but sinners' (verses 10- 13).

Luke describes Levi-Matthew as providing a great feast in his house. In Matthew's gospel, the location is slightly more ambiguous, but it could have been in Jesus' house that the meal was taken for Matthew describes the home at Capernaum as the home of Jesus (Matthew 4:13).

This meal was the occasion for another confrontation with the Jewish leaders. The first confrontation had been *with the scribes* in 9:3 who were concerned that Jesus was blaspheming because He forgave the sins of the man who was paralysed. Now it was *with the Pharisees* who could not understand why Jesus was associating with what they regarded as undesirable people, and lastly in this chapter, there was the confrontation *with the unhappy confused disciples of John*, needing to know about fasting in the life of a disciple. Jesus uses each episode to teach His disciples important truths about Himself and His coming kingdom.

So here, in the episode following the calling of Matthew (verse 10), the problem for the Pharisees was the company Jesus kept. If He was who He said He was, why did He not recognise that those people with whom He was reclining at table were absolutely beyond the pale? The question of table fellowship was so important to the Jews. Interestingly, they did not question Jesus directly, but turned to His disciples (of whom there were now five!) 'Why does *your* teacher eat with tax collectors and sinners?' (verse 11). The emphasis on 'your' teacher reveals the gulf they perceived between Jesus and themselves. It was greater than they realised, for He was indeed 'Son of God' and 'Son of Man'. Though the question had been addressed to the disciples, Jesus Himself answered their question, justifying the presence of the tax collectors and sinners.

Sinners was the term used pejoratively of those who were or had been pagan Gentiles, or who were careless about obeying the finer points of the Mosaic Law as interpreted by the Rabbis. Jesus uses medical terminology for the condition of both the tax collectors and the Pharisees. He describes the tax collectors and sinners as sick and in need of a physician, for it was assumed in those days that there was a causal relationship between sin and illness. They needed a physician, not just to cure the body, but to deal with the cause of the illness, sin. And here before them is the great Physician!

But surely the Pharisees do not need a physician? They are righteous! There *is* a righteousness for those who fulfil all the teachings of the law. Paul speaks of his personal righteousness under the law, and says that he was blameless (Philippians 3:6). But righteousness under the law is not enough. Paul knew that he needed a personal encounter with the Lord Jesus, which was given to him on the road to Damascus (Acts 9:1-9). He needed the gift of righteousness based not on obedience to the law, but on the gift of God which became his through faith in Christ, who loved him and gave Himself for him (Philippians 3:9; Galatians 2:20).

This was exactly what the Pharisees needed. The distinction between the tax collectors and sinners and the Pharisees was that the former knew they were sick and needed Jesus. The Pharisees thought that they were beyond the realm of sickness for they were righteous. They were perfectly well. They did not need Jesus. How infinitely sad that this put them beyond the possibility of being healed, and liberated, by Jesus. Jesus said,

'I came not to call the righteous but sinners to repentance' because He knew that without repentance there was no hope for these so-called religious people (Matthew 9:13). There has to be an acknowledgement of their status as sinners; then comes repentance, then the joy of entering into fellowship with the Lord Jesus. The joy of being His disciple. The joy of being *His*!

Jesus says to the Pharisees, 'Go and learn' (verse 13) which they would recognise as a typical Rabbinic command. As a Rabbi with his students and followers, Jesus was inviting them to learn from Him. He says, 'Go and learn what this means, "I desire mercy and not sacrifice",' a quotation from Hosea 6:6. Mercy, 'chesed' in Hebrew, can also be translated as 'lovingkindness', 'steadfast love'. This is the hallmark of those who follow Jesus, who are His disciples. They are learning mercy, lovingkindness, the steadfast love of the Lord. The sacrificial system has now become obsolete, for Jesus is the last, final, and ultimate sacrifice, the sacrificial Lamb of God, who takes away the sin of the world (John 1:29), the One who has come to give His life a ransom for many (Mark 20:28).

The abundant life of which Jesus spoke, does not depend on offering up gifts on the altar. God demands mercy and not sacrifice. Jesus Himself is the altar upon which/whom all the sacrifices representing all sin, was laid; becoming indeed the embodiment of all the sacrifices ever made, none of which could take away sin (Hebrews 10:12). In Him, and in Him only, was the LIFE, and the life was the light of men (John 1:4).

How little of this pronouncement could have been understood at the time, for He had not yet gone to the cross. Jesus Himself said, 'I have many things to say to you, but you cannot bear them now. But when He, the Spirit of truth is come, He will guide you into all truth' (John 16:12).

Matthew 9:14-17. The disciples of John

Then the disciples of John came to Him saying' Why do we and the Pharisees fast, but your disciples do not fast?' And Jesus said to them, 'Can the wedding guests mourn as long as the

Bridegroom is with them? The days will come, when the Bridegroom is taken away from them, and then they will fast. And no one puts a piece of unshrunk cloth on an old garment, for the patch tears away from the garment, and a worse tear is made. Neither is new wine put into old wineskins; if it is, the skins burst and the wine is spilled and the skins are destroyed, but new wine is put into fresh wineskins and both are preserved'.

John the Baptist was now in prison, for 'Herod had seized John and bound him and put him in prison for the sake of Herodias, his brother Philip's wife, because John said to him, "It is not lawful for you to have her" (Matthew 14:3,4).

Then the disciples of John came to Jesus saying, 'Why do we and the Pharisees fast often, but your disciples fast not?' (Matthew 9:14).

As frequently, behind the question raised by John's disciples lies a whole raft of uncertainties. Must their spiritual lives now be modelled on that of the Pharisees, who appear to be so vigilant in upholding the law, and in almsgiving and fasting, or should they be following the example of this new prophet and His disciples? They are drawn to Jesus. They remember that John the Baptist had said to them, 'There is One coming after me who is greater than I, the latchet of whose shoes I am unworthy to unloose' (Matthew 3:11). They remember that John had warned them about the Pharisees and Sadducees whom he denounced as 'vipers' (Matthew 3:7). Could it be that they should now transfer their allegiance to Jesus? And was fasting indicative of this?

In His inimitable way, Jesus led them away from the meaning of fasting, which Isaiah explains that for the Jews was a humbling of themselves before God, bowing down their head like a rush, spreading sackcloth and ashes under them. Isaiah 57:3-5 emphasises that fasting is an attempt to make their voice to be heard on high, to reach the ear of God, to mourn so that God would hear them.

Jesus was leading them from that position to another which was altogether different, but actually answered the question which they had been unable to ask. What do we do now that John, our leader, the one whom we were following, is in prison?

Jesus speaks of the wedding guests who do not mourn as long as the bridegroom is with them (verse 15). He could be speaking *parabolically* about any wedding which in the time of Jesus was a highly ritualised ceremony, and sometimes lasted many days. Or He could be speaking *prophetically* as Himself being the Bridegroom who had come to earth seeking a Bride, His church, which He loved and was going to present to Himself as without spot or wrinkle or any such thing (Ephesians 5:27) until the time when she comes to Him out of Heaven, as a Bride adorned for her Husband (Revelation 21:2) at the end of time.

What joy there will be when the Bridegroom is able to enter even more fully into His relationship with His Bride! In two parables, Matthew 22:1-4, and Matthew 25:1-3, Jesus speaks of weddings, that of the wedding feast of the king's son, and that of the wise and foolish virgins who went out to meet the bridegroom. Both of these parables enable us to see Jesus as the Messianic Bridegroom anticipated prophetically in Psalm 45; God, thy God has anointed *You'*, (whom we understand as the Bridegroom) with the oil of gladness above your fellows (verse 7). The 'king's daughter', whom we understand as the church, is all-glorious within (verse 13), and she shall be brought to the king (verse 14). This is not an entirely foreign concept in the Old Testament. We also note Hosea 2:16-20. 'In that day says the Lord, you will call Me, my Husband. I will betroth you to Me forever,' and Isaiah 54:5, and 62:4, 'Your maker is your Husband, the Lord of Hosts is His Name', and 'As the bridegroom rejoices over the bride, So shall your God rejoice over you'.

These verses describe *the relationship of God to his people in terms of marriage*. Here in the Old Testament, God is expressing His desire towards HIs people, the deep yearning of His heart for the closest possible relationship with them. These Old Testament verses are also prophetic, for they understand that though this is a prophecy yet to be fulfilled, the accomplishment of it can only be achieved when He, the Messiah, the Anointed

One is incarnated, not only as Son of God, but also as Son of Man. Jesus comes to earth as a bridegroom seeking His bride.

Jesus can now put the fasting of the disciples of John and the non-fasting of His own disciples into perspective. The time will come when the Bridegroom is taken away from them, and then they will fast (verse 15). Jesus is referring to the time of HIs passion and death, a time yet to come when He will be taken away from them, and of which His disciples at that time had no knowledge, for He had not yet begun gently to prepare them for what He knew had to be. His time on earth had a projected span. He would not always be with them as He now was, but would send the Holy Spirit, the Comforter, to them (John 16:7). He would not leave them comfortless, desolate, orphans (John 14:18), He would come to them.

But when He is taken from them, then they will fast (Matthew 9:15).

Jesus wants to make it clear that there is a difference between the Old and the New. When He makes the point about the bridegroom, and by implication, the bride, He is careful to explain in terms that they can understand, that putting a new patch on an old garment and new wine into old wineskins does not work. We can imagine Him at home in Nazareth, watching Mary as she undertook to mend one or other of the childrens' clothes. Or watching Joseph, carefully decanting the new wine into new wineskins, like all the other mothers and fathers in the village.

God is doing a new thing, as He promised in Isaiah 43:19. Jesus has announced it, the Kingdom of Heaven is at hand (Matthew 4:17). Those who have entered that kingdom, the realm where the manifestation of Divine sovereignty and authority have drawn near, have entered into that realm through repentance and faith, and are represented by the *new piece of cloth* (verse 16). The old cloth cannot contain it. Those in whom the *new wine* of the Holy Spirit has come to dwell (John 14:17b) cannot any longer be bound by the old wineskins (Matthew 9:17). They must seek new wineskins and then the old wineskins will be preserved (9:17) because God has not cast off His people, the old wineskins whom He foreknew (Romans 11:1), but wants them to return to Him through faith in His beloved Son.

The fundamental incompatibility between the new and the old is reconciled in Jesus, the old represented firstly by the scribes (verse 3), then the Pharisees (verse 11), and lastly, the disciples of John (verse 14), The new is represented by those newly entered into a relationship with Jesus through repentance and faith, *the embryo church, the embryo bride,* His new disciples; a group which by the grace of God will hopefully, in the ensuing days, include scribes, Pharisees and the disciples of John as they all too urgently recognize their need of Him.

Jesus is not at this juncture spelling out what a new wineskin will consist of, but already a new community is beginning to be established, all those whose lives are beginning to be transformed by their faith in Jesus.

John's disciples have a choice. Jesus did not by any means undervalue John. He said, 'Among those born of women there has not arisen one greater than John the Baptist' (Matthew 11:11) He was the forerunner, prophesied by Malachi (Malachi 3:1]) and Isaiah (40:3) and endorsed by all four evangelists (Matthew 3:3, Mark 1:2, Luke 3:4, John 1:23) as the voice of one crying in the wilderness, 'Prepare ye the way of the Lord.' And he suffered a cruel and terrible, humiliating death. *But he was the end of the Old, just as Jesus was the beginning of the New,* and this was what his disciples needed to recognise.

Even in John's lifetime, there were those of his disciples who had seen in Jesus the Lamb of God who takes away the sin of the world, for so John had described Him, and they followed Him (John 1:37) to John's complete and utter satisfaction and with his blessing, for he said, 'He must increase, and I must decrease' (John 3:30). John says, 'He who has the bride is the bridegroom, but *the friend of the bridegroom, John himself,* who stands and hears him, rejoices greatly at the bridegroom's voice; therefore, this joy of mine is now full' (John 3:29). These former disciples of John, when they became full of new wine, the wine of the Holy Spirit, would be poured into new wineskins.

Several hundred years earlier, Isaiah had seen in the Suffering Servant the *agent of the New. This was the New Covenant,* which God had in mind. He says, 'Behold, the former things have come to pass and *new* things I now declare. Before they spring forth, I tell you of them. Sing unto the Lord a new song!' (Isaiah 42:9-10). And we do, rejoicing in Him who is the ultimate Suffering Servant, the One who took a towel and girded Himself and washed His disciples' feet, (John 13:4); who said, 'Lo I come to do Thy will O my God' (Hebrews 10:7) for His only desire was to do the will of His Father, to be obedient to Him, and to serve the purposes of God both in His life and in His death. We worship Him.

Matthew 9:18-26. An interrupted miracle: The healing of two daughters

> While He was yet speaking at the feast to the disciples of John, behold a ruler approached and worshipped Jesus, kneeling before Him and saying, 'My daughter has just died, but come and lay your hands on her, and she shall live.' And Jesus rose, and followed him, with His disciples (Matthew 9:18).

> And behold, a woman who had suffered from a haemorrhage for twelve years came up behind Him, and touched the fringe of His garment, for she said to herself, 'If I may only touch the fringe of His garment, I shall be made well'. Jesus turned, and seeing her He said, 'Take heart, daughter. Your faith has made you well'. And instantly, the woman was made well (Matthew 9:18-21).

In Mark's recounting of this earlier episode, the ruler is described as Jairus, a ruler of the synagogue, and the child described as being at the point of death, i.e., not yet having died (Mark 5:21-43). These details are also included in Luke's account, and in addition that Jairus' daughter was 12 years of age (Luke 8:41-56).

Matthew's telescoping of the incident focuses attention on Jesus, on His authority not only to heal, but to raise from the dead. Since all scripture is given by inspiration of the Holy Spirit (2 Timothy 3:16) how gracious of Him to give us three viewpoints on this precious work of the Lord Jesus, individual pictures of Him which are complementary rather than contradictory and emphasise the reality of who He is, and how we may have an understanding of Him. Though John does not record this incident, his gospel gives a further dimension to the Lord's teaching; and status as the Son of God.

So, in God's economy, we have a divine revelation. Jesus, the Lamb of God who takes away the sin of the world, has come down to us in human form, to live among us, His glory veiled, under the anointing of the Holy Spirit, to minister His grace to all who will receive Him. Jesus said to John's disciples, 'Go and tell John what you hear and see; the blind receive their sight, the lame walk, lepers are cleansed, the deaf hear, the dead are raised up and the poor have good news preached to them' (Matthew 11:4-6). The gospels give us the whole picture, but each gospel writer gives us a different emphasis in fundamental harmony with Jesus Himself, and with each other. This is the One who should come, and there was no need to look for another (Matthew 11:3).

The purpose of Matthew's abbreviated version is part of what he is demonstrating throughout chapters 8 and 9. The theme of *faith*, the use of the word *'following'* to indicate discipleship, the use of the word κύριος, *Lord,* to show the Christological aspect of Jesus' ministry in 8:2; 6-8, 21, 25; 9:28, 38; and His absolute authority over all conditions of men and women, and even nature itself.

Matthew omits the name Jairus, using the title *ruler* ἄρχων, archon. This title could be used of any prominent civil or religious person in the community and which therefore could include a synagogue ruler, as in Luke, the person who presided over synagogue worship. The ruler could have been an aristocratic person, perhaps a high official, as in John's gospel (John 4:46), but when he comes to Jesus he comes as a worshipper, kneeling before Him as a distraught father on behalf of his little daughter. 'My daughter has just died, but come and lay your hand on her, and she will live' (verse 18). And Jesus rose, for presumably He was still sitting/reclining at table with Matthew, and followed him (verse 19). How tender was His response to this poor despairing father. Jesus immediately does what he asks, accompanying him on the way to his house with His disciples.

But *behold*, a woman who had suffered a haemorrhage for 12 years (the little girl was 12 according to Luke) came up behind Him and touched the fringe/tassel of His garment, for she said to herself, 'If I only touch His garment, I shall be made well.' Rev. Alec Motyer says, 'When you see the word, 'behold' it means 'stop, consider this'. Verse 18 says, 'Behold a ruler came'. Now in verse 20, 'Behold, a woman.' There is a link between these two needy people, the important ruler, and the unclean woman (for the issue of blood made her ritually unclean as all menstruating women were ritually unclean) (Leviticus 15:19, 25).

How different were these two people in every respect except one, that whether high or low, respected or feared as unclean, as man or woman, they both needed Jesus. They needed Him to turn the situation around, and He did, and in doing so, did so much more. We can understand a little of the man's despair, his love for his little daughter, his desperation as he comes to the only Person who can help him. We can imagine a little of the woman's desperation too, as she tried to get near to Jesus as He walks beside the child's father, knowing that the law forbids it because she is losing blood, and because of that, coming behind Him and secretly touching the tassel of his garment, the tassel which all Jews wore as a sign that they were remembering to obey all God's commandments, that they were holy, separated unto God (Numbers 15:37-4; Deuteronomy 22:12).

It may be that touching His garment in that way was a plea from the woman. 'I want to be holy too, for I too am a daughter of Israel. Please Lord, take away from me that which makes me unholy in the eyes of the law.' And Jesus turned and said, 'Take heart, daughter, your faith has saved you' (verse 22). And instantly she was made well. Again, Jesus is not merely saying, 'Cheer up!' Jesus reaches down into the very heart of this woman; He sees all the pain and discouragement over many years, all the ostracism, the exclusion from the Temple, even from the Court of the women, let alone the Holy Place; the exclusion from society, even perhaps from her family. Jesus saw it and knew it all. So, He says to her, 'Take heart,' θαρσεω, be of good courage, just as He had said to the paralysed man. Just as He knew all about the man, so Jesus knew all about the woman, her social exclusion, her desire to be clean. He says, 'Take heart,' then calls her, 'Daughter!' She is received back into all her heritage as a child of the covenant, a true Israelite, and yet something more, ransomed, healed, restored, forgiven. 'Her faith has made her well'.

Matthew uses the word σωσο, save, your faith has 'saved' you, translated here as 'made well' in verses 21 and 22. Jesus' healing of her was so much more than giving her back her health. He 'saved' her, recognising her faith. 'Be of good courage daughter, your faith has *saved* you' (verse 22), and instantly, in that hour – από της ώρας εκείνης, she was made well, she was saved, a unique healing that was a concrete expression of the salvation by faith that is always real, faith that is something active, that takes risks, that puts unlimited trust in Jesus, as she had done.

Jesus always responds to such risks, ambiguous though they may sometimes be, as in this case. Saving is something concrete; it includes healing and goes hand in hand with faith. His name is Jesus, Saviour from sin, for He saves His people from their sins (Matthew 1:21) and gives them new life in Him (John 3:16), for He came to seek and to save those who were lost (Luke 19:10) and to give His life a ransom for many (Matthew 20:28).

So, Jesus comes to the home of the other daughter, the little girl who has died, where the usual accompaniments to mourning were going on, the flute players, the people, usually women, paid to cry and weep to express the grief of the family, for this was the custom in that culture.

'When Jesus came' (verse 23) to that home, everything changed, as it always does when He comes. Jesus will not allow the wailing, grieving crowds to share in the miracle that is about to take place, and says, 'Depart, for she is not dead, but sleeps' (verse 24), and they mock Him, laugh Him to scorn. Again, there is a strong note of His authority, His knowledge, for *He knew what He would do*. The crowds leave, and Jesus enters the room where the little girl lies, takes her *by the hand* and raises her up.

We hear no more about the father. In Matthew's version, all the emphasis is on Jesus, and the disciples Peter, James and John are not included in the witnessing of the miracle, neither are the father and mother of the child as in Luke's account. Matthew is continuing his emphasis on Jesus, Jesus as the ultimate authority, as the sole authority, who heals every illness and condition of men and women, who forgives sin, who has power over all natural phenomena, who even has power over death, Jesus, Son of God and Son of Man, whose nail-pierced hands are even now extended to all those who in faith receive Him, welcoming them into His kingdom, embracing them in His love. *The hands of Jesus*. And the report of Him went through all that district (verse 26).

Matthew 9:27-31. The healing of two blind men

And as Jesus passed on from there, two blind men followed Him, crying aloud,' Have mercy on us Son of David.' When He entered the house, the blind men came to Him and Jesus said to them,' Do you believe that I am able to do this?' They said to Him, 'yes, Lord.' Then He touched their eyes, saying, 'According to your faith, be it done to you.' And their eyes were opened. (Matthew 9: 27-29).

Jesus passed on from there (verse 27), passed on from the home of the now rejoicing family whose little daughter was alive and well, back to the house He had left (verse 18), and He was followed by two blind men crying aloud, 'Have mercy on us, Son of David' (verse 27). Possibly they had heard of all that He was doing (verse 26), or had an instinctive feeling that the cure for their blindness could only be found in the Son of David, Jesus.

Following, as we have seen, indicates discipleship. How or whether they had come to be disciples, we are not told, only that they had a measure of Messianic understanding, that God's whole covenant with David, as a man whose son would sit upon his throne, pointed prophetically to Jesus, the incarnate Son of God who would indeed fulfil the Davidic covenant, and provide a Messiah for His people, One who would bear their griefs and carry their sorrows, who would be wounded for their transgressions and who would be healed by His stripes (Isaiah 53:4, 5).

God was doing a new thing through His covenant with David. He was promising a Son who would sit on His throne, an Anointed One, the Messiah, the King, forever ruling and caring for His people (2 Sam 7:4; Psalm 89:3, 20, 34; Psalm 78:70). Throughout the writings of the prophets, from Isaiah to Malachi, there is a longing for the fulfilment of the promise of that covenant to come to pass. And here, in Jesus' day, there was still a longing in the heart of the people for the healing, governing presence of 'the One who should come' (Matthew 11:3) as John the Baptist so poignantly phrased it; an intense Messianic expectation. As Jesus rides into Jerusalem for the last time before His death and resurrection, the crowd throw palm branches on the road before Him, calling out, 'Hosanna to the Son of David! Blessed is He who comes in the name of the Lord!' (Matthew 21:3) greatly disturbing the chief priests and scribes (21:15) who could not believe that Jesus was indeed the Messiah.

As with all the titles given to Him, Jesus was indeed the Son of David by genealogical descent (Matthew 1:17) and also by the fulfilment of God's covenant with David, but He was so much more than that. And between following Jesus on the way to the house, and coming into the house where Jesus was, these two blind men, these disciples had a mighty revelation. *He was LORD!* Jesus said, 'Do you believe that I am able to do this?' And they reply, 'Yes, Lord!' And with His gentle touch upon their eyes, their blindness left them. They saw the Lord!

Not high and lifted up, His train of angels filling the Temple, as Isaiah had seen (Isaiah 6:1), but as a Man, like themselves, but clothed with all the full authority of God, come down to earth in human likeness to show men and women the true, loving, forgiving nature of the One whom they worshipped. They saw the Lord! Their eyes were opened, and they could look upon Him, the first Person they saw. How wonderful to see the Lord. Was it almost worth the years of blindness? To feel His touch upon their face and to see His face? The promise is in Revelation 22:3, that His servants shall serve Him, and they *shall* see His face.

This Son of David in the biological sense was Solomon, but in the covenantal sense, He was Jesus. Jesus was genealogically the son of David (Matthew 1:4,20), but *prophetically* He was the Son of, and fulfilment of, the Davidic covenant, the purpose of God that His Son would be King of Kings and Lord of Lords; yet also be the One who heals the sick and the lame, the blind and the deaf, Israel's Messiah, but even more than that, the Lord of the world. It is only in the miracle stories of the gospel that He is known as the Son of David, but *all* messianic hopes are fulfilled in Jesus. He is the Christ, the Son of the living God. This was the Father's revelation to Peter (Matthew 16:16). And on that Rock, that revelation, that declaration, that He is the Christ, the Son of the living God, Jesus said He would build His church. Jesus leads the blind to see, through His healing, transforming love.

Those who had heard the report that went abroad about the child who had been raised from the dead (verse 31) had conceivably thought that was the ultimate miracle, a man who could bring life out of death. But Matthew's chronology is very careful. Jesus' message is not only resurrection life for those who believe in Him, but enlightenment. As Paul writes, 'Having the eyes of your heart *enlightened*, that you may know what is the hope to which He has called you, and what the riches of His glorious inheritance in the saints' (Ephesians 1:18). Paul describes our former state as being 'blind' defined in Romans 10:2-4 as ignorance of the righteousness that comes from God, seeking to establish our own righteousness. So, in a sense, the healing of two blind men becomes allegorical. No one could have doubted the reality of the healing which had taken place, but Matthew has a positive message which he wants to convey. First life, then enlightenment.

There is a spiritual blindness which will not let us see our need of Jesus, our need of His touch upon us, which does not allow us to see Him as He is and ourselves as we are, without hope and without God in the world (Ephesians 2:12). He wants to open our eyes that we may behold all the wondrous things that He does, that He says (Psalm 119:8). There is a song which begins: 'Open my eyes Lord, I want to see Jesus.' We do want to see Him and one day will see Him fully, face to face (1 Corinthians 13:12). That day will come. As Jesus said to the blind men, 'According to your faith, be it done for you' (9:29).

Matthew 9:32-34. The healing of a dumb man

And as they were going away, behold a dumb demoniac was brought to Him. And when the demon had been cast out, the dumb man spoke; and the crowds marvelled saying, 'Never was anything like this seen in Israel'. But the Pharisees said, 'He casts out demons by the prince of demons.'

The final scene in the drama of chapter 9 comes with Jesus healing the dumb demoniac. The Greek word κωφών indicates that he was a deaf mute, both deaf and dumb. A child who was born deaf at that time could very seldom learn to speak, and it has been noted that in that culture, all illness was thought to be the result of demon activity. Matthew was following the cultural trend when he called him a dumb demoniac.

With Matthew's theme of faith running through chapters 8 and 9, it is interesting to observe that this man did not even come of himself to Jesus, but was *brought* (verse 32). He could not speak to Jesus, he could not say as the blind men had said, 'Have mercy on me' (verse 27). He could not call Jesus 'Son of David', let alone 'Lord'. Here was a man who had absolutely nothing; he was totally and completely vulnerable. If he had faith, it was undiscernible, yet Jesus cast out the demon and the dumb man spoke (verse 33), proof that he had been healed by Jesus.

How important this is for us to learn. We can bring nothing to Jesus. *Nothing in my hand I bring, Simply to Thy Cross I cling* (A.M. Toplady). The experience of the hymn writer has to be ours too. We come to Jesus as the paralysed man did, unable to walk in step with Jesus. We come to Him in desperation as the father of his dead daughter did, knowing that nothing he could do would restore her to life. We come to Him as *an* outcast, having a long-term incurable illness called sin, which only He can heal. We come to Him as blind and deaf and dumb. Jesus, our only hope. But whoever we are and whatever our circumstances, we may respond to His invitation to leave them at His feet and by His healing and saving power, to receive from Him LIFE, eternal life.

The crowds marvelled, and this comes as no surprise, for indeed nothing like this had ever before been seen in Israel (verse 33), though surely some, or even many, had seen and believed that this was He that should come (Matthew 11:3), the One whom the prophets foretold, the Messianic expectation that He should be the One on whom the Spirit of God, the Holy Spirit would rest.

But the Pharisees proved that they were indeed blind, blind guides as Jesus called them in Matthew 23:16, blind fools (verse 17), blind men (verse 19) and deaf to the voice of God speaking through Jesus; spiritually disabled because they were unwilling to view Him as the fulfilment of the prophetic scriptures. They attributed His authority to the 'prince of demons', perhaps Beelzebub, Lord of the Flies, as in chapter 10:25, as we shall discover later.

Matthew 9:35-38. The compassion of Jesus

And Jesus went about all the cities and villages, teaching in their synagogues and preaching the gospel of the kingdom, and healing every disease and every infirmity. When He saw the crowds, He had compassion for them, because they were harassed and helpless, like sheep without a shepherd. Then He said to His disciples, 'The harvest is plentiful, but the labourers are few. Pray therefore the Lord of the harvest, to send out labourers into His harvest.'

The opposition of the Pharisees did not prevent Jesus from doing what He had done in 4:23, going about in all the cities and villages, teaching in their synagogues, preaching the gospel of the Kingdom, and healing every disease and every infirmity (verse 35).

But this time there was a difference. Jesus recognised the enormity of the task of reaching these precious sheep with the gospel. They needed shepherds. Perhaps also, those who had come to Him in faith needed to *learn* to be shepherds, too. So He said to His disciples, 'The harvest truly is plentiful, but the labourers are few. Pray therefore the Lord of the harvest, that He may send forth labourers into His harvest' (verse 38). A prayer that the church has been praying ever since, and which leads us into Jesus' second discourse in Chapter 10. But first a summary of chapter 9 would be helpful.

Matthew 9:1-38. Summary of the importance of faith

Chapter 9 begins with scribes questioning Jesus' authority to forgive sins (verse 3). Then the Pharisees query His table fellowship (verse 11). It is becoming increasingly obvious that not just a division, but a huge gulf is opening up between the religious leaders and Jesus, an antagonism which eventuates in His trial and death.

The 'crowd' of this chapter represents a different reaction to Jesus from that of the Pharisees and scribes. The contrast could not be more stark. Their amazement at what Jesus is doing does not necessarily equate with faith, but it does indicate a positive reaction, a willingness to at least try to understand how the power of Jesus to perform miracles could influence and impact their own lives. When they say, 'Never was anything like this seen in Israel,' they are acknowledging the Messiah's healings as for, and in, His people Israel.

This division created by Jesus between the people and the scribes and Pharisees will conclude with His rejection by Israel, and Matthew's report of this division is seen progressively throughout his gospel. But he does not conclude chapter 9 with the Pharisees, but with Jesus' compassion for the crowds because they were 'harassed and helpless', like 'sheep without a shepherd' (verse 36).

'Then He said to His disciples' (verse 37). This appears to be the first time that Jesus differentiates between the new disciples who had repented 'for the kingdom of heaven is at hand' (4:17), and who had sat at His feet on the mountainside to hear His first sermon, and those who were close to Him, His inner circle, those whom He was about to designate as 'apostles', sent ones, in verse 2 of chapter 10. These men were to be the spearhead of the new movement which would later include the many labourers sent into His harvest (verse 3). Jesus was building His church. There were many new disciples, and there were the Twelve, and from the Twelve, there were those who were closest to Him, Peter, James, and John. Many 'labourers' were to come from the new disciples, but the Twelve had a special place in His ministry on which He elaborates in chapter 10.

From chapters 5 to 9, Jesus has been declaring what the gospel of the kingdom is like, and how He, as Israel's Messiah, fulfils the law and the prophets, not only in His teaching but also in His healing activity as He traverses all the cities and villages of the region. Quite openly, for this was not done in a corner, all men and women could hear Him and see Him and make their own decision about how this new prophet, this long-awaited Messiah, could transform their own lives. Jesus urges them to respond, to repent and believe the gospel, to receive from Him eternal life, and many, many do respond, but some doubted, and some rejected Him. So, there is an urgency about Jesus' word to His disciples. 'The harvest truly is great,' He says. He has already begun the harvesting. He explains to His disciples in chapter 10 how the harvesting may be continued by them under His delegated authority.

In chapters 8 and 9, Matthew has given us individual examples of the gospel of the kingdom in action; Jesus coming to individuals at their time of greatest need, and bringing them into the complete reality of freedom, the liberation which the gospel provides. They come to faith, to discipleship, even if their understanding of Jesus is limited.

From these examples of the love of the Lord Jesus in action, men and women all down the centuries have taken the stories of these miracles into their personal experience. Jesus, who performed those miracles so long ago is the same Jesus who is alive today and living in His world, Jesus Christ, the same yesterday and today and forever (Hebrews 13:5). His power is without limit of time or space or historical continuum. Many who come to Him may not be blind or deaf or dumb or paralysed physically, but spiritually they may be hopelessly in need of a Saviour. And they may be physically in need too.

Can we still expect Jesus to do miracles for us? Or perhaps more acutely, for our loved ones? God has provided us with a natural law without which it is impossible for life to exist, for example, the law of gravity. A miracle disobeys the natural law. It is a supernatural intervention. It can and does happen, but rarely, for if it were to become an ordinary happening or expectation, it would cease to be a miracle. The miracles of Jesus are special deeds, special actions that are not consistent with normal experiences of reality. They arise out of His compassionate concern for individuals, sometimes but not always in response to faith. He does not break the natural law, He supersedes it. He breaks the power of the devil over human suffering, fear, and blindness. He describes this as 'the kingdom of God come among you' in direct and powerful contradiction of what has become the norm in the world (Matthew 12:28).

The miracles of Jesus are real, historically real, but they represent an alternative reality, a glimpse of the time when there will be no more sin, or grief, or crying or sorrow; when Christ will be all in all, for He is greater than all, above all. We long for that day to come, our beloved Jesus, God's beloved Son, raised by Him to be far above all, seated at God's right hand (Ephesians 1:20,21). Even so, come Lord Jesus. We need to pray, 'Thy will be done, as in heaven, so on earth,' for we do not always know what the will of the Lord is, though we know that whatever His will is, is for our good, and for His blessing of us. Sometimes, what we perceive to be a blessing is withheld for our good. Suffering can teach us many things we would not otherwise learn, and for which in time to come we may give grateful thanks.

But when miracles do happen, Heaven is breaking into earth, Eternity is breaking into time, and Jesus is glorified!

Matthew Chapter 10

Matthew 10:1-23. The second discourse:
The mission to the twelve

And He called to Him his twelve disciples and gave them authority over unclean spirits, to cast them out, and to heal every disease and every infirmity. The names of the twelve apostles are these: first Simon, who is called Peter, and Andrew his brother; James the son of Zebeddee, and John his brother; Philip and Bartholomew; Thomas and Matthew the tax collector; James the son of Alphaeus, and Thaddaeus; Simon the Cananaean, and Judas Iscariot who also betrayed Him. These twelve, Jesus sent out (verses 1-5).

The second discourse is addressed to the twelve disciples and could be understood as the disciples' discourse. Jesus' *first* discourse, the Sermon on the Mount, proclaimed a life lived on the basis of the gospel of the kingdom. This, the second one, is a sending discourse, extending the ministry of Jesus ultimately to the church, delegating His authority to those chosen by Him to continue His activity.

The concept of discipleship under these terms frames the discourse from the beginning (9:37 – 10:1), in the middle (10:24-25) and at the end (10:40-11:1). This concept of discipleship is effective both for *itinerant* and *settled* believers, understood as not without cost materially and familially, yet always under the protecting power of the Father and the presence of the Lord Jesus that defines them as His (10:40).

Jesus called to Him His twelve disciples and gave them authority (10:1). The twelve, whose names follow, were *called out ones* and were given a specific vocation as also *sent* ones, *apostles* ἀπόστολος. The church has never been without some persons holding specific authority and responsibility,

These twelve He sent out on a mission of compassion to 'the lost sheep of the house of Israel' (verse 6), to preach that the kingdom is at hand, to heal the sick, raise the dead, cleanse lepers and cast out demons (verse 7). Freely you have received, freely give, Jesus says to them. You receive without paying, give without pay (verse 8).

Having described for them the purpose for which He was sending them, Jesus then got down to the practical details of what they should take with them and where they should receive hospitality, followed by the warning that this was a dangerous project to be engaged upon (10:16). As He amplified the details of the persecution which would in all probability accompany their mission, Jesus also spoke prophetically of the countless attempts on their lives there would be throughout the years to come, throughout the period until He comes again at the Parousia (verse 23). There would be innumerable attempts to carry out the vocation which He had given to the Twelve. There would be many labourers who would be recruited to the task of preaching the gospel of the kingdom with His own love and compassion for the sick, the distressed, the underprivileged. But He always revealed the cost of discipleship.

We know so little of these twelve men. Philip and Andrew have Greek names and were from Bethsaida, a Hellenistic town (John 1:44). But Peter, also from Bethsaida, Andrew's brother, was also known by the Semitic name of Simon.

Bartholomew is identified with Nathanael (John 1:45) of whom Jesus said, 'An Israelite indeed in whom is no guile,' no Jacob (John 1:47) and who had breakfast with the other disciples at the Sea of Tiberias/Galilee after Jesus' resurrection from the dead, where he is described as being from Cana of Galilee.

Thomas, also known as the Twin, was also with them at that special breakfast after his doubt had turned from doubt to glorious faith when he beheld Jesus for himself after His resurrection. He is coupled with Matthew in Matthew's account in Matthew 10:3, but this need not mean that Matthew was his twin. Matthew tends to position these disciples as two together.

When going on such a mission as prescribed for them by Jesus, how precious to have your brother disciple alongside!

After Matthew and Thomas comes James, known as 'the less' to distinguish him from the brother of John, and Thaddaeus.

Last comes Simon the Cananaean, otherwise known as Simon the Zealot as Luke describes him (Luke 6:15) and finally the last in all four lists of the disciples of Jesus, Judas Iscariot who betrayed Him.

The four lists, Matthew 10:1-4, Mark 3:16-19, Luke 6:13-16, and Acts 1:13 do not entirely agree. There is agreement in Matthew and Mark, but in Luke, Thaddaeus is missing and replaced by a second Judas who naturally enough also appears in Acts 1:13 since Acts was written by Luke. Thaddeus is alternatively called Lebbaeus in some early manuscripts, and in none of the lists is Nathanael mentioned by name. It is interesting to note that whereas Matthew and Mark refer to Judas as the one who betrayed Jesus, Luke 6:16 says, 'Judas Iscariot, who became a traitor,' implying that right up to the end, Judas had a choice about whether or not he would betray Jesus.

Philip's Greek name may have encouraged the Greeks who came up to Jerusalem to approach him, rather than any of the other disciples, saying, 'Sir, we would see Jesus.' Philip went and told Andrew, and they told Jesus (John 12:20-22).

As always, Jesus had a purpose in HIs choosing of these twelve, although we know so little about them. They were to be pioneers of the heavenly way. The number twelve is significant, immediately suggesting a connection with the twelve tribes of Israel, so that the disciples may be said to represent the new Israel, the new people of God. Through the gospel of the kingdom, God is inaugurating a new and living way by which to come to Him. These twelve 'called out' ones declare that not only is God doing a new thing, initiating a new Israel, but that He is doing it in love and compassion for the descendants of the 'old' Israel. This is why Jesus says to them, 'Go nowhere among the Gentiles and enter no town of the Samaritans, but go rather to the lost sheep of the house of Israel (verses 5, 6), and preach as you go saying, "The kingdom of heaven is at hand' (verse 7).

Under Jesus' authority, this is what the disciples are called to do, and under that authority they become *'apostles', sent ones.* The focus shifts from their appointment as disciples, those learning about the ways of Jesus, Jesus' inner circle of friends, to their ministry as apostles, ministering the gospel, the good news of repentance and faith, the good news of healing and deliverance, even as Jesus had been doing, but first to the lost sheep of the house of Israel. It is not until Matthew 28:19, that the disciples receive the commission, 'Go therefore and make disciples of *all* nations.'

The lost sheep, shepherdless as Jesus describes them in Matthew 9:30, suggests that they are that despised group within the nation who fail to observe the rabbinic tradition closely. Galilean Jews were often despised, as Galilee was some distance from Jerusalem, and it was more difficult for this agrarian community always to attend the three more significant 'feasts of the Lord', Passover, combined with the feast of unleavened bread; the Feast of Weeks; and the Feast of Booths; otherwise known as Succoth, which it was incumbent upon all Jews to observe three times a year in Jerusalem (Deuteronomy 16:16). Galilee was where Jesus was preaching, teaching, and healing when He spoke those words, but they probably had a greater reference than that, for the whole Jewish people were like lost sheep, needing to hear, to see, to believe and to be healed by Jesus.

We are reminded of Ezekiel's beautiful passage in Ezekiel 34, where God denounces the shepherds of Israel who do not look after His people, His sheep, and declares, 'I myself will search for my sheep and will seek them out' (Ezekiel 34:11). And they shall know that I, the Lord their God, am with them, and that they, the house of Israel, are my people, says the Lord' (Ezekiel 34:30). I will send down the showers in their season, they shall be showers of blessing (Ezekiel 34:26).

These promises are about to be fulfilled for Israel. The gathering together of the lost sheep is the dawn of the new age, the Messianic age, the age of salvation.

We thank God that it is no longer limited to Israel, for Jesus also had His church in view when He sent out His twelve disciples, to learn the way of the kingdom. He transformed them into apostles who were sent to share the life of the kingdom with so many others, bringing into existence the church which is built upon the foundation of the apostles and the prophets, Christ Jesus Himself being the chief cornerstone (Ephesians 2:20). He is the Lord of the Harvest, and He urges His disciples to *pray* that He will send forth labourers into His harvest, for prayer is fundamental to, and the basis for, the apostolic ministry, bringing them into the will of God as they pray, 'Thy will be done,' uniting them together in the One who was also 'sent', who said, 'As the Father has sent me, so send I you' (John 20:21). The writer to the Hebrews, with some perspicacity, some revelation, calls Him 'the Apostle and High Priest of our confession', the Apostle, the One sent from God, and the One who is able for all time to save those who come unto God by Him, since He always lives to make intercession for us as our great High Priest. (Hebrews 3:1; 7:25). Therefore, as the Holy Spirit says, 'Today, when you hear His voice, do not harden your hearts' (Hebrews 3: 7) but joyfully enter into all the work of the ministry which He has for you, for He is still calling labourers into His harvest, to share in His authority, to share in His joy over one sinner that repents.

Matthew says, 'The names of the twelve apostles are these: *first* Simon who is called Peter' (verse 2). Does this refer to the fact that he was the first disciple to be called by Jesus as he mended his nets by the Sea of Galilee (4:18)? Or does it make him the first among equals? Or does it make him the representative disciple/apostle?

'First among the apostles, but not above the apostles. Is this the Pope of Rome?' asks a theologian called Bengel (quoted by U. Luz p68), for this has been the interpretation of this verse by the Roman Catholic church. A more acceptable view to Protestants is that Jesus gives the disciples *first* His authority and *then* sends them out, and this is borne out by verses 1-4. In what follows, He gives them timeless instructions about their mission.

This mission is not going to be a comfortable one, but on the contrary self-sacrificial, for Jesus begins with several prohibitions. *First,* they may take no money with them, not gold or silver, or even small change, for the gospel of the kingdom is a free gift to all and cannot be bought or sold for money. They may accept hospitality, but not money, and the hospitality they are given is given from the heart, out of love for the brethren, without charge. *Secondly,* they must not take a bag of provisions, a bag for carrying food to eat along the way. *Thirdly,* they may not take a second tunic as a change of undergarment, or for additional warmth. *Fourthly,* they may have no footwear for protection of the feet. And *lastly,* they may have no staff to help over difficult terrain, or to ward off unwelcome attention from stray dogs or worse.

They must rely on the protection and provision of their heavenly Father, who will guide them to a home in the village or town where there is a 'worthy' person, possibly someone who is seeking after the truth, or a disciple who has already heard and responded to the good news of the kingdom, and where the disciples can stay until going on to the next city, village or town, wherever people need to hear about Jesus.

The disciple goes bearing peace to that house, but there will be some who reject it, and the disciple must then shake off the dust from his feet as he leaves that place with sorrow in his heart, for he recognises that on the day of judgement, that place, those people, will be judged because they refused the gift of salvation which Jesus came to give.

These conditions demonstrate two things; the *willingness* of the disciples to follow Jesus' commands no matter what the cost, and the *authority* of Jesus, that even when that authority is delegated to ordinary human beings it still remains the authority of Jesus, for without Him they can do nothing (John 15:5). This is such a safe place to be, and ensures that all the glory goes to Him. Jesus had gone through towns and villages, preaching the gospel of the kingdom, healing the sick,(Matthew 4:23, 24, 9:35, 36), and they now know the joy of following in Jesus' footsteps, but not in their own strength but in His power to preach and heal, under the divine blessing of peace.

Matthew 10:16-23. The persecution of the disciples

Behold, I send you forth as sheep in the midst of wolves, so be wise as serpents and harmless as doves. Beware of men, for they will deliver you up to councils and flog you in their synagogues and you will be dragged before governors and kings for My sake to bear testimony before them and the Gentiles. When they deliver you up, do not be anxious how you are to speak or what you are to say for what you are to say will be given to you in that hour, for it is not you who speak but the Spirit of your Father who is speaking through you.

In this central section of His discourse Jesus moves on to a further test of the disciples' integrity, loyalty, and commitment. As before, Jesus never underestimates the cost of discipleship. Whenever the kingdom of heaven is at hand (verse 7), there will be wolves who come amongst the sheep. The disciples who have recently been called to be apostles, the ones sent by God, are now described as 'sheep'; not 'lost sheep', but 'found sheep', those who had come to love the Good Shepherd who gave His life for the sheep (John 10:11).

Jesus warns that that very blessing of being called by God, is going to be challenged by the wolves who come to destroy the flock, who will deliver up the sheep to unmentionable torture and harm, but that this in itself will give an opportunity for the disciples to testify before 'governors and kings' (verse 19) 'for Jesus' sake' (verse 18). Their sphere of ministry has certainly increased, but so also has the antagonism to the message. Above all, the commission to the disciples is reinforced. Jesus says, *'Behold I, your Lord, send you out,'* in verse 16. When we read the accounts of how the apostles suffered in the Acts of the Apostles, we note how absolutely accurate was this description from Jesus of what life was going to be like for the young growing church, and then for the church down through the years. There have always been believers who have suffered in a similar way for their faith in Jesus.

This passage beautifully includes the specific ministry of all Three Persons of the Godhead, for Jesus 'sends them', the Holy Spirit speaks through them as they bear witness before governors and kings (verse 20), and Jesus declares that their heavenly Father cares so much for them, that just as not one sparrow falls to the ground without your Father's will (verse 29), so they need not fear, for to the Father they are of more value than many sparrows (verse 31). This is the gracious loving care of their heavenly Father.

Three times Jesus tells them, 'Do not fear' (verse 26, 28 and 31). The governors and kings are Gentiles, so, in a sense, the gospel is being extended from Israel to the Gentiles. But these are hostile people, enemies of the gospel. We cannot help but think of the apostle Paul who had this experience of persecution in full measure, and especially of his trial and examination before Festus the governor, and Agrippa the king. Paul was on trial for his life, but was still taking the opportunity to speak clearly to these men of the resurrected Jesus, and the transformation He makes in the lives of those who trust in Him. Agrippa said to Paul on that occasion, 'Almost thou persuaded me to be a Christian' (Acts 26:22 A.V.). How wonderful for that faithful apostle it would be, if his persecution allowed even one of his persecutors to come to Christ in faith. And that may have been the case with many who persecuted Jesus' disciples, His apostles, His sent ones.

What could have been an even greater burden for the disciples to bear was the division it caused within their own families. Jesus warns them, 'Brother will deliver up brother to death and the father his child, and children will rise up against parents and have them put to death' (verse 21) and this awful catalogue is continued in verses 35-37, concluding with, 'A man's foes will be those of his own household' (verse 37).

Not everyone in a family who hears the gospel receives it, and there is a great gulf fixed between those who believe and those who do not, for discipleship involves a complete change of heart and mind and way of life, and those who do not or will not receive the good news of the kingdom, the way of salvation, the intimacy of life lived in relation to the Lord Jesus and his heavenly Father, do not understand, and may even become the 'foes' of those whom they love.

Jesus recognises this. He recognises the temptation to renounce faith in order to live peaceably within the family, but Jesus says, 'This is not the peace I came to give, for I came not to bring peace on those terms, but a sword' (verse 34). Jesus is speaking metaphorically of a sharp instrument that cuts through all the grey and indistinct and ensures that the issue is seen as black and white. 'He who is not with Me is against Me,' He says (Matthew 12:30). This is a hard saying. Who can bear it? said His disciples on another occasion (John 6:60). Can Jesus really mean that there is no room for compromise, no discussion of how to make these completely disparate positions reach some kind of understanding? The way is hard, the gate is narrow, that leads to life (Matthew 7:13), but unless Jesus is Lord of all, He is not Lord at all.

This is surely what He means when He tells His disciples to take up his cross and follow Him (verse 38). The disciple who does this, who humbles himself even as Jesus did when He became obedient to death, even death on a Cross, who is prepared to lose his life for the sake of Jesus, will find it (verse 39), though he may lose everything that would otherwise, and legitimately, make life apparently worth living.

We are not all called upon to make such sacrifices in such a vivid way though we must all deny ourselves and *daily* take up the cross (Luke 9: 23) if we are to follow Him, counting all things but loss for the excellency, the surpassing worth, of knowing Christ Jesus as Lord of our lives (Philippians 3:8). Many disciples of the Lord Jesus have undoubtedly suffered many things on behalf of the gospel.

All down the ages, others have been called to suffer for their Lord, and it may be that Jesus is anticipating this and speaking eschatologically, for He says, 'You will not have gone through all the towns of Israel before the Son of Man comes (verse 28).

By the time we get to Matthew 24, the disciples have some understanding that conditions before the coming again of Jesus could be difficult. They say to Him, 'What will be the sign of your coming and of the close of the age?' (Matthew 24:3). And Jesus tells them of the great tribulation that will precede His coming.

Here in chapter 10, He gives them a foretaste of what they can expect. The incredible, almost unbelievable truth is that none of the disciples, the Twelve, returned from following Him, or refused His conditions. For His sake, they were prepared to suffer all things, relying on His precious word to them, 'He that endures to the end, the same shall be saved' (verse 22). For the Twelve, it really does not get any better as they return to accompany Jesus during the rest of Matthew's gospel. As He had warned the disciple in chapter 8:30, 'foxes have holes and the birds of the air have nests, but the Son of Man has nowhere to lay His head'. Like Him, they have no established place of residence.

How can *we* follow this teaching of Jesus on mission? on seeking the lost for Him? We have homes and various buildings at our disposal in which we can meet together as a church. Most of us have enough food and clothing, and income which we are glad to share with others. Can we justify ourselves by saying that the mission on which Jesus sent His disciples was unique? On practical grounds, we may believe so, for otherwise the nation would be overwhelmed, swamped by itinerant preachers all wanting to live up to the highest form of discipleship there could possibly be.

In verses 24-28, our gracious Lord Jesus gives a certain other perspective to His teaching, for He talks about the master of the house and his servants (verse 24) and the members of his household (verse 25). This is surely an indication of *settled* discipleship, men and women living in settled conditions, yet still able to live as disciples of the Lord Jesus. Even though Jesus is speaking of the servant being as his master, and of the accusation which the Pharisees had levelled against Him of being Beelzebul, and therefore ending with the conclusion that those of the household of the master would be maligned in the same way, He is surely setting forth a principle here.

There have been many who throughout the ages have gone out to all the four corners of the earth, like Abraham, not knowing whether they went, but knowing that God was calling them to a particular form of evangelism; and many, perhaps thousands, will give eternal thanks for their ministry. For all those dear ones, who are now serving their Lord in this way, we too give eternal thanks for their ministry; we give thanks to God for them.

Sent by Jesus, their ministry will glorify Him. Under His authority, they will endure to the end, and poverty, vulnerability and defencelessness will not deter the proclamation of the gospel, but will in fact enhance it, for Jesus had said, 'The Spirit of the Lord is upon Me, *and He will anoint you.* He has anointed Me to preach the gospel to the poor (to have no shoes is an expression of acute poverty) to proclaim release to the captives, recovery of sight to the blind, to set at liberty those who are bound, to let the oppressed go free, to proclaim the acceptable year of the Lord' (Luke 4:18), and *these servants of the Lord Jesus are doing exactly as their Lord had done under the anointing of the Holy Spirit.*

Matthew 10:1-11:1. Summary of the second discourse

Jesus' *identification* with His people could not be questioned, and the identification of *the disciples* with Jesus gave them their authority and their endurance. It makes very significant the words of Jesus in verse 24, 'A disciple is not above his master.' That is the safest place of all to be.

But to understand that settled discipleship is *also* a safe place, is also to understand that it too can be an option for serving Him, in the acknowledgement that this is consistent with the calling of God upon one's life, *His will.* This is a great comfort to those who truly want the highest and best in terms of loving Him and His way in their lives. These may be the ones to give the cup of cold water to the little ones (verse 42) (not an inconsiderable mercy in the heat of the day in the Middle East). They serve Him in the ordinary and the domestic. They are salt and light in the community in which they live. God never made clones, all His children are individuals, unique.

Is one calling higher than the other? No. What is important is living in the will of God and being faithful to Him whatever the circumstances. 'Be faithful until death and I will give you the crown of life.' Revelation 2:10 is a promise both to those who suffer for the gospel's sake, whether they are taking part in an extraordinarily difficult time of ministry, or are going about their ordinary lives, also in difficult times. They are faithful to Him whatever their circumstances, because they love Him.

With the disciples we take great comfort from the Lord's words, 'You will not have gone through all the cities of Israel *before the Son of Man comes*' (verse 23) an event which is nearer to us now than when we first believed (Romans 13:11). 'He is coming! And every eye will see Him and those who pierced Him, and we shall be with Him forever' (Revelations 1:7).

Amen, even so, come Lord Jesus.

Matthew Chapter 11

Matthew 11:2-15. Messengers from John

And when Jesus had finished instructing His twelve disciples, He went on from there to teach and preach in their cities.

Now when John heard in prison about the deeds of the Christ, he sent word by his disciples and said to Him, 'Are you He who is to come, or shall we look for another?'

Jesus concludes the discourse of chapter 10 as He does every one of the five discourses recorded by Matthew with the words, *kai egeneto, It came to pass.* So, chapter 11:1 reads: *And it happened or, and it came to pass,* when Jesus had finished instructing/ giving His commands to His disciples. But there is a difference between the ending of the first discourse, the sermon on the mount (Mathew 7:28) to the 'crowd' of new disciples, and the ending of this, the second discourse (Matthew 11:1) which was for the Twelve.

Matthew 13:53; 19:1; 26:1; are the endings of the further three discourses of the Lord Jesus and all contain the word 'finished'. These discourses are complete in themselves. As the Psalmist said 'Thy word is settled in heaven' (Psalms 119:89 A.V.), Jesus' word is just that, settled, complete and cannot be added to or taken away from. And having explained to His disciples the itinerant ministry which had been given to them and having foretold all the suffering which they would endure for His sake at the ending of the discourse, Jesus now goes on to do exactly as He had asked them to do, fully aware of the suffering which it would eventually cause Him: 'He went on from there to teach and preach in their cities' (11:1).

Luz (pp 124-128) believes that the twelve disciples represent the embryo church, that there is in these verses the implication of the concept of discipleship for the understanding of the church, and that therefore, Matthew 9:26-28 to Matthew 11:1 becomes an ecclesiological discourse, mandatory on the church. The discourse begins with discipleship, μαθηνης, it occurs at the beginning (9:37, 10:1), in the middle (10:24-25), and at the end (10:42, 11:1) and this reveals a fundamental ecclesiological concept, for the *church consists of those called into discipleship* through repentance and faith, called into the kingdom of God. The church is essentially a group of disciples. This church is not an intellectual or institutional entity, but under the authority of Jesus, is a lived and suffered obedience to Him.

This is how Matthew understands the church, not as a discussion about sanctification, or the administration of the sacraments, important though these may be, but as followers of Jesus, depending on Him and His compassion for the mission to the world, taking on His lifestyle of poverty and vulnerability, sharing His suffering, continuing the earthly life of Jesus. 'It is enough for the disciple to be like his teacher, and the servant his Master' (Matthew 10:25).

These are the characteristics of the church, obedience, righteousness, and above all, love, followed by the consequences of these deeds of love and righteousness, which often become hostility, suffering, death. The church exists in a world which generally speaking, rejects it, refuses its message, has nothing for it but contempt, or at least, indifference.

In the Creed, we say that we believe in the church's unity, holiness, catholicity, *and apostolicity*, one holy, catholic and apostolic church. The church is *sent out* into the world to proclaim love and forgiveness. When it no longer does this, it loses its apostolicity, its 'sentness'. Church is not simply '*is*' but '*becomes* church when it recognises Jesus' authority. When Jesus shares His authority with His disciples. It demonstrates that it is His church by its deeds, by its activity. But its underlying purpose is not just what it does, important though that is, but in its fundamental relationship with Jesus, loving Him, following Him, worshipping Him, enjoying intimacy with His Father, looking unto Jesus the author and finisher of faith (Hebrews

11:1), with brothers and sisters, the true family of Jesus who do the will of the Father (Matthew 12:50). In chapters 13 and 18, Jesus develops for the disciples their understanding of the dynamism of the church, expanding the implications of following Him.

Here in Matthew 9:37 to 11:1, Jesus is showing His disciples the *cost of discipleship,* the cost not only individually, but corporately as His family, as the church, for it is the church together in its mission, its faithfulness to the gospel that lifts Him up, drawing men and women to Himself as the exalted Son of God. He was lifted high upon the Cross. He is also lifted up in the hearts of His redeemed ones as they follow in His steps.

Matthew 11:1-6. The messengers from John the Baptist

And when Jesus had finished instructing His twelve disciples, He went on from there to teach and preach in their cities.

Now when John heard in prison about the deeds of the Christ, he sent word by his disciples and said to Him, 'Are you He who is to come. or shall we look for another?' And Jesus answered them, Go and tell John what you hear and see: the blind receive their sight, and the lame walk, lepers are cleansed and the deaf hear, and the dead are raised up and the poor have good news preached to them. And blessed is he who takes no offence in Me'.

The beginning of chapter 11 concerns the imprisonment of John the Baptist, and also marks a new phase in the ministry of Jesus. Until now, His words, accompanied by His works of healing, have been received by the people in repentance and faith as they entered into the life of the kingdom of heaven. Now, a change has occurred. As He has gone through the cities of Galilee (Matthew 11:21), Chorazin, Bethsaida, Capernaum, preaching, teaching, and healing, many have not repented, and Jesus has faithfully warned them that the alternative to repentance on hearing His word, is judgement. This situation, however, has not yet arisen; judgement is reserved for verses 20-24.

Although John has been arrested and put in prison, his disciples have been allowed to visit him. Perhaps this too is part of Herod's cruelty. This strong man with his powerful message to which so many have responded is now living, or barely living in a dungeon, deprived of light and air; a hard experience for one who had lived in the open. Possibly he is chained, like Peter in Acts 12:6, and Paul and Silas in Acts 16:24, 26, perhaps having to rely on his disciples to bring him food. How devastating for the disciples, and how humiliating for John to be in such a position, all part of Herod's cruel treatment of him and them.

But the worst thing for John was not his imprisonment but his disturbed faith, for *doubt is not unbelief,* but *disturbed faith.* He had lived close to God all his life, ever since his miraculous birth to Zacharias and Elizabeth. He was filled with the Holy Spirit even from his mother's womb (Luke 1:15), 'living in the wilderness till the day of his manifestation to Israel' (Luke 1:80) until the time when he knew from God that he should start preaching, 'Repent, for the kingdom of heaven is at hand' (Matthew 3:1). Had he made a dreadful mistake? All those years spent preparing for what he believed was the coming of the One who was mightier than he? (Matthew 3:11). He remembered all the men and women whom he had indeed baptised as they repented. He remembered the wonderful experience of baptising Jesus, and seeing the heavens opened, and the dove alighting on Him, and hearing those powerful and significant words from heaven, 'This is my beloved Son in whom I am well pleased' (Matthew 3:17), the very voice of God Himself acknowledging Jesus as His Son.

How could he have been so foolish? Was all this for nothing? How could he have wasted so many years of his life when he could have had a life like other men, a wife, a home, a family? What if he had led these loyal men, his disciples, astray? But what if Jesus really was the Messiah, the One sent from God for His people Israel?

'Are you He that should come, or shall we look for another?' (Matthew 11:3) was the agonised message he sent to Jesus, conveyed to Him by John's disciples. And Jesus was quick to reply, 'Go and tell John what you hear and see' (11:4). They had seen the signs of the Kingdom of Heaven at work. With the coming of the kingdom *at hand* (Matthew 3:2), as John had prophesied, the blind receive their sight, the lame walk, lepers are cleansed, and the deaf hear, and the dead are raised up and the poor have the good news preached to them' (Matthew 11:4-6).

These are the deeds of the Spirit anointed prophet in Isaiah 61:1-3 and fulfilled, repeated, and enlarged in Luke 4:18; Jesus as the fulfilment of Isaiah's prophecy. Yet Jesus was someone who was not only a Prophet, but the Spirit filled Servant of God, for Messiah or Christ means 'Anointed One', anointed by the Holy Spirit. And Jesus adds, 'Blessed is he who takes no offence at Me' (Matthew 11:6).

Jesus says, Blessed is he who does not take offience at Me; who does not find in Me a stumbling block. How could Jesus be an offence, a stumbling block to John? To anyone? Isaiah speaks of 'a stone of stumbling and a rock of offence' (Isaiah 8:14), and that 'there is no beauty that we should desire Him' (Isaiah 53:2). We find that difficult to comprehend. Not desire Jesus? On whom our very life depends? Whose love and compassion towards us has changed us utterly from the sin-burdened, oppressed, persons we were, to the joyful, rejoicing free people we are in the process of becoming, and for which He was prepared to give up His very life, pouring out His precious blood upon the Cross, to bring us near to God.

For John the Baptist, of course, the Cross had not yet happened. For him, the stumbling block could be that he wanted so much to see in Jesus the fulfilment of all the Messianic prophecies. There would be many that would be fulfilled at a later date. Jesus was reminding him that all the prophecies about Him were equally valid, but at this point in His ministry, the prophecies regarding His earthly life and His ministry of healing and teaching was the confirmation that He was indeed the Messiah, He that should come.

'And there is blessing for you John, because that is what you believe, and you are not offended in Me' (verse 6). The 'stumblers', those who find Jesus to be a stumbling block and offensive to them, are those who are unable or unwilling to recognise His mission and ministry as that of the Messiah. And as the disciples of John went away, back to the prison to tell John what Jesus had said, Jesus began to talk to the crowd about John, for they too had to make a decision, for or against Jesus.

Matthew 11:7-19. The testimony of Jesus to John

As they went away, Jesus began to speak to the crowds concerning John: 'What did you go out into the wilderness to behold? A reed shaken by the wind? Why then did you go out? To see a man clothed in soft raiment? Behold, those who wear soft raiment are in king's houses. Why then did you go out? To see a prophet? Yes I tell you, and more than a prophet. This is he of whom it is written, Behold, I send My messenger before Thy face who shall prepare Thy way before Thee. Truly, I say to you, among those born of woman there has risen no-one greater than John the Baptist, yet he who is least in the kingdom of heaven is greater than he'.

Jesus gently asked two questions of the crowd. He knew that many, perhaps most of them, had gone down to the River Jordan, and had seen John baptising those who came to him, may even have been baptised themselves, while John explained to them that though he baptised in water, there was one coming after him who would baptise them in the Holy Spirit (Matthew 3:11). Jesus asked these people, first, 'What did you expect to see?' And then, 'Why did you go?'

There were reeds growing on the banks of the river, responding to every breath of wind, wavering, swaying, moving, shaking. Jesus asked them, did they expect John to be like a reed, unstable, insecure? Was this what they expected to see? Someone who appeared to be like the reeds at the water's edge? unstable?

Secondly, *why* did they go? Did they expect to see an important person, dressed like those who had access to authority, perhaps a courtier in one of Herod's palaces? (He had four, one in Jericho, Cyprus, Masada and Machaerus on the east side of the Dead Sea, where according to Josephus (Antiquities 18:2), John was imprisoned. If the dungeons at Machaerus were indeed his prison, then John's disciples had had a long walk to bring John's message to Jesus).

Were the people surprised to see him dressed not as a court official, but as a prophet, in a garment of camel's hair, with a leather girdle around his waist? Or did they go hoping to see a prophet? Jesus says, 'Yes, I tell you and more than a prophet' (verse 9), an emphatic statement as He goes on to quote the prophet Malachi, 'Behold I send my messenger before thy face, who shall prepare the way before thee' (Malachi 3:1). Jesus continues, 'Amen, translated as' Truly,' Amen, I say to you,' a statement with all the authority and power of God behind it; 'Amen I say to you, among those born of women there has arisen no-one greater than John the Baptist' – this we can accept, but He then goes on – 'Yet he who is least in the Kingdom of Heaven is greater than he' (verse 11).

What can Jesus possibly mean by these inscrutable words? John has stood on the very threshold of the Kingdom of Heaven. He is Jesus' forerunner, the one who has gone before Him to prepare His way in fulfilment of Isaiah's prophecy in Isaiah 40:3. 'A voice cries in the wilderness, prepare the way of the Lord. Make straight in the desert a highway for our God'. Who could have a greater destiny than John's? He has ushered in a new dispensation, a new phase of God's desire for a people who may be given the privilege of living in an intimacy with Him that only comparatively few were able to enjoy under the old dispensation.

Now Jesus has come, come in human likeness, come as Son of God and Son of Man to live among human beings, to give them the right to become children of God, even to those who received Him, who believed in His Name (John 1:11). These, though the least in the kingdom, have an experience which John did not enjoy. John had announced that the Kingdom of Heaven was 'at hand' (Matthew 3:1), but these 'least' had *entered in* to that kingdom, even though ever since John, there had been violent people, who by their violence had tried to prevent those who wanted to enter, and this violence was still going on even as Jesus spoke. He said, 'From the days of John the Baptist even until now, the kingdom of heaven has suffered violence, and men of violence take it by force' (verse 12). And we might say, even until now, in the 21st century.

Jesus reminds the crowd about Elijah, who also suffered violence in his ministry, and identifies John with Elijah. Every Old Testament prophet of God suffered. Suffering becomes proclamation, as the prophets knew; it becomes testimony to the claims of God. John who is a witness to Jesus also suffers.

The special place that John has is that 'all the prophets prophesied until John' (verse 13) but John is the last in that wonderful chain of prophecy that God initiated in order to bring His people near to Himself. Elijah's call was to 'repent', his call to Israel to acknowledge that they were 'halting between two opinions' (1 Kings 18:21), whether to worship God or the god Baal. Elijah brought them to the place on Mount Carmel where they had no choice but to say, 'The Lord, He is God, the God who answers by fire, He is God' (1 Kings 18:24-39). This is John's call to Israel too.

What makes John 'more than a prophet' (verse 9) is that he has the *fulfilment* of all the prophecies, *JESUS,* standing among the people. He saw what the prophets of old had longed to see: Jesus, the Son of God. 'Behold the Lamb of God, who takes away the sin of the world' (John 1:29), John had said. What an amazing revelation!

No wonder then that Jesus was gently trying to encourage these crowds to understand about John, that this man whom they had seen or heard about, the one who was baptising in the River Jordan, whom they had hurried down to investigate, perhaps from a hope that he might indeed be the Christ (John 1:20) was not the Christ but was the forerunner of the Christ, the One foretold by God through His prophets to be the Messiah, the Anointed One of God.

John was a true envoy, an ambassador of the kingdom. John was the one who called the people to repentance in preparation for the coming of the King, the Messiah. Were these people expecting John to be the Messiah or the Christ, the Anointed One whom they had been expecting for so long? No, for this man, John, though not the Christ, was nevertheless the one who ran ahead of the Christ, the one who would prepare the way before Him.

Jesus however does not equate these people with the crowd which had surrounded Him before. He calls them, 'this generation'. He says, 'To what shall I compare this generation?' (verse 16). They are like children who are not satisfied with their play, whether they play at 'weddings or funerals' as children tend to do.

John's asceticism had not appealed to them. It was like a funeral where nobody knew how to mourn properly. Jesus' more social behaviour did not impress them either. It was like a wedding where no one bothered to get up and dance; in fact, they thought Jesus was a glutton and a drunkard because He was befriending those traitorous tax collectors and those obvious sinners. In their estimation, Jesus was ceremonially contaminated.

'This generation' had responded neither to John nor to Jesus. Jesus compares them to children who do not know what they want, but are disgruntled, not satisfied with either alternative. The term 'this generation' indicates that they are *contemporaries* of John and Jesus, but they do not appreciate or understand how blessed they are. Perhaps they are seeking wisdom to know exactly what is going on between what John was doing before his incarceration and what Jesus is doing now.

Jesus says, 'Wisdom is justified by her deeds' (verse 19). If nothing else, they are spectators of all these wonderful happenings, these deeds, and could be recipients of all the wisdom passed down to them through the generations, the wisdom who *is* Christ. But they do not see in Him the epitome, the apex, the eternally superior and above all, God's wisdom, which is personified in Jesus. Proverbs 8:22-31 speaks thus prophetically of Him, and this is taken up by Paul in

1 Corinthians 1:30, for *He is wisdom,* and wisdom is justified by her deeds (verse 19).

'This generation' regard Jesus as a man who carouses and drinks, like any other human being. Jesus clearly states that He is the Son of Man, the One who will one day rise in judgement (verse 19). He also identifies Himself as the Wisdom of God, incarnated wisdom, through His works. All the works or deeds which Jesus does, He does in wisdom; the works and deeds which only He could do.

These verses indicate a new phase in Jesus' ministry as noted earlier. There is a growing rejection of Him, of which He is aware. Yet Jesus' words and works among them justify Him, bear witness to Him (verse 19), and contradict all the criticism against Him.

Matthew 11:20-24. The reproach of Jesus on the cities of Israel.

Then He began to upbraid the cities where most of His mighty works had been done, because they did not repent. 'Woe to you Chorazin! woe to you Bethsaida! for if the mighty works done in you had been done in Tyre and Sidon they would have repented long ago in sackcloth and ashes. But I tell you, it shall be more tolerable on the day of judgement for Tyre and Sidon than for you' (Matthew 11:20-24).

Matthew 11: 1 has described how Jesus went 'to teach and preach in their cities' after He had delivered His teaching to His disciples on the cost of discipleship.

Now, having borne testimony to John the Baptist, He reports on this latest mission. He had been to Chorazin, a Galilean city about two miles north of the Sea of Galilee, and Bethsaida, east of the point where the River Jordan flows into the Sea of Galilee, and to Capernaum, Jesus' home town (Matthew 4:13), His message had not changed. He had done 'mighty works' in these towns (verse 20), and preached repentance, but they had not repented.

Jesus had warned His disciples in 10:11-15, that there would be a day of judgement, and that those who refused their message would be judged. He now applies that same message of judgement to Chorazin, Bethsaida, and Capernaum, for they had rejected Him and must bear the consequences. He says, 'Woe to you, Chorazin; woe to you Bethsaida; for if the mighty works done in you had been done in Tyne and Sidon, they would have repented long ago in sackcloth and ashes.'

These cities were cities universally despised by Israel because they had been part of Philistia, heathen cities, Gentile cities, Philistine cities against which many of the Old Testament prophets had pronounced judgement (Isaiah 23, Ezekiel 26-28, Joel 4:4, Zechariah 9:2-4). Jesus says, 'If the mighty works done in you Chorazin and Bethsaida, had been done in Tyne and Sidon, they would have repented long ago in sackcloth and ashes' (Matthew 11: 21).

And His word to Capernaum intensified and heightened His disappointment. This city, His city, He compared with Sodom, a place renowned for its wickedness. 'Woe to you,' He says of Capernaum, 'you will have sorrow upon sorrow, for you have rejected God in rejecting Me' (Matthew 10:40).

The miracles He had done were signs of the presence of God among them, but they did not recognise them as such. Jesus was not just preaching an emotional, sentimental gospel of love, but a loving gospel which had consequences of judgement for those who rejected it.

There was only one alternative to entering the Kingdom of Heaven via repentance and faith; and that was not entering in, leading to judgement. God could only say to such people on the Day of Judgement, 'Why did you reject My Son?' Isaiah saw God as holding out His hands all day long to a disobedient people (Isaiah 65:2, Romans 10:21). Jesus was holding out His hands to the people of these Galilean cities. 'Come to Me,' He was saying, 'Come to Me and I will give you rest' (Matthew 11:28). *But they would not.* Perhaps these are some of the most serious words in the English language. *They would not.* They had used the free will which God had given to men and women at their creation to turn against Him. They had said, 'We will not have this Man to reign over us' (Luke 19:14).

Both Matthew and Luke recall an episode in the life of Jesus when He drew near to Jerusalem and wept over it, saying, 'O Jerusalem, Jerusalem, how often would I have gathered your children together, as a hen gathers her brood under her wings, *and you would not* (Matthew 23:27, Luke 13:34, 19:41). 'Behold, your house is left unto you desolate' (Matthew 23:27 A.V.) and we detect that same desolation in the voice of Jesus as He weeps over these cities of Galilee, longs for them and eventually dies for them.

But this is not the end, for the apostle John saw a new heaven and a new earth, and the holy city, new Jerusalem coming down out of heaven from God, prepared as a Bride adorned for her Husband (Revelation 21:2). This new Jerusalem, the Bride of Christ, is composed of those who are clothed with fine linen, for fine linen is the righteous deeds of the saints (Revelation 19:8), a great multitude whom no man could number from every nation, from all tribes and peoples and tongues, worshipping God and the Lamb, Jesus (Revelation 7:9). Our Lord Jesus, crowned with glory and honour. This is the new heaven and the new earth prepared for those who have entered into this new and intimate relation with Him.

Many have not responded to His invitation, 'Come to Me,' but many, many, have, and have known His rest, and the ease of the yoke, and the lightness of the burden; and the joy of being part, even a very small part, of that multitude which no man could number; the new Jerusalem, the Bride of Christ.

Matthew 11:25-30. The gentleness of Jesus towards His disciples.

At that time, Jesus declared, 'I thank thee, Father, Lord of heaven and earth, that thou hast hidden these things from the wise and understanding, and hast revealed them to babes; yes Father, for such was Thy gracious will'. All things have been delivered to Me by My Father, and no-one knows the Father except the Son, and anyone to whom the Son chooses to reveal Him.

Come to Me, all who labour and are heavy laden, and I will give you rest. Take My yoke upon you and learn of Me; for I am gentle and lowly of heart and you will find rest to your souls. For My yoke is easy, and My burden is light.

'At that time' (verse 25), while Jesus was receiving opposition from those who would not acknowledge either Him, or John, or His disciples, Jesus was constantly aware of the presence and closeness of His Father. He says, 'No one knows the Son except the Father, and no-one knows the Father except the Son' (verse 27). This mutual knowledge between Father and Son is the constant underpinning and foundation of the life of the Son of God as He speaks in gratitude to His Father for the revelation He has given to His disciples whom He describes as the 'babes' (verse 25), for they were still young in the faith; and the revelation of divine gentleness to those newly come to faith in Jesus; and above all, the revelation that 'all things have been delivered' to Him by His Father (verse 27).

In spite of all the rejection of Him and His words among some of the people, and the sorrow He has as He reminds them of the judgement consequent upon that rejection, Jesus does not despair, for He still recognises that His Father is 'Lord of heaven and earth' (verse 25), the One ultimately in control. Jesus has been revealing Himself as the Messiah to 'the crowds' and to 'this generation', but only 'the babes' have understood that 'all things have been delivered to Him by His Father' (verse 27). Though they have a lot yet to 'learn of Him' (verse 29), they will grow in their understanding. They have entered into life with Jesus, and He does not promise that this will be an easy journey, quite the reverse, but as they come to Him, and learn from Him, they will find rest for their souls.

A yoke upon the shoulders of two oxen pulling together means that the responsibility is shared. The yoke that Jesus graciously shares with His 'little children' does not mean that they do not have the labour, the burden, but that He comes alongside, places His shoulder next to theirs in His yoke and shares it with them, for His yoke is easy and His burden is light (verse 30). These are indeed 'comfortable (and comforting) words' (B.C.P. Holy Communion). As babes, as little children, we come to Him, learn of Him, learn His gentleness and meekness, and grow up in Him, 'Grow in the grace and knowledge of our Lord and Saviour Jesus Christ' (2 Peter 3:18) while we rest in Him.

At His invitation, we 'come to Him' and all the rest, the refreshment, becomes ours. The 'wise', the religious aristocracy, the scribes and the Pharisees, receive the same invitation, for Jesus excludes no-one, and we do hear of people like Nicodemus and Joseph of Arimathea, members of the Sanhedrin, who respond to the call of Jesus.

But here again, we have the stark alternatives of those who follow Jesus, and those who reject Him.

Those who follow Him, though but 'babes' (verse 25), infants, simple and devoted followers of Jesus, have received their revelation of who He is from the Father. Jesus is conscious that He is not alone, but that He and the Father are workers together in the salvation of men and women; a concept highly developed by John in his gospel, for example, John 6:37, where Jesus says, 'All that the Father has given me will come unto Me, and him who comes to Me, I will in no wise cast out'. And in John 10:30, 'I and the Father are One.'

What the Father and the Son have between them is that intimate, special knowledge. 'No one knows the Father except the Son, and no one knows the Son except the Father' (verse 27) is an absolutely unique statement, and yet They want to share that knowledge 'with those to whom the Son 'chooses to reveal' the Father (verse 27), drawing simple human beings into relationship with Them. The longing in the heart of Jesus is evident; as He says, 'Come to me' (verse 28). It is the grace of the Lord Jesus, who, though He was rich, became poor, that we through His poverty might be made rich (2 Corinthians 8:9).

There is a sense in which all the epistles are commentary on the gospels.

In Matthew 11:27 Jesus says, '*All things* have been delivered to Me by My Father.' In Matthew's gospel, at the time of His arrest in the Garden of Gethsemane, before His trial and subsequent execution, He declared that even at that time, He could have called upon more than twelve legions of angels to rescue Him, to deliver Him, but then how should the scripture be fulfilled? (Matthew 26:53). His Father was in control and His will was being done, and Jesus and His Father were one in their determination to bring men and women into fellowship with Them.

So, He left His Father's glory, and did not count equality with God a thing to be grasped, but emptied Himself, taking the form of a servant, being made in the likeness of men, being born as a man (Philippians 2:6-8). But in the emptying, the *kenosis*, of Himself of glory, He did not empty Himself of His special unique relationship with Father, nor of the authority which He possessed as Son of the Father, but being born as a man, He became utterly human, with human needs of food and clothing and shelter, exemplifying to human beings the entirety of the provision of God and the certainty of living life in entire dependence upon Him.

This is what the Son is, *essentially*. In His very essence, He is God, and yet He is also Man, and without Him there is no way to the Father. 'He who comes to God must believe that He is, and that He is the rewarder of those who diligently seek Him' (Hebrews 11:6). And as we come to Him, we receive from Him the message of grace, not cheap self-evident grace, but that grace of which 2 Corinthians 8:9 speaks; costly grace, the love of God in action. Though He was rich beyond all imagining, for our sake He became poor. For us His grace connected with our attitude of childlikeness, humility before God as a child, as we read His word, praying to Him yet knowing, and aware of, our inability to understand anything at all of Him whom we love, except for what we receive of the gracious work of the Holy Spirit in revelation.

'All things' have undoubtedly been delivered to Him by His Father. But only the Father, who knows the Son, is able to know the cost of the sacrifice which enables Him to say, 'Come to Me'. How great is the Father's love for us, how vast beyond all measure. How precious the words of the Lord Jesus to His Father, 'Lo, I come to do Thy will' (Hebrews 10:7). 'Let this cup pass from Me, nevertheless, not as I will but as Thou wilt' (Matthew 26:39). The whole gospel is summed up and established in these verses (Matthew 11:25-30). It is reminiscent of John's gospel. Because of who He is, because of who the Father is, Jesus can and does issue this invitation to all. 'Come to Me and I will give you rest.'

Matthew Chapter 12

Matthew 12:1-8. The disciples are hungry on the Sabbath

At that time, Jesus went through the grainfields on the Sabbath; His disciples were hungry, and they began to pluck heads of grain, and to eat. But when the Pharisees saw it they said to Him, 'Look, your disciples are doing what is not lawful to do on the Sabbath.' He said to them, 'Have you not read what David did when he was hungry, and those who were with him? How he entered the house of God and ate the bread of the presence which it was not lawful for him to eat nor for those who were with him, but only for the priests?'

'At that time' Jesus went through the grain fields on the Sabbath; His disciples were hungry, and they began to pluck heads of grain and to eat (Matthew 12:1).

Again, Matthew uses the phrase, 'At that time'. This was no accidental happening or event, but was purposeful, purposed by Jesus, not only for the enlightenment of the Pharisees, but more importantly for His disciples. It is quite possible that the disciples often knew hunger. Jesus had been open with them about the life to which they were committed if they followed Him. Perhaps they had had no breakfast, or even supper the previous evening. On one occasion when they had forgotten to take bread (Matthew 16:5), Jesus reminded them of the experience they had of the five loaves which fed the five thousand and the seven loaves which fed the four thousand, and therefore how faithless they were to be concerned that He might rebuke them for not having brough bread with them.

But Jesus never used His power lightly or indiscriminately. There is purpose in all He does. He wants His disciples to get

223

to a place where they trust Him completely, whatever the circumstance, and all His miracles, and all His teaching of them is to that end. So, this section of Matthew's gospel begins with the significant phrase, 'at that time', for Jesus used every circumstance, every experience, to demonstrate that He was in complete control, and could even use the disciples' hunger purposefully.

At the end of chapter 11, Jesus had invited them to come to Him and rest. Jesus had spoken of His rest as something which went on in their hearts and lives, taking His yoke upon them and learning of Him. The Jewish concept of rest had been rightly concerned with the Sabbath, the day of rest which God had commanded for His people, which together with circumcision, was a sign of the covenant between Him and them. God said, 'Remember the sabbath day to keep it holy. Six days shall you labour and do all your work, but the seventh is a sabbath to the Lord your God... for in six days the Lord made heaven and earth, and rested the seventh day, therefore the Lord blessed the seventh day, and hallowed it' (Exodus 20:8).

This is the fourth commandment of the ten which God gave His people. In Exodus 31, 12-17, God explains to Moses that keeping the sabbath is a sign that His people are special to Him, sanctified, set apart for Him, and are in a perpetual covenant with Him; and an acknowledgement that He is creator and sovereign Lord. Not only were the people to rest but also the domestic animals, the ox and the ass, any stranger that might be with them and even the slaves or servants might be refreshed (Exodus 23:12). A fully comprehensive day of rest (Deuteronomy 5:12).

And into this minefield walked Jesus with His disciples.

They were on their way to the synagogue and were passing through the grain fields. It was harvest time, and the grain was in the ear. Under biblical teaching, it was permissible to walk through a grainfield, and to pluck and eat the grain, crushing it with the fingertips, but not to use a tool (Deuteronomy 23:26). But this day was a Sabbath day, and therefore the Pharisees,

THE KING AND THE KINGDOM

watching on the sidelines to see what Jesus' disciples would do, interpreted it as 'work', work which was forbidden on the Sabbath day.

The Sabbath, the day of rest. Is this the rest that Jesus wants His disciples to enter into when He says, 'come unto Me and rest.'

The Pharisees were correct in that the Sabbath is a day of rest, commanded by God, but they had overlaid the simple, understandable words of the commandment with much that was petty and trivial. What had been a day of liberation and freedom had become a day of intricate observance, a burden to be borne, not a day to rejoice in the goodness and provision of the Lord and relax with one's family. And yet the Pharisees really conceived of the Sabbath as a great blessing. In their view, Jesus was undermining something really precious to them, a commandment which set them apart from all other nations, for to none of them was one day of the week more special than any other according to their religious traditions.

Jesus' emphasis was not so much on the commandment as on the God of the commandment. He gave rest to His people because He *is* Rest. When He rested after the creation on the seventh day, He rested completely, eternally. He has never stopped resting. All that He does He does from a position of rest. We cannot imagine God becoming fractious or irritable or anxious or despairing. This is why Jesus can say, 'Come unto Me and rest,' because in close and intimate relationship with His Father, *He too is rest,* a position which John the apostle fully recognised as he rested on Jesus' breast at the last supper (John 13:23).

The Pharisees accuse Jesus, 'Behold, *your* disciples are doing what is not lawful to do on the Sabbath': identifying Jesus' disciples with Him, and changing the emphasis from the disciples' hunger to the question of the Sabbath (verse 2).

God had offered His people Sabbath rest as an example of the rest which was to be continually theirs as they entered into the rest of God through faith. But Hebrews tells us that because of their disobedience (Hebrews 3:15), their rest was forfeit. Psalm 95:7-11 is quoted by the writer to the Hebrews four times as he pleads with his readers not to harden their hearts but to enter into God's rest through faith (Hebrews 4:1), for it is only through faith (Hebrews 4:4) that 'We who have believed enter that rest,' the rest of the God who has never ceased to rest since He created the world; entering God's rest, ceasing from our labours as God did from His (Hebrews 4:10).

All our labour is subsumed under the rest of God. Just as death comes under the authority of life, and darkness under the authority of light, so labour comes under the authority of rest. So Jesus can say, 'Come unto Me all you who labour and are heavy laden and I will give you rest' (Matthew 11:28), a perpetual and continual Sabbath, a Sabbath rest for the people of God (Hebrews 4:9) as we cease to make any attempt to struggle to achieve sufficient righteousness to satisfy a Holy God, but are able to draw near to the throne of grace to receive mercy and find grace to help us in time of need (Hebrews 4:16). His yoke is easy, and His burden is light.

If living from a position of rest is not the case in our present experience, maybe disobedience or rebellion has crept in somewhere? And we need to come again to the throne of grace, to find again that mercy, and that help in time of need, the place where the Lord Jesus deals with all that would make for unrest in our daily experience.

In trying to help the Pharisees to understand God's purpose in commanding that the Sabbath be a day of rest, Jesus refers them to an episode in their history when David had to flee from Saul with his men (1 Samuel 21:1-6). David came to the Tabernacle, where was the Table of the Shewbread, bread which spoke to the people of Israel of the presence of God and sometimes known as the Bread of the Presence. David took the bread and both he and his followers ate of it. David did not ask permission of the priest, Ahimelech. He and his men ate the loaves because they were hungry. They had a need which superseded Leviticus 24:5, which states that the bread was for the priests alone to eat in the holy place. The shewbread had become a merciful provision for hungry men.

For mercy is at the heart of the observation of the Sabbath. The 'rest' of the Sabbath was for the poor, the downtrodden, the outcast, the hungry, the slaves, even the animals (Deuteronomy 5:14-15). Jesus is suggesting to the Pharisees, by referring again to Hosea 6:6, as He had in Matthew 9:13, that the phrase 'I desire mercy and not sacrifice' indicates that the Sabbath commandment is fundamentally subordinate to the love commandment, for the word translated 'mercy' may also be translated as lovingkindness, or steadfast love. Jesus says that the two commandments which sum up the whole purpose of God in the life of His people are firstly the love of God and then the love of one's neighbour. 'On these two commandments depend all the law and the prophets' (Matthew 22:40). We cannot therefore leave someone lying in a ditch because to use a ladder or a rope would be to work, and entail disobedience to the Sabbath law, as the Essenes, a pious Jewish sect, did (Luz p184). That is not mercy, or love for one's neighbour.

Jesus goes further and reminds the Pharisees that on the Sabbath day the priests work twice as hard as they do on any other day in order to prepare the offerings made by fire to the Lord (Deuteronomy 28:3,9-10), and are guiltless (Matthew 12:5) although by so doing they could be said to be profaning the Sabbath and the Tabernacle, and later in the Israelites' history, the Temple. Jesus affirms, *something greater* than the Temple is here (Matthew 12:6).

What does He mean by something greater? Different theologians employ different exegesis of this verse. Gundry (p 223) thinks that Matthew with his Christological emphasis, ensures that greater '$\mu\varepsilon\iota\xi o\nu$' refers to Jesus. Though the disciples, like the priests, had profaned the Sabbath, they were guiltless, because just as the greatness of the Temple is greater than the greatness of the Sabbath, so much more is the superior greatness of Jesus, a greatness that surpasses the greatness of the Sabbath. An argument from the lesser to the greater requires the acceptance of the lesser.

David Hill (p 211) offers the view of T. W. Manson (BJRL p 191) that 'something greater' is the community of disciples who with Jesus constitute the corporate Son of Man. It is the view of Lohmeyer (Temple p 67, 69), that the something greater is the Kingdom of God present in the eschatological community.

These views have much to recommend them, but perhaps do not do complete justice to the text.

A third view is presented by Luz (p 180). He argues that: verse 1 emphasises the disciples' hunger, in verse 2 the Pharisees protest the disciples behaviour and, in verses 3 and 4 Jesus gives a threefold answer; the story of David's visit to the priest Ahimelech; the Sabbath sacrifices performed by the priests in the Tabernacle/Temple which invalidate the Sabbath commandment (Numbers 28:9-10) and that something greater than the Temple is here.

Therefore, mercy and not sacrifice is that which is greater.

The word used for greater μειξον is neuter, some *thing*, so we cannot interpret verse 6 Christologically. Jesus does not say He is greater than the Temple. Nor may we insert here the concept of the Kingdom of God. Instead, Jesus quotes again Hosea 6:6, 'I desire mercy and not sacrifice.' *If one is allowed to violate the Sabbath, it must be on the grounds of mercy. Mercy is the greater thing.*

This is Jesus' interpretation of the will of the Father. Mercy is more acceptable to His Father than sacrifice, and is greater than the Temple. Mercy is *not a substitute* for the sacrificial tradition. After the destruction of the Temple in AD 70, sacrifices were no longer possible. Mercy is *more* than the sacrificial tradition because it is at the centre of God's will completely fulfilled in Jesus, not as an ethical principle, but as an outworking of His love for His Father.

The Pharisees should have been merciful towards the hungry disciples. Then they would have obeyed the chief demands of the law, described by Jesus in Matthew 23:23 as 'justice, mercy and faith'. The hunger of the disciples has a meaning far beyond the transgression of the law regarding the Sabbath. It exposes what God desires, the centre of His will, 'Be merciful, even as your Father in heaven is merciful' (Luke 6:36). *This is the 'something greater'.*

Mercy, steadfast love, is the centre of God's will expressed in the Law, the Torah, and He will not abolish it, as believers come into a new experience of the love and wisdom of God expressed in the New Covenant. Jesus had already stated this in Matthew 5:43. He had said, 'Do not think I have come to abolish the law and the prophets. I came not to abolish but to fulfil.' 'Love your enemies,' He said, 'pray for those who despitefully use you and persecute you, so that you may be sons of your Father who is in heaven. You have heard it said, love your neighbour, *but I say unto you,* love your enemy. You therefore must be perfect (in mercy and love) just as your heavenly Father is perfect' (Matthew 5:43-48).

The sovereign Lord Jesus is saying, 'But I say unto you' (Matthew 5:44). He is expressing the same sovereignty when He says, 'The Son of Man is Lord of the Sabbath' (Matthew 12:8) for everything He said or did, He said it or did in love, at rest in His Father's will.

Mercy, love, the biblical commands of mercy become the greatest commandments; greater than the Temple. The Sabbath is a precious gift, given to His people by God, and because it exists for the poor, the hungry, the slaves, it certainly includes mercy. If therefore it becomes representative of a law or commandment which *excludes* mercy, it negates its own purpose and its own principle, the principle of love.

In this principle, the people of God were commanded to live, not for one day of the week only, but as the centre of the life that God desires for His people. The Sabbath rest for the people of God is entering into that life of love, love of the Father, love of the Lord Jesus, love of the Holy Spirit, love for one another, even love for our enemies, being perfect in love even as our heavenly Father is perfect. We come into that life through God's mercy to us, by faith, in humility of spirit, pleading, 'God, be *merciful* to me, a sinner.' And He always is. And we are at rest.

Sunday is not the Christian Sabbath

The Christian church understood Sunday, the first day of the week on which Jesus rose from the dead, as the day of rest, in contrast to the Jewish Saturday. In that sense, as a day of rest, the Sabbath was abolished for Christians. Sunday, resurrection day, became the day of the worship service in the early church. Worship in the life of the church was pre-eminent, but was also the day for Christian teaching for the ordinary people, and especially important on the physical level for some whose daily work was hard. In the New Testament the references relevant to the church on the issue of the understanding of its worship day include 1 Corinthians 16:2 'on the first day of the week, each of you is to put something aside, as he may prosper, so that contribution need not be made when I come'. Acts 20:7, 1 Corinthians 11:18,33, Revelation 1:10, and Hebrews 10:25 also suggest the first day of the week as the day for Christians to gather together.

Christians are liberated from the law, so the Sabbath commandment may be said to be no longer valid for them. Yet a day of rest, based on the principle of mercy, is a very precious development in the life of the church. Many Christians do work on Sunday, for economic reasons, or caring for others, or because they live in a place where Sunday is not allowed to be a day of rest, and must choose other opportunities of meeting with others, and spending time with their families.

In this country, we are blessed that there is a recognition that political decisions are made notionally on the basis of the well-being of the people. Traditionally, we seek to keep Sunday special, not for Christians only, but for protection from an unmerciful and destructive way of life for all people, for all need the provision of a day of rest.

Mercy is at the centre, the focus of a life lived in accordance with the will of God. Mercy is also at the heart of the Christian Sunday, just as it was for the Jewish Sabbath, an opportunity for worshipping our loving God, and for encouragement of one another on the journey of faith, resting on Jesus as He has invited us to do.

Matthew 12:9-16. The man with the withered hand

*And Jesus went on from there and entered their synagogue.
And behold, there was a man with a withered hand. And they
asked Him, 'Is It lawful to heal on the sabbath?' so that they
might accuse Him. He said to them, 'What man of you, if he
has one sheep, and it falls into a pit on the sabbath day will not
lay hold of it and lift it out? Of how much more value is a man
than a sheep! So it is lawful to do good on the sabbath'. Then He
said to the man, 'Stretch out your hand.' And the man stretched
it out, and it was restored while, like the other.*

Jesus and His disciples now enter the synagogue, where there
was a man with a withered hand.

In spite of the controversy about the Sabbath which Jesus
had had earlier with the Pharisees, they were there in the
synagogue, waiting to accuse Him of violating the Sabbath (verse
10), for they wanted a reason to destroy Him (verse 14). Jesus
had already spoken to them of the need for mercy, and that the
basis of all God's dealings with His people rested on mercy. True
to His teaching, and His compassion for all human disability,
when He saw the man with the withered hand, His compassion
went out to the man, asking him to stretch forth his hand, and in
so doing, the man's hand was restored 'whole like the other'
(verse 13).

But the central focus of this episode is not the healing of the
man with the withered hand, but that the healing should have
taken place on the Sabbath. It appears that the Pharisees have
learned nothing from Jesus' explanation to them that the fourth
commandment was subordinate to the love commandment.
Their opposition to Him was greater than any concern they may
have had for the man with the withered hand, whose whole life
and livelihood was affected by his disability.

Jesus graciously uses the opportunity to give the Pharisees
some further teaching about the Sabbath, giving the example of
a sheep that has fallen into a pit. Some of the poorer people
possessed only one sheep. It was the only asset they possessed.

It represented all their worldly wealth. Jesus says, 'If a man has only one sheep and it falls into a pit on the Sabbath, will he not lay hold of it and lift it up? Of how much more value is a man than a sheep!' (verse 12).

The implication of this short parable was lost on the Pharisees. Matthew had already highlighted the gulf between Jesus and these religious leaders by using the term *'their synagogue'* (verse 9) indicating that by this point in His ministry, Jesus and His disciples no longer had any affinity with Pharisaism.

It is unlikely that Jesus was surprised by the question they asked, 'Is it lawful to heal on the Sabbath?' (verse 10), a pre-prepared question to trap Him 'that they might accuse Him' (verse 10). They understood by the example which Jesus gave of the lost sheep, that Jesus was using the common practice of the ordinary people with regard to their sheep, as an argument for a mild, minor infringement of the Sabbath commandment. They also understood that healing the man's withered hand was an example of what it meant to do good on the Sabbath day (verse 12), a concrete example of love, of mercy. But more important to them was the preservation of their status as the guardians and custodians of the Torah. As they saw it, Jesus was subverting everything they stood for. He had to go. 'They went out and took counsel against Him, how to destroy Him' (verse 14). For the first time in this gospel, the death of Jesus comes into view, the determination of the rulers of God's people to destroy God's Son. A terrible darkness had fallen upon Israel, a division that could not be healed, yet, as always, God has a remnant, those who still honour His Son.

Matthew 12:14 says, 'The Pharisees went out'. This of course means, 'out of the synagogue', yet we could read a deeper meaning into it quite legitimately, for their decision to kill Jesus had created an unfathomable distance which could never be reversed.

These verses have been interpreted as having an anti-Jewish bias on the part of Matthew but he writes only what was becoming ever more obvious. There is an echo here of the Last

Supper which Jesus had with His disciples, when, after Jesus had given the sop to Judas Iscariot, it is said, 'He, Judas, went out, and it was night' (John 13:26-30).

The same could be said of the Pharisees. For them, it had become night. There is a development running through from this verse to Matthew 22:15; when 'they sought to entangle Him in His speech'; to Matthew 27:1, when 'they took counsel together against Jesus to put Him to death'; and then to Matthew 28:12, when, after His resurrection, 'They gave a sum of money to the soldiers and said, "Tell people the disciples came by night and stole Him away while we were asleep."' It was, and still is, unusual to be given a reward for dereliction of duty. Soldiers do not sleep on duty, on pain of severe punishment.

How could the Pharisees not see that Jesus was not creating a crisis, but only placing love, mercy, at the centre of their traditional understanding of the scriptures? They may have reasoned among themselves, could Jesus not have postponed the healing of the man to another day? No, for He wanted to challenge their understanding, not only of the scriptures, but of their own religious identity, in the name of love.

They could not accept the challenge. It would have altered their whole life, their own *raison d'etre*. For them, the only solution to what they saw as the problem of Jesus was His death.

Jesus came to seek and to save that which was lost (Luke 19:10), to bring mercy and love to those with withered hands; and hearts, that they might be healed, even on the Sabbath day, as they stretch out their hands to Him. Aware, yet again, of what the Pharisees were planning to do, Jesus withdrew from there (verse 15), for His hour was not yet come (John 2:4; 7:6; 8:20), and many followed Him and He healed them all (verse 16). *All* the sick, exemplary of Jesus' compassion for *all*.

The Pharisees had asked the question, 'Is it lawful?' (verse 10). Jesus replies with a counter statement. 'It *is* lawful' (verse 12). It is lawful to do good on the Sabbath day. The law is fulfilled, the majesty and all-embracing complexity of the law is fulfilled in the healing of one man with a withered hand. Yet, Jesus does not end there, but heals the many who follow Him, multiplying the effect of the happy outworking of the law which Jesus fulfils in the lives of many. To make His point, Jesus could have healed only one man and it would have been enough. But others also needed Him. Jesus goes beyond and above discussion of the law. His love and compassion both then and now, knows no bounds.

Jesus ordered the people not to make Him known (verse 16), because His hour was not yet come. He had many things to say to them, and much to show them, and comparative obscurity would shield Him from too much attention from the religious authorities. He had withdrawn from the synagogue and the Pharisees to give His disciples time for reflection on what had transpired on that unique Sabbath harvest day; the purpose of the controversy with the Pharisees which had ensued and the threat of the coming crisis for which the Pharisees were planning. There was going to be trouble ahead. Jesus needed to withdraw in order to be in touch with His Father, and for Him to spend time alone with His disciples. But the time, though precious, was limited by the arrival of those wanting Him to heal them too. He did not turn them away, but healed them all (12:15).

Matthew 12:17-21. Jesus, the servant of the Lord

Jesus, aware that the Pharisees took counsel together that they might destroy Him, withdrew from there. And many followed Him and He healed them all. and ordered them not to make Him known (Matthew 12:14).

This was to fulfil what was spoken by the prophet Isaiah: Behold My Servant whom I have chosen, My beloved with whom I am well pleased. I will put My Spirit upon Him and He shall proclaim justice to the Gentiles. He will not wrangle or cry aloud or cause His voice to be heard in the street. He will not break a bruised reed, or quench a smouldering wick till He brings justice to victory; and in His Name will the Gentiles hope (Matthew 12:17-21).

Jesus had withdrawn from the synagogue. Many had followed Him and He had healed them all, but He had ordered them not to make Him known. Matthew uses Isaiah 42:1-4 as an explanation of Jesus' behaviour through prophetic fulfilment. Isaiah's prophecy in Isaiah 42 is fully fulfilled in Jesus. Isaiah records God as saying 'Behold My servant whom I have chosen, My beloved in whom I am well pleased. I will put My Spirit upon Him, and He shall proclaim justice to the Gentiles. He will not wrangle or cry aloud, nor will anyone hear His voice in the streets. He will not break a bruised reed or quench a smouldering wick till He brings justice to victory. And in His Name will the Gentiles hope.'

Matthew has no problem in identifying and associating the Servant of the Lord in Isaiah with Jesus. In fact, Isaiah describes Jesus perfectly, the Chosen Servant, the Beloved One with whom God is well pleased, the one anointed with the Holy Spirit (Matthew 12:18), whose ministry is to Gentiles as well as Jews in terms of justice and quiet healing until the time of His glorious victory, bringing hope to the Gentiles who were formerly without hope.

This is the *sixth* of the *ten* quotations from the Old Testament used by Matthew throughout his gospel to demonstrate that Jesus acts in accordance with scripture and God's will, as simultaneously the scripture is fulfilled. All that Jesus does fulfils God's intention, His Father's will implemented as men and women enter into relationship with Him through faith in Jesus.

Matthew's quotation of Isaiah 42:1-4 not only declares that the Christological significance of Isaiah's text is to be found in Jesus, but also predicts that His followers too will suffer persecution. These disciples who are Gentiles will have justice proclaimed to them, the justice of justification through faith (verse 18), but not by loud and public exhortation, for Jesus understands how they have suffered. They have become a *'bruised reed'* and a *'smouldering wick'* whom Jesus treats with great tenderness, so that His Name means everything to them. In that Name they have hope, a glorious hope that one day He will be vindicated by His victory.

Thus, Matthew's quotation becomes an explanation that God has everything under control. No matter how it looks to an uninstructed observer, Jesus, the Messianic King is pursuing His plan of salvation, a plan that ultimately cannot fail, even though there is great suffering to be endured before the final denouement, by the One who is Peace, who does not cry aloud or wrangle in the street (verse 19), the peaceful and humble *Son, and Servant* of God.

These few verses, verses 18-21, are designed by Matthew to demonstrate that the whole of Jesus' life is the story of Jesus as Son of God, Immanuel, God with us, and a preview of what is to come as the Gentiles are also drawn to Him. Matthew is drawing aside, like a curtain, that which would obscure God's ultimate purpose in the sending of His Son, so that the readers of his gospel can see something of the glory of the Son, not as the disciples saw Him on the Mount of Transfiguration (chapter 17:1-8), but as the One on whom the Spirit rests (verse 18), the One who is gentle, merciful, kind, non-violent, full of love: the Prince of Peace.

The situation with the Pharisees had come to a head. Jesus' death had been decided upon, yet His only concern is to express once again His obedience to the Father, and His loving graciousness to all who come to Him.

This is the way victory comes!

Matthew 12:22-37. A further confrontation with the Pharisees.

Then a blind and dumb demoniac was brought to Him, and He healed him, so that the dumb man spoke and saw (Matthew 12:22).

We have already noted that in the culture of Jesus' day, demon activity was thought to be the cause of illness. Matthew recounts this episode as a healing rather than an exorcism. It is not until a few verses later that Jesus deals with the question which the Pharisees raise about Jesus casting out demons by the prince of demons, Beelzebul (verse 24). Nevertheless, as always, Jesus had a purpose in healing this man at this time, for He wanted to continue to instruct the Pharisees about many things. It seems that His patience with them was unlimited, while their opposition to Him grew ever more caustic, ever more bitter.

Like the paralysed man in Matthew 9:2, and the dumb man in Matthew 9:32, this blind and demoniac man was brought to Jesus for healing through the kindness of others; we are not told by whom.

In chapter 9, the accusation against Jesus had progressed from blasphemy (Matthew 9:3), through His table-fellowship with sinners and publicans (Matthew 9:11), to association with the prince of demons (Matthew 9:34). Here, in chapter 12, the Pharisees have gone further. They are even more explicit as they attempt to build up a case against Him so that He can be 'destroyed' (Matthew 12:14). 'Destroyed', destruction; these are powerful words to use in connection with the strategy they are deploying to bring about their purpose.

Seeing the healing of this poor blind and dumb demoniac man, the crowd were again amazed. It is slowly dawning on them that this is possibly the Son of David, the Messianic King of whom their scriptures spoke so clearly. Like John the Baptist they were saying 'Is this He that should come? Can this be the Son of David?' (verse 23) No such exegesis of the scriptures bothers the Pharisees. Eager to refute what the people were saying, their immediate response was, 'It is only by Beelzebul, (known to the Pharisees as the prince of demons), that this man casts out demons' (verse 24), thereby making Jesus an accessory to Beelzebub; or Beelzebul; a god of the Philistines also otherwise known as the Lord of the flies (2 Kings 1:2).

Jesus' reply to the Pharisees appears enigmatic. To start with, Matthew again puts Jesus firmly in charge of the situation by affirming that, 'Jesus, knowing their thoughts' (verse 25) gave them a political answer. The Jews were living under Roman occupation. The Pharisees, perhaps rather unwillingly, accepted the limitations of their power over the people, but it still rankled as the Roman authorities imposed more and more restrictions upon them. It was why, in the end, it was not they who had the authority to crucify Jesus, but Roman soldiers. The Pharisees knew all about the division caused by those Roman foreigners; division of loyalties, of families, as people were conscripted to serve the occupying power, of wealthy people who became wealthier, while the poorer people became poorer. It was an iron yoke they bore.

Jesus, knowing their thoughts, their preoccupation with trying to maintain their biblical heritage, their special destiny as the chosen people of God, under such conditions; Jesus, knowing and understanding all this, used the example of the present political situation, Jews against Romans, Romans against Jews to remind them of another and more potent alternative example of division and conflict; the Kingdom of Satan opposing the kingdom of God. Jesus, the word made flesh, had come, and it was now more difficult for Satan to maintain what hold he had over human beings. This division was caused by the many who were finding that life in the *other* kingdom, the kingdom of God, was the one that gave them joy and peace, and a relationship with their heavenly Father which they had not had before. If Jesus was acting on Satan's behalf, as the Pharisees claimed, by casting out demons, then Satan's kingdom is doomed, for it would be Satan acting against himself, and as we know from the example of Rome and Israel, the kingdom would no longer exist. But, referring back to His anointing by the Holy Spirit (verse 18), Jesus says, 'If I, by the Spirit of God, cast out demons, then the Kingdom of God has come upon you' (verse 28).

Jesus then gives a masterly description of His exorcisms under the anointing of the Holy Spirit. The one who is troubled by a demon is like a house occupied by a strong man. The person is troubled, wants to be rid of the strong man who is plundering his goods (verse 29), taking away from him his peace, his joy, all that makes life endurable. Jesus has the answer. By the Spirit of God, He binds up the strong man so that he can do no more damage, plunder no longer. Then He Himself enters the 'house', the person of the troubled man. The man is free from the domination of the demon represented by the strong man.

Whether or not the Pharisees were convinced by Jesus' exposition, He then gives them a solemn warning. 'He who is not with me is against me, and he who does not gather with me scatters' (verse 30). 'Therefore, I tell you' (verse 31, a strongly imperative phrase); 'Therefore I tell you, every sin and blasphemy will be forgiven, but the blasphemy against the Spirit will not be forgiven' (verse 31).

It is helpful to understand the spiritual world as divided into two kingdoms, the Kingdom of Satan, and the Kingdom of God. Through transgression, disobedience, rebellion, iniquity, people owe allegiance to the Kingdom of Satan, until *by faith* they make the transition to the Kingdom of God. This absolutely puts *faith* into a different perspective. 'For by grace you have been saved through faith; and this not of yourselves: it is the gift of God' (Ephesians 2:8). How powerful is the act of faith, which liberates a person from the Kingdom of Satan to the Kingdom of God! And we would say, impossible but for the atoning power of the Lord Jesus who came to take away sin by the sacrifice of Himself upon the Cross. More, *so much more,* than a cerebral agreement, is faith.

How could anyone ever come to faith except by the work of the Holy Spirit? It is He who convinces men and women 'concerning sin, because they do not believe in Me, concerning righteousness because I go to the Father and you will see Me no more, concerning judgement, because the ruler of this world is judged' (John 16:8-11). This is the work of the Holy Spirit, the Comforter, the Counsellor, the Paraclete, the One who comes alongside men and women and points them to Christ, interceding for them with sighs too deep for words (Romans 8:26), witnessing to them of the Saviour's love, always glorifying Jesus (John 16:14).

And the miracle happens. They respond in that faith, which is the gift of God, and are adopted into His family, and learn to cry, 'Abba, Father!' (Romans 8:15), while the Holy Spirit witnesses with their spirit that they are children of God (Romans 8:16). No wonder Paul writes, 'I consider that the sufferings of this present time are not worthy to be compared to the glory that is to be revealed to us' (Romans 8:18). This is at least, the beginning of glory, to be delivered from the dominion of darkness and translated (A.V.) to the Kingdom of His beloved Son, the Son of His love (Colossians 1:13). And accepted in the Beloved (Ephesians 1:6 A.V.). Amazing grace, amazing love, amazing work of the Holy Spirit.

The Pharisees had deeply perverted the action of Jesus in healing the blind and deaf man by claiming that it was by some kind of collusion with Beelzebul that Jesus acted in this way. Jesus was far removed from that. It was as though they saw in Jesus Satan himself, which was why He said, 'If Satan casts out Satan, he is divided against himself; how then will his kingdom stand?' (verse 26). Everything that Jesus did, all His derived power and authority from His Father was directed towards people who were suffering, who needed His healing touch on body, soul or spirit (1 Thessalonians 5:23).

Jesus turns the argument against them by declaring that there can only be one way of casting out demons, and that is by the Spirit of God, and if He has cast out a demon from the blind and deaf man, 'Then the Kingdom *of God* has come upon you' (verse 28) that is, upon the Pharisees. That kingdom which is now, and not yet, which they too may enter by repentance and faith if they allow someone stronger than the strong man who owns the 'house', Jesus, working under the anointing of the Holy Spirit, to enter the house, to bind the strong man by someone stronger than he, and give liberation to the one under whose cruel regime he had lived.

And Jesus adds, that when this happens a decision has to be made. The person who has been delivered from the strong man, Satan, the Adversary of God, now has to choose. He may have been blind, but now he sees; he may have been dumb, but now has speech to be used for the glory of God. Now he has to choose, for Jesus says, 'He that is not with me is against me' (verse 30) probably the most important decision that person will ever make, to choose to be with Jesus. Nobody is neutral in the Kingdom of God. There is no intermediate position.

Jesus is offering the Pharisees the gift of being with Him, of 'gathering' with Him the lost souls under the domination of Satan. His defeat is already beginning to take place through Jesus' exorcisms. There will come a time when he will be bound (Revelation 20:2). Jesus' work through the Holy Spirit, means that God has already begun the work of establishing His eschatological Kingdom of God. How could the Pharisees continue to obstruct Him? To want Him killed? But they did.

Matthew 12:31. The blasphemy against the Holy Spirit

Therefore I tell you, every sin and blasphemy will forgiven men. But the blasphemy against the Holy Spirit will not be forgiven. And whoever says a word against the Son of Man will be forgiven, but whoever speaks against the Holy Spirit will not be forgiven, either in this age, or in the age to come.

Here again, in these verses we see the love between the members of the Trinity. In John's gospel, it is very clear that the object of all that the Holy Spirit does is to glorify Jesus (John 16:14). In Matthew 12:31, it is equally clear that the Lord Jesus will not allow any kind of sin of blasphemy against the Holy Spirit. Jesus expressly says: 'Therefore I say to you (verse 31) every sin and blasphemy will be forgiven against men, but the blasphemy against the Spirit will not be forgiven. Whoever says a word against the Son of Man will be forgiven, but whoever speaks against the Holy Spirit will not be forgiven either in this age or in the age to come' (verse 32). *Never!*

Of what does the blasphemy against the Holy Spirit consist? Jesus is saying, 'People can speak against me if they wish (verse 31) and they can be forgiven, but there are accusations against the Holy Spirit which they may not make under sentence of judgement.

Jesus made Himself of no reputation (Philippians 2:6). Though He was in the form of God, He did not count equality with God, a thing to be grasped, but *emptied* Himself, taking the form of a servant. And being found in fashion as a man, He humbled Himself (Philippians 2:7,8). In one sense, He had nothing to lose, for He refused all the glory that was rightfully His by coming to earth as a child and then a Man. This is the humility of Jesus. So not on His own account, but on behalf of the Holy Spirit, He warns that judgement will come upon anyone who blasphemes the Holy Spirit (Matthew 12:31). Speaking against Jesus was forgivable, although for every idle word that men shall speak, they will give account on the day of judgement (Matthew 12:36 A.V.).

The Pharisees blasphemed the Holy Spirit through their stubbornness to recognise that, as Jesus said, the blind and dumb man was delivered of his demon by the Spirit of God (verse 28). They were accusing Jesus of delivering, healing the man through Satan. Jesus knew that He was doing it through the operation of the Holy Spirit, and therefore logically, they were equating the Holy Spirit with Satan. They were saying that the Holy Spirit is not Holy, but equivalent to Satan, the Adversary of God, the one who through rebellion against God entered the world, the one who holds human beings in an intolerable bondage. If what the Pharisees had been saying was true, the conclusion would be that the Holy Spirit could not be part of the ineffable Godhead of Father, Son and Holy Spirit. This is blasphemy indeed, first to intimate that He is not Holy, and then to suggest that He is therefore not of the Godhead.

There is a love that shines forth from Jesus as He goes about Galilee healing all that come to Him, inviting them to come to Him, and receiving His rest, for His yoke is easy and His burden is light. This love is the same love expressed within the Three Persons of the Trinity for each other, and gloriously extended to human beings. Jesus acknowledges that it is 'through the Spirit of God' (verse 28), the anointing that He received from the Holy Spirit, that He is able to love people into the kingdom, and every time we use His title, Jesus the Messiah, Jesus Christ, which means the Anointed One, we acknowledge it too. We underestimate the precious work of the Holy Spirit at our peril.

This episode in Jesus' ministry is a clear revelation of *His* deity, but Jesus' concern is with the work of *the Holy Spirit*, because He knows that the time will come when He will return to Father, and the Holy Spirit will then continue the work of Jesus upon the earth. Jesus says, 'If I go, I will send Him to you' (John 16:7). 'I will not leave you comfortless without the Comforter, desolate, orphans, I will come to you!' (John 14:18).

To Jesus, the contrast is obvious between what is the work of the enemy of men and women's souls, and the life affirming work of the Holy Spirit. He says that there are good trees which have good fruit and there are bad trees which have bad fruit (Matthew 12:33).

The fruit is that by which we distinguish them. If this is the fruit which the Pharisees are manifesting, a denial of what the Spirit is doing through Jesus, then they are a *'brood of vipers',* poisonous creatures who can only do harm (verses 33, 34), and it is necessary to discern all they are saying because everything they say comes from an evil heart, 'For out of the abundance of the heart, the mouth speaketh' (verse 34). There is good treasure within some people, and there is evil treasure within others, and we know which it is by the way they speak. We may discern whether they are good or bad trees, says Jesus. How important it is, therefore, how you speak, and what you say, because your words will either justify you or condemn you on the day of judgement (verses 26, 37). Every idle word that men shall speak, they shall give account of on the day of judgement (verse 38).

Matthew 12:31-33. Blasphemy in the Hebrew scriptures

And whoever says a word against the Son of Man will be forgiven but whoever speaks a word against the Holy Spirit will not be forgiven, either in this age, or in the age to come.

In Leviticus 24:15-16, we learn that blasphemy was more than not having respect for God. *Misuse of God's name* is condemned in the Ten Commandments. 'You shall not take the name of the Lord your God in vain, for the Lord will not hold him guiltless who takes His name in vain' (Exodus 20:7), and in Leviticus 22:28, 'You shall not revile God, that is, curse Him or use His name in a curse.' In Leviticus 24:15-16, the consequence of doing so is made quite clear. 'Whoever curses his God shall bear his sin,' so he will not be atoned for on the Day of Atonement. 'And he who blasphemes the Name of the Lord shall be put to death; all the congregation shall stone him.'

This is not just disrespect, it is profanity, and as such was punishable by death. Because Stephen was considered to have blasphemed, he was stoned to death (Acts 6:11) demonstrating that even as late as the first century A.D., this punishment was still thought to be appropriate for the sin of blasphemy. Dishonouring the Name of the Lord was a serious matter, and the person who committed this crime must bear the consequences (Leviticus 24:14).

The importance of the Name of the Lord rested in the Person, Character and Presence of the Lord. To take His Name in vain was to impugn His character, to deny that He was holy, to deny His existential presence as the 'I AM' (Exodus 3:13). That is why the church baptises in the *Name* of the Father, Son and Holy Spirit, His Name (Matthew 28:19). We honour God when we acknowledge Him as Sovereign Lord. The person being baptised is being incorporated into the Body of Christ, the church, through the death and resurrection of the Person of Jesus Christ Himself, but as part of the Godhead, the character, the being, the Name of God.

The Jews were of course monotheistic. 'Hear, O Israel, the Lord our God is *One Lord,* and you shall love the Lord your God with all your heart, and with all your soul, and with all your might' (Deuteronomy 6:4). The Pharisees did not recognise in Jesus the second person of the Trinity, for they were monotheists, though many may have heard the voice from heaven, 'This is my beloved Son,' at the time of His baptism in the River Jordan (Matthew 3:17) and perhaps may even have seen the Dove alighting upon Him. Even though the Holy Spirit was spoken of in their scriptures, e.g. Genesis 1:2, Isaiah 61:1, they perhaps had a hazy idea of Him as representative of God, though without the recognition of Him as the third person of the Trinity, or rather, believed these references to be to that of God Himself, which of course in a sense, they were.

Jesus was not denying the scriptures, the scriptures as they understood them. He was explaining that He was the fulfilment of the scriptures. He had been with His Father from the beginning (Proverbs 8:30) as had the Holy Spirit (Genesis 1:2), in the creation of the world. The healing of the blind and deaf man, Jesus declared to them, was the work of the Holy Spirit through Him. He was offering them the way into the kingdom which, He said, 'has come upon you' (verse 28). *But they would not.*

In the person and activity of Jesus, the sovereign authority of God had been manifested through the executive agency of the Holy Spirit. The Pharisees' reaction to Jesus, accusing Him of being in league with demonic power revealed that their attack on Jesus was not accidental, but came from the heart. Surely they could not truly believe that the wonderful work that Jesus was doing was the work of Beelzebul (verse 27). But they were blind.

Jesus said 'Out of the abundance of the heart the mouth speaks' (12:34). Out of what they are, in their innermost being, come the words they say. They had not learnt that, 'the Name of the Lord is a strong tower. The righteous man runs into it and is safe' (Proverbs 18:10), or how great is the gift that Jesus has given us to be able to say, 'Our Father in heaven, *hallowed be thy Name'* (Matthew 6:9).

Matthew 12:38-42. The sign of the prophet Jonah

Then some of the scribes and Pharisees said to Him, 'Teacher, we wish to see a sign from you.' But He answered them, 'An evil and adulterous generation seeks for a sign, and there shall no sign be given it but the sign of the prophet Jonah. For as Jonah was three days and three nights in the belly of the whale, so will the Son of Man be in the heart of the earth.'

Was this the same group of Pharisees which now included scribes? They call Him 'Teacher', 'Rabbi', which is a term of respect, but they may have been using it ironically. The sign they requested was a cosmic sign. They had already seen Jesus perform many miracles. The sign they wanted was a demonstration of Jesus' cosmic power. Had not Elijah prayed that it would not rain, and the Lord withheld the rain from the land for three and a half years? (1 Kings 17:1; James 5:7). Had not Moses lifted up his rod and the waters of the Red Sea parted? (Exodus 14:21). Had not Jacob rested his head on a stone pillow at Bethel and seen the angels of God ascending and descending to heaven? (Genesis 28:12).

What exactly did they want? Jesus answered them, 'An evil and adulterous generation seeks for a sign, but no sign shall be given it except the sign of the prophet Jonah' (Matthew 12:39).

Perhaps Jesus' mind was still running on the Person of the Holy Spirit, for Jonah means 'dove', and the dove often symbolises the Holy Spirit in scripture, as was indeed the case at Jesus' baptism (Matthew 3:16). Jesus was about to explain the significance of Jonah's experience in terms of death and resurrection, and Paul explicitly states that it is through the Spirit of Holiness that Jesus was raised from the dead (Romans 1:4). As always there was so much more to what Jesus was saying than appeared on the surface, different levels of understanding to those with eyes to see and ears to hear what Jesus was saying and doing.

What Jesus did was always in obedience to Father's will. He says, 'I do always those things which please Him' (John 8:29 A.V.). Undoubtedly, He had power and authority, as He had already demonstrated, but He never used His power for anything but altruistic reasons, but always on behalf of others, and always in obedience to His Father's will.

What the Pharisees were asking for was an authentication of Jesus' authority, but nothing that He could have done would have convinced them for they did not want to believe that He was indeed the Messiah. They asked Him again in Matthew 16:1, and His answer was the same. There shall no sign be given except the sign of the prophet Jonah (16:4).

Perhaps Jonah was last on their list of people who were moved by God to do great things or have supernatural manifestations. What did Jesus mean by choosing Jonah, of all people? They were experts in the Old Testament. It was their field of expertise and they wanted to see a sign from Him. Were they expressing antagonism because He had just spoken to them of judgement? (verses 25-37). It was a demand, 'We want to see!' (verse 38), 'we want to see a sign from you!' a demand for evidence, for more than the legitimating miracles of the eschatological prophets.

Mark's version of this episode tells us that Jesus sighed deeply in His Spirit as He answered them (Mark 8:11), by saying, as Matthew also tells us, 'An evil and *adulterous generation* seeks for a sign' (verse 39). This generation, these contemporaries of Jesus, are adulterous, not in terms of marital infidelity, but infidelity towards God. The prophets had consistently spoken against the tendency of Israel to be unfaithful to God, and to His covenant with them; Hosea especially (Hosea 3:1-3). And 'evil', the adjective describing this generation, carries the weight of that which God condemns on the Day of Judgement, as in verses 34-35.

Jesus unconditionally refuses their demand for a sign σημεῖον from Him. yet subtly refers them to the sign of the prophet Jonah. 'For as Jonah was three days and three nights in the belly of the whale, so will the Son of Man be three days and three nights in the heart of the earth (Matthew 12:40, Jonah 1:17). Jonah was delivered by the Lord from the belly of the whale, just as He will deliver Jesus from death, for the whole of the second chapter of Jonah emphasises that his rescue from the whale has the significance of a rescue from death, even though in the case of both Jonah and Jesus, the death has not yet taken place.

There is no tension for Matthew between the three days and three nights and the third day. He records the Pharisees as saying to Pilate, 'We remember that that imposter said while He was still alive, "After three days I will rise again." Therefore order the sepulchre to be made secure until the third day.' (Matthew 27:62-64). In Jewish thought, three is a symbolic number, for example, Genesis 42:17-18, Exodus 19:11,16, Hosea 6:2. Matthew, as a Jew has little interest in the exact timing, but more in the event which Jonah typologically provides and prefigures in his deliverance from death. In the resurrection of Jesus, God will Himself provide the promised sign. The sign is Jesus, 'designated Son of God in power according to the Spirit of Holiness by His resurrection from the dead' (Romans 1:4).

Jonah was called by God to preach repentance to Gentiles, to the men of Nineveh (Jonah 1:2) on the ground of the resurrection through which he had just symbolically passed, though of course, unlike Jesus, he would eventually die. This is the glory of the resurrection of Jesus, the glorious revelation of His resurrection, that though Jesus dies, inevitably through execution, He will rise again from the dead. He is also glorying in the fact that the Kingdom of Heaven will also be extended to *Gentiles*. The Ninevites, Gentiles, repented and turned to God. Jesus is also proclaiming repentance through the gospel to Gentiles as well as Jews but with an even greater impact on their lives than that of Jonah, for those who repent and come to Him by faith have entered into the Kingdom of Heaven.

The scribes and the Pharisees have asked Jesus for a sign, but *Jesus Himself is the Sign, the* sign of the Son of Man (Matthew 24:30). His intention is that all shall have the opportunity to hear and respond to the gospel of the kingdom. The Ninevites repented. The Queen of the South came from the ends of the earth to hear the wisdom of Solomon, and behold, something greater than Solomon is here (verse 41,42). Greater than anything the scribes and Pharisees could possibly imagine is the whole plan of deliverance and salvation which God had purposed in His Son, salvation freely offered and freely received whether by Jew or Gentile. Something greater is *here,* Jesus tells them, standing before them reaching out to them, for it was not His will that any should perish, but that they should all come to eternal life (John 3:16).

Matthew 12:43-45. The return of the unclean spirits

When the unclean spirit has gone out of a man, he passes through waterless places seeking rest, but he finds none. Then he says, I will return to the house from which I came. And when he comes, he finds it empty, swept and put in order. Then he goes and brings with him seven other spirits more evil than himself and they enter and dwell there. And the last state of that man is worse than the first. So shall it be with this evil generation.

If only the Pharisees could acknowledge it, they had already seen, if not *'the'* sign of the Son of Man, according to Matthew 24, but undoubtedly, *'a'* sign in the healing of the deaf and dumb demoniac man which led to Jesus' teaching about the Holy Spirit through whom He had performed the sign, the sign that His authority penetrated even into the kingdom of darkness, which Jesus explicates in these following verses, 43-45.

Jesus is warning them against complacency. Even after such an experience of deliverance from an evil spirit, such a person needs to walk softly. Jesus is concentrating on the 'house', the person out of whom the spirit was cast. The house had indeed been 'swept and put in order' (verse 44), but vigilance has to be maintained constantly so that the unclean spirit does not return, and especially, that he does not bring seven other spirits with him.

It appears that spirits have different functions. This one is described by Jesus as unclean. Paul, writing to Timothy (2 Timothy 1:17) speaks of a spirit of fear. We can recognise such in some who need the healing, cleansing power of the Holy Spirit in their lives and long to help them. How much more does Jesus want them to turn to Him, to be delivered and set free from all that oppresses them.

Jesus is warning that the person who has been cleansed and healed has an even greater need to stay close to Him, in fellowship and communion with Him and His Father, in utter dependence upon the Holy Spirit, so that his last state does not become worse than his first (verse 45). The Holy Spirit 'casts out' uncleanness. He 'casts out' fear. The person from whom this has been completely eradicated has a responsibility to maintain the work which the Holy Spirit has done. There has to be no escalation of uncleanness in his life. This is impossible without constant referral to, and dependence upon, the Holy Spirit.

Jesus spoke to the man at the Pool of Bethesda whom He had healed saying, 'Go and sin no more, lest a *worse* thing befall you' (John 5:14). This is also a warning to those who, *under Jesus' authority,* cast out demons, the authority exemplified in that delegated to His disciples in chapter 10:8.

Perhaps we could think of a person who has recently experienced such a mighty turnaround of their whole life as being in what could be described as a state of convalescence. For them, it is essential that they receive the whole-hearted support and comfort of the fellowship of the church. The church is challenged too in its walk with God and its subservience to His will under the authority of the Holy Spirit, in its pastoral ministry. Together with those cleansed and renewed, the church becomes a sign of the presence of Jesus among His people.

Zwingli (U. Luz p223) is reported as saying, 'Those who demand signs after the truth is proclaimed show that in reality they resist the truth.' As Matthew's gospel unfolds it becomes increasingly evident that resistance to the truth which Jesus is proclaiming is intensifying among the scribes and Pharisees.

Matthew 12:46-50. The true family of Jesus

While He was still speaking to the people, behold His mother and His brothers stood outside, asking to speak to Him. But He replied to the man who told Him, Who is My mother and My brothers?' And stretching out His hand toward His disciples, He said, 'Here are My mother and My brothers! For whoever does the will of My Father in heaven is My brother and sister and mother.'

It may be that because of the resistance of the Pharisees to the truth of what Jesus is saying, and their perceived persecution of Him, that Jesus' mother and His brothers rush to His defence, standing outside, wanting to speak to Him (verse 47); perhaps to advise Him that if He continues to preach like this, He is likely to find Himself in deep trouble. 'While He was still speaking to the people, behold His mother and His brothers stood outside, asking to speak to Him' (verse 46).

This verse immediately stirs up a juxtaposition between the people to whom He had been speaking, and His earthly family. He had apparently been unaware of them until He received the message from 'the man who told Him' (verse 48) that they were 'outside' (verse 46).

It is inconceivable that they would have had anything but love for this gentle eldest son and big brother with whom they had lived for thirty years. Mary had given birth to Him, washed Him, dressed Him, fed Him, potty trained Him, and watched Him grow into a young man who was always kind and careful to everyone. While working in the carpenter's shop with Joseph, He still had time for His younger siblings, looking after them, listening to their woes, comforting them.

How could He now say, 'Who is my mother? And who are my brothers?' (verse 48) to this messenger from them. Does the very fact that they had sent an anonymous individual to ask Him to speak with them, already indicate that they understood that He was growing away from them, that the call of God upon His life was separating them from Him in some way? Harsh though His words may have appeared to them, perhaps they had some premonition that this was to be the case from now on.

But what He was really doing was giving them an invitation. 'He stretched out His hands to His disciples (verse 49) and He said, "Here are my mother and my brothers! For whoever does the will of my Father in heaven is My brother, and sister, and mother" (verse 50). "My earthly family is precious to me, and always will be, but there is a new family who have a Father in heaven, God the Father, and *that* is the family to which I long that *you* should be a part of, too."'

Could the Lord Jesus have anything but love in His heart for His mother and brothers? He wanted for them the very best, and that was that they too should come into the Kingdom of Heaven, where the will of the Father in heaven was operating, and was paramount.

Even as He was dying on the Cross, He made provision for His mother, committing her into the loving care of John the beloved disciple (John 19:26,27). It could not be that He could ever be thought to have abandoned or rejected her. She and His brothers had been 'outside' (verse 46). Now Jesus was inviting them to come 'inside', to become part of the true family, the family of God. They too will know and probably not for the first time, His hands stretched over them in love and protection (verse 49), even as He did to His disciples.

The true family of God has at last come into existence, and the test is whether its members do the will of the Father in heaven, live in obedience to Him (verse 50). The two aspects are here set forth: coming under the protection of His Son while being obedient to the Father's will. These are the criteria of discipleship (verses 48, 50), the conditions under which disciples live.

Protected and obedient, the disciples of Jesus are brothers, sisters and mothers (verse 49), as they stand under His protective hand. We venerate Mary, even as Jesus did, and are glad that she became, and is, together with His brothers and sisters, part of the family of God (Acts 1:14).

Matthew Chapter 13

Matthew 13:1-17. The third discourse:
The parables of the Kingdom

*That same day, Jesus went out of the house and sat beside
the sea, and great crowds gathered about Him so that He got
into a boat and sat there, and the whole crowd stood on the
beach. And He told them many things in parables (Matthew
13: 1-3).*

Unlike the Sermon on the Mount of chapters 5-7, the discipleship
discourse of chapter 10, the ecclesiastical discourse of chapter
18 and the eschatological discourse of chapters 24-25, this
discourse is an *interrupted* set of teaching by Jesus. The parables
are presented as having been spoken to *the crowds* with
interpretation being given *privately* to the disciples, for to them
'it has been given to know the secrets of the Kingdom of Heaven'
(verse 11).

Matthew 13 marks a turning point in the gospel. The
attitude of people to Jesus as recorded in the earlier chapters of
the gospel has been a positive one; but here, in chapter 13, they
are portrayed as people who do not understand, who are
hardened and unresponsive, in contrast to the disciples who do
respond. This is an echo of 11:25, Jesus' thankful cry to His
Father, 'You have hidden it from the wise and understanding
and revealed it to babes'. Jesus gives thanks to His Father for
the revelation He has granted to 'babes', those early disciples
without preconceived ideas or prejudices. But there are now
others, people who have listened to the teaching of Jesus, but
whose hearts are hardened, who lack understanding (Matthew
13:13).

Changes in location and personnel make this a unique
discourse among the discourses of Jesus. According to the

narrative, Jesus is where He was at the end of chapter 12, in the home at Capernaum. It appears that, almost casually, He left the house to go and sit beside the sea, and was immediately surrounded by a large crowd (13:2).

It appears from the comments made to His disciples in verse 10 that this was a different crowd from the earlier crowds whose response to Him had been positive.This is why Jesus says to His disciples, 'To you it has been given to know the secrets of the Kingdom of Heaven, but *to them it is not given,*' and in verse 34, 'He said nothing to them – the people – without a parable.' Nevertheless, Jesus never neglected an opportunity to speak to them about the Kingdom of Heaven and as they crowded around Him, He got into a boat and sat there so that they could hear Him more distinctly and to emphasise His didactic authority, for in such a way did the Rabbis teach, sitting before their disciples.

'And He told them many things in parables' (verse 3). Maybe there were more than the seven recorded for us in this chapter. Jesus had not previously spoken to them in parables, and when questioned by the disciples as to why He used this method of teaching, He referred them to the prophet Isaiah who said to the disobedient people of Israel, 'You shall indeed hear but never understand, you shall indeed see but never perceive. For this people's heart has grown dull, and their ears are heavy of hearing, and their eyes they have closed, lest they should perceive with their eyes and hear with their ears and understand with their heart and turn for Me to heal them' (Isaiah 6:9-10).

How unutterably sad that Jesus already knew that much of the seed which He is about to sow as 'the sower who went forth to sow' (verse 3) was going to fall on stony ground, and not going to bring forth any harvest. Jesus knew that so much of the seed of the word of the gospel of the kingdom which He was sowing would not be understood because of their hardness of heart.

Understanding is a key theme of chapter 13, being mentioned six times, but not previously in this gospel. These people are blind and without understanding and will come to judgement (verse 41). Until this point in Jesus' ministry the people had still been open towards Him, but now there is a change. There will still be a high percentage of seed falling on good ground and bringing forth grain, some, a hundredfold, some sixty, some thirty (verse 8), but the time is coming, at the end of the chapter, when He could not do many mighty works there because of their unbelief (verse 58).

A hardening of heart had befallen them because of their unbelief. This is why Jesus speaks to them in parables, and when the disciples ask the question, 'Why? Why do you speak to them in parables?' (verse 10), He answers 'To you it has been given to know the secrets, the mysteries of the Kingdom of Heaven, but to them it has not been given' (verse 11).

A parable is a truth embodied in a tale, a story drawn from nature. or from human life, an embodied myth, an illustration of spiritual truth whose meaning is not on the surface, but which makes one main point.

In the case of these parables of Jesus in chapter 13, the point concerns the Kingdom of God. The followers of Jesus have entered the Kingdom of Heaven through repentance and faith. *But what is the kingdom? What is it like?* Jesus is going on to explain to them that it is the mysterious working of the reign of God in human hearts until the glorious consummation when He is all in all, and His kingdom reigns over all. The Kingdom of God is 'within you' and also 'in the midst of you' (Luke 17:21). And the time is coming when men and women will see the whole purpose of the Kingdom in action, when the Son of Man comes in a cloud with power and great glory to receive His kingdom in all its fullness, when all the world will acknowledge Him as their King (Luke 21:27). We need to watch and pray for the ultimate coming of the kingdom.

But all these mysteries of the kingdom were only gradually being given to the disciples, as we see in Matthew 13:36-52; 15:10-12; 16:9-11,21; and 17:1-13. There was so much more to come. And these mysteries could not be given to the crowd of people on the seashore, for they lacked the capacity to hear and see, to understand and perceive, as Isaiah had foretold in Isaiah 6:9-10, even though the Lord yearned for them to turn to Him so that He could heal them (verse 15).

Indeed, many prophets and righteous men, men with no qualification other than the desire to be obedient to God, had longed to see and hear what the disciples were presently experiencing, and did not see it or hear it (verse 17). How privileged were the disciples, and how privileged are believers today, to hold this gospel in their hands, and to be able to respond to all that they read there of the Lord Jesus and His wonderful compassion towards the people of His day, people like them.

To the followers of Jesus, the disciples, it had been given to know γνῶναι the mysteries of the Kingdom of Heaven (13:11), the rule of God Himself. There was a distinction in those who were able to understand, and those with an inability to understand, these parables of Jesus. Jesus says, 'He who has ears to hear, let him hear' (13:9).

Those who have their inner being tuned to what Jesus is saying, and to be obedient, are the ones with ears to hear, and these are the ones to whom knowledge is given. But they are not specially gifted people. Jesus' invitation to come to Him and learn of Him is open to everyone. Jesus says 'To him who has more will more be given, and he will have abundance, But from him who has not, even what he has will be taken away (verse 12). These are difficult verses. David Hill, p227, suggests that what they will be deprived of is all that goes within the keeping of the law as an expression of righteousness, because they have resisted the call to repentance.

But many of those who follow Jesus do respond to Him and bring forth fruit, some thirty, some sixty and some a hundredfold. Jesus wants His followers to live fruitful lives.

Matthew 13:1-23. The parable of the sower and the interpretation

'Behold, ειδον, a sower went forth to sow' (Matthew 13:1). As we have noted, 'behold' indicates 'stop', 'listen', 'pay attention'. This first parable of the kingdom provides the key to all the parables in this chapter, while each has its own particular emphasis.

When Jesus was asked by the messengers of John the Baptist, 'Are you He that should come?' (Matthew 11:3), one of the criteria He gave as to His ministry was that the poor had the good news preached to them (Matthew 11:4). This is what Jesus had been doing and was continuing to do, for faith comes by hearing, and hearing by the word of God (Romans 10:17). They were hearing the good news, the gospel of the kingdom, through His preaching.

Jesus' parable of the sower was very simple. The people would have been familiar with the sight of the sower who went forth twice a year before the rains came, 'the early and the latter rain', to sow his seed. With the basket of seed supported by his left arm, he would use his right hand to take handfuls of seed from the basket and scatter it before him as he walked along. Inevitably, it did not always fall on the recently ploughed land. Some would fall on *the path* where the birds would fly down and take the seed. Some would fall on land which could not be ploughed adequately because it was *rocky,* and where there was no depth of soil. The seed would germinate and send up little shoots, but because it had no depth of soil, they would flag and die when scorched by the midday sun. Other seed would fall on *thorns* which choked the seed, so that it could not grow at all.

But some seed fell into *good ground,* with all the right conditions for growth, and brought forth grain, some a hundredfold, some sixty and some thirty.

This parable must have seemed puzzling to the people gathered around him, 'What does Jesus mean?' Jesus says, 'He who has ears to hear, let him hear' (verse 9), which makes it more puzzling still. Even the disciples did not understand, and interrupted His discourse to ask Him. Luke tells us, 'The seed is the word of God' (Luke 8:11), and Matthew later in the chapter says, 'He who sows the good seed is the Son of Man' (13:37), when referring to a later parable.

Having made the point that understanding comes only by divine revelation, for understanding comes from hearing and hearing comes by the word of God, Jesus goes on to explain the meaning of the parable to His disciples. The 'word of the Kingdom' (verse 19), is being spoken by the King.

And the gospel is concerned with what happens to the seed when it is sown in the human heart. Is the seed taken away by Satan, represented by the birds of the air? (verse 19). Is it unable to grow because the heart is 'rocky'; the person has no root in himself and although he received the word with joy, yet *when his faith is tested* by persecution or tribulation, he falls away from the truth and does not continue in the faith? (verse 20). Is it the thorns which prevent the seed from growing in the heart, *the* cares of the world and the deceitfulness of riches choking the seed so that it cannot grow? (verse 22).

How precious it is when the seed is received into the good soil of an *understanding heart* (verse 23). Nourished by the good soil, growing up straight and tall in the wind and the rain and the sun, in time it will bring forth grain, some more, some less; Jesus is concerned more with the production of the fruit than its quantity. The seed which fell on the path, or the rocky ground, or on thorns bears no fruit at all.

These mysteries or secrets which are revealed to those who follow Jesus are not only spiritual, but have a practical dimension. This is the conclusion towards which the parable is aiming. The Kingdom of God is here, already here, and already opposition has risen against it. And already individual members of the crowd are challenged. To which of these categories do I belong? These are heart-searching questions.

Jesus says to His disciples, 'Blessed are your eyes for they see, and your ears, for they hear' (verse 16). Like people in the crowd they have seen Jesus healing many people. The disciples have heard Him preach the gospel of the kingdom. And they have made their choice; and the eyes and ears of the heart have begun to function in response to what Jesus is doing and saying. They have become an understanding people. It is true that their understanding is progressive, as we see in 13:36,51; 15:10,12-20; 16:5; 17:13; but Jesus said to His disciples, 'To you it is given to *know*' (verse 11). What *has* been given to them is the beginning of the understanding of the Kingdom of God. What *will* be given is a growing understanding as they continue with Him. There is understanding only through Him; so that the fruit which grows through the activity of the word of God in the human heart belongs only to Jesus. There is no room for boasting. All is of Him.

Matthew 13:24-30. The wheat and the tares

Another parable He put before them, saying, 'The Kingdom of Heaven may be compared to a man who sowed good seed in his field. But while men were sleeping, his enemy came and sowed weeds among the wheat and went away' (Matthew 13:25).

We have noted that each of these parables recorded for us in chapter 13 of Matthew's gospel expresses some truth about the Kingdom of Heaven. This is the second parable, *'another* parable' Jesus put forth before them, that is, the crowd. As in the parable of the sower, Jesus Himself is the sower, sowing 'good seed' on His land (verse 24). But He has an enemy who sows seed that appears similar to the good seed, as the weed darnel does to the seed of the wheat. He sows his darnel at night, at a time when no-one is watching, 'while men were sleeping' (verse 25). The enemy's seed, the seed of the darnel, develops a fungus which is poisonous when it becomes mature.

The servants of the master of the field recommend that they go and pull up the darnel, but the master says, 'No, let both grow together until the harvest' (verse 30).

As with all agricultural procedures, there is an end in view, an inevitable end when everything in the field will be taken up. Then the master will send reapers into the field who will make the tares, the darnel weeds, into great bundles and throw them into the fire, but gather the wheat into the barn.

Matthew 13:31-33. The Mustard Seed and the Leaven

The parable of the wheat and the tares is followed by the parable of the mustard seed.

Another parable Jesus put before them, saying, 'The Kingdom of Heaven is like a grain of mustard seed which a man took and sowed in his field. It is the smallest of seeds, but when it has grown it is the greatest of shrubs and becomes a tree, so that the birds of the air come and make nests in its branches.'

This parable was followed by another. 'He told them another parable' (verse 33). The Kingdom of Heaven is like leaven which a woman took and hid in three measures of flour until the whole was leavened.

Jesus' first parable recorded in this chapter was that of the sower, and Matthew then follows that by a quotation by Jesus from Isaiah 6:9-10. 'You shall hear and not understand, you shall indeed see but never perceive. For this people's heart has grown dull, and their ears heavy of hearing, and their eyes they have closed, lest they should perceive with their eyes and hear with their ears, and understand with their heart and turn for Me to heal them'.

We see here an unfolding of the process by which men and women turn away from God. First they hear the word, but they allow their ears to become 'heavy'. They lack any motivation to take in what they have heard. They may begin to see something of what they have missed through their lack of concentration, by not paying attention to what they have heard, but this is the danger point, for a hardening of the heart has already begun. There is still time, but in his prophecy, Isaiah is fearful that it is becoming increasingly difficult for them to turn to the Lord that He might heal them. Isaiah's concern for his people is reflected in the concern which Jesus has for these people gathered around Him.

These following three parables of the wheat and tares, the mustard seed and the leaven are followed by a quotation by Jesus from Psalm 78:2. Almost as a counter to Isaiah's prophecy, Jesus says, 'I will open my mouth in parables, I will utter what has been hidden since the foundation of the world', taking upon Himself words spoken prophetically by the psalmist Asaph.

Though Jesus knows that the people are hard of hearing, His proclamation to them of what has been hidden from the foundation of the world could have the effect of causing them to turn again to Him. Matthew again substantiates the ministry of

Jesus as the fulfilment of scripture. The word which was spoken by the prophet to his people in Psalm 78 (traditionally Asaph, 1 Chronicles 25:2; 2 Chronicles 29:30), was given in parable form as quoted by Matthew. What was spoken by that prophet so long ago and recorded in the scriptures was fully fulfilled in Jesus, for He says nothing to the crowds 'without a parable' (verse 34).

But as before, the disciples were puzzled, especially by the parable of the wheat and the tares, and as He left the crowds and went into the house, His disciples came to Him for an explanation. They already had an intimation that this parable expressed a truth which Jesus had already touched upon in the sermon on the mount. There are those who enter the Kingdom of Heaven by the narrow gate and the hard way which leads to life, and those who choose the wide gate and the easy way which leads to destruction (Matthew 7:13). And there are those who build their lives upon the Rock, while others who build on sand (Matthew 7:24).

In the discipleship discourse of chapter 10, Jesus warned His disciples that many would not accept the gospel of the kingdom which they brought to their towns and villages (Matthew 10:11); and neither would the governors and kings before whom they were brought to witness their faith in Christ (Matthew 10:18). In chapter 11, He upbraided Chorazin and Bethsaida and Capernaum for their lack of repentance (Matthew 11:20).

But here, in chapter 13, Jesus makes the future destiny of those who do not repent and believe the gospel, more explicit. 'At the close of the age will be a time of judgement when the Son of Man will send His angels, and they will gather out of His kingdom all causes of sin and all evildoers, and throw them into the furnace of fire' (verse 41). All those tares gathered together and thrown into the fire represent unrepentant hearts and lives which do not belong in the 'barn' (verse 30) of the future glorious kingdom when the Son of Man comes.

Jesus, the sower of the word, had sowed good seed in His field, but Jesus has an enemy, all that rebels against God. The seed sown by the enemy may be indistinguishable from the true seed as it grows, but it will be condemned at last, for there is a harvest coming.

The reapers are angels (verse 39), heavenly messengers, sent by God to gather together the wheat, the fruit of the passion and resurrection of His dear Son, the Bride coming down from heaven, prepared as a Bride adorned for her husband (Revelation 21:4). But first, the angels have to gather together the tares, for nothing unclean can enter into that kingdom, but must be destroyed (Revelation 21:7).

The gates of the city of God are indeed closed to sin, but not to those who have been to Jesus for His cleansing power, the forgiveness of sins made possible by the sacrifice for sin which He made on the Cross, the shedding of His Blood, for without the shedding of blood there is no remission (Hebrews 9:22). To say, 'Thank you, Lord Jesus,' barely seems adequate, but we do thank Him from the bottom of our hearts, for all He accomplished on the Cross: for the means of grace and for the hope of glory. Thanks be to God for His unspeakable, inexpressible gift (2 Corinthians 9:15).

The disciples were familiar with the concept of harvest as judgement from their scriptures (Joel 3:13; Jeremiah 51:33; Hosea 6:11) and the entire prophecy of Zephaniah is a warning against the judgement to come. Jesus gives *no explanation* of the parables of the *mustard seed* and *the leaven*, but it is easy to see that as the mustard seed begins as a tiny seed, which grows into a tree, so the Kingdom of Heaven may have a tiny beginning and yet grow into something immense. This one seed, which a man sowed (verse 31), may grow into a tree potentially to a height of 8-12 feet in Palestine, large enough to provide lodging for birds. Jesus has in mind a great kingdom, large enough to accommodate Gentiles as well as Jews.

The fact that it was only *one* seed, sown by the Man who of course represents Jesus, emphasises the uniqueness of Jesus' teaching of the Kingdom of Heaven. There never has been, or ever will be, teaching quite like it. The wheat and tares parable marks the distinction between those who hear and believe the gospel and those who do not. It is followed by the parable of the mustard seed, which envisages the momentousness of the kingdom that is to come. So, sequentially, we have the beginning of the kingdom in the human heart, and its final glorious consummation at the end of time. Jesus taught His disciples to pray, 'Thy kingdom come' (Matthew 6:10). There can be only one seed because there is only one kingdom, inclusive and yet exclusive at the same time. Jesus has moved from the personal and diverse to the integrated whole, 'a plan for the fullness of time, to *unite* all things in Christ, things in heaven and things on earth, to bring all things under *One Head*' (Ephesians 1:10, R.S.V. and A.V.).

The Kingdom of Heaven is available to all, but there is only one way into it, the bowing of the neck to King Jesus, the humbling within each individual, leading him or her to realise that there can be salvation in no other. 'For there is none other name under heaven given among men, whereby we must be saved' (Acts 4:12).

The parable of the *leaven* hidden in the dough expresses a further truth about the Kingdom of Heaven. However small the amount of leaven and however large the quantity of dough, the leavening process goes on until the whole is leavened. The Kingdom of Heaven, the leaven, is at work silently, secretly, in the hearts and lives of men and women until the time of its final consummation. When that time comes, will we discover that we are too late? The gospel says, *'Today,* when you hear His voice, do not harden your heart' for it is the Holy Spirit who is speaking (Psalms 95:7; Hebrews 3:7,15).

These are great underlying truths about the Kingdom of Heaven, expressed in these four parables, but more is to come.

When the Greeks came to Philip, the disciple with a Greek name, wanting to see Jesus, Philip took Andrew with him and they went and told Jesus. The Greeks had said to Philip, 'Sir, we would see Jesus,' (John 12:21), and Jesus had answered them, 'The hour has come for the Son of Man to be glorified. Truly, truly, amen, amen I say to you, unless a grain of wheat falls into the ground and dies, it remains alone. But if it dies, it brings forth much fruit' (John 12:23). In the parable of Matthew 13, the mustard seed, the *seed is the Kingdom of Heaven*. In the image in John's gospel, the *seed is the Lord Jesus,* the *king* of the Kingdom of Heaven.

John gives us the identification of the king with His kingdom; the One who was the Seed (who died and was buried and rose again, 'bearing much fruit' (verse 24) in the lives of men and women. The King Himself is the corn of wheat falling into the ground and dying. Though the image of the seed is different, the long awaited and anticipated outcome is the same, 'Where I am, there shall my servants be' (John 12:26), both in the future, and also in day to day living. In the kingdom, with the king, we observe the *'now'* and *'not yet'* of the Kingdom of Heaven.

When we come to the parable of the leaven, it has been suggested (Luz, p262) that the use of the image of salt would have been more appropriate than the image of yeast, leaven; for a tiny amount of salt could change the dough, and leaven may represent something evil.

In Exodus 12, Moses prepared the people of Israel for the night of the Passover when the angel of death would pass over the houses of the Egyptians so that the first born of the Egyptians died. The houses of the Israelites would be safe, because on the doorposts and lintels of their homes they had the blood of the Passover lamb that had been sacrificed. And when Pharoah and the Egyptians rose up in the night to find their first born dead, they implored Moses to take the Israelites and leave Egypt immediately, which they did, taking their unleavened dough with them.

So great was their deliverance from Egyptian slavery, which had lasted for four hundred years, that the Passover was celebrated every year by the Israelites; on the 14th day of the first month, followed by the Feast of Unleavened Bread on the 15th day. For seven days, no leaven was to be found in their houses (Exodus 12:19). Leavened bread is described in Deuteronomy 16:3-4 as the bread of affliction, for the Israelites had indeed suffered affliction at the hands of the Egyptians. The Feasts of Passover and Unleavened Bread were designed by the Lord to encourage their remembrance, the remembrance of all they had suffered, and remembrance of their miraculous deliverance.

The symbolism of leaven is not elaborated upon in the Old Testament, but 1 Corinthians 5:8 describes leaven as the 'old leaven', the leaven of malice and evil, in contrast to the unleavened bread of sincerity and truth. The Passover rituals would suggest that leaven is unacceptable.

But leaven is a living organism, unlike salt, as Luz suggests, and may be good or bad as in all living organisms, or perhaps rather, may induce good or bad outcomes. Its very hiddenness in the flour of the parable adds to the image of its powerful activity until all is leavened. Eventually it becomes bread, the Bread of Life as Jesus described Himself to be (John 6:35). How many millions of people down through the ages and even to the present day, have fed upon Him in their hearts by faith and with thanksgiving; the King making Himself available to all those who have entered His kingdom of love and joy and peace. Jesus also gave His disciples the prayer, 'Give us this day our daily bread' (Matthew 6:11), the faithful provision of their heavenly Father which we may legitimately regard as spiritual as we look in thankfulness to Him, as well as materially meeting the needs of our bodies.

These three parables Jesus had spoken to the crowd, and Matthew brings this part of the discourse to a close quoting Psalm 78, as we have seen; and Jesus' explanation of His teaching method. Jesus has nothing more to say to the unresponsive crowd. These final parables are meant for the understanding of the disciples.

Matthew 13:44-45. The treasure in the field and the pearl of great price

The kingdom of heaven is like treasure hidden in a field, which a man found and covered up; then in his joy he goes and sells all that he has and buys that field.

Again, the kingdom of heaven is like a merchant in search of fine pearls, who on finding one pearl of great value, went and sold all that he had and bought it.

Jesus has yet more to say to His disciples. The narrative has moved *from* Jesus' public teaching of the crowds about the Kingdom of Heaven, *to* intimate revelation to His disciples. 'He left the crowds and went into the house' (verse 36). In verse 44, He speaks of the treasure hidden in a field which a man found and covered up; then in his joy he goes and sells all that he has and buys that field. Then *'again'*, verse 45, the Kingdom of Heaven is like a merchant going in search of fine pearls, who, on finding one pearl of great value, went and sold all that he had and bought it.

At first sight, these two parables appear to run along parallel lines, but closer inspection discovers that the Kingdom of Heaven is likened as *treasure* hidden in a field in the former parable, and as the *merchant,* not the pearl in the latter. Though Jesus gives no explanation of these two parables, the *identification* of the kingdom with the king again becomes clear.

Matthew 13:44. The hidden treasure

The kingdom of heaven is like treasure hidden in a field.

How great is the contrast between those who have rejected the claim of Jesus on their lives, and those who have embraced it with all their being. So important was the finding of the treasure of the kingdom to this man that he was prepared to sell all that he had in order to acquire it. It might cost him everything he had, but it was worth it, because so great is the treasure of the kingdom. Economic security was exchanged for economic sacrifice. Nothing was too great or too important to surrender for the sake of finding the Kingdom and entering into all its fullness of joy.

The hiddenness of the treasure like the hiddenness of the leaven emphasises its personal nature. Just as the man hides the treasure until his sacrifice is complete, so the woman hides the leaven (verse 33). The dough and the field demonstrate that though to those involved, the man and the woman, the kingdom may be seen as comparatively small and domestic, yet the kingdom is far greater than anyone could envisage. Earlier, Jesus had said, 'The field is the world' (verse 38), by no means a small area to cover, and in Luke's gospel 15:7-10, Jesus declares the cosmic significance of 'the joy in heaven over one sinner who repents, more than over ninety nine persons who need no repentance.'

No wonder that the man 'in his joy', goes and sells all that he has and buys that field (verse 44), expressing the joy of those who receive the word of the gospel (verse 20). This is the mark of true discipleship. Though it may cost everything a man possesses, yet the intense overwhelming joy of finding that treasure more than compensates for the sacrifice. We must be careful however that another's life experience is not compromised by our satisfaction at finding the treasure of complete abandonment to God.

The frequency of invasion often led people to bury their treasure in the ground, and in Jesus' day, Palestine was infested with brigands and rapacious soldiers. Comparing the Kingdom of Heaven to hidden treasure draws attention to the huge value of what the man has found and his determination at any cost to secure it for himself.

The followers of Jesus have entered the kingdom through repentance and faith, not always appreciating how vast is the kingdom. There may be much digging in the field and the economic sacrifices may be enormous, yet this doesn't compare with the overwhelming joy which comes with whole-hearted response to the gospel, a response which leads to understanding; understanding the words and works of Jesus. Again, we think of the apostle Paul, who wrote, 'I count everything as loss because of the surpassing worth of knowing Christ Jesus as Lord. For His sake I have suffered the loss of all things, and count them as refuse, in order that I may gain Christ and be found in Him' (Philippians 3:4-11).

Matthew 13:45-46. The pearl of great price

When we come to the parable of the merchant seeking goodly pearls, the emphasis is different. Pearls were highly valued in the Middle East. They were often imported from India. They were fished for in the Indian Ocean, the Red Sea, and the Persian Gulf. Since the time of Alexander the Great, they had been considered as the very essence of luxury. This is why the pearl could be used as an image for something priceless.

The pearl merchant had probably spent his entire life in the search for the perfect pearl. Though he had many 'goodly pearls' (verse 45) when he found the 'one pearl' he went away and sold everything he had in order to buy it. He now has only one pearl for which he had given everything.

Why does Jesus, the merchant, keep only one pearl and sell all the others? What is the Lord Jesus seeking? What is He searching for? He has come preaching the Kingdom of God from the very beginning of His ministry (Matthew 4:17), offering the rule and reign of God as of preeminent value in the lives of men and women, holding out to them the blessings of forgiveness and acceptance as they open themselves up to the power of the love of God through Him, as they turn around completely from the former direction of their lives in repentance, to a child-like dependence upon God in faith, yielding to the demand of Jesus that they became converted and become like little children (Matthew 18:3).

As they enter the Kingdom of Heaven, they are utterly dependent on Him, looking forward to the ultimate fulfilment of the promise of the Kingdom of Heaven when all is summed up in Christ, and He is the Head of all things (Ephesians 1:10,22); They are anticipating a time of rejoicing but also a time of judgement of all that is rebellious against God

This is what the Merchant was seeking. As He went about all the cities and villages, teaching in their synagogues and preaching the gospel and healing every disease and every infirmity, He was also the Shepherd looking for His sheep. He had compassion on them because they were harassed and helpless, like sheep without a shepherd (Matthew 9:35). Surely many people, lost and bewildered, confused and afraid, turned to Him, found in Him that peace and security which was missing in their lives. But they were still diverse, separated one from another.

What Jesus was searching for was One Pearl, the many becoming One in the dispensation of God; a people united under One Head, a gathered out and gathered together group of people: In other words, *a church, εκκλησία,* which means gathering. Ephesians tells us that Christ loved the church and gave Himself up for her, that He might sanctify her, that He might present her to Himself (Ephesians 5:27).

The pearl of great price is the church for which the Lord is seeking, for which He went the way of the Cross, what Paul describes as Christ's afflictions for the sake of His Body, that is the church (Colossians 1:24). Being found in fashion as a Man, He humbled Himself, He, the Son of God, humbled Himself and became obedient to death, even death on a Cross (Philippians 2:8). This was the price He was prepared to pay so that He could bring many sons to glory (Hebrews 2:10), so that He could call them brethren (Hebrews 2:12), so that they could become one with Him and with each other in the family of God.

This is what it cost the merchant to find the Pearl. It cost Him everything. And He found it. He has found those who gather together to love and worship Him who has done so much for them, to praise Him, to rejoice in His love, to thank Him for all the blessings He showers upon them, to come alongside others to share the good news of the kingdom, to witness to an alternative way of living, simply looking to Jesus (Hebrews 12:2), this same Jesus who was taken up into heaven, and who will come in the same way as the disciples saw Him go into heaven (Acts 1:11 A.V.).

The Pearl illustrates what the Lord of the church wanted the church to be, a radiant and radiating organism, rather than an organisation, radiating the love and grace of its Head, beautiful, glowing with the presence of Jesus, attracting others to Him.

There is, however, another interpretation of this wonderful parable. Early on in Christian theology, Christ became both the pearl and the treasure. The treasure in the field is interpreted as the Christ hidden in the scriptures, or His divinity hidden in the flesh. And perhaps even more telling, the Pearl is Christ for whom the seeker after Him gives up everything in order to find

Him, the Pearl of great price. This interpretation too is a potent symbol of the one who will not stop searching until he has found what he has been searching for all his life. The Kingdom of Heaven is Christ. He is the kingdom, or rather, *the kingdom is HIM;* and full satisfaction, fullness of life, is only to be found in Him, the Pearl of great value. The seeker has found Him. No wonder the hymn writer can say,' I've found the Pearl of greatest price, my heart doth sing for joy'! He is the One Pearl, the pearl of greatest price.

That the merchant discovers the *one* pearl is relevant; the one pearl for which he has given everything, so great is his desire and longing. There is only one way, one Jesus, who said, 'I am the way' (John 14:6), through whom we receive salvation, by whose grace we live. We do not judge others, but are so glad when we find others, brothers and sisters, who have also found the Pearl of great price, even though it has cost them everything too. As Jesus prayed to His Father at the end of His life (John 17:11) that they may be *one,* even as We are one.

So we can see that both interpretations of this parable are valid, and feed into one another.

Jesus said to his disciples at the end of these parables, 'Have you understood all this?' and they said, 'Yes,' for they were beginning to understand without explanation what He was saying to them (verse 51). And Jesus reminded them later that the Holy Spirit, whom the Father would send in the Name of Jesus would teach them all things (John 14:26).

So we worship Him for who He is, for what He has done, and for fellowship, communion with all other sinners, saved by grace (Ephesians 2:5; Romans 5:8).

Matthew 13:47-50. The Dragnet

Then again, the Kingdom of Heaven is like a net which was thrown into the sea and gathered fish of every kind. When it was full, men drew it ashore and sat down and sorted the good into the vessels, but threw away the bad (Matthew 13:47,48).

This final parable of the Kingdom of Heaven repeats Jesus' previous warning of judgement, as He speaks of that which is to come. The angels are once more called into service as they separate the evil from the righteous (verse 49) and throw them into 'the furnace of fire' (verse 50). As people realise the enormity of what they have done, or neglected to do, they weep and gnash their teeth in an agony of repentance and frustration, but it is too late.

This is the third compassionate warning that Jesus has given, the warning that judgement awaits those who have chosen not to respond to the offer of new life in the new kingdom where Jesus is king. His compassion was also an incentive to His disciples to seek the wanderers and bring them home. How great is the contrast between those who have rejected the claim of Jesus on their lives, and those who have embraced it with all their being, as we saw in the parables of the treasure and the pearl.

Is Jesus not being too severe as He speaks of the final judgement? Is He not setting up a separation between the people and the disciples? Between the saved and the unsaved? All around us are the signs, in climate change, in population explosion, in natural disasters, that the world is not what it was. It appears that judgement may be coming.

The Lord is not willing that any should perish (2 Peter 3:9), but that all should come to repentance; but He has given free will to human beings for them to choose the way they should go, and He cannot allow anything that defiles, or anything that speaks of rebellion against Him, in His new heaven and His new earth. So Jesus, in His compassion for men and women, warns them of the judgement to come; and speaks of it to His disciples that they also may warn the people of what is to come. The issue is not how one lives, but whose one is, to whom one belongs. They may be confused or deceived by the delight in riches even though that includes the cares of this world (verse 22), or they may respond to the call of Jesus to 'come to Him' (Matthew 11:28).

Jesus' message is always, 'Come to me, you that are weary and heavy laden and I will give you rest.' All He can do is offer the invitation. It is for the individual to respond. It is of His mercy that we are not consumed (Lamentations 3:22 A.V.), but the steadfast love of the Lord never ceases. Wherever people will be in the future lies entirely in their hands, for those who seek Him will find Him when they seek Him with all their heart (Jeremiah 29:13). Paul speaks of 'the Son of God who loved *me* and gave Himself *for me* (Galatians 2:7), and many would share his wonder, and worship Him for what He has done in giving Himself for them. But the individual's response is completely voluntary. Choose *you* this day whom you will serve. The choice is ours (Joshua 24:15).

Matthew 13:1-52. Summary of the third discourse

Chapter 13 brings together seven parables for Jesus' third discourse, parables of the Kingdom of Heaven. His speaking in parables is the fulfilment of Old Testament prophecy and also points to the *understanding* of His teaching by His disciples, but *non-understanding* on the part of the crowds because of the hardness of their hearts (verse 13). He says, 'He that has ears to hear, let him hear' (verse 9) thus making a distinction between those who are open to Him, and those who have closed their minds to Him, 'Lest they should perceive with their eyes and hear with their ears and understand with their heart, and turn to me that I should heal them' (verse 15) quoting Isaiah 6:9-10.

Because of this distinction between those with understanding, and those with hardened hearts, this discourse happens in different locales.

Jesus begins to teach the crowds while seated in a boat beside the sea. He had left the house, and the crowds quickly gathered about Him on the seashore to hear His teaching.

Jesus' first parable about the Kingdom of Heaven did not fall exclusively on deaf ears, for there were some who received the word and 'brought forth fruit' (verse 23). But the explanation and interpretation of the parable of the sower was given not to the crowds but to the disciples who came to Him privately. So, some of His teaching was in public, and some in private to His disciples.

The parable of the wheat and the tares, the mustard seed, and the leaven, were all given publicly, but the time came when again He needed to speak privately to His disciples. 'He left the crowds and went into the house' (verse 36). And His teaching becomes utterly serious as He explains to them the meaning of judgement to come in the parable of the wheat and the tares, following it up with the cost of discipleship in the parables of the treasure and the pearl, giving up everything for the sake of entering the Kingdom of Heaven, and a final warning of judgement to come in the parable of the dragnet.

Jesus spoke to the crowds publicly in parables, and to the disciples privately because the message of the Kingdom of Heaven could only be received by faith. Faith comes through hearing, and hearing by the word of God (Romans 10:17; Luke 8:11). This is why to the disciples 'it was given to know the mystery of the Kingdom of Heaven' (Matthew 13:11). It could only be received by faith.

It was the seeing of the eye of faith, the hearing by faith that made the interpretation possible of acceptance. Abraham believed God at the age of 75 that he would have a son, and his faith was counted to him for righteousness, even though the promise was not renewed until he was 99, and he was 100 when Isaac was born (Genesis 15:6; 17:9; 21:5). He was convinced that God was able to do what He had promised (Romans 4:21 R.S.V), that what He had promised, He was able also to perform (A.V.). Faith had come to him by hearing, and hearing by the word of God.

And these things were written for our sakes who believe in Him (Romans 4:23,24). Not to all were the mysteries of the kingdom given, but only to those who received the blessing of enlightened eyes and opened ears (verse 16), the blessing that comes from faith.

For the disciples, the discourse has a discernible *progress,* from the sowing of the seed of the kingdom (13:3), to its current dissemination (13:24-36) to its consummation (13:47-50). God is moving on. He has His purpose in view. His Son is already King of Kings and Lord of Lords, but the time is coming when everyone will bow the knee and recognize Him as King of Kngs and Lord of Lords, when time will be no more and He will receive the acknowledgement of His kingship throughout heaven and earth, 'the voice of a great multitude crying Hallelujah!, for the Lord our God, the Almighty reigns. The marriage of the Lamb has come and His Bride has made herself ready!' (Revelation 19:6,7,16).

Matthew 13:51-5. The new and the old

Therefore, every scribe who has been trained for the Kingdom of Heaven is like a householder who brings out of his treasure what is new and what is old.

Just as there were Jewish scribes who had been trained under the Old Covenant, skilled in exegesis and knowledge of the law, so the Lord Jesus says there are scribes who have been trained for the Kingdom of Heaven. He used the metaphor of the master of a house, who does not use his precious treasures all the time, but when the occasion demands, will bring out of his treasure store, treasures both old and new. This is such an encouraging word for the disciples, and for us. Though not everyone would claim to be a scribe, trained for the Kingdom of Heaven, these disciples have answered *'yes'* to Jesus' question as to whether or not they had understood His parables and His interpretation of them. They are being trained for the Kingdom of Heaven by Jesus. They are using their spiritual storehouses for the safe bestowal of their spiritual treasures, treasures which they can use not only for their own encouragement in the life of faith, but also to help and comfort others.

Old treasures are perhaps early experiences of the love and compassion of God in their lives; testimony to His mercy and grace in time of need. *New treasures,* are perhaps for those same acts of mercy, still occurring day by day as the disciples hear and receive His word, and commit their lives to Him in obedience and worship. His mercies are new every morning, great is His faithfulness (Lamentations 3:23).

A scribe is a disciple who is learning new things all the time about the Kingdom of Heaven; that people are so often comfortless until they learn of the comfort which Jesus came to give them through the Holy Spirit, the Comforter (John 14:16 A.V), the Counsellor (R.S.V.), the Paraclete, the One who comes alongside, the Spirit of Truth, of reality (John 14:17). And that they can declare to all the mighty works of God as they trust Him to help them teach others more and more of His ways.

A scribe is a disciple who is always learning. The old understanding makes the new understanding possible, and both are valuable as they go on in the life of the kingdom, and share with others what God has done, and what God can do.

Scribes appeared in Judaism after the Exile. They were not merely copyists, or secretaries, but experts in the Law, authorised Rabbis, or commissioned theologians. They were interpreters of the ancestral law (Hill p 240) and formed a group in the time of Jesus dedicated to preserving the Mosaic tradition. They were generally also Pharisees, rather than Sadducees, descended spiritually if not biologically, from those who had stood in the breach and defended the Temple at the time of its desecration under Antiochus Epiphanes.

How do scribes in the Kingdom of Heaven compare with the Jewish scribes of Jesus' day?

The Jewish scribes are living in the past glories of God's dealings with His people, a time of God's longing for a people dedicated to Him alone, a people who are living in constant fellowship with their Creator and Redeemer. But God is doing a new thing. He has sent His Son to be the Saviour of the world which He so loved, that whoever believes in Him should not perish but have everlasting life (John 3:16). As followers of Jesus, we thank God for the past, and all God's ways described and ascribed to Him in the Old Testament, for the evidence of His everlasting love, of His lovingkindness which He poured upon the children of Israel who found grace in the wilderness (Jeremiah 31:2,3) and still pours upon us and them today. The ancient Old Testament promises are for us too, for God never changes, He is unchangeable in His love, in His mercy (Malachi 3:6).

But in that love, that mercy, He has now, by the presence of Jesus in our lives, given us a fresh, active, personal and relevant experience of Himself. Things old and new are insisting by their presence in the storehouse that they are evidence of the faithfulness of God, ready to be taken out for the comfort and encouragement of others, ready to be relied upon once again as we live in the sunlight of a new experience of everlasting, eternal love.

In identifying His disciples as scribes in the kingdom of heaven, is Jesus suggesting in some way that there are experts in His Kingdom just as the Jewish scribes were experts in the law? That would suggest a self-reliance incompatible with living life, not in dependence on Him but on ourselves. But it is possible to use the treasures of the past, and God's provision for us and His guidance of us, to enlighten and perhaps justify the present. Or, for example, as they read the scriptures, a personal understanding of redemption from slavery which had happened to the Israelites in the past could now become real for the disciple who has been delivered by God from some form of bondage. Or, for example, just as Daniel had been delivered from the lions, so a follower of Jesus could interpret that for themselves as a real way in which God could act in their lives also to find deliverance from those who were hostile to them.

Whatever the meaning of the old and new treasures in Matthew 13:52, the issue is the Kingdom of Heaven, and especially whether the disciples had understood Jesus' teaching and could say 'yes' to Him. Understanding is what Jesus wants for His disciples, that they should not drift through their Christian lives, but see Him, and the outworking of His loving will for them in all that they go through of sorrow, illness, bereavement, persecution, and so much more.

We saw from the beginning of chapter 13 how important the concept of understanding was. The people in the crowd had no understanding, because they had hardened their hearts; so Jesus turned to His disciples, and by the end of His discourse they could say 'yes', they understood what He had been teaching them.

With this final metaphor, of the old and new treasures, Jesus has brought His third discourse to a close.

Biblical literacy is very important, but personal experience of intimate fellowship with God, both in the past and in the present, is the gift which Jesus offers to all who come to Him. The reality of the 'now' lived in daily, homely fellowship with Him is His gift to us, and also distinguishes the 'new' scribe from the 'old', and the new treasure from the old. Of course, as in all the precious gifts that He wants to give, people may, and can, refuse. Not all disciples want to become scribes in the Kingdom of Heaven, but what a blessing for those who do.

We know that Jesus fulfils the law and the prophets (Matthew 5:17), and that He is the continuity between 'then' and 'now'. He is also the continuity in our lives as His followers. He combines the Old and the New in His Person and we live by the revelation of who He is in any situation. This is the Treasure which we have in Him.

Like so much else, Jesus redefines the concept of the scribe. Humble as we are content to be, rejoicing in what He has given us, we yet aspire to being one of those privileged ones who take from their storehouses treasures new and old to glorify the Giver of such munificence, our precious Lord and Saviour, Jesus.

Anselm says rightly that faith comes before understanding. To put understanding first is the wrong way round. Faith is the medium in which we live. But understanding is the method, the means by which we come, the rational mind which is being renewed day by day (Ephesians 4:23), as Paul writes: *Be renewed in the spirit of your minds and put on the new nature (R.S.V.) the new man (A.V.) created after the likeness of God.* What a privilege! to be able to say 'yes' to Jesus, and to live in His 'now'.

Matthew 13:53-58. Back at Nazareth

And when Jesus had finished these parables, He went away from there, and coming to His own country, He taught them in their synagogue (verse 53).

As we saw at the end of the Sermon on the Mount (Matthew 7:28), and the discipleship discourse of chapter 10 (Matthew 11:1) Matthew uses the word 'finished'. Jesus had fulfilled, finished, completed, all that He had to say for the time being concerning the Kingdom of Heaven, allowing His disciples to reflect, and ruminate on what He had taught them. Like the growth and development of children which often comes in spurts, the disciples needed to have time to think, to coalesce with their hearts and minds the implication, not only for them, but for the training they were receiving for the benefit of others, of what Jesus was conveying to them of His purpose and plan of salvation.

Jesus goes back to the beginning; to His own country, to 'their' synagogue to which He would so often have gone as a boy with His mother and earthly father, His brothers and sisters.

The use of the word 'their' indicates already a separation between Jesus and the teaching of the synagogue, yet He had been asked, as the custom was, to read part of a precious Hebrew scroll, and teach them from it. So He acceded to their request. They were 'astonished' at His teaching (verse 54), but they could not accept it, or Him. They said, 'Where did this man get this wisdom and these mighty works?' (verse 54). 'Who does He think He is? Is He better than we are? He is only the carpenter's son. We know Mary His mother. We know James and Joseph and Simon and Judas, His brothers, and we know His sisters. Where did he get all this information from?'

Perhaps Jesus had been expecting such a reaction. He identified Himself with a long line of prophets who had also been rejected by their own people. He says to them, 'A prophet is not without honour except in his own country and in his own house' (verse 57). But because of their rejection of Him, and their unbelief in Him as the Messiah, the One sent from God, there were many who were in great need of His ministry who remained unhealed, or discouraged, or lacking the peace and joy which He came to give because of their unbelief (verse 58).

The word ἀπιστία – *apistia* – *unbelief* is found only here and in Mark 6:6, and Mark 9:24 where the father of the epileptic boy pleads with Jesus to heal him, and in answer to His question as to whether the man has faith, says to Jesus, 'I believe; help my unbelief!'. Matthew says of his own country of Nazareth, 'He did not do many mighty works there, because of their unbelief' (Matthew 13:54, 58).

Unbelief is more than inability to believe; it is *wilful refusal* to have faith in Jesus. It could not be more serious, for the Lord Jesus earnestly desires that we should have faith in Him, and that He is then able to do many mighty works among us. By faith, we cooperate with Him, yield to Him any resistance we may have, place ourselves entirely in His will, and trust Him for what can only be His blessing of us.

We know from Matthew 4:13 that Jesus had moved His home to Capernaum from Nazareth, but Nazareth remained the place of His upbringing, and where it appears that His earthy family remained throughout His ministry. This may be confirmed by the incident recorded in John's gospel (John 7:1-10); when His brothers had gone up to Jerusalem from Galilee to the Feast of Tabernacles. They had spoken to Him before they left that He should go too, so that the works that He did should be on public display, and be validated. The sad note of this incident comes in John 7:5, 'For even His brothers did not believe in Him'.

It is also possible that they were at the marriage at Cana in Galilee, where His mother also was, and where He changed water into wine (John 2:1,3). How His brother James came not only to be His disciple, but to be the leader of the church in Jerusalem after His death and resurrection (Acts 15:13) we are not told. Perhaps His other brothers too became part of the Jerusalem church, or leaders of churches elsewhere. We find it hard to believe that having lived with Jesus as His younger brothers and also His sisters, they had not come to the truth of who He was.

But we do have the letter of James which appears to be a commentary on Jesus' teaching, particularly on the Sermon on the Mount. The ways of the Lord are mysterious. Why does one child in a family respond to the working of the Holy Spirit in their lives, causing them to seek after and follow Jesus, while others seem to miss the mark? Or we could say, 'Why me Lord? As the first letter to Timothy expresses it, 'Christ Jesus came into the world to save sinners, with Paul's addendum, 'Of whom I am chief' (1 Timothy 1:15. A.V.), a claim which many of us would dispute, for we know our own hearts.

We can only thank Him and praise Him for His grace towards us, and pray for others; pray for the power of God to move upon them; pray that they might come upon someone in their lives: friend, neighbour, colleague, who will show them the way, who will discover Jesus to them, for Jesus is the way, the truth and the life (John 14:6). And pray that that someone could be me; us.

Matthew Chapter 14

Matthew 14:1-12. The death of John the Baptist

At that time, Herod the tetrarch heard about the fame of Jesus, and he said to his servants, 'This is John the Baptist, he has been raised from the dead, that is why these powers are at work in him.'

For Herod had seized John and bound him and put him in prison for the sake of Herodias, his brother Philip's wife, because John had said to him, 'It is not lawful for you to have her.' And though he wanted to put him to death, he feared the people, because they held him to be a prophet (Matthew 14:1-4).

In these few words, we see not only the burden of guilt which Herod carried for his beheading of John the Baptist, but also his supernatural fear of the consequences, that perhaps John was not indeed dead, but had achieved a resurrection body. This resurrection body was now known as Jesus. It was as though Jesus was using John's persona. This superstition had become for Herod the explanation of why Jesus did so many works of power.

The following verses give us an abbreviated account of this tragedy, a tragedy for John of course, but for Herod also; an example of, and result of, his irrational behaviour, for the event became common knowledge and he would not be able to repudiate it, but would carry the memory of it to the end.

Herod Antipas was an Idumean, not Jewish. He was the tetrarch (a quarter) of Galilee from 4 B.C. to 39 A.D. He was the son of Herod the Great, 37 B.C. to 4 B.C., who killed all the little boys under two because of his fear that little Jesus might be a rival for his throne and become king (Matthew 2:1,19).

In his antagonism towards John, Herod Antipas takes after his father, Herod the Great, who tried to kill Jesus. Herod had two brothers, Philip who was tetrarch of Idumea, 4 B.C. to 34 A.D., and Archelaus, ethnarch (puppet king) of Judea, 4 B.C. to 6 A.D. (Matthew 2:22). Jesus called Herod Antipas 'that fox' (Luke 13:32).

Anticipating the history of this family slightly, we know that Herod's grandson, Herod Agrippa I, king from 41-44 A.D., killed the apostle James, and shortly after was killed by an angel of the Lord when the people proclaimed him 'to be a god, and not man' (Acts 12:2,22).

His son, Herod Agrippa II (c.50-63 A.D.) was invited by Festus to hear Paul's defence before he was sent to Rome for trial. At the end of Paul's testimony, Agrippa said to Paul, 'Almost thou persuadest me to be a Christian' (Acts 26:28 A.V.). Agrippa and his sister Bernice would have been content to release Paul had he not appealed to Caesar (Acts 26:32). Herod Agrippa II was the last of the Jewish kings.

How mysteriously God moves in the lives and hearts of men and women, whether kings or commoners. Like Paul, we pray for one another, and for them that have the rule over us, that they might become such as we are, followers of the Lord Jesus, 'except for these chains' as in the case of Paul (Acts 26:29).

Our present concern is with Herod Antipas, son of Herod the Great. He first married the daughter of the Arabian King Aretas. Later, he married Herodias, his brother Philip's wife, and was rebuked by John on the grounds that he was committing incest according to Leviticus 18:6 and 20:21. Herod, like other members of his family who governed Jewish communities, posed as a conforming Jew, and could therefore be rightly criticised by John on the grounds of the Hebrew scriptures. One can also imagine how this condemnation of her marriage to Herod infuriated Herodias, as Mark in his gospel explains (Mark 6:19) and it is Herodias who suggests to her daughter that she asks for the head of John the Baptist 'here, on a platter' (verse 8) as a reward for pleasing the guests at Herod's birthday celebration with her dancing (Matthew 14:8).

Like his father before him, Herod Antipas was a man of fear. Herod had ordered the death of John by beheading (a practice favoured by the Romans, but forbidden by the Jews. The Romans believed that decapitation prevented ghosts from returning to haunt the living); and we have noted that Herod believed that although he had indeed commanded that John should be beheaded, yet because of the mighty works being done by Jesus, Jesus was John the Baptist risen from the dead. The Pharisees had a belief that someone risen from the dead would be able to do miracles. Herod also 'feared the people, because they held John to be a prophet' (14:5).

Herod's theological thinking was somewhat muddled. And he was also distracted by this beautiful young woman who entertained the guests at his birthday celebration by dancing before them. She was a princess, the daughter of Philip and Herodias, and should not have been dancing like a courtesan, but she was urged on by her mother. Herod had promised 'with an oath' (verse 7) to give her anything she might ask as a reward, and prompted again by her mother (verse 8) she had asked for the head of John the Baptist.

Herod was sorry (verse 9) but was reluctant to go back on his word before his guests, so he had sent and had John beheaded in the prison. We can imagine the soldiers marching into John's dungeon cell, carrying the axe with which to behead him, and John falling to his knees as he lifted up his eyes to God and prayed, 'into your hands I commend my spirit'. This murder did not solve Herod's or Herodias' problem, however. It only increased Herod's fear of Jesus, and his fear of retribution.

Of all the gospel writers, Luke is the only one who recalls another incident between Jesus and Herod. At the end of His life, Jesus was brought before Pilate who when he heard that Jesus was a Galilean sent Him to Herod, possibly with the view that as Herod knew more about Jewish law than he did, he might be able to determine whether Jesus was innocent of the charges brought against Him by the scribes and Pharisees (Luke 23:6). Perhaps Herod believed that Jesus could absolve him in some way for all the crimes he had committed, but absolution can only come from deep heartfelt repentance, and Herod was not prepared to go that far.

At His trial before Herod, Jesus was silent. As Isaiah had prophesied, 'He was oppressed and He was afflicted, yet He opened not His mouth. Like a lamb that is led to the slaughter, and like a sheep that before her shearers is dumb, so He opened not His mouth' (Isaiah 53:7).

Luke tells us that Herod was glad to see Him because he was hoping to see some sign done by Him. Since Jesus did not display His power and authority in that way, Herod treated Him with contempt and mocked Him, thus demonstrating the kind of person he was who had had John beheaded and was now treating another innocent victim in the same way (Luke 23:15). There have been many, before and since, for whom the exercise of power has resulted in deeds of cruelty and oppression.

John's faithful disciples were allowed to take John's body and bury it and then went and told Jesus.= (Matthew 14:12).

Matthew 14:13-21. The feeding of the five thousand

Now when Jesus heard this, He withdrew from there in a boat to a lonely place apart. But when the crowds heard it, they followed Him on foot from the towns. As He went ashore, He saw a great throng, and He had compassion on them and healed their sick. When it was evening, His disciples came to Him and said, 'This is a lonely place, and the day is now over. Send the crowds away to go into the villages and buy food for themselves.' Jesus said, 'They need not go away. You give them something to eat.'

How the account of John's death must have burdened the heart of Jesus, and how He must have wanted to escape for a little while to a lonely place so that He could talk to His Father about it and receive His comfort.

With sorrow in His heart, Jesus left, and withdrew from Capernaum in a boat to a lonely place between Capernaum and

Bethsaida (Luke 9:10). Matthew uses the word 'withdrew' to indicate Jesus' desire for a time of personal and intimate fellowship with His Father.

However, it appears that someone had seen Him, and alerted others to the 'lonely place'. And when the crowds heard it, they followed Him on foot from the towns. Alas, the time of fellowship with His Father was limited by the crowds that followed Him. Matthew calls them a great throng, verse 14. And as He went, He had compassion on them, as He always did, healing their sick. 'And when the crowds heard it, they followed Him on foot from the towns' (verse 13). So Jesus came ashore, full of compassion for them, and healed their sick.

It appears that this ministry of healing took some time, for 'when it was evening' (verse 15), the disciples, who had apparently also followed Him on foot, came to Jesus and suggested that as it was late, and this was a lonely place, the people should be advised to go to the villages around to provide food for themselves.

Jesus' reply was impossible, extraordinary. He said to His disciples, 'they don't need to go away. You give them something to eat.' We can imagine the look of blank surprise and astonishment on the faces of the disciples. How were they to obey this command from Jesus? And we can imagine a certain oscillation, a certain quivering between faith and doubt as they say to Him, 'We have only five loaves and two fish' (verse 17). 'Bring them here to Me,' He said.

And as the Lord was the Host at this meal, He ordered the people to sit down on the grass. When they were all comfortably seated, He took the five loaves and looking up to His Father in heaven, He blessed and broke the loaves and gave the loaves to the disciples to give to the people, and the fish also. And they all, five thousand men as well as women and children, ate and were satisfied. When they could eat no more, the disciples gathered up what food remained into twelve baskets. This food may well have been taken to those villages so recently recommended as a source of provision. Jesus knew He could trust His heavenly Father to provide.

All four gospels recount this incident. In John's gospel, the loaves are described as barley loaves, the common food of the people, indicating that this was the time of the barley harvest, the time of Passover. This may have gone some way to interpreting the miracle of the feeding of the five thousand in Eucharistic terms, likening it to Holy Communion, or the Lord's Table. John's gospel explicitly states, 'the Passover, the feast of the Jews was near' (John 6:4), at the beginning of his account of the feeding of the five thousand.

Passover was the occasion of the Last Supper that Jesus had with His disciples, when He took bread, blessed it and gave it to them saying, 'Take, eat, this is My body.'

And He took a cup, and when He had given thanks, thanking His Father that He had given Him the privilege of laying down His life for their sakes, He gave it to them, saying, 'Drink this, all of you, for this is My blood of the New Covenant, which is poured out for many for the forgiveness of sins' (Matthew 26:26).

The Passover alluded to by John was however the second Passover mentioned by him in his gospel (John 2:13; 6:4; 11:55), the occasion in chapter 6 corresponding to the second of the three years of Jesus' ministry, and not to the third Passover which saw the trial, death and resurrection of Jesus.

Because of what follows in John chapter 6 of Jesus' teaching about the Bread of Life, and this teaching occurring subsequent to the miracle of the feeding of the five thousand at the time of the second Passover, according to John, some Biblical scholars have linked this miracle as recorded in the synoptic gospels with the Last Supper and given it an Eucharistic interpretation, especially as Jesus is described as using similar vocabulary as He breaks the bread and gives thanks to His heavenly Father.

But further scrutiny of John 6 will reveal that Jesus did not interpret the miracle in this way. He used the occasion simply to describe Himself as the Bread of Life, the Manna sent down from heaven, which was greater than the manna enjoyed by the Israelites in the wilderness (John 6:51). Jesus is the living Bread sent down from heaven: 'if anyone eats of this Bread, he will live forever, and the bread which He will give for the life of the world, is His flesh'. The 'flesh' of Jesus *is* the manna sent down from heaven to feed the people of the new covenant, the covenant in His blood. This is so that a man may eat of it and never die (John 6:50). Eating His flesh and drinking His blood through faith is the way to abiding in Him, for unless they eat of His flesh and drink His blood they have no life in them (John 6:53, 54).

Many of His disciples, when they heard this, said, 'This is a hard saying. Who can listen to it?' Understand it?

It is certain that in Matthew's account of the feeding of the five thousand, the phrase 'He blessed, broke, and gave the loaves to His disciples', echo the words of institution at the Lord's Supper (Matthew 26:26), but whether this was intentional on the part of the Lord Jesus would be hard to establish or verify. In a sense, all our eating becomes sacramental as we pray over our food, giving thanks for all His provision for our needs, following His example. But our remembering of Him and His sacrifice for us at His Table is especially precious.

One further truth which the disciples were given to understand at this miraculous feeding of the five thousand deserves consideration. The disciples were there to feed the people after that the Lord had given thanks. Jesus said, '*You give them to eat*' (verse 16(. It is the responsibility of those who have been called as undershepherds of Christ's flock, to feed them with the Bread of life. Obediently, the disciples do as He commands them, following His example. Sharing His compassion, they distribute food to the hungry, an inexhaustible supply until all are satisfied. Jesus said to Peter after His resurrection, 'Feed My sheep, feed My lambs,' And He had in mind more than bread and fish, for their needs were not only physical but also and especially, spiritual (John 21:15-17).

In the new kingdom of Heaven, which Jesus has come to establish on earth, there are men and women who are hungry for Him. When the miracle takes place of finding Him, putting their trust in Him, they find others who have also come to love

Him. And so they gather together in His presence, eating together as followers of Jesus, remembering Him as they eat the bread and drink the cup. The crowd of the miracle is completely representational, gathered together and nourished by Jesus; men and women, young and old, husbands and wives and children, nourished not only physically, but spiritually by the King in His Kingdom. They are feeding not only on bread and fish, but on Him, in their hearts by faith and with thanksgiving.

John's gospel takes the feeding of the Five Thousand out of the context of the Lord's Supper and makes it an ordinary or extraordinary picnic meal by Lake Tiberias, the Sea of Galilee (John 6:1), *because the life, eternal life, is not in the ritual of Holy Communion but in Jesus; His broken Body; the Bread of Life sent down from heaven.* Yet the reality behind the ritual is clear as we eat the Bread, symbolic of His Body, and drink the Cup, symbol of the life poured out; as we proclaim His death, the atoning power of His Cross, until He comes again, and the offer of eternal life is at an end.

We remember Him: not that we ever forget Him, for He is our Life, but in that brief moment as we take the bread and drink the cup His presence is exquisitely sweet and near, near to us and to all who share the moment with us.

They all ate and were satisfied (Matthew 14:20). All together in that one place, all together satisfied, not with the food alone, but with the presence of Jesus, the knowledge of His compassion and love. Jesus.

Matthew 14:22-33. Jesus walks on the water

Then He made the disciples get into the boat and go before Him to the other side, while He dismissed the crowds. And after He had dismissed the crowds, He went up on the mountain by Himself to pray. When evening came, He was there alone (Matthew 14:22-23).

Jesus was longing to be alone, to spend time with His Father. He had sent the disciples to the boat, to go to the other side of the Sea of Galilee (Josephus tells us that the Sea of Galilee was about four and a half miles wide). This must have taken an appreciable amount of time, as the people would have wanted to stay with Him, thanking Him for their healing and their food, but at last, here He was, communing with His Father, sharing the burden and the joy of the day with Him in precious fellowship.

Meanwhile, the boat containing the disciples, some of whom were experienced fishermen, was now some distance from the land (verse 24). The Sea of Galilee was noted for the storms that suddenly arose, and the boat was 'beaten by the waves, for the wind was against them' (verse 24). It was now the fourth watch of the night (verse 25). The Romans had divided the 12 hours of the night, from 6 p.m. to 6 a.m. into four periods, or watches, and the fourth watch would have been between 3 a.m. and 6 a.m.

Jesus, aware of their situation, came to them, walking on the sea (verse 25). Was it that, lost in contemplation and prayer, He had not noticed the passing of time, or was it that, purposeful as His actions always were, He wanted to teach His disciples something more about Himself? Perhaps these two explanations are not incompatible. But when they saw Him they were terrified (verse 26), saying, 'It is a ghost!' for of course men and women do not walk on water. It was a logical deduction to make of something they could not possibly understand, but they were crying out from a position of fear.

Jesus spoke to them 'immediately', (verse 27) saying, 'Take heart, it is I; have no fear.' He did not want them to remain in this state of incomprehension and especially not in the grip of fear. His words have been translated as, 'Take heart, it is me! Stop being afraid!' But in the Greek it is ἐγώ εἰμι, translated, 'It is I', or more accurately, 'I AM'. Where fear comes in, Jesus speaks as one with the Father. When He speaks as *Yahweh, I Am!* fear leaves, the storm subsides (Exodus 3:14). And Peter responds by saying, 'If it is you, bid me come to you on the water' (verse 28). Jesus never says, 'No,' to faith. He says to Peter, 'Come. (verse 29). So Peter got out of the boat and walked on the water and came to Jesus.

Paul speaks of those who are 'weak in faith' (Romans 14:1), and perhaps this was the case with Peter at that time, although afterwards, it was noted by the Jewish leaders, that, 'When they saw the *boldness* of Peter and John, they recognised that they had been with Jesus' (Acts 4:13).

Peter had faith, he was learning quickly what it meant to walk with Jesus, but he still had much to learn. When he sees the wind, he becomes afraid and begins to sink, and does the only sensible thing he could do. He cries out to Jesus, 'Lord! Save me! And *immediately,* Jesus reached out his hand and caught him saying, 'O man of little faith, why did you doubt?' (verse 31). 'And when they got into the boat, the wind ceased' (verse 32).

Peter learned a lesson that day that the other disciples missed. Impulsively, he had climbed out of the boat to come to Jesus, walking on the water, keeping his eyes on Him. It was when He took his eyes off Jesus and 'saw the wind' that he began to sink.

'Lord, increase our faith,' pleaded the disciples on another occasion (Luke 17:5). Was it an increase of faith that Peter needed at that time? Only if his increased faith had constrained him to keep his eyes on Jesus, 'Looking into Jesus, the author and finisher of faith' (Hebrews 12:2), and not at the raging storm or the terrifying mountains of water.

How sensible of the other disciples to remain in the boat while the storm raged about them. But how much they missed by not doing as Peter did; walking, going towards Jesus in the midst of a storm, for in a storm, He is the only safe place. Like Peter however, they too came to the same affirmation. 'Truly, you are the Son of God' they say (verse 33) and they worshipped Him. Peter had already confessed Him as 'Lord', calling out to Him for salvation. 'Lord, save me!' he cries (verse 30). Now the disciples too had a recognition, a revelation of who Jesus was, 'Truly, you are the Son of God' (verse 33). Not a ghost, not some ethereal, phantasmic manifestation, but the Son of God in human flesh, who exercises His authority over illness; and hunger; and the forces of nature, in perfect love. No wonder they worshipped Him.

This was the first time in the gospel that the disciples had made this confession, a confession closely connected with Peter's question, *'If it is you'* (verse 28) and Jesus' reply, *'It is I.'* Peter's question *'Lord if it is you', 'κύριε εἰ οὐ εἰ,'* followed by, *'ἐγώ εἰμι,' It is I. I am,'* and Jesus' outstretched hand to Peter, saying to him, 'O man of little faith, why did you doubt?' Even a little faith causes Jesus to respond to those who are sinking. Again we remember Paul's words, 'He that is weak in faith, receive him, welcome him' (Romans 14:1 A.V. and R.S.V.). Jesus does not require of us that we have great faith before He reaches out His hand to us, to save us, knowing that as we learn to trust Him, faith will grow. Our faith may be small, but it is faith in a great Lord.

Peter's confession of Jesus as Lord becomes for the disciples, 'Truly, You are the Son of God' (verse 33), an intensification of his confession. So, weak as our faith may be, it could enable others to come to a place of greater understanding of the precious gift of Jesus Himself.

Walking on water, it is clear, is a solely divine ability. Human beings cannot do it; for them it is completely impossible, so the fear of the disciples when they saw Jesus walking on the water is entirely justifiable. It is when they hear the word of Jesus to them, 'It is I, the I Am, be not afraid' and recognise this as being the Name of God that worship takes the place of fear. They cannot avoid the equivalence of the 'I Am' with 'Son of God'. It is more than a revelation, it is an epiphany. They will never be the same again.

Peter knows as well as the disciples that to walk on water is impossible, yet he says, 'If it is you, bid me come to you on the water' (verse 28). It was all he wanted, the only desire he had. The wind and the waves meant nothing to him. He wanted to come to Jesus. And Jesus gives him the answer he asks for: 'Come'.

On that word alone, impossible though he knew it to be, he could step out of the boat and come to Jesus (verse 29). But he suddenly perceives what he has done, and looking at the water instead of looking at the Lord, knows that he is threatened with insecurity, danger, injury, death.

291

How necessary under these circumstances becomes the outstretched hand of Jesus, that he should not drown but that he should experience the saving presence of the Lord. Peter, moving out from all the experience of his life so far, had moved into the marvellous insecurity and joy of being in the storm with Jesus. When Jesus said 'Come', he had obeyed, taking the risk of obedience to Jesus. Though he had subsequently failed in his faith, he had learned something precious, that obedience to Jesus does not necessarily obviate life's storms, but gives us the joy of going through them with Him. Though for a little while, he doubted, until Jesus caught him (verse 31), Peter's experience is not unlike the experience of many believers. Doubt becomes part of faith until we lay hold of the hand outstretched to save and doubt is overcome by faith, for even faith is the gift of God (Ephesians 2:9). Faith is the victory which overcomes everything which does not put Jesus first, and which we call doubt.

The story of Jesus as recorded in this gospel has this episode as a distinctive evaluation of the Person and work of the Lord Jesus. As His life was a personification of the love of the Father for the Son, and the Son for the Father, bound together in the love of the Holy Spirit, so out of that love, They, the precious members of the Trinity, designed and purposed the sharing and including of that love with human beings, human hearts.

The members of the Godhead all say, 'Come'. Jesus' love and obedience to His Father shines through as Immanuel, God with us (Matthew 1:23). This gospel is the story of the Son of God, who is God with us. This is the context, the surrounding framework of the whole gospel, the context of the entire story of Jesus. Peter's response to Jesus, 'Bid me come,' and his obedience in coming, is the way for all to come, and for all to experience the way of love, the way of being carried by Him, even as God the Father and God the Son intended from the beginning. With Peter and the other disciples, we too worship Him.

Matthew 14:34-36.The healing of the sick in Gennesaret

And when they had crossed over, they came to land at Gennesaret. And when the men of that place recognised Him, they sent round to all that region and brought Him all that were sick and besought Him that they might only touch the fringe of His garment, and as many touched it were made well, διεσώθησαν – were saved.

After the disciples' confession (verse 33), 'Truly, you are the Son of God,' a high point in the disciples understanding of who Jesus was, we might expect a subtle change in the narrative, but no, Jesus carried on as He has always done, because He has always been the Son of God, only formerly they had no recognition of Him as such.

But it seems that 'the men of that place', Gennesaret (verse 35), near the western shore of the Sea of Galilee, did have some recognition of Him as the Healer, and how quickly they sent round to all that region and brought to Him all that were sick (verse 35). Since it could have been early dawn when Jesus got into the boat with his disciples and crossed over to land at Gennesaret (verse 34), the men of that place could have already started their working day, making use of the daylight hours; while the women were engaged in domestic duties.

The strange thing about this healing, however, was that having brought the sick to Jesus, they asked to be permitted to touch the fringe, the tassels on the edge of His garment. And all that touched it were made well, were saved.

All the miracles point to the living reality of who Jesus is. In Matthew 9:20, a woman came to Jesus with an unclean illness and after touching the tassel on His garment, was made whole. There is no indication that those who came to Jesus on this occasion for healing were ritually unclean as was the woman with the haemorrhage in chapter 9, so why do they too want to touch the fringe of His garment?

The tassels represent a devout Jew, worn to remind the wearer of his obedience to the law. They are attached to the four corners of the garment and are normally between three and nine inches in length. Numbers 15:41 states, 'The Lord said to Moses, speak to the people of Israel, and bid them to make tassels on the corners of their garments... it shall be to you a tassel to look upon and remember all the commandments of the law, to do them, not to follow after your own heart and your own eyes, which you are inclined to go after wantonly. Be holy to your God. I am the Lord your God.' And Deuteronomy 22:12 also has the same commandment. We are expected to take note when something is repeated.

When these people came to Jesus, were they expecting more than just healing? They were encouraged to touch His garment, and the very act of touching represented faith. As with the poor woman in chapter 9, did they feel estranged from the commonwealth of Israel? Made to feel less than they should as the people of God, partly because of their masters, the Romans, and partly because of the high standards of righteous behaviour imposed by their leaders, the chief priests and members of the Sanhedrin, the Jewish ruling body? How could they hope to draw near to God, when there were so many obstacles to overcome as an agrarian community before they could even manage the journey to Jerusalem at the time of the sacrifices, to receive God's mercy, His direction for their lives.

But here is a pious Jew; some think He is a prophet (Matthew 16:14), who is not sitting up there in the Temple, demanding of the people what they should do, but one who has come to them. His garment may not be the cleanest; He has just come through a storm with His disciples, but it has the tassels on it which speak of the Covenant which God made with Israel all those centuries before, and His healing power proclaimed that He had a special ministry amongst them, for whether they recognised it or not, He was the Son of God. They will not only be 'healed', but 'saved', rescued, delivered, from all that would prevent them from being acknowledged as people of the covenant, people of God.

This is the significance of this particular instance of Jesus' healing ministry. The verbs Matthew uses explains all. The men 'recognised' Him, they 'brought' to Him all that were sick, they *'besought'* Him that they might only touch the fringe of His garment, and as many as *'touched'* it were saved.

Jesus came to save His people from their sins (Matthew 1:21). His healing power extends not to their physical illnesses only, but to all that would separate them from His Father. Jesus, Saviour from sin, Saviour of all, who is the Restorer of His people, not only restores them to the Old Covenant but brings men and women into the New Covenant through His sacrificial love for them.

As followers of Jesus, we no longer need to wear tassels on our clothes, for we have the witness of the Holy Spirit, witnessing with our spirit that we are children of God, and if children, then heirs, heirs of God and fellow-heirs with Christ, provided we suffer with Him in order that we may also be glorified with Him (Romans 8:16,17). As many as touched his garment were made well (verse 36).

Matthew Chapter 15

Matthew 15:1-20. The tradition of the elders

Then the Pharisees and scribes came to Jesus from Jerusalem and said, 'Why do your disciples transgress the tradition of the elders? For they do not wash their hands when they eat (verse 1, 2).

He answered them, And why do you transgress the commandment of God for the sake of your tradition? For God commanded, 'Honour your father and your mother', and 'He who speaks evil of father or mother, let him surely die'. But you say, If anyone tells his father or his mother 'what you would have gained from me is given to God,' he need not honour his father. So, for the sake of your tradition, you have made void the word of God.

Although we do not know the extent of the time span between the end of chapter 14 and the beginning of chapter 15, Matthew is always careful to provide a link, this time between the healing at Gennesaret and Jesus' present disputation with the religious leaders.

It appears that the Pharisees and scribes came to where Jesus was, possibly still at Gennesaret, from Jerusalem; always an ominous sign; with the intention of questioning Jesus and His authority over the very thing that had been troubling the men and women of Gennesaret.

Did the disciples eat with unwashed hands? Washing the hands before meals had become for the Pharisees the mark of those who were devout, who were serious about obeying the law. But Jesus points out that this was not the Mosaic law as inspired by God and handed down through generations of His people, but 'the traditions of the elders' (verse 2) that is, commentary on the commentary of the text. As Jesus says in chapter 23:4, 'The scribes and Pharisees bind heavy burdens hard to bear, and lay them on men's shoulders,' and in doing so had manufactured a two-tier system of religious belief, one for themselves as the 'elite' and one for the 'ordinary' common people. This was what the men of Gennesaret had been troubled with. May God preserve us from any such attitude in His church.

There was no scriptural injunction about the washing of hands; though of course there were about clean and unclean foods (Leviticus chapters 11, 15, 16), and about *ceremonial* uncleanness. Though subscribed to by the Pharisee and scribes (though not the Sadducees) these traditions were arcane. They were later written and codified by Rabbi Judah ha Nasi 135-220 A.D. and formed the Mishnah (Hill p 251). But there was a scriptural injunction about the attitude of children to their parents which had also become tradition, and this was the one about which Jesus was more concerned.

Like so much else, the traditions of the elders originally arose from a sincere desire for scrupulous obedience to what was perceived as the will of God. Though the Israelites did not have the sophisticated access to clean water which we enjoy, washing played an important part in their faith. In both the Tabernacle and the Temple, a laver was provided for the priests to wash in, both before and after they performed their ministry at the altar. Exodus 30:17 and Deuteronomy 21:1-6 give instructions as to the cleansing procedure when an unidentified man is found slain. A heifer is slain in the place of the killer, and the men of the city wash their hands over the heifer, proclaiming that they had no part in the death, an action which possibly gives rise to an assertion still heard sometimes, 'I wash my hands of the whole affair!'

We may also note Deuteronomy 20:1-10, Exodus 19:10, and Leviticus 13:6,34, 14:9, 15:11. These are but a few examples among others, but the washing of the hands before food in Jesus' day had become *de rigueur*, the removal of ceremonial defilement caused by contact with things unclean.

Even before the discovery of bacteria, this would seem a reasonable and sensible thing to do, to have a finger bowl of water on the table, especially before the invention of forks (in 15th century Florence). It therefore appears to be a fairly innocent question that the Pharisees posed to Jesus, 'Why? Why do your disciples transgress the tradition of the elders? For they do not wash their hands when they eat.'

What is a matter of ceremonial purity to them carries with it a whole background of casuistry, rules and regulations to which the average working man or woman would never be able to aspire. A man may well come in from the field where he has been working, and lave his face and hands from the sweat of the day, but that water has come from a communal well such as the one at Sychar in John 4:4, where the women of the village have queued up in the morning to fill their water jars before carrying them home. It becomes a real act of generosity to give a cup of cold water to a passing child (Matthew 10:42).

In the view of the Pharisees, the disciples had committed a transgression, and their accusation requires an answer from Jesus. But Jesus answered them, 'Why do *you* transgress?' (verse 3). He implies, 'My disciples may be transgressing your tradition, but you are transgressing the commandment of God by not obeying His word concerning the honouring of father and mother.'

The Pharisees needed saving just as much as the men and women of Gennesaret, saving from the hypocrisy of the lives they were living. Instead of the commandment of God, they were obeying the traditions of men. On Mount Sinai, God had said, 'Honour your father and mother' (Exodus 20:12). This was the fourth commandment. with an additional clause to the commandment in Leviticus 20:9 'He who curses father or mother shall be put to death,' and the curse is described as the result of a son or daughter dishonouring father or mother in Deuteronomy 27:16.

This is serious. So how were the Pharisees dishonouring their parents? Jesus was aware that they were refusing to help them, from the context it appears financially, because that which could have been given to the parents was 'given to God' (verse 5), an offering to Him. Both in the money given as an offering to God (which was likely to win them much appreciation in the Temple), and in the ritualistic hand-washing, the Pharisees were claiming a special understanding of the Torah, the law of Moses Interpreted by the Mishnah, which evidently the disciples of Jesus did not have.

But Jesus recognises, and tries to explain to them, if only they would listen, that in so doing they were nullifying the Torah altogether, for they were over-interpreting it, and in so doing were actually emptying it of its essential content. The love of God for His people and His desire that they should love one another and perhaps especially older members of their own family, was the greater commandment. And together with the commandment to love the Lord their God with all their mind, soul and body, all others were rendered subordinate to it. This the Pharisees failed to understand.

This is why Jesus reminds them of Isaiah 29:13-19. 'These people honour me with their lips, but their heart is far from me; in vain do they worship Me, teaching as doctrines the precepts of men' (Matthew 15:8,9). What a terrible indictment of all that the Pharisees are doing. He says, 'in vain do they worship me.' There was no substance in all that they sought to do in the temple, and in the synagogues, nothing that God could describe as worshipping Him. They have subordinated the love commandment of Deuteronomy 6:4, 'You shall love the Lord your God, with all your heart and with all your soul and with all your strength', all that comes from the heart towards God and their fellowmen, into an empty, formulaic system. This was transgression of an extremely virulent kind.

This system, like their misunderstanding of the Sabbath in chapter 12, makes nonsense of what they regard as their special relationship with their God, and leaves them open to all sorts of ritualistic practice which will never give them peace of mind. Under this system, they will never know when they have done enough, and will never have a heart satisfied by the welcoming presence of God.

And not only were they themselves not satisfied, but they were laying this dreadful burden on the shoulders of others. Jesus had so much to say to them concerning this in chapter 23.

Meanwhile, the disciples were intrigued by Jesus' words concerning cleanness and defilement. He had called the people to Him (verse 10) to explain to them why He called the Pharisees hypocrites, people who speak one way and act another. He had diagnosed them as having made void the word of God by their traditions (verse 6), and made clear that what defiles a man is not what goes into the mouth, but what comes from it (verse 11).

Perhaps the disciples were worried that the Pharisees were offended by what Jesus was saying. But Jesus was not concerned about the Pharisees' attitude towards Him, for He was only too aware of their desire to destroy Him (12:14), and was leaving it to His Heavenly Father to root up every plant which He had not planted (verse 13). This unconcern He recommends to His disciples. *'Let them alone,'* He said, 'they are blind guides, and if a blind man leads a blind man, both will fall into the pit' (verse 14); the terrible pit of the catastrophe of missing the will of God by failing to distinguish the unimportant from the necessary.

Peter persists however in asking Jesus about cleanness and defilement. The explanation which Jesus gives appears so logical and rudimentary. Jesus says, 'Whatever goes into the mouth passes into the stomach, and so passes on. But what comes out of the mouth proceeds from the heart, and this defiles a man. For out of the heart come evil thoughts, murder, adultery, fornication, theft, false witness, slander (verse 19). Quite a list! These are what defile a man, but to eat with unwashed hands does not defile a man' (verse 20). Jesus is not suggesting that the Pharisees are guilty of all these dreadful things, but that what is in the heart is expressed through what is said – and sometimes acted upon. How important is the heart before God! The Psalmist says (Psalms 108:1 A.V.) *My heart is fixed, O my God, fixed on Thee.* There may be times of testing, like Peter on the water, when faith wavers, but Jesus remains the guiding star, the light in which we walk, the knowledge of the love that surrounds us. We rest in Him.

But there is a warning too, for followers of Jesus. There has to be a distinction between what God has commanded in His word, and the additional habits which accrue to us and which we call 'Christian'. We justify the use of them by the interpretation we have given to the scripture, things we do because they are the Christian thing to do.

Christ has set us free from the law, which becomes the law of sin and death if we remain bound by it. Iconoclasm never did get rid of icons. Being eradicated from one area, they spring up in another. It is so easy for us to be seduced away from the truth, to find and employ substitutes for the living but invisible God.

The Pharisees did not have a monopoly on this. We humbly come to Jesus, and pray for Him so to fill us with Himself, that there is no room for anything that is not Him, that we are genuinely free from anything that would hinder our obedience to the love commandment, to love Him, and to love our neighbour as oneself. We were created for worship, only let it be the worship of the One, Triune, God, and not some imitation of Him. It is not a distinction between morality and ritual purity, as though the act of worship had some intrinsic value of its own, and it is not a rejection of that which makes worship meaningful, for there is much in the Torah, indeed in all the Old Testament, which is valid as an expression of worship. How often do we find ourselves going time and again to the Psalms, which put into words that for which we cannot find expression.

But in this there is a warning for followers of Jesus. Jesus came to fulfil the law, not even to re-interpret it, but to fulfil it (Matthew 5:17]), for He was the only one who fully obeyed it. There was no sin, no disobedience found in Him. In Him was life, and the life, a life of total obedience to His Father, was the light of men (John 1:4). And that life He came to give us. The question of purity, uncleanness under the law is superseded once again by Jesus' cry in Matthew 11:28. 'Come to me, all you who labour and are heavy laden!' In addition to all other burdens, Jesus takes away the burden of conformity to human traditions that do not carry the weight of the authority of God, and do not express His divine person and character, the character of unending, enduring, everlasting love. Then the words of Isaiah 29:13 will be reversed. Then we *shall* be people who *do* honour Him with our lips, and not only with our lips, but with our hearts in close proximity to His, as we worship Him.

This also takes away all the bases on which we judge others. We do not judge them on the grounds that they eat only vegetables (Romans 14:2) or esteem one day better than another (Romans 14:5) or abstain from food (Romans 14:6). Paul writes, let us not pass judgement on one another or put a stumbling block in the way of a brother, 'For I am persuaded that nothing is unclean of itself but it is unclean for anyone who thinks it is unclean... do not let what you eat injure the person for whom Christ died, for if you do so, you are no longer walking in love'. For the Kingdom of God is not food and drink, but righteousness and peace and joy in the Holy Spirit (Romans 14:17).

We cannot make what is clean or unclean for us a condition of fellowship with other believers. We welcome them and respect their conscience, because Jesus does. We identify ourselves with Christ within us, believing that He will take care of the asceticism, legalism, inclination to idolatry of others or ourselves, for we live by faith, the faith that sets us all free, free to love Him and love our brethren under the lordship of our One Lord.

None of us lives to himself and none of us dies to himself... whether we live or die, we are the Lord's (Romans 14:8) Rupert Baxter, a leading Puritan clergyman (1615-1691) wrote: *In essentials, unity. In non-essentials, liberty. And in all things, charity.*

Matthew 15:21-28. The faith of the Canaanite woman

And Jesus went away from there and withdrew to the district of Tyre and Sidon. And behold, a Canaanite woman from that region came out and cried, 'Have mercy on me O Lord, Son of David; my daughter is severely possessed by a demon.' But He answered her not a word. And His disciples came and begged Him, saying, 'Send her away for she is crying after us' (verse 21, 22).

The link between this episode and the previous one is not hard to find. The Pharisees had spoken of uncleanness of hands. Jesus had spoken of uncleanness of heart. In this narrative we discern the Pharisaic evaluation of a human being. Does he or she belong to the 'house of Israel' (verse 24) or are they Gentiles, and therefore pagan, and not entitled to the benefits of those who belong to Israel? This is the distinction made by the Pharisees. Nowhere is the woman described as unclean, but the impression given is of one who does not have the entitlement afforded to Jews.

Can this possibly be the view of Jesus? Jesus had a purpose in mind when He went away from what appeared to be Gennesaret, and withdrew to the district of Tyre and Sidon, on the Mediterranean coast, an area some miles northwest of Galilee in Syro-Phoenicia. This is why Mark calls her a Greek Syro-Phoenician woman (Mark 7:26). Phoenicia is the Greek equivalent translation of Canaan.

In both of the accounts, by Matthew and Mark, it appears that having healed her daughter, Jesus returned to Galilee, which would suggest that He made the journey to Tyre and Sidon, specifically for the needs of this woman, and to emphasise a new aspect of His teaching.

The word 'withdrew' also suggests this, for every occasion when Matthew uses this term of Jesus' activity, there is some fundamental reason for doing so. In Matthew 12:15, He withdrew from the Pharisees, who wanted to destroy Him. In 14:13 again He withdrew from the crowds so that He could commune with His Father. In this present instance, Matthew 15:21, again He withdrew from the debate arising from the conduct of the Pharisees so that He could heal the demon possessed daughter of a Canaanite woman. It has been suggested that on each occasion, He withdrew from fear of the Pharisees (see Luz p190). But surely this is not the case. Jesus is aware of the conspiracies of the Jews. He is not fearful, but the object of *their* fear and complete misunderstanding of who He is. His utter obedience to the will of His Father would preclude Him from doing anything that would deny His utter dependence on Him, whatever the circumstances. In Luke's gospel, we have the ultimate 'withdrawal'. In the Garden of Gethsemane, 'He withdrew from them about a stone's throw and knelt down and prayed, "Father, if Thou art willing, remove this cup from me, nevertheless not my will but Thine be done"' (Luke 22:41).

The woman needed Him and in obedience to His Father's will, He went to find her.

In the region of Tyre and Sidon, the woman came out to Him. She cried, saying, 'Have mercy on me, Lord, Son of David, my daughter is severely possessed by a demon' (verse 22). How extraordinary, that such a woman, presumed to be an outcast from Israel, should address Jesus not only as Lord, but as Son of David. She was recognising Him as the Messiah, She was saying, 'The Messiah is here! And He has the power and authority to heal my daughter!' But Jesus answered her not a word' (verse 23).

When He had healed so many who came to Him, including a Gentile centurion's servant in chapter 8:13, why did He not heal her daughter immediately? Why did He allow her to persist in crying after Him? (verse 23). Why did He not do as His disciples suggested and send her away? His answer to the disciples seems unutterably bleak as He says, 'I was not sent but to the lost sheep of the house of Israel' (verse 24).

Can this be the same loving, caring, healing Lord Jesus whom we have encountered in these first 15 chapters of Matthew's gospel? Has He ever before refused one who came to Him for blessing? And as she came and knelt before Him, prostrating herself in worship at His feet (verse 25), she was acknowledging His Lordship. But He said to her, 'It is not meet to take the children's bread and throw it to the dogs. '

He was making a distinction, the same distinction between her as a Gentile, and someone who was of the house of Israel, as the Pharisees had made, and also between themselves and the ordinary people; as though some people were more worthy of the mercy of God than others. So she was doubly excluded. She was a Gentile, and also 'ordinary' like the ordinary Jewish people, someone who did not follow the teaching of the Torah.

Jesus had indeed come for them, for the house of Israel, but He had come for her and her daughter too, what could be described as an 'ordinary' Gentile family, people who had not had the privilege of being born 'of the house of Israel'.

This Syro–Phoenician woman had dimly understood this. Nationality, race, does not determine our relationship with God. Jesus was using the example of children sitting at the table to represent Israel, and the little (Greek or Gentile) dogs who had probably come in from the street, looking for crumbs, which always fall from the table when children are eating.

Her reply was surely inspired. 'Yes Lord, yet even the dogs eat the crumbs that fall from their master's table.' The bread may not be on the table, but it is the same bread, though in crumbs, and equally acceptable as life-giving food. She was not seeking a place at the table, but only the privilege, the right, to partake of the crumbs.

Then. How wonderful to her was that 'then'. Then Jesus answered her and said, 'O woman, great is your faith! Be it done for you as you desire.' And her daughter was healed *instantly* (verse 28), healed by the mighty power of love for her and her mother. Nothing more is said of the disciples' reaction, but surely they learnt an unforgettable lesson. *No one,* whether Jew or Gentile, or whatever their background, is beyond the reach of the love of God. That is the *first* lesson. And the *second* was this. Jesus' plan of salvation extended far beyond the boundaries of Israel, both geographically and spiritually. It began with the Jews, for that was where Jesus was, and it reached far down the avenue of time to include Gentiles. Long ago, God had promised to Abraham that through his posterity, all the nations of the earth would be blessed (Genesis 12:3, Galatians 3:3), and He never breaks His promise.

This mighty and life-giving plan of salvation, reaching down through the ages, this *heiligeschict*, holy history, is exemplified by one mother and her concern for her daughter in a remote part of Palestine, but a mother who was not afraid to acknowledge that she had seen in this itinerant preacher the longed for Messiah, and was not afraid to identify herself as a little dog under the table searching for crumbs if that meant sharing in what the Messiah had come to give.

No wonder Jesus said, 'O woman, great is your faith!' (verse 28) She had seen something which the disciples had failed to see, though she was a Canaanite, a Gentile, an outcast, in Pharisaic terms, unclean. Her faith *'great faith'* (verse 28) had saved both her and her daughter and provided an insight, a revelation, to the disciples.

Her faith in Jesus as Lord and Son of David is confirmed by the concrete experience of the healing of her daughter. Undoubtedly encouraged by the woman's faith, Jesus later created another table, a table at which all could eat of the Bread that He provided, the bread which was His Body, broken for all who come to God by Him.

Matthew 15:29-39. The healing and feeding of the four thousand

And Jesus went on from there (from the region of Tyre and Sidon) and passed along the Sea of Galilee. And He went up on the mountain, and sat down there. And great crowds came to Him, bringing with them the lame, the maimed, the blind, the dumb, and many others, and they put them at His feet, and He healed them (Matthew 15: 29, 30)

It appears that having returned to Galilee from the Gentile Syro-Phoenicia to which He had gone for the exclusive healing of one little girl and the spiritual enlightenment of her mother, Jesus now goes up on to the mountain and sits down there. He is the Teacher at rest, waiting for His disciples to come to Him.

But what actually came was the crowds, 'great crowds' Matthew tells us. Perhaps they were wanting to learn from Him, but wanting even more the relief of His healing power on those they brought with them. The precious refrain echoes throughout Matthew's gospel, 'And He healed them' (verse 30). Not one person would have left that mountain unhealed, or suffering from lameness, or still crippled, or blind, or deaf, or dumb.

He healed them all, as many as needed Him. They had been put at His feet to signify His Lordship and as their Lord, He healed them all and they worshipped Him. 'And they glorified the God of Israel' (verse 31).

This phrase 'the God of *Israel*' has been interpreted by some biblical scholars to indicate that these people were Gentiles for whom the God of Israel was not automatically acknowledged as their God. Jesus, 'passing on from there' (verse 29) that is, from Tyre and Sidon, to the Sea of Galilee, would have arrived at an area where there were many non-Jewish settlements along the eastern shore of the Sea of Galilee, and that the crowd who glorified the God of Israel were not themselves of Israel (Hill p 55).This phrase therefore established a Gentile setting to the incident. If this is so, it is typical of Matthew's gospel that Jesus should move from one Gentile woman and her daughter to four thousand Gentile people, all needing His healing and HIs compassion.

Only in Matthew and Mark is the feeding of the four thousand mentioned, emphasising the Christological significance of Jesus as King in Matthew, and Jesus as the Servant in Mark. How grateful we are that God has given us in His word these different aspects of the ministry of His Son. *Jesus, the Servant King.*

If they were indeed a Gentile crowd, this could be an anticipation of the mission to the Gentiles which occurred after Pentecost, following the commission of Jesus to the disciples as He ascended back to heaven after His resurrection to be with His Father. 'Go therefore and make disciples of *all* nations' (Matthew 28:19) He said to His disciples as He was taken back into heaven, and this is what they did after they had received the Holy Spirit on the Day of Pentecost.

The feeding of four thousand Gentiles anticipates the Gentile mission, as the feeding of the five thousand had anticipated the gathering in of the Jewish people in chapter 14:13-21; those who were open to Jesus, those who were *'the remnant'* spoken of by Isaiah in 6:13, 10:37, 37:32, in Jeremiah 44:12 and by Paul in Romans 9:27, 11:5. Those Jewish people, the remnant, who had come by faith in Christ into the Kingdom of

God, into the family of God would be part of the marriage supper of the Lamb in Revelation 19:7. God has not cast off His people whom He foreknew (Romans 11:2).

But God also had a place for the Gentiles. Jews and Gentiles, all together, all one, all ransomed, healed, restored, forgiven, living in the love of God the Father and of His Son, Jesus Christ. Neither Jew nor Greek, neither bond nor free, but all one in Christ Jesus (Galatians 3: 28).

This is what was in the heart of God. And this compassion for the crowds was in the heart of Jesus, for what was in the heart of God was in the heart of Jesus too. 'I have compassion on the crowd, because they have been with me now three days, (that was how long it had taken to heal all these people), and have nothing to eat, and I am unwilling to send them away hungry, lest they faint on the way' (verse 32). Even though the geography of the place, and their reaction to Jesus, were indications that they were Gentile people, Jesus had compassion on them.

Once again, the disciples baulk at the task of feeding so many. Is it possible that Jesus had made a mistake? Although they had been with Him at the feeding of the five thousand, surely He can't go on feeding people like this? And anyway, where is He doing to get the food from? And doesn't He know that these people are Gentiles?

Jesus' answer is so simple. 'How many loaves have you?'

Did it matter whether these people were Jews or Gentiles? Yes, it did. The disciples needed to learn that Jesus' love extended to everyone, of every tribe and nation. He came to seek and to save the lost, not only the lost sheep of the house of Israel, though He had come for them first (Matthew 15:24), but the lost of every nation, every generation.

So, in the same way that He had fed the five thousand, He fed the four thousand. With seven loaves and a few small fish in His hands, He gave thanks to His Heavenly Father, broke the food and gave it to His disciples to distribute to the waiting people, seated on the ground (verse 35). And they all ate and were satisfied (verse 39). And they took up seven baskets full of the broken pieces left over (verse 37), broken in the hands of Jesus as He gave them what they needed to enable them to get back to their homes, surely saying to each other, 'We have seen great things today.'

And Jesus, sending away the crowds, got into a boat and went to an unidentifiable place called Magadan (verse 29).

This was the second time such an event as the feeding of a large number of people had taken place. When something is doubly reported in the scriptures, especially when it concerns the Lord Jesus, it is doubly important, 'Take note of this.'

This story therefore reveals four things. Firstly, that Jesus is full of compassion for any group of people, Jew or Gentile, not as a group, but as individuals within the group. Every person within this crowd received individual healing and individual sustenance for the journey home, even though they were part of a greater number. The individual matters to God.

Secondly, that for Jesus; compassion is not abstract, but is demonstrated concretely, physically as He feeds them with 'real' bread and 'real' fish, and by His healing power takes away real disability, real pain, real discomfort.

Thirdly, that He has passed this compassion on to His disciples. Whatever their personal views had been as to what was to happen, they engaged in the work that Jesus had given them to do, out of compassion for those who had been with Him for three days and had nothing to eat.

And so fourthly that compassion led to obedience. Whether Jew or Gentile, whatever their background or status in society, these people were hungry, a basic human need which Jesus was able to satisfy out of His compassion for them through the cooperation of His disciples. Leadership in the church that He is building must always be on the ground of compassion. Without compassion, leadership becomes manipulation.

How much Jesus was teaching His disciples, and how much do we need to learn from Him. 'Learn of me,' He said, 'for I am gentle and lowly in heart, and you will find rest for your souls' (Matthew 11:29).

Matthew Chapter 16

Matthew 16:1-4. Another demand for a sign

And the Pharisees and Sadducees came, and to test Him they asked Him to show them a sign from heaven. He answered them, 'When it is evening you say, "It will be fair weather, for the sky is red." And in the morning, "It will be a stormy day for the sky is red and threatening." You know how to interpret the appearance of the sky, but you cannot interpret the signs of the times (Matthew 16: 1-3).

It appears that Jesus went alone in a boat to the region of Magadan (chapter 15:39), and that the disciples did not join Him until verse 5 of chapter 16, having crossed the Sea of Galilee to meet Him.

Meanwhile, the Pharisees and the Sadducees came to Him, seeking a sign from Him to test Him. Though the Pharisees and Sadducees were hostile to each other, holding different interpretations of scripture particularly over resurrection (Acts 23:8, Matthew 22:23), yet on this occasion they came together against a common enemy, Jesus, just as they had against John the Baptist in Matthew 3:7.

Some of the scribes and Pharisees' (Matthew 12:38) had already asked Him for a sign from heaven, a cosmic sign. Whether these were the same Pharisees who had formerly come to Him along with their scribes, and now came accompanied by Sadducees, we cannot determine, but their question was the same, and Jesus' reply was the same. He says, 'There shall no sign be given this evil and adulterous generation but the sign of the prophet Jonah'; the sign that as Jonah was in the belly of the whale for three days and three nights until he was delivered by God; in this way providing an image of death and resurrection; so Jesus too would be 'three days and three nights in the heart of

the earth, but would come forth from death to resurrection'
(Matthew 12:40).

This, Jesus knew, would not be enough to satisfy them, for
they had developed a habit of interpreting their scriptures to
suit their own preconceived ideas and prejudices (Matthew 12:3-
8). So He called their attention to something they did regularly.
By observing the sky, they were able to forecast what the weather
would be, a fine day or a stormy one.

Jesus' comment was, 'You know how to interpret the
appearance of the sky, but you cannot interpret the signs of the
times' (verse 3).

They asked for a sign from heaven. What they really needed
to see was not some cosmic happening, but what God was doing
here and now before their very eyes; and what Jesus had told
them about what His Father was going to do in the future,
beginning with the sign of Jonah; the life of Jesus, His death and
resurrection, progressing to the revelation of His power and
glory and judgement at the end of time.

Of course, He had not yet died and risen again. That sign
will be given to them in the future. But everywhere around Him
were the signs of His Messiahship. *He was the Messiah,* sent
from God to His people. They knew the scriptures. Could they
not see in Him the fulfilment of them? Many of the ordinary
people did as He healed them and fed them and had compassion
on them.

But He was bringing in a new age, a new era, a time of change
to the status quo. He offered to them a place in the new kingdom,
for He excluded no one. But as He had already told them, the way
into the kingdom was through repentance and faith, a complete
turn-around from everything they had ever known.

This they could not do. They felt they had too much to lose.
Jesus said, 'Whoever loses his life for my sake will find it'
(Matthew 10:39). It was a huge step to take, to lose one's life, to
lose all that one holds dear and upon which he or she has built a
life whether as a simple artisan, or a fisherman, or a mother of a
family, or a Pharisee. But the reward of knowing and following
Jesus is great.

Jesus' compassion extended even to these enemies of His, for this was one of the principles of the kingdom. 'Love your enemies' (Matthew 5:43). These are decisive days for the Pharisees and Sadducees, just as they had been for the Ninevites in the time of Jonah, who had repented at the preaching of Jonah (Matthew 12:41). If they could but see it, Jesus was Himself the sign.

Jesus now left them and departed (Matthew 16:4). He would not speak to them again until He had left Galilee and travelled to Judea (Matthew 19:3). He continued compassionate, but they continued obdurate, and He was still thinking about them when the disciples rejoined Him, according to verse 5.

Matthew 16:5-12. The leaven of the teaching of the Pharisees and Sadducees

When the disciples reached the other side, presumably by boat, 'they had forgotten to take bread' (verse 5). Jesus said to them, 'Take heed and beware of the leaven of the Pharisees and Sadducees.' And they discussed it among themselves saying, 'We brought no bread' (Matthew 16:5-7).

Presumably too, they had not supplied themselves from some of the bread left over from the feeding of the four thousand, for all that food had been given to the people to take home to their families, a not inconsiderable gift given the circumstances endured by many of the poorer people of Jesus' day. He said, 'The poor you always have with you' (Matthew 26:11).

How surprised they must have been when Jesus said to them, 'Take heed – listen carefully – beware of the leaven of the Pharisees and the Sadducees' (verse 6). Associating the word 'leaven' with 'bread', they said, 'It is because we have forgotten to bring bread.'

Though it is impossible to believe that Jesus was exasperated, how sad He must have been at their lack of understanding. They had been with Him at the feeding of the four thousand. They had been with Him at the feeding of the five thousand.

How could they not perceive that He was not talking to them about bread, bread He could so easily provide for them if it was within His discipleship of them, but about leaven, the leaven of the teaching of the Pharisees and Sadducees?

As we saw in the parable of the Kingdom of Heaven, of the woman who took leaven and hid it in three measures of flour until the whole was leavened, (Matthew 13:23), leaven was a neutral substance, neither positive nor negative, but had the capacity to represent both (1 Corinthians 5:8). But in this case, Jesus was warning them against the teaching of the Pharisees and Sadducees, a much greater problem than lack of bread.

As Jesus had demonstrated in His teaching about the Sabbath in chapter 12:1-8 and the washing of hands before eating in chapter 15:1,2; and especially when compared with the greater transgression of not honouring one's parents, the 'tradition of the elders' was not based on love or mercy (15:2; 12:7). Thus, Jesus says, the Pharisees, the scribes and the Sadducees had made void the word of God. They had emptied it of its main and most important constituent, love; the love of God for His people, and the yearning of His heart that they should love Him with all their heart, mind and soul, and should love each other as themselves (Deuteronomy 6:4).

This is the leaven, the teaching of the Pharisees, which Jesus wants His disciples to beware of, the leaven of not honouring the character of God by whose Word they believed themselves to be living. Above everything, this was HIs desire, that they should love one another as He loved them (John 15:12). Apart from Him, we can do nothing (John 15:5), but His love has been shed abroad in our hearts by the Holy Spirit, who has been given to us, and would be for them if they had come to Him in repentance and faith (Romans 5:5).

The teaching of the Pharisees and Sadducees is destructive leaven, because it is entirely and totally antipathetic to the teaching of Jesus, and His love, compassion and concern for all who come to Him. The teaching of the pre-eminent Teacher, Jesus, runs contrary to all that these religious leaders taught. Discipleship, learning from and of Him, both then and now, means sitting at His feet, listening to Him, and rising to transform His words into deeds, His words of love into deeds of love. The leaven of the teaching of the Pharisees and Sadducees was destructive because it was empty of the character of God, of His love for His people, of His faithfulness, of His mercy, attributes of God seen and made apparent throughout their scriptures and yet unrealized by them. How different was the teaching of Jesus.

Matthew 16:13-20. The second 'Son of God' confession and the promise to Peter

Now, when Jesus came into the district of Caesarea Philippi, He asked His disciples, 'Who do men say that the Son of Man is?' And they said, 'Some say John the Baptist, others say Elijah, and others, Jeremiah or one of the prophets!' He said to them, 'But who do you say that I am?' Simon Peter replied, 'You are the Christ, the Son of the living God' (Matthew 16:13-16).

And Jesus answered him, 'Blessed are you Simon Bar-Jona! For flesh and blood has not revealed this to you, but my Father who is in heaven. And I tell you, you are Peter, and on this rock I will build my church, and the powers of death (Hebrew R.S.V.), the gates of Hades (Greek) shall not prevail against it (verses 17, 18).

Here we have a different location. Caesarea Philippi was situated on the slopes of Mount Hermon, and near the source of the River Jordan. As an area, it was associated with apocalypticism, a place of revelation and a meeting place for the upper (mountainous) world, and the lower (watery abyss) world (Hill p262).

The city Caesarea Philippi was built by Herod Philip and named Caesarea in honour of the Roman emperor, and the addition of Philippi distinguished it from the other Caesarea, the seaport on the Mediterranean coast. It was situated 25 miles north of the Sea of Galilee (Hill p259; Gundry p329). This was a long way for Jesus and the disciples to travel on foot, but it gave an opportunity for much teaching from Jesus for the disciples and an opportunity for them to be with Him and their fellow disciples.

Just as Matthew 13 had been a pivotal time in the teaching of Jesus, so now in chapter 16, we reach another pivotal moment in Jesus' earthly life, and a complete declaration of what He will experience in the days to come (verse 21) days which would have their own impact on the lives of the disciples.

There is a sense that the drama is drawing to its close. Jesus is on a predetermined path, determined from eternity. He lives His life in utter dependence and obedience to the will and purpose of God, in the foreordained salvation and redemption of men and women back to Himself. It is the will of His Father in heaven that governs every moment of Jesus' life.

After this revelation, the disciples can never be the same again, especially when they see Him transfigured before them on the mountain in chapter 17:2. Yet they still have much to learn in the time they have left with Jesus before these things come to pass.

As they come into the district of Caesarea Philippi, Jesus says to them, 'Who do *men* say that I am? That I, the Son of Man, am?' (16:13). They tell Him that some, including Herod, believe that He is John the Baptist risen from the dead; others believe that He is Elijah, for had not Elijah gone straight to heaven in a chariot of fire without dying? Making it easy for him to return? Yet others would think He was Jeremiah, restored to them, that great prophet who defied all the religious and political leaders of his time; or even one of the other prophets of Israel, unafraid to speak out the word of the Lord to His people, even when it was unpopular, in an effort to remind them that they were in a covenant with Him as their God, and to seek to bring them back into a holy relationship with Him.

Though this was of course, nothing but speculation by the people, yet it was revealing. It showed that they were taking Jesus seriously, in the limited fashion of which they were capable.

But the disciples were different. They had lived close to Him, seen Him in ways which other people had not, and in close personal proximity to Him had discovered that He was indeed all that He claimed to be, Son of Man, Son of God. So perhaps it was no surprise to them when He said, 'But who do *you* say that I am?' (verse 15).

Apparently without hesitation, Simon Peter replied, 'You are the Christ, the Son of the living God.'

And Jesus answered him, 'Blessed are you, Simon Bar-Jona! For flesh and blood has not revealed this to you, but my Father who is in heaven' (verse 17). 'And I tell you, you are Peter, and on this rock I will build my church, and the gates of hell shall not prevail against it' (verse 18).

The question of Jesus' identity is an important one. Jesus has been fond of His self-referential title, Son of Man, God revealed as one with His people, humanity and deity in perfect balance. But from now on, He uses it only when speaking to His disciples. Now, they will see more of what and who He is. He has already declared in chapter 11:22, 'No one knows the Son except the Father, and no-one knows the Father except the Son, and anyone to whom the Father chooses to reveal Him.' It is always a matter of revelation.

Peter's confession, 'You are the Christ, the Son of the living God,' has not come to him through logical deduction, or rational analysis. It has come to him by revelation. Jesus says, 'Flesh and blood, human endeavour, human ability, has not revealed this to you, but my Father in heaven (verse 18). How blessed you are Peter! It seems that their heavenly Father is never far away from what is going on in the hearts and minds of the disciples as they walk and talk with Jesus.

The knowledge that Jesus is the Son of God comes only by divine revelation. The disciples on a boat in a storm, rescued by Jesus as He walked on the water towards them, also worshipped Him saying, 'Truly you are the Son of God' (Matthew 14:33). This too was revelation of a distinct kind, bound up in the miraculous stilling of the storm; 'The wind ceased' (14:32).

Peter's was not a greater revelation. He had been in the same incident, the same boat with Jesus as He entered it. This revelation, however, was more explicit. 'You are the Christ, the Messiah, the Anointed One, for so long foretold by the prophets. The coming One has come! And you are the Son of the living God! God alive and dwelling with us, Immanuel, God with us! All this is implied by Peter's answer. And Jesus said to him, 'You are Peter, Petros, and on this rock, Petra, I will build my church, and the gates of hell will not prevail against it' (verse 19).

Discussion of the import of these verses is a well-known phenomenon which has gone on for many years, and interpretation of them reveals the interpreter's theological predilection. We must receive our interpretation from the text itself and not from another's interpretation of it. However, it is well known that the Roman Catholic church recognises Peter as the 'rock' upon whom Jesus says He will build His church, and because we do not lightly reject that church's interpretation of Matthew 16:18, we need to look at these verses openly and without prejudice, bearing in mind that the strength of any hermeneutical study relies upon the witness of the entire gospel, and indeed, the whole of the New Testament.

There is a distinction to be made between, *'You are Peter,* and upon this rock I will build my church,' Jesus' words in verse 18, and Peter's confession of faith in verse 16, *'You are the Christ,* the Son of the living God.' The distinction lies in where the emphasis falls. 'You are Peter'/'You are the Christ.' Peter's confession brought forth from Jesus the words, *'Blessed are you,* Simon Bar-Jona' (verse 17).

In what did Peter's blessing consist? Surely that to him had been given a revelation from the Father in heaven concerning the identity of the Lord Jesus, 'You are the Christ, the Anointed One, the Messiah, the One who should come, the Son of the God who is living, who has life in Himself and passes that life on to His Son, living, active, purposeful God. Alive and well and living in us through Jesus.'

What an astonishing revelation!

Protestant believers regard Peter's confession as the rock upon which Christ builds His church, and so great is this confessional foundation that all the powers of death and hell ranged against it cannot overcome it or prevail against it. All the 'gathered out' ones who comprise the Ἐκκλησία, the church, are safe, protected by the purposeful building of His church by Jesus. It is not the church of Peter, but the church of Jesus, and the New Testament bears witness to this, Paul even describing the Rock as Christ in 1 Corinthians 10:4.

Historically then, we turn to the subject of the papacy. The Roman Catholic Church, as we have observed, regards the Bishop of Rome, the Pope, as a successor to Peter. Peter was understood to be the representative disciple, the first among equals, the first among his brethren who became the bishop of Rome.

Origen, (c.185-253/4 A.D.) an early church father, understands Peter as the prototype disciple who comprehended the building of the church.

Tertullian c.160-240 A.D., who together with Origen c.200-248 A.D. and Cyprian were the three North African fathers of the western churches, also interpret the authority given to Peter, the keys of the Kingdom of Heaven (Matthew 16:19) as a mark of high office in the church. But not until the post-Constantinian period (Constantine c.273-337) of the mid to late third century was the Roman congregation legitimated with Matthew 16:17-19. By the third century, Rome was the capital of a powerful empire. The church in Rome was large and important. It was the centre of Christian orthodoxy. It had the tomb of Peter. And it was a divided church.

The political climate of the time encouraged and required a monarchical head of the church, corresponding to the hierarchical structure of the empire. A rupture had occurred in the church. Under one head, the church could be united again (Luz p370-373). Only relatively late were the beginnings of the supremacy of the Roman church and its bishop connected with Matthew 16:18. It was a new interpretation, and in reality was a retro-legitimising of the Roman claim to leadership in the church.

It has often happened that the shape of Protestant churches too has been determined by historical accidents and not by the Bible. How often and how easily has the church accepted conditions and evaluations of people and circumstances without discussion or reference to scripture even though it claims the principle of 'sola scriptura'. There are examples even in our own time.

The papal interpretation of Matthew 16:18 remains only one among others. Peter as the Bishop of Rome could be accepted. But the conferring of this eminence upon *future* bishops of Rome as under apostolic succession was not acceptable either to Eastern or Reformation churches, preferring the interpretation which speaks of Christ as the fundamental rock of the church, the foundation on which it is built, and Peter's confession of faith as compliant with it.

Augustine (354-430 A.D.) writes that upon this foundation Peter himself was also built. For indeed, no one can lay another foundation besides that which has been laid, which is Christ Jesus (1 Corinthians 3:11). Peter is not the rock upon which the church is founded, but in an account of the primacy of the apostleship, he serves as the representation of the church, says Tertullian.

Matthew 16:19. Christian leadership

Christian leadership is exemplified by Peter, but not only Peter, but by all the disciples in the authority given to them by Jesus (Matthew 18:18). If we accept that Peter is the rock, the foundation of the church, the community, we are declaring that Jesus built His church on Peter. It becomes Peter's church, not the church of Jesus.

To interpret the 'rock' as something *other* than Peter's person, that is, on that which was *revealed* to him, makes Jesus, the Christ, the Son of the Living God, as Peter confessed, both the head of the church and its foundation, with which the teaching of the New Testament agrees (1 Corinthians 3:10-17; 1 Peter 2:6-7; Ephesians 2:20). Jesus is the Rock!

Peter declares 'Thou art the Christ!' 'Christ' has already appeared in Matthew's gospel, in Matthew 1:1,2; but Matthew

16:18 is the first time His title has come to open expression by Jesus' disciples. 'Christ' is unquestionably a high title for Jesus, recognising His essential deity as the Anointed One, the Messiah; and Peter's additional title for Him as the Son of the living God declares an annunciation of His particular place in the Godhead; as the One through whom the redemption of sinful men and women is assured. How quickly after Pentecost, Jesus is referred to by the disciples as Jesus Christ, indicating not just a kind of surname for the Lord, but a recognition of the saving grace of God wrought through Him (Acts 2:31,36,38; 3:6,18,20; 4:10).

The church, happily and with adoration and worship, confesses Him as the Christ, the Son of the living God. And to Peter is given the keys of the Kingdom of Heaven (verse 19). Jesus has already spoken of the 'gates of Hades' (verse 18). It is not for these gates that Peter is given the keys, but the gates of the Kingdom of Heaven. We sometimes sing of Jesus, *He only could unlock the gates of heaven, and let us in.* So what does this authority given to Peter signify?

It may be possible to understand it in conjunction with the commission which Jesus gave to Peter on the seashore after His resurrection. 'Feed my lambs' (John 21:15), 'Tend my sheep' (John 21:16), 'Feed my sheep' (John 21:17). The lambs and the sheep have come to the sheep fold. How are they to get in? Peter is there with the keys. He is the facilitator, more importantly, he has been given a shepherd heart. He provides for them, helps them, encourages them. The sheepfold is a microcosm of the church. Jesus says, '*My* lambs, *my* sheep.' Peter is looking after those with tender loving care those who, like him, have come to recognise in Jesus, the Christ, the Son of the living God.

But Jesus is going back to heaven to be with His Father, and so He has entrusted His servant with the shepherd heart to represent Him here on earth; opening up the Kingdom of Heaven to all believers.

Perhaps it is no accident that the Bishop of Rome is called Pope, Father, as representing the Father heart of God. This is what Peter is being called by Jesus to do in chapter 16 of

Matthew's gospel, just as he will be on the seashore after Jesus' resurrection. A shepherd heart, a father heart, a servant heart. This is the pattern of all Christian leadership, exemplified by Peter, but not only him, for all the disciples were given the authority to 'bind' and 'loose' in chapter 18:18.

Jesus says to Peter, 'Whatever you bind on earth shall be bound in heaven, and whatever you loose on earth shall be loosed in heaven. This appears to be an extreme delegation of Jesus' authority. Whom or what shall they bind? Or loose?

To the disciples has been given the gift of discernment, of discerning where the kingdom lies, how it is operating in the lives of men and women, not only as a glorious freedom and liberty from all that previously bound them, but as a spiritual enabling and principle for all future living, a new life. Life in the kingdom is life with the King, a life such as they had never before known. But for some, maybe for many, there could be obstacles in the way of fully entering into the glorious liberty of the children of God (Romans 8:21). Perhaps they could not fully repent, or fully believe or were fearful of the impact of such a decision not only on their lives, but on the lives of others for whom they had responsibility. Matthew 13:22 speaks of the cares of this world and the deceitfulness of riches which choke the word of the gospel. These things, among others 'bind' men and women to the earth, and to the disciples Jesus is giving the ability to recognise through the discernment given to them that this is so, and this is ratified in heaven.

But there will be others who live 'loose' to this world's goods and values. And the disciples will discern that this decision on their part to live wholly for the kingdom on earth will also be ratified in heaven. Heaven is the seal, the rubber stamp that what takes place here on earth is recognised and taken account of in heaven. And the disciples, and Christian leaders, have a part to play in this guidance and exhortation for they are those whom Jesus has appointed. Peter is not alone in being given a shepherd heart. To all the disciples was given the mediating role of compassion and encouragement and guidance and to rebuke where necessary, that which would 'bind' people and prevent them from coming to faith, to proclaim that through the gospel, Jesus has the power to deliver men and women from the dominion of darkness, and transfer them to the kingdom of His beloved Son (Colossians 1:13).

How could Christian leadership exist without that discernment? And how important that they should live under the authority of 'Christ, the Son of the living God' (verse 16). And this, not for them only, but for all who love Him and seek only to do His will.

Matthew 16:20. The command to keep silent

Then He strictly changed the disciple to tell no one that He was the Christ (Matthew 16:20)

Did He not want people to know that He was the Christ? Yes, of course He did. But just as the revelation had come from God the Father to Peter and to the other disciples, so He wanted this knowledge of HIs appointed position as the Christ of God, to come to those who were seeking God through revelation; seeking as they were for the joy and peace which only Jesus could give as the Anointed One, the Messiah, the Christ; seeking for Him, in their lives, in their daily experience; Jesus being revealed to them in all His fullness as the Christ. He wanted this glorious truth to come to them through revelation so that they could enter all that He had for them. Their prayer would be 'open my eyes, Lord, I want to see Jesus'.

The people had seen the miracles that He did. They had seen the fulfilment of Isaiah 61 before their eyes. 'The Spirit of the Lord is upon me, because He has anointed me to bring good tidings to the poor. He has sent me to bind up the broken hearted, to proclaim liberty to the captives and the opening of the prison to those who are bound... to comfort all who mourn...' (Isaiah 61:1, 2).

He had told them that the sign of Jonah was the sign of the intervention of God in human history, God speaking again through His servant just as He had in the time of Jonah, God speaking to the Ninevites on the grounds of resurrection, of risen life. But here is something greater than Jonah for the Lord Jesus transcended all the prophets including Jonah. Though Jonah had been in the belly of the great fish for three days and three nights, God had provided for him a way of escape through the fish spewing Jonah out upon the dry land, an allegory of resurrection. Jonah was resurrected to human life. Jesus was resurrected to sit again at the right hand of the Father, from which happy position He could once again distribute life and light and love and joy and peace to all those whom He had chosen, and who had chosen Him (John 15:16).

A greater than Jonah was here, in front of them. But the revelation as to His identity as the Christ came from His Father, from a personal encounter with 'the Son of the living God', God in His mercy meeting the emergent, compulsive desire of a man or woman for an unveiling to their own heart of the satisfaction of new life in Jesus. To tell the people that He was the Christ would have pre-empted the revelation. It would have been of the head, not the heart, for when Christ enters, He comes not only as Saviour, but as Lord, Jesus the Anointed One, Christ (Matthew 1:1, 21). And through the operation of the Holy Spirit, God does the ever-astounding miracle of bringing men and women into fellowship with Himself.

Matthew 16:21, 22. The Suffering Servant

But as always, there was a cost involved.

> From that time, Jesus began to show His disciples that He must go to Jerusalem, and suffer many things from the elders and chief priests and scribes, and be killed, and on the third day be raised (verse 21). And Peter took Him and began to rebuke Him saying 'God forbid, Lord! This shall never happen to you. But He turned and said to Peter, 'Get behind Me Satan! You are a hindrance to Me; for you are not on the side of God but of men' (Matthew 16:22).

For many of us, our reaction would have been the same as Peter's on hearing these terrible words, a total abhorrence that this could possibly happen to this One whom he had grown to love so dearly. Ignoring the promise of the resurrection, Peter took Him and began to rebuke Him, saying, 'God forbid Lord! This shall never happen to you!' not knowing what he was saying.

Jesus was preparing His disciples for what was to come. He knew that the way would be hard for them, as well as for Himself. Only a few years later, in 44 A.D., Herod laid violent hands upon some who belonged to the church and killed James the brother of John, and son of Zebedee, with the sword (Acts 12:1). Jesus knew that following Him would be a costly undertaking. But that was the way He had to go, not for them only, but for the redemption of the whole world. Perhaps they had forgotten the words which John the Baptist had spoken when they first saw Jesus, 'Behold the Lamb of God who takes away the sin of the world' (John 1:29). But to stand in His way was the work of Satan, the adversary of God, for that is what Satan means. Satan would do all he could to frustrate the purposes of God, and would even seek to use this precious disciple as an instrument, distorting even his love for his Master as a weapon against Him.

Which is why, at this moment in time, Jesus could say to Peter, 'Get behind me, Satan. You are a hindrance to Me, for you are not on the side of God but of men' (verse 23), for He knew the wiles of the devil and how he was trying to use Peter to obstruct God's plan of salvation.

Jesus has a sure way of dealing with this. And He expands and repeats for all His disciples what He had previously intimated to them in His discourse on discipleship (Matthew 10:38). 'If any man would come after Me, let him deny himself and take up his cross and follow Me. For whoever would save his life will lose it, and whoever will lose his life for My sake, will find it. For what will it profit a man if he gains the whole world, but loses his soul? (A.V.) Forfeits his life? (R.S.V.). Or what shall a man give in exchange for his soul, life? Do not fear those who kill the body, but are unable to kill the soul, but rather fear Him who is able to cast both body and soul in hell (Matthew 10:28).

This amazing transaction which had gone on in the lives of the disciples is replicated in the lives of all those who would seek to follow the Lamb wherever He goes (Revelation 14:4), to take up His cross and follow Him. Do we save our lives or lose them for His sake? A choice which many have had to make as the ultimate choice, but which has reverberations in many of the lesser decisions for believers, perhaps on a daily basis. Do we deny ourselves or indulge ourselves? Do we embrace the effect of the Cross on our lives or reject it? What does it really mean to take up His cross and follow Him? (Matthew 10:38). What is the cost of true discipleship?

The cross indicates suffering. There is a strong thread running through these verses linking the suffering of Jesus to the suffering of the disciples to the final coming of the Son of Man (Mathew 16: 21, 24, 27, 28). This is the totality of discipleship, an acceptance of what it means to suffer for His sake, (Matthew 16:25), but also *looking ahead* to the coming of the Son of Man in glory with His angels (Matthew 16:27); *then* a period of judgement (Matthew 16:27), and *finally* the promise that some among them 'will not taste of death until they see the Son of Man coming in His Kingdom' (Matthew 16:28).

From the beginning of this section of the gospel, from verse 13 to verse 28, the emphasis on *the Son of Man* has been a framework, for it speaks of His humanity. He is the Son of God, yes, and how precious to us is the knowledge of His deity. He was, and is, God, but He was also Man. 'Who do men say that I, the Son of Man, am?' says Jesus (Matthew 16:13). And in these last verses of the chapter, Jesus again uses the title. 'The Son of Man is to come with His angels' (Matthew 16:27), 'The Son of Man coming to His kingdom' (Matthew 16 28). How precious to Jesus appears to be this His own title, Son of Man, comprehending all His earthly life and His great mission of salvation for all who believe. The Kingdom of God becomes the Kingdom of the Son of Man; Jesus has announced to His disciples His suffering, death and resurrection, and He will repeat it several times before HIs arrival in Jerusalem (Matthew 17:12, 22, 20:17-19).

Matthew says, 'From that time' (verse 21), from that specific point in HIs ministry, Jesus began to show HIs disciples that He must go to Jerusalem and suffer many things from the elders and chief priests and scribes. Although this has been divinely ordained, it does not remove the culpability from the Jewish leaders, who out of their own fear of Him and their malice towards Him are planning His execution. But as always, there was a cost involved. From that time, Jesus began to show His disciples that He must go to Jerusalem and suffer many things from the elders and chief priests and scribes, and be killed, and on the third day be raised (Matthew 16:21).

So Jesus repeats and expands for all His disciples, not just Peter (though including and exonerating Peter for He knew the battle for men's souls which goes on), those words which He had previously said to them in His discourse on discipleship (Matthew 10:38). 'If any man would come after me, let him deny himself, say no to himself and take up his cross and follow me. For whoever would save his life will lose it, and whoever loses his life for My sake will find it.'

Jesus is aware of the future coming distress, both His and theirs, and out of compassion for all that will come upon the disciples when these things come to pass, He wants to show His disciples, firstly what will happen to Him, and secondly that He willingly and knowingly goes that way in obedience to His Father's will and on behalf of all mankind. It is important that they understand that He is in control of the situation at all times; that nothing that will happen either to Him or to them is outside His Father's overseeing of all things.

Nevertheless, there is now a shadow cast over Matthew's narrative, the shadow of the Cross.

Peter had replied to Jesus' declaration of His future suffering, 'God forbid, Lord, this shall never happen to you!' (verse 21). 'God will be merciful to you! He will never allow this to happen to you!'

This is what we often feel about the suffering of fellow Christians. This suffering cannot be of God! He would never allow His servants to suffer in this way! Suffering is part of the human condition on so many levels: hunger, poverty, illness, disability, bereavement, persecution historically and still extant in many places of the world and even at home. But suffering for a Christian is part of the discipline which a disciple undergoes, spoken of in Matthew 16:24; but defined by Jesus as the taking up of the cross becomes an altogether different experience.

Paul writes in Romans 8:17, 'If children, then heirs, heirs of God, and joint-heirs with Christ, provided we suffer with Him, in order that we may be glorified with Him'. We do not suffer on our own, we suffer with Him. And especially when we suffer with others, we identify their pain as our own as together we look to Jesus. Paul again writes, 'I consider that the sufferings of this present time are not worthy to be compared with the glory that is to be revealed to us' (Romans 8:18). And the writer to the Hebrews concludes, 'My son, do not regard lightly the discipline of the Lord, nor lose courage when you are chastened by Him, for whom the Lord loves He chastens' (Hebrews 12:5).

That which befalls all humankind also comes to Christians. They are not immune from the trials and tribulations of the world, living in a little bubble of being special to God. They have suffering to endure like others, and in some cases, persecution for their faith as well. Paul, in his second letter to Timothy, is very plain. He says, 'If we endure, we shall also reign with Him. If we deny Him, He will also deny us. If we are faithless, He remains faithful for He cannot deny Himself' (2 Timothy 2:12). This is the mercy of the Lord to us, that we can trust Him completely to bring blessing out of sorrow, good out of evil, peace out of fear.

Our whole attitude to the suffering, the problems and the difficulties of this present life is changed. It is an opportunity to lean yet more on the everlasting arms of our heavenly Father, Deuteronomy 33:27, the arms of our Lord underneath us, protecting, supporting, loving us, to experience once more that God is our refuge and strength, a very present help in time of trouble (Psalms 46:1). Taking up one's cross is not some trivial annoyance, but something we suffer for His sake, believing in

His perfect will, bound up in His eternal love, trusting that through it all we are brought closer to Him, the precious reality of being a disciple, a believer, a child of God. We may not literally take up the horizontal bar of a cross, carry it through the streets from the place of judgement to the place of execution, enduring the insults of people along the way as Jesus did. Any suffering we may endure will certainly not have the redemptive power of the Cross of Jesus upon whom at His crucifixion came the sins of the whole world. But Jesus knows what we suffer. He says, 'I have said this to you that in Me you may have peace. In the world you will have tribulation, but be of good cheer, I have overcome the world' (John 16:33).

Matthew 16:24. Christ's invitation to 'come and die' (Dietrich Bonhoeffer)

Then Jesus told His disciples, 'If any man would come after Me, let him deny himself, and take up his cross and follow Me. For whoever would save his life will lose it, and whoever loses it for My sake will find it. For what will it profit a man if he gains the whole world and forfeits his life? Loses his soul? Or what shall a man give in exchange for his life, his soul?'

Jesus calls us to take up our cross and follow Him, for He knows about the identification of our spirits with His, the life that He gives being the only life that has eternal value because it lives in the hope of His coming glorification. And the instrument which performs this miracle is the cross which we take up, in our total surrender to whatever He has in mind for us, to His praise and glory.

May the Lord enable us to 'take up the cross' for His sake (verse 25). The gaining of the whole world is not to be compared to it (verse 26). We offer up our suffering to Him as an oblation of worship, and in return He gives us Himself.

Jesus is looking forward, forward to the Cross, but also forward to the coming of the Kingdom of the Son of Man. Without the Cross, there would be no way forward, but three times we see a reference to the Son of Man; the *angels* of the Son of Man (verse 27), the *Father* of the Son of Man (verse 27) and the *Kingdom* of the Son of Man (verse 28). Through His humbling of Himself, claiming no equality with God but taking upon Himself the form of a servant, being found in fashion as a man, Jesus as Son of Man has inaugurated the Kingdom of Heaven, and has also inaugurated a company of believers who are beginning to know the glorious humiliation of being like Jesus through the transforming power of taking up their cross and following Him.

There will of course be a final enactment of that glorious kingdom of which He speaks in Matthew 24. But even now, the disciple can look forward to the Son of Man coming into His Kingdom after His resurrection, when the Holy Spirit is poured upon His waiting church, when the Royal Commission is about to be fulfilled. 'Go *therefore* and make disciples of all nations' (Matthew 28:19), 'Go *into all the world* and preach the gospel' (Mark 16:15), and, 'Lo, I am with you always, even unto the end of the world, the close of the age' (Matthew 28:20).

'Truly', Jesus says, 'Amen I say to you, there are some standing here who will not taste of death before they see the coming of the Son of Man in His Kingdom' (Matthew 16:28). They were that close to the coming of the Kingdom. On that very first day of the outpouring of the Holy Spirit, the Day of Pentecost, there were added to them about three thousand souls (Acts 2:41). We do not know when the final glorious consummation is to be. But we do know that it is nearer than when we first believed. Even so, come Lord Jesus (Revelation 22:20).

Matthew Chapter 17

Matthew 17:1-8. The transfiguration of Jesus

The event of the transfiguration of Jesus has become so familiar to us, that perhaps we have lost the impact that such an event should have. These verses should be read on the knees of the spirit. It speaks of our beloved Jesus, robed in the glory which He had with His Father before the world was. The disciples were allowed to have a glimpse of that glory, the glory He had before He took upon Himself the likeness of a man. No wonder they fell on their faces and were filled with awe and fear, and needed the touch of Jesus upon them before they could rise.

After six days, Jesus took with Him Peter and James and John, his brother, and led them up a high mountain apart. And He was transfigured before them, and His face shone like the sun, and His garments became white as light (Matthew 17:1, 2).

After six days, after a week (this is presumably the seventh day) when the disciples had had an opportunity to digest all that Jesus had said to them on the way to Caesarea Philippi of His person, His suffering, His death and resurrection, Jesus takes three of His disciples up a mountain.

This is variously identified as Mount Hermon, or Mount Tabor, but as is usual with Matthew, the actual mountain is not significant. What is significant is Jesus' purpose in going up to a place apart, for it is necessary for them to see His glory, and it is necessary for them to hear the voice of His Father acknowledging and substantiating all that Jesus is and has been, not only from the beginning of His ministry when He had submitted Himself to be baptised by John in the River Jordan, but from the beginning of time. 'In the beginning *God*' (Genesis 1:1), 'In the beginning was the Word, that which was the dissemination of God from God Himself, and the word was *with* God, and the word *was* God' (John 1:1). And they called His name, Jesus.

Jesus had fully fulfilled His destiny and purpose as *the Son of Man,* in His total activity as Healer and Teacher. His whole life had been given in compassionate service to others. And He knew there was much more to come in terms of suffering and death. But God the Father had seen all this and more. Jesus' self-designation as Son of Man was very precious to Him. But the voice that came from heaven proclaimed, 'This is *my beloved Son,* with whom I am well pleased. Listen to Him' (Matthew 17:5). Jesus is not only the earthly Son of Man, tremendously important though that is. He is also the exalted Son of God.

'Son of Man' is a horizontal title. It speaks of Jesus as He lives among men and women, drawing them to Himself, into the fellowship with His Father that He enjoys, so that they can pray 'Our Father', giving them new life, eternal life. It expresses His desire for the universal experience, for all people everywhere, out of every kindred tribe and nation, that they shall come into the glorious Kingdom of the reign of God.

Jesus is the Son of Man.

He is, however, also 'Son of God', a vertical title. It allows us another perspective, lets us see Him in His divinity, to see the progress of Him who came down from heaven, the earthly Jesus, through His Cross and Resurrection to His Exaltation as Judge and Ruler of the universe in awesome majesty.

Jesus is the *Son of God,* God Himself revealing Jesus as the Son of God.

God had already revealed this to the disciples on the stormy sea when Jesus came to them walking on the water. 'Truly' they said as they worshipped Him, 'Truly, you are the Son of God' (Matthew 14:33). He had also revealed this to Peter on the road to Caesarea Philippi, and Peter had confessed 'You are the Christ, the Son of the living God' (Matthew 16:16).

This was a different kind of revelation on the mountaintop. Jesus was transfigured, changed, metamorphosed before them. This was a different Jesus from the one they knew and loved. No wonder they were afraid as they entered into the cloud that overshadowed them. They saw their Lord clothed in dazzling white raiment, His face shining like the sun. When Moses and Elijah joined Him, Peter's immediate response was to offer to build three booths, three dwelling places, one for Jesus, one for Moses, and one for Elijah. Once again, he had completely misunderstood *the* purpose of what Jesus was doing.

Both Moses and Elijah, on Mount Sinai and Mount Carmel respectively, though differently, had mountain top experiences; Moses at the giving of the law to the people of Israel, Elijah as he took on the battle for the souls of the people against the idolatry of Baal (Exodus chapters 19, 20; 1 Kings 18). These humble servants of God, whom He had used for the enlightenment of His people, also had a different experience of death. Moses was buried by the Lord somewhere 'in the land of Moab opposite Beth-peor and no-one knows the place of his burial to this day' (Deuteronomy 34:6). Elijah was provided by the Lord with chariots of fire and horses of fire, and 'went up by a whirlwind into heaven' (2 Kings 2:11).

But God had foreordained for Jesus, His Son, His beloved One, something completely unique.

Luke tells us that Moses and Elijah appeared in glory and talked with Jesus, speaking of His departure, His exodus, which He was to accomplish at Jerusalem (Luke 9:31). They were there to encourage Him and support Him in the tremendous ordeal which awaited Him. Jesus was not going to be whirled away like Elijah, or buried in an unknown grave like Moses. What Jesus was going to accomplish was the salvation, the redemption of the whole world, to restore a fallen humanity to God's original purpose: that God should have a family of sons and daughters like His own dear Son; that Jesus should have His church, His Bride whom He could love and cherish; and that the Holy Spirit would have the wonderful task of so working in the lives of men and women that this could all be brought to fruition as He glorified Jesus.

Luke also gives us the insight that Peter suggested the three booths, 'not knowing what he said' (Luke 9:33), for Moses and Elijah were not in any sense going to be living permanently on the mountaintop. Their lives of obedience and service to God on earth were over, and we do not know what function they enjoyed in heaven, although we can speculate that it involved worship. They were returning to heaven. They were evidence that there was life after death even though they had not been resurrected as Jesus was going to be.

But the fulfilment of Jesus' life was yet to come, what is described as 'His exodus which He was about to accomplish at Jerusalem'. The waters of death, like the Red Sea of Moses' experience, would not overwhelm Him. The evil forces of sin and idolatry and faithlessness to God which was challenged by Elijah on Mount Carmel would not overwhelm Him. That which the Father had determined would come to pass.

Matthew tells us that while Peter was yet speaking, still considering what could be done for the heavenly visitors, a bright cloud overshadowed them (verse 5) and a voice from the cloud said, 'This is my beloved Son, with whom I am well pleased. Listen to Him.'

So powerful was this voice that the disciples fell on their faces to the ground in fear and awe. This voice which came from the glory of the cloud enveloping them was still ringing in their ears, when a touch and a voice which they knew and loved, someone whom they could see without fear came to them saying, 'Rise, be not afraid' (verse 7). This is no longer the heavenly, transformed, transfigured Jesus. They 'lifted up their eyes, and saw no-one but *Jesus only*' (verse 8), their 'normal' beloved companion and friend.

Moses and Elijah had fulfilled their function and departed. Just as Jesus had spoken to his disciples of the prophet Jonah in terms of resurrection life, so now the living presence of Moses and Elijah, also 'resurrected' to their heavenly existence, reinforced Jesus' teaching that His rising again after death was not only possible but certain. The disciples needed to know that the suffering and death which He would undergo would not be the end. Like all human beings, they knew about death, may even have experienced bereavement in some sense themselves. But they had not experienced resurrection. This was a concept totally unfamiliar to them.

Jesus was allowing them to see that death was not the end for Him. He would overcome death for death had no power over Him as the *Te Deum* has it. 'When Thou hadst overcome the sharpness of death, Thou didst open the kingdom of heaven to all believers' (*B.C.P. Morning Prayer / Matins*). Death could not hold Him. Hell could not hold Him. We worship a living Lord who has overcome sin and death, who is now alive and reigns with His Father and the Holy Spirit, and who will come again and receive us to Himself that we may be with Him forever. 'Therefore, comfort one another with these words' (1 Thessalonians 4:18).

Matthew 17:9-13. Coming down from the mountain

And as they were coming down from the mountain, Jesus commanded them, 'Tell no man of the vision until the Son of Man is raised from the dead.' And the disciples asked Him, 'Then why do the scribes say that Elijah must first come?'

The transfiguration of Jesus was not just a vision, an hallucination, a theophany such as Abraham experienced in Genesis 18, or Moses in Exodus 3, or Jacob in Genesis 28, or Gideon in Judges 6, or the parents of Samson in Judges 13, or Ezekiel in Ezekiel 2, or Daniel in Daniel 9, or others throughout the Old Testament.

This was real, a real seeing of Jesus transfigured, transformed before then, a real cloud overshadowing them like the Shekinah, which stood over the Tabernacle In the wilderness (Exodus 40:34), the cloud which protected the children of Israel as they journeyed through the wilderness, and guided them to the Promised Land (Exodus 40:36).

And it was a real voice speaking to them. The disciples, Peter and James and John had been given the privilege of seeing Jesus as God saw Him, the reality of who Jesus is; and hearing the voice declaring that He was the Son of God.

Confused, ecstatic but happy, they came down the mountain with Him. But Jesus told them to tell no-one what they had seen 'until the Son of Man be raised from the dead' (verse 9).

This was too precious a revelation to be made a common thing to be talked about, discussed, interpreted, questioned, re-interpreted, denied, explained away. It could not be allowed to be as it was on the day of Pentecost when the disciples were accused of being full of new wine, although it was only nine o'clock in the morning, when what they were full of was the Holy Spirit. Jesus says that after His resurrection, which Jesus again reminds them is going to happen, then they may speak of this that they have not so much experienced as endured. How wise is Jesus in all His dealings with them. He knows that when they see His resurrection Body, the impact on them will be great, but there will at least have been preparation for Peter, James and John, preparation for an even greater transfiguration.

Going over in their minds all that had happened, the disciples were intrigued by the presence of Elijah on the mountaintop. The scribes, experts in the law, had said that before the Messiah comes, Elijah must first come (verse 10). And because they believed that Elijah had not yet come, it followed that Jesus could not be the Messiah. But Jesus says, 'I tell you that Elijah has already come, and they did not know him but did to him whatever they pleased' (verse 12). Then they understood that He spoke to them of John the Baptist, that John had taken on the mantle of Elijah and become the forerunner of the Messiah (Malachi 3:1; 4:5). And Jesus warns them that just as John had suffered at their hands, so also would He, the Son of Man suffer (verse 12).

Though unrecognised by the Jewish leaders, the plan and purpose of God would go forward. There would always be some who mocked, scorned, doubted and tried to frustrate the purposes of God, but ultimately, they would not succeed, for *His purposes cannot fail. He is God.*

It is *necessary* as Jesus says in chapter 16:21. He *must* go to Jerusalem and suffer many things, and it is a *certainty* that He will do so. The Son of Man will suffer at their hands (17:12) but God is in control. Through it all His will will be achieved because of the love that He has for all mankind, and because of the Son who is utterly obedient to His will. Jesus says, 'I and my Father are one' (John 10:20). Perfectly one in power and love, and righteousness. United in their love for One Another, and for the fallen race of mankind.

The voice from Heaven said, 'Listen to Him' (17:5), 'to the Son of Man who is also Son of God, revealed in glory on the mountain top, who is prepared for humiliation and suffering, but who will not dwell in a booth on a mountainside, distinct from those He came to save, but who will dwell in their hearts and lives. For He also said in His prayer to His Father, 'I in them and Thou in Me.' I pray for those who believe in Me through their (the disciples) word, that they may all be one, even as Thou Father art in Me and I in Thee, that they also may be in Us, so that the world may believe that Thou hast sent Me, and hast loved them even as Thou hast loved Me' (John 17:22). And all made possible through the Cross.

No wonder the Psalmist wrote, 'Such knowledge is too wonderful for me. It is high. I cannot attain unto it' (Psalms 139:6).

In Colossian we read 'for in Him dwells all the fullness of the Godhead bodily: And you are complete in Him', or 'for in Him the whole fullness of the deity dwells bodily: and you have come to fullness of life in Him' (Colossians 2:9. A.V.; R.S.V.). 'And having spoiled principalities and powers, He made a show of them openly, triumphing over them in the Cross'. He disarmed the principalities and powers and made a public example of them, triumphing over them in the Cross (Colossians 2:15 A.V.; R.S.V). This was what happened as Jesus hung on the Cross. Paul makes it very personal. He says the Son of God who loved me and gave Himself for me' (Galatians 2:20). And every believer is entitled to have the same testimony.

αμήν λέγω υμίν

Matthew 17:14-21. The epileptic child

And when they came to the crowd, a man came up to Him and kneeling before Him said,' Lord, have mercy on my child, for he is an epileptic and he suffers terribly; for often he falls into the

fire, and often into the water. And I brought him to your
disciples and they could not heal him (Matthew 17:14, 15).

The transfiguration of Jesus had been an unforgettable experience for these three disciples. Peter is still living in the good of it when he wrote in his second letter that they had been eyewitnesses of the majesty of the Lord Jesus Christ when He received honour and glory from God the Father, and heard the Voice which was borne to him on the Majestic Glory. 'This is my beloved Son, with whom I am well pleased' (2 Peter 1:16, 17).

Perhaps Peter and James and John would have loved to stay on the mountainside with Jesus. But how could they, as created beings, live for long in uncreated light, the possibility of a recurrence of the pure white light from which they had been protected by the overshadowing cloud. Could they live in the presence of a God who might continually break out in glory, the glory of His Son whose face shines like the sun, even whose clothes are radiant?

Besides, at the bottom of the mountain, something extraordinary had been going on, which required that the Lord Jesus should once again appear as One among us, no longer clothed in glory but a Man like any other man, and yet how different.

And when they came to the crowd, a man came up to Him, and kneeling before Him said, 'Lord, have mercy on my son, for he is an epileptic and suffers terribly; for often he falls into the fire, and often into the water. And I brought him to your disciples, and they could not heal him' (17:14-16)

God had been speaking of His Son. How poignant that this man should be speaking of his son; that special relationship between Father and Son, between father and son.

There is a much fuller treatment of this narrative in both Luke and Mark (Luke 9:37-43 and Mark 9:14-27), where the emphasis is on the healing of the epileptic boy. In Matthew, the real centre of the story focuses on faith, faith in the compassionate Son of God, and in His delegated authority.

Matthew's abbreviated, more concise version of this episode begins with Jesus coming down from the mountain to the crowd (verse 14) followed by the father bringing his epileptic son (verse 15) and ending with Jesus casting out the demon (verse 18). In addition, there is the father's statement about the inability of the disciples (verse 16) and Jesus' response of reproach to them (verse 17).

We now have a medical explanation for epilepsy. In antiquity, it was regarded as a 'holy' illness, a state of being possessed by a divine power. This later became possession by any supernatural power, including demons, and in the Palestine of Jesus day, this was the explanation given. Jesus was content to go along with the contemporary theory, for His purpose in healing the boy was not just for the relief of the boy and his father, important though that was, but also to reinforce all that He had taught His disciples earlier of the meaning of faith and their exercise of the authority He had delegated to them in chapter 10:1. The healing of this damaged child gave Him the opportunity He needed, and besides, He never missed an opportunity to exercise His compassion on all who were troubled or sick in body or in mind. Not only the boy, but his father, longed for the miracle that apparently only Jesus could perform.

The disciples, the nine left at the bottom of the mountain, clothed though they were with Jesus' authority, and no doubt full of compassion for the child, could not heal him, (verse 16) could not give him relief from his terrible suffering. 'For often he fell into the fire and into the water' as the father thus described his son's suffering. But compassion alone was not enough' (verse 15).

Jesus curtailed the father's plea for mercy by turning to His disciples. His tone was harsh and penetrating, as it needed to be, yet we hear behind the words He spoke something of the sadness He must have felt that they had so soon neglected to live in the good of all the authority He had given them.

This was not peculiar to them. Jesus gave the same rebuke to the two disciples on the road to Emmaus after His resurrection. 'O slow of heart to believe, to understand' (Luke 24:25), and had we been there, it is doubtful whether we would have been any different.

Bring him to Me,' said Jesus. And Jesus rebuked the demon and it came out of him, and the boy was cured instantly' (verse 18), causing the disciples to come to Him privately and say to Him, 'Why could we not cast it out?' (verse 19) Jesus had already spoken to them after the father's heartbroken cry, 'I brought him to your disciples and they could not heal him' (verse 16). Jesus had turned to His disciples and said, 'O *faithless* and *perverse generation,* how long am I to be with you? How long am I to bear with you?' (verse 17).

We noted earlier that Jesus used the term 'generation' when speaking to the crowds who would not take seriously the preaching of John the Baptist, nor listen to the preaching of Jesus (Matthew 11:6). They were those who not having repented and believed the gospel, were faced with the alternative of facing the day of judgement; facing it moreover without the rest which Jesus grants to all who come to Him weary and heavy laden (Matthew 11:28).

Another use of Jesus' term, 'this evil and adulterous generation' (Matthew 16:4), refers to the Pharisees and Sadducees who could forecast the weather, but with all their education and knowledge of the scriptures, could not accept Him as the promised Messiah. Jesus would not accede to their demand for a 'sign from heaven' as a legitimation that He was indeed the One foretold by the prophets of old. The sign that would prove that He was indeed 'He that should come' was His rising again from the dead. They would eventually see their sign, though even then they would not believe.

Was Jesus then equating the disciples with the unbelieving crowd? Or the unbelieving Jewish leaders? The nine disciples who were left at the bottom of the mountain while Jesus went up with Peter, James and John had often seen the presence and power of God as Jesus had moved among the people. The father of the child had called Jesus 'Lord', κύριε, 'Lord, have mercy on my son' (verse 15). The disciples knew that He was indeed the Lord. How could they possibly assume that they could do the same as He had done so often? Yet Jesus had said to them, 'I give you authority over unclean spirits, to cast them out, and to heal every disease and every infirmity (10:1), followed by a list of every one of the twelve disciples whom He also called apostles (10:2), 'sent ones'. Not one disciple was excluded.

This was a crisis of faith for them all. It is obvious that they did not, could not, believe Jesus' word. He had given them authority, but they were afraid to use it. They were disobedient to His word. On that level, they were identified with the crowd of 11:6, and the Jewish leaders of 16:4. Disobedience is unbelief because it queries the authority of the person who gives the authority to act, and in so doing, also questions the delegation of that authority.

But all is not lost. They came to Jesus privately, saying to Him, 'Why could we not cast it out?' (verse 19). In this they were unlike the crowd and the Jewish leaders. They were all too aware of their failure, and this is the first step towards reinstatement.

And Jesus replied, 'Because of your little faith' (verse 20).

Did He really intend that they should heal the sick? Cast out demons? Did He mean what He said? They had repented and believed the gospel, they had entered into a relationship with God as their Father through the Lord Jesus, but it was not yet a wholehearted faith. They had not yet learned to cast themselves upon Him and His word, to trust Him utterly and completely no matter the outcome, to rely on His power in their lives, and not their estimation of His power and their own inability.

The father of the child had said, 'They were *not able* to heal him' (verse 16). The disciples said, 'We were *not able* to cast it out' (verse 19). Jesus says, 'If you have faith, *you will be able*. Nothing shall be impossible to you' (verse 21).

There will be a steep learning curve. Jesus says, 'How long will I be with you? How long am I to bear with you?' (verse 17). Their time with Him will be limited. Already He is warning them yet again of His approaching 'delivery into the hands of men' (verse 22) who will kill Him and He will be raised on the third day' (verse 23). No wonder they were greatly distressed (Verse 23). But He had given them a word of hope. 'Truly, *Amen,* I say to you, though you have only little faith, faith as a grain of mustard seed, you will say to this mountain, 'Move from here to there,' and it will move, and nothing will be impossible to you' (verse 21). It takes only a little faith to move mountains, whether literal or metaphorical, because the power lies *not* in the quantity of faith, but where the faith lies. The power always rests with God. After His resurrection, Jesus says, 'All authority in heaven and upon earth is given to Me' (Matthew 28:18), and then He says to His disciples, 'Go therefore' (verse 19). He is allowing them to cooperate with Him in His tremendous work of reconciling men and women to God, and this sometimes, perhaps often, requires the kind of faith that removes mountains.

It is the faith and not the mountain that is at issue here, the participation in the omnipotence, the power of God, not to display their faith, but as a witness to His *infinite* love and care and forgiveness. The whole of chapters 12, 13 and 14 of 1 Corinthians, Paul's wonderful exposition of the gifts of the Holy Spirit, the charismata χαρίσματα given to the church, rests upon one pronouncement, one sentence. *Jesus is Lord* (1 Corinthians 12:3). We cannot equate faith with power though faith is one of His gifts. Not everyone who has an inability to do miracles is of little faith; not every act of healing presupposes great faith on the part of the person who has been instrumental in the healing. *All comes under the Lordship of Jesus. Jesus is Lord.*

The gifts of God are His to give to whom He will (1 Corinthians 12:11), and the greatest gift of all is love (1 Corinthians 13:1-13). And the gifts are distributed by the *Holy Spirit*. The essence of faith is laying hold on the promises of God, both initially when we first come to Him, and subsequently as we walk with Him. What we cannot, He can do, and sometimes He allows it to be done through us.

Faith is believing in His absolute trustworthiness. 'God is not a man that He should lie, or a son of man that he should repent. Has He said and will He not do it? Or has He spoken and will He not fulfil it?' says Balaam in Numbers 23:19.

What He *says* He will do, He will do. *Because we know* that He loves us, *we believe* that all He says and does is for our blessing, and even for the blessing of others. We believe that all things work together for our good, the good of those who love Him (Romans 8:28). We are persuaded that nothing, *nothing*, can separate us from His love (Romans 8:38). So faith is grounded in love. Underlying all the authority that Jesus gave to His followers is the absolutely necessary, the absolutely essential gift of love. Love causes us to trust Him. It lets God be God. It allows His servants to be a channel of blessing to others as they live their lives in obedient faith, responsive to the claim of God's power to activate the impossible.

God is light and in Him is no darkness at all (1 John 1:5).

God is love, and they who dwell in God and God dwell in them (1 John 4:16).

These profound verses, from a mature and ageing beloved disciple, about to be incarcerated on the Isle of Patmos, summarise everything that Jesus is wanting to share with His disciples at the foot of the mountain.

The light which is God is *reflected* through Jesus, the light of the world, and then through His followers, for those who follow Him will not walk in the darkness but will have the light of life (John 8:12).

The love which is God is *personified in Jesus*, who took a towel and girded Himself and washed His disciples' feet so that they could learn to love one another even as He loved them. 'By this shall all men know that you are My disciples, if you have love one for another' (John 13:4, 14, 35). Mutual love, reflecting the love of the Father through the Son, to the loved disciples. *Agape love.*

Matthew 17:22-28. Jesus again foretells His death and resurrection

> *And as they were gathering in Galilee, Jesus said to them, 'The Son of Man is to be delivered into the hands of men, and they will kill Him, and He will be raised on the third day. And they were greatly distressed' (Matthew 17:22-23).*

This is a change of location. Caesarea Philippi is the far north of the country, where the River Jordan rises from Mount Hermon before flowing down to the Dead Sea, a most beautiful part of the country. Now Jesus wants to return to Capernaum, by the Sea of Galilee, for the last time before He goes on to Jerusalem. Galilee has always been important as a place of Jesus' healing and teaching activity, as the place of the calling of the disciples, and as the place where many had responded to His call for repentance and faith, and their entrance into a new relationship with God. He returns once more to Capernaum (verse 24). But His ministry in Galilee is soon coming to an end.

For the sake of His disciples, these words of Jesus concerning future events in Jerusalem are very clear, concise and decisive. He had already 'begun to show them' (16:21) that He must go to Jerusalem and suffer many things from the elders and chief priests and scribes, and be killed and on the third day rise again. He had reminded the three disciples on their descent from the mountain that this would be so. It will not be until chapter 19:1 that 'He went away from Galilee' but He takes the opportunity to remind them that the journey to Jerusalem is predetermined and will eventually come to pass. At the same time, He is in control of His own destiny, for apart from that which He will undergo in Jerusalem, it could be said that there was no need to go there.

He had formed a company of disciples, a group of leaders to whom He had given much teaching. Many others had come to accept His teaching as the way of life, built on compassion and love. Surely that was enough? A new ethics, a new way of behaving towards God and each other? And plenty of people through whom this wonderful ethical teaching could be implemented?

Matthew's gospel could have ended right there. Jesus had given us a wonderful example to follow. Could we not be content with that? Surely there was no need for Him to die? For His martyrdom? No, even a higher morality was not enough. Once again Jesus had to remind His disciples that He '*must* go to Jerusalem' (16:1). All that He had so far done for people was not enough. He was indeed 'the Lamb of God who takes away the sin of the world' (John 1:29) even as John the Baptist had declared when the disciples first saw Him. And knowing their scriptures they would have understood the reference to the *redeeming blood of the lamb* laid on the doorposts and lintels of the homes of the Israelites, so that they did not endure the loss of their beloved first born as did the Egyptians when the angel of death 'passed over' in Exodus 12. Or the many sin offerings and guilt offerings, animals offered in sacrifice as commanded in the book of Leviticus, especially on the Day of Atonement (Leviticus 16), when the sins of the people were laid on the scapegoat as he was sent away into the wilderness.

God was providing for His people, not a morality, or code of ethics, but a life free from sin, for 'without the shedding of blood there is no remission,' no forgiveness of sins (Hebrews 9:22). By the shedding of Christ's own blood, we have redemption, we are redeemed. By the blood of Jesus, God has opened up for us a 'new and living way' (Hebrews 10:19). We have been sanctified through the offering of the body of Jesus Christ once and for all (Hebrews 10:10). Sanctification through identification with Jesus.

How glorious is the reality of the Lamb of God, who is Jesus, going not into the wilderness, as had the scapegoat for the children of Israel, for He had already been there and overcome all the temptations of the devil, but to Jerusalem, the city where God had put His name, the city of Zion (1 Kings 8:9, Psalms 132:13). Jesus said, 'It cannot be that a prophet should perish outside of Jerusalem' (Luke 13:33). Jesus was a prophet, for a prophet is one who conveys the word of the Lord to the people in the name of the Lord. But He was more than a prophet, significant as that aspect of His ministry was. He was the Son of the Most High God, and only He could suffer and perish in Jerusalem, bearing upon Himself the sin of the whole world, reconciling men and women to God, and subsequently taking His place as the Lamb upon the throne (Revelation 5:6, 12).

Just as He loved the title 'Son of Man' while on earth, it is indubitably so that He also loves the title 'Lamb of God' in heaven as He continues His work of redemption.

Although Jesus had already begun to show His disciples what was going to happen in Jerusalem, Matthew says, 'They were greatly distressed' (verse 23) indicating that they understood what Jesus was saying to them, and the implication yet again of two different worlds, the world of the Son of Man, and the world of men. He was 'in the world, but not of it (John 17:14-16).

As they were gathering in Galilee (verse 22) for the last time Jesus said to them, 'The Son of Man is to be delivered into the hands of men' (verse 22).This indicates an ambiguity. When Jesus says 'delivered', He could be suggesting human involvement, being delivered by human agency But He could also be suggesting divine intervention, being delivered according to the foreknowledge and plan of God. Isaiah 53:6 says, *'The Lord* has laid on Him,' His obedient servant, 'the iniquity of us all. This destiny which belonged to Jesus alone was the sure purpose and plan of God for the salvation not only of His chosen people but for all men and women of all time everywhere. 'God was in Christ, reconciling the world to Himself' (2 Corinthians 5:19 A.V.). And this supreme revelation is being given to His disciples; the will of the Father merged, melded together with the will of His beloved Son. 'Father, let this cup pass from Me. Nevertheless, not as I will but as Thou wilt', He said (Matthew 26:39).

What could we do with our sin if Jesus had not taken it away from us, nailing it to His Cross? (Colossians 2:1).

Matthew 17:24-27. The Temple Tax

When they came to Capernaum, the collectors of the half-shekel tax went up to Peter and said, 'Does not your teacher pay the tax?' He said, 'yes.' And when he came home, Jesus spoke to him first, saying, 'What do you think Simon? From whom do the kings of the earth take toll or tribute? From their sons or others? And when he said, "from others," Jesus said to him, 'Then the sons are free.' (Matthew 17:24-26).

Jesus and the disciples were going to spend one last time at home in Capernaum (Matthew 4:13). With what relief they must have entered the town after all that they had seen and heard, a respite from all the pressure caused by the needs of the ordinary people, even when they rejoiced with them over the new life, physical and spiritual, enjoyed by them after their encounter with Jesus. There was the pressure too caused by the malice and opposition of the Jewish leaders.

But for a time, they were going to be alone with Jesus, listening to His wonderful teaching as He spoke to them of their life together as a community, what has been described as the ecclesial discourse of chapter 18, the discourse concerning the gathered together ones, the church, the ἐκκλησία. But almost on the doorstep they were greeted by the collectors of the half shekel Temple tax, who went up to Peter and said, 'Does not your Teacher pay the tax?' (verse 24).

What may seem a simple question is actually loaded. This was the Temple tax introduced after the post-exilic rebuilding of the Temple at Jerusalem from 538-515 B.C. (Nehemiah 10:32) and was to be paid annually by all males over 19 years old. The distance to Jerusalem (from Capernaum to Jerusalem is 90 miles) and the cost of taking time off from their ordinary labour in order to visit the Temple meant that the people of Galilee were seldom able to make that journey, and some resistance was observable among the Galileans, that they should have to pay an annual tax for its upkeep, symbolic though it was of their Jewish faith, and proud as they were of their Jewish origins.

To the question of the tax collectors Peter replied 'yes', probably without any idea how they were going to raise what amounted to a substantial sum of money for men living on the fringes of poverty. Perhaps the earlier phrase applied to Peter could be true here, 'He knew not what he said' (Luke 9:33). But we prefer to think that he is beginning to believe that though he does not have the money to grant their request, yet Jesus would know what to do.

Jesus apparently knew that Peter had been questioned, and He had a question of His own for Peter. As Peter came into the home (verse 25), Jesus spoke to him first, saying, 'What do you think Simon?' (His lovely Semitic family name). 'From whom do kings of the earth take toll or tribute? From their sons or from others?' And when he said, 'From others,' Jesus said to him, 'Then the sons are free' (verse 26).

Almost without exception, Jesus' statements and questions have so much more behind them than appears on the surface. Here, Jesus is apparently claiming that because His disciples are not of the earthly present political scheme of things, but belong to another Kingdom of which they are the sons, they are free. They no longer have an obligation to pay toll, a local tax, or tribute, a state tax, or a tax to the Temple, an institution which is now regarded by Jesus as not part of the Kingdom of God; nor to the state, for this is to support a regime in opposition to all that the Kingdom of God stands for.

But though the sons of the Kingdom of God are free, Jesus says they do not give offence to the ruling power. Jesus says to Peter, 'Go to the sea and cast a hook, and take the first fish that comes up, and when you open its mouth you will find a shekel: take that and give it to them for Me and for you' (verse 27).

Peter did so, and the Temple tax was paid, and no offence to the Temple authorities given.

But what about the toll or tribute of which Jesus speaks? These are imposed by the state, as we have seen. Jesus is not only concerned with His disciples' attitude to the religious power, but also to that of the political power. *Because* of their sonship, as sons of God, and not as if they were 'sons of the kings of the earth', members of the ruling political family or its courtiers (verse 23), they are exempt.

But *because* they are sons of God, they submit to paying the temple tax, and the toll and tribute, in order not to give offence.

Time and time again, we see the principles which Jesus laid down in His first sermon, the sermon on the mount, enlarged and expanded and brought into the experience of these 'learners', these disciples. Jesus said, 'Love your enemies, do good to them that hate you, pray for those who persecute you' (Matthew 5:44; Luke, 6:27-28). The tax collectors had described Jesus as '*Your Teacher*', implying that even they recognised that there was likely to be a conflict between the task they had been given to do, and the behaviour recommended to His disciples by Jesus.

There was no conflict. Jesus is the Prince of Peace. He would not have His disciples look upon anyone as beyond His compassion and saving power.

But there is a greater offence, the offence of the Cross.

Σκανδαλισμένος, scandal, is the word used for the stumbling block of the Cross (1 Corinthians 1:25), the stumbling block to the Jews, and folly to the Gentiles, for those who will not believe. This is the offence, the stumbling block, the scandal, which separates men and women from God. Jesus will do for them all that He can, teaching them, healing them, and all that He does will be gladly accepted by them. But the Cross, that dreadful cruel place of torture, of suffering, of humiliation. Can they follow someone who in their eyes is so weak, so helpless, so ineffectual? The innocent victim of Jewish malice, of Roman cruelty? Who comes into Jerusalem, not as a warrior, a revolutionary, riding on a warhorse, but on a pitiful, humble donkey? It is laughable, even more, it is inconceivable that such a Person should claim to be all that the prophets had foretold of the Messiah that was to come.

To people who thought like this, the Cross, and Jesus upon the Cross, was a scandal indeed, and by the payment of the Temple tax the minor offence is contracted within the greater. Nothing but faith, the opening of the blind eyes, the work of the Holy Spirit in the hardened hearts of those who are disobedient, can set people free from such a misconception, and there will always be other stumbling blocks to faith. Jesus' words to Peter about the Temple tax have the merit of removing one of them.

The word of the Cross is folly to those who are perishing, but to us who are being saved it is the power of God and the wisdom of God (1 Corinthians 1:18).

Paul writes, 'I rejoice in my sufferings' (Colossians 1:24) and many have suffered for the sake of Christ, for the scandal of the Cross. Paul's principle of action was, 'I determined to know nothing among you except Jesus Christ and Him crucified' (1 Corinthians 2:2). Grounded in that assurance, he could 'press on toward the goal, the prize of the high calling of God in Christ Jesus' (Philippians 3:14). There is so much more for those who are prepared to go the way of the Cross with Jesus.

So, Jesus said, to Peter, 'Take the shekel you will find in the mouth of the fish and give it to them for Me and for you' (verse 27), so that we do not give offence to them. How much more serious is it going to be in the future when Peter has to confront the greater offence, the offence of the Cross, those who will not bow the knee to the One who has come to pour out His life for them upon the Cross.

Matthew Chapter 18

Matthew 18:1-35. The community discourse

At that time, the disciples came to Jesus saying, 'Who is the greatest in the kingdom of heaven?' And calling to Him a little child, He put him in the midst of them, and said 'Truly, I say to you, unless you turn and become like little children, you will never enter the kingdom of heaven. Whoever humbles himself like this little child, he is the greatest in the kingdom of heaven' (Matthew 18:1-4).

What is known as the community or ecclesial discourse is also the briefest discourse in Matthew's gospel. Exploring the gospel, we have come to recognise that each of the discourses of Jesus has its place within a narrative. Jesus' emphasis is always on discipleship, that is, learning. There is a superficial level of meaning in all that Jesus says and does, but there are deeper levels of understanding not immediately obvious which Jesus wants to reveal to His disciples.

Each discourse is set within the narrative of the life and ministry of Jesus, even as the narrative itself also conveys meaning. This discourse follows on from the episode of the Temple tax, during which Jesus had made a clear distinction between the Kingdom of God, and the kingdom of men, clearly describing the sons of God's kingdom as free. Prior to that, Jesus had been speaking of His death and resurrection, to the distress of the disciples. They already knew themselves to be separate from the world because of their relationship to Jesus. Soon they were to know the cost both to Him and themselves of that relationship.

This discourse offers them a vista of life beyond the cross, although only made possible through the cross. The cross for Jesus is not the end of the journey. Jesus has in view a community of those who have come into the good of all that He suffered; a gathered community, what became the church, not by any means always a perfect group of those who love Jesus, but sometimes as a community that struggles to live as those who are part of something so much greater than themselves.

It was God's design and intention that His Son should have a Body of ransomed, restored, forgiven people through whom His love could be demonstrated to the world; to whom He would be as a Bridegroom to His Bride, loving, cherishing her, sanctifying her, even as He had given up Himself for her (Ephesians 5:23; John 3:29).

This was not just an ideal, an aspirational way of conducting their lives for the disciples. This was working through, in the everyday ordinary circumstances of life, the principles that Jesus had given, and which became enlarged upon as together they sought to follow Him. It was important that each one *individually* should know and experience a relationship with the Lord Jesus, made real and actual by the wonderful cooperation of the Holy Spirit on the grounds of Jesus' death and resurrection. But it was also important that His disciples, and all followers of Jesus should recognise and enjoy the life they had *together*. It was one of the defining features of the believers after Pentecost, that 'they were together and had all things common' (Acts 2:44), caring for one another, worshipping together (Acts 2:45, 46). And the Lord added to their number day by day those who were being saved' (Acts 2:47).

Matthew 18:1 begins, 'At that time', or an alternative translation, 'In that hour', which had seen the return of the disciples to Capernaum, hoping eagerly to be able to settle down to hear the precious teaching of their Lord, for they longed to know more of what He taught them; and so this discourse is inaugurated by the disciples, and not by the Lord, although He had much to say to them about their future life together.

At that time, the disciples came to Jesus saying, 'Who is the greatest in the Kingdom of Heaven?' (Matthew 18:1).

If this had been their intention, to learn more from Jesus about the life of faith, what made them ask such a question? Was there some rivalry between them? Some jealousy, as some have interpreted it. Or perhaps we could more charitably regard it as wanting to be the best they could be for Jesus' sake? To be great for Jesus?

This gospel portrays Peter as a representative rather than as a dominant personality, and there is no indication that any one of the disciples regarded himself as greater than any other at this stage (but see Matthew 20:20). In addition, Jesus had been describing them *all,* in the previous discussion about taxation, as 'sons, free sons of the king' (17:26). Surely they do not now want to know about questions of rank, or hierarchy?

Jesus called to Him a little child and put him in the midst of them (18:2). Jesus always cared about children. He is not thinking only of His present audience, but of the larger audience that is to come in the future, when His followers form the church. This little child in the midst of them represents the humble members of that church, the ones with no power, no influence, nothing to recommend them save innocence, lack of pretension, unconcern with status, humility. Jesus says, 'Whoever humbles himself as a little child, he is the greatest in the Kingdom of Heaven' (18:3).

This is the condition for entry into the Kingdom and this is the condition of those who live in the Kingdom. There is no rank, only equality. One who has repented 'turned' (verse 3), 'changed direction and conduct, is the one who also becomes a little child, in humility. Humility is required in Jesus' name, because of Him; because He has commanded it. The 'little ones' of the church are the ones whom Jesus places in the midst of them as of special importance, because of their special quality of being in need of care and protection and the self-sacrificial love of their brothers and sisters. It is the privilege of others in the church to receive 'one of those little ones who believe in Me' (verse 6), because in so doing they receive Jesus. Not to receive one of these little ones or to cause one of these little ones to sin, receives such a reaction from the Lord as to suggest that a millstone be hung around the neck of the perpetrator, and that he should be thrown into the depths of the sea (verse 6).

This judgement truly reveals the seriousness of not receiving the 'little ones'. Though children were not regarded too highly in the world of Jesus' day, in contrast with the western culture of today, children were always loved by Jesus. He says, 'Whoever humbles himself like this child,' whom He had set in the midst of them, 'he is the greatest in the Kingdom of Heaven' (verse 4). Humility is of great value, perhaps of supreme value in the church of which Christ is the Head, the One who humbled Himself, and made Himself of no reputation even though He was Lord of all (Philippians 2:7). So Paul concludes, 'In humility count each other better than yourself' (Philippians 2:3).

Jesus recognizes that temptation to sin was not only a hazard for one of the little ones. Jesus says that temptation is a necessary concomitant to living. But woe to that man through whom temptation comes (verse 7). Though the temptation to sin may be inevitable, judgement on the one who tempts another is also inevitable. Even should they cut off the hand, or the foot, or pluck out the eye, which causes another to sin, this would be better than to endure the 'Gehenna of fire' (verse 8, 9) reserved as eternal punishment, separation from God. To sin oneself is serious enough, but to cause another to sin entails the greatest condemnation of all.

Such temptation may well lead a brother or sister in the church to stray and Jesus regards those who deliberately or inadvertently place such temptation in the way of others as looking upon the little ones with disdain, contempt, and despising them (verse 10). This is totally reprehensible to Jesus. Do these so-called disciples, members of His church, not understand, not realise, that the angels of these little ones 'always behold the face of my Father which is in heaven?' says Jesus (verse 11). In despising these little ones, they despise Him, they do not bring honour to His Name but contempt, and accusation against His protection of them.

Jesus continues, if a shepherd has a hundred sheep, carefully counting them into the sheepfold at night for protection from predatory wolves, and realises that one is missing, will he not search for the one that is lost, that has gone astray? And when he finds it, will he not rejoice over it more than over the ninety nine who never went astray? (verse 13). So your heavenly Father goes after those who go astray, for He is not willing that one of these little ones should perish (verse 14) Truly, I say to you,' says Jesus (verse 13). This is Jesus speaking with full authority. Truly, I say to you that these are reasons why you should not despise these little ones. And why they should be valued in the church. How greatly must their heavenly Father value them that He allows their angels to behold His Face! They are precious to Him, and therefore especially precious in the church (verse 10).

It is not only the little ones who may go astray (verse 12). Any member of the church, any brother or sister may sin against another. There may be a serious rift between them. How to maintain harmony in the church? Jesus says, 'If your brother sins against you, go and tell him his fault between you and him alone. If he listens to you, you have gained your brother (verse 15). This too requires humility on the part of both the one who had committed the sin, and the one against whom the sin had been committed, and is in no way an easy option. It requires, also, a level of trust in one another, and above all, it requires love between these brethren. Jesus' supreme desire for His disciples, the members of His church, was that they should love one another even as He loved them (John 15:12). So much so that they should 'abide', remain, dwell, *live in His love* (John 15:4, 12). As the Father has loved Me, so I have loved you, abide in my love. Continue in My love (John 15:9).

To have a rift between brothers and sisters is to have temporarily lost the bond that links them to each other. How necessary it becomes to go to one another in humility, trust and love in order to heal the breach. But what if the rift between them is so great that this approach fails? Then, Jesus says, take another brother or sister with you, a neutral person who will listen to both sides, who will weigh up the evidence and try to resolve the dispute between you; on the principle that at the mouth of two or three witnesses, every word may be established (Deuteronomy 19:15), and on the additional principle that you should love your neighbour as yourself (Leviticus 19:18).

It would have been better if the so-called wronged person had 'not let the sun go down upon their wrath' (Ephesians 4:26) but had been kind, tender-hearted, forgiving, even as Christ had forgiven them (Ephesians 4:32). But this is perhaps a counsel of perfection, and not many of us could claim to have got there. Perhaps some of us some of the time, perhaps all of us some of the time, but perhaps not all of us, all of the time.

But this situation is continuing and worsening. The person who has apparently sinned has not been willing to listen, either in the first place to the brother whom he has wronged, or the deputation of those who had tried to heal the breach between them. It has now become so serious that the matter has to be taken to the church.

This must be the extreme, the most extreme of any situation, that it has been allowed to get thus far. What kind of sin against one's brother or sister could provoke such a serious solution? Something that has to be resolved by the whole church? The sin in question is not specified. Would *forgiveness* on the part of the brother or sister, so hurt and wounded that the matter had been taken so far, have prevented such a situation arising? We remember the words of the Lord Jesus as He hung upon the Cross, 'Father, forgive them, for they know not what they do' (Luke 23:34).

O let us not be weary in well-doing for in due season we shall reap what we have sown. Let us sow to the Spirit, and let us not lose heart. (Galatians 5:9).

What Jesus desires above all for His church is that they should agree. 'If two of you agree on earth about anything they ask, it will be done for them by My Father in heaven. For where two or three are gathered together in My Name, there I am in the midst of them (verse 19, 20). Agreeing together before God is not a passive acquiescence to each other's ideas or practices. Such agreement could be detrimental to the life of the church, leading it into many different avenues of heresy and total misunderstanding, at best, of what the Lord has sanctioned in areas both of belief and practice.

Agreement by the church as they gather in love, and in the Name of Jesus, accepting His will and His guidance in all things, praying in His Name as they gather together, and recognising, rejoicing in the fact that He is in the midst of them; this is the practise which Jesus is encouraging for His sons, His daughters, His family, His disciples, the family of brothers and sisters, united in love to one another, and to Him.

Then Peter came up and said to Him, 'Lord, how often shall my brother sin against me and I forgive him? As many as seven times? Jesus said to him, 'I do not say seven times, but seventy times seven' (verse 21, 22).

Dear practical Peter, who so liked to get things right. He was right in calling Jesus 'Lord' and acknowledging the Lordship of Jesus. He was right in acknowledging that his fellow believers were his brothers, but how limited was his conception of forgiveness. But his question gives Jesus the opportunity to underline what He has been saying to them, that forgiveness is the key to a healthy, functioning, loving church community. Whatever sin my brother has committed against me, or I against him, both of us are in need of the loving forgiveness of the Lord. We need each other, we need Him. We could adapt Matthew 10:8 A.V. to read, 'Freely as you have received forgiveness, so freely forgive,' or repeat again with total sincerity, 'Forgive us our sins, as we forgive those who sin against us' (Matthew 6:12), the prayer which Jesus gave us. Forgiveness is the foundation of all the interaction which we have together as members of the church which is His body, the fullness of Him who fills all in all (Ephesians 1:23).

Beloved, let us love, for love is of God, and he who loves is born of God and knows God (1 John 4:7). He who loves not knows not God for God is love (verse 8) Beloved, if God so loved us, we also ought to love one another (verse 11).

Matthew 18:23-35. The parable of the unforgiving servant

Jesus said, 'Therefore, the kingdom of heaven may be compared to a king who wished to settle accounts with his servants. When he began the reckoning, one was brought to him who owed him ten thousand talents, and as he could not pay, his lord ordered him to be sold, with his wife and children and all that he had, and payment be made.'

So the servant fell on his knees, imploring him, 'Lord, have patience with me and I will pay you everything.' And out of pity for him, the lord of that servant forgave him the debt.

Jesus went on to tell them more about forgiveness in the parable of the unforgiving servant. *Therefore*, the Kingdom of Heaven may be compared to a king who wished to settle accounts with his servants (verse 23). As always, when we see a 'therefore', we want to know what it is there for. So we see a link between what the Lord Jesus is teaching through this parable, life in the kingdom of heaven based on forgiveness and also forgiveness on a larger scale. In Peter's eyes, the question of forgiveness of sin had become a domestic matter. 'How often shall *my brother* sin against me and I forgive him?' (verse 21). It concerns the relationship broken through sin of brothers and sisters, and requiring reconciliation, the renewing of the bond of love. But Jesus is also setting the scene for the forgiveness of sin in our relationship with others.

Jesus is always aware of His Jewish heritage, the importance of being, by His human birth, part of what God has done for His people down the centuries, taking out of the nations a people for Himself, acting in a covenant relationship with them as He moves towards the apex of His plan of salvation for all people, everywhere; forgiveness for all who come to God through Him.

After Jesus' resurrection, two disciples, travelling from Jerusalem to Emmaus, a distance of seven miles, found that a stranger had joined them as they were talking about what had happened in Jerusalem; how Jesus of Nazareth had been condemned to death, and how some women of their company did not find His body within the tomb, but saw a vision of angels who said He was alive! In their confusion, Jesus had come to these weary, hopeless disciples, and now He said, 'Was it not necessary that the Christ should suffer these things and enter into His glory?' And beginning with Moses and all the prophets, He interpreted to them in all the scriptures the things concerning Himself (Luke 24:26-27).

What would we not have given to hear that exposition of 'all the scriptures'. How precious, and how significant that the Lord Jesus should acknowledge Himself to be the fulfilment of all God's purposes, and plans and activity, not only on behalf of the people of Israel, but Gentiles too.

Of course, forgiveness of sins was of the utmost, highest importance in the life of the church, as it had been in the life of the Israelites. But Jesus was going beyond even the church as He spoke of the parable of the king who forgave his servant.

Once again, Peter had begun his question with κύριε, *Lord*, a recognition of Jesus' Lordship, of His absolute authority and a firm belief that what He said indeed was, and could not be otherwise. No doubt the other disciples were there too, anxious to learn what was Jesus' reply to Peter's question, and perhaps equally surprised by this parable which Jesus told, which, when first listened to, appeared to have little to do with loving relationships within the church; or the attitude of the disciples to those outside the church.

Jesus' parable begins with an oriental king who has the power of life and death over his servants. This king had a sudden whim to determine whether or not his accounts were in order and is chagrined to discover that one servant owes him the equivalent of a billion pounds. How could the servant ever repay what he owes? The king could sell him, after all, he is only a slave. He could sell his wife and his children and all that he possesses, but that would not be enough to repay the debt. The terrified servant throws himself on the ground before the king, pleading for mercy, and miraculously, the king takes pity on him, and forgives him all that debt.

Leaving the royal presence, the servant goes outside and finds one of his fellow servants who owes him the equivalent of four or five pounds. Seizing him by the throat (verse 28), he says,

'Pay what you owe.' So his fellow servant fell down and besought him saying, 'Have patience with me and I will pay you all' (verse 29). But he refused and put him in prison till he should pay the debt (verse 30), which of course he could not do while he was in prison and unable to earn money to pay, though his family may have been able to raise the money and ransom him.

Outraged, his fellow servants reported this to the king who summoned the man, saying to him, 'You wicked servant, I forgave you all that debt because you besought me, and should you not have had mercy on your fellow servant as I had mercy on you?' (verse 33). So he was thrown into jail and the other servant was released from jail.

How do we understand this parable? How does Jesus want us to understand? There could be alternative interpretations concerning the church and society at large, but the overriding insight concerns forgiveness. We are not looking here at an end-time parable of the day of judgement, for forgiveness had already been given to the servant who was in debt; judgement has already taken place. This is a present day reality, but not in terms of money. Jesus uses the metaphor of money to express and represent something infinitely more important.

The Father in heaven (verse 35) is also God the King, both literally and metaphorically in this parable, as is indicated by the word προσκυνέω, as the debtor *prostrated* himself before the king, a position customary in the East before both rulers and gods, even as Muslim men do today. The debt of the servant has been discovered. It is far more than he can ever repay, just as the sin of which the supplicant is all too aware, is far greater than he can make atonement for. What can he do but throw himself on the mercy of the king? And spectacularly, miraculously, the king forgives him all that debt.

'Debtor' and 'to owe' have the meaning for Aramaic speaking people of both monetary debt and sin, as we saw in different translations of the Lord's prayer. 'Forgive us our sins,' or, 'Forgive us our debt' (Matthew 6:12). The man had asked for a reprieve. 'Have patience with me and I will pay you what I owe' (verse 26), he pleaded. But the king did so much more than expect to be paid back. He forgave him all that debt (verse 27) This is the greatness of the mercy of the king, the mercy of God.

The servant should have imitated the king in granting mercy to his fellow servant. If the granting of mercy to the first servant was incomprehensibly amazing, so must have been the incomprehensible behaviour of that same servant to his fellow servants, and intolerable in the light of the forgiveness which had been extended to him. No wonder the other servants were distressed and reported to their lord all that had taken place (verse 31). Sometimes, when we see that a great injustice has been done, that is the best thing to do: go and tell our Lord above about all that has distressed us.

Jesus had spoken earlier in the chapter about church discipline when one member sins against another, and the church is called together to mediate between these brothers or sisters. Some interpreters have used the following verse, 'If he refuses to listen even to the church, let him be to you as a Gentile and a tax collector' (verse 17) as permission, or instruction even, to excommunicate such a person from the church.

But as Matthew the former tax collector can testify, such a person may need extra help, such as would be given to those who at present believe themselves to be totally outside the realm of the kingdom of God's love. Even tax collectors and Gentiles may become disciples, members of the church. Repentance and faith is still open to all. Jesus said, *'Him that cometh to Me I will in no wise cast out'* (John 10:37).

Here, the Lord, the King, is approached by the fellow servants. It is a situation they cannot deal with. They must come to Him. Any judgement that is given, any punishment meted out, must be at His command and on the grounds of His knowledge, His will, His mercy.

But there is a warning here for the disciples too. In their time with Jesus, they have experienced His overwhelming and underserved forgiveness. This forgiveness has been extended through the new relationships they have with one another, and how precious their love for one another has become. Now they perceive that there are others who need their forgiveness, not just that this is something they do because they belong to Jesus, but 'from their heart' (verse 35), not just outward reconciliation but *affirming* them as those who too can become brothers, sisters, for the mercy of God is inexhaustible. He does not wish that any should perish but that all should come to repentance. (2 Peter 3:9). As far as the east is from the west, So far has He removed our transgressions from us. As a father pities his children, so the Lord pities them that fear Him. For He knows our frame; He remembers that we are dust. (Psalms 103: 12-14) I have blotted out, as a thick cloud your transgressions, and as a cloud your sins. (Isaiah 44:22).

Mathew 18: 1-35. Summary of the fourth discourse.

Brother, sister, community, are not just words. They express human relationships, valuable in themselves, but chiefly valuable in what they express of the relation of each other to God the Father. Sin against one's brother or sister therefore constitutes also sin against God, for it denies that relationship. It challenges the existence of the church at all, or at the least makes the church of none effect, for the foundation of the church is based upon love. Fellowship is only possible on the basis of love, fellowship with each other and the exalted Lord in the midst (Matthew 18:20). We do not just 'associate' with one another, we are a community of faith and love, where each one is accepted for who they are, where God's love is experienced in human love, where grace becomes the experience of all.

This is not self-deception, not something that the church chooses for itself. This is what the church received from Jesus, as John expresses it, *'That which we have seen and heard* we proclaim also to you that you may have fellowship with us; and our fellowship is with the Father, and with His Son Jesus Christ' (1 John 1:3).

'If we walk in the light, as He is in the light, we have fellowship one with another, and the blood of Jesus, His Son cleanses us from all sin' (1 John 1:7).

This is how the church lives in the world, as a witness to the love of God in redeeming power. And as lovers of the Lord Jesus find themselves loving one another, they extend that love to those who do not yet know Him. Their sin may be apparently very great; or it may appear to be not so great. But sin of any dimension is rebellion against God, disobedience to His will, idolatry of someone or something other than Him. It is a barrier, an obstacle, setting up a human will against the will of God from fear of allowing Him to take control. Lying, adultery, murder, covetousness are but expressions of that underlying disposition. This may be construed as debt for which men and women need forgiveness.

The church demonstrates that far from being a restriction, coming to the Lord Jesus and prostrating oneself before Him as the King, as the first servant did, receiving His forgiveness, His mercy, is coming into liberty, freedom, the liberty of the children of God. Glorious liberty (Romans 8:21), joy unspeakable and full of glory (1 Peter 1:8 A.V.). Free to love Him, to serve Him, to become part of His family, part of what He is doing in His world. To have a higher purpose in living, knowing that this life is not the end, but that there is a sure and certain hope of the life to come, tremendous compensation for the giving up of one's own life for the indwelling life of Jesus.

Truly, the witness of the church to the forgiveness shown by members of the church, not only to each other but to everyone inside or outside the church, is a powerful declaration. Openness to God, openness to one another and openness to friends and neighbours and strangers, should be the hallmark of any community which claims to be the church of Jesus Christ. This is how the church should understand itself. This should be its lived and experienced reason for being. When the church is not community, it is not the church as Jesus meant it to be. The church of Jesus is based on humility, lowliness, renunciation of power, wealth, rank, self-promotion; recognition of one's own fallibility, reaching out to other members of the family, taking seriously the 'little ones' and those who go astray and those who have been injured in any way, constantly 'looking unto Jesus' (Hebrews 12:3).

Again we may say with the Psalmist, 'This is high, I cannot attain unto it' (Psalm 139:6), and Jesus understands that, and that is where His wonderful grace and forgiveness is extended to us once again. How blessed we are in His love.

Matthew Chapter 19

Matthew 19:1-2. Jesus leaves Galilee on the way to Jerusalem

Now, when Jesus had finished these sayings, He went away from Galilee and entered the region of Judea beyond the Jordan, and large crowds followed Him, and He healed them all (Matthew 19:1, 2).

Their period of rest and respite over, the disciples accompany Jesus as He begins to leave Galilee, and, as He had told them, begins the journey to Jerusalem. He decides to go through Perea, beyond the River Jordan. This common route avoided Samaria.

The word translated 'Now' in the R.S.V. is translated, 'And it came to pass,' in the A.V., καὶ ἐγένετο. The same expression which introduces 7:28, 11:1. 13:53 and 26:1, begins this chapter. Matthew is introducing the fifth section of his gospel with this phrase, the section which encompasses 19:1 to 26:2. The journey of Jesus to His death and resurrection has finally been determined. Jesus is leaving Galilee for good. It has come to pass.

But to begin with, all seemed to be as it had been throughout Jesus' ministry. Again, 'large crowds followed Him and He healed them there' (verse 2). But it was not the same; a shadow hangs over the disciples as they remember what Jesus had told them of what awaited Him in Jerusalem.

When the Pharisees approached Him, there must have been some anxious foreboding as to what would happen next. Although Jesus, the healing Messiah is surrounded by all the people who so need Him, and to whom He is faithful to the end, the disciples know that the Pharisees only ever come with questions intended to trap Him, to tempt Him into expressing what they would regard as an heretical opinion, for they had been seeking to destroy Him from as far back as Matthew 12:14.

Matthew 19:3-9. Teaching about divorce

And Pharisees came up to Him and tested Him by asking, 'Is it lawful to divorce one's wife for any cause?' (Matthew 19:3).

Jesus is not concerned with the malicious motives or intentions of the Pharisees, for He knows that His heavenly Father has it all in hand. He will not allow the Pharisees to touch Jesus until the appointed time, and Jesus rests in His Father's will. Nevertheless, He uses the Pharisees' question to teach His disciples about marriage and divorce.

And Pharisees came up to Him and tested Him by asking, 'Is it lawful to divorce one's wife for any cause?' (verse 3). The question implies that the practice of divorce was widespread, with quite a liberal interpretation of the grounds for divorce. Jesus completely ignores their question, together with the implied debate that was ongoing at this time between different religious/Jewish groups. (The school of Rabbi Hillel emphasised a lenient standard for divorce, even simple dissatisfaction with one's wife; on the contrary, the school of Rabbi Shammai emphasised the 'scandalous' nature of divorce, permissible only for adultery).

Jesus brings them back from endless religious disputations to the scriptures of which they aspired to be experts. "'Have you not read?'", He asks them (verse 4). As always He is not concerned with debate, but with the effect that such debates have on the lives of men and women, in this case, those who find themselves married to someone whom they cannot trust, who has become unfaithful.

What better way to help them than to point them to God's intentions for marriage 'from the beginning', ἀρχῆς (verse 4). 'He who made them from the beginning made them male and female. For this reason a man shall leave his father and mother and be joined to his wife, and the two shall be one. So they are no longer two, but one' (verse 5).

Jesus understands Genesis 1:27 and 2:24 in terms of marriage, the union of two human beings resulting in a new reality. And since God has thus ordained marriage, human beings should not dissolve their union.

As with His earlier treatment of the law in chapter 5, so with this treatment of the law concerning divorce, the law as set out in Deuteronomy 24:1. Jesus does not advocate a departure from the Mosaic Law, but an intensely radical interpretation of it. That is why He goes back to the very beginning, to God's intention when He created a man and a woman and gave them to each other. God took a rib from Adam's side in order to create Eve, 'not from his head so that she should rule over him, not from his body that she should be subservient to him, but from his side so that she should be equal with him' (source of quotation unknown). God's intention in creation outweighs, though it does not annul, the ordinance given to Moses by God; but fulfils them. He fills them full of what the joining together of two human beings could and should ultimately be.

The Pharisees spoke of divorce, 'Is it lawful to divorce one's wife for any cause?' (verse 2). Jesus' reply was, 'From the beginning it was not so' (verse 8). The Pharisees regarded this as a 'test' of Jesus' authenticity as a teacher. Did He subscribe to the easy view of divorce, that because a man's wife did not please him in some way he should divorce her and take another, or was He of the school of thought that denied all grounds for divorce except on the grounds of unchastity (verse 9), *porneia*, by which is meant adultery or unchastity. The Pharisees had entirely missed the point; that marriage in the sight of God and under His direction and blessing, is a holy estate, the sacramental union of two people in the eyes of God.

It has been noted that there is a distinctly anomalous position here. In the Palestine of Jesus' day, under the Law of Moses, no indication is given that the wife might actively not only resent, but potentially be at risk, from the adulterous behaviour of her husband, and wish to divorce him. In our society had his behaviour been adulterous he would certainly be allowed to be divorced by her., but there was no such facility for women at that time. It is in this context that we must view the issues of divorce for our own day, and perhaps our concern for people whom we know and love who have endured this experience.

The Pharisees had no doubt that the interpretation of Deuteronomy 24:1 gave them immutable grounds for divorce according to Mosaic Law. Jesus insists that it was because of their hardness of heart that Moses allowed divorce, and additionally, that same hardness allowed that the only condition for divorce was *the wife's immorality*.

Jesus also insists that if a man divorces his wife, he may not marry again. If he does, he commits adultery (verse 9). Jesus is not just identifying adultery as grounds for divorce. He goes back further to their hardness of heart (verse 8), as the source of all they attempt to justify to themselves, the source of the complete misunderstanding they have of all their study of the scriptures, for they were concerned only with what was 'lawful' and not 'merciful', representative though they should have been of the mercy and love of God towards His people (Matthew 12:2, 7).

They were happy to apply the seventh commandment, 'Thou shalt not commit adultery' to others, but the episode of the woman taken in adultery in John chapter 8 is a strong indication that the Pharisees viewed quite differently their own adultery as compared with that of the woman whom they wanted to stone. ``Let him that is without sin among you cast the first stone' said Jesus (John 8:7), and when they heard it, they went away, one by one, beginning with the eldest (John 8:9). We can assume that Jesus knew that though these were privileged men in this situation, they had been guilty of the same sin for which they were stoning her, and that was why they crept away one by one.

In Matthew's gospel, the Pharisees attempted to trap Him by referring to the Law of Moses, doubting His ability to understand the law adequately. 'Is it lawful?' they say (verse 3). 'Do you know enough about the law to tell us what is the right interpretation of Moses' views on divorce?' And in Jesus' riposte to them, 'Have you not read?' Jesus takes them back further than Moses, He takes them back to God. 'He who made them from the beginning made them male and female. What therefore God has joined together, let no man put asunder' (verse 4, 6). A man shall leave his father and mother and cleave unto his wife, and the two shall be one (verse 5).

This answer does not satisfy the Pharisees. 'Why then did Moses command one to give a certificate of divorce and to put her away?' (verse 7). They are setting their own view of the Mosaic Law against that of Jesus. They are appealing to Deuteronomy: Jesus is appealing to Genesis, thought by many scholars to have been written later than Deuteronomy. Jesus is not denying that Moses gave this commandment concerning divorce, but He gives the reason why this is so. 'Because of your hardness of heart, Moses allowed you to divorce your wives' (verse 8).

It is not a question of correct or incorrect interpretation of the scriptures as permitting divorce. God's original intention against a man and woman being 'put asunder' (verse 6), is harmonised by God's allowing Moses to provide divorce 'because of the hardness of your heart' (verse 8). What a man or a woman may do outside of marriage, extramarital affairs, they may call 'falling in (or out of) love', but true love has nothing to do with it. Jesus calls it hard heartedness, for it is self-indulgent, in not regarding the damage done either to his extramarital partner or his wife, or her husband or children. Love is not a matter exclusively of the emotions, but a consistent intention of the will.

Because of your hard heartedness God has allowed you to put her away. Divorce hurts. It hurts men and women and the children born to them. It is anathema to God. Hard heartedness describes the inner dimension of sin, reflecting an unwillingness to repent, being closed to God, stubbornness. Yet men and women can be hard-hearted even when staying within marriage. Domestic abuse, domestic violence, perhaps in wilful ignorance of what such a commitment would impose upon them, two people living together in perpetual incompatibility, rather than entering into divorce, even though divorce is permissible on the grounds of hardheartedness.

Can this possibly be the outcome of Jesus' words? Because of their hard heartedness, they could either allow the marriage to end in divorce, or they could stay together, without love, without the care for one another which Jesus has so obviously taught is the way for His children to live?.

Something of this comes across in the disciples' reaction to what Jesus is saying. 'If such is the case of a man with his wife, it is expedient not to marry' (verse 10). But what appears to be a concession on Jesus' part is in reality a different way of living. 'Not all men can receive this saying, but only those to whom it is given' (verse 11).

Jesus seems to realise the extreme intolerability for some of this teaching on divorce and remarriage. Though this way is not easy, for either the husband or wife, when such a life is lived by believers in obedience to Christ, it surely excludes the violence and adultery, which require repentance, that is, a 180-degree turn around, facing in the opposite direction, for that is what repentance is. Love is of the will as well as of the emotions.

Still, Jesus knows that 'not all can receive this saying', of enduring either the loveless marriage or the option of living alone, 'but only those to whom it is given' (verse 11). Is He then only referring to the marriage of believers? Disciples? He never gave false expectations of life lived in obedience to Him. He says in verse 23, 'He who is able to receive it, let him receive it.' And if a man cannot receive it, he must live as a eunuch, not because of congeniality, or castration, but because having divorced his wife on the grounds of immorality, he has chosen to become a eunuch of the Kingdom of Heaven.

Such an act of discipleship is required of men whose wives have committed adultery. We have seen that there was a failure in Jewish society of the time, to give women the right to divorce their husbands, though even being given that right, women would have found it very difficult to become a virtual widow; to live without the support of a husband. But we have to conclude that within the constraints of discipleship, what applied to men applies equally to women, as they live a difficult and perhaps lonely life in obedience to God.

God does not require from men and women what is beyond their capacity and through Moses He has adapted the institution of marriage to human need, so that there is no distinction between God's will at creation, and the law of Moses. Nevertheless, adultery signifies the breaking of a contract between a man and a woman, and cannot be regarded lightly. It is a legal contract, a social contract, as well as, for Christians, a sacred contract, as they promise to keep each other only to themselves as long as they both shall live. Marriage is ordained of God. It is the bedrock of society, and when there appear to be difficulties in the marriages of those whom we love, we must help and support them as much as possible, giving them time and space, and privacy.

But what if he or she is coercive or a bully or uses threatening behaviour? And cannot be won to love however hard the other tries? Then the societal contract is broken. And the sacred and solemn promise to love and honour the other is broken and the marriage made null and void. Entering into the marriage covenant continues to be a solemn undertaking. But commitment of one's whole life into the hands of another is to be undertaken joyfully, where there is love for each other, understanding of each other, and a determination to fulfil the oath and commitment given.

Even then, marriages break down, a tremendous sorrow to those who love them. May the Lord in His mercy come to all those whom we know are presently suffering in this way, and pour in the oil and wine of His comforting presence.

The coherence of Jesus' teaching cannot be denied, but in the context of the 21st century environment where marriage is not perceived as necessarily being one man, one woman for life, Christians may find His teaching difficult to assess. Many Christians are themselves divorced and remarried, or have parents, sons or daughters, who are. How to reconcile their belief in the inerrancy of scripture, their desire to follow the teaching of Jesus, with the choices they have had to make in order to lead ordinary, societally acceptable lives, requires an ultimate belief in the grace and mercy of God, a faithful God who was once a human being, tempted as we are, yet without sin

(Hebrews 4:15), who 'knows our frame who remembers that we are dust'. Like as a father pities His children, so the Lord pities them that fear Him (Psalms 103:13, 14). The unchanging lovingkindness of our God (Malachi 3:6; Psalms 102:27).

We mourn for those whose marriages appear to fail to come up to the ideal set before us by Genesis 2:24, for whatever reason. Are they then a travesty of what God wants to His people? No, for we see much love, self-sacrificial love and honouring of one another as well, and we rejoice with them that they have found what is perhaps more than happiness, contentment. And contentment is a great gift.

God in His mercy, so often gives us another chance. This is what John is writing about in his first letter, 'If we walk in the light as He is in the light, we have fellowship one with another, and the blood of Jesus His Son *goes on cleansing* us from all sin (1 John 1:7). We constantly come to Him in repentance, asking for forgiveness. He constantly restores us, cleansing us from all sin. He is able to restore, to do exceedingly more than we can ask or even think. To Him be the glory forever (Ephesians 3:20).

Matthew 19:13-15. Jesus and the children

Then children were brought to Him, that He might lay His hands on them and pray. The disciples rebuked the people; but Jesus said, 'Let the children come to Me, and do not hinder or prevent them; for to such belongs the Kingdom of Heaven.' And He laid His hands on them and went away (Matthew 19:13).

That the blessing of children should succeed, follow on from, the teaching of Jesus on marriage is perhaps not coincidental. Children in that society were not regarded particularly highly and mortality was relatively high. But these 'people' (verse 13), whether parents, grandparents, guardians, cared enough about these children to want to bring them to Jesus.

Why did the disciples rebuke them? Were they so impressed with Jesus' teaching that they thought that a great teacher would have no time for children? Were they trying to protect Jesus from too much stress, from becoming too tired or exhausted by the many calls upon Him?

Jesus had already taken a child and put him in the midst of them when He was teaching them about the community which He was beginning to establish. He had been urging them to humility, represented by the child, and stressing the importance of receiving and caring for not just children, but 'little ones' within the Christian community, those who were without any pretence of greatness or influence, or position. It may be that these 'people' had seen Jesus with the child and longed that their children should be blessed by Him too. Jesus was pleased that other children had come to Him for blessing. He did not want them sent away.

How often had He laid His hands on people for healing! There was the leper, cleansed by Jesus as He stretched out His hand and touched Him (Matthew 8:3), or Peter's wife's mother, whose fever left her when Jesus touched her (Matthew 8:15), or the little daughter of the ruler, whose healing had been interrupted by the woman who had been haemorrhaging for 12 years, but who rose up when Jesus took her by the hand (Matthew 9:25, 9:25) or the blind men whose eyes He touched (Matthew 9:29).

This was a different kind of touch. Jesus laid His hands on the children, wanting to protect them from anything that would prevent them from coming to Him.

We do not know how old these children were, but some expositors have used this incident as intended to relate to the baptism of infants. This text has been used in justification of the practice; a position thoroughly investigated by Ulrich Luz (p 504). He concludes that ultimately there is no convincing reference in the New Testament for the baptism of small children. It is simply a blessing rather than baptism that Jesus gives to the children. In early Christianity there could have been a rite for the blessing of children, and children were no doubt present at the regular worship of the church. Luz says that Jewish children began reading the Bible, the Hebrew Scriptures, at the age of five and the Mishnah at the age of ten, and we cannot but remember that many Christians (like John and Charles Wesley) were encouraged to do the same.

The more positive conclusion we can draw from the blessing of the children by Jesus is the acceptance of these small people in church, in main corporate worship and not 'given their own space' elsewhere, ostensibly for Bible teaching according to their intellectual ability, when what they truly need is to see the church 'in action', during worship, and to discover the blessing of being together, part of the community of the church for themselves, and helping to shape and share in its worship as they grow more and more into the knowledge of the presence and love of the Lord Jesus.

How blessed are those children whose parents encourage them to come to Jesus in their earlier years, so that as they develop physically and emotionally, they also develop a trusting relationship with Him. How precious they are to us and how much more precious to Him. And how great our privilege and responsibility to bring them up 'in the nurture and admonition of the Lord!' (Ephesians 6:4 A.V.). 'Nurture'; what a beautiful word. To nurture them in Jesus, to love them, guide them, pray for them, even as He does (Romans 8:25,26; Hebrew 7:25).

Matthew 19:16-30. Jesus and the rich young man

And behold, one came up to Him and said, 'Teacher, what good deed must I do, to have eternal life?' And He said to him, 'Why do you ask Me about what is good? One there is who is good. If you would enter into life, keep the commandments' (Matthew 19:16-17).

Matthew often uses ἰδών, *behold,* as an interjection, drawing attention to the continuity of the text, in this case between the blessing of the children (verses 13-15) and the rich young man (verses 16-26). Behold, look attentively, intensely! 'Behold' is also a commandment. This is something that you must see and understand.

We see this particularly in narrative sections of the gospel where Matthew connects various events focusing on Jesus' authority, so that one episode sheds light on another; as we have seen for example in chapter 9 where Jesus healed the daughter of the ruler, the woman with a haemorrhage, and the dumb demoniac (9:18; 9:20; 9:32).

Now, when the young man 'came up to Him' (verse 13), Jesus, through Matthew's narrative text, is making a connection with husbands and wives (19:3-12), with children (19:13-15) and now, the rich young man(19:20). The family is complete. Jesus has consideration for the ultimate blessing of each individual person, and this young man's desire to find eternal life summarises what Jesus wants to give to each one.

'Teacher, what *good* deed must I do to have eternal life?' (verse 16) he says. 'Good?' says Jesus, 'What is good? Only God is good. If by good you mean righteous, God has given you the commandments. You have only to be obedient to them and you will enter into life. The young man said, 'I have observed all the commandments but there is still something lacking, there is a deficiency in me somewhere, somehow'. And Jesus, with His compassionate insight into the young man's aspiration 'to be perfect' (verse 21), says to him, 'Go, sell what you possess and give to the poor and you will have treasure in heaven, and come, follow Me' (verse 21).

But when the young man heard this, he went away sorrowful, for he had great possessions. Yes, it would be a great thing to follow Jesus, but to give up all he had? That was too great a price to pay. Wealth gave him status. It gave him the opportunity to spend time obeying the commandments which being poor would not do. Poverty often causes people to lie, to steal, sometimes on behalf of others, it means not being able to honour father or mother as much as one would want to. There are so many temptations associated with poverty. Vagrants at a crime scene are always the first suspects. To give up his possessions would put the young man into that place of temptation. Perhaps he had seen what poverty could do to a man.

Jesus is not advocating poverty as a way of life for His disciples, although it was indeed the case that He Himself had no possessions. What He is insisting upon is total, wholehearted following of Him.

Riches can be an idol, something that gets in the way of total commitment to Jesus, something that is worshipped instead of Him. To feel the need to be totally righteous can also be an idol, because the righteousness becomes more important than God who requires it. The effort, the struggle, to be more and more righteous becomes the object of desire; the worship of God neglected, or made to become only a part of the pathway to that goal. But not only the young man's desire to inherit eternal life but also the part that riches played in his life as he sought to be perfect (verse 21) caused Jesus to say, 'Truly I say to you, my disciples, it is hard for a rich man to enter the Kingdom of Heaven. Again, I tell you, it is easier for a camel to go through the eye of a needle than for a rich man to enter the Kingdom of God' (verse 24).

Jesus uses what may be an ancient proverb, as He speaks of the eye of the needle. Or He may be referring to what has also been described as a gate in and out of the city called 'the Eye of the Needle'. The camel, laden down with the goods of its master, attempts to get through the gate but cannot until the load is reduced.

The young man has loaded himself twice, once with his possessions, but also with his law-based righteousness. Of this, he has become aware when he says, 'What do I still lack?' (verse 20). What he lacks is *faith-based righteousness*, which can only be his as he follows Jesus.

It is possible to have life under the law. Leviticus 18:5 says, 'You shall therefore keep my statutes and ordinances, by doing which a man shall *live:* I am the Lord.' But no-one could keep the law. We hear Paul's cry in Romans 7:24, 'O wretched man that I am! Who will deliver me from this body of death?' followed by his cry of assurance, 'I thank God through our Lord Jesus Christ.'

Romans 10:4 tells us that Christ is the end of the law. He has fulfilled both law-based righteousness and faith-based righteousness (Matthew 5:17). He has fulfilled both. And this life of righteousness He lives in us. He is made to us wisdom and righteousness and sanctification and redemption, all that we cannot have apart from Him (I Corinthians 1:30).

All who are in Him live His faith-based righteousness. The righteous shall live by his faith (Romans 1:17), faith which is the gift of God (Ephesians 2:8). Paul comes to the conclusion that the only way to live is to confess 'that It is no longer I who live, but Christ who lives in me, and the life I now live I live by the faith of the Son of God who loved me and gave Himself for me (Galatians 2:20).

This is the life which Jesus is offering the young man if he follows Him. He went away sorrowful (verse 22), but had he known the extent of what he was rejecting his sorrow would have been infinitely greater. Jesus had said to him, 'If you would be *perfect,* sell what you possess and give to the poor' (verse 21). To be perfect is to be complete. He was unfulfilled, incomplete. Jesus had taught His disciples in the Sermon on the Mount, 'You therefore *must* be perfect, even as your Father which is in heaven is perfect' (Matthew 5:48).

There may well be an incompleteness about life until a person comes to the Lord Jesus. This young man had accurately diagnosed it when he said to Jesus, 'What do I still lack?' (verse 20). Something was missing.

Matthew chapter 5 stresses love over and over again; love for your brother, love for your wife, love for your enemy. Love is the fulfilment of the law (Romans 13:10), the love which God is, the God who is rich in mercy, and for the great love wherewith He loved us, even when we were dead in our trespasses and sins, has made us alive together in Christ (Ephesians 2:4). To be perfect is to love with the love of God, even as He loves. To 'give to the poor' (verse 21) as Jesus recommended to the rich young man, could be the beginning of the expression of that love.

How unbearably sad that this prospect was denied to this young man, and how astonished were the disciples when they heard Jesus saying, 'It is easier for a camel to go through the eye of a needle than for a rich man to enter the Kingdom of Heaven' (verse 24). 'Who then can be saved?' they said (verse 25). If someone with all the wealth and position and privilege and status which the young man undoubtedly had was disadvantaged by all this in his struggle for perfection, what hope was there for the poor and vulnerable in society?

Jesus had already given them the answer. He had said, 'Follow Me,' to the young man, an impossible step for the young man apparently to be able to take. But Impossible also to people who were poor and needy, for even they had something precious of family or home, which the prospect of potentially losing them in order to follow Jesus would cause them to think hard before responding to Jesus' invitation to 'Come, follow Me.'

But Jesus said, 'Impossible with men, but not with God, for with God all things are possible' (verse 26).

Peter reminded Jesus, 'Behold, we have left all and followed you' (verse 27). Will there be a reward for us? A special blessing? Because we have left all to follow you? On this day of surprises, Jesus' answer must have been the greatest surprise of all. There is going to be a new world Peter, when God fully establishes His Kingdom on earth, 'When the Son of Man shall sit on His glorious throne and you who have followed Me will also sit on twelve thrones, judging the twelve tribes of Israel' (verse 28) God's throne of glory they could perhaps faintly grasp, for Peter and James and John had seen Him glorified on the Mount of Transfiguration. But that they should have a part in reigning with Him, ruling His covenant people, the twelve tribes of Israel, how are they to understand that?

So often had Gentiles come to Jesus, and He had healed them all. Of the Gentile centurion, He had even said, 'Truly I say to you, not even in Israel have I found such faith' (Matthew 8:10). Jesus' message of new life in Him, of entering into the life of the Kingdom of Heaven through repentance and faith was open to all; none were excluded.

But that did not mean that God had cast off His people whom He foreknew (Romans 11:3). Jesus was aware that much that went on among the Jewish leaders of His day had become a denial of the Torah in its essence, the teaching of the law and of all that it stood for, which made the request of the young man to know how he could inherit eternal life even more remarkable.

But God's chosen people includes all those who by faith have responded to Jesus, Jews, but Gentiles as well. Amongst the twelve tribes were going to be many in this new world of faith and trust in Jesus, who were acknowledging the Lordship of the Son of Man as He was gloriously enthroned, with those by His side who had been among the first to acknowledge His Lordship, His entitlement as the Son of God as well as the Son of Man, a position they could only have come to by faith.

Peter says they had left all to follow him (verse 27). Jesus says, 'Everyone who has left houses or brothers or sisters or father or mother or children or lands, for My Name's sake, will receive a hundredfold, and inherit eternal life'. A fully comprehensive list of self-sacrifice, self-abnegation.

Did Jesus mean literally? That we could only inherit eternal life on the basis of all that we had left behind?

We have seen from the conversation that Jesus had with the young man that there is a tension between the owning of worldly possessions and his question to Jesus, 'What good deed must I do that I might inherit eternal life?' (verse 16). Eternal life is not just the future coming of the Kingdom of God, but the experience of day to day living in the good of all that Jesus *has* done, and that God *is* doing, both in individual lives and in the community which Jesus is establishing significantly under the leadership of the encircling Twelve.

But, yet again, the Lord Jesus includes not only the disciples, but πᾶς ὅστις – *everyone* – who leaves everything for His Name's sake – will receive eternal life. (verse 29).

In the Middle Ages there arose the Consilium Evangelicum, the doctrine that the way of perfection for the believer consisted in *poverty* (Matthew 19:22), *chastity* (Matthew 19:10) and *obedience* (Matthew 19:21). But this meant that there became two ways of living the Christian life, for such commitment was not open to everyone. It was creating a two-tier system of Christianity.

But as we have seen, Jesus was not advocating poverty or chastity or obedience, for its own sake, but only that people with a determination to follow Him would prefer poverty to a life of riches, possessions, culture of body or mind, or anything which might become a hindrance or an obstacle to uninterrupted fellowship with Him; or cause them to move from a position of obedience to the will of their heavenly Father to disobedience, developing their own path without reference to His purpose for them. If riches get in the way of devotion to Jesus, they must go.

Jesus was saying that anything or anyone at all that becomes a hindrance to total commitment to Him, to a life lived 'for His Name's sake' (verse 19) has to be left behind, abandoned. Only so, could a believer move into the full purpose of God for his or her life, eternal life, life lived not on the basis of the here and now, although that is important, but on the ultimate clear, satisfying purpose of the will of God, utter subjection to His will, even as Jesus prayed in the Garden of Gethsemane, 'Not My will, but Thine be done' (Matthew 29:39; Luke 22:42; Mark 14:36).

John says, 'We know Him who is true and we are in Him who is true, in His Son Jesus Christ. This is the true God and eternal life.'Little children, Keep yourselves from idols (1 John 5:21), from anything that would get in the way of your commitment to Him.

Jesus says *'many'* – πολλοὶ - that are first shall be last, and the last first (19:30); a cryptic statement that He will enlarge upon in the following chapter.

Matthew Chapter 20

Matthew 20:1-16. The labourers in the vineyard

Although introduced by the statement, 'Many that are first will be last, and the last first' (Matthew 19:30), at first sight this parable which Jesus told appears to be concerned with the difference between the mildly affluent and the abject poor, continuing the discussion about possessions and wealth in chapter 19. But Jesus has something more radical in mind.

Jesus says, 'The Kingdom of Heaven is like a householder who went out early in the morning to hire labourers for his vineyard' (Matthew 20:1).

The owner of the vineyard does not keep slaves. Slaves are expensive to buy, require shelter but are always available for work that needs to be done. But perhaps for compassionate reasons, the owner prefers to employ day labourers, for there were many unemployed free people needing work.

The vineyard owner gets up at sunrise, 6 o'clock, to hire day labourers to work in his vineyard. Already they are there, waiting to be hired. He chooses as many as he needs and takes them to the vineyard. We do not know of what the labour of the day will consist — hoeing, pruning, harvesting, but these men have made an agreement with the owner, and will do a full day's work for a full day's pay, a *denarius*. Just a subsistence wage not easily translated into present day currency, but money which would only be sufficient for one day's needs, and hardly that if one had a family of little mouths to feed. Such a labourer would also be dependent on being able to be hired on subsequent days.

This was a conscientious and assiduous owner. He goes out to the market place again at 9 o'clock in the morning, the third hour (verse 3) and sees other workmen standing idle, and to them he said, 'You go into the vineyard too, and whatever is right I will give you.' So they went (verse 4).

He goes out again at 12 o'clock, the sixth hour, and 3 o'clock in the afternoon, the ninth hour. At 5 o'clock in the afternoon, the eleventh hour, he went out for the last time, and still found men waiting, and he said to them, 'Why do you stand here idle all the day?' They did not try to defend themselves from the change of idleness, but simply said, 'Because no-one has hired us' (verse 7). He said to them, 'You go into the vineyard too.'

When evening came, 6 o'clock, the end of the day's work, the owner said to the steward, 'Call the labourers together and pay them their wages, beginning with the last, up to the first' (verse 8).

This was unusual. Normally, those who had been hired first would be paid first. But Jesus was here making an important point in His parable. It was necessary that those who had been hired at the beginning of the day should witness the payment of the latecomers. How surprised they would have been to see the recently employed labourers receive a denarius! Surely the denarius was for the workers who had worked all day, in 'the burden and heat of the day' (verse 12). Perhaps when it came to their turn, they would receive more? After all, these men who had been hired last did not deserve a whole day's wage if they had not worked a full day.

When their turn came to be paid, they grumbled. They were dissatisfied with the money they had been given. When one of them spoke to the owner, he did not use a polite address to him, but complained about the unfairness, the lack of justice on his part. Should they not have been given more than those who had worked fewer hours, less time?

The owner responded by calling him 'friend' (verse 13). 'Friend,' he said, 'I am doing you no wrong; did you not agree with me for a denarius? Take what belongs to you and go; I choose to give to this last as I give to you. Am I not allowed to do what I choose with what belongs to me? Or do you begrudge my generosity?' (verse 15). So, Jesus concludes, the last will be first and the first last, echoing His statement at the end of chapter 19.

Jesus specifically states that this is the reason and explanation of the parable, linking it to what He had told the disciples in chapter 19 of God's design and purpose at the end of time when His Son would be sitting on His glorious throne, surrounded by these disciples whom He had chosen to reign with Him, men who had left all to follow Him. Many others, Jesus knew, would do the same. They would leave houses, brothers and sisters, mothers and fathers and children and lands, for His Name's sake, and would inherit eternal life. But there would be a distinction between them. Some would be 'first' and some 'last'. Surely there cannot be some kind of pecking order, some kind of hierarchy in the Kingdom of Heaven? Jesus had already dealt with that when He spoke of eunuchs for the Kingdom of God's sake, and He will reinforce that with the comments He makes to the mother of the sons of Zebedee, Jesus and John, later on in the chapter (Matthew 20:20).

There have been many interpretations of this parable. One interpretation calls it 'the gospel *in nuce*', the gospel in a nutshell, as it bears witness to the mercy and righteousness of God against human understanding of mercy. None of us deserves anything. Whatever we are given is given to us by the mercy of God, whether we come to it late or early (Luz p 527).

A similar interpretation suggests that some arrogantly suppose that because they have worked hard for the kingdom, they will be adequately rewarded, whereas those who on the contrary, do not arrogantly suppose that they deserve or have earned anything will actually be rewarded. Those who claim to be exalted shall be brought low, and those who consider themselves low will be raised up as in Mary's prayer of Luke 1:57-53.

Others suggest that the parable magnifies God's graciousness and generosity, not exclusively to those who have laboured for Him, and not as a reward for their 'works', but to all human beings apart from works, 'Not of works lest any man should boast' (1 Corinthians 1:29). The parable shows the difference between 'law' and 'grace'. They cite the case of the thief on the cross, who had nothing to bring to Christ but his repentance.

Yet others, building on that, say that it is possible to come to Christ, even at the 'eleventh hour', on one's deathbed, after living a life of self-indulgence, and nevertheless to be accepted by Him.

Another suggests that the parable concerns the difference between the law and the gospel, that is those who, under the law, expect to be paid for their spiritual accomplishments, and those others who know that they have no claims before God, but come to Him by faith. The parable declares that there is no meritocracy before God.

There is merit in all these attempts to understand the parable, but surely the focus becomes, firstly, the understanding of reward, and secondly, the relationship of the parable to Judaism.

It is accepted in all exegesis of these verses that the owner of the vineyard is God, an owner who graciously goes beyond all that is required of Him, and all that justice requires of Him too. As the Owner of the Vineyard, God does not need a reason to be gracious. He just is. And He thereby disrupts our understanding of what justice is.

The psalmist cries out when he is in trouble, 'Has God forgotten to be gracious? Has He in anger shut up His compassion?' (Psalm 77:9). To which of course the answer is, 'No!' It is His nature to be gracious, to be compassionate. But He is also free to bestow His graciousness where He will. We cannot assume a universal validity.

There are those who would make God's justice the benchmark of His graciousness, as if His graciousness depended on the principle of justice as dominant. They would speak of unequal pay for unequal work, a calculation as to how much graciousness someone is entitled to. But God said to Moses, 'I will be gracious to whom I will be gracious, and will show mercy on whom I will show mercy' (Exodus 33:19). Unearned, undeserved graciousness, unearned undeserved mercy for those who have nothing to offer, nothing to bring, the least, the lowest. Jesus speaks of God's grace without undermining the principle of God's justice. No one can lay claim either to His Justice or His mercy to it. We cannot depend on our works for our salvation. Whether first or last, we can only depend on the love, compassion, and mercy of our God.

The second problem then arises. Is Jesus thinking of Jews and Gentiles when He refers to the first and the last? It is true that He uses the metaphor of the vineyard, and His heares would immediately have recognized the scriptures that speak of Israel 'as the vineyard of the Lord of Hosts' (Isaiah 5:7; Jeremiah 12:10; Song of Songs 8:12). Jesus Himself uses the metaphor again in Matthew 21:28.

There is justification in viewing the parable as having a reference to seeing the early workers in the vineyard as the people of *Israel,* as the many people, both prophets and priests and 'ordinary' people, who in spite of so much idolatry and unbelief around them still pursued their relationship with God. There are of course many examples, such as David's cry to God when he was in the wilderness of Judah, 'O God, Thou art my God, early will I seek Thee, my soul thirsts for Thee, my flesh faints for Thee as in a dry and thirsty land where no water is!' (Psalm 63:1). Surely God was gracious to such men and women as these who lived, as David did 'under the shadow of Thy wings' (Psalm 63:7) It is equally certain that they craved no reward. God Himself was enough.

But Jesus has come: the One sent from God to witness to a new covenant between God and men and women, whether they be Jews or Gentiles, a new experience of entering into a relationship with God, and that includes the poor and needy of any ethnicity, who have not had the advantage which the Pharisees and scribes, the religious leaders of the people, have had, but who have seen in Jesus something precious of the love and mercy of God.

These are the latecomers, those who may not have power and privilege, or those who are not politically or religiously very important, but whoever and whatever they are, have become labourers in the vineyard of the Kingdom of God. They may have been labouring in the vineyard only for a short time, and the Owner of the Vineyard recognises this, nor does He despise those who have worked hard, for a long time, in His Kingdom. The use of the word 'Friend' as Jesus addresses the spokesman of the labourers is an expression of kindness to him for all that he had done.

But we must accept that God is God. He will be gracious to those to whom He will be gracious, and merciful to those to whom He will be merciful. Without His grace and mercy, where would any of us be? We may be the last, both in historical terms, and as present-day labourers, but we have every confidence that God will be gracious to us.

Paul writes, 'To me, who am less than the least of all the saints, was this grace given, to preach to the Gentiles the unsearchable riches of Christ' (Ephesians 3:3).

None of us can lay claim to anything from God. Nothing we can do, nothing we can bring to Him is deserving of anything but His grace, His love, His continuing faithful presence with us. Yet He pours upon us all these gifts from His generous, bountiful store.

To be thankful is good. But we are only too aware that it is not enough. We just want to yield ourselves to Him in love and devotion and worship for all that He is to us — and even that is not enough. Faithful, unchanging God.

It is really so simple. We need Him so much, so badly, and He is prepared to need us, to use us as labourers in His vineyard. This is His grace and love.

Matthew 20:17-19. The ascent to Jerusalem

And as Jesus was going up to Jerusalem, He took the twelve disciples aside, and on the way He said to them, 'Behold, we are going up to Jerusalem; and the Son of Man will be delivered to the chief priests and scribes and they will condemn Him to death, and deliver Him to the Gentiles to be mocked and scourged and crucified, and He will be raised on the third day' (Matthew 20:17-19).

Jesus is on His way to Jerusalem with His disciples. This is the life of discipleship for them, walking with Jesus wherever He may go. He has yet to go through Jericho on His way to Jerusalem

384

(verse 29), and He still has much to teach them. From Jericho to Jerusalem is a distance of about 18 miles. Matthew's topographical details help us to visualise His life, His journey.

There would have been much conversation during this journey. Matthew gives us three instances in this chapter. The most significant episode above all others is His drawing the disciples 'aside' (verse 17), in order to deliver for the third time His prediction concerning His death and resurrection, the others being as we have seen, in Matthew 16:2 at Caesarea Philippi, and in Matthew 17:22 after they had descended from the Mount of Transfiguration.

The prediction of Jesus' death and resurrection in Matthew 16:21 and 17:22 had been given to the disciples in summary form. Here in chapter 20, Matthew is introducing the final section of his gospel, the final journey to Jerusalem at the end of His three-year ministry. And it is time for Jesus to announce to His disciples in some detail the individual stages of His suffering, *firstly* at the hands both of the chief priests and scribes (verse 18), and *secondly,* also at the hands of the Gentiles, the Romans (verse 19). What the Romans do, mock Him, scourge Him, crucify Him, is the consequence of what the Jewish leaders have already determined, and which Jesus assures His disciples will surely come to pass.

But the *third* glorious stage will be, 'He will be raised on the third day' (verse 19). His death and passion are inevitable, irreversible. The term 'will' has about it the aura of the divine passive. 'Thy will be done,' as Jesus had taught his disciples to pray, for He knew His Father's will would prevail, of course to His suffering, but ultimately to their blessing.

For the first time the word 'crucify' appears, revealing that this will be, not a summary execution, but a full trial, for only the Romans had the authority to crucify. Yet they will not have the last word. The last word is 'raised'. God's will again intervenes. The crucifixion is not the final objective. God has something more wonderful in view, the glorious resurrection of His crucified Son! He will raise Jesus on the third day.

The focus therefore for the disciples becomes, of course, Jesus' death, as they continue on their journey to Jerusalem, but also pre-eminently, God's plan for Him. God Himself has set His purpose for mankind in motion. His Son, out of love for His Father, and love for the humanity which They have created, is prepared to go this way of suffering and death, so that humanity may be redeemed, restored, forgiven and given eternal life, life lived in proximity to, and close relationship to, their Redeemer.

Though the disciples may not have fully understood all the implications of what Jesus was sharing with them, they remembered that He had already intimated that they too would have a share in that suffering, in Matthew 10:17-22; 10:38 and 16:24-26 He had told them that they too must go the way of the cross.

So the disciples may have had some delicate appreciation of the future cost to them personally, of following Jesus, some understanding of what was to come. This is revealed to them more clearly in verses 20-28.

Matthew 20:20-28. Suffering and service: the request of James and John

Then the mother of the sons of Zebedee came up to Him with her sons, and kneeling before Him, she asked Him for something. And He said to her, 'What do you want?' She said to Him, 'Command that those two sons of mine may sit one at your right hand and one at your left, in your Kingdom' (Matthew 20:20,21).

There are two aspects to this section of Matthew's gospel. The *first* is introduced by the mother of the sons of Zebedee. It begins with a question from their mother, and a definitive answer from Jesus, directed firstly at her, but continuing to the brothers. The *second* aspect concerns His words to the other disciples, indignant at the request of the mother of James and John. The disciples are challenged about their relationship to one another, and their understanding of who Jesus is, and the purpose of His coming amongst them.

Between the two aspects of these verses, Jesus is giving His disciples the privilege of sharing His *'cup'* with them.

Comparison of Matthew 20:20 with Luke 24:10, Mark 15:40, John 19:25, and Matthew 27:55, may indicate that the wife of Zebedee was Salome and that she was the sister of Jesus' mother, Mary. She was one of many women who followed Jesus from afar, ministering to Him (Matthew 27:55).

She may well have caught something of the importance and significance of Jesus' ministry, recognising that it would not end in despair and frustration, but had a higher purpose, and would end in His glorification. When that time of glorification came, she wanted her sons to be part of it. Her great faith that it would be so, that Jesus would enter into His glorious kingdom, persuaded her that this was indeed going to be the case, and she wanted them to be included and preferably in a prominent position. What mother does not want the very highest and best for her children? She kneels before Jesus in silence and worship, and He encourages her to speak to Him.

It is noteworthy that Jesus did not rebuke her. Though great, her understanding was limited. Did she not realise that the way to glory was through the cross? That was the way He had to go. Though of course for James and John the way of the cross was not the way for the redemption of mankind as it was for Jesus, yet for them too it was a bitter cup.

He turned to them and said, 'Are you able to drink the cup that I am to drink?' (verse 22). And then their answer, 'We are able,' which demonstrated completely their misunderstanding of what would be involved in that cup, but also their abandonment and willingness to suffer with their Lord.

Then He gently said to them, 'You will drink My cup, but to sit at my right hand and at my left is not mine to give, but it is for those for whom it has been prepared by my Father' (verse 23).

What did He mean by 'His cup'? Psalm 75:9 speaks of a cup in the hand of the Lord which is a cup of judgement for the wicked. Isaiah 51:17 speaks of the cup of the wrath of the Lord, which in verse 22 He takes away from His people to give to their tormentors (verse 23). Jeremiah 25:15 also speaks of the cup of the wine of the Lord's wrath which Jeremiah was to give to all the nations to drink as a punishment (verse 29), including Judah and all the inhabitants of Jerusalem who have not turned away from their evil ways (verse 5, 7).

When Jesus says, 'Are you able to drink the cup which I am about to drink?' (verse 22) does He have the imagery of the Old Testament in mind? The cup is a symbol of judgement, of testing through extreme circumstances. Jesus says to them, 'You *will* drink my cup' (verse 23). Jesus has an affirmation for these two treasured disciples that they will go all the way with Him into suffering and death. Jesus never coerces anybody, but how He rejoices when someone takes that step of faith. In another context He declares that there is joy in heaven over one sinner who repents. Perhaps He might have added, over one follower of Mine who is prepared to go all the way with Me (Luke 15:7, 1). In these events, Jesus finds great joy.

Suffering and death are something in their future which James and John and in some measure, all the disciples, will endure. They will experience the judgement of people unqualified to judge, people whose power lies in oppression and cruelty and torture. James' will have a martyr's death at the hands of Herod in 44 A.D. (Acts 12:2) and for John, incarceration on the Isle of Patmos. There are also traditions concerning the death of John of which the New Testament does not speak.

We know the story of the Passion, and that all the disciples 'forsook Him and fled' (Matthew 26:56). But when James and John made their declaration, of being able to drink that appalling cup, they were totally sincere and committed to that declaration.

Perhaps many of us recognise that determination to follow Jesus all the way, and how often we fail. We have no claim before God, only the plea to His mercy, a mercy which never fails. We do not look for seats of honour, only for the privilege of being able to see His Face, the Face of the Judge whom we know as our Saviour, Jesus, and His Face is the face of love.

The cup of judgement has become for us the cup of blessing which we bless (1 Corinthians 10:16) the precious promise of forgiveness through His blood, for the judgement fell on Christ instead of on us who deserved it (1 Corinthians 11:25). Jesus has transformed the cup of judgement into something precious, a way of remembering Him and His death 'until He come' (1 Corinthians 11:26). It has become for us participation in the body of Christ, the cup of the New Covenant in Hs blood,

When the other disciples heard what James and John had said, they were indignant (verse 24), even though Jesus had made it clear that positions in the Kingdom of Heaven were not in His gift, but in the gift of His Father.

This verse among others had been used in what is known as the Arian controversy to explain that Jesus was subordinate to His Father, as a lesser God to a higher God. But Jesus had declared, 'I and my Father are One' (John 10:30). Such a (mis) understanding of the Trinity would not have occurred to Matthew, who identified Jesus as Immanuel, God with us, both functionally and ontologically, and for whom any other identification would have self-evidently impugned the authority and majesty, the God likeness, of Jesus.

Jesus knows what is going on in the hearts and minds of these possibly temporally rebellious disciples, who have heard Salome's words. He gently calls them to Him (verse 25), for He has something of tremendous importance to say to them. Do they really want to be great? He says, 'Look at the Gentile rulers; they are not able to do as they think best because they have lords who rule over them. That kind of greatness is not what I want for you, which in the end only becomes an evil and tyrannical authority, an authority of oppression. The greatness which I want for you is the greatness of service, that you should be servants one of another, caring for one another, even as a slave cares for his master. 'The first among you must be your slave' (verse 27).

This is what Jesus came to do, and be. He came to serve, not to be served, and in the end this took Him to the cross, where He gave His life as a ransom for many (verse 28). And we serve each other as slaves in the church, giving up all right to ourselves, our time, our ability if only we can serve another. How the Lord does persist in turning things upside down! Just as He did in the challenge to become like little children in Matthew 18:1-4.

Of course, there needs to be leadership in the church. But these leaders who would be first πρῶτος, among you (verse 27) have an ever greater responsibility to be servants of all, for even the desire to be great corrupts genuine service.

In this way, as in many other instances throughout this gospel, the church becomes a counter culture, subverting the 'natural' order of things in the world. And Jesus reinforces these sayings in Matthew 23:8-12. We are given the privilege of being servants of the servants of the Lord, *servus servorum Dei*.

Jesus is not speaking here of secular authority, those who would be great in the world, which is of fundamental difference from the church. Without the transforming power of the gospel, human beings will not go down the route of self-subordination if it is avoidable. What the church must do is what Jesus has done. Jesus, using once again His self-designation of Son of Man, which includes all His earthly activity of healing and teaching, His death and resurrection and future exaltation — Jesus says it is as the Son of Man that He came to seek and to save that which was lost; as the Son of Man that He came not to be served, but to serve, and to give His life as a ransom for many (verse 28).

Jesus is interpreting His death as λύτρον, ransom. Ransom is the price paid for slaves, or the ransom money paid in place of capital punishment (Exodus 21:30). Jesus has ransomed believers from slavery to sin. He has paid the price for us. We are His. He has become a substitute, vicariously suffering the death, which was our due, because of the sin which we had committed.

As so often, we turn again to Isaiah 53: When He makes Himself an offering for sin, He shall see His seed, He shall prolong His days. The will of the Lord shall prosper in His hand and He shall see the fruit of the travail of His soul and be satisfied (Isaiah 53:10-11). This is love, not that we loved God, but that He loved us, and sent His Son to be the expiation, propitiation, atonement for our sins. Beloved, if God so loved us, we also ought to love one another (1 John 4:10, 11).

Matthew 20:29-31. The healing of two blind men

After the profound thoughts of Matthew 20:20-28, it seems a bit of an anti-climax to come to the healing of the two blind men. But as we have seen so often, Matthew's contextualisation of his passages of healing with passages of narrative and teaching fulfil a very distinct purpose.

As they went out of Jericho, a great crowd followed Him. And behold, two blind men sitting by the roadside when they heard that Jesus was passing by, cried out, 'Have mercy on us, Son of David!' The crowd rebuked them, telling them to be silent, but they cried out the more, 'Lord, have mercy on us, Son of David!' And Jesus stopped, stood still and called them saying, 'What do you want Me to do for you?' They said to Him, 'Lord, let our eyes be opened.' and Jesus in pity, filled with compassion touched their eyes, and immediately they saw again, and followed Him. (Matthew 20: 29-34).

In Matthew's gospel, this is the last recorded miracle that Jesus performs before entering Jerusalem in the last week of His life. Jesus and His disciples had got as far as Jericho on their journey to Jerusalem. It was now time to leave Jericho for the last lap of the journey, to Jerusalem. Suffering and death await Jesus, and confusion, dismay and betrayal await the disciples, but there is no sense either of rush or delay but the same steady rate of progress, inevitably followed by the crowd.

And behold, two blind men sitting by the way, οδόν. For us, the word 'way' has overtones, it being the first name by which Christians were called (Acts 9:2; 19:9,23; 18:26; 22:4), and a sense that the blind men were almost waiting for Jesus' call to follow Him. But we almost feel as if we could pause on every word of the gospel. Matthew again uses 'Behold!' We have understood 'behold!' as a stop sign, 'look, be attentive. Here are two blind men sitting by the way'! We have also seen what the way might mean in terms of discipleship. The way of faith, the way of repentance.

These men were sitting, waiting for Jesus. They wanted to receive their sight, yes, but they wanted so much more than that. 'Have mercy on us, Son of David!' they cried. They believed Him to be the Son of David, the fulfilment of all the Messianic prophecy, perhaps He could be merciful to them, give them a life of following Him, an inner life of trust and faith, eternal life, not just a life which would go on forever, but a *quality of the eternal,* here and now; the eternal which could only come from an eternal God, not confined by time but outside of time, where He dwells in eternity. So perhaps they were inadvertently asking for this life, which He gives to all who come to Him in penitence and faith.

The crowd rebuked these two men (verse 31). Like many crowds everywhere, they failed to see what was going on here. They had no idea what was going on in the hearts and minds of these men, even on the practical level of how disabling it is to be blind. The *vox populi,* the voice of the people so often gives advantage to the many at the expense of the minority. Undeterred, the blind men 'cried out the more' (verse 31), this time using the title, 'Lord', '*κύριε*'. Lord, have mercy on us, Son of David! This was an insight the crowd did not have, that the Messiah, the Son of David, was also the Lord.

Such a revelation to these men caused the Lord Jesus to stop in His tracks, yet His words to them were simple, 'What do you want Me to do for you?' (verse 32). For us there is an echo of the question to the mother of James and John, 'What do you want Me to do for you?' (verse 21). What she had wanted was a position of greatness for her sons. What they wanted was vision.

The mother of James and John, and in fact all the disciples, had been blind as to their conduct, to their behaviour in the fellowship they had with each other, until Jesus had opened the eyes of their understanding. All that these two blind men were asking for was sight, ability to see, but behind that request was all the longing for a different life, a life of following Him. 'Lord, let our eyes be opened,' they said to Him (verse 33), and Jesus, in pity, in compassion, touched their eyes, and immediately they received their sight and followed Him (verse 34).

Not all the opposition of the crowd could prevent the mercy of the One who came not to be served, but to serve, from reaching these two men. This was an historical act of Jesus, witnessed by two men. At the mouth of two or three witnesses every word shall be established was a strong principle in the time of Jesus (Deuteronomy 17:6, 7; Matthew 18:16).

But we can also understand the story metaphorically. We ourselves are blind, sitting by the wayside, urgently and incessantly calling out to God for mercy, to the Messianic Son of David for healing, the One who will shortly enter the Holy City of Jerusalem in the Name of the Lord, where the crowds will shout, 'Hosanna to the Son of David, blessed is He who comes in the Name of the Lord' (Matthew 21:9).

It appears hopeful that when He enters Jerusalem the crowds will have come to some recognition of who He is, possibly through the witness of these formerly blind men. But Jesus will receive a cold reception in Jerusalem from the 'blind' Pharisees and scribes (23:16) for they do not recognise Him as Lord as the blind men did. Beginning with the very first chapter of the gospel, it is evident that 'the Son of David' refers to all the prophecies, all the promises of a new reign under a new King. Using His title 'Lord' brings the past into the present.

There is no doubt as to the authority and presence of Jesus as Lord, for He utterly and completely fulfils all the prophecies, actively preparing for the final fulfilment of them in Jerusalem. Jericho, the city of the moon, receives its light from the sun, and He 'passes by' (verse 30) in all His humanity, yet also in His deity. He stands still in His impermanence, in His passing, (verse 32) and calls the blind to Him that they might change to a new life, receive their sight, freeing not them only, but all who come to Him, from their blindness.

He is unchanging. He will always be there, willing to change the lives, the future, the principles by which men and women try to live, to living in the light of the Son of Man. 'A light to lighten the Gentiles and the glory of His people Israel' (Luke 2:32).

Matthew Chapter 21

Matthew 21:1-11. The triumphal entry into Jerusalem

And when they drew near to Jerusalem and came to Bethphage, to the Mount of Olives, then Jesus sent two disciples, saying to them, 'Go into the village opposite you, and immediately you will find an ass tied, and a colt with her; untie them and bring them to Me' (Matthew 21:1-2).

Jesus enters Jerusalem from the east, from Jericho, and comes near to Bethphage, a village on the slopes of the Mount of Olives, in effect, a suburb of Jerusalem. Many pilgrims would have taken that route, especially at the three Feasts of Tabernacles, Dedication of the Temple and Passover; coming from the east, from Jericho, and passing through Bethany and then Bethphage, just across the Kidron valley from Jerusalem.

Jesus' arrival in Bethphage indicates that the other village 'the village opposite you' (verse 2) to which Jesus sends His disciples for the loan of the donkey, could have been Bethany. Bethphage, the 'House of Figs' was less than a mile from Jerusalem itself.

Jesus is about to make His entry into Jerusalem, although His goal is not at present the city but the temple. Jerusalem is 'the city of the great king' (Psalm 48:2). Jerusalem is often identified as Zion in certain poetic writings, especially throughout the Psalms, especially in relation to the period when the Ark of the Covenant had been brought up out of the city to the Temple. Zion is 'the city of our God', the place where God has said that He would put His Name there (1 Kings 8:29), built on Mount Moriah where Abraham so sacrificially offered up his son Isaac to God until prevented by the voice from heaven (Genesis 22:1-14). Zion was the city of David, won from the Jebusirtes by David for God (2 Samuel 5:6-9;

2 Chronicles 27:3; 33:14) Zion, the most significant of all the sacred places to the prophets (Isaiah 4:5; Jeremiah 31:6; Zechariah 8:2,3).

'Zion' stands for the whole of Jerusalem, the religious capital of the people of the Lord (Psalms 48:2; Isaiah 28:16; Romans 9:33). In other places in the Old Testament it stands symbolically for the tribes or land of Judah, or for the whole of Israel, because it represents God's presence with His chosen people, and their duty of dependence on Him.

It is of extreme significance that Jesus rides *publicly* into Jerusalem. Until now, He has often asked that His identity be kept secret or at least contained, saying to those who were healed or blessed 'to say nothing to anyone' about who He is (8:4), or see that no-one knows it of His activity among them (9:3), or 'ordering them not to make Him known' (12:15), or in the case of His wonderful transfiguration before the disciples. 'Tell no one the vision until the Son of Man be raised from the dead' (17:9).

But Jesus enters Jerusalem publicly, for as He said, 'It cannot be that a prophet should perish away from Jerusalem' (Luke 13:33). A prophet speaks what he has heard from God. He is the messenger whom God has chosen to convey to the people His plan and purpose for them, and that they need to hear, and respond to.

Jesus was prophet, priest and King.

He enters Jerusalem riding on a colt, which along with its mother has been borrowed from some unknown disciple, one who eagerly responds to the two disciples' request for the animals, ending in a phrase with which the unnamed disciple cannot fail to cooperate. 'The Lord has need of him' (verse 3).

So the owner unties it, and it is brought to Jesus, and the disciples put their garments on it, to comfort it. It is apparent that it has not yet been broken in, for a colt that had been broken in would no longer be with its mother.

Luke tells us that it is a colt 'upon which no-one has ever yet sat' (Luke 19:30) yet the colt does not rear or become fractious when Jesus sits on him. In another context, Isaiah says, 'The ox knows its owner, and the ass its master' (Isaiah 1:3). This young donkey apparently knows or senses that it has its Creator upon its back, the kindest, most loving, most understanding of anyone it has yet encountered, and responds by being utterly calm in spite of the crowds shouting, 'Hosanna to the Son of David! Blessed is He who comes in the Name of the Lord' (verse 9), spreading their garments on the road before its hoofs, waving branches which they had cut from the trees and scattering them on the road; palm branches according to John's gospel (John 12:13; Matthew 21:8).

What was the point of this public entry into Jerusalem that Jesus was trying to make, both to His disciples, and to the crowd? For nothing He ever did was without purpose. Jesus was coming into His own city as a King. He was quite obviously not coming as a conquering king who would ride a warhorse. He was indeed a coming king, but what kind of king comes in humility, on an animal which is not even His, on a lowly donkey?

Throughout this gospel we have noted Jesus' love and compassion as a defining characteristic of His ministry. Surely this attribute of humility is the very foundation of all that He came to do. Again, we turn to Philippians 2:6-8. Though He was in the form of God, He did not count equality with God a thing to be grasped, but emptied Himself, taking the form of a servant, being born in the likeness of men. And being found in human form *He humbled Himself* and became obedient into death, even death on a cross.

'Thou shall call His Name Jesus, for He shall save His people from their sins', is such an important theme in Matthew's gospel (Matthew 1:21). A time for judgement must surely come, but not until there has been a time for repentance, an opportunity to respond, to be given the gift of an open heart before God, an uncovering of the ears of the deaf and the eyes of the blind to see the wonderful salvation which Jesus offers.

Some aspect of this is to be observed in the acclamation of the people, 'Hosanna to the Son of David! Blessed is who comes in the Name of the Lord!' (Matthew 21:9). They at least realised His kingship when they clamoured, 'Hosanna to the Son of David!' David, the greatest king they had so far had. How much more wonderful will be their appreciation of Him when they realise that this kingship is a foretaste of what God has for them as they come to Him and receive Him into their lives, as they submit themselves to the King.

John 12:15 quotes Zechariah 9:9. 'Fear not, daughter of Zion, behold your king is coming, riding on an ass's colt'. Matthew also quotes Zechariah 9:9, making it very clear that this entry into Jerusalem was a fulfilment of Old Testament prophecy; a Messianic fulfilment, introducing it with a quotation from Isaiah 62:11. 'Say to the daughter of Zion, behold, your salvation comes. Behold, His reward is with Him, and His recompense before Him. Isaiah 62:2 is full of promises of what the Lord has in mind, 'For Zion's sake, for Jerusalem's sake. How unutterably sad that the Jewish leaders (Matthew 21:15), those who represented the Lord before His people should be the very ones to reject Him.

Zechariah as well as Isaiah had a vision of 'the king coming to you, triumphant, humble and riding on an ass, and on a colt the foal of an ass. Therefore, rejoice, greatly, O daughter of Zion! Shout aloud, 0 daughter of Jerusalem!'

The contrast of a victorious, triumphant king, yet humbly riding into Jerusalem, is almost a contradiction in terms. How could He be both victorious and triumphant, and yet humble? This is Jesus, the Messianic King. This is the reality of who He is. The future for Him and for His people lies not through some military conquest, but through the conquest of all that militates against the compassion and love of God, and its transforming power.

It is noteworthy that from this point on, Jesus has no further dealings with the chief priests and the scribes alone.

Truly, this took place to fulfil all that was spoken by the prophet (verse 4). Truly this was a destiny that could only lead to 'rejoicing greatly, O daughter of Zion' (Zechariah 9:9). Even though there will be many who reject Him. God will never cast off His people when He foreknew (Romans 11:2). The sadness comes in the parable which Jesus will tell in this same chapter, when the owner of the vineyard sends His Son to receive the fruit of the vineyard saying, 'They will reverence My Son,' but whom they cast out of the vineyard and killed (Matthew 21:28). Always, God has His Son in view, and many, indeed, multitudes, have turned to Him, but there will always be those who turn away from Him.

Jesus has come to the end of His earthly ministry, though He still has much to teach His disciples. Jesus is giving the crowds a last opportunity to recognize Him as the fulfilment of all their scriptures, and to turn to Him and receive His salvation. All those in Jerusalem that day could have seen Him. But the challenge, as always, comes to every individual, every man, every woman.

As He entered Jerusalem, all the city was stirred, shaken, σείεται like an earthquake, saying, 'Who is this?' And the crowds said, 'This is the prophet Jesus from Nazareth of Galilee' (Matthew 21:10, 11).

Many of the prophets of the Old Testament had amazing things happen to them, but this prophet was outstanding. It may seem incredible that a whole city was so stirred that the effect was that of an earthquake under their feet, there was a shifting of all that was usual and normal, just because someone had ridden into their city on a donkey. Was it something to do with what they had been shouting? 'Hosanna, Hosanna to the Son of David! Blessed is He who comes in the Name of the Lord' (Matthew 21: 9).

It was a shout of jubilation. But it was also a shout of purpose, an anticipation of what the prophet from Nazareth was about to do. He was going to enter Jerusalem 'in the Name of the Lord' (verse 9), carrying with him all the might and power of God, God's whole character, all that He is or ever will be, the One who rules from eternity over all the nations upon earth, who dwells in eternal light, whom no man ever saw or can see, who is above and beyond all human knowing. All this is represented by the Name of the Lord. And all this, and more, is in Jesus.

God was in Christ, reconciling the world to Himself (2 Corinthians 5:19). We read this and believe, because it is the only thing we shall ever read which makes sense of everything else.

We see God in Jesus.

The Jewish leaders are ignorant of who Jesus is. The crowds know a little and rejoice in what they know. We too know a little and long to know more and more of this remarkable and wonderful Person who manifests God to us, a part of whose Body we are, redeemed, restored and forgiven through the shedding of His precious blood upon the Cross. May God be gracious to us, and bless us, And cause His face to shine upon us, That His way may be known upon earth, His saving power among all nations. Let the people praise You, O Lord. Let all the people praise You! As they did when You rode into Jerusalem (Psalm 67 1-3).

Matthew 21:12-17. The cleansing of the temple

And Jesus entered the temple of God and drove out all who sold and bought in the temple, and He overturned the tables of the money changers, and the seat of those who sold doves. He said to them, 'It is written, My house shall be called a house of prayer, but you make it a den of robbers' (Mathew 21:12,13).

The first temple had been built on the threshing floor of Ornan the Jebusite after the Lord stayed the plague from Jerusalem when David interceded for the people. It began as an altar to the Lord, which David built, offering burnt offerings and peace offerings and cereal offerings, which God answered with fire from heaven upon the altar. And this altar became the place of sacrifice for the nation. David said, 'Here also shall be the house of the Lord God, and here the altar of burnt offering for Israel (1 Chronicles 21:18-21; 2 Samuel 15-25).

But Solomon, David's son, built the first temple, the house of the Lord in Jerusalem, on Mount Moriah where the Lord had appeared to David his father, at the place that David had appointed, on the threshing floor of Ornan the Jebusite (2 Chronicles 3:1).

This temple was destroyed by Nebuchadnezzar in 587 B.C. and the people taken in captivity to Babylon (2 Chronicles 36:19,

20; 2 Kings 25:9). But when Cyrus became king of Persia in 559 B.C., he proclaimed that the Lord, the God of heaven, had charged him to build Him a house in Jerusalem. This was accomplished by Ezra and Nehemiah and completed in 515 B.C. (Ezra 6:14-23) under Darius the king, and according to the promise made by God to Zerubbabel (Haggai 2:9).

This temple, sometimes known as the Zerubbabel temple (as opposed to Solomon's temple) was the one so largely restored by Herod the Great. It stood for 420 years until 70 A.D.

Following its conquest by Alexander the Great, Judea became part of the Ptolemaic kingdom of Egypt until 200 B.C., when the Seleucid king Antiochus III Epiphanes of Syria defeated Ptolemy V at the Battle of Panion. Judea then became part of the Seleucid empire. The temple was looted, and its services stopped.

In 167 B.C. Antiochus Epiphanes ordered an altar to Zeus to be erected in the temple. He also banned circumcision, and ordered swine to be sacrificed on the altar of the temple.

Following the Maccabean revolt against the Seleucid Empire, the second temple was rededicated and became the religious pillar of the Jewish Hasmonean Kingdom. This rededication is associated with the Jewish festival of *Hanukkah*.

Reconstruction of the temple began under Herod the Great with a massive expansion of the Temple Mount, generally dated from 20-19 B.C. If the Lord Jesus was about 30 years old when He began His ministry, having been born in about 4 B.C. the Jews were correct in stating that the Temple had been 46 years in building by that time (John 2:20).

Religious worship and temple rituals continued during the reconstruction process. Later, the sanctuary shekel of Exodus 30:13 was reinstated to support the temple as the temple tax. Pilgrims coming to the Feasts of the Lord in Jerusalem from distant parts of the Roman Empire needed to change their currency from the profane standard Greek or Roman coinage for Jewish or Tyrian money, for only the latter two were considered religious. Then the pilgrim would be able to purchase sacrificial animals, a pigeon or a lamb, in preparation for the following day's sacrifices.

The first thing would be to enter the temple at the south side, then visit a *'mikveh'* where they would ritually wash and cleanse themselves. Retrieving their sacred animals, they would then proceed to the Count of the Gentiles. This had become primarily a bazaar, an emporium with vendors selling souvenirs as well as sacrificial animals and food, and also accommodated currency changers because the Jews were not allowed to coin their own money and viewed Roman currency as an abomination to the Lord.

At Passover time, there could be as many as 3,000-4,000 pilgrims.

The meetings of the Sanhedrin were held on the upper floors.

To buy sacrificial animals actually in the Temple itself was essential because only in this way could worshippers be certain of the necessary ritual purity of the animal. But the money changers would impose a high commission, perhaps 2% or 4%. This was especially hard on those poor enough to be able to afford only a pigeon or dove.

Mark, though nor Matthew, also speaks of those who carried things through the temple (Mark 11:16), using the temple as a shortcut, as some water carriers did.

Jesus was quoting Isaiah 56:7 when He said, 'My house shall be called a house of prayer' (verse 13). The din of commerce would have made it difficult for Gentiles to pray in the outer court, the court of the Gentiles. Jeremiah 7:11 speaks of the Lord protesting the use to which 'this house, which is called by My Name' is being put, saying, 'Has this house become a den of robbers?'

The priests had made the temple a place from which they could carry on a business to make a profit, while misusing their calling to celebrate public worship, prayer and sacrifice. They commit something frightful. They put God at the service of sin.

It is true that Matthew uses the word ἱερόν – temple precincts rather than ναός – inner sanctuary (verse 12), the place where God said He would meet with His people. Nevertheless, Jesus accuses the traders of making the house of prayer into a den of thieves, οἶκον ἐμπορίου – a house of merchandise, emporium. The chief priests and scribes, using the traders in merchandise even when honestly conducted, are depriving the Temple of its right to be called a house of prayer.

And Jesus entered the temple of God, and drove out all who sold and bought in the temple, and He overthrew the tables of the money changers, and the seats of those who sold doves, saying to them, 'It is written, My house shall be called a house of prayer, but you have made it a den of robbers' (verse 13).

Why did Jesus find it necessary at this point in His ministry to enter the temple in this authoritative way? And to drive out the money changers and those who sold sacrificial animals? He had but recently arrived in Jerusalem. Did He feel it was necessary to establish at the outset that the time of the New Covenant that God was making with mankind had begun? That the Old Covenant, including the temple, was passing away, with all its ritual and sacrificial ethos, and that the New would be ratified in the once-for-all sacrifice which would be made (Hebrews 10:10), not on an altar in a building, however beautiful, but on a bleak hillside outside Jerusalem, exchanging the altar for the cross. This was the point in time to which Jesus was progressing, but which had been determined from eternity. All the altars, from Abel and Noah and Abraham onward, were anticipations of the final altar, the cross.

The chief priests and the scribes had already schemed, planned to destroy Him, and showed, once again, their contempt of Him when 'the blind and the lame came to Him in the temple, and He healed them' (verse 14). This was the temple, the house of prayer where inability to *walk* God's way, to *see* with God's vision, had been so obvious to Him, and so overlooked by the religious leaders, proving just how 'lame' and 'blind' they were in God's sight, with all their knowledge of His word, the scriptures.

Have you never read?' said Jesus to the scribes and Pharisees, 'that out of the mouths of babes and sucklings, Thou hast perfected praise?' (verse 16; Psalm 8:2). They had become indignant that the children in the temple were crying out, 'Hosanna to the Son of David!' The children could appreciate what the religious leaders could not, that a Messianic King had come among them. The babes and sucklings could have been children as young as three, for it was not unusual in those days for children still to be nursed at that age. How wonderful to hear children at any stage of their development praising the Lord! It is not Israel's leaders who represent the true Israel, but the formerly blind, the formerly lame (verse 14), the children, who represent the true people of God. These are the people who are welcome in His house, His home. They are His loved ones, His family. The temple will one day cease to be, but His love for His own will never cease.

With what relief Jesus left the crowded, noisy city of Jerusalem and went out of the city and lodged in Bethany (verse 17). Bethany was about two miles outside Jerusalem. We would love to speculate that He went to the house of Lazarus, Martha and Mary, but we have no evidence for that.

When the temple was destroyed in 70 B.C. the religious ritual of the temple passed not to the synagogues, important though they were, but to the Jewish home, for the temple had been the Lord's home here on earth, the place where He delighted to be with His family. They became, not the people of the temple, with its sacrificial rituals but the people of the Book, their sacred Hebrew scriptures, while so much of their religious experience was confined to the home.

A transaction had taken place at the cross. Paul, writing to the Christians in Corinth (1 Corinthians 3:16), says, 'Do you not know that *you* are God's temple, and that God's spirit dwells in you? And in 1 Corinthians 6:19, 'Do you not know that your body is a temple of the Holy Spirit within you, which you have from God? You are not your own, you were bought with a price. So glorify God in your body.' In these passages, as also in John 2:19-21, 2 Corinthians 6:16, Ephesians 2:19-21, Revelation 21:21, the Greek word ναός – inner sanctuary is used rather than ἱερόν, the temple precincts, the other Greek word for temple.

This is the new thing that God is doing. Jesus has been made to us wisdom, righteousness, sanctification, and redemption

(1 Corinthians 1:30). He has come to baptise us, immerse us, in His Holy Spirit (Matthew 3:11; John 1:33). He has come to make His dwelling in us. Within us is the inner sanctuary in which God loves to dwell by His Spirit. We are His temple. We are not our own. *We are His.*

Matthew 21:18-22. The withered fig tree

In the morning, as He was returning to the city, He was hungry. And seeing a fig tree by the wayside, He went to it, and found nothing on it but leaves only. And He said to it, 'May no fruit ever come from you again!' And the fig tree withered at once (Matthew 21:18-19).

This episode, probably relying on Peter's comment in Mark 11:21, has been variously described as 'the cursing of the fig tree' (Hill, Luz, Gundry).

The use of the word curse/cursing indicates a solemn utterance or imprecation, intended to inflict destruction or punishment, according to the Oxford dictionary. But to assume that Jesus would curse a fig tree just because He was hungry and the fig tree had no figs would seem petulant to a degree, and unlike the character of Jesus so far revealed to us in the gospel.

So what was the purpose of Jesus speaking (not cursing) to the fig tree? For we have also discovered that He does nothing without a purpose even when passing judgement upon a fig tree. As with all Jesus' miracles, this miracle points beyond itself.

The vine was an established metaphor for Israel in Old Testament texts, but this could not be said for the fig tree, though it is sometimes mentioned in conjunction with Israel (Jeremiah 24:10; 8:13; Hosea 2:14; 9:10; Joel 1:7; Micah 7:1).

So is the Lord Jesus thinking of judgement upon Israel, or perhaps especially of Israel's leaders, since He has so recently cleansed the Temple both symbolically and actually? There is nothing in these verses to suggest such an explanation, though undoubtedly He did want to see 'fruit', the fruit of righteousness in those chosen to be the shepherds of God's people, to use another metaphor.

Jesus was fully human, as well as fully divine. He wept at the grave of Lazarus (John 11:35). He fasted for 40 days in the wilderness and afterwards was hungry (Matthew 4:2, 11). When He hung upon the Cross, He said 'I thirst' (John 19:28). As well as being the Son of God He was just as truly the Son of Man, made like His brethren in every respect, yet without sin (Hebrews 2:17; 4:15) Hunger may have been the trigger for the miraculous withering of the fig tree, but Jesus had a stronger reason than that for He wanted His disciples to learn something of extreme importance.

After His cleansing of the Temple in verse 12, He had declared, 'It is written, My house shall be called a house of *prayer.*' He would enter the Temple again in verse 23, but at this moment He is walking toward Jerusalem from Bethany, where He, and presumably also the disciples since they were with Him (verse 20), had lodged overnight. Walking along the road, two miles into Jerusalem, there would have been many trees, but Jesus chose this particular sterile tree to teach His disciples about faith, and about prayer.

And seeing a fig tree by the wayside, He went to it, and found nothing on it but leaves only. And He said to it, 'May no fruit ever come from you again!' And the fig tree withered at once (verse 19). The disciples were astonished! They marvelled, saying, 'How? How did this fig tree wither at once?' And here we have one of the Amen sayings, implicating the whole purpose and character of God, for it is the name of Jesus (Revelations 3:14). 'Amen, I say to you, if you have faith and never doubt, you will not only do what has been done to the fig tree, but even if you say to this mountain, "Be taken up and cast into the sea," it will be done. And whatever you ask in prayer, you will receive it, if you have faith' (verses 21, 22).

Jesus is teaching His disciples; if your prayer rests on divine faithfulness (Lamentations 3:22), you can say to those obstacles which stand in the way of true obedience, of true discipleship, 'Be taken up and cast into the sea.' Faith is perfect confidence in the nature and ability of God, a confidence which induces even the weakest of us to surrender to Him, and His perfect will for us, and for those for whom we pray.

So, faith is surrender. It is saying, 'Our Father, Thy will be done.'

Fig trees and mountains which get in the way of the Father's will, will be removed if we have faith as we pray. Prayer and faith are inextricably linked. Prayer without faith is empty. Faith without prayer is impossible.

This was what the Jewish leaders had not understood, or they would not have allowed the temple, the dwelling place of God, to become a mere bazaar, a den of thieves, instead of the meeting place between God and men and women it was intended to be.

But buildings, however, extensive and beautifully constructed, are not the only places where prayer can be made to a loving Heavenly Father. Buildings are not the precondition. Faith is. Jesus says, 'If you have faith'. In faith, come to Him, and whatever you ask in prayer you will receive, if you have faith (Matthew 21: 22).

Jesus had shown His disciples the impossibility of causing a fig tree to wither and then the possibility of speaking to it on the grounds of faith. Jesus had become for them a paradigm in the exercise of faith. Even mountains, excessive examples of difficulty must yield to the will of God expressed in prayer. The steadfast love of the Lord never ceases, His mercies never come to an end. They are new every morning. Great is Thy faithfulness (Lamentations 3:22). However great or weak our faith, however hard we pray or however difficult we sometimes find prayer, we thank God that the answer to prayer lies not in our faith, but on His faithfulness, He who is the Amen of God.

Whatever we ask in prayer, we shall receive, if we have faith (verse 22). More important than the loss of a fig tree was the purpose of the Lord Jesus in showing His disciples the nature of the relationship between faith and prayer. Faith is the predisposition of the disciple. Without it he cannot come to God, for he that comes to God must believe that He is (Hebrews 11:6 A.V.) Prayer is the expression of that predisposition.

How can a child not want to come and talk to her father? No more can a child of God not want to come and talk to her, or his Father. And what father does not delight to listen to his child? Even so, our Father delights to hear us when we talk to Him. And when we have spoken with Him, He then gives us authority to deal with the fig trees and mountains in the lives of ourselves and others.

It's so simple really. Wesley is right. Love is at the root of all. His love for us, our love for Him. 'Give me the childlike praying love, that longs to build Thy House again. Thy love, let it my heart o'er power and all my simple soul devour.'

Matthew 21:23-22:46. The authority of Jesus questioned

And when He entered the temple, the chief priests and elders of the people came up to him as He was teaching (Matthew 21:23).

This section of Matthew's gospel records events which took place in the temple, giving it added significance. It is remarkable in at least two ways. Firstly, how amazing that after cleansing the temple on the previous day, upsetting the usual business of the court of the Gentiles, releasing the doves, overturning the temples of the money changers, Jesus was allowed to sit quietly in the temple and teach all and any who came to Him, as any rabbi would do.

Why was He not arrested at this point and taken off to some dreadful place of torture and interrogation? Because His hour had not yet come (John 2:4; 7:6, 30; 8:20). This is the additional factor. There is no doubt that He is in control, that nothing can happen to Him without His express permission. He is allowing the chief priests and elders of the people to question His authority because He still has something to teach them.

So these verses give us an introduction to this whole section of Matthew's gospel, from 21:33 to 22:46. They derive their importance not only from what Jesus is wanting to teach them, but also from their proximity to the culminating events of His life, for He has chosen this Passover to fulfil His destiny as the Lamb of God, who takes away the sin of the world (John 1:29)

John records Him as saying, 'No man takes my life from Me, I lay it down of Myself. I have power to lay it down and I have power to take it again. This I have received from My Father' (John 10:18). In such a short while, the laying down of His life is what Jesus will do, so we take even more seriously what He is teaching in these chapters. This is the *first* remarkable thing to notice, that Jesus is in complete control in each of these events leading up to His death.

Of course He has always been, throughout all the circumstances of His ministry, but this is the point at which all the malice and rejection of the leaders of God's people is aimed at Him, their compulsion and determination to destroy Him, the one whom their God, whom they purported to serve, had sent to deliver them from their bondage to sin and the law. This is He whom all the prophets in the scriptures of which they were so knowledgeable, had prophesied would come, and they did not recognise Him. He came into His own and His own received Him not (John 1:11).

The *second* thing to notice is the emphasis on Jesus' authority. But to as many as received Him, who believed in His name, He gave power, *exousia*, deferred authority, to become children of God (John 1:11).

There are five recorded controversies in these chapters, and a trilogy of parables. The controversies all centre around the understanding of the Jewish leaders of their religion and are presented in the form of question and answer, a method used in rabbinical schools, highlighting the fact that though Jesus was not (probably) an ordained rabbi, yet they recognised the quality of His teaching.

But did this give Him the competence to act as He did in this way; entering the city on a donkey? Or cleansing the temple? Was His authority to do these things from God, from men, or from Himself? He has regularly taught the people in the synagogues (4:23; 9:35; 13:54), now in the temple He is encroaching on the domain of the chief priests and elders of the people (verse 23), the representatives of the high priestly families, the highest representatives of the temple and the nation, that combination of His opponents who rule Jerusalem and will bring about His execution.

Elders of the people is a term used specifically as appropriate to the temple because of its biblical historicism (Exodus 17:5; 19: Numbers 11:16, 24; Ruth 4:4, Isaiah 3:14, Jeremiah 19:1). It will be repeated in the passion narrative (Matthew 26:34; 27:1), drawing attention to the hostility of these religious leaders, who now, in spite of their privileged position, are leading the people of whom they are the 'elders', astray.

These are the opponents who now want to inquire of Jesus' authority. 'Who gave you this authority?' (verse 23), they say. They do not deny that He has authority. They are just concerned with its origin. In spite of the undoubted authority which they possess by reason of their elevated position as chief priests and elders of the people, they cannot 'do these things' which Jesus is doing (verse 23). They are referring not primarily to His teaching but to His miracles, His driving out of the sellers and changers of the money in the temple; His healing of the blind and lame. Their query is a serious one, for they believe that all authority must be legitimated by them.

What is the answer of Jesus to their questions? What can He say in answer to these questions, 'By what authority do you do these things? And who gave you this authority?

These questions actually enable Jesus to answer their questions with one of His own. He makes His answer to them conditional on their response to His question. 'I also will ask you a question, and if you tell me the answer, then I also will tell you by what authority I do these things. The baptism of John, whence was it? From heaven or from men? (verse 24, 25)

To answer one question with another is typical of rabbinical debate. It does not necessarily mean avoiding the issue, but can be a means of clarifying it, and coming to a rational conclusion, or an exposure of your opponents point of view as irrational.

Jesus posed His question, involving an inevitable alternative. Was His authority from God or man? But He went further. John the Baptist's ministry, was *it* from God or man? (verse 25). They say, 'We do not know' (verse 27).

Because of their reaction to John's ministry, for they were unable to accept that he was indeed sent from God to proclaim repentance and forgiveness; and because of their fear of the multitude who believed that John was indeed a prophet, (verse 26), they could not give Jesus an answer. If they had confessed that John's authority to perform baptism for repentance came from God, they would have called attention to their own negative reaction to John's ministry. They did not respond to John's teaching, which is why he called them a 'brood of vipers' (Matthew 3:7).

They cannot give the wrong answer 'from men', because of the multitude.

They cannot give the right answer 'from God' without exposing themselves as disobedient to the prophet whom God had sent and invested with authority.

They say, 'We do not know' (verse 27).

Therefore, Jesus refuses to answer their questions.

Jesus asks the question about John's baptism because of the voice of the Father from heaven, 'This is my beloved Son, with whom I am well pleased' (3:17), and the corresponding descent of the Dove, the Holy Spirit upon Him at His baptism. The voice from heaven inaugurated Jesus' ministry as the Messiah, the Anointed One, the Christ, for He was indeed God's beloved Son. If John's ministry was in doubt, it gave the religious leaders justification for believing that Jesus' ministry was also in doubt. But they cannot escape the conviction that their policy of political expediency reveals and intensifies their guilt. They feared that the appropriate reply to them from Jesus would be, 'Why then did you not believe him?' (verse 25). In spite of all their importance as religious leaders, they could only say, 'We do not know' (verse 27).

And He said to them, 'Neither will I tell you by what authority I do these things' (verse 27).

Matthew 21:28-32. The parable of the two sons

But Jesus still has something to say to the chief priests and elders of the people (verse 23) in answer to their questions about His authority, and invites their consideration of the problem by means of a parable of which this is the first of three. He says to them, 'What do you think?' (verse 28), inviting them to listen carefully to what He has yet to say to them.

He said, 'A man had two sons, and he went to the first and said, "Son, go and work in the vineyard today." And he answered, "I will not," but afterward he repented and went. And he went to the second and said the same, and he answered, "I go, sir," but did not go. Which of the two did the will of his Father?'

To His listeners, the answer seemed obvious. 'Of course it was the first son,' they said (verse 31).

The difficult part of the interpretation comes next. Who are represented by these two sons? We must remember that we are still in the context of the discussion about the ministry of John the Baptist, and the authority of Jesus.

Jesus says, 'Amen I say to you, the tax collectors and the harlots go into the Kingdom of God before you' (verse 31). What a dreadful thing to say to them. They are upright people, obeying the law in every particular. Should they not be prioritised? Be the first to go into the kingdom of God? Jesus is not speaking about priority in time however, but exclusive displacement in eternity, in the eschatological future. The tax collectors and the harlots are represented by the first son of the parable for they were obedient to the preaching of John the Baptist. John came to them in the way of righteousness (verse 32). He had lived an impeccable life before God, in total obedience to what God had shown him to do. But he had not imposed that way upon those who had lived a very different kind of life, but rather showed them how they too could enter the Kingdom of Heaven through repentance and confessing their sins (3:6).

Jesus does not here use the term 'Kingdom of Heaven' as so often in Matthew's gospel, but 'Kingdom of God'. These people who had repented and confessed their sins had entered into, not a space, even a sacred space, and not a state of being, a state of grace, living under the reign of heaven, though they had done all those things, but emphatically they had entered into a relationship such as they had never enjoyed before, being as they were, outcasts from society. They had entered into a relationship with God.

This was a relationship with a totally satisfying, totally reliable, totally trustworthy Person, who just happened to be the creator of the universe. They had entered the Kingdom of God, the Kingdom of God the Father. For them, it could have been a tough decision on all sorts of levels. There could well have been a hesitation to commit oneself to what was so obviously the calling of God through the words of John. Perhaps at first it was easier to say to God 'No, I will not' as in verse 29, but afterwards, they repented, for a greater than John was here.'

But what of the second son?

Just as the Sadducees and Pharisees did not believe that John's ministry was from God, and even when they did see John's as the way of righteousness, they were disobedient to his preaching and did not repent, so in the parable, they as representatives of the religious establishment, symbolised the second son who replied to his father on receiving the command to go and work in the vineyard, 'I go, sir,' but did not go.

How terrible, how devastating, that they had said 'I go, sir,' to God, but they did not go. They were upright leaders of the people and had tried so hard to obey every jot and tittle of the law, but they failed to enter the Kingdom of God. God had sent John to them, a voice crying in the wilderness, 'Prepare the way of the Lord', (3:3) and the Lord had come to them, but they believed neither John nor the Lord, satisfied as they were with their meagre ability to be righteous outwardly, yet never coming to repentance, the gateway to eternal life, life in the kingdom, for with all their efforts, we are told, 'There is none righteous, no, not one' (Romans 3:10). God has concluded all under sin, that He may have mercy on all (Romans 11:32).

The only one who ever completely fulfilled the law was the Lord Jesus, as He said, 'I came not to abolish the law, but to fulfil it' (Matthew 5:17). John had shown them the way of righteousness, obedience to God, but they were not willing to accept it. These upholders of the law preferred to rest in their own perceived righteousness, rather than to see what John and later the Lord Jesus were inviting them to experience, the love and mercy of God as they came to Him acknowledging their need of the righteousness which only He could give, the imputed righteousness (Romans 3:22) of the One who bore all our sins in His body on the Tree (1 Peter 2:24) and that we being dead to sins should live to righteousness. By whose stripes we are healed.

And Jesus said to them, even when you saw the way of righteousness, you did not afterwards repent and believe him (verse 32). God had given them a second chance, or perhaps even a third or fourth chance, to hear what John was preaching, but they still would not believe John's message.

It is only repentance and faith that marks the difference between somebody who had previously lived an immoral or amoral life, and a righteous person, according to the law, who had shunned the very idea of repentance. Jesus says, 'The tax collectors and the harlots go into the Kingdom of God before you;' those who have been only too aware of their unrighteousness (verse 31), for these were the ones who had obeyed and repented.

Did the chief priests and the elders afterwards believe what Jesus was telling them? We want to believe that some at least who listened to these words of Jesus did respond to Him. 'Amen, I say to you.' Jesus is giving them yet another chance. It is the grace and mercy of God to them, but they still reject Him.

Matthew 21:33-46. The parable of the vineyard

Jesus said, 'Hear another parable. There was a householder who planted a vineyard, and set a hedge around it and dug a winepress in it, and built a tower and let it out to tenants, and went into another country. When the season of fruit drew near, he sent his servants to the tenants to get his fruit; and the tenants took his servants and beat one, and killed another and stoned another.

Again he sent out other servants, more than the first, and they did the same to them.

Afterward he sent his son to them saying, they will respect my son. But when the tenants saw the son, they said to themselves, "This is the heir; come let us kill him and have his inheritance." And they took him out of the vineyard and killed him' (Matthew 21: 33-39).

What a truly distressing story. Knowing of course the truth behind the parable, Jesus must have found it almost unbearable to tell. What care this indescribably patient owner had taken over his vineyard. He had supplied it with everything needed to ensure a good harvest of fruit from his vineyard, protecting it with a hedge, providing it with a winepress and even setting up a watchtower, so that it was constantly being guarded.

The chief priests and the elders were listening intently to this parable. Their minds, well versed in scripture would have been challenged by Isaiah's use of the metaphor in Isaiah chapter 5, when the prophet likened the nation of Israel to God's vineyard; obviously the owner of the vineyard represents God.

But something does not quite accord with their understanding. Surely, the vineyard is Israel, but Jesus is telling the story in such a way that it seems as though the *tenants* are representative of Israel. When the time of harvest approaches, the absent owner sends a group of his servants to receive his fruit from the tenants, but the servants are treated brutally. They are beaten, they are killed, some are even stoned to death.

What can the owner do? He will try again, sending another group of his servants to receive what is his. But these servants were treated in the same way.

At last, the owner decides on a completely different approach. He sent his son to them saying, 'They will reverence my son'.

By now, the chief priests and the elders are beginning to realise that Jesus is telling this story against them. They had been God's vineyard, His own possession. He had cared for them. He had called them His beloved, but they had turned away from Him. He had sent His prophets, time and time again, to bring them back to Himself, and His prophets had been treated cruelly, some were killed, some were stoned. Now He was sending His Son. His Son will carry with Him all the Father's authority, and will give the tenants the opportunity to repent, for surely this is what they will be swift to do when they see the Son. But the tenants are interested only in the inheritance. They were ambitious for the position of ownership, when they could have their own way. They see the Son coming and their malice and resentment knows no bounds. They say, 'This is the heir. Come let us kill him and the inheritance will be ours.' And they took him and cast him out of the vineyard and killed him.

What can the father in the parable do? Those wicked tenants must be punished. Jesus says, 'When therefore the owner of the vineyard comes, what will he do to those tenants?' Caught up in the story, even the chief priests and elders recognised that retribution was necessary. They said to Him, he will put those wretches to a miserable death and let out the vineyard to other tenants who will give him the fruits in their seasons'. They had apparently forgotten what Jesus had said about the bereaved father losing his son. They certainly did not identify themselves as those who are hostile to the son as those tenants were. And yet their answer is so terribly apposite. The vineyard will be taken away from them and given to others. They are pronouncing their own judgement.

Jesus has another question for them which concerns the Son whom they neglected to consider. Jesus said to them, 'Have you never read in the scriptures, 'the very stone which the builders rejected has become the head of the corner? This was the Lord's doing and it is marvellous in our eyes?' (Matthew 21:42). Jesus Himself is the chief cornerstone. He was the Son for whom they were even now attempting to find reasons of heresy or blasphemy against Him, so that He might be charged and executed. They are the builders who have rejected the most important stone who will become the head of the corner, on the very highest elevation. But Jesus goes on to say 'therefore I tell you, the kingdom of God will be taken away from you, and will be given to a nation producing the fruits of it'. As wicked tenants, of course they must be replaced, not by other tenants, or, in the context of the interpretation of the parable, different chief priests and elders, but by 'a nation producing the fruits of it'.

The use of the term 'nation' is interesting. Jesus is stating that under the Old Covenant, Israel possessed the kingdom of God, which would now be taken away from them and be given to another nation. The vineyard had represented the kingdom of God, God's vineyard, where His people are under His direct rule and governance, where He is sovereign Lord. But this prospect of being the kingdom of God, will now be taken away from them, for by their conduct they have forfeited their right to be the leaders of God's people.

God has another 'nation' in view, a people who will bring forth the fruits of the kingdom of God; the fruit of the Spirit, love, joy, peace; living humbly and contentedly in the will of God.

At last, the chief priests and the Pharisees understood. They perceived that He was speaking about them. But when they tried to arrest Him, they feared the multitudes, for they held Him to be a prophet (verses 45,46). Out of his own mouth, they had heard Him claim to be the Son of God (verses 37, 38), and perhaps that they are about to lose their status as God's chosen people, His nation. But God was not casting off His people whom He foreknew (Romans 11:2). He was granting them the opportunity of entering into a new relationship with Him through His death and resurrection. Though this was still future for these leaders of Israel, Jesus was still inviting them to come to Him, to that living stone, rejected by men but in God's sight, chosen and precious, and to be part of that chosen race, that royal priesthood,' a holy nation, God's own people, 'that you may declare the wonderful deeds of Him who called you out of darkness into His marvellous light' (1 Peter 2: 4, 9). And to them who received Him, He gave the right to become children of God, even to them who believed on His Name (John 1:12).

Matthew Chapter 22

Matthew 22:1-14. The parable of the marriage feast

And again, Jesus spoke to them in parables, saying, 'The Kingdom of Heaven may be compared to a king who gave a marriage feast for his son, and sent his servants to call those who were invited to the marriage feast, but they would not come' (Matthew 22:1-14).

For the third and last time in this final confrontation with the Jewish leaders, Jesus speaks to the chief priests and the Pharisees (Mathew 21:45) parabolically, and for the third time, He is speaking in terms of the father/son relationship.

The first father had two sons, representing the Old and New Covenant people of God, and a strong invitation to the people of the Old Covenant (the first son) to become people of the New Covenant (the second son) through entering by faith into the life of the people of God which He provided in His Son Jesus.

The second parable concerned the father whose one beloved son was thrown out of the vineyard, highly suggestive of the nation of Israel, and was killed, causing the vineyard to be given to others. If the first vineyard tenants were recognised as Israel, then the second could only refer to the church, rising up on the death and resurrection of the Son, the Lord Jesus, those 'called out' ones, *ecclesia,* who became the new 'Israel of God' (Galatians 6:16).

Here in this third parable, we have a father who is a king, and whose son is entering into a very special relationship with his bride, and who wants to include everybody in the marriage feast to celebrate.

What a wonderful feast he has prepared for them! A feast which in the Palestine of those days could well last several days.

417

And when the feast was ready he sent out his servants to those invited to the feast. In those clockless days, too, the servants have the task of announcing to the guests when the time has come, 'Come to the marriage feast, everything is now ready!' (verse 4).

What a privilege to be honoured with an invitation to the marriage feast of the king's son! But they made light of it (verse 5) they were indifferent to this honour that was being paid to them, they had more pressing, more important things to do. One person went off to his farm, another to his business, and even more reprehensible, others seized his servants and treated them shamefully and killed them (verse 6).

What was the king to do? This was more than an insult, this was rebellion, treason. The king could not allow this to pass without some retribution, and that had to be in proportion to the offence. Twice he had sent his servants with the invitation to the banquet. Twice the invited guests had ignored them, going about their own affairs, and even murdering his servants. The king was angry, and he sent his troops and destroyed those murderers, and burnt their city (verse 7).

Then the king had another thought. This has not solved the problem of the marriage feast, which was still ready for the guests who never came. He said to his servants, 'The wedding is ready, but those invited were not worthy. Go therefore to the thoroughfares, the places where people meet together in the city, and invite to the marriage feast as many as you can find' (verse 8). The servants did as they were bidden to do. They went out into the streets and gathered all whom they found, both bad and good πονηρούς τε καὶ ἀγαθούς (verse 10), whatever their spiritual condition.

So the wedding hall was filled with guests (verse 10). No precondition was necessary. They did not have to be important people, nor those regarded by the elite as negligible. They did not have to be great philanthropists, or poor unemployed people hoping for someone to employ them. They did not need to be seen as 'righteous', as opposed to those people regarded as 'sinners' (Luke 15:2; 5:29, 30). All they needed to do was accept the invitation to the wedding of the king's son. 'And the wedding hall was filled with guests' (verse 10).

But what is this? A man at the feast who has no wedding garment. All those people who had responded to the wedding invitation had come in their ordinary clothes. They had not had the time to go home and find their best clothes, or go to the dressmaker for something new and suitable for a wedding, especially a royal wedding where the bridegroom had been waiting so long.

This difficulty had been overcome by the king providing wedding garments. As the guests approached the wedding hall, they found someone standing there who gave them a wedding garment to put on.

But as the king, as the host, moved amongst his guests, he saw a man there without a wedding garment. He addressed the man as 'friend', for it was possible that there was a reason for this. He was giving the man an opportunity to explain why he felt no need for a wedding garment. 'Friend,' he said, 'how did you get in here without a wedding garment?' (verse 12). The man was speechless. He had nothing to say, no excuse to give. He had ignored the provision of a garment by the king. Perhaps he thought his own clothes were good enough, and he did not need to come down to the level of everyone else. Perhaps he had not come to the entrance of the wedding hall where wedding garments were being distributed to the other guests, but had come in through another door.

He had nothing with which to answer the king, no excuse to make, no reason to give, no repentance. He was speechless.

Then the king said to the attendants, 'Bind him hard and fast and cast him into outer darkness; there men will weep and gnash their teeth. For many are called, but few are chosen' (verses 13, 14). Was this not harsh on the part of the king? Why was such a punishment necessary? The man had actually chosen his own fate when he refused the provision that the king had so graciously given to all the guests.

To understand, we must go back to the beginning of the parable, and indeed back to the first parable, for as we have noted, this is one of three which are directed at the chief priests, the elders of the people, and the Pharisees (21:23, 45), and provides a progressive revelation of who Jesus is. They needed to know who this One is whom they are intent on destroying. They also need to know that the door is not yet closed to them.

For these men, the crucifixion of Jesus on the cross has not yet happened, but they have had the immense privilege that only the few thousands who lived in Palestine at the time of Jesus had. That was His own presence with them. The glorious Son of God, not yet gone to the cross, but living a life among them of perfect obedience to His Father, God incarnate, God with us, Immanuel, carrying with Him the whole purpose of God.

This was what He wanted them to see, that everything that was written about Him in the law of Moses, and the prophets and the Psalms had to be fulfilled (Luke 24:44). And in spite of all their knowledge of the scriptures, they were blind. In rejecting Jesus they were rejecting God. They acknowledged that Jesus was speaking about them in these parables (21:45), but instead of responding to the mirror He held up to them, showing them where their true motivation and attitude to Him lay, they were still unwilling to turn to Him, only regretful that their hands were tied because of their fear of the multitudes who held Him to be a prophet (21:46).

The first parable in this sequence had focused on the ministry of John the Baptist and had recalled the inauguration of Jesus' ministry endorsed by the voice of the Father in heaven and the descent of the Holy Spirit like a dove (21:20-33).

The second parable had emphasised the mission of Jesus, sent by His Father to establish a community, another 'vineyard', the true Israel of God of which they too could become a part by repentance and faith.

The third parable looks forward to the marriage banquet of the Son, when all believers are gathered together, clothed in the garment of righteousness which He supplies, celebrating with the Father and the Son over the fulfilment of what They had desired from the beginning of time, a people near to Them.

Moses recognises this when he said, 'What people has a god so near to them as is the Lord God to us, whenever we call upon Him?' (Deuteronomy 4:7). 'This,' says Jesus, 'is what the Kingdom of Heaven is like. The people of God seated around the table of the King, celebrating the marriage supper of the Lamb and His Bride, the church' (Revelation 19:7, 8). The marriage of the Lamb has come, and His Bride has made herself ready. It was granted to her to be clothed with fine linen, bright and pure, for fine linen is the righteous deeds of the saints, those who are sanctified, for Christ has become their wisdom and righteousness and sanctification and redemption (1 Corinthians 1:30). They are separated from the world, set apart for God. Clothed in His righteousness alone. Faultless to stand before His throne and to sit at His table and worship Him.

This is indeed a parable of the Kingdom of Heaven. God, seated on His throne, rejoicing that His Son has found a Bride, inviting all and sundry, everyone, to rejoice with Him in His Son's marriage, even providing them with the robes of righteousness that they so desperately need.

Of course, there will be many who refuse His invitation, for whatever reason. Luke gives some in addition to those given by Matthew in his rendition of the story (Luke 14:18-20). But the excuses, or the reasons are unimportant. The refusal is, for yet again Jesus is giving to these chief priests and elders and Pharisees, an opportunity to come into His Kingdom, to be part of the banquet of God. All they need is the wedding garment provided for them by Jesus, His righteousness in response to their repentance, but they prefer their own garment, the garment of their own self-righteousness which will never earn them a seat at the marriage supper of the Lamb.

All three of these parables are a cry from the heart of Jesus, metaphorically holding out His hands to them, saying, 'Come!' to them. But they would not. And this proclamation of grace is coming right at the end of His earthly life. They will not have another opportunity of hearing Him speak in quite this way, though He still has much to say to His disciples about them and warnings to give them in chapter 23. When He wept over Jerusalem, crying, 'O Jerusalem, Jerusalem, how often would I have gathered your children together, as a hen gathers her brood under her wings, and you would not' (23:37), we feel sure that He included all these stubborn, malicious leaders of the people in that cry of lament.

There is an ultimate banquet, the marriage supper of the Lamb laid up for all believers. All are welcome, all are invited to the feast; but all have the right to refuse the invitation. God never coerces anyone. He has given free will, freedom of choice, to everyone. But He goes on inviting people to come to Him and receive all the blessings of the Kingdom of Heaven, where He is king, where His Son reigns in utter and absolute love. The identification of Jesus as Bridegroom has already been adumbrated in Matthew 9:15 and will be repeated in Matthew 25:1-3. 'Behold, the Bridegroom comes!' (25:6). Even so, come Lord Jesus (Revelation 22:20).

Jesus concludes this parable with the strong assertion, 'Many are called, but few are chosen' (22:14). All are invited, but only a few are saved. All have free choice, but in His omniscience, God knows what the outcome will be, that not everyone will respond to the gospel message.

At issue is not the doctrine of divine election, but the calling, 'Come to Me', neglected by the many, but embraced gratefully by the few who recognise all too clearly their need of a Saviour, and to be clothed in the white garments of His righteousness, for they acknowledge that they have no righteousness of their own. Paul too has a cry from his heart, 'O that I might gain Christ, and be found in Him, not having a righteousness of my own, but that righteousness which is through faith in Christ!' (Philippians 3:8, 9).

In Zechariah 3:3-5, we see an acted parable in a vision that Zechariah saw. Joshua, the Old Testament equivalent of Jesus, being stripped of his filthy High Priestly garments, representing the sins of the people for whom he was high priest, and being given the rich apparel of righteousness, God having replaced the sins of His people with the robe of righteousness, a purpose that had always been in His heart to accomplish.

It could only be partially accomplished through the prophetic high priestly ministry of the Old Testament, but here we have Jesus. The Lord Jesus allowed Himself to be clothed with all the dirty rotten clothes of sin, the sin of the whole world. He did not hang there naked on the Cross. His High Priestly garments were also filthy, because they represented the garments of the people whom He came to save. This is why He cried out in great distress to His loving heavenly Father, 'My God, why have you forsaken Me?' (Matthew 27:46). How could God bear to look upon His beloved Son, clothed with the sin of the whole world? For He is of purer eyes than to behold evil (Habakkuk 1:13)

But when He was about to yield up His spirit at the point of death, He could say, *'It is finished.'* He had done what He came to do, taken upon Himself the sin of the world, taken it down into death. (John 19:30). And when He was in the realm of death, all that sin died with Him. Over sin He had conquered. Over death He had conquered, nailing our sin to the cross (Colossians 2:14). He was clothed with the rich apparel of His resurrection glory, resurrected from the dead by the Holy Spirit of God (Romans 1:4), having accomplished all that He set out to do, having a new Body, yet with the recognisable scars of His suffering (John 20:27), but untrammelled by the laws of nature, able to go through closed doors, to appear and disappear at will until He was received up to heaven, taking with Him the marks of His humanity (Acts 1:9). Our great High Priest, ever living to make intercession for us (Hebrews 7:25), dispensing His righteousness to all who come unto God by Him.

The death He died, He died to sin, but the life He lives He lives to God (Romans 6:10).

Revelation 3:5 says, 'He who overcomes shall be clothed in white garments... and I will confess his name before My Father, and before His angels.' This is what the Spirit is saying to the churches (Revelation 3 6). This is what He is seeking, a Bride pure and holy, those who belong to Christ alone.

By grace we will answer His call, 'Come my love, my fair one, come away, for lo, the winter is past, the rain is over and gone, the flowers appear on the earth, the time of the singing of birds has come, and the voice of the turtle-dove is heard in our land' (Song of Songs 2:10). The One whom we love is the chiefest of ten thousand (Song of Songs 5:10). He is the altogether lovely One (5:16). We worship Him.

Matthew 22:15-22. Paying tribute to Caesar

Then the Pharisees went and took counsel on how to entangle Him in His talk. And they sent their disciples to Him, along with the Herodians, saying, 'Teacher, we know that you are true, and teach the way of God truthfully, and care for no man, for you do not regard the position of men.' Tell us then, what you think. Is it lawful to pay taxes to Caesar, or not? (Matthew 22:15).

This is the second of the controversy stories in this section of Matthew's gospel, that is, the section comprising chapter 21:23 to 22:45.

The first was the controversy over Jesus' authority. 'By what authority do you do these things, and who gave you this authority?' they say to Him (21:23). It continues here with the discussion over paying taxes to Caesar (22:15-22), followed by their misunderstanding of resurrection (22:23-38), the status of the Great Commandment (verses 34-40), and the identity of the Son of David (22: 41-46).

The Pharisees, the Herodians, and the Sadducees were all involved, and though the Pharisees are explicitly described as wanting to set a trap for Him, to entangle Him in His talk, (verse 15), this is patently the motivation of each group of His opponents. Wanting to enslave Him belongs to all groups, and so in a sense they are unified. We already know from Matthew 21:46 that they want to arrest Him, the Pharisees and scribes being specifically mentioned, and when they themselves are too susceptible of the indignation of the people, they send their disciples, along with the Herodians to do the work for them (22: 16); or alternatively, a lawyer (22: 33).

However, in every question they challenge Jesus with, it is He who takes the initiative, and it is they who are trapped. At the end of this chapter they are rendered speechless. 'And no-one was able to answer Him a word, nor from that day did anyone dare to ask Him any more questions' (22:46).

There is a sense that everything is moving towards a finale, not just between Jesus and the Jewish rulers, but towards the great purpose of His earthly life which Jesus is about to consummate. It is in this atmosphere of building suspense towards the final conclusion of the drama that Jesus had given them the three parables of the two sons, the vineyard and the marriage feast, highlighting the invitation to come to Him, to share in the Kingdom of Heaven, and to share in the marriage feast, if only they had ears to hear what He was saying to them.

But ignoring all that He was trying to show them, intent on His destruction, the Pharisees 'took counsel on how to entangle Him in His talk' (verse 15) together with their disciples and the Herodians. They come up with an ingenious answer to the problem of how He could be charged simultaneously with both civil disobedience, and disobedience towards God. The choice was a stark one, either to be obedient to the demands of the state, or to be obedient to His religious and spiritual heritage. The choice is a stark one for they apparently believe that an individual cannot do both.

With barely disguised sycophancy they speak to Him, saying, 'Teacher, we know that you are true, and teach the way truthfully, and care for no man, for you do not regard the position of men. Tell us then, is it lawful to pay taxes to Caesar, or not? (verses 16, 17).

It was true that Jesus indeed taught the way of God in truth. It was true that He was not dependent on the opinions of others, but nevertheless, their challenge immediately strikes a warning note.

The Pharisees hated paying taxes as a subject people to an occupying power. The Herodians, supporters of Herod Antipas, son of Herod the Great, who ruled over territories in Galilee and Perea, had probably come to Jerusalem for the Passover Feast.

Herod held his power under Roman authority, and the Herodians would naturally favour payment of taxes to Rome.

So these two opposing groups are unified against Jesus. Jesus, aware of their malice, said, 'Why put Me to the test, you hypocrites? Show Me the money for the tax' (verses 18, 19).

He knows that if they see that He favours the tax, He will immediately become very unpopular with the people, for all hated paying the tax, and if the people turn against Him, then the Pharisees will be able to arrest Him with impunity. If however, Jesus opposes paying the tax, the Herodians can haul Him to the Roman authorities on a charge of sedition, for after a revolt of the Galilean named Judas in 6 A.D., the refusal to pay taxes meant a call to revolution, according to Josephus in his history of the Jewish war (Luz p36).

The way Jesus responds to this apparently reasonable and gentle confrontation but with all its hidden animus behind it shows His absolute mastery of the situation. He knows that they are not genuinely wanting His view on taxes, that they are hypocrites (verse 18). He says, 'Show Me the money for the tax.' And they brought Him a coin. And Jesus said to them, 'Whose image and superscription is this?' They said, 'Caesar's' (verse 20).

Portrayed on the front of the Tiberius denarius used in Palestine was the head of the emperor, with the imperial mother, Livia on the reverse side. The inscription includes the words, '*divus et pontifex maximus*' indicating that Tiberius Caesar regarded himself both as a god, *divus,* and as a cultic high priest of the Roman pantheon. The Jews would see this as being in direct opposition to their first commandment. 'You shall have no other gods before Me' (Exodus 20:3). This was the money they had to use in direct contravention of their sacred scriptures.

But Jesus was saying to them, 'Render to Caesar the things that are Caesar's, and to God the things that are God's' (verse 21). How amazing was that! How simple when they thought about it! When they heard it, they marvelled, and they left Him and went away (verse 22).

He had successfully foiled the attempt to entrap Him, but what did He mean by rendering to Caesar the things which are

Caesar's and to God the things that are God's? There is always so much more behind the words of Jesus than appear on the surface.

These two opposing forces, the kingdom or empire of Tiberius, a man claiming to be a god, and the Kingdom of God, will always symbolically and in fact, be, in opposition to each other. How many people around the world, daily remember Tiberius? And how many remember Jesus? Tiberius is typical of many who have gone before him, and come after him, assigning to themselves a position and power, which does not belong to them. At the very beginning of the Psalms (Psalm 2), the psalmist recognises this to be the case, 'Why do the nations rage, and their people imagine a vain thing? The kings of the earth set themselves, and their rulers take counsel together against the Lord and his Anointed (Psalm 2:2). This is how serious it is; claiming to be a god, to be in a cultic succession of idolatrous practice will doubtless have consequences.

What is God's reaction to those who incur His wrath, who attempt to take upon themselves *His* anointing? 'He who sits in the heaven *laughs;* the Lord has them in derision (Psalms 2:4), for His purpose is firm, 'I have set My king upon My holy hill of Zion' (verse 6), and no one can thwart His will. This we believe, and this we rejoice in. The Anointed Son of God reigning as King in His Kingdom.

Does this mean that as followers of the Lord Jesus we do not pay taxes, because in doing so we are supporting a regime antithetical to the reign of God?

We are in the world, but not of it (John 17:11, 14). We are part of society, and have a duty towards that society by paying taxes, which are used to support the weak, the elderly, the infirm, the destitute, the unemployable, and ensure good government. This does not commit believers to an idolatrous system, conformed to the objectives and aspirations of worldly government. Believers may not be *conformed* according to some outward reality, but *transformed* by the renewing of their mind to understand what the will of the Lord is (Romans 12:2), and to appropriate His will spiritually; the outward form as expressive of the inward reality. This is what becomes the opposition for the believer; the outward form of reality versus the inward expression of the true reality, which is, 'Christ in you, the hope of glory' (Colossians 1:27).

In spite of what is going on in the world around, the believer is constantly alive to instances of genuine, infinite, eternal worth. He does not allow the cares of this world to deprive him of the spiritual riches, those riches which do not deceive (Matthew 13:22).

Galatians 1:4 reminds us that, 'Our Lord Jesus Christ gave himself for our sins to deliver us from this present evil age,' and Colossians 3:2, that therefore, 'we may set our minds on those things which are above, not on things of the earth, where Christ is, seated at the right hand of God.' This is how we live, looking to Jesus the author and finisher of our faith (Hebrews 12:2), that we might be conformed to His image, the image of His Son (Romans 8:29).

All human authority and power is under the supreme authority of God. We know that our God reigns. We are content to be part of the society in which we live, trusting not in those who are set over us, but in God who holds all things in the hollow of His hand (Isaiah 40:12). We render unto Caesar the things that are Caesar's, but do not neglect to render unto God the things that are God's.

He has made us salt and light to those around us (Matthew 5:13,14), and we seek to draw all men and women into the Kingdom of God, to be partners with Him in what He came to do, to fill up that which was lacking for His Body's sake, that is, the church (Colossians 1:24). But together with Peter and John, we must say, 'We must obey God rather than men' (Acts 5:29).

Jesus never promised His followers an easy life. He said to His disciples, 'In the world you will have tribulation, but be of good cheer, I have overcome the world' (John 16:37). There is a principle of evil in the world (John 17:15), but Jesus says His followers are not of the world, but He has chosen them out of the world, and that explains why 'the world hates you' (John 15:19).But we also have those wonderful promises of John 14:27.

'Peace I leave with you, My peace I give unto you. Not as the world gives, give I to you. Let not your heart be troubled, neither let it be afraid.' We render to God that which belongs to God, but how much more He gives us in return.

Matthew 22:23-33. The question about the resurrection

The same day, Sadducees came to Him who say that there is no resurrection, and they asked Him a question saying, 'Teacher, Moses said, "If a dies, having no children, his brother must marry the widow and raise up children for his brother. Now there were seven brothers... In the resurrection, to which of the seven will she be wife, for they all had her."' (Matthew 22: 23-28).

Each day is becoming more precious as Jesus moves towards His passion and death. On this day, He has already dealt with the question raised by the disciples of the Pharisees and the Herodians. Now, 'the same day' (verse 23). He is dealing with the Sadducees' question regarding the resurrection.

The Sadducees believed that only the Torah, the five books of the law, were canonical, authoritative. The Pharisees found scriptural evidence for the resurrection of the dead in Isaiah 26:19, and Daniel 12:2. Speaking prophetically to God, Isaiah says, 'Thy dead shall live, their bodies shall rise. O dweller in the dust, awake and sing for joy!' Daniel, writing apocalyptically, speaks of the end of time, when, 'Many of those who sleep in the dust of the earth shall awake, some to everlasting life, and some to shame and everlasting contempt. And those who are wise shall shine like the brightness of the firmament, and those who turn many to righteousness like the stars forever and ever' (Daniel 12:2-4).

The story the Sadducees tell Jesus is an unlikely one, told with great cynicism and arrogance, in an attempt to prove how much more pragmatic and superior they were to the Pharisaical teaching. They claimed to be speaking for Moses, for they ignored the other 34 books of the canonical scriptures 'Teacher,' they say, as if conferring on Jesus some recognition in which they did not truly believe. 'Teacher, Moses said, "If a man dies having no children, his brother must marry his widow and raise up children to his brother"' (verse 24). Deuteronomy 25:5-6 shows that this was in fact true. This is known as levirate marriage, from 'levir', Latin for husband's brother, brother-in-law of the widow, and was an attempt to continue the name of the family through the generations. It could be said to be an attempt at eternal life. As long as children, grandchildren, great grandchildren continued to arrive, there was a human legacy, a continuity of the family name. This was apparently the only kind of eternal life the Sadducees could envisage, for they regarded the idea of resurrection as absurd.

Deuteronomy 25:5-6, where it speaks of levirate marriage, and Genesis 38:8, where Judah is described as having married his daughter-in-law Tamar, gave them some foundation for their views. But these Sadducees were taking the words of Moses and carrying them to an absurd length, a *reductio ad absurdum*, in order to trap Jesus. Supposing there were seven brothers and after the first one died, his wife was left as a chattel to be inherited one after another by each of the other brothers in turn, until she herself died, not having produced any children.

This is a totally abhorrent marital situation to us in a more liberal society, even as a fable, but the emphasis for the Sadducees is not on marriage, but on resurrection. In Deuteronomy, there is a get out clause. The brother may not want to marry his brother's wife and there is provision for such an eventuality. The Sadducees ignore this, wanting to make the point that because the idea of resurrection makes nonsense of human relationships, it is not, therefore, a valid hypothesis, and no one has ever come back to tell us what happens after death.

Jesus answers both these fundamental objections to the idea of resurrection from the dead with such a seemingly simple explanation for them, one that is so obvious, they must have wondered why it had not occurred to them before.

As to marriage, Jesus explained that in heaven there is neither marriage nor being given in marriage. Every one, as an individual, and not one of a partnership, is responsible before God for the life they have lived. Just as angels neither marry, nor are given in marriage, so it is with human beings. There is no marriage in heaven between angels, and neither is there marriage between human beings.

This is another area of controversy for the Sadducees, for they do not believe in angels either (Acts 23:8).

As to the resurrection of the dead, Jesus says again, 'Have you not read?' This was a question He had already asked the Pharisees in 12:5; 19:4; and 21:16. We are beginning to think that these so-called experts in the law lacked understanding of what they read, or applied their own understanding, bringing their own fragility, their own experience or indeed inexperience of the reality of the origin of the word of God, God Himself, to the interpretation of His word.

Jesus answered them, 'Have you not read what was said to you by God? I AM the God of Abraham, of the God of Isaac and the God of Jacob. He is not God of the dead, but of the living (verse 32; Exodus 3:6). A living God, surrounded by living beings who once walked the earth, not only the patriarchs, but all who lived the life of faith and who died in faith (Hebrews 11:13). I AM, YHWH. God's Name as it was revealed to Moses at the burning bush (Exodus 3:1).

The author of Hebrews goes on to say, 'We are surrounded by so great a cloud of witnesses' (Hebrews 12:1) through this thin veil which separates this world and the heavenly world where God is. 'We look not at the things that are seen, but at the things that are unseen through this thin veil, for the things that are seen are transient, but the things that are not seen are eternal' (2 Corinthians 4:18).

It is hard to give up a cherished belief, but this is what Jesus is asking them to do. *Firstly,* because faith does not depend on reason, even though the life of faith is a more rational way of living, and *also* because it relies on the revelation of the absolute faithfulness of God. Faith comes not by reason, but by epiphany, by revelation, by hearing and absorbing the word of God, receiving it into our very being.

Belief is not faith. Belief is a set of propositions by which it is possible to live rationally and within our own cultural circumstances. But sometimes we have to give up our beliefs for the truth. We have to live our lives from within. Paul writes, 'The outer man, the outer nature is wasting away (2 Corinthians 4:16), for a deeper purpose, so that the inner man, the inner nature may daily be renewed by the Holy Spirit, for the inner man is where faith lies.'

What a relief, that our faith does not lie in our outward circumstances, nor in our ability to reason from the scriptures, but just to live in the glorious hidden life from within, the life of the Holy Spirit within us, whose temple we are (2 Corinthians 6:16).

This is what Jesus is recommending to the Sadducees, that they give up belief for faith, not having their own righteousness, their own rightness of doctrine and behaviour, but the righteousness, which is of God by faith (Romans 3:22). How difficult for them to acknowledge this, rejecting the whole basis upon which their lives were founded. How amazed were the crowd when they heard His teaching. How wonderful it would have been if a few at least of those who heard it were able to turn their lives around on that day, and come to put their faith in Jesus, the Author and Finisher of faith (Hebrews 12:2), the Alpha and Omega of faith, the first and the last, the beginning and the end (Revelation 22:12).

Faith is an active spiritual force which rises up within us in response to the immeasurable riches of the grace of God to us. Faith is not of ourselves, it is the gift of God, not of works of righteousness that we have done, lest anyone should boast (Ephesians 2:7-9).

Our need meets His grace, and faith, His gift to us, rises up within us to meet Him, to share in His great love with which He loved us (Ephesians 2:4). We who were dead in our trespasses and sins are made alive together with Christ (Ephesians 2:5). We no longer live to ourselves, but to Him who died and rose again.

This is resurrection life; not the pallid possibility which the Sadducees were trying to refute, but the glorious liberty of the children of God, alive to God through the Lord Jesus Christ, walking by faith not by sight (2 Corinthians 5:7) looking unto Jesus, the author and finisher of our faith, for He who began a good work in us will complete it to the end (Philippians 1:4).

Jesus said, 'I am the Resurrection and the Life' (John 11:25). We live in Him. We do not wait until we die. Here and now we can live the resurrection life of Christ, and when we eventually die, to live with Him in heaven, a continuation of the life lived in the world, except that we shall see His face, face to face with Christ our Saviour (1 Corinthians 13:12).

Jesus said to the Sadducees, 'You are wrong' (Matthew 23:29). Not just, 'you are mistaken', but 'you are wrong, because you know neither the scriptures nor the power of God'.

This is a salutary lesson for us who love and study the scriptures. We love the word of God because it reveals Jesus to us; it helps us to understand a little of God's purposes towards mankind, His great love and compassion and mercy towards fallen human beings, His never-ending faithfulness, *hesed*, the Hebrew word for mercy and loving kindness, God's mercy and loving kindness towards us, portrayed so carefully in the two covenants, the old covenant in the blood of bulls and goats (Hebrews 10:4) superseded by the new covenant in the blood of Jesus (Luke 22:20), for without the shedding of blood there is no remission or forgiveness of sins (Hebrews 9:22)

All this wonderful panorama of the grace of God, and the life of God, revealed in His Son, and in the people who call upon His Name, is of infinite worth, and worthy of careful study. But without the power of God, and reliance on Him to show us from His word what we need to know as part of our daily living, our daily dependence on our living, loving Lord, all our study is in vain. So we come to His word in deep humility of spirit, in awe and reverence, recognising that we stand on holy ground, so, so thankful that the Lord Jesus told His disciples that the Holy Spirit whom He would send in His Father's name, would teach them all things (John 14:26).

FLOWER

How we need the Holy Spirit, the Counsellor, the Controller, the Comforter, the One who comes alongside, the Paraclete. Jesus has made this wonderful provision for us, and we are so grateful, for the Holy Spirit came to glorify Jesus, and to lead us into all truth (John 16:12, 14). Paul writes 'The resurrection life I live, I live by the faith of the Son of God who loved me and gave Himself for me' (Galatians 2:20).

Matthew 22:34-40. The great commandment

But when the Pharisees heard that He had silenced the Sadducees, they came together. And one of them, a lawyer, asked Him a question, to test Him. 'Teacher, which is the great commandment in the law?' And He said to Him, 'You shall love the Lord your God with all your heart, and with all your soul, and with all your mind.' This is the great and first commandment. And a second is like it. You shall love your neighbour as yourself. On these two commandments depend all the law and prophets (Matthew 22:34-40).

This is the *fourth* controversy the religious leaders have with Jesus in this section of Matthew's gospel, in these last days of His earthly life, and it demonstrates an escalation, not only of the impossibility they assume of His being able adequately to answer them, but because they still want to test Him (verse 35), to entrap Him, to enslave Him, to entangle Him in His talk (verse 15). He has so far more than adequately answered each controversial question. The question of the origin of His authority, the political question which turned out to be a spiritual question after all, about tribute to Caesar, and the absurd question about marriage which had ultimately been discovered as a question about living in the good of the resurrection life which Jesus promised to His followers.

But here is a question of the gravest importance because it concerns the very foundation of the lives of these religious people; an escalation even on those questions which had gone before. It required an encyclopaedic knowledge of their

434

scriptures, but even more than that, it required an incisive appreciation of what lay behind and beyond the text, to the Author of the text.

Every law, rule, regulation, command or suggestion referred back to Him, to the Lord their God, their Redeemer from slavery, the Holy One of Israel, but even more than that, to the Creator of the universe, the true and living God, omnipotent, all powerful, omniscient, all seeing, all loving, faithful and true. *GOD.*

Did they fully recognise the God with whom they have to do? How to describe Him? In the Old Testament, Isaiah and many of the Psalms had made heroic attempts. The epistle to the Hebrews in the New Testament describes Him as a consuming fire (Hebrews 12:29) but also as the God of peace (Hebrews 13:20).

So we look at the scriptures which Jesus so loved, and knew so well, and see this wonderful picture of God there displayed before us, but apparently unknowable. The people of God can worship Him with reverence and godly fear. How are they going to know Him?

Even in the Old Testament, God had provided a way. He said to them 'Hear, O Israel. The Lord our God is One Lord; and you shall love the Lord your God with all your heart, and with all your soul and with all your might' (Deuteronomy 6:5). You shall love the Lord your God with all that you have, with every fibre of your being, and the love that you have for Him will connect with the love that He is, and that He has for you, for God is love.

This is what Jesus came to show us. The way to the Father is through love. Jesus is the image of the invisible God. He bears the very stamp of His nature (Hebrews 1:3) He reflects the glory of God. And He is love. When Jesus knew that the time had come for Him to depart out of the world to the Father, having loved His own who were in the world, He loved them to the end, to the uttermost (John 13:1).

This is not just something read in a book, even such a book as the Word of God. This is reality. We love Him because He first loved us (1 John 4:19). This is His gift to us, His new covenant people, even as it was to those under the old covenant. *Through this gift, we can know Him,* even if now we see in a glass darkly or in a mirror dimly (1 Corinthians 13:12, A.V., R.S.V.), the day will come when we shall see Him face to face.

'You *shall* love the Lord your God.' This is command, but it is also permission. God gave to His people long ago permission to love Him, to serve Him, to have a relationship with Him. All the other laws in the Torah, the law book of Israel, rested on this. Each of the laws shows the compassion of God for men and women in their relationship with Him and with each other, and even for the animals which were so much a part of their economy. As an example we think of Exodus 34:26, 'You shall not seethe/boil a kid in its mother's milk'. The Lord God carried them all the days of old, and there was not one feeble amongst them, for He said, 'Surely they are My people' (Isaiah 63:8, 9). He never changes. He is the same God today as He was then, and will be forever. He says, 'I am the Lord, I change not' (Malachi 3:6).

And Jesus is the same, yesterday, today and forever (Hebrews 13:8).

We can rely utterly on Him, secure, safe, loved. We do not need to 'know' God in order to love Him. The psalmist says, 'Such knowledge is too wonderful for me. It is high, I cannot attain it' (Psalm 139:6). But some may say, 'How can I love someone whom I cannot see?'

Is love an intellectual rather than an emotional experience? Is Deuteronomy's emphasis on loving God purely a matter of the will? Or an ethical dimension to life? If this were so, then love becomes a matter of duty laid upon His people by God, to love someone they cannot see, to worship someone who therefore may or may not even exist.

Is this too great a burden to lay on the shoulders of fallible human beings? Often, their response could be just a response of gratitude, because life at the moment is good. Do they assume that the good things happening at the moment come to them from a Supreme Being? Or is it just good luck, good fortune? The reverse of this thinking implies that when bad things happen, this is just the way things are, just bad luck. Then the response may be not gratitude but indignation, anger, the 'why me?' question, indifference, fatalism. Are men and women justified in feeling this way? Could their experience cause them to think of a loving God or are they satisfied with the reassurance that this is just life? The question is how could they love and trust a God whom they have not seen. Is He expecting too much of them?

John, the beloved disciple, gives us a clue. He says, 'He who does not love his brother whim he has seen, cannot love God whom he has not seen' (1 John 4:20). How can he? John is of course speaking of the love each member of the fellowship of the church has for each other. This is John's supreme concern, that we should love one another as God has loved us (1 John 4:11), that he who loves God should love his brother also.

But we can access John's 'clue' differently. John's clue is that we know how to love God, because we know how to love one another. Who can deny the love a mother has for her child. Can a woman forget her suckling child, that she should have no compassion on the son of her womb? Even these may forget, yet will I not forget you,' says the Lord to Zion (Isaiah 49:15). Who can deny the love of a husband for his wife (Exodus 5:25), or for brothers and sisters in a family (Genesis 50:20), or for friends, as David and Jonathan were? (1 Sam 18:1).

Love is not unknown to us on a horizontal level. Why should it be impossible on a vertical level, as we look up to our heavenly Father, not just because in giving us Jesus He gave us all things (Romans 8:33) but because He is who He says He is, the God of all grace, the God of all mercy, the God who is love.

No one has ever seen God (1 John 4:12; John 1:18), but we have seen His face in the face of Jesus Christ, as 1 Corinthians states (1 Corinthians 4:6), 'the light of the knowledge of the glory of God in the face of Jesus Christ.' We see God through Jesus. Through the light of His face we see the Father. He is the light of the world. Through Him we see everything else or we are blind. How can we help but love Him?

Jesus says, 'This is the great commandment. But the second is like it. You shall love your neighbour as yourself' (Matthew

23:39). Does this mean that we can only love in community? The saints of God gathered together in perfect harmony?

This second of the double commandment, says Jesus, is *like* the first, but not the *same* as the first. The love with which we love God is of the whole person, body, soul and spirit, 'With all your heart, and with all your soul, and with all your mind' (Matthew 22:37).

The second is like the first in its emphasis on love, in loving one's neighbour as oneself, but to God alone is the love due that involves the whole person, otherwise, 'love of the neighbour' would become idolatry, putting someone else in the place of God.

Then, 'Who is my neighbour?' as the lawyer asked Jesus in Luke 10:29. Jesus is not suggesting to the lawyer a kind of Christian humanism, a kind of one-dimensional morality or a kind of Christian socialist behaviour, which wants to put the world to rights. These ideologies have their place, and the lives of many would be poorer, literally, without them. But we cannot see the world outside of us as one entity, experienced as 'the world'. The world is composed of human beings. As human beings, we are not necessarily very lovable, not renowned for our goodness or generosity, not very beautiful and sometimes not even socially acceptable. None of this matters. What matters is that we are neighbours, neighbours because we share in our equality before God, and because God loves us and wants us to love Him and our neighbour, and sometimes, the way that He can convey His love to them is through the love shown to them by His lovers.

It is so easy to allow the need of a person to become the dominant factor; for the need to be met but the love to be missing; the activity on another's behalf to become purely a moral exercise. This can be the motivation behind good works, charitable giving, which have very little of the true 'caritas' of which Paul speaks in 1 Corinthians 13, behind it. Yet God may well use it for the blessing of others.

We wonder what motivated the Good Samaritan? The illustration which Jesus gave to the lawyer in Luke 10:25-37 about loving your neighbour compares the unwillingness of the priest and Levite, to show love, mercy, to the poor wounded man on the way from Jerusalem to Jericho, with the love shown to him by the good Samaritan.

We may have many reasons for not wanting to show love to people. As Jesus is speaking these words in Matthew 22:37-29, He is perhaps addressing another lawyer (or even the same one) representing the religious leaders of the day. It is significant that the lawyer to whom He gave the parable of the good Samaritan would also be aware of the problem which the priest and the Levite would have had as they passed by on the other side, the problem of whether to prioritise religious and ritual defilement over against mercy, for as priests they were not permitted to go near the body of a dead man, and there was every possibility that the man had been killed by these robbers who had beaten him, leaving him half-dead (Numbers 9:6; Leviticus 21:1). Free from any dilemma concerning ritual defilement, the Samaritan gladly showed mercy to the man.

And Jesus replied to the lawyer who had asked the question, 'Who is my neighbour? 'Go and do likewise!' The Samaritan had demonstrated love for his neighbour, showed him mercy even though he did not have the benefit of being of the household of God for whom the second commandment was given.

Is Jesus suggesting that we can ignore scriptural injunctions? That the priest and the Levite should have ignored the limits set upon them by their priestly function? No, but we ourselves must obey the higher laws of love towards God, and love towards our neighbour.

There are so many who do wonderful acts of charity. We are blessed in this country by having so many organisations who help the poor and needy, the destitute, the dispossessed. And some of them are Christian charities, basing their work on Jesus' words in Matthew 25:45. 'In as much as you did it to the least of these My brethren, you did it to Me.'

The conflict arises when morality, moral activity or ritual observance become identified with religious faith and faith gets lost, swallowed up in the legitimate doing of good works, for

Jesus also said, 'The poor you have always with you' (Matthew 26:11). Religion, relationship with God is relegated to some background position, as the Pharisees discovered. Charitable works, even when based on religious observance are good, but not necessarily, and not always what Jesus meant when He said, 'Love your neighbour as yourself.'

The *first* and great commandment comes first. You shall love the Lord your God. The *second* commandment comes after that, springs from that. You shall love your neighbour as yourself. This self-effacing love is an echo of the first love. It is the love of God shed abroad in our hearts by the Holy Spirit (2 Corinthians 5:8). It is a reflection of the love poured out upon us through the Lord Jesus Christ, reflecting back to Him in love and worship, and reflecting back to others in care and compassion. Without the first commandment, the second commandment loses its impetus. We love others, because we first loved Him.

'On these two commandments hang all the law and the prophets,' said Jesus (Matthew 22:40). Jesus called them great for there is nothing outside of them. All other laws are subsumed under them, and all scripture must be interpreted in the light of them, all the law, all the prophets. All are related to the great commandments of love of God and love of neighbour. They support all that was revealed to Moses on Mount Sinai, all that God was speaking to His people through the prophets.

The Jewish people had these wonderful truths within their Torah, their sacred scriptures. They knew that they had to trust in the Lord with all their heart and lean not unto their own understanding (Proverbs 3:6). Jesus came to show them, and us, that. What could devolve into mere theory was actualised, fulfilled, compelling in Him, and through Him could be the motivation of our lives too. The self-absolutism of our modern society, a temptation even for Christians, must give way before His assertion of what was fundamental; the difference between love of God and love of neighbour, and simultaneously, the inseparability of love of God and love of neighbour.

This is the witness and testimony of the whole Bible, Old and New Testaments, Old and New Covenant. It is the word of God.

Matthew 22:41-46. The identity of the Son of David

Now while the Pharisees were gathered together, Jesus asked them a question, saying, 'What do you think of the Christ? Whose son is He?' They said to Him, 'The Son of David.' He said to them, 'How is it then that David, inspired by the Holy Spirit, calls Him 'Lord', saying: "The Lord said to my Lord, Sit at My right hand till I put Thy enemies under thy feet."' (Psalm 110:1).

This is the fifth and final controversy that Jesus had with the religious leaders in Jerusalem before His arrest, torture and execution. It could be said to be His final invitation to them to recognise who He was, and to come to faith in Him.

It has been apparent from the beginning, going back as far as John's baptism of Jesus in the River Jordan, that the Pharisees and Sadducees and scribes have a deep problem. Not only for them, but for the whole of the known world, religion was important. It was the atmosphere in which people lived their daily lives. The Greeks had their pantheon, the Romans had theirs, the ancient religions of the Indian sub-continent and China all dominated the lives of men and women.

For the Jewish world of Jesus, it was important to recognise the distinction between their religion and what they would regard as false religion. They worshipped the One true and living God, but there was false religion, the worship of gods who were so absolutely unlike Him, for the gods of the nations were but idols. The Jewish people were in the unique and happy position of having a Law passed on to them by their living God, a precious gift to them, which no other nation had. This had become for their leaders a matter of the utmost concern, for their purpose was always to obey the Law, to do the right thing in the right way, always to observe all the commandments, however detailed and complex, for that was their salvation.

There had been periods in their history when this had not been the case; when the Israelite people had failed to observe the law, had resorted to the worship of idols, and had suffered a terrible downfall, at one time being taken into captivity for seventy years, a long and terrible exile, not only from their homeland, but from their temple, and all that it stood for.

This folk memory was deeply ingrained in every Jew. Though they were now under subjection to Rome, at least they were in their own land, with their own temple. They could not afford to jeopardise their position by neglecting any jot or title of the law. They had become legalistic. Their religion had become a ritualistic legalism, and the more sincere they were, the more legalistic they became.

They found Jesus' teaching to be outrageous. They believed He was undermining their whole way of life, for what He taught made the carefully elaborated system by which they lived only an outward show. They were even more incensed when He said He did not come to abolish the law but to fulfil it. He says, 'I am the fulfilment of the law'. How dare He, when He considers the prayer of a man who beats upon his breast crying out to God, 'God, be merciful to me, a sinner!' of more value to God than the prayer of the Pharisee (Luke 18:9), a man dedicated to keeping the law. How dare He, when all the years they have spent in reading and learning and discussing and debating the whole text can be summarised by Him in two short sentences. 'You shall love the Lord your God with all your heart, with all your soul and with all your mind, and your neighbour as yourself.'

They were seeking certainty, the certainty that they were right, righteous even. Jesus had challenged this perception of themselves. He is saying, 'I am Immanuel, I am God with you. Come to Me and you will find rest for your souls. You are burdened with much learning, with much piety. Come to Me, for My yoke is easy and my burden light, and you will find rest from all your trying. It is not try, but trust. From generation to generation, you have kept the flame alive as the people of God, and I have come to fan the flame, to increase the knowledge of God, the true God, not only for you, My chosen people, but throughout the world.'

'You have been custodians and interpreters of the Law, but I will show you a new and living way. Follow Me, I have provided something better for you, an entrance into the Kingdom of God, an awareness, a palpable awareness of His presence and His purpose for your lives. Come to me.'

This was their last opportunity before His death, though after His resurrection, when they began to be troubled by His disciples who would insist on proclaiming that He had been raised from the dead, and were doing so much in the name of Jesus, they, like Gamaliel, a teacher of the law, may have come to see that if this new way of living were from God, they should not oppose it, in case they were found to be opposing God (Acts 5:39).

But this episode is before His death and resurrection. The Pharisees were now gathered together (verse 41) and it was Jesus who asked the question, 'What do you think of the Christ? Whose son is He?'

At last, He has the Pharisees on their own, not represented by disciples or lawyers. The scribes, most of whom belonged to the Pharisaical party, and the Herodians, are also not mentioned in this final confrontation between Jesus and the Pharisees. Jesus needs them to recognise His Messianic claim that as son of David, using David's own words, recorded in Psalm 110 and, inspired by the Holy Spirit, He is also Lord (verse 43). Jesus says to the Pharisees, 'How is it that David, inspired by the Spirit, calls Him Lord, saying, "The Lord said to my Lord, sit at My right hand until I put your enemies under your feet."' If David calls Him Lord, how is He his son?' (verse 45). A son does not normally call his father 'Lord'. If then the Lord calls him' My Lord', a new dimension is being introduced into the conception of who this Son would be, the concept of deity.

The Pharisees had known and accepted that the Messiah, the Christ, the Anointed One, would come and that He would be a son of David (Isaiah 11:1; Jeremiah 23:5). If only they could accept that this Anointed One was also 'the Lord' as David's psalm prophetically assumes, that the psalm equating the 'Lord' with the Messiah, is in fact equating the Messiah with deity. A greater than a son of David is here, even as a greater than Solomon, or Jonah is here (Matthew 12:6, 41) It is the Lord!

The One whom they have been worshipping through all their ritualism, all their learning.

'What do you think of the Christ?' says Jesus to the Pharisees, and upon their answer to this question, hangs all of their future destiny. 'Whose son is He?' It was the Pharisees who said to Him, 'He is David's son' (verse 41, 42), thus introducing David into the discussion.

We know that Jesus is God's Son. Twice God had spoken from heaven saying, 'This is my Beloved Son in whom I am well pleased,' at His baptism and at His transfiguration (Matthew 3:17, 17:5). We also know that humanly speaking, Jesus is descended from David, from Matthew's first chapter (1:6). Both are true, for in Jesus, humanity and deity combine. He is Son of Man, and Son of God, and although what the Pharisees see before them is the man, Jesus, what they see, veiled in flesh, is the incarnate Deity, pleased as Man with man to dwell, Jesus our Immanuel.

Jesus is making a huge claim here. The old has gone. The new has come. No matter what happens in the future, either to Him or them, this is undeniably an incalculably prestigious moment. 'What do you think of the Christ?' says Jesus (verse 41). One can almost believe that the angels are peering down from heaven to hear what is going on, to hear the answer of the Pharisees to the greatest question of all.

Jesus was hoping to have from the Pharisees the answer He had had from Peter at Caesarea Philippi, 'You are the Christ, the Son of the living God' (Matthew 16:16). What might have been in the future for the Jewish people if they had had the same revelation! Jesus had said to Peter, 'Blessed are you Simon bar-Jonah, for flesh and blood has not revealed this to you, but My Father who is in heaven.' (Matthew 16:17). Had the Pharisees been willing for all the consequences of receiving that revelation, the 'loss of all things that they might gain Christ (Philippians 3:8); had they been willing, the Father would have revealed this also to His ancient people, the Jews, and the whole of Jewish history could have been so different from that time on.

The moment passes. The time for revelation is over and gone. They have rejected the Son of God. And yet it was an impressive silence that followed Jesus' words. 'And no-one was able to answer Him a word, nor from that day did anyone dare to ask Him any more questions (verse 46). There is still tension in the hearts and minds of the Pharisees.

Jesus had quoted Psalm 110:1 in full: *The Lord said my Lord, Sit at My right hand till I put Thy enemies under Thy feet.* How terrible to suppose they had become the enemies of the Lord after all their hard work at attempting to be righteous? After all their self-justification? But they had determined their course of action, and in Matthew 26:3, the chief priests and the elders of the people gathered in the palace of the High Priest, who was called Caiaphas and took counsel together in order to arrest Jesus by stealth and kill Him. But they said, 'Not during this feast, lest there be a tumult among the people'. They were determined on His death, but God was also determined that this was indeed the time *He* had chosen, as His Son gave His life into His hands, to become the Saviour of the world.

The Lord had made a covenant with David, that he would have a son to reign on his throne forever (Jeremiah 33:21). He would be a righteous Branch springing forth from David, and the name by which He would be called was Jehovah-Tsidkenu, the Lord our Righteousness (Jeremiah 33:15, 16). This covenant is confirmed as an 'everlasting covenant', even the sure mercies, the steadfast love for David (Isaiah 55:3. A.S.V., R.S.V.).

It began in 2 Samuel 7, when David explained to Nathan the prophet that he wanted to build a house for the Lord, a place where the Ark of the Covenant, the symbol of the presence and glory of the Lord, dwelling in the midst of His people, could be safely kept. This was such a passion for David, that he says in Psalm 132 that he would give no sleep to his eyes, or slumber to his eyelids until the Ark came into its resting place within the House of the Lord. Speaking on behalf of the Lord, Nathan assures David that although he himself will not build a house for the Lord, yet the Lord's intention is that *He will build David a house,* that is, a generational family (2 Samuel 7:11), from which one would come who would be His Son, and for whom God would be His Father.

This was God's promise to David. It was the Davidic covenant, a sovereign statement of divine intent. Consequent upon David's oath to God that he would build Him a house (which he did, that is, through his family), came God's oath to David. In Psalm 89 two promises were covenanted to David, that he would reign over the whole created world (verses 24-27), and that his throne would be everlasting (verses 28-29). These promises were of course fulfilled in David's greater Son.

But the revelation to Isaiah goes further, that the Davidic king, the king of David's line, is also the suffering servant; that the covenant with David is an everlasting covenant, made on the basis of the sure mercies, the steadfast love for David, but extended into the future. 'Behold, My Servant,' says the Lord in Isaiah 52:13, the One despised and rejected of men, a Man of sorrows and acquainted with grief (Isaiah 53:3). He is the Davidic king. He is also the suffering servant, the specially anointed servant of the heavenly King, the Messiah, the Sent One, the humble one. The Servant and the Messiah are one. Isaiah 42:1 says: Behold, My Servant, whom I uphold, My chosen in whom My soul delights, I have put My Spirit upon Him'.

God has anointed His servant. He is the Anointed One, He is the Messiah, the Christ. And He is the Son of David. The Lord swore unto David a sure oath from which He will not turn back. 'Of the seed of your body, I will set on your throne' (Psalm 132:11). I will not violate My covenant or alter the world that has gone out of My lips. Once have I sworn by My holiness. I will not lie to David. His line shall endure forever, his throne as long as the sun before Me (Psalm 89:34-36).

God promises to David world rule and an enduring throne (Isaiah 55:4,5), promises which could only be fully realised in Jesus, the Son of David. Because they consistently go on studying the Davidic psalms (9:11, 18:49, 57:9-11, 108:4-5, 145:21), and the references to David throughout the prophetic writings (Isaiah 4:2; Jeremiah 23:5; 33:15; Zechariah 3:8; 6:12; 2 Sam 7:11; Psalm 89; Psalm 132; Isaiah 9:7; 22:22; 55:3; Jeremiah 30:9; Hosea 3:5;

Amos 9:11), looking for a future fulfilment of the promise to David, the Jewish leaders were still looking for a Messiah, a king in David's image who would come and lead them into a new era of peace and prosperity. They failed to see in Jesus the One who should come.

The Servant is the Messiah who through His dying and living again will grant them all the blessings of the Davidic covenant, the blessing of entering into a new relationship with God which transforms personal experience, even as it did with David, through the moral and spiritual experience of returning to God (Psalm 51).

It is hardly surprising that after Jesus had recalled to the Pharisees all that was understood in their scriptures of the relationship between the Messiah, the Christ, and the Son of David, and His own proof of Himself as Messiah by His words and works, that they had nothing more to say. This was what He had explained to John's disciples in Matthew 11 when John had sent his disciples to Jesus with the question, 'Are you He that should come, or do we look for another?' (Matthew 11:2-6). They too had nothing more to say. Suppose it was true? That He was indeed the One foretold, the Christ?

He is the Christ. It is His title, not His name, for His name is Jesus. But how we rejoice in calling Him 'Christ', that which expresses to us all that He is, the Anointed servant of God, all that He had accomplished; great David's greater son, risen, ascended, glorified. Jesus wants the Pharisees to recognise that He is the Son of David. He is the Suffering Servant. He is the Messiah, the Sent One. Each of these titles speak of His atoning work. They cannot be conflated, for each speaks independently of He who is, 'highly exalted, and given the Name which is above every name, that at the Name of Jesus, every knee shall bow, and every tongue confess that He is Lord, to the glory of God the Father' (Philippians 2:9-11). Jesus Christ is Lord!

Matthew Chapter 23

Matthew 23:1-39. Warning against the Pharisees. Introduction to the fifth discourse

Then Jesus spoke to the crowd and to His disciples, saying, 'The scribes and the Pharisees sit on Moses' seat, therefore all that they tell you to do, do and observe, but do not do according to their deeds, for they say things and do not do them' (Matthew 23:1-3).

Jesus has not yet left the Temple to which He was heading at the beginning of chapter 21. He has ridden into Jerusalem on a donkey, cleansed the Temple, received the acclamation of the crowds (verse 9), healed the blind and the lame and received the acclamation of the children.

The fig tree had withered at His command when He returned to Jerusalem the following morning, entering the Temple once again, confounding the chief priests and elders of the people as He spoke three parables to them, and confronting them as they sought to entangle Him in His talk (22:15) asking Him questions about paying taxes to Caesar, about the question of the resurrection of the dead from the Sadducees, about the great commandment from the lawyer, and about Jesus as the Son of David, from the Pharisees.

Following on from His confrontation with the Pharisees and Sadducees, Matthew 23 has become, at the beginning of this discourse from the Lord Jesus, an introduction to what Jesus has to say about the end of time in chapters 24 and 25. At first reading, this chapter reads as an introduction; it seems an unlikely prequel, but as the chapters unfold, we see the relevance of what Jesus is saying in chapter 23, as He mourns over a Jerusalem forsaken and desolate, its destiny foretold.

'Then,' said Jesus to the crowds and to His disciples, 'the scribes and Pharisees sit on Moses' seat, so practice and observe whatever they tell you, but not what they do, for they preach but do not practise. They bind heavy burdens, hard to bear, and lay them on men's shoulders, but they themselves will not move them with their finger. *They do all their deeds to be seen by men'* (Matthew 23:1-5).

Jesus is not speaking directly to the Pharisees at this point. He has already done so, pointing out to them in His love and in His mercy that His gospel is for them too, if only they would accept it.

Here He is speaking to the crowds and to His disciples (23:1). He can see the teaching of the Pharisees and scribes as a dark and terrible abyss. Far, far from drawing men and women to God, it has the potential to lead them away from Him, making them to be 'twice as much a child of hell as themselves' (verse 15).

We see much of chapter 23 adumbrated in the Sermon on the Mount, the first great discourse. Jesus has not altered His teaching, only intensified it. This fifth and last discourse balances it; in its length, in its association with a mountain (24:3) in Jesus taking the seated position of a teacher (24:3), in the contrast between the 'woes' and the 'beatitudes' and in the closing scenes of judgement when the exalted Jesus says, 'I never knew you, in Matthew 7:23, and 'Depart from Me', in Matthew 25:41; seriously, so seriously and so faithfully is Jesus warning His listeners, as He did in Matthew 6:1-8, of the dangers of a religion which panders to the worst offence possible, to interpreting the loving laws which God had provided for His people, to keep them safe in their relationship to Him; into a yoke, a burden not to be borne, a travesty of all God's purpose for them, and a complete denunciation of all that He was wanting to show them in visual form of the meaning behind all the ritual sacrifices which spoke of His Son, the Lamb of God who takes away the sin of the world (John 1:29).

Even now, so many hundreds of years after Moses, God's people had failed to understand all His purposes for them. But here is Jesus, the Son of God, Immanuel, 'God with us'. On the mountain of transfiguration, another mountain experience, God had said, 'This is my beloved Son. Hear Him' (Matthew 17:5). The Pharisees had refused to 'hear Him', but there were surely many in the crowds, and especially the disciples, who were only too anxious to hear, and to obey, what He had to say to them.

It was as if He was clearing the ground for action, as He first analysed and laid bare for them just how pernicious the teaching of the Pharisees could be. Jesus said, 'They sit on Moses' seat' (verse 2). They have the privilege of sitting on his seat, yet they do not do as Moses commanded. 'Moses seat' was not simply a metaphor. In every synagogue there was a seat on the raised dais at the front where the authoritative teacher, usually a scribe, sat next to the ark containing the scrolls of the Hebrew Scriptures, the Old Testament. The teacher sat on this seat to expound the law. Jesus said, 'Practise and observe whatever they tell you; but not what they do' (verse 3).

Sitting in Moses' seat does not guarantee authenticity of interpretation if the teacher, scribe, rabbi, does not appreciate the status of the Giver of the Law, His holiness, His transcendence, the everlastingness of His covenant with His people ratified in the shed blood of the sacrifice made on the altar, first in the tabernacle which God commanded Moses to set up, and then in the temple. Though well educated in the letter of the law, they needed the revelation which came by faith, as to who God is, and what His purpose concerning His people. This liberating understanding of the scriptures which would cause His people to walk in joy and gladness towards their synagogue week by week, rejoicing in their God-given freedom to follow Him in justice and mercy with each other and 'the stranger within their gates', had been replaced by the burdensome rules and regulations which they found impossible to keep.

Jesus could see the burdens on the faces of the people. He wanted to restore to them the 'joy of their salvation', going even further than that expressed in Psalm 51. He was not speaking only to the disciples here, but also to the crowds (Matthew 23:1). This was the last opportunity the crowds had, as well as the final opportunity given to the religious leaders in chapters 21:1–22:46, to hear what Jesus had to say about the ritualistic religion into which they had been brought by the teaching from 'Moses seat'.

How typically compassionate was Jesus when He described them as children of Jerusalem needing to be snuggled under His wings in the terrible time to come (verses 37, 38), just as a hen gathers her brood together.

The religious leaders believed it was necessary to make their superior status as distinctive as possible to the ordinary Jew; so they made their phylacteries broad, and their fringes, or tassels, long (verse 5). This religious ostentation was expressed in going further than the law demanded. It is true that Moses, speaking on God's behalf, recommended to the people that as a memorial, a remembrance of being rescued from Egypt, they should have as a sign of their remembrance 'a sign on your hand, and as a memorial or frontlet between your eyes' (Exodus 13:9, 16; Deuteronomy 6:8; 11:18).

The Jews called these their 'tefillin', prayer bands, phylacteries. They were small cases or boxes, made of parchment or leather on a leather strap, and contained texts of the law (Deuteronomy 11:13-32; Exodus 13:9). They were tied to the forehead and/or the left arm (the one nearest the heart) and the broader strap which the Pharisees used was to show just how religious they were.

Similarly, tassels, or fringes on the corner of the outer garment were worn in accordance with Numbers 15:38 and Deuteronomy 22:12 as a reminder of all the commandments of the Lord. Jesus Himself wore them according to Matthew 9:20, and 14:36, but the Pharisees lengthened theirs in order to draw attention to their piety.

This self-identification of themselves enabled them to claim the place of honour at the feasts and the best seats in the synagogues (verse 6). They would receive salutations, greetings as they went shopping in the marketplace (verse 7). They would be called 'Rabbi', commonly used as a term for 'Teacher', but having at its Semitic root the idea of 'great one'(verse 7).

This was total anathema to Jesus. His disciples were to understand that humility was the true mark of a servant of the

Lord. 'He who is greatest among you shall be your servant; whoever exalts himself shall be humbled, and whoever humbles himself shall be exalted (verses 11, 12). And you are not to be called 'Rabbi', for you have one teacher, and you all are brethren (verse 8). And call no man your father on earth, for you have one Father who is in heaven (verse 9), Neither be called 'master', for you have one Master, the Christ (verse 10).

Matthew 23:13. Jesus condemns the Pharisees

But woe to you scribes and Pharisees, hypocrites! because you shut the kingdom of heaven against men; for you neither enter yourselves not allow those who would enter to go in. Woe to you scribes and Pharisees, hypocrites! For you traverse sea and land to make one proselyte, and when he becomes a proselyte, you make him twice as much a child of hell as yourselves (Matthew 2313-15).

These three are honorific titles, Teacher, Father, Master. They are intended as descriptive of the *function* which each of these people known as father, Rabbi, master, perform. If they truly fulfilled these functions, being spiritual fathers, or teachers, or masters, they would enjoy the blessing of honour on all their endeavours.

But Jesus calls the Pharisees 'hypocrites' (verse 13). The children of God needed those who would lead them into a closer relationship with Him, but these Pharisees compounded the felony of sitting on Moses' seat and bringing people into bondage and legalism, with not even themselves practising what they preached. They were hollow, shallow teachers of the law. 'Woe to you, scribes and Pharisees,' says Jesus, 'because you shut the Kingdom of Heaven against men, for you neither enter yourselves nor allow those who would enter to go in' (verses 13, 14). 'Woe to you, scribes and Pharisees, hypocrites, for you traverse sea and land to make a single proselyte, and when he becomes a proselyte, you make him twice as much a child of hell as yourselves' (verse 15).

Paul writes in Romans, 'The law is holy, and the commandment is holy and just and good' (Romans 7:12). Hebrews 11 gives us many examples of those who lived under the law, and walked by faith, and were acceptable to God, as to righteousness under the law, blameless (Philippians 3:6). It was said of David that He was a man after God's own heart, who would do all His will, (Acts 13:22) and that 'Moses and Aaron were among His priests, and Samuel among those who called on His Name. They cried to the Lord and He answered them' (Psalm 99:6). There were many, known and unknown to us through the scriptures, who found in the Lord their God the satisfaction of all the longing of their hearts.

So what did Jesus mean when He said, 'I am come that they might have life, and have it more abundantly' (John 10:10) since they could have been already in possession of so much mercy and grace and compassionate love? Of what were the Pharisees so completely unaware?

The letter to the Galatians asserts that the law was our custodian, our guardian, our schoolmaster, to bring us to Christ (Galatians 3:24). They, the Jewish people, were like children, even as we are, helpless, dependent, ignorant, but having a desire for righteousness and truth. How often were they led astray to dumb idols! (1 Corinthians 12:2) to following the gods of the nations round about them. Isaiah however is convinced that there was always 'a remnant', who did not follow after strange gods. In Isaiah 6:13, he speaks of a tenth of the people as a tithe to the Lord of all who remain faithful to Him. A remnant will return, he says, a remnant of Jacob to the mighty God (Isaiah 10:21), whose desire is to worship the Lord in the beauty of holiness (Psalm 96:9 A.V.) The psalmist cries from the bottom of his heart, 'O come let us worship and bow down, let us kneel before the Lord our Maker!' (Psalm 95:6).

Yet here is this man Paul, who describes himself as having the righteousness of the law, blameless according to its prohibitions (Philippians 3:10), who confesses that apart from the law he had not known sin. He delights in the law of God in his inner man (Romans 7:22), but cannot prevent himself from

453

doing the very thing which he hates (Romans 7:15). 'O wretched man that I am,' he cries. 'Who will deliver me from this body of death?'(Romans 7:24) and comes up with this reassurance 'I thank God through our Lord Jesus Christ' (Romans 7:25).

Paul, and we who trust in Jesus, may be set free from our apron strings, from the childhood of the law which holds us in its power, the guardian of Galatians 3 which has kept us so long until now. We recognise that we cannot keep the law that leads to righteousness. As James reminds us, even if we are only guilty in one particular instance, we are guilty of all (James 2:10).

Paul writes that the law was our custodian, our guardian keeping us safe until Christ came, until we realised that our only hope of satisfying the demands of the law was to fling ourselves on the only one who was sinless, and on His mercy, the mercy of Jesus, to find in Him forgiveness and new life, eternal life, in Him (Galatians 3:24). Now faith has come, faith in the risen Christ who shed His blood on the Cross for us to free us from our sin, that faith which gives us justification, the imputed righteousness that we have by faith in Christ Jesus (Romans 3:22), and now we are no longer under a custodian, no longer under the law.

So, Paul continues his argument, do we need the law anymore? All we desire of righteousness, of right living and believing in the eyes of a Holy God, has been granted to us through the sacrifice of Christ on the cross, where He paid the price for all our sin, by cleansing us. What then, are we to sin, because we are no longer under the law, but under grace? By no means, God forbid! (Romans 6:15).

We were once slaves to sin, but now are free from sin. We have been redeemed from the curse of the law, the curse of knowing that we could not keep the law. The price has been paid. We are free *not* to sin. And the Holy Spirit intercedes for us with groans that cannot be uttered, with sighs too deep for words (Romans 8:26. A.V.; R.S.V). If we sin we have an advocate with the Father, Jesus Christ the righteous, and He is the propitiation for, the expiation of, the atoning power for, our sins (1 John 2:1).

This is what Jesus had in mind for us, when He says He is come to give us life, and to have it more abundantly. This is what He is offering to the Pharisees, the scribes, the Sadducees, the crowds, the disciples. This is why He has to reveal the end result and consequence of the hypocritical attitude of the Pharisees to the precious law given to Moses, the law of God, law built on the never failing faithfulness, the total holiness of the character of God, a law which the Pharisees have utterly traduced, making it a chain, a bondage, to enslave God's people, rather than a pathway to loving God, at least in part, until the promised One should come; the One who would come to judge the world with righteousness, and the people with His truth (Psalm 96:13), the One who *is* the Truth, *and* the Way, *and* the Life (John 14:6).

How they needed Him to speak to them of a higher way, a way which God was about to implement through the willing offering of His Son to come down to earth, to become a man, to die as a man in great pain and suffering as He took upon Himself the sins of the whole world. And He was here, with that life changing message, but they would not accept Him or His message. Though at this point in time, all had not yet been fulfilled in Him and by Him, here He was amongst them. They were seeing the Son of God face to face, hearing His voice inviting them to come to Him, Jesus, Immanuel, God with us.

We find it unbelievable, incredible that they did not fall in worship at His feet, except that the Son of God was so truly 'veiled in flesh', and only a few saw Him as the 'incarnate Deity, pleased as Man with Man to dwell, 'Jesus our Immanuel', as Wesley so exactly put it.

Jesus uses strong words about the teaching of the Pharisees, and the contradiction between what they said and what they did, so anxious was He that these people, the crowds and the disciples of Matthew 23:1, should at least have a glimmer of understanding of this wonderful alternative way of living, that could be theirs, if only they would turn, and repent of their sin, and believe the gospel which He had brought to them, pointing out the contrast between what their religious leaders were advocating, and the source of His life, the life with the Father in the Kingdom of Heaven.

'Woe to you, scribes and Pharisees, hypocrites,' He says six times, in verses 13, 15, 23, 25, 27 and 29. 'And woe to you, blind guides,' He says once in verse 16. Seven woes altogether. 'Hypocrites' are play actors, playing at being something or someone they are not; usually quite legitimately. 'Blindness' is also something Jesus has so often intimated is the spiritual state of the Pharisees. To be a hypocrite, a spiritual hypocrite may only affect oneself, self-deception. It becomes more serious when it affects the spiritual lives of others. How careful we need to be, to be absolutely transparent in our dealings with others, to ask for wisdom when we lack spiritual insight and discernment, to have our eyes open if there is an attempt to pretend a too-easy way out of a situation.

Jesus called the Pharisees blind guides because they said it was all right to swear by the temple on the altar, but not by the gold of the temple or the gift on the altar (Matthew 23:16). Both the temple and the altar were symbolic of the Lord's presence with His people, but the religious leaders were blind to their significance, treating them as superstitious objects. Jesus says there are even some who swear by heaven, not understanding that they swear by the throne of God, and He who reigns from it, seeking to draw God down to their level if that were possible. They are indeed 'blind guides' having no understanding of the sacredness which intrinsically adheres to these concepts, objectivising them to their own eventual judgement (Matthew 23:16-22); and neglecting its effect on the lives of others.

These *others* may very carefully weigh out the herbs used in cooking, making sure they give a tenth of them to God, while neglecting justice, mercy and faith (Matthew 23:23), neglecting respect for the rights of others; or fidelity to the trustworthiness of God's will. They carefully filter the wine through a cloth to avoid 'unclean insects', while neglecting these weightier matters of the law. They strain out a gnat, but swallow something much worse, 'a camel', a metaphor for a beast of burden. And how burdensome is all their occupation with the letter of the law!

Yet *others* (Matthew 23:25), make sure the outside of the cup is clean, but ignore the fact that the 'inside', the contents, come to be there as a result of 'extortion and rapacity' (verse 25), robbery, or greed, or self-indulgences. It is the inner life of a man that counts, not what can be seen from the outside. If someone is living in obedience to God, then his outward behaviour and inner status before God will also be 'clean', compatible. Jesus calls them 'blind Pharisees' (verse 26) as if they were not even aware that there should be some sort of correspondence between outward piety and inner purity, not even being aware of the contents of the cup being extortion and rapacity.

Jesus is saying that they need to get rid of what is inside the cup, using the metaphor of the cup for the whole person, and the inside of the cup as the inner part of the person. Only the cleansing of the heart will produce a discernible difference in the behaviour of the whole person. Jesus says, 'First cleanse the inside of the cup and of the plate, that the outside also may be clean (verse 26).

Jesus continues this theme in verse 27. 'Woe to you, scribes and Pharisees, for you are like whitewashed tombs' (R.S.V.), 'whited sepulchres' (A.V.), which outwardly appear beautiful, but within they are full of dead men's bones and all uncleanness. So you also appear outwardly righteous to men, but within you are full of hypocrisy and iniquity, lawlessness, ἀνομίας (verses 27, 28).

David Hill, p313, comments that sepulchres were whitened each year before Passover, in order that passers-by should not inadvertently come into contact with them and thereby contract ceremonial impurity (Luke 11:44). Sometimes this was a lime wash, but it could be replastering.

But these beautifully preserved tombs of the prophets and monuments of the righteous (verse 29) do not mask the reality that within them is corruption and all uncleanness. However beautiful the Pharisees may have looked on the outside, only God knew of the corruption within, in German 'außen hui und innen pfui'. Jesus called them hypocrites and we sense an intensification of the cup metaphor. But Jesus goes on to make an even more serious accusation against them. Not only do they *adorn* the monuments of the righteous, but they *build* the tombs of the prophets, saying, 'If we had lived in the days of our fathers, we would not have taken part with them in shedding the blood of the prophets' (verses 29, 30).

This self-justification is the exact opposite of what they are claiming. Jesus says they are witnessing against themselves. They may not have done any actual building of the tombs or shedding of the blood of the prophets, but they were 'the sons of those who murdered the prophets' (verse 31). The martyrdom and location of the graves of Isaiah, Jeremiah, Ezekiel, Micah, Amos and Zechariah was well known. The righteous ones' were possibly those of the Maccabean period and also well known. Peter mentioned the tomb of David on the Day of Pentecost (Acts 2:29). These were indeed monuments to Israel's past history.

To describe themselves as being 'sons of their fathers' implies not a continuity of guilt, but a ploy, a stratagem to honour belatedly those who had been martyred, in order to distance themselves from the actions of their predecessors, and in some measure atone for what had happened in the past.

But their attempts at self-justification become self-incrimination. Jesus knows the thoughts and intents of their hearts. He knows that they plan to kill Him, and He knows that after His death, many of the prophets, wise men and scribes who come in His Name will be martyred for His sake, scourged in their synagogues, and persecuted from town to town (verse 34). And upon them will come all the blood guiltiness of all the righteous bloodshed, from A-Z, from Abel to the prophet Zechariah, the son of Barachiah, last but one of the Old Testament prophets in the canon (verse 35).

Jesus says to them, 'How will you escape the judgement of hell? Do you understand what you are doing, and its consequences? Hell is not only inevitable separation from God, but from all that you profess to hold dear. Are you willing to go down that route, to incur the judgement of God? For judgement is surely coming, when your house will be left to you forsaken and desolate (verse 38). You are going to fill up the measure of your fathers (verse 32), complete the terrible work which they had begun, and the time will come when you will not be building their beautiful tombs but will be hounding men and women to death, 'killing the prophets and stoning those who are sent to you' (verse 37). Woe to you indeed!

Matthew 23:34-39. The lament of Jesus over Jerusalem

Therefore I send you prophets and wise men and scribes, some of whom you will kill and crucify and some you will scourge in your synagogues and persecute from town to town that upon you may come all the righteous blood shed on earth (Matthew 23:34).

Behind this apocalyptic oracle of Jesus and His final denunciation of all that the Pharisees and scribes, and Sadducees stood for, Jesus says, 'All these things will come upon this generation' (verse 36).The context presupposes the term 'generation' to refer to the Jewish religious leaders, but Jesus has them and others too in this apocalyptic statement. He has more than His contemporaries in mind. He has laid out in no uncertain terms what is happening and has happened in the religious life of the Jewish community. And this has become a bridge into what He has to say about the future, not only of His precious city of Jerusalem and what it will have to suffer, but of the final Parousia when He will come again 'in power and great glory' (Matthew 24:30).

'O Jerusalem, Jerusalem, killing the prophets and stoning those who are sent to you! How often would I have gathered your children together as a hen gathers her brood under her wings, and you would not!' (verse 37).

This is one of the most powerful laments in the whole of the scriptures, revealing in its intensity the absolute agony Jesus felt as He contemplates the terrible destiny awaiting Jerusalem. How often had the prophets' warnings been ignored. How often had His Father's compassion gone out to them, but they 'would not' (verse 37), they were unwilling. 'Behold, your house is left to you forsaken and desolate' (verse 38).

But, there is hope. But, the time will come, when you will say, 'Blessed is He who comes in the Name of the Lord (verse 39). He is the Coming Son of Man, Son of God; their God who at sundry times and in several different ways has spoken through the prophets to His people, but had, during the last three years of Christ's ministry, spoken to them by His Son (Hebrews 11:1), God bearing witness to Him by signs and wonders and various miracles, and by gifts of the Holy Spirit distributed according to His own will (Hebrews 2:4). And He will come again! (Matthew 24:27).

Many received the word with joy (Acts 17:11 A.V.), leaving all to follow Jesus, including the Twelve who are here with Him in the temple, hearing what He has to say about the scribes and Pharisees, and their rejection of Him and His teaching. The division between these disparate groups of people has been increased and enhanced by Jesus' words. What were the disciples to make of it?

Jesus now left the temple (chapter 24:1), never to return, and was going away when it occurred to His disciples that His assessment of the future for Jerusalem would probably also include the buildings of the temple. And so, Jesus enters into the second part of the last discourse He will ever give to His disciples, chapter 24 and 25.

Matthew Chapter 24

Matthew 24:1-2. The destruction of the temple foretold

Jesus left the temple and was going away when His disciples came to point out to Him the buildings of the temple. But He answered them, 'You see all these do you not? Truly, I say to you, there will not be left here one stone upon another, that will not be thrown down' (Matthew 24:1-2)

In abandoning the temple, Jesus is moving away from polemic to apocalyptic, from the indictment of the scribes and the Pharisees and their history to the future destiny, not only of the Jewish people, but of the whole world.

Jesus' departure from the temple constitutes its being forsaken (23:38), but in addition to that, there will not be one stone upon another that will not be thrown down (verse 2). This prediction is fulfilled in A.D. 70 along with the razing to the ground of the rest of Jerusalem under Vespasian and Titus with their Roman armies.

The lament over Jerusalem in the previous chapter (23:37-39), and the prediction over the temple causes the disciples to ask Jesus for clarification. Is this part of all the prophecies they have read and heard about the coming of the Messiah, the coming of Jesus – *'your coming'* (verse 3), for they had an understanding of who Jesus was – and of the close of the age?

Jesus too knows the prophecies like Micah 3:12 which says that Jerusalem will become a heap of ruins. Jeremiah 26:6,18 has the same prophecy. But He wants to distinguish between the *soon coming* destruction of Jerusalem, and the cosmic catastrophes which will herald *the final and complete renewal of the world;* the new heaven and the new earth; the consummation of all things.

Jesus has in view the whole of salvation history, encompassing all His knowledge of the purposes of God when speaking earlier of the hypocrisy of the Pharisees, right up to the last judgement of Matthew 25:31, an exposition of the theme of the Kingdom of Heaven until 'the Son of Man comes in His glory and all His angels with Him. Then He will sit on His glorious throne, and before Him will be gathered all the nations, and He will separate them one from another, as a shepherd separates the sheep from the goats.' Our great and glorious Shepherd King!

Jesus' *first* discourse described the righteousness of the Kingdom of Heaven, of life lived in relationship with the Father in heaven (chapters 5-7). The *second* discourse concerned the proclamation of the gospel of the Kingdom, not only to the lost sheep of the house of Israel, but to the whole world (chapter 10:7,8). The *third* discourse was about the secrets, the mysteries of the Kingdom of Heaven, mysteries provisionally hidden, and subsequently revealed through faith to His devoted followers, (chapter 13). The *fourth* discourse was concerned with brotherly relations between those who now belong in the Kingdom of Heaven (chapter 18).

And now, in the *fifth and last* discourse, Jesus is revealing a cosmic crisis which will eventually be manifested before the whole world (Matthew chapter 24), and the active, compassionate preparedness of those who look for the total, absolute complete reign of the Kingdom of God, the end of all things summed up in Jesus.

Matthew 24:3-25:46. The end time, eschatological discourse

Jesus and His disciples had now left the temple, but not the city. They have gone to the Mount of Olives, and 'as He sat there, they came to Him saying privately, 'Tell us when will this be, and what will be the sign of your coming and of the close of the age?' (Matthew 24:3-4).

The disciples have linked together the destruction of the temple, the return of the Lord Jesus and the end of the age; its

462

consummation; indicating that by this stage in His ministry, and in their discipleship, they had reached an understanding of who Jesus truly is, and were ready for the revelation which He was about to give them.

In response to their question, the first thing Jesus says is, 'Take heed that no one leads you astray. Be careful that you are not deceived (verse 4), for many will come in My Name saying, "I am the Christ," and they will lead many astray' (verse 5).

This statement tells us at least two things. *One,* that Jesus is making it absolutely certain for them that He will come back again to the world He is leaving, and *secondly,* that there will be many who believe that such an event is more than a possibility, but they are deluded into thinking that the anointing of the Holy Spirit, the 'Christ-ing' rests on them. They believe themselves to be anointed without the witness of their spirit that they are the children of God, a witness that no one could miss if they truly knew the indwelling of the Holy Spirit. They are deceived to such an extent that they believe themselves to *be* the Christ, the One who has returned to His people. Jesus says, 'Many will come in My Name, and they will lead many astray' (verse 5), They are deceived. They may also be involved in the deception of others, because of the power it brings them.

But Jesus says, 'You, My disciples, must not be deceived, for the end is not yet' (verse 6). So much needs to happen before 'the glorious coming of the Son of Man' (verse 30).

Then He turns from the individual to the national and international. 'You will hear of wars and rumours of wars' (verse 6). Nation will rise against nation and kingdom against kingdom. There will be famines and earthquakes in various places, and this is but the beginning of the birth pangs (verse 8). But the end is not yet (verse 6).

Interpreting His Master's words, Paul comments, 'The whole creation groans and travails in pain until now' (Romans 8:22) but the sufferings of this present time are not worthy to be compared with the glory that is to be revealed to us (Romans 8:18). And in this hope we are saved (Romans 8:24).

This hope and expectation is the theme of the whole discourse. Terrible things may well happen to the children of God. They will be delivered up to tribulation, they will be put to death, they will be hated of all nations, for His Name's sake (verse 9), and worst of all, such persecution will be too much for some of the followers of Jesus. They will cease to follow Him. They will betray others who do, so that they are not themselves under the suspicion of having once followed the Lord. There will be false prophets, against whom Jesus had already warned His disciples in chapter 7, who pretend to have a life affirming trust in Jesus, even to the extent of prophesying in His Name, casting out demons and doing many mighty works in His Name, but to whom Jesus declared, 'I never knew you, depart from Me' (Matthew 7:22, 23).

And then this terrible consequence, that because there is so much wickedness, 'The love of many will grow cold' (verse 12).

The tension between Christian believers and the outside world leads to much tribulation. How much worse is tension between those who claim to belong to the same Lord, that the way the world relates to the church, and to others, infects and surfaces in the way brothers and sisters in the church find themselves relating to one another. Jesus says, 'Many will fall away, or stumble, and betray one another, and hate one another'. (verse 10), the complete antithesis of what He wants for His beloved church, a company of those who love one another as He has loved them. (John 15:12).

But as always, 'Jesus tempers the wind to the shorn lamb.' There *will* be those who endure to the end, and they *will* be saved. (verse 13). And even the persecution and diaspora of Christians will be used to spread the gospel, for the gospel is a testimony, a witness that the flame of love which the Lord Jesus has kindled will not be put out, will not grow cold. And when the gospel has been preached throughout the world, then shall the end come (verse 14), the Coming, the Parousia, παρουσία, the second coming of Jesus, and this time as the heavenly Judge. (1 Thessalonians 2:19; 3:13; 4:15; 5:23; 1 Corinthians 15:23; and many relevant passages also in 2 Thessalonians, James, 1 John, 2 Peter).

'Then shall the end come,' says Jesus (verse 14), the end, the τέλος, the fulfilment and completion of all things, just as Jesus said in His last words on the Cross, before bowing His Head and yielding up His spirit to His heavenly Father saying, 'It is finished', τέλος, the work of atonement for the sins of the world is finished, completed. (John 19:30). Nothing that happens, either in the world, or more especially, in the life and death of Jesus, is without significance. Everything constitutes purpose in the mind and heart of God. And all of history is under his control.

Jesus goes on to remind His disciples of what happened in the temple at the time of Antiochus Epiphanes in 168 B.C., when a pagan altar was set up on which swine were sacrificed; a desolating sacrilege. (Matthew 24:15). Jesus knows that this was not the first time nor would it be the last, that the temple, the meeting place of the Lord with His people, was to be desecrated. In 40 A.D. Caligula had a similar idea, and in 66-70 A.D., the Emperor Vespasian and his son Titus completely destroyed the temple, as we have noted.

These terrible events, prophesied by Daniel in 9:27, 11:31, and 12:11, indicated that there was always, in the perception of those invading Palestine, a compulsion to destroy the worship of the One True God. (verse 15). The very presence of the temple, and more especially, the altar, proclaimed the special relationship that the unseen but all-prevailing Presence of God had with the people who served and worshipped Him. The invading armies under their idol worshipping kings, attempted to oust Him by setting up their own gods, or destroying everything that pertained to Him, yet they could not doubt His reality. Why would they bother to try to destroy something or someone which was not real? Without meaning? Or power?

There have always been such. Psalm 2 describes it so well. 'Why do the heathen rage, and the peoples plot in vain? The kings of the earth set themselves, and their rulers take counsel together against the Lord, and against His anointed, saying, 'Let us break their bands asunder and cast away their cords from us.'

He who sits in the heavens shall *laugh,* the Lord shall have them in *derision.*

It had happened time and time again, in greater or lesser measure, and just for a period of time, that God has allowed such desecration of the holy place. But Jesus is speaking here of 'great tribulation, such as has not been seen from the beginning of the world until now'. (verse 21). God has allowed this great tribulation because He is working towards the end. This is not the end, but it is the beginning of the end, when the tribulation will be so great that the only resource is to flee. When you see the desolating sacrilege, the sacrilege especially of the altar, then if you are in Judea, says Jesus, flee to the mountains, as people have always done, the rugged Judean wilderness where the cave-filled mountains were a traditional place of safety (Ezekiel 7:16). If you are on the top of your house, do not go down into it to retrieve your possessions, but flee! (verse 17). If you are working in the field, do not go home to pick up your cloak (verse 18) which keeps you warm at night, but flee!

It will be difficult for those who are pregnant, and therefore slower, and for those who need to stop to feed their babies, so pray! And pray also that your flight may not be in winter, (verse 20), when the winter rains make travelling difficult, or on a Sabbath when markets with their supplies will be closed, and there will be a greater danger of being exposed as a Christian because Christian and Jewish people follow restrictions on travel on the Sabbath. Jesus is conflating A.D.70 with the last tribulation, as the double fulfilment of prophecy, for prophecy stretches from the more immediate future to the mysterious forth-telling of the distant time to come.

Daniel 12:1, had spoken of a time of trouble, of tribulation. Jesus says, 'This will be a time of *great* tribulation and unless it had been shortened no human being would be saved, but for the elect's sake, those called to follow Jesus, those days would be shortened. (verse 22). And *'then'*, Jesus says, will be the most dangerous time of all, following on from His 'then' in verse 9 describing what will happen after the international wars, famines and earthquakes.

Jesus is prophesying the chronology of this. Event follows event, just as God has ordained. Nothing is outside His control, everything is necessary for the future conquest of all that is, or has become, evil, in the world which He had created as perfect, and which by man's disobedience and rebellion against Him has been corrupted.

And this first dangerous, dreadful thing is the imitation, falsification and denigration of Christlikeness by people calling themselves Christ. These false Christs, false prophets (verse 24) will do all kinds of marvellous signs and wonders, for only so can they lead people astray, so much so that even the elect, God's chosen people, may be deceived. Some of these false Christs will go into the wilderness, expecting many people to follow them, some will be hidden away in 'inner rooms', secret buildings. (verse 26).

But Jesus says, 'Do not believe it'. (verse 26). These people make a pretence of being the Christ. For all their apparent ability to do signs and wonders, do not believe it. Nothing that Jesus says or does is done in a corner. When He does return, it will be like lightning, lightening the world from one corner of it to another, from the east to the west. This will be the coming, the Parousia of the Son of Man. (verse 27).

Behold, He is coming with the clouds and every eye shall see Him, and those who pierced Him and all the tribes of earth shall mourn because of Him, even so. Amen. (Revelation 1:7; Zechariah 12:10).

And what of these false Christs and false prophets when He makes His appearance? Just as vultures gather round their prey, so Jesus says, these people will gather around those who have deceived them. And because of their presence there, they will be known and acknowledged for who and what they are, and those who did not recognise their assertion that they were the Christ, will be vindicated.

For there is yet more to come. Jesus says (verse 29). '*Immediately*, after the tribulation of those days, there will be cosmic disturbances.' Some exegesis has claimed that immediately means '*suddenly*', but there is a distinction here. Immediately suggests a time pattern being followed, and in such a way that no human participation is involved, that God alone is in control. 'Suddenly' suggests a chaotic state of affairs, brought to an end by further intervention by God, almost taking Him by surprise!

We may truly believe that God knows what He is doing, has planned it from eternity, even if, as many said in the time of Peter, 'Where is the promise of His coming?' (2 Peter 3:3), Peter, speaking as he was moved by the Holy Spirit, (2 Peter 1:21), gave as the explanation, 'The Lord is not slow concerning His promise, but is forbearing towards you, not wishing that any should perish, but that all should come to repentance. (2 Peter 3:9). Even God's forbearance and mercy towards sinful men and women is accommodated into His plan for the end of time, and for the new heaven and the new earth in which righteousness dwells. (2 Peter 3:13).

The end begins with the darkening of the sun and moon, and the stars falling from heaven, and the powers of the heaven shaken. (verse 29). Earthly history has come to an end, and the entire cosmos is drawn into the event, an event which at last conveys the conviction that this indeed is the fulfilment of God's plan for the restoration of all things, and particularly the restoration of His beloved Son to His proper status and position. (verse 29, 30).

All the tribes of the earth will mourn for Him, for they had been slow to accept the final consummation. (verse 30). And now they will see Him as He is, for *then* shall appear the sign of the Son of Man in heaven, coming on the clouds of heaven with power and great glory (verse 30), using His angels to gather together all His beloved ones from the four winds, from one end of heaven to the other. (verse 31). His divine power δύναμις, His divine glory δόξα universally established, universally acknowledged, no longer limited by His earthly Body, which was so precious to Him because it was indicative of the fact that by flesh and blood He was made 'like unto His brethren' (Hebrews 2:17), partaking of human nature (Hebrews 2: 14), that He might become a merciful and faithful High Priest in the service of God, understanding human temptation because He Himself has suffered and been tempted, yet without sin, and so is able to make expiation for the sins of the people (Hebrews 2:17,18).

The work is done, the Redeemer, the Saviour. Immanuel came and delivered all those who all their lifetime were subject to bondage. (Hebrews 2:15) and now He comes again to gather together His elect, His chosen ones. (Matthew 24:31). Blessed hope of the coming of the Lord!

The disciples had asked, 'What will be the sign of your coming?' (Matthew 24:3). Jesus says, 'After you have witnessed these cosmic events, then will appear the sign of the Son of Man in heaven' (Matthew 24:30). This is the final sign. There will be no more 'signs and wonders'. *Jesus Himself is the ultimate sign,* the sign that Jesus is reaping the harvest He has sown. As a corn of wheat, He fell to the ground and died (John 12:24), and in rising again He brought forth much fruit, men and women who would share with Him in His glory, who would sit with Him at His wedding banquet as His Bride, clothed in garments white and pure, the fine linen which is the righteousness of the saints. (Revelation 19:7,8) His beloved, His gathered elect ones, a multitude which no man can number, from every nation, from all tribes and people and tongues, standing before the throne of God and before the Lamb, serving God day and night in His temple, those who have come out of the great tribulation and have washed their robes and made them white in the blood of the Lamb. (Revelation 7:9,14,15).

Matthew 24:32,34. The lesson of the fig tree

Jesus is aware yet again, that He is speaking to these beloved learners, disciples, who are not quite up to the revelation of all things which will come to pass in God's own economy, His own time, time which He measures by eternal dimensions. So He uses a homely example, which being easily understood, will encourage them to realise the tremendous significance of what He has been telling them.

To the disciples He says, 'From the fig tree learn its lesson. As soon as its branch becomes tender, and puts forth its leaves, you know that summer is near. So also, when you see all these things, you know that He is near, at the very gates. (Matthew 24:32)

Most of the Palestine trees are evergreen. But the almond and fig trees are deciduous. The almond tree loses its leaves in winter and sprouts new ones in early spring. The fig tree also loses its leaves in winter, but it is late spring before it produces new ones, so that when its new leaves begin to appear, summer is approaching. In ancient Hebrew there are only two terms for the seasons: winter and summer.

Jesus says, like the approach of the summer, which we recognise by the new tender growth on the fig tree, 'So also when you see all these things, you know that He is near, at the very gates'. (verse 33).

This is not a trivial saying, a trivial example, but a solemn warning. Jesus continues with another solemn 'amen' warning. 'Truly, amen, I say to you, *this generation* will not pass away till all these things take place. Heaven and earth will pass away, but My words will not pass away'. (verse 34, 35).

There has been some controversy over what Jesus meant by 'this generation'. Did He mean that He would return in the lifetime of these disciples? Could He, as some affirm, have made a mistake? He never makes a mistake. Looking more closely at the word generation, it appears that although it could refer to all the people born at a particular time (e.g. the use of the term' the millennial generation; or 'your father's generation'); it could mean the procreation or propagation of a *species,* or in human terms, generating though the act of begetting. (Oxford English Dictionary, 9th edition).

The generation of the disciples, and of all who are born again, or anew, in John's terminology, are those who are begotten, born of water and the Spirit, without which none can enter the Kingdom of God. (John 3:5). John's precise reporting of the words of Jesus help us to understand His use of the word generation, for an almighty miracle has taken place when that which is born of the flesh (verse 6) is 'born anew', born again (John 3: 3) by the Spirit of God, and enters into the kingdom of

God, where God reigns in the life of that person, and where believing in Jesus means entering into eternal life (verse 15), into the resurrection life of the Son of God, as Peter also reminds us (1 Peter 1:3,23).

God has 'generated' new life in that person, and 'that generation' comprises all those who are so generated, born again by the Spirit of God, who live by the faith of the Son of God, who loved them and gave Himself for them. (Galatians 2:20).

'This generation' is the church, waiting and longing for the return of their Lord, convinced that heaven and earth will pass away, but that the words of Jesus will never pass away for *He is the word, the Logos.* As the creative power behind the First Creation, it is not a huge step of faith to believe, to know, to understand, to appreciate, that He will also be the Word who ushers in the New Creation.

In chapter 12:39, Jesus had spoken of an evil and adulterous generation, a generation generated from, or by, or with evil. There have always been such, But Jesus had referred to the prophet Jonah even to these people, a prophet who models the precious reality of resurrection as he is released from the belly of the whale after three days and three nights (12:40). As the Lord acted on behalf of Jonah, even though he had disobeyed God, so God who is a merciful God, will listen to the crying out to Him of all who are in any kind of trouble, and He will deal with the evil. He is the God of restoration, and where there is repentance, He will lead in the paths of righteousness for His Name's sake. (Psalm 23:3)

To these too, this generation, Jesus gives the opportunity to repent, for the unclean spirit, the evil which motivates them, to be cast out of them. But their responsibility is to ensure that it does not return. Even the most obdurate, rebellious sinner may come to the cross of the Lord Jesus and find forgiveness, healing and new life in Him. The Ninevites repented at the preaching of Jonah (Jonah 3:10). A greater than Jonah is here and the Holy Spirit is doing the work He loves best, generating new life in men and women, convicting them of sin, and righteousness and judgement, bringing them to new birth and glorifying Jesus, (John 14:8, 14).

The Arian Heresy

But here again, Jesus interposes a warning word of caution.

'But of that day and hour, no-one knows, not 'this generation', not even the angels of heaven, nor the Son, but the Father only. (Matthew 24:36).

Only the Father knows.

Jesus wants His disciples, and the generation of believers who come after them, to know how vital it is to be ready for Him when He returns. This is the ultimate event in the history of mankind, entirely dependent on the Father for the time of its fulfilment, His perfect timing. But for some who have heard or read His words, there is a problem; it is that only *the Father* knows the time of the Parousia, and that not even Jesus knows. Does this mean that He occupies a subordinate position in the Godhead?

There was a time in the fourth century when Jesus was viewed as subordinate to His Father. This was the Arian heresy. It shook the church to its foundations because it implicated the whole doctrine of salvation.

Arius was a priest and pastor in Alexandria c250-336. He was much loved for his asceticism and care of others. His much learning encouraged him to believe that Christ was subordinate to the Father. He wanted to emphasise the unity and simplicity of God. He did not believe in a hierarchy of divine beings. He was a radical monotheist and concluded that the Father alone is God. The Son is the one through whom God created the universe, but He is only a creature, a created being. He is not eternal but had a beginning. Arius says, 'There was a time when He was not.' This teaching is found today in the teaching of Jehovah's witnesses.

This teaching might seem to us today to be remote and obscure. But it is fundamental, and central to Christian faith. Without the deity of Christ, there is no revelation of God. God was in Christ, revealing Himself to the world, reconciling the world to Himself. (2 Corinthians 5:19). There would be no reconciliation if the One who had gone to the cross was not the Son of God but just a being created from nothing, who had a beginning and was not therefore eternal as God is, was not part of God's eternal covenant.

Arius raised an important question, but came up with a controversial answer. The Council of Nicea convened in *325,* produced an anti-Arian creed, stating:

We believe in God, Father almighty, Maker of all things visible and invisible. And in one Lord Jesus Christ, the Son of God, begotten of the Father, that is from the substance of the Father. He is God from God, light from light, true God from true God, begotten not made, of one substance (homousious) with the Father.

This creed was established more fully at the Council of Constantinople in 381 and today is known as the Nicene Creed with additional phrases concerning the Lord Jesus Christ and the Holy Spirit. The Council was convened to deal with Arianianism once and for all, to affirm that Jesus Christ was both fully God and fully man, to protect not just the doctrine, but the *fact* of the Incarnation. (The Lion Book of Christian Thought, Tony Lane, p 34).

Why then does Jesus say, 'But of that hour of My coming again, no-one knows, not even the angels of heaven, nor the Son, but the Father only?'

How often do we turn to Philippians 2:6, and the revelation of the self-limiting Son of God, who, though He was in the form of God, did not count equality with God a thing to be grasped, but emptied Himself, taking the form of a servant, being made in the likeness of men.

When Jesus lived among men and women as the Son of Man, identifying Himself with their humanity, He lived his life out from God, in prayerful dependence upon His Father. He refused to exercise the omnipotence which was legitimately His, not even changing stones into bread when He was hungry after a fast of 40 days. (Matthew 4:3), or throwing Himself down from the pinnacle of the temple to prove that He was greater than the temple, that He was the Son of God. (Matthew 4:6). He was utterly dependent on the will of His Father, and not only at that crucial time in the Garden of Gethsemane when He prayed, 'Not my will but Thine be done', but throughout His earthly life. (Matthew 26:39).

The love of and for his Father was the guiding, determining principle of His life. What He could have done because He was the Son of God did not determine what He actually did as Son of Man, because that was the will of the Father. The incarnation did not destroy His power as Son of God. It caused Him to limit Himself to human capabilities, and yet capabilities indwelt and inspired by the Holy Spirit, because He was the Anointed One, the Messiah, the Christ. The Spirit of the Lord God was upon Him (Isaiah 61:1), full of grace and truth (John 1:14). This is the inexpressible, the unknowable mystery which leaves us breathless. Jesus was truly God and truly Man.

But in declaring that 'of that day and of that hour, no one, not even the angels in heaven, nor the Son', (verse 36) knows when the whole of creation will be rolled up 'like a scroll' (Revelation 6:12–17), Jesus is making a further comment aimed at caution.

Because not even the Son knows when He will come again, it is absolutely necessary for His people to be watchful, to be prepared. Uncertainty surrounds the coming again of the Son of Man, (verse 36). No-one knows. Jesus says, '*You* do not know. Watch therefore, for you do not know on what day your Lord is coming'. (verse 42). The watchword is vigilance, but vigilance centred on complete trust in the Father, who *does* know and will achieve the absolute universal recognition of His Son in His own appointed time.

Jesus says, 'Watch therefore'. Do not be taken by surprise, or by dangerous people who think they know. Your Lord is coming. Your uncertainty is balanced by your heavenly Father's certainty, but you need to be ready, ready for the unveiling of all that God has been working towards, the unveiling of His purpose regarding His beloved One, the Son of his love, with whom He has a unique relationship, the One who alone knows Him, (Matthew 11:27).

What example can Jesus give to His disciples to help them to understand what He has been saying about this uncertainty, how to help them to be ready and expectant in the face of all that appears contrary to this wonderful event, that He will come in an hour when they think not.? (Matthew 24:44).

Perhaps the most obvious Biblical incident of which Jesus could remind them was the Flood. Though Noah had spent many years building the Ark, routinely watched by people who mocked him as they continued eating and drinking, marrying their wives and giving their daughters in marriage, (verse 38), they were still unprepared when the flood came and swept them all away. (verse 39).

Jesus reminds His disciples that in the days before the flood, people were ignorant of the judgement to come. In Genesis 6:5,6, we read 'the Lord saw the wickedness of man, that it was great upon the earth, and that the thoughts of his heart were only evil continually. And the Lord was sorry that He had made man on the earth, and it grieved Him to His heart'. God's judgement on the people, blotting out both them and all living things upon the earth, (Genesis 6:7) was absolutely in line with justice. It was the 'ius talionis', the punishment exactly matching the crime of destroying/ corrupting the earth. (The Hebrew word 'sāhat has the double meaning, destroy/corrupt). Genesis 6:11-13, 17).

Watching the Ark being built by Noah and his sons inclined the people more to mockery of what they were doing than recognition that they could be right, that a flood was indeed about to happen, and so it will always be. But Noah found favour in the eyes of the Lord (Genesis 6:8). Noah walked with God, a righteous man (verse 9). After the Flood, God made a covenant with Noah and put a bow in the clouds as a sign of the covenant (9:13), the earliest covenant which God made with mankind; and He said, 'Never again shall all flesh be cut off by the waters of a flood, and never again shall there be a flood to destroy the earth'. (verse 11).

But the judgement of those mocking people was assured. The words of Jesus concerning His coming, the final time when

God judges the earth, the day of the Lord, enable us to understand that judgement is coming. It will come like a thief, and then 'the heavens will pass away with a great noise, and the elements will melt with fervent heat, and the earth and the works upon it will be burned up,'(2 Peter 3:1). In the last days, judgement will be, not by water, but by fire.

Inherent in Jesus' reference to Noah, is the theme of judgement. The coming of the Son will be a time of division. There is something threatening about the idea which Jesus goes on to reveal, of two men working side by side in a field, when suddenly, one of the men is taken away, and one is left. Perhaps they are friends, perhaps they are members of the same family, father and son, brothers, or even master and servant. There will be the catastrophe of not knowing where the other has gone, the catastrophe of being left behind. (verse 40).

In verse 41, the same is true of two women, friends, or mother and daughter, or two daughters, two sisters, doing the work of the home together, in this case grinding flour from the wheat between two heavy circular grinding stones set on a central fulcrum; heavy and exhausting work indeed, but easier when done together. We can imagine the shock, the anguish, the despair when one is taken and the other left.

These people have been going about their daily routine activities, just as the antediluvian people had been, and are suddenly separated, one from the other. It is happening, not to special people, but to ordinary men and women. It could happen to you, or to me. We need to be watchful, for we do not know 'on what day your Lord is coming,' says Jesus. (verse 42).

The uncertainty of the time of the end is fundamental to the teaching of Jesus, not only about His coming again, but the judgement that will follow. He wants us to be ready for Him, waiting for Him, watching for Him, even as we go about our daily lives, longing for His return while rejoicing and trusting in the knowledge of His present reign, His power in holding all things together. (Colossians 1:17). For in Him all things consist, and in Him all the fullness of God was pleased to dwell, and through Him God was able to reconcile to Himself all things,

whether on earth or in heaven, making peace through the blood
of His cross. (Colossians 1:19,20). And when He appears, we also
will appear with Him in glory. (Colossians 3:4). Wherefore,
comfort one another with these words. (1 Thessalonians 4:18).

Matthew 24:43-44. The first watchfulness parable.
The householder and the thief

*Therefore be alert, for you do not know on which day your Lord
is coming. But be sure of this, that if the owner of the house had
known at what time of the night the thief was coming he would
have been on his guard and would not have allowed his house
to be broken into. (Matthew 24:42).*

Jesus gives an example of watchfulness in a first parable about
His coming, that of the householder whose home is in danger of
being broken into by a thief at night. The householder naturally
wants the burglary to be prevented, but cannot watch because
he does not know at what time the thief will arrive, and of
course, cannot spend all or every night watching.

Jesus, having exhorted His disciples to be watchful at all
times, is making a different point here. He is saying that because
some do not know the time, they conclude that they are unable
to watch, and become careless about the Lord's coming. They
lack constancy. They are not committed to watching and waiting
for His return. Just as a burglar does not advertise in advance
when the burglary will take place, when he does come, it will be
when the householder is not expecting him, is not ready and
waiting for him, that Jesus will come.

So the 'not knowing' of the Lord's return causes His faithful
followers to be always ready for Him, always looking forward to
His imminent arrival. Because we do not know the hour or the
day is not a reason to be careless and unwatchful; but actually to
have more reason to be looking for His coming.

To watch, to be awake, γρηγορειν, is evidence of a relationship
with the living Christ. It was His word to the disciples in
Gethsemane. Watch and pray. (Matthew 26:41). Watch for Him,

watch for His activity in the world and pray for His return, gladly, constantly, for the Day of the Lord will come as a thief in the night. (2 Peter 5:2). So be diligent in your daily walk with God, but keep your eyes fixed on the horizon, the horizon of His coming.

Matthew 24:45-51. The second watchfulness parable. The chief steward

Who then is the faithful and wise servant whom his Master has set over his household to give them their food at the proper time? Blessed is that servant whom his Master when he comes will find so doing. (Matthew 24: 45, 46).

Jesus goes on to extend the example of the householder in the first watchfulness parable. In that parable, the householder is responsible only for his own home and contents. In the second one, the emphasis is on that of a steward, responsible for his master's household and for his fellow servants.

At first, the servant is faithful and wise, and though his master is from home, continues to do his duties faithfully, providing for the needs of his fellow servants. But the days and weeks go by and still the master does not come. He does not see how well his household is being run. Gradually all the discipline which had guaranteed the wellbeing of the other servants begins to break down. If the steward is annoyed with the servants, he will have them beaten. If they continue to flatter him, to be sycophantic, to share with him in overeating or even to get drunk with them, he will sink to their level. (verse 49).

His Master had so trusted him that he had intended to increase his responsibility and set him over all his possessions. (verse 47). But he had abused his Master's trust. He says, 'My Master is delayed.' (verse 48). He will never know and why should I worry about something in the future which may never happen? I know I am self-indulgent, but I am enjoying myself, and why should I not? These other servants and me, what did we ever gain by being faithful and obedient? I know that but for me, they would have remained faithful to the Master, but we are having such fun! And those killjoys, who wouldn't join in. They deserved all that beating, they deserved all they got. That was fun too! To see them squirm under the lash!

But the day of reckoning was nearer than he thought. On a day when he was not expected, the Master came. (verse 50).

Judgement is immediate and clear. He is a wicked servant and must bear the consequences of his wickedness. Not only has he himself become corrupted as he waits for a Master who delays his coming, but he leads others into corruption also. There is only one punishment adequate for such behaviour. He has behaved like a hypocrite, appearing to be a good and obedient servant but in reality being disobedient when it suited him, and leading others into disobedience, so he will receive the same punishment as the hypocrites. He will be cast out with them. There will be weeping and gnashing of teeth. (verse 51).

He had begun as a faithful and wise servant. (verse 45). He had become unfaithful and foolish. Of course when the Lord Jesus comes, He will come as the Judge of the world, but there are not two judgements but only one, the judgement of the individual. Romans 14:10 reminds us that we must *all* stand before the judgement seat of God and *each of us* shall give account of himself to God.

There is more than a suggestion in the story that watching for the return of the Master is a shared responsibility, that even though encouraged by the steward to excessive behaviour, the other servants too had a responsibility to be ready for their Master's coming. Some of their fellow servants, as we have seen, will have suffered for their obdurate recognition that when he comes, they do not intend to be found wanting.

But others have been quite content to allow the responsibility of their action to fall on other shoulders, in this case, that of the chief steward. For while each servant had the ultimate responsibility to be true and faithful to their absent Master, the chief steward had the greater responsibility. It is not just for himself, but for these others, that he has the responsibility of ensuring that the discipline of daily work and daily meal times is maintained. This rests with him, so that when the Master returns, he will find his servants ready and waiting with hearts full of expectation and joyfulness at his coming. Instead, the Master finds his household awry, his servants drunk, his steward behaving abominably.

Responsibility may be delegated, but not accountability. So the question is, for whom do we have responsibility, responsibility towards those whom we should implore, should impress, the need that as servants of the Lord Jesus, we must be watching and waiting for His return.

Particularly, this must be so in the church. The coming of the Lord must not be neglected, or passed over lightly. We must constantly remind ourselves and others that the Day of the Lord is near, and for those in positions of leadership, there is even more need.

By this reasoning, the parable speaks to us as representing the Master's household as the church, the steward represents leadership in the church, the one responsible for giving his fellow servants spiritual food. (verse 45).

'He is coming!' Is the watchword of the church! His delay does not give the church a reason for unacceptable behaviour. That way lies grief and hopelessness, for judgement and punishment are inevitable. There will be weeping and gnashing of teeth, eternal pain, of being outside the Kingdom of God, shut out from Him (8:12, 13:42,50, 22:13, 25:30).

The parable surely demonstrates that the relationship of believers to one another is decisive for the coming of the Lord. Expecting His return means the correct ordering of the church, and especially the spiritual feeding of believers, to give them their food at the proper time (verse 45), in due season (A.V.). It means that while waiting for Him, there should be no violence against one's brothers and sisters, no using of His resources, of that which belongs to the Lord, unworthily. It means working together. It means love.

It is incumbent on all the members of the church to be actively watching and waiting for their Lord, but for the church leaders, there is a special requirement to encourage this expectation while protecting believers from falling into the awful trap of allowing their behaviour to demonstrate that the coming of their Lord means nothing to them.

There could be many reasons for judgement to descend on the church, and on its leaders. But watching and waiting for the Lord's return is a sure way of establishing that His people are walking humbly with their God. Watching and waiting throw a gentle light over all their activities. Whatever they do comes within that light. They might want to give as a criterion for their actions, 'Is that what I want to be doing when the Lord comes?'

Thus, all life is judged in the light of His near return, not just on the basis of the terrible judgement upon those who despise the day of His coming, (Matthew 3:2), but on the persistent desire of every heart to see Him, for when He appears we will be like Him, for we shall see Him as He is. And everyone who hopes in Him purifies himself even as He is pure. (1 John 3:2,3). Behold, what manner of love the Father has bestowed upon us, that we should be called children of God! (1 John 3:1). And such we are! This is our motivation. Love for the Father, love for His Son, love for each other, and a longing to see Him return, that every knee should bow to Him and every tongue confess that He is Lord, to the glory of God the Father, (Philippians 2:11), our living, loving Lord.

The true significance of human behaviour lies here. There is before God no ethical neutrality. There is only 'Yes' to Him and implied obedience, or 'No'; implied disobedience. He says, 'Watch therefore', (Matthew 25:13), and we watch and are obedient, or we do not watch and incur judgement on our disobedience.

These parables of watchfulness which Jesus told are not intended merely or only what He wants for His people, but are designed as *applications,* as definitive *instruction* leading to new attitudes towards behaviour, towards Kingdom living, living in the light and love of God as Matthew 25:1 goes on to say, 'This is what the Kingdom of Heaven is like.' Confessing Christ as Lord can only be authentic on the grounds of obedience. And for this there is grace.

Matthew Chapter 25

Matthew 25:1-13. The third watchfulness parable. The ten virgins

Then the Kingdom of Heaven shall be compared to ten maidens who took their lamps and went to meet the Bridegroom. Five of them were foolish, and five were wise. For when the foolish took their lamps, they took no oil with them, but the wise took flasks of oil with their lamps As the Bridegroom was delayed, they all slumbered and slept. But at midnight there was a cry, 'Behold the Bridegroom! Come out to meet him!' (Matthew 25:1-6).

In the New International Version and the Authorised Version of the New Testament, these ten people are called 'virgins'. In the Good News Bible, the word is translated 'girls', and in the Revised Standard Version, 'maidens'. All these are translations of the Greek word παρθένης each expressing a different role which these young women played in the parable.

The third parable which Jesus then told them was of a supremely important occasion. It was a wedding day, the day when the bridegroom was coming to take his bride to his home. As was usual in that society, the bridegroom, not to seem too eager to see his beautiful bride, delayed his coming until the evening, when it was getting dark. Waiting for him were ten virgins, young women who had not yet married, though it was customary for all women to be married, and to be married when quite young. These young women were ready and waiting for the bridegroom with their lamps burning so that they could accompany the bride to her new home. They had gone out to meet him, (verse 1), but he was apparently delayed. Eventually they could resist the desire for sleep no longer, but suddenly, at midnight they heard the cry! *The Midnight Cry!*. Behold, the bridegroom is coming! (verse 6).

Quickly gathering up their lamps to light the bridegroom to the bride's house, they went to greet him. But only five of them had oil in their lamps. The oil in the lamps of the others was going out. They had no light in their lamps, and no oil in their vessels with which to obtain more light.

The first resource was to the other young women, 'Please could we have some of your oil'? they said. At first, this would seem to be a sensible thing to do, to share what they had. But the other virgins had the importance of the occasion in view. 'Perhaps there will not be enough for us both. It would be a tragedy if the bridegroom had no light to light him on his way. Why do you not go to the shopkeeper and buy some more'?

Accepting this suggestion, the five foolish virgins went off to try to find someone who would supply them with oil. But they were too late. While they were away, the bridegroom came. Those who were ready with oil in their lamps went with him to the marriage feast, and the door was shut. (verse 10). Hurrying back, the five foolish virgins found the door shut. What could they do? In desperation they cried out, 'Lord, Lord, open to us!' But he replied, 'Truly, amen, I say to you, I do not know you.' (verses 11, 12). Their cry of, 'Lord, Lord,' is not quite how a bridegroom is normally addressed. Something of the recognition of who the Bridegroom is has entered into the parable. Neither does an earthly bridegroom usually reply with the word, *'Amen'*, the Amen of God with all God's character and purpose behind it.

The joyful wedding has become a portrayal of judgement. As in the allusion to the two men working in the field, and the two women grinding out the flour, a separation, a distinction had been made between the five wise and the five foolish young women.

The hour of the heavenly Bridegroom's arrival is unknown. How necessary then to be always ready; to have our vessels full of oil, full of the Holy Spirit, for the oil, the anointing oil, represents the Holy Spirit. He who is our Bridegroom can come at any time, and the door may be shut. May we with our lamps trimmed and burning brightly, be ready to welcome Him our returning Lord. Above all other judgement, all other punishment, would be the utter devastation of hearing Him say, 'I do not know you.'

May He help us to heed His words. 'Watch therefore, for you know neither the day nor the hour when your Lord will come', (verse 13), and to heed his warning. 'Be careful lest the light which is in you be darkness', 'for if the light that is in you be darkness, how great is that darkness.' (Luke 11:35).

1 Peter 2:9 records how God has called us out of darkness into His marvellous light, and Ephesians 5:8 reminds the believer that once you were darkness, but now are light in the Lord; walk as children of light. Believers carry within them the light of the glorious gospel of God in the face of Jesus Christ. It has shined in their hearts, (2 Corinthians 4:6). And by that light they witness, not only to His presence, but to His coming again. The light of the presence of the Bridegroom is enough for all. And the virgins themselves are the Bride waiting for the heavenly Bridegroom, Christ, with their lamps burning, rejoicing in the reality of His near return

Matthew 25:3,4,8. The Significance of the Oil

What appears to be the significant aspect of the parable which Jesus told is the presence of absence of oil in the lamps of these ten young women.

While we do not wish to over-interpret this parable which Jesus told, we are reminded of the place given to oil in the Old Testament scriptures, with which He was so familiar. We want to learn from Him, and do not want to miss anything He wants to teach us.

In Exodus 28:41, and 29:7; and Leviticus 8:12, we read of the anointing oil which was placed on the head of Aaron the High Priest, to consecrate him to that office, to set him apart even from the other priests, to represent God to His people, and His people to God, not as a mediator, but as an instrument of His salvific purpose concerning them, the one who through whom they could receive atonement for their sins on the

Day of Atonement, as Aaron sent the scapegoat away into the wilderness, sacramentally carrying away the sins of the people.

The anointing oil was also placed on the head of Kings, as in 1 Samuel when Samuel anointed Saul – twice – as the King of Israel. (1 Samuel 10:1, 11:14, 12:5).

The oil of gladness, the anointing oil is also placed prophetically on the head of the King as he goes forth to meet his Bride, the one who is all glorious within. Psalm 45:13 A.V. is indubitably a prophetic reference to Christ, (verse 6) as He comes for His Bride in Revelation 19:7.

As He says in Luke 24:27, in all the scriptures we see the things concerning Himself, for He is prophet, priest and king and coming Bridegroom.

But surely, even more significant than all these references to the holy anointing is Isaiah 61:1. The Spirit of the Lord God is upon Me, because the Lord has *anointed* Me. (A chapter of Isaiah that concludes with the Bridegroom.) This passage from Isaiah, which had been extensively interpreted as referring to Zion, or to the nation of Israel, is here authoritatively taken over by the Lord Jesus in Luke 4:16-22 as referring to Himself. Isaiah is displaying here a Messianic Person, and Jesus is confirming it as applying to Himself, expressing His own understanding of what the will of the Father was for him in succeeding verses, prophecies which He more than fulfilled in his earthly ministry.

But for the purpose of understanding the parable about the ten virgins, it is important to recognise the identification of the anointing, the anointing oil of Exodus, Leviticus, 1 Samuel, Psalm 45 and 23, and others, with the Holy Spirit. The Spirit of the Lord is upon Me, because the sovereign Lord, Adonai, Yahweh, has anointed Me. (Luke 4:18). His Spirit alighting as a dove upon him at His baptism. (Matthew 3:16).

In this precious anointing, the oil of gladness of Psalm 23:5, and Psalm 45:7,8, explains the different life enjoyed by the king, a life of joy, a life *which may be passed on to His followers*. Jesus said, 'I will pray the Father, and He will give you Another comforter, another one to come alongside you, another Counsellor, the Paraclete, and He will be with you forever, even the Spirit of Truth, whom the world cannot receive because it neither sees Him or knows Him. You know Him, for He dwells *with* you, and will be *in* you. I will not leave you orphans. I will come to you.' (John 14:16-18).

Apparently, the parable of the ten virgins has as its interpretation the wonderful joy of belonging to Jesus, of having the oil of the Holy Spirit in their lives. And there was surely no harm in taking time to sleep while they waited for the Bridegroom for He intends that we continue to lead normal lives while waiting expectantly for His return. But somehow, when the foolish virgins arose to trim their lamps, they discovered that they had not enough oil.

Is this possible? Does the Holy Spirit limit Himself to those who are truly and fully dedicated to following Jesus? Do we limit ourselves to how much we allow the Holy Spirit to lead us, guide us, intervene in our lives? Or is it only those who are constantly aware of the near return of the Bridegroom who can be said to be fully filled with the Holy Spirit? (Ephesians 5:18). Jesus Himself said, 'I am the light of the world. He that follows Me shall not walk in darkness but shall have the light of life' (John 8:12). The corollary of that saying of Jesus would indicate that those who are not following Him are exactly that, walking in darkness.

We are not told if, or in what way, those foolish virgins were not following Jesus as they should. But Jesus, the Bridegroom, knows, and He knows too that there are times when He has to shut the door and say, 'I do not know you.' He described Himself as the Bridegroom in Matthew 9:15, and He described John the Baptist as the friend of the Bridegroom. Again, He told the parable of the King who gave a wedding feast for His Son in Matthew 22:2, as a strong indication that He Himself was the Son for whom the wedding feast was prepared.

Here in chapter 25, we have the Bridegroom coming for His Bride. This is an occasion when the place should be filled with light and joy, but because of the unpreparedness of five people, the light was less and the joy was less. They failed to keep oil in their lamps because they took no account of the possibility of the delay of the Bridegroom. They were no longer living in the light. John takes this up in his first letter where he says, 'Walk in the light as He is the light and you will have fellowship with one another, and the blood of Jesus, His Son, will cleanse you from all sin. (1 John 1:17). It is sin that puts the light out. But there is a remedy in the precious blood that was shed to put away sin.

But sin cannot enter that place where the Bridegroom is enjoying the marriage feast with those who have kept their lamps burning, who have not allowed the light to go out. The door is shut. Jesus says, 'Make sure you are on the guest list. Watch therefore for you do not know either the day of the hour.' (Matthew 25:13). We may well sing *Give me oil in my lamp, keep me burning; keep me burning till the break of day'.* We need the Holy Spirit to keep us burning until He comes.

Matthew 25:11,12. A final thought on the parable of the ten virgins

The parable of the ten virgins describes the future fulfilment of the Kingdom of Heaven. Jesus says, 'The Kingdom of Heaven is like ten virgins who took their lamps and went out to meet the bridegroom' (Matthew 25:1). The parable concerns the coming of the Bridegroom to take His Bride, and to take His power and reign.

As lovers of the Lord Jesus, we are waiting for this wonderful consummation, for the final and complete fulfilment of the Kingdom of Heaven when the Bridegroom who is also the King will come into His KIngdom. Do we belong to the wise or foolish virgins? The apocalyptic thought of the return of the Lord Jesus is empowering. As we look ahead to the final consummation of all things, we have a perspective on history, on present world affairs and on the future. It is not for us a dark unknown, but an increased and increasing realisation of the freedom we have in Christ, to orientate our lives in relation to one another and to Him, lives full of purpose because we have at least a primitive perception of God's purpose for us. We cannot change the world, but we know who can. Perhaps we cannot change our circumstances, but we know the One who gives us the ability to endure them 'until He come'.

This does not do away with the day of reckoning, the day of judgement. But we do know the Judge. He is the One who has comforted us in our distress, who has sustained us when we were in need. So far from being indifferent to us, He knows us through and through, and judges us seriously, as individual persons, not merely as people who had never experienced His grace and lovingkindness.

We look into His face as Judge and we see there the face of Jesus, our beloved Lord and Saviour.

He will come. And He will judge. Because in the New Heavens and the New Earth, there will be, could only be, righteousness, the righteousness which originates with, and is identical with, a right relationship with God. (2 Peter 3:13). This had been God's design and purpose from the beginning, when He first created the heaven and the earth. (Genesis 1:1). He had looked for a perfect world in which the will of the men and women, whom He had created with free will, could live in harmony with His own will. The will of God would be their 'law', their reason for living, for doing everything they did. In being disobedient to God's will, in choosing their own way, they negated the purpose of their own lives.

How different was the One who came and said, 'I do only those things that please Him'. (John 8:29). He could have said, in truth, 'I *choose* to do only those things that please Him'. This was His will, identical with His Father's. 'Lo, I come to do your will, O My God' (Hebrews 10:7). This was the One who came to seek and save that which was lost, because that was the will of His Father, (Luke 19:10), to restore that lost relationship, to provide again for that life lived in harmony with the One who became as beloved to them, as He was to His Father, the One acclaimed by His Father as His Beloved Son, the Son of His love. And the nearer His coming again, the more our hearts rejoice, for when He appears, we shall be like Him, for we shall see Him as He is. (1 John 3:2).

There is so much we do not know, but the limits of our knowledge do not preclude the precious elements of our expectation. How important, how very important, is the expansion of our thought into the beginning and end of history.

In the chronology of Matthew's gospel, the suffering and crucifixion and rising again of the Lord Jesus are soon to take place. These are passages which we read on the knees of the spirit, as we contemplate what it cost Him to make a path for us into the will of God, and ultimately into His presence as the Bride of Christ. We can perhaps imagine to some extent the suffering, the pain inflicted on a human body, of being subjected to the scourging and the humiliation, and the agony of being left hanging on a Cross to die, but no imagination could cope with the absolute devastation of bearing the sins of the whole world in that same body, the same sinless body, the devastation expressed in those awful words, the cry from the heart of the faithful Son to His faithful Father. 'My God, why have you forsaken me?' (Matthew 27:44; Mark 15:34). The terrible separation from His Father was almost more than He could bear. But He knew why His Father had forsaken Him, for He was the embodiment in that fraction of time of all the sin of all the world being laid on Him, for the Lord laid on Him the iniquity of us all, the sacrificial Lamb of God who takes away the sin of the world. (Isaiah 53:6; John 1:29).

Death could not hold Him, because death is the consequence of sin, (1 Corinthians 15:56). and He knew no sin (Hebrews 4:15), so He was raised from the dead on the third day by the Spirit of holiness. (Romans 1:4). And how glad they must have been to be with each other, the Resurrected Lord Jesus, and the Resurrecting Holy Spirit, as they contemplated what Christ had achieved on the cross.

But we anticipate, for Jesus has yet something more to teach His disciples before the end of this eschatological discourse.

Matthew 25:14-30. The fifth eschatological discourse. The Parable of the Talents

For the coming of the Son of Man will be as when a man going on a journey called his servants and entrusted to them his property. To one he gave five talents, to another two, to another one, to each according to his ability. Then he went away. He who had received the five talents went at once and traded with them, and he made five talents more. So also, he who had the two talents made two talents more. But he who had received the one talent went and dug in the ground and hid his master's money. (Matthew 25:14)

Jesus is giving His disciples another parable concerning a master and his servants. This master too is going on a long journey. Who is to look after his property while he is away? For he is a very rich man, and needs servants who will serve him faithfully and well.

To the first servant he chooses, he gives five talents. This is a great deal of money. A talent equals 60 minas (pounds in Luke 19:13). One mina equals 100 denarii. One denarius is the daily wage of one labourer. It would probably take a labourer about 75 years to earn that amount of money.

To the second servant he chooses, he also gives a great sum of money, though rather less than the first one. He gives him two talents.

And to the third servant he gives one talent. Still a considerable sum, but adapted to what he regards as the abilities of the servants.

And then he goes away.

He must have been away for a very long time. When he gets back he calls his servants to him so that they may give account of their stewardship of his money. During that long time, the first servant had increased his five talents by trading with them, and had made five talents more (verse 16). So also, the servant with two talents came forward bringing with him the two extra talents that he had made. To each of these faithful servants the master said, 'Well done good and faithful servant. You have been faithful over a little, I will set you over much. Enter into the joy of your master.' (verses 21, 23).

Lastly, the third servant came forward with his one talent which he gave to his master. Presenting the one talent to him, the third servant began to explain why he had not traded his talent, but had buried it in the ground to protect it from robbers, to keep it safe against his master's return. 'I was afraid,' he said, 'not so much of the robbers, but of you, for I know that you are a hard man, and I wanted to return your money to you intact.' Using the common imagery for judgement, he went on, 'I know you reap where you do not sow, and gather where you have not scattered. I was afraid. Please receive back what is yours.' (verse 25).

it appears that the third servant is not expecting condemnation from his master. But these excuses carry no weight with the master. 'You have condemned yourself out of your own mouth,' he says, 'you wicked and slothful servant. You knew that I reap where I have not sowed, and gathered where I have not scattered. You knew that a judgement day was coming when I would return and claim back what is mine. The least you could have done was to place my money with the usurer, and at my return I would have received my own with interest.'

He said to the bystanders, 'Take his talent away and give it to the servant with ten talents. For to everyone who has, more will be given, and he will have abundance, but from him who has not, even what he has will be taken away. And cast the worthless servant into the outer darkness. There men will weep and gnash their teeth.' (verse 30).

So that with which the servant was entrusted is taken away from him, and he is taken away to the judgement of separation from God, to the place which describes the torment of being separated from God as a place of outer darkness. for the parable clearly suggests that Jesus is the long-delayed Master, and His servants those who care for that which belongs to Him, until He returns.

If this seems a harsh judgement, giving credence to the third servant's estimate of his master as a harsh, severe man, we need to examine more closely what is at stake here.

Can we assume that the first and second servants gained their extra money by putting it out at interest? Although the third servant is challenged by the master as to why he did not use the banking system of his day, it is not clear that this applied to the earlier servants. There were other ways of making a profit with one's money, for example, dealing in commodities, as in buying and selling, or speculating in land.

We are not told how these servants increased the money entrusted to them by their master, but only concerned with his acknowledgement, 'Well done, good and faithful servant. You have been faithful over a 'little'. I will set you over much. Enter into the joy of your master.' (verses 21, 23).

However many talents they had been given, to their master it counted as 'little'. The point was not that they had been successful, but that they had been faithful, and the reward was that they entered into the joy of their master.

Did the third servant's unsuccessfulness amount to unfaithfulness? He guards the money carefully, finding a safe place in which to hide it, but ultimately taking no responsibility for it, for to watch a safe place continually would have naturally aroused suspicion that something of value had been hidden. There it was, and there it would remain until his master returned.

What was it that caused the third servant to be afraid? 'I was afraid,' he said, 'because I knew you were a hard man, a severe man. I hesitated because I did not want to lose your money. I did not know what you would do to me if I lost it. I was afraid that I would not succeed, that I would fail to be able to give you back what is yours, but here it is, intact. Look, you have what is yours.' (verse 25).

The master does not object to himself being described as a hard man, gathering where he had not sown, reaping where he had not scattered. 'But why,' he said, 'did you not take the money to the bank? At least then I would have gained some interest on my money.' (verse 27).

Though the third servant had given his motivation as fear of his master, we see that his motives were more complex. The master had given him an opportunity to prove himself, to take on a responsibility and to fulfil it while waiting for his master's return. The master had given him an opportunity to show himself as reliable and faithful, as he had the other servants. The test had not proved inconclusive. It had demonstrated the true nature of the third servant. He had been unfaithful. He had not taken on the responsibility that had been entrusted to him. And above all, he had not trusted his master, but in fact blamed his master for his unfaithfulness, saying, in effect, that he could have been a better servant had his master been a better master.

Jesus, as the Master, is seeking faithfulness in His servants, and when much has been given to them, and they have proved faithful, then He will give them much more. But those who prove unfaithful to Him will lose what they enjoyed in the first place.

Hypocrisy, unfaithfulness, and unreadiness for the Lord's return result in judgement, that severe judgement of being separated from their Lord into a place where He is not. Indeed, that place is a place of weeping and frustration, sorrow and gnashing of teeth. (verse 30).

'Talents' has been interpreted as the God-given personal attributes that people have, and they are many and varied. But He has given so much more than that. To some He has given social position, wealth, influence, good health. Others may have none of these things, but they may have been given the privilege of serving Him in the leadership of the church, or as a humble believer seeking to live in the good of what their Lord has given to them as in the previous parable of the master and his servants. (Matthew 24:45-57). Of the stewardship of all these gifts, men and women have to give an account of themselves to God.

But to those who love Him, who have committed their lives to Him, who have entered through that narrow door into the Kingdom of Heaven where He is, and where He reigns, He has given joy unspeakable and full of glory. (1 Peter 3:8 A.V.) He has given grace. He has given above all His Holy Spirit. Everything that they have they have received from Him and His mercy, an innumerable number of 'talents'. His grace enables them to be faithful to Him; their faithfulness to Him as they wait for His coming is what He receives from them.

How little we can give the Lord for all that He has given us. We echo Christina Rosetti's, 'What can I give Him, poor as I am?' But we can give Him hearts that love Him, and wills that are obedient to Him, and lives that seek to glorify Him.

Talent has come to mean 'aptitude', ability. We have to admit with Paul in Romans 7:15 that in me, that is, in my flesh dwells no good thing. We have no ability in ourselves, but 'can do all things through Christ who strengthens me', as Paul also said. (Philippians 4:13). He is our ability. He is our strength. The steadfast love of the Lord never ceases, His mercies will never come to an end. They are new every morning. Great is thy faithfulness. (Lamentations 3:22). What an amazing reversal, His faithfulness to us enabling our faithfulness to Him. But whatever we have as gifting from the Lord will be refined, (Malachi 3:3), pruned as the branches of the vine are pruned that they might bring forth more fruit. (John 15:3).

This is what Jesus had in mind when He encouraged His disciples to pray, 'Lead us not into temptation'. (Matthew 6:13). 'Bring us not to the test'. For the testing is the proof of our discipleship. Hebrews goes so far as to say that just as a father disciplines his children, so the Lord our heavenly Father disciplines us, for the testing, the discipline are proof of our discipleship, a proof of our relationship to Him as children of our Father that He allows us to go through times of testing. 'For the Lord disciplines him whom He loves and chastises everyone whom He receives.' (Hebrews 12:6). He tests even the talents, the gifts, the charismata, which He has given.

Of the three servants who were tested, two proved faithful to their Lord. In the testing times and experiences through which our heavenly Father allows us to go, may we too be faithful to Him, trusting that we too might receive the commendation, 'Well done, good and faithful servant, precious child. Enter into the joy of your Lord.' The greatest gift of all, to enter into His joy; to be with Him where He is.

These are the alternatives. This is the judgement. To be with Him – *joy*. Not to be with him – *outer darkness*. While we naturally abhor the prospect of outer darkness, all our longing, our desire, is to be with Him where He is, and for the prospect of that great reward to endure all the rest, however difficult it may be.

God grant that we may be among those who hear the invitation. 'Enter into the joy of your Lord. When we feel our faith will fail *He will hold us fast'. Thy right hand shall hold me.* *(Psalm 139:10).*

Matthew 25:31-46. The final teaching of Jesus. The Last Judgement

When the Son of Man comes in His glory and all the angels with Him, then He will sit on His glorious throne. Before Him will be gathered all the nations, and He will separate them one from another as a shepherd separates the sheep from the goats, and He will place the sheep at His right hand, but the goats at His left. (Matthew 25:31-33).

This section completes the eschatological discourse of Matthew 24:3 – 25:46, the comprehensive teaching of Jesus about His second coming, and the fulfilment of all God's purposes since time began.

In verse 31, we see Jesus, adorned with glory and honour, and with all his angels with Him, seated on His glorious throne with all the nations gathered before Him. This is our Shepherd, King and Judge, for this is the throne of judgement.

Though this passage has been referred to as a parable, it cannot altogether be regarded as such, although it may have parabolic associations such as the use of the terms Shepherd, the sheep, the goats. Instead, it is so obviously the reality of what will happen at the end time, as revealed to the disciples.

Although 'all the nations' are gathered before Him, sentence is being passed by the Judge on individuals, for due to the great tribulation of Matthew 24:9 endured by the followers of Jesus, and their constancy and faithfulness as they witness to Him through all their suffering, the gospel has been preached 'throughout the whole world' (24:14), and now the end has come. The whole world, all the nations, are before Him.

Judgement in effect has already begun to take place, for we see the 'sheep' on His right hand and the 'goats' on His left. Now we are given the explanation as to why they have been separated. Once again, with the sheep on His right hand and the goats on His left, the Son of Man takes on His identification as Shepherd.

It was common to have a mixed flock of sheep and goats in the Palestine of Jesus' time, and He always used examples with which His disciples would be familiar. The shepherd may well have taken care of both sheep and goats during the day, but in the evening they would need to be separated. Goats must be kept warm and sheltered at night, unlike sheep with their heavy fleece. Goats are also destructive of pasture. While sleep graze happily on grass, goats tend to eat the plant down to the root, from which it cannot easily or quickly recover (Ezekiel 34:17,18). This may have entitled the 'sheep' to be at the Shepherd's right hand, the place of honour.

The identification of the Lord God as Shepherd over Israel, His flock, is a familiar one in the Old Testament. It is not surprising that in His last discourse, He Himself, the Good Shepherd of the sheep in John 10:1-30 and in Luke 15:3-7, is the One seated on the throne of judgement, the One who is the Lord. He is the Messianic King and Shepherd of Ezekiel 34:23, caring for His sheep. In Isaiah 40:11, He is the One feeding His flock like a shepherd, gathering the lambs in His bosom, and gently leading those that are with young. In Psalm 80:1 He is called the Shepherd of Israel, the One who leads Joseph like a flock, the tribes of Ephraim and Manasseh who are eventually constituted as the Northern Kingdom of Israel.

For David, He becomes 'my' shepherd, (Psalm 23:1) because of whom he could never be in want as He made him to lie down in green pastures and beside still waters, protecting him with him with His rod or club, and guiding him with His staff, as a Shepherd with His sheep. And Hebrews calls Him 'that great Shepherd of the sheep, by the blood of the eternal covenant'. (Hebrews 13:20) a concept which deserves more exposition than is possible here.

As a Shepherd King, a Shepherd Judge, we would expect that Jesus, the Son of Man would be merciful. We might also expect Him to want to know the spiritual credentials of those whom He is sitting to judge. But this is no ordinary trial. There is no defending or prosecuting counsel, no jury. It appears that people are judged entirely on their acts of love and charity, that is, love in action, which they have inadvertently performed during their lifetime, with no thought of recompense or reward.

Jesus says, 'Come, O blessed of My Father, inherit the Kingdom prepared for you from the foundation of the world. For I was hungry and you gave me food, I was thirsty and you gave me drink, I was a stranger and you welcomed Me, I was naked and you clothed Me, I was sick and you visited Me, I was in prison and you came to Me (Matthew 25:34).

This is the destiny of the sheep.These are the blessed of the Father. They will inherit the kingdom prepared for them from the foundation of the world.

Since these are the sheep, followers of Jesus, disciples, Jesus does not need to ask such questions as, 'Have you repented? Have you received eternal life?' He assumes this to be so, otherwise, they would not be His sheep. His sheep are those who hear His voice (John 10:27). His sheep are those who once were lost, far away from the flock, until Jesus, the Good Shepherd (John 10:11), went after them into the wilderness that He might find them, and having found them, put them on His shoulders and brought them home rejoicing, calling together His friends and neighbours and saying to them, 'Rejoice with Me, for I have found the sheep which I had lost.' (Luke 15:3-7).

These sheep are easily distinguished from the goats because of the love they have for the One who rescued them, delivered them, redeemed them, and because of the great cost of their redemption, because of the Shepherd's great mercy to them, they are merciful to others. Because they are the blessed of His Father, (Matthew 25:34), they are a means of blessing to others. God always knew that there would be such, and from the foundation of the world He has made provision for them, (Matthew 25:34), preparing a kingdom for them to inherit, a kingdom where He is unassailably and universally acknowledged as King, and where eventually there will be no more crying or tears, no mourning or pain, for the former things will have passed away. (Revelation 21:4).

But while waiting for Him to 'make all things new' (Revelations 21:5), there are many who need food and drink to assuage their hunger and thirst, they need garments to cover their nakedness, they need the provision of medical help and comfort to those who are sick and encouragement and help to those in prison either to lead a better life, or for the comfort of fellowship especially if they are imprisoned for the sake of the gospel and their witness to Jesus. Perhaps also as prisoners they need basic supplies of food and the necessities of life even as Paul did when in a Roman prison (Philippians 4:10-19) for the prisons of that day, and even until modern times (e.g. Newgate Prison in Victorian London) did not always supply even minimum sustenance for the prisoners.

But *'when?'* they say. 'Lord, when did we see you hungry and feed you, or thirsty and give you drink? When did we see you a stranger and welcome you or naked and clothed you? And when did we see you sick or in prison and visit you?' (Matthew 25:39).

In all these instances, Jesus was identifying Himself with the sufferers. It was not enough for Him to identify Himself as Shepherd, as King, as Judge. 'Those whom you have blessed are My brethren,' says Jesus. They may be the least, the most apparently insignificant of My brethren, but *inasmuch* as you have served or ministered to one of them, you have ministered to Me.' (Matthew 25:40).

That wonderful word, 'inasmuch', found in the Authorised version of the Bible, but left out of many other translations, means so much. This one word (Matthew 25:40) has become more important for the care of the poor and the needy than whole systems of worldly maxims, whole volumes of theological sociology. It is love, expressed only for its own sake without any motivation of reward, for if such motivation had inspired the action, it would not have been love, it would no longer have been love for others. When they call Him 'Lord', *'Lord,* when did we see you in need?', they are indicating that they are in a relationship with Him. This excludes general humanitarianism, praiseworthy though that is. Jesus' reply of, 'Amen, truly I say to you,' (verse 40) carries with it all the authority and character of

THE KING AND THE KINGDOM

Jesus, not only as the Son of Man, but the Son of God. 'Truly I say to you, inasmuch as you did it to the least of these My brethren, you did it to Me'. (verse 40). And those who have shown in this way their love for Christ are unaware that they have done so.

Of course, they have shown mercy, not least to Jesus' brothers and sisters, the Christian family, but also to those who do not recognise Him as their Saviour, those outside their community, the 'heathen', or 'Gentiles' in the time of Jesus, who would probably now prefer to be called humanists or unbelievers, or even atheists, or 'not very religious'. They have shown mercy to strangers who may or may not become brothers or sisters, simply because the love of God has been shed abroad in their hearts by the Holy Spirit, (Romans 5:5), and they share that love with all or any who cross their path, the overflowing love of God to all, without qualification.

Since we do not have the ability or the wisdom to judge what goes on in a human heart, (Matthew 7:1), and cannot distinguish between what has been described as the deserving or undeserving poor (a term of complete anathema to any loving heart) we have the privilege of sharing the love of Christ with all.

2 Corinthians 5:14 says the love of Christ controls us, (R.S.V.) or constrains us (A.V.). In Christ, God was reconciling the world to Himself, and entrusted to us the ministry of reconciliation (2 Corinthians 5:19). To be His hands and eyes and ears to those who sit in darkness and in the shadow of death, and to guide their feet into the way of peace, as Zechariah prophesied of his son, John the Baptist (Luke 1:79), is to receive a calling to be a prophet of the Most High, in the sense of preparing the way of the Lord. (Luke 1:76). The Lord needs 'preparers' of His way.

What of the judgement of the 'goats'?

Then Jesus says to them, 'Amen, Truly I say to you. Verily I say unto you, inasmuch as you did it not to one of the least of these, you did it not to Me' (Matthew 25:45). 'Depart from Me, go from Me, you cursed, into the eternal fire prepared for the devil and his angels. Go!' (Matthew 25:41). For I was hungry and you gave Me no food, I was thirsty and you gave Me no drink. I was a stranger and you did not welcome Me, naked and you did not clothe Me, sick and in prison and you did not visit Me'.

'Depart from Me'. And they will go. (verse 46). Their destiny also is assured.

To go away from Jesus is eternal punishment, especially when contrasted with the eternal life for the righteous (verse 46). The parallel points up the unrighteousness of the goats and the righteousness of the sheep, and recognises the absolute seriousness of proclaiming Jesus as LORD. 'Lord, when did we see you hungry or thirsty,' is the question asked in verses 37, and 44; by both the sheep and the goats.

In another context, Jesus says, 'You call me Lord, but you do not do the will of My Father who is in heaven. You call me Lord, and tell Me of all the mighty work you have done in My Name. But I declared I never knew you. Depart from Me you evil doers, workers of iniquity.' (Matthew 7:21-23). The Lordship of the Lord Jesus is paramount.

JESUS CHRIST IS LORD, to the glory of God the Father. (Philippians 2:11)

What chaos there would be if He were not in control, working beside His Father as a master workman, daily His delight, rejoicing before Him always. (Proverbs 8:30). The manifestly plural God, Father, Son and Holy Spirit, Elohim, the plural Hebrew word for God; God who is the Father; the Son who is the Word, the Logos; the Holy Spirit, the Ruach, the breath of God moving in the beginning over an earth without form or void, brooding over the face of the waters. And gloriously, the chaos is resolved, for God decreed it so. (Genesis 1:1,2). *And God said, His word, His Logos, His Son.* For God there is no gap between thought, word and result. God said, and it was. (Genesis 1:3). And God saw that it was good, perfectly conformed to His will, exactly as He intended it to be. (Genesis 1:4).

This same God is now upon the throne of judgement in the person of His Son, and dare these 'goats' address Him as Lord when they contravene the very rationale of the whole creation, the master workman rejoicing in his inhabited world and delighting in the sons of men, (Proverbs 8:31), the rationale of the Elohim, the Godhead, Father, Son and Holy Spirit, whose overflowing love for Each Other initiated the creation of a whole world of people over whom this love could flow, and overflow.

The only possible destiny for that which either denied that Lordship or misinterpreted it, was *fire*. Fire is cleansing, purging, burning away all the dross, all that would render that love null and void. This is the judgement which of necessity has to take place before God can create a new heaven and a new earth within which dwells righteousness, and only righteousness. (2 Peter 3:13).

Beloved, let us love one another, for love is of God. (1 John 4:7). Beloved, let us love all those whom the Lord causes us to be with, to speak to, to serve, day by day. Let us show forth His love not only in our speech but in our service to others, daily offering up our lives to Him, to be channels of His blessing. As He is, so we are, and so shall we be, by His grace, in this world. (1 John 4:17).

Matthew 24:1-25:46. Summary of the fifth discourse

In the parable of the talents, we noted that the two faithful servants 'came forward', (verses 20, 22), not expecting commendation, and in the same way, the unfaithful servant 'came forward', (verse 24) not expecting condemnation.

In this final teaching which Jesus is giving to His disciples, He is characterising the criteria for true discipleship. He has given a hint of this in the story of the talents. Here in verses 31-46 He expounds for them the reasons why eternal punishment (verse 46) has to be the destiny of those who subvert His teaching to their own ends; why His judgement is absolutely consistent with all that He has been sharing with His disciples over the last three years. He will still have a little time with them before His death, but never again will they be able to sit at His feet in quite the same way and hear His words.

As we would expect, His final message to them has described what will happen at His coming in glory. (Matthew 25:31). From the beginning of His ministry, we have seen the 'now' of the Kingdom of Heaven working out in people's lives. This final message is that the *'not yet'* of the Kingdom will become the *'now'*, the fulfilment of all that Jesus had in mind for His beloved followers as they made their way through all the vicissitudes of human life. Eventually, Jesus is saying, the Kingdom of Heaven will be seen to be here, and the Son of Man will be seen to be seated on His glorious throne, and all His angels with Him. (verse 31).

This is absolutely consistent with all His teaching, for throughout Matthew's gospel, beginning with 4:17, the theme of His teaching has been the Kingdom of Heaven, and that the way into the Kingdom is through repentance and faith, with the outcome in Kingdom living being summed up in the Great Commandment, 'You shall love the Lord your God with all your heart and with all your soul and with all your mind; and the second which is like it, you shall love your neighbour as yourself'. (Matthew 22:37-39).

The gospel begins with the birth of Jesus as a king, descended from David's line, being worshipped by wise men from the East who had come to worship Him (Matthew 2:2). It has now come to that place in the gospel where Jesus, the Son of Man, is seated on His throne as King and Judge of the nations, before the gospel describes the greatest of all His acts of Kingship, the laying down of His life, (Matthew 27:50) for those blessed of His Father, that they might inherit the kingdom prepared for them from the foundation of the world, (Matthew 25:34), and then taking His life again that He might rise from death in glory. (Matthew 28:1-11). Here in His final teaching, we see the culmination of all that Jesus has been saying, not only in this eschatological discourse, but throughout His ministry.

As we consider Matthew 25:32, it appears that a time will come when all the nations are gathered before Him in judgement. This would suggest universality but in fact it is individuals who are judged. The greater truth is that in all the nations are those who have confessed Christ, as we learn from Matthew 24:14. These are the ones being judged, not pagan

502

peoples, many of whom have been considerate in their acts of charity. The basis of judgement for those is whether they have heard the gospel, and having heard it, whether it has caused them to seek after God, and find in Jesus their salvation.

The basis for judgement for believers who have trusted in Christ is whether they have performed acts of mercy, acts of love, not because they hope for a reward, for they are ignorant that such exists, but simply that in living close to Jesus, and inspired by the love of the Holy Spirit, they see the needs of people and respond. How surprised they are when Jesus says, 'Inasmuch as you have done it to the least of these My brethren, you have done it to Me.' (verse 40). How astonished when Jesus identifies Himself with 'the least of these My brethren'. (verse 40). They say, 'Lord, when did we see you hungry and feed you, or thirsty and give you drink? And when did we see you a stanger and welcome you, or naked and clothe you? And when did we see you sick or in prison and visit you? `

This is at the heart of the teaching of Jesus and it is completely appropriate that it should come right at the end of His teaching ministry.

Out of every tribe, and tongue, and nation (Revelation 7:9), there will be those who have turned to Christ in repentance and faith and entered the Kingdom of Heaven. And some, perhaps many, because they have seen Jesus in His followers. They have seen that to enter the Kingdom of Heaven is to submit one's life to the King. When He enters a human life, He enters it not only as Saviour, but as Lord.

To enter into the Kingdom is also to enter a realm where we encounter others who have also entered it. To all these repentant, saved and delivered men and women, the Lord has given these other believers who love Him, who when they pray, say, 'Our Father'; for they have become a family of sons and daughters of the King, brothers and sisters in His Kingdom. And love for one another, service to one another is the true manifestation of who they truly are, for the Lord Jesus wanted them to have as a guiding principle of life, 'if you love Me, you must love your brother also. (John 14:15; 15:17).

So we conclude that this Gospel is about the King and His Kingdom in the hearts and lives of believers.

But is it possible to summarise Jesus' teaching throughout the Gospel? Perhaps the expanse is too great. Matthew has faithfully conducted us from the Baby born to be King to this point where He, the incarnated Son of God is seated on His kingly throne; and of course Matthew has the precious but unenviable task of setting forth His last hours upon the earth which He had created and so loved, in chapters 26 and 27.

For Matthew, the key theme of all this amazing revelation has been 'Immanuel, God with us'. (Matthew 1:23). Throughout his Gospel, he has shown Jesus as the Son of Man, healing all who came to Him, showing them the way to God, being there for them, and not just for His disciples but even for those who were not in the privileged position of being of the nation of Israel. *JESUS, IMMANUEL,* God with them and with us.

In Matthew's first chapter, two names are given to Jesus. Immanuel was the title given to Him long ago when His birth was prophesied, and now the prophecy is fulfilled. (Isaiah 7:14). Behold, a virgin shall be with child, and shall bring forth a son, and they shall call His Name Immanuel, God with us. (Matthew 1:23). But the Name which the Angel revealed to Joseph was, 'JESUS, for He shall save His people from their sins.' (Matthew 1:21).

The precious truth of Immanuel is with us right to the end of the Gospel. 'Lo, I am with you always, even unto the end of the world. (Matthew 28:20). But before that, in verses 18 and 19. Jesus says to His disciples, 'Go therefore, and teach all nations, baptising them in the Name of the Father, the Son and the Holy Spirit.'

God is calling out a people for Himself, from all nations, a people who have been brought to the realisation that they need Jesus; men and women with a great desire for the One who will save them from their sins. Jesus came to teach them that this same God had a great desire too; a desire for those who would know Him as Father, just as His Son did. (Matthew 6:45, 48). Jesus came to reveal God to them as Father, to introduce them to the kingdom where He was King; to encourage their daily living; to walk close to their Father; to reflect the love they had for Him to others, the essence of true discipleship; and then to be sent by Him to go and make disciples who would also become part of the family of God, sons and daughters of the Great King.

All the teaching of Jesus culminated in His going to the Cross, where men and women were reconciled to a Holy God by His death and resurrection, and from which point He could implement His great desire, 'I will build My church, and the gates of hell shall not prevail against it.' (Matthew 16:18). His gathered ones, His *ekklesia*, living in union and perfect harmony with each other and with the Father.

Salvation history takes on human shape in the Gospel of Matthew; Jesus, Son of Man, clothing Himself with human likeness to satisfy the desire of His Father for a people like His own glorious Son, even though it meant suffering and death on a cross.

He laid down His life that He might take it again and pass on that eternal life to all believers through the saving power of the blood of the Cross. And as He is now eternally with His Father, so too He is with those who believe in Him, 'Lo, I am with you always, even into the end of the world', (Matthew 28:19). They are bound up with Him in the same bundle of life; (1 Samuel 25:29b A.V.) with the Father, and with the Son, under the anointing of the Holy Spirit.

Matthew Chapter 26

Matthew 26:1-27. The Passion Narrative

And it came to pass, when Jesus had finished all these sayings, He said to His disciples, 'You know that after two days the Passover is coming, and the Son of Man will be delivered up to be crucified.'(Matthew 26:1,2).

Jesus ends His eschatological discourse formulaically, using the formula which has ended the first one, the sermon on the mount, (Matthew 7:25); the second, the commissioning of the disciples to the task of mission,(11:1); the third, the parables of the Kingdom (13:53); the fourth, life and discipline among believers (19:1); and lastly, the fifth, this last one in which Jesus has taught them about His coming and the end of the age. (26:1) Mathew writes this phrase with little variation at the end of the discourses of Jesus, 'and it came to pass, when Jesus had ended all these sayings', thus providing connecting links in the chronology and continuity of Jesus' ministry.

With chapter 26:1, we come to the beginning of Matthew's account of the days immediately preceding the foreordained but nonetheless sorrowful and distressing death of Jesus, and look forward with anticipation because we know that this is not the end of His earthly story, and that He will rise from the dead as portrayed so vividly in chapter 28.

Up to this point, Jesus still has all His disciples with Him, those whom He has taught and nurtured over three years, sharing with them all that they are going to need to know after He leaves them until the Holy Spirit comes to them to guide them into all truth, (John 16:13), and bring to their remembrance all that He has said to them. (John 14:26). He pre-visions with them what it will mean to be His church, His gathered-out and gathered-together ones. He will lose Judas in 26:25, and we have the heart-rending comment in 26:56 that 'all the disciples forsook Him and fled'. But even this was in the Divine will, for what Jesus was about to go through, to accomplish, He had to go through alone as the Son of God (26:64), and Son of Man (26:2; 26:64).

Matthew 26:1 begins with the formulaic 'And it came to pass, when He had finished *all* these sayings'. *All* could allude to the previous two chapters when He had spoken to them in some detail of the end of time; what would happen before and after His coming again to take up His rightful position as King and Judge.

There is also some justification for applying the 'all' to all the five discourses which He has given to His disciples, for each one had and has its own importance in developing in those privileged to have entered into the Kingdom of Heaven through repentance and faith, a blueprint for their future, lived in holy union with their heavenly Father and with one another.

Not one word that He ever spoke fell on deaf ears, but was treasured up and repeated. We can imagine the disciples saying to each other after Pentecost, 'Do you remember when He said...?' Precious indeed, to them and to us, are the words of Jesus.

But now He has something of tremendous importance to tell them. 'You know that after two days is the Passover.' Yes, they knew that, but were devastated when He added, 'And the Son of Man will be delivered up to be crucified.' (verse 2). They knew that such an event was coming, for He had told them so in 16:21 at Caesarea Philippi, in 17:22-23, after His transfiguration; and in 20:18-20 when He had been speaking about the behaviour of His disciples to one another and especially in 20:19, saying that the method of His death would be by crucifixion. But now they had to face the prospect that such a horrific death was only days away, probably only hours away. Matthew does not share with us their reaction to Jesus' words, but they may have gained some comfort from the complete sense they had that Jesus was in control. This is confirmed by verse 3.

Matthew 26:3. The plot of the Sanhedrin against Jesus

Then the chief priests and the elders gathered in the palace of the High Priest, who was called Caiaphas, and took counsel together in order to arrest Jesus by stealth and kill Him. But they said 'Not during the feast, lest there be a tumult among the people.' (Matthew 26:3).

These important religious people, the chief priests and the elders of the people and even Caiaphas the High Priest have gathered together in the palace of the High Priest as the Sanhedrin. They were the ruling body of the Jewish people, not politically, for political government had been taken over by the Romans, but in practising their religion, and they met together to discuss, not only that they needed to arrest Jesus and kill Him, but to kill Him *secretly*. They had decided however not to kill Him during the approaching Feast of the Passover because they suspected that there would be a riot among the people.

Jesus overturned all their careful plans. He had already decided on the timing of events. He had decided that His death could not be more public although they had wanted secrecy. He was in complete control, and the disciples' understanding of His control over every detail was a comfort to them, even though their faith wavered in the Garden of Gethsemane when the soldiers came to take Him away. (verse 26).

But first, Jesus decided to accept the invitation from Simon the leper for Himself and His disciples to enjoy a meal at his house. This may seem extraordinary. With all that He has in view for the salvation of the world by giving up His life, He has time to go to the home of a previously unknown person for supper? But as always, there will be an event of tremendous significance awaiting Him, and by extension, His disciples.

Matthew 26:6-13. The anointing at Bethany

Now when Jesus was at Bethany in the house of Simon the leper, a woman came up to Him with an alabaster flask of very expensive ointment, and she poured it on His head as He sat at table. (Matthew 26:6,7).

Each episode of this chapter, leading on to the cross of the Lord Jesus as it does, is loaded with eternal verities, tremendous insights.

This episode is echoed with some variation in Matthew 14:3-9; Luke 7:30-38 and John 12:1-8. The account most consistent with Matthew's is Mark. Luke's account is placed in Capernaum, not Bethany and in the house of a Pharisee. If the Simon of Matthew and Mark's gospel were a leper, he would not have been allowed to be a Pharisee, though there is a possibility that he may have been a leper until healed by Jesus. This may also indicate the possibility of there being two such incidents.

There is no indication in Matthew or Mark that the host at this meal had forgotten the duties of a host in giving his guest the opportunity to wash his feet after walking along a dusty road in sandals, as in Luke's gospel, and no indication that Jesus used the event to tell the story of the two debtors. In addition, the woman of Luke's gospel not only anointed His head with the ointment, but also washed His feet with her tears before anointing them and kissing them. This extravagant love for Him caused Jesus in His loving compasion for her to say, 'Your sins are forgiven.' (Luke 7:48). and 'Go in peace, your faith has saved you.' (Luke 7:50).

We conclude that Luke's account, though similar in many respects to that of Matthew and Mark, and even John, may have been of a separate occasion.

As for John's gospel, John specifically states that it was six and not two days before the Passover in Jerusalem, but such a discrepancy is not really germane to the purpose which Jesus had in allowing the anointing of Himself. However, John's account suggests certain elements which agree with Matthew and Mark but not with Luke, reinforcing the possibility that there may have been two occasions when a woman came to Jesus in this way.

In John's gospel, the house to which He had come was in Bethany, just outside Jerusalem, the home of Mary and

Matthew and Lazarus, whom He had raised from the dead. Matthew and Mark had called the host in their account Simon the leper, but the word Lazarus is also associated with leprosy. The O.E.D. defines a lazar as a poor or diseased person, especially a leper, probably taking its meaning from the name Lazarus in Luke 16:20; but in the medically limited time of Jesus, any skin disease could be nominated as leprosy as in Leviticus 13 and 14.

There were many lepers in the time of Jesus, as we understand from the leper who came to Jesus in Luke 7:22 and the ten lepers who were cleansed by Him in Luke 17:12, and together with the blind receiving their sight, the lame walking, the deaf hearing, the dead being raised up and the poor having the gospel preached to them, Luke includes the lepers who are cleansed, as a witness to John the Baptist's disciples that Jesus was indeed He that should come (Luke 7:18-23). Surely this must have been a great comfort to John in prison. Matthew also records this in Matthew 11:2-6. And Matthew and Luke both identify Jesus' declaration of His healing ministry to John, as the substantial justification of John's ministry, in Matthew's case of John being the one the one who would prepare the way of the Lord as prophesied by Isaiah 40:3 (Matthew 3:3) and especially in response to John's heartfelt cry, 'Are you He that should come or do we look for another?'(Matthew 11:3).

In Matthew's gospel, Jesus is in Bethany in the house of Simon the leper. (Matthew 26:6). These are all the details we have in this gospel, for, as always, Matthew is consistent in His purpose to put Jesus centre stage, to demonstrate who He is, and to eliminate any unnecessary details.

Here is a woman. Who was she? In John's gospel she is Mary, the sister of Martha. In Luke, she is a sinner, (7:37), who nevertheless 'loved much'. In Matthew and Mark, no identification is given of her, and so for all women everywhere and down the centuries, she has been their representative. No doubt, she has been taken as the representative of men too, for women do not have the monopoly of 'loving much' when confronted with their living, loving, Lord.

As Jesus reclined at table, she approached Him with an alabaster flask of very expensive, very costly ointment, 'and she poured it on His head. (verse 7). According to John, the house was filled with the fragrance of the ointment'. (John 12:3). The disciples were indignant. 'What does she think she is doing? Why this waste? This ointment might have been sold for a large sum and given to the poor. (verse 8,9).

Those dear disciples. After all their time with Jesus, they still did not recognise the significance of what she had done.

Jesus, 'aware of this', (verse 10) said to them, 'Why do you trouble the woman?' It must have been a trouble to her to realise that her great gift of precious ointment, perhaps something she had inherited, perhaps something she was saving up for her own burial, or the burial of someone dear to her, had been completely misunderstood.

But Jesus understood. He always does. He says to the disciples, 'She has done a beautiful thing to Me. You always have the poor with you but you will not always have Me. In pouring this ointment on My body she has done it to prepare Me for burial. Truly, I say to you, wherever the gospel is preached in the whole world, what she has done will be told in memory of her'. (Matthew 26:11, 12).

She had anointed Him, not only with the ointment, but with her love for Him.

As we saw earlier, oil or ointment is a very precious reminder of who Jesus is. Priests, prophets and kings were anointed with oil, and Psalm 45:6 speaks of the oil of gladness with which God has anointed the One who sits on the Divine throne. Did the woman's gift speak to Him of the joy which was His as He did the will of His Father? Or of the Holy Spirit with whom He had been anointed? Such recognition of who Jesus is, is at the heart of the woman's adoration and worship of Him, but recognition too that His Kingship will soon be tested beyond all human endurance, as He dies and is buried. She had been instrumental as no-one else in Jesus' circle of friends and disciples had been, in preparing His Body for burial after His death.

Even as He hung there on the cross, so soon after her act of anointing Him, the fragrance of that ointment would still be there, under the crown of thorns which they had so cruelly placed over it. Inadvertently, without knowing it, they had pressed that awful crown down upon the anointing. But Jesus knew, and how precious to Him was the encouragement that this was not the end, but that in the will of His loving heavenly Father, He was moving into the furtherance of all that They had planned together of the salvation of men and women from the tyranny of sin.

He was Prophet, and Priest, but above all the Anointed One, the Christ, the Messiah, the King. Anointed by the Holy Spirit as Isaiah so wonderfully proclaims, 'The Spirit of the Lord God is upon Me, because the Lord has anointed Me.' Isaiah 61:1. Anointed Him to bring good tidings to the afflicted, to bind up the broken-hearted, to proclaim liberty to the captives, and the opening of the prison to those who are bound, to proclaim the year of the Lord's favour and the day of vengeance of our God. To comfort all who mourn in Zion, to give them a garland of beauty for ashes; the oil of gladness instead of mourning; the mantle of praise for a spirit of heaviness; that they may be called trees of righteousness, the planting of the Lord, that He may be glorified.

It is probable that each one of us comes in one or more of those categories, afflicted, broken hearted, enslaved to someone or something, imprisoned in some way. How precious is the anointing of the Lord Jesus as Christ. Through that anointing He has accomplished so much for us. He is God's answer to the needs of the whole world. Whatever the question, it is probable that Jesus is the answer.

It is probable too that the woman had none of this in mind when she lovingly approached Jesus with her precious ointment. But she too was open to the intimations of the Holy Spirit that that was what she was going to do today, and did it, and brought great gladness to the heart of Jesus by her obedience and love for Him. The woman, however dimly, recognised His Anointing, and what she had done would be told in memory of her. (Matthew 26:13).

Matthew 26:14-16. The treachery of Judas

Then one of the twelve, who was called Judas Iscariot, went to the chief priests and said, 'What will you give me if I deliver Him to you?' And they paid him thirty pieces of silver. And from that moment, he sought an opportunity to betray Him. (Matthew 26:14-16).

What a contrast between the woman at Bethany and Judas Iscariot! She had poured upon Jesus ointment which was reckoned as amounting to the value of 300 denarii, in John 12:5, a year's wages for a labourer. (But who could put a price on what she had done?)

The chief priests paid Judas only thirty pieces of silver to betray Jesus, indicating how much they thought His life was worth. But also, they did not realise that they were fulfilling scripture, the prophecy of the shepherd in Zechariah 11:12. 'And they weighed out as my wages thirty pieces of silver', for Jesus is shepherd too as He had reminded them in Matthew 26:31 'It is written, I will strike the shepherd and the sheep of the flock will be scattered". (Zechariah 13:7).

Why did Judas do it? What made him want to betray someone who had always loved him, included him, trusted him with the money bag (John 12:29) from which the disciples and many others were supplied.

In verse 14 Matthew uses the word 'then'. Then Judas went to the chief priests. It happened directly after the anointing of Jesus that Judas went to them and said. 'What will you give me if I deliver Him to you?' And they paid him the price of a slave, according to Exodus 21:33. They knew who Judas meant by 'Him', the one who would be delivered to them. 'And from that moment, he sought an opportunity, a convenient time to betray Him'. (Matthew 26:14-16).

It would appear that the anointing of Jesus at Bethany was the final straw for Judas. He was disappointed in Jesus. He had perhaps expected that Jesus would join the not inconsiderable group of those who were in rebellion against the Roman occupation of their country. The whole of the Sanhedrin had conferred, had consulted together to arrest Jesus and kill Him, for they recognised in Him something more than a rebel leader; but their intention was that it should be done in secrecy All that planning had now gone by the board, for they were putting their confidence in a disillusioned and disappointed disciple of Jesus who would deliver Him up at an opportune time which *He* would decide. The chief priests do not even have the ability to carry out their own determined plan.

Jesus will be delivered up in order to be crucified, but it will be at a time in complete agreement with God's plan. In the fullness of time, God's time, God sent forth His Son, and in the fullness of time, God's time, God will receive Him back into the glory He had with Him before the world was. (Galatians 4:4; John 17:4). He Himself is complete Master of the situation, and the beginning of His suffering is also the beginning of His victory over sin and death.

But both Jesus and His Father knew that there was in the heart of Judas an undisciplined unwillingness to subject himself to all that he had seen and heard since responding to Jesus' call to follow Him. There is a contrast between the absolute, total, devotion to Jesus of the woman, the total commitment of herself to Him who is going to His death, and the attitude of Judas, who not only regarded the pouring out of the ointment a waste of money, but a complete waste of the time he had spent in following a Man who did not fulfil his expectations.

She had a relationship to Christ. In spite of everything, In spite of daily contact with Jesus. Judas had somehow missed out on that special relationship. He could never have brought himself to such a display of devotion. She recognises who He is, nameless though she herself was. Judas did not have that recognition. He judged Jesus by his own prejudices and by his own dislike of the Roman regime under which they were forced to live.

And the information he is about to give the chief priests well deserves the reward of thirty pieces of silver, in his view.

Is it then that he is greedy? Avaricious? Does he value Jesus so little? For it is certain that the information the chief priests are expecting from him will at the very least lead to His arrest and imprisonment, and perhaps more, for Jesus had predicted that He would be 'delivered up' in 17:22; 20:18; and 26:2, and Judas is here offering to deliver Him up. (Matthew 26:15). Is this an indication that Jesus had always known that Judas would betray Him, that perhaps unknowingly, he was to be the instrument of the will of God?

But this does not eliminate his guilt, for he had free will and wanted to act on his own initiative. 'From that moment, he sought an opportunity to betray, and possibly, destroy Him'. (Matthew 26:16). Judas is setting the story of terrible darkness in motion, he who was, perhaps we should now say, he who had been, one of the special circle of the Twelve disciples of Jesus.

But this is the story of Jesus, not Judas. Jesus is at the centre of all that darkness, all that suffering and He it is that drives the narrative forward, for everything that happens has been predicted by Him, and is therefore happening in God's will and according to His timing. He can use even the despair, even the desperation of a man who had possibly hoped at Jesus' triumphal entry into Jerusalem for a political uprising of the people against their oppressors – even that He can use to fulfil the purpose which He had in view before the world was.

Under God, Judas had initiated a train of events, so similar and yet so different from what he had envisaged. Matthew's narrative continues with its unrelenting progress to 'on the first day of Unleavened Bread', the Feast of the Passover which heralded all that was about to be prophetically fulfilled, all the *eternal* preparation now coming to fulfilment. (verse 17). Judas had made his preparations. Jesus had also made His. He knew that the time was at hand. (verse 18).

Judas sought an opportunity εὐκαιρία, a good time, an opportune time, to betray Him. (verse 16). Jesus knew that the time καιρός, His time, had come (verse 18).

Matthew 26:17-19. Preparation for the Passover

Now on the first day of Unleavened Bread, the disciples come to Jesus saying, 'Where will you have us prepare for you to eat the

515

Passover?' He said, 'Go into the city to a certain one and say to him'. The Teacher says, 'My time is at hand; I will keep the Passover at your house with My disciples.' And the disciples did as Jesus had directed them, and they prepared the Passover.

This was the third and last Passover which Jesus was going to share with His disciples. The three are clearly set out in John's gospel. The *first* one, in John 2:13 occurred when He had cleansed the Temple of those who sold doves, oxen or sheep for sacrifice, and poured out the coins of the money changers, over-turning their tables, (John 2:14-15), prior to the visit of Nicodemus by night, presumably Passover night, when Jesus said to him, 'You must be born again'. (John 3:7). And how much there is to learn from those verses.

The *second Passover* of Jesus' earthly ministry according to John's gospel occurred at the time of the feeding of the five thousand in John 6:4, when He spoke to the people, the Jews and His disciples of Himself as the Bread of Life (John 6:35), and then to His disciples of Himself as the flesh and blood which they were to eat and drink that they might have eternal life. (John 6:54). At this second Passover, though His teaching concerned so many of the elements of what became the Lord's Supper, He did not actually institute it. That was to be reserved for the *third* Passover meal according to the synoptic gospels.

Yet, in John's gospel, the third Passover in John 13:1 is concerned not with the bread and wine, but with the expression of love for His disciples which Jesus demonstrated by the washing of their feet. Before the feast of the Passover, when Jesus knew that His hour had come to depart out of this world to the Father, having loved His own who were in the world, He loved them to the end. (verse 1). And He rose from supper, laid aside His garments and *girded himself with a towel* (verse 4) and began to wash the disciples' feet as an expression of His cleansing love for them and of His Servanthood, a servant to them as He wanted them to be to each other.

And yet He no longer called them servants, for the servant does not know what His Master is doing, but Jesus called them friends, for all that He had heard from His Father He had made known to them. His commandment was that they should love one another as He had loved them (verse 12), the cleansing love of the Lord for them, and the cleansing love they were to have for each other.

So in John's gospel we note a sequence from these three Passovers. Those who are born of the Spirit of God, (John 3:5) feed upon the Bread of Life, the life of the Lord Jesus, (John 6:51) and relate to one another in cleansing love. (John 13:14,15). And all within the typological interpretative context of the Passover, the Lamb sacrificed for their deliverance from sin, from chains which would bind them to the world, even as the Israelites were delivered from Egypt, from the place of suffering and slavery.

Only on the basis of the Lamb of God who takes away the sin of the world (John 1:29) can this freedom be offered to all men and women everywhere. But His eternally valid sacrifice sets men and women free to love Him and to love one another. Bread and wine, or foot-washing? Surely both are important for believers.

Matthew, Mark, Luke and John all suggest different understandings of this important event, the last Passover in the life of Jesus. All imply obedience to His word to them.

Matthew celebrates the Christological overtones of all that Jesus says and does in his gospel. In 26:17 we read 'on the first day of Unleavened Bread', the alternative title for the Feast of Passover. We are left in no doubt as to the timing of what Jesus is about to do.

The Feast of Unleavened Bread celebrated annually by the Jews comprised eight days beginning on the 14th Nisan, the day and the month on which the Passover lamb was slain, and the feast prepared, and ended eight days later, during which time the Jews ate only unleavened bread. The leaven symbolized evil, possibly the evil of slavery in Egypt, as in 1 Corinthians 5:7, 'For Christ, our Passover Lamb has been sacrificed for us. Let us therefore keep the feast, not with the old leaven, the leaven of malice and evil, but with the unleavened bread of sincerity and truth'. Hundreds of years later, a grateful nation still remembered the night of their deliverance from Egypt, and kept the feast of sincerity and truth. The first letter to the Corinthians reminds us that we too were once enslaved, but the blood of the Lamb of God, the Lord Jesus has set us free, and we too may keep our own feast, when we remember Him at His Table, and the remembrance of being set free from that which is evil, not sincere, not pure, not of the truth.

The children of Israel had been enslaved in Egypt for four hundred and thirty years. (Exodus 12:40). Now God had decreed their deliverance, that He would deliver them from Egypt. He had promised the children of Israel that if they put the blood of the lamb on the doorposts and lintels of their houses, the angel of death would *pass over* them, and their firstborn would be safe. This had indeed happened. The homes of the children of Israel were protected by the blood of the lamb, but the Egyptian families were in deep distress because they had not put the blood of the lamb on the lintels of their houses, and when the angel of death *passed over*, all the firstborn had died.

The children of Israel had to leave Egypt fast before the Egyptians realised what was happening and set off in pursuit. There was no time to bake their bread. All they could do was to bake unleavened bread of the dough which they had brought out of Egypt. They had no opportunity to leaven their bread. (Exodus 12:39). This was why the feast was called not only Passover, when the angel passed over them, but also the feast of Unleavened Bread. And at this special Passover time, the last one Jesus would share with His disciples, Jesus knew that He was about to set people free from all that Egypt represented of slavery; the slavery of sin, the slavery to death, those who through fear of death, were all their lifetime subject to bondage. (Hebrews 2:15)

In the Jewish understanding of time, the day began at sunset. So the day of preparation, the Day of Unleavened Bread of Matthew 26:17 was the 14th Nisan, becoming the 15th Nisan at sunset, the day of the Passover, when the Lord Jesus was about to share the Passover with His disciples. It was so important that the institution of His Supper should correspond, concur with the Feast of the Passover; as we shall see.

The preparation for this special Passover had been thoughtfully pre-arranged with an unknown person, probably a disciple. Jesus said to His disciples, 'Go into the city to a certain one and say to him, "The Teacher says, 'My time is at hand'. I will keep the Passover at your house with My disciples'. (verse 18). Mark designates this as 'two disciples to go into the city. (Mark 14:13). Luke describes Jesus as sending Peter and John. (Luke 22:8). But Matthew just uses the term 'the disciples' emphasising once again that the chief and most important protagonist in this drama is Jesus Himself.

Jesus says 'Go' to these disciples, whether they were two or twelve, and they immediately obey, finding the man as Jesus had said they would, speaking authoritatively as they pass on Jesus' message. 'The disciples did as Jesus had directed them, and they prepared the Passover, (verse 19), and when it was evening He sat at table with the twelve disciples. (verse 20).

Why was it so important for Jesus to celebrate the Passover with His disciples? And why did He use this particular feast of remembrance in the Jewish calendar to institute a special remembrance of Him in the breaking of the bread and the drinking of the cup?

These are important questions. But first we come to His betrayal by Judas.

Matthew 26:20-25. The betrayal

When it was evening, Jesus sat at table with the twelve disciples, and as they were eating, He said 'Truly, one of you will betray Me'. And they were very sorrowful and began to say to Him one after another, 'Is it I, Lord?. He answered, he who has dipped his hand in the dish with Me, will betray Me. The Son of Man goes as it is written of Him, but woe to that man by whom the Son of Man is betrayed'.

Part of the message from Jesus to His provider of their accommodation for the feast emphasised, 'My time καιρός has come'. (verse 16). He is the Lord of time, and He is actively participating in the shaping of God's plan.

Here, as the disciples dip their bread into the common dish, we see the difference and yet the similarity between Judas and the other disciples. In preparing for the Passover, the disciples had acted immediately in complete obedience to the command of Jesus. But one disciple was about to relinquish that honourable description. Discipleship belongs to the family of those who do the will of their Father who is in heaven. (Matthew 12:50). After tonight, after he has dipped his morsel into the common dish, Judas will no longer be able to consider himself part of that happy, privileged community.

As they were eating, Jesus said, 'Truly, I say to you, that one of you will betray Me' (verse 21). The disciples were already sorrowful because they knew, because He had told them, that 'the Son of Man will be crucified', (verse 26), and that 'the time was at hand.' (verse 18). How could their distress be any greater than it was? But a dreadful thing was about to happen. As they were eating, Jesus said, 'Truly, I say to you, one of you will betray Me'. (verse 21).

Betray? Betray Him? Betray Jesus?

How could He even think it?

And yet perhaps they had not always and in every circumstance been faithful to Him, or understood what He was trying to do. They searched their consciences. One by one they began to say to Him, 'Lord, is it I?' And He answered, 'It is one who has dipped his hand in the dish with Me'. (verse 23).

He does not name the individual because he is a friend, as is shown by his eating from the common bowl, but he is a deceitful, hypocritical 'friend', for what friend would do what Judas was planning to do? How exact were Jesus' words, 'The Son of Man goes as it is written of Him, but woe to that man by whom the Son of Man is betrayed! It would have been better for that man if he had not been born'. (verse 24).

Stimulated at last into his own question, 'Teacher, is it I?' Judas is revealed to the other disciples as the one who should betray Jesus, as He said to him, 'You have said so'. (verse 25). Jesus wanted Judas to confess, to 'say so', for confession may lead to repentance and repentance to forgiveness. Jesus, the pastor, the true shepherd of this little flock, wanted Judas to know there was still time for him to change his mind.

We do not know from Matthew's account at what point Judas left the room. In this gospel, we do not meet him again until verse 47 after Jesus' agony in the Garden of Gethsemane, but John's gospel says, 'After receiving the morsel which Jesus handed him from the bowl, he immediately went out, and *it was night.* (John 13:30). Darkness had descended, not only on the world, but on the heart of Judas.

Did Judas partake of the Last Supper? The breaking of the bread, signifying the breaking of His Body, the drinking of the cup, signifying the New Covenant in His Blood. Was he there? Matthew does not tell us, but Luke seems to think that he was there. (Luke 22:20,21).

This has been a matter of some controversy historically. Some church leaders have interpreted the text as indicating that we should be tolerant of those in the church who may not be fully committed followers of Jesus, and yet who want to partake of Holy Communion. We cannot judge of another's commitment to Jesus. Paul's advice is very personal. Let a man examine himself and so eat of the bread and drink of the cup. (1 Corinthians 11:28).

It is noteworthy in this connection that when asking Jesus, 'Is it I?' they used His title 'Lord', 'κυριος'. 'Lord, is it I?' The confession of Jesus as Lord is the word of faith and the means of justification according to Romans 10:8-10. Judas does not use the title 'Lord' for Jesus, but calls Him 'Teacher', Rabbi, reminding us of chapter 23:8, for 'rabbi' is used by the people, the Jews, of the Pharisees, and also by the Sadducees and lawyers as they came to Jesus, trying to entangle Him in His talk in Matthew 22:15, 23, 24. 'Rabbi'.Teacher', can be a loaded word.

To the other disciples, He is Lord. To Judas, He is merely 'Teacher'. This may be the perspective he had given himself as to the ministry of Jesus and why he thought it was reasonable to betray Him.

In John's account, Jesus has a specially important aspect to the lives of the disciples as they share the Passover together, that He wants to impart to them; the absolute preeminence of love.

At this Passover time He gives His disciples a new commandment, that they should love one another even as He had loved them, so they should also love one another. (John 13:34). It was that love which was missing in Judas, and which Jesus displayed to the utmost by hanging on a cross to take away sin by the offering of Himself for their sakes; (and ours). (Hebrews 10:10). He opened His arms wide upon the Cross, that He might embrace all who come to Him; and that great love wherewith He loved us, (Ephesians 2:4), has been poured into our hearts through the Holy Spirit whom He has given to us, (Romans 5:5), so that we might love one another as He has loved us.

How incredible, unbelievable, that in that atmosphere of such intense love, Judas still felt that he could betray Jesus, and how Judas could not receive that love is a complete mystery. He had free will, but used his will in opposition to the greater will, the will of God concerning His Son, just as Eve and then Adam had done in the Garden of Eden, asserting their will in defiance of God's word to them.

The only answer for men and women is to see in Him a faithful God, whose will is perfect, and whatever the circumstances of life, apparent or real, desires only good for His children. Somehow, Judas had missed out on that revelation, having allowed himself to be preoccupied with political expediency. Perhaps some of the saddest words in the gospel was Jesus saying to His disciples, 'Rise, let us be going, My betrayer is at hand. (Matthew 26:46). Judas, so privileged, and so lost. Judas, no longer a disciple, but a betrayer.

Matthew 26:26-29. The Last Supper

Now as they were eating, Jesus took bread and blessed and broke it and gave it to the disciples and said, 'Take, eat, this is My Body.'

And He took a cup, and when He had given thanks, He gave it to them saying, 'Drink of it, all of you; for this is My Blood of the New Covenant, which is poured out for many for the forgiveness of sins. I tell you I shall not drink again of this fruit of the vine until that day when I drink it new with you in My Father's Kingdom.'

This was the last meal as a human man Jesus would ever have, and certainly the last time He would eat with His disciples before His death. As the meal proceeded, Jesus took bread, and blessed and broke it. They had been eating (verse 20) before the distressing announcement that one of them, Judas, was a betrayer. Now, in the absence of Judas, verse 26, they resume their meal.

This has turned out to be a more momentous occasion than they had anticipated, for Jesus now has something of tremendous significance to give them. His gift was a Remembrance meal. In time of course, this became liturgical as His followers broke bread together in remembrance of Him whenever they gathered in His Name. This ritual meal however was very simple. It did not have all the detailed dialogue and actions of the Passover meal, (Exodus 12:24-27) but Jesus used the framework of the Passover to underline and draw significant parallels with what He was about to do.

As the host, Jesus presides over the meal, as a Jewish father at home with his family would do. It is a family meal. And the Last Supper when members of His Body, the church, gather together to remember Him, is a family meal. On one occasion, Jesus had said to the people, 'Who is my mother and who are my brothers? For whoever does the will of My Father in heaven is My brother, and sister, and mother (Matthew 12:49-50). He said this while stretching out His hand towards His *disciples*. He so wanted His mother and His brothers and sisters to be part of the family of God and He was inviting them to be part not only of His earthly family, which they were, but part of the greater Family also.

Of course, we cannot but assume that Mary was already His devoted follower, right from the beginning when the angel appeared to her, announcing the conception of the child Jesus. But we understand the point which Jesus was making. We too needed to become part of that family of Jesus, and by His grace we have responded to His invitation. We break bread *together* as part of that family as we share in the remembrance of His death and His risen life, and worship Him who gave His life for us.

Jesus took bread. Just some bread, unleavened bread of course, which had been before them on the table.

But this was the Passover meal. Why then not a piece of lamb? Or some bitter herbs? Or a sprig of hyssop? Items of food, each with its own spiritual significance, readily available at this meal. Surely, as John would later write of the revelation given to John the Baptist, He was the Lamb of God who takes away the sin of the world. (John 1:29). Would not a piece of the broken lamb be more appropriate?

But Jesus took bread. Bread was, as it still is in many societies, the staple of their diet. From the highest in society to the lowest, bread was the one item of food which was common to all, and if it was out of reach of the very poorest, then their poverty was great indeed.

Jesus knew this. He had given them this prayer to pray to their heavenly Father. 'Give us this day our daily bread'. (Matthew 6:11). That prayer of course has many overtones, of trust in our heavenly Father, of spiritual food as well as material food, but Jesus uses bread in this prayer, as in other instances, such as the feeding of the five thousand, as a basic requirement for living; and a declaration that the one who is praying 'Give us this day our daily bread' is totally dependent on his or her heavenly Father for the necessities of life; and faith that in His own way, their heavenly Father will provide.

And with this in view, Jesus had described Himself as the Bread of Life, that food without which we cannot live. (John 6:35). In that chapter, John had described how Jesus had reminded the Jews of the manna that had miraculously fed the Israelites as they wandered in the desert, after they had been delivered from Egypt. Psalm 78:25 says, 'Man ate of the bread of the angels. He rained down upon them manna to eat.' And in Psalm 105:40,'He gave them bread from heaven in abundance'. Jesus says, 'I am the living Bread which came down from heaven.

If anyone eats of this bread, he will live forever, and the bread which I shall give for the life of the world is My flesh'. (John 6:57,52).

Jesus was not only or even symbolically representing Himself as Bread. He *was* Bread, the Bread of Life, the sine qua non of life. '*I AM* the bread of life,' He said. Without Him, we have no life, not the reality of life as it has been given to us to live. As we are reminded in Ephesians 2:1, until we are made alive in Christ, we are dead, dead in our trespasses and sins. 'But God, who is rich in mercy, even when we were dead through our trespasses, has made us alive together with Christ'. (Ephesians 2:4). How appropriate then, that Jesus is represented by Bread in this most solemn and sacred meal. This is the life He gives to us. We feed on Him in our hearts by faith, with thanksgiving; we receive His life as we eat.

But at this Passover meal, this is Broken Bread. Jesus took bread and blessed, and broke it, and gave it to the disciples and said, 'Take eat. This is My Body.' The blessing which He pronounced over the bread was the same blessing which He had used in Matthew 14:19 when He was distributing the five loaves and two fish to the disciples, to feed the hungry crowd of five thousand men besides women and children. What a story those children would have to tell their grandchildren! Matthew 14:19 says, 'He looked up to heaven and *blessed and broke and gave* the loaves to the disciples.' In chapter 15:36 we have a similar incident. 'He took the seven loaves and the fish, and *having given thanks, He broke them and gave them* to the disciples, and the disciples gave them to the crowds.'

From these two accounts, we may assume that the 'blessing' of the bread at this significant Passover meal may be identified with the giving of thanks, the εὐχαριστία, the Eucharist, the giving of thanks with the εὐλογιά, the blessing.

But there was a difference here. This was the unleavened bread of the Passover, pure and unadulterated, free from the symbolic evil of the leaven, totally symbolic of the purity of the life of Jesus who was completely free from the leaven of evil. It was not the normal everyday barley bread used by the ordinary people of Palestine, which was baked with leaven to make the dough rise, but unleavened bread.

In addition, the two occasions of providing bread and fish for the hungry multitudes, and the wine for the marriage at Cana in Galilee (John 2:7) were miracles of supply, as He took the food in His hands, or spoke His authoritative word over pitchers of water to change them into wine.

But at this Passover meal, when Jesus took the bread in His hands and broke it, He was not increasing its volume. This bread had a different purpose, a different significance. It was for the disciples to understand that His was to be a broken body. He says, 'This is My body, broken for you' (verse 26) Not, 'This will *become* My Body,' or, 'This *represents* My Body,' but this *is* My Body. The former statement, that the bread *becomes* the body of Christ, allows the transubstantiation doctrine of the Roman Catholic Church. The representative statement, that the bread *represents* His Body, is the doctrinal position of the Reformers of the 15th, 16th, and 17th centuries. Jesus says 'this *is* my Body'. And we understand by this that because we are feeding on Him in our hearts *by faith,* we are acknowledging that we have taken Him into our very being; that He lives in us and we in Him; His Body, broken for us.

What did Jesus mean as He held up before His disciples the broken bread? Jesus is holding His own life in His hands. But this is a life He wants them to have, to participate in. How do they receive that life? By His Body being broken and His life poured out. 'Take, eat,' He says to them. I want you to share in My life, and I know that you can only do that if My body is broken and My life poured out for you.

His blessing of the bread was not only thanksgiving to the Father, the Eucharist, but it was also the blessing, ευλογιά, of the disciples who were to receive it, and especially the blessing of God Himself. How often do we read of blessing the Lord in the Psalms, for example, 'Bless the Lord, O my soul, and all that is within me, bless His holy Name'. (Psalm 103:1). The Hebrew root of the word for blessing is to kneel down and worship. To bless the Lord is to *review* Him, to *consider* all His ways with us, to be thankful for His mercy, for His holiness, for being who He is, to bow down in worship to Him, and to know that His love and His presence with us is mediated to us as our blessing, His blessing of us.

So what is the equivalence of our blessing of Him and His blessing of us? For He cannot worship His creation.

When He blesses us, it is also a review, a review or consideration of our inadequacies, our failures, but to have a perception, a foreknowledge that we may become *not* what we are in ourselves, but *may become* in His Son. By His mercy, and according to His holiness, *His sufficiency makes up our deficiency. We are blessed.*

All this is implied in Jesus' blessing of the bread. He loves us as we are, but does not want us to stay as we are. As we eat the bread and drink the cup, as we partake of His risen life, we remember that it was a life laid down for us. His life becomes our life. We live by the faith of the Son of God, who loved us, and gave Himself for us (Galatians 2:20).

Jesus took the bread, and blessed it, and gave it that we might receive it, this precious, unaccountably precious, gift of Himself. 'Take, eat, this is My Body.' (Matthew 26:26). 'This is what it means to be a part of Me'.

There have been various interpretations of these words of Jesus. But the beginning of understanding what Jesus was doing is not an interpretation but an event. It is something which as lovers of the Lord Jesus we *do*. There is a ritual of taking, breaking, distributing, eating, and we do it prophetically, a symbolic action expressing a fundamental truth.

Εὐχαριστῶ, thanksgiving includes the word χάρις, grace. An outward visible sign of an inward invisible grace, a sacrament. St. Augustine says that the reason why the bread and the wine are called sacraments is that one thing is seen in them, but something else is understood. That which is seen is bodily appearance. That which is understood is spiritual fruit. The Apostle Paul teaches, 'We are many but we are one loaf, one body'. (1 Corinthians 10:17). We do not see ourselves visibly as the Body of Christ, but that is what we are, invisibly, spiritually.

Bread is not made from one grain of wheat, but from many. Augustine says, when you were baptised, you were moistened. When you received the fire of the Holy Spirit, you were cooked! Many grapes hang in a cluster, but their juice is mixed in unity. So the Lord has set His mark on us, wanting us to belong to Him. (Sermon 272, Bettenson. The Later Christian Fathers p 245).

There are seven feasts of the Lord set out for the Israelites in Leviticus 23, including the Sabbath, and all have tremendous spiritual significance in the lives of the Jewish people. They are distributed throughout the year, and the most significant are the Day of Atonement, the 10th Elul, corresponding to our September/October; the Passover or Feast of Unleavened Bread on 14th Nisan, corresponding to our March/April; and Pentecost, or Feast of Weeks, seven weeks or fifty days after Passover. All the feasts of the Lord, as they came round annually, were a reminder to the children of Israel of their tremendous inheritance; how God had intervened in their history, in their lives, how He had brought them through and provided for them, their merciful and faithful God.

Just as the people of Israel associated their deliverance from bondage in Egypt with the Passover meal, so Jesus took bread and broke it, thus declaring that for His disciples, as they took the bread and ate it, they too were delivered from slavery, just as the children of Israe had been. *They were free through the offering up of the Passover Lamb, the Lamb of God who takes away the sins of the world.* His disciples had entered into the glorious liberty of the children of God. (Romans 8:21). His broken Body accomplished their deliverance, they were free to live to Him, to offer up their lives to Him, even if it meant suffering and death. As they ate the unleavened bread and drank of the cup, they were entering into a sacred commitment, not now for them the commitment of remembering the cost of their deliverance from Egypt, but the remembrance of the unique sacrifice which Jesus was about to make, and not for them only, but for the whole world. They were indeed thankful.

Jesus was lifting the Passover onto a different plane, not suspending it, for God had indeed accomplished a mighty deed of deliverance for His people; but extending it, filling it out, and when He comes to the cup, He speaks of the New Covenant in His blood.

Matthew 26:27-28. Jesus took the cup

Imperatively, Jesus has commanded the disciples to 'take, eat.' Now He commands them to drink, 'Drink of it, all of you.' In breaking the bread, and distributing fragments of it to all the disciples, He is creating table fellowship. In the drinking of 'all of you' from the same cup, He is establishing that the table fellowship rests upon the New Covenant in His Blood.

And He took a cup, and when He had given thanks He gave it to them saying, 'Drink of it all of you, for this is My blood of the covenant which is poured out for many for the forgiveness of sins' (Matthew 26:28).

Matthew omits the word 'new' in relation to the covenant, perhaps understanding that this covenant, *the* covenant ratified in the blood of Jesus, surpasses all the covenants which God had previously made, with Noah, and Abraham, through Moses, and with David. It was in fact a summation of them all but went far beyond them, as God strove to have a relationship with His people, Each one looked forward to the only covenant made possible by the shedding of the blood of His Son, whereby the cross became an altar upon which He died to take away sin by the offering of Himself once for all, (Hebrews 10:10), opening up a new and living way to God. (Hebrews 10:20).

For Matthew, this is not only a covenant, but the *Only Covenant* which from henceforth draws men and women into relationship to God through the sacrifice of His Son. Without the shedding of blood, there is no forgiveness of sins. (Hebrews 9:22), and without forgiveness of sins, men and women cannot draw near to a Holy God. But we may draw near with a true heart in full assurance of faith (Hebrew 10:22) when we have been to the foot of the Cross and there received the precious gift of justification, the righteousness of God through faith in Jesus Christ. (Romans 3:22).

So, Jesus says, 'This is My blood of the covenant which is poured out for many for the forgiveness of sins'. (verse 28). The one cup is passed around all the disciples, for all are to drink of it. A corresponding command for the bread had not been necessary, for the bread was broken into pieces by Jesus as it was distributed to them all.

But why was the Cup so important?

As we have seen, the One Cup, was based upon His death, His blood, the one atoning sacrifice.for sin.There was no other good enough to pay the price of sin. His blood alone atones for the guilt-ridden soul. There is only one sacrifice, only one way to the Father, and it is through the death and atoning blood of the sacrifice of His Son when He said, 'I come to do your will, O God.' (Hebrews 10:7). 'I lay down My life that I might take it again'. (John 10:17). 'This command I have received from My Father' (John 10:13).

It is the blood of *JESUS* that is being shed, poured out *for many, περί πολλών* for the forgiveness of sins (verse 28). And this is the reason for the outpouring of the blood. Forgiveness of sins is at the very heart of all that Jesus came to do, and be, for us. Even His Name, Jesus, given to Him at His birth (Matthew 1:21) was prophetic of what He came to do. 'You shall call His Name Jesus, for He shall save His people from their sins.' So the word becomes a promise for all, 'My blood, poured out for many for the forgiveness of sins' (Matthew 26:25). In sharing in the Cup, the disciples and all who follow after are proclaiming that the promise is for them, that they may by faith enter into the saving power of Jesus' death.

The Cup declares it. Their faith makes it real. It is His final gift to them before He suffers. Paul writes, 'The cup of blessing which we bless, is not a participation in the blood of Christ?' (1 Corinthians 10:16). Participation is κοινωνία, fellowship or communion. The Cup declares that it is a holy communion; a holy participation. Jesus has given us the privilege of drinking His Cup in fellowship with others, in celebration of our oneness in Him, our unity in the fellowship of the church.

Jesus' 'last supper' with His disciples was not a Christian modification of the Passover meal. It was a new understanding of the Passover. The Passover of the Israelites in Exodus 12 led them on to the 'Old' covenant which Moses mediated between them and their Redeemer, their Deliverer, at Mount Horeb-Sinai, in Exodus 20, and reiterated for them in Deuteronomy 5:2, their deliverance from slavery into a covenant with a God who loves them, whom God has chosen to be a people for His own possession, the faithful God who keeps covenant and steadfast love with those who love Him. (Deuteronomy 7:6,8,9).

Here Jesus is instituting a new covenant, but God's intention has not lessened. He still desires a people for His own possession, a people 'holy to the Lord your God,' (Deuteronomy 7:6), those who will follow Him, love Him and represent Him to those who have yet to know Him. Jesus is instituting a new covenant, prophesied all those centuries ago by Jeremiah in 31:31. 'I will make a new covenant with the house of Israel... I will put my law *within* them', not a law which is peripheral to their understanding of who I am, but a law which I will write on their hearts; and 'I will be their God and they will be My people... and they will all know Me, from the least to the greatest', says the Lord, 'for I will forgive their iniquity, and I will remember their sin *no more*'. (verse 34).

Ezekiel also speaks of the inward transformation which the new covenant will bring. 'A new heart will I give you, and a new spirit will I put within you... and I will put My Spirit within you.' (Ezekiel 36:26).

The precious law, the ten commandments which God had given to His people, was placed within the Ark of the Covenant in the Tabernacle in the wilderness. But God knew that His people could not keep the law, and so He placed the Mercy Seat, the covering of the Ark, on top of the Ark guarded by two cherubim. Mercy covered the law, the mercy of a loving God towards His people. But God said, 'In My new covenant I will put My law *within them*. And they will know me, just as I know them, for the obstacle to their knowing Me will be taken away. I will forgive their iniquity and I will remember their sin no more'. (Jeremiah 31:34).

How precious is the covenant with God into which we have entered through 'My blood of the covenant' as Jesus said. It is an eternal covenant, and by it the God of peace has brought again from the dead that great Shepherd of the sheep, the Lord Jesus, the shepherd and bishop or overseer of our souls, that we may do His will as He works in us that which is well-pleasing in His sight, to whom be glory for ever. (Hebrews 13:20, 1 Peter 2:25).

Matthew 26:29 Until that day

I tell you, said Jesus, I shall not drink again of the fruit of the vine, until that day when I drink it new, with you, in My Father's kingdom.

How solemn has been this precious time of fellowship with His disciples! And as they begin to think of leaving this holy time, Jesus has something more to say; His final Kingdom saying, 'I tell you, I shall not drink again of the fruit of the vine until that day when I drink it new with you in My Father's kingdom'. (verse 29).

The cup has been symbolic of death, of the life of Jesus poured out even while establishing the new covenant of new life in Jesus, His children ransomed, healed, delivered, restored, forgiven. This is the word of *promise*. But Jesus' death is imminent.

As always, Jesus balances for them the horror of what is to happen immediately, with the subsequent blessing of that which is to come, of new life in the kingdom, for Jesus is speaking prospectively of a banquet which is to take place in the kingdom where His Father reigns, and in which both He and they, will share. 'I *will* drink the fruit of the vine *with you* in My Father's kingdom'. (verse 29).

The disciples will continue to drink of the wine together in remembrance of Him, the fruit of the vine, for the fulfilment of all that Jesus has in mind is not yet. But He is looking forward, emphasising that it is His Father's kingdom that He has in view, and that those who follow Him will be with Him at that banquet.

As the bread had symbolised His Body, so the cup, the wine in the cup had symbolised His Blood. This was not the blood of a sacrificial animal as in the Passover, but the blood of *JESUS* which the disciples were symbolically sharing in, the blood which ushered in the New Covenant for the forgiveness of sins. Forgiveness of sins had always been the centre of Jesus' ministry. How often had He said to a suppliant for His healing power, 'Your sins are forgiven you'. The earliest account of His preaching ministry in Matthew 4:17 tells us that Jesus began to preach saying, 'Repent, for the Kingdom of Heaven is at hand', for without repentance there is no forgiveness of sin. The cup, symbolising His blood, throws light on the means whereby forgiveness of sins can take place, the divine authority, $\varepsilon\xi o\upsilon\sigma\iota\alpha$ given to Him. (Matthew 9:6).

These forgiven ones will be the ones who enjoy the final consummation of all things in the coming kingdom. This is not a funeral meal, but a joyful prospect of greater glory to come for the Lord whom they have loved so long, enjoying fellowship with Him and with each other. Jesus says, 'I will drink wine *with you* in the Kingdom.' Just as His emphasis on repentance and forgiveness reflect Matthew 1:21, 'He will save His people from their sins', so His 'with you' reflects Matthew 1:23, 'Immanuel, God with us'. As He was with His disciples in His earthly activity, so He will be with them always, even to the end of the age. (Matthew 28:30).

In this Eucharistic meal, Jesus is combining both of these elements of His life among them, and their future life together as His followers, as they remember Him in the breaking of bread and the taking of the cup, proclaiming His death *until He come,* until the glorious consummation of all things when He is seated at His Father's right hand, enjoying the everlasting banquet with them. These are not abstract deliberations, definitions of biblical texts, but ongoing salvation-giving emphasis to the valid experience available to all who come to Him in faith. The basic conditions of Eucharistic fellowship are written here for all to see.

The outcome is glorious! Jesus is with us and will be to the end. And will we not remember Him when all we have is of His grace, When life itself we take from Him, and have no light but in His face.

And on this joyful note, singing a hymn, they went out to the Mount of Olives. (verse 30).

Matthew 26:31-35. Peter's denial foretold

And when they had sung a hymn, they went out to the Mount of Olives. Then Jesus said to them, 'You will all fall away because of Me this night, for it is written, 'I will strike the shepherd ποιμένας and the sheep of the flock will be scattered. But after I am raised up, I will go before you to Galilee.' (Matthew 26: 30-32).

The disciples had left their temporary home, the upper room where they had shared with Jesus His last precious meal with them, an experience which was to become so important to them in retrospect in the future, when they remembered all that Jesus had said and done at the Last Supper.

They were singing, probably Psalms 113-118., (Greek N.T. p103), as was usual at the end of the Passover meal, making their way to a place called Gethsemane, or 'olive press,' (Matthew 26:36), a place to which Jesus often went with His disciples, (John 18:2), so that they were totally unaware of the significance to which they would attach this place in the future.

They were crossing the Kidron valley, making for the garden, (John 18:1), when Jesus said a troubling thing. 'You will all fall away because of Me this night, for it is written, I will smite the shepherd and the sheep of the flock will be scattered.' He was quoting from Zechariah 13:7, again establishing that what He was about to go through, and indeed, what was going to happen to them, was no accident, no coming together of the malicious conspiracy of the religious leaders, but a fulfilment of God's plan of redemption, prophesied in His word.

The joyful ending of the meal they had enjoyed together had become something extremely serious. Jesus had said, *'This night'*. (verse 31). They knew that terrible things, terrible events were coming, for He had told them so. But so soon? How that must have shocked them.

But the worst was to come. 'You will all fall away because of Me'. (verse 31). The word 'fall away' or 'stumble' is a translation of σκάνδαλο χεσθαι (verses 31, 33) from which we get our word 'scandal'. Luther translated the word as 'offence'. He called it the 'offence of the cross'. 'You will all be offended because of Me this night'. (Luz p388). But Jesus' word is much stronger than that. The crucifixion will be scandalous, the scandal of the cross. For the disciples, already confused and distressed, Jesus' death will become, for them, a scandal. They will be scandalised by it. Indeed, they will all 'fall away' because of Him, but Jesus in His loving mercy tells them that this is not the end. He will be raised up. And He will go before them into Galilee. (verse 32).

Peter cannot focus on the ultimate triumph of Jesus' resurrection. Resurrection is totally outside of his experience. He has never seen anybody resurrected, though he had seen a child raised from the dead by Jesus who would ultimately die again. (Matthew 9:23-25). Though Jesus had repeatedly told them that He would rise from the dead, to the pragmatic Peter, this was an unknown. His thoughts were concentrated more on what Jesus had said about the disciples falling away because of Him.

Peter declared to Him, 'Though they all fall away because of you, I will never fall away.' (verse 33).This was not some kind of hubris. He genuinely believed that his love for His Master was strong enough to overcome any temptation to traduce Him, to deny Him. Jesus was quite straight with him. He knew the heart of Peter. He also knew the wickedness, the brutality which could be inflicted on Peter if even those of the High Priest's household somehow discovered that he had been with Jesus.

Jesus understood all this, and knew that Peter would not be able to stand the test. He said to Peter, *'Amen, truly'* speaking with all the authority of His Father behind what He was saying. 'Truly, I say to you, Peter, this very night, before the cock crows, you will deny Me three times.' (verse 34).

Peter could not, would not, take this in, although Jesus Himself had said these words to him. How could he contemplate denying his Master? It could never be. He said to Jesus, 'Even if I must die with you, I will not deny you.' (verse 35). And in alignment with Peter, also dreading the prospect of denying the One in whom they had placed implicit trust, and had come to love so much, all the disciples said the same thing (verse 35). Jesus knows that because of His suffering and death, because of Him, Jesus says, 'You will stumble and fall, and in the case of Peter, utter words of denial'. But because of His resurrection, their special relationship with Him will be restored. To deny means to disown. They may disown Him, but He will never disown them.

He has spoken of Himself in reference to Zechariah 13:7 *as* the Shepherd and His disciples as the flock. (verse 31). Palestinian shepherds normally walked behind the flock and drove them. Jesus, the Good Shepherd, (John 10:10) is the shepherd who *leads* His flock. Isaiah 40:11 says, 'He will feed His flock like a shepherd. He will gather the lambs in His arms. He will carry them in His bosom and gently lead those that are with young.'

Jesus comforts His disciples as He says, 'I will go before you to Galilee' (verse 32) 'Your risen Lord, *leading* you to the place where I will be with you *forever,* even unto the end of the age' (Matthew 28:20).

Jesus is always in control of events. He is not a helpless victim of circumstances, but knows and accepts the sacrifice He must make in total conformity and accord with His Father. He has revealed this to His disciples, but they are still focussed, understandably, on the suffering which He has told them He must undergo. The present moment carries more weight with them than the future justification, by means of the resurrection, of all that Jesus will endure. Their forsaking of Him (verse 56), known beforehand to Jesus, is not a meaningless abdication of faith, but a serious reaction to an immediate threat. The disciples may even have considered that with their Leader dead, they could somehow cobble together a 'Jesus movement', an attempt to carry out His ethical teaching which they obviously could not do if they themselves came into conflict with the authorities, a cruel and brutal regime which regarded human life cheaply.

But yet in attempting to defend them, we cannot help but be astonished that these men who had lived, loved, talked with Jesus on a daily basis for three years, could deny Him. How reassuring are Paul's words to Timothy in 2 Timothy 2:13. 'If we are faithless, He remains faithful, for He cannot deny Himself.'

Peter and the other disciples needed to know the measure of their own weakness, their own ability or more accurately, their inability to endure. Faced with the ultimate test which anyone who loved Jesus would ever have to face, they nevertheless had a great devotion to Him, and unquestionably were totally sincere in their declaration that they would die rather than deny Him. (verse 35).

But they were still disciples, still learning, and even at the late hour, Jesus was still teaching them. They had to learn that they could never rely on themselves, their own faith, their own love for Him even. Jesus knew that after His death and resurrection His disciples were going to experience great hardship, great persecution, as indeed were all who followed Him. They would constantly fail if they looked only to themselves.

The Apostle Paul speaks powerfully to this. He records that Christ spoke to Him saying, 'My grace is sufficient for you, for *My strength* is made *perfect* in weakness' (2 Corinthians 12:9), and when in prison wrote, 'For His sake, I have suffered the loss of all things, and do count them but refuse that I might know Him, and the power of His resurrection, being made conformable to His death.' (Philippians 3:8, 9, 19).

Soon after Jesus' death and resurrection there was a great persecution against the church in Jerusalem. (Acts 8:1). But by this time, the disciples had received the Holy Spirit (Acts 2), the One whom Jesus had promised would come alongside them, the Paraclete, and when the religious authorities 'beheld the boldness of Peter and John, and perceived that they were uneducated, common men, they took knowledge of them that they had been with Jesus'. (Acts 4:13).

Quite obviously something had happened to Peter and John. Jesus promised that He would send His Holy Spirit to them after He had ascended to His Father. (John 14:26, 28), and this promise had been fulfilled at Pentecost. The Holy Spirit had brought them into such a relationship with their Risen Lord, that they could even say to the High Priest, 'We must obey God rather than men'. (Acts 5:29) Nothing is wasted in the economy of God. He makes even the wrath of man to praise Him. (Psalm 76:10). As a father pities his children, so the Lord pities them that fear Him. For He knows our frame, He remembers that we are dust. And gives us His Holy Spirit to come alongside us. (Psalm 103:13,14). Even some of those who have received His Holy Spirit sometimes fail. But the steadfast love of the Lord never ceases. His mercies never shall come to an end. They are new every morning. Great is your faithfulness, O Lord. (Lamentations 3:22).

Jesus had warned His disciples in John 15:5. 'Without Me you can do nothing. Abide in Me, and I in you. (verse 4). The disciples have to learn the hard way what it means to abide, remain, stay, in Jesus, to abide in His love, just as He had kept His Father's commandments and abided in His love (verse 10). There is no safer place.

Jesus abided in His Father's love by constant and close communion with Him, by referring everything in His life to the will of His Father, by doing always those things that pleased Him. (John 8:29). What a tremendous prospect He was holding out to His disciples! To abide, remain always in the love of God. To know the love flowing between them and their heavenly Father, and between them and one another, like sap flowing in the branches of the Vine. (John 15:1). He is going to send the Comforter to them, (John 14:16, 15:26), the Holy Spirit who will take of Jesus and reveal Him to them. (John 16:14. A.V.). He knows that in the world they will have tribulation, but He says to them, 'Be of good cheer, take heart, I have overcome the world. Let not your heart be troubled, neither let it be afraid. (John 14:27).

Matthew has not recorded all this for us in the way John has. But Matthew's assurance is equally comforting to these distressed disciples. 'I go before you, says Jesus. (verse 32). Even in the most dreadful events yet to come, they may rely on Jesus' words. They are about to witness in the garden of Gethsemane, to which they have now come, the most tremendous spiritual battle the world has ever seen, and their part in it will be shameful, disgraceful indeed, but the end is not yet, but a prelude to something greater.

Matthew 26:36-46. The prayer in Gethsemane

Then Jesus went with them to a place called Gethsemane, and He said to His disciples, 'Sit here, while I go yonder and pray.' And taking with Him Peter and the two sons of Zebedee, He began to be sorrowful and troubled. Then He said to them, 'My soul is very sorrowful, even to death. Remain here and watch with Me. And going a little farther, He fell on His face and prayed, 'My Father, if it be possible, let this cup pass from Me. Nevertheless, not as I will but as Thou wilt.' And He came to His disciples and found them sleeping.

The disciples are still 'with Jesus' (verse 36), and yet how far away from Him they had become. It is now past midnight, the watch of the night between 12 and 3, the time at which the cock will crow. The disciples have had a long day. They are tired and emotionally drained from all that has occurred.

Jesus has one further request to make of them, and He takes Peter and James and John with Him a little apart. 'I am going yonder to pray,' He says to them. 'Will you sit here, watch, keep awake while I spend time with My Father?'

His prayer was very troubled. He began to be very sorrowful as He prayed in an agony that this might pass from Him. Even at this late hour, could His Father change His mind? Could there be some other way of redeeming a people to Himself in holiness and righteousness? Must He go through with it, this act of renunciation of His own life, and especially for that period of time when He who knew no sin would be made sin for the sake of those who loved Him, that they might become the righteousness of God In Him? (2 Corinthians 5:17); that the whole burden of the sin of the world would be laid upon Him that He might bear the iniquity of us all? (Isaiah 53:6) not only being made sin but being forsaken by His Father? (Matthew 27:46).

Nevertheless, Jesus says, 'Not as I will but as Thou wilt' (Matthew 26: 39)

Though physically only a short distance away from Jesus, Peter, James and John were an eternity away. Huddled up in their cloaks to keep warm, and resting, lying with their backs against a rock or the trunk of an olive tree, they had absolutely no conception of the agony He was going through. He came to the disciples and found them sleeping (verse 40).

As Jesus approached them, Peter looked up at Him as He said to Peter, 'Could you not watch with Me one hour? Watch and pray that you may not enter into temptation: the spirit indeed is willing, but the flesh is weak'. (verse 41).

Jesus had recommended that they sit. 'Sit here,' He said, 'while I go yonder and pray' (verse 36). But they were lying down, sleeping. How often our posture indicates what is going on in our hearts. 'The flesh is weak,' says Jesus (verse 41). They had augmented the sorrow which Jesus had as He contemplated the events of the next few hours, with the sorrow He felt that they could not watch with Him for one hour (verse 40). Such was His sorrow and distress that He had fallen on His face as He prayed to His Father (verse 39), a Man of sorrows and acquainted with grief. (Isaiah 53:3).

Would He have been a little less sorrowful if He had been aware that His disciples were at least concerned, at least awake and watching with Him, even though they could not possibly have known even a little of the eternal, cosmic significance of what He was about to do. Yet eternally and cosmically significant though it was, three times He uses that precious title for God, 'My Father'. (verses 39, 42, 44). This was not the imposition of the will of a mighty, all-powerful God on the will of a humble servant. Jesus had indeed taken on the form of a servant for the benefit of the Incarnation, (Philippians 2:7), but His precious relationship as Son to His Father was never more precious than now. There was a sense in which He never had to declare His

Sonship of God. Everything He said and did proclaimed it more loudly than any words He could utter. But now, in this last extremity, it is the only word He has for God. 'My Father', if it be possible, *let this cup pass from Me.* (verse 39).

For the second time He went away and prayed, 'My Father, if this cannot pass away unless I drink it, Thy will be done' (verse 42). And again He came and found them sleeping, for their eyes were heavy. (verse 43). He went away the third time, saying the same words. Then He came to the disciples and said to them, 'Are you still sleeping? and taking your rest?'(verse 45). Jesus' second and third prayer echo the first.

This cup which He is about to drink is necessary for the salvation of the world. Unless He drinks it, (verse 42), the future of the whole human race is in jeopardy. We read in John 3:16 that God so loved the world, that He gave His only Son. That world is condemned to live forever in disobedience to the will of God, in having no ability to approach a Holy God, of death without hope, of life without peace, if Jesus does not drink of that cup.

Jesus could have died normally and gone straight to His Father. He said He had power to lay His life down and He had power to take it again. This He had received from His Father (John 10:18). There was no compulsion from His Father to go to the Cross. God was not insisting on the sacrifice. But Jesus said, 'I and My Father are One' (John 10:30). One in loving purpose, in perfect harmony as they contemplated the need of men and women for love, for forgiveness, for life, abundant eternal life. (John 10:10) which could only be supplied to men and women on the basis of the sacrifice which Jesus was about to make.

Jesus knew the cost of the cross. He said, 'Now is my soul troubled. And what shall I say? "Father, save Me from this hour"? No, for this purpose I have come to this hour. Father, glorify Thy Name.' (John 12:27, 28). Then a voice came from heaven 'I have glorified it and I will glorify it again'. The crowd standing by heard it and said that it had thundered. It was indeed the thunderous word of God, validating and endorsing and sharing with His Son all that He was going through.

He chose to go His Father's way, the way of His love for the whole world, (John 3:16), to bear in His own Body on the Tree the sins of the world, (1 Peter 2:24) that men and women might die to sin and live to righteousness. By His wounds we have been healed.

There is a sense in which Gethsemane was the hardest part for Jesus. It was the point of no return. It was certainly excruciating as He contemplated what He was determined to do for love of His Father, and love for the whole of mankind. What came afterwards, Jesus had already contemplated, accepted, and settled in His mind, because He knew that His Father knew best, and that there was no other way.

Hebrews 12:2 says that for the joy that was set before Him He endured the Cross, despising the shame, and the joy that was set before Him was that He would bring many sons to glory (Hebrews 2:10), as the author of their salvation. (Hebrews 2:10 A.V.). In Gethsemane, Jesus could have decided not to go through with the terrible experience of taking upon Himself the sins of the whole world. But His love for His Father, and His love for men and women lost in sin, walking in darkness and in the shadow of death, caused Him to go that way for us. The spiritual battle was cosmic in its outworking, and He went through it alone.

It was truly said of Peter, and indeed could be said of all the disciples, 'the spirit is willing but the flesh is weak'. (verse 41). Jesus knew how willing they were, but how much they missed by allowing the weakness of the flesh, the needs of the human body, to overtake His desire for them. He wanted them to understand more perfectly that this was not ordinary prayer, the constant referral of all things to His Father, but the pouring out of His heart and soul in utter subjection, in total conformity with God's purpose, and in absolute confidence that He was at the focal point of history.

The cross of the Lord Jesus looked back to all God's dealings with men and women since the dawn of time, and looked forward to all God's dealings with them in the time to come, until the creation of a new heaven and a new earth. So perhaps it was appropriate that this amazing giving of Himself up to His Father's will should be a private, alone-time with His Father, for no-one, not even the disciples, could enter even a little into the tremendous spiritual battle for the whole world which was going on in a garden outside Jerusalem in a place called Gethsemane.

Because Jesus was the Son of God, the salvation of the world could only be accomplished through Him. Because He was also the Son of Man, He trembles when faced with suffering and death. *As to His divinity, He was the Son of God. As to His humanity, He was the Lamb of God, who takes away the sin of the world.* Jesus, in Gethsemane.

His prayer was not in vain. Though God did not 'save him from death,' (Hebrews 5:7). Jesus was heard for His godly fear, His reverence and awe and respect for the will of His Father.

God did not abandon Him in the garden. He heard the cry of His beloved Son, and Jesus knew that He had been heard. At the grave of Lazarus, He had cried, 'Father, I thank Thee that Thou had heard Me. I knew that Thou hearest Me always.' (John 11:41). And having completed His prayerful submission to His Father with strong crying and tears, (Hebrews 5:7 A.V.), He arose from the ground and came to the disciples and said, 'Are you still sleeping and taking your rest? Behold, the hour is at hand, and the Son of Man is betrayed into the hands of sinners. Rise, let us be going. Behold, my betrayer is at hand. (Matthew 26:45,46). Strengthened and comforted by His trust in His Father, Jesus says, 'Father, the hour is come. Glorify Thy son that the son may glorify Thee.' (John 17:1)

And in the strength of that commitment, and in the knowledge of the glory to come for His Father, He went forth to meet His betrayer.

Matthew 26:47-56. The betrayal and arrest of Jesus

Then He came to the disciples and said to them, 'Are you still sleeping and taking your rest? Behold, the hour is at hand, and the Son of Man is betrayed into the hands of sinners.' Rise, let us be going. See, behold, My betrayer is at hand.

While He was yet speaking, Judas came, one of the twelve, and with him a great crowd with swords and clubs, from the chief priests and elders of the people. (Matthew 26: 47)

Jesus had passed through a time of agony, but He had come through into a strong place. There was a steadfastness in His voice as He said to His disciples, 'Behold, the hour is at hand. Behold, the Son of Man is betrayed. Rise, come with Me,' He says this as Judas approaches Him. He sees the group of people with Judas, a crowd with swords and clubs. Gundry p.537 suggests that these may have been people camping out on the Mount of Olives during the feast of Unleavened Bread. There were also the chief priests and elders of the people. Scribes are not mentioned, indicating that these people coming towards im, were acting in a political rather than religious capacity.

But Jesus sees only Judas.

With sorrow in His heart, He says. Behold, My betrayer is at hand. This one individual, whom He had loved and spoken with and shared His life with. And He reproached him with the word 'Friend'.

Amongst all these people, it was important that Judas should have a pre-arranged signal, so that no mistake could be made as to which of these men was the one they sought when they came to arrest Him. The signal was a kiss, often given, not as a gesture of affection, but as a salutation of honour, or sometimes in Jewish culture, of family solidarity. Judas' greeting, 'Hail, Master!' (or literally Rabbi) confirms this. Judas came up to Jesus and kissed Him. His words to Judas were so gracious. There was no condemnation, no questioning of his loyalty, but only the question, 'Friend, why are you here?' (verse 50), or an alternative translation, 'Friend, do that for which you have come.'

Twice Jesus had used the word 'behold' to His disciples. 'Behold, the hour is at hand;' 'Behold My betrayer is at hand.' Behold' means more than just 'look'. It means take special notice, something important is going on. Jesus was not altogether unaware of the approaching crowd, and His 'behold' heightened His emphasis on its constituent members, so that the disciples knew that their own people, the people of Israel, were rejecting Him, just as those of the occupying power, the Gentiles, were about to reject Him. He was indeed despised and rejected of all men, a Man of sorrows and acquainted with grief. (Isaiah 53:3).

But still, His present thought was of Judas. Could not at least some of the blame be on the shoulders of those who had covenanted with Judas for thirty pieces of silver if he would betray Jesus to them? Jesus' compassion was boundless.

At the same time, all had rejected Him and were therefore in rebellion against God, not only the ordinary people, but the religious authorities. All needed to be redeemed. His sacrifice was for all. To as many as received Him, He gave the right to become children of God, even to them who believed on His Name (John 1:12 A.V.).

And having seen the signal given by Judas, the kiss which betrayed Him to them, the chief priests and elders of the people, totally complicit in their rejection of Him, came up to Him and laid hands on Him and seized Him. (verse 50). There was a temple guard attached to the temple in Jerusalem; under the auspices of the Sanhedrin, suggesting some formality in the arrest of Jesus. John describes them as 'officers of the chief priests'. (John 18:3).

Confronted with this crowd of people, one of those who were with Jesus stretched out his hand and struck the slave of the high priest and cut off his ear. (verse 51). John informs us that this perpetrator was Simon Peter, and that the slave's name was Malchus. (John 18:10). Luke the beloved physician tells us that Jesus 'immediately touched his ear and healed him'. (Luke 22:51). According to John 18:16, John was familiar with the High Priest's household., and would no doubt have known the name of Malchus the slave.

Peter's violent reaction however, draws a rebuke from Jesus, 'Put up your sword into its place, for all who take the sword will perish by the sword. Do you think that I cannot appeal to My Father, and that He will at once send Me twelve legions of angels? But how then shall the scriptures be fulfilled, that it must be so? (Matthew 26:52,53).

John's description bears the same message. Though he omits the saying of Jesus about the support of the angels which Jesus could ask of His Father, John's gospel says, 'Put your sword into its sheath.The cup which My Father has given Me, shall I not drink it?' (John 18:11).

Jesus has entered into a state of utter defencelessness and rejection of violence because of His trust in His Father and He recommends the same to His disciples and Peter; for Him and them, radical, uncompromising trust in God. The importance of 12 legions of angels (a legion is 6,000) cannot compare with one trustful heart, determined on accepting the will of God in absolute obedience.

But it does highlight for the disciples that Jesus is irrefutably the Son of God, for which of them – or us, could ask, and receive, such intervention? Though, or because, He was the Son of God, He was obedient to His Father's will. He would not go against that will, with or without the help of the angelic host. The will of God, revealed throughout scripture which had arrived at this point of culmination, was paramount; the fulfilment of the purpose of Father, Son and Holy Spirit.

Indeed, the hour had come (verse 45), as Jesus had said, and He had entered fully into that hour. And at that hour, Jesus challenges the crowd. 'Why did you not seize Me when I sat day by day teaching in the temple?' (verse 55). He did not go to the temple as a robber, for them they would have been justified in arresting Him, but He went as a Rabbi. As a Rabbi, He had taught them much. He had taught them their scriptures, and He had taught them that the scriptures of the prophets must be fulfilled. (verse 56). Why did they want to do Him harm? They had not understood that the whole history of Jesus from beginning to end was the fulfilment of prophecy.

The crowds did not rise to the challenge.

But *all* the disciples πάντες μαθηταί forsook Him and fled. (verse 26). Jesus must suffer alone. The horror of this night has been too much for the disciples. The shepherd has now been smitten and the sheep scattered, the natural consequence of all that has happened. (26:31).

And in spite of everything, Jesus is still Master of the event, the Sovereign Lord in control. Sovereign in relation to Judas, sovereign in relation to the intentional zeal of His disciples, as they seek to defend Him with swords, sovereign in relation to the men armed with swords and clubs who would arrest Him, sovereign in trust in God, in the divine power which He could command at will and refuses to do so.

The majestic figure of Jesus commands the narrative, the obedient Son of God about to give His life as a ransom for many. (Matthew 20:28; Isaiah 53:10)

Matthew 26:57-66. Jesus before the Sanhedrin

Then those who had seized Jesus led Him to Caiaphas the high priest, where the scribes and the elders had gathered. But Peter followed Him at a distance as far as the courtyard of the High Priest, and going inside he sat with the guards to see the end. Now the chief priests and the whole council sought false testimony against Jesus that they might put Him to death, but they found none, though many false witnesses came forward.

Now the temple guard seized Jesus and led Him away. At this stage, there was no violence against Jesus for they were taking Him for what they assumed to be a formal trial. This appeared to have been decided by the religious authorities to be convened at the house of Caiaphas the High Priest, and it is remarkable that the scribes and elders had already gathered, (verse 59), possibly on the understanding that Judas' identification of Jesus would be certain, and that there would be little or no resistance from the followers of Jesus, which was indeed the case. Though 'all the disciples forsook Him and fled', (verse 56), Peter fled only as far as the courtyard of the High Priest's house, and going inside he sat with the guards, believing this to be *'the end'.* (verse 58).

The 'whole council' (verse 59) of the Sanhedrin comprised the elders, the chief priests, (with former chief priests and their families) and the scribes who were mostly of the Pharisaic party though some were Sadducees.

The Sanhedrin numbered 71 members, but required only 23 to form a quorum. It seems improbable that all 71 members would be available in the middle of Passover night, a Passover which they would have shared with their families, and which in any case would be illegal according to Jewish law, for a trial had to take place in daylight hours, and to be in session for two days, together with the *private* interrogation of witnesses.

The trial before the Sanhedrin was not legal by Jewish standards, and the public testimony against Jesus inadmissible especially on a capital charge, for the Council was determined on finding Jesus guilty of blasphemy, a capital offence.

Had the witnesses been suborned earlier? To be on standby for the trial to come? This too was a travesty of Jewish law, for the Jewish juridical system was very clear about the assessing of evidence against the accused.

In this trial of Jesus, the court of judgement acts both as prosecutor and judge, contrary to normal Jewish legal practice. Most trials would have been conducted against people like Barabbas, convicted of robbery and murder, or of even relatively minor infringement of the law. In Matthew 26:57, it was important that the scribes should be present at this trial, for the issues were theological. Jesus was going to be tried on the grounds of His Messiahship and divine Sonship, that is, according to their assessment of Him, as a blasphemer. But there is no mention of these charges after verse 56, and the reference to the chief priests drops out after verse 59, for it is obvious that it is Caiaphas who is being highlighted as the prosecutor, indeed, the enemy, of Jesus. Yet though Caiaphas Is the chief prosecutor, he is not alone, for in verse 59 it is the whole council who seek false testimony against Jesus, that they might put Him to death.

With all the many trials in which Caiaphas had taken part, he had never seen an accused person like Jesus. Jesus stood quietly before him as witness after witness came forward with their false testimony that they might put Him to death. (verse 59). But none of this false testimony could stand up in this false court. Eventually, 'at last' (verse 60), two witnesses came forward and said, 'This fellow said, "I am able to destroy the temple of God and to build it in three days."'

This was indeed partly true. According to John 2:19 Jesus had said something like that, but of course they had interpreted His saying literally, when He had intended it allegorically. John tells us that Jesus meant it allegorically, that He was telling them that His Body was the temple of God, the temple in which God dwelt, and that it would be destroyed by the Jews whose temple in Jerusalem He had just cleansed, but that in three days, the temple of His Body would be resurrected. 'When He was raised from the dead, His disciples remembered that He had said this.' (John 2:22). The temple of which He spoke was His Body.

The distorted truth of these witnesses was more damaging than the testimony which was actually false. The Sanhedrin had sought false testimony and found it to be true, but it was a compromised truth. Nevertheless, it was sufficiently serious to give a reason for putting Jesus to death, though this was going to be a problem, for under Roman occupation they had no right of execution, as John states in 18:31. The Jews said to Pilate, 'It is not lawful for us to put any man to death.' This was to show by what death Jesus was to die, for under Jewish law, death for the crime of blasphemy would have been by stoning. Under Roman law, death was by crucifixion for rebellion and revolt against the state.

Caiaphas the High Priest was satisfied that these two witnesses had made the case against Jesus. He stood up and said to Jesus, 'Have you no answer to make to these men? What is it that these men testify against you?' (verse 62).

The witnesses had said of the words of Jesus, 'I am able, I have the power to destroy the temple of God'. (verse 61). This Caiaphas chose to understand as a claim that Jesus was setting up in opposition to God, that Jesus believed He could destroy God's temple. There was indeed some opposition on the part of Jesus to what the temple in Jerusalem had become, which was why He had just cleansed it, quite possibly for the second time. His Father had wanted the temple to be a house of prayer for all nations, but they had made it a den of robbers. (Matthew 21:13; Isaiah 56:7; Jeremiah 7:11).

Generally speaking, people expect that things are as they are, and will not change. Change involves adjustment and they prefer the stability of circumstances remaining unchangeable. These Jewish people had no idea of the dreadful changes that would be coming upon them and their city, when Vespasian and Titus razed it almost to the ground, when their temple was destroyed. They could not foresee this. Neither could they believe that when this came to pass in A.D. 70, the only temple to which they could run and hide was the temple that was Jesus, resurrected and glorified.

This was 40 years into the future, but many of them would still be alive at that time. And they did not need to wait that long to find that reassurance in Jesus, for His hands were always outstretched to those who recognised in Him the answer to all their needs of forgiveness, of holiness apart from the law, of peace in their hearts.

It was recorded for us only once, but it was the constant cry from the heart of Jesus, 'Come unto Me, all you who are weary and heavy laden and I will give you rest. Take my yoke upon you, and learn of Me, for I am meek and lowly of heart and you shall find unto your souls'. (Matthew 11:28).

This important man, Caiaphas who was standing before Jesus, like Gallio, cared for none of these things, (Acts 18:7), not for Jesus' ministry of healing of which he must have heard, nor of the invitation to come to Him which Jesus held out to all. And yet prophetically, as the High Priest that year, he had said, 'It is expedient for you that One Man should die for the nation and that the whole nation should not perish. (John 11:50). John's editorial comment was that Caiaphas did not say this of his own accord, but being High Priest he prophesied that Jesus should die for the nation, and not for the nation only, but to gather into one the children of God who are scattered abroad. (John 11:52).

This same Caiaphas now had this same Jesus of John 11:50 in front of him, and who, in spite of his questioning of Him, remained silent. If Jesus had attempted to explain to him the correct interpretation of the words reported by the false witness, would Caiaphas have responded? It seems unlikely.

But then Caiaphas did an unforgivable thing. He adjured Jesus, he wanted Him to swear an oath, that He was indeed the Christ, the Son of the living God (verse 63); to swear an oath by the living God. In His sermon on the mount, Jesus had prohibited swearing (Matthew 5:33-37). ὅλως! Do not! Swear not at all!

Caiaphas is tempting Jesus to swear by the living God. (verse 63). This Jesus could not do. No one can have direct knowledge of God's being and nature, though He reveals much of Himself to us. To use the divine Name as an oath reduces God to human level and in effect desecrates and defiles His Name and His Nature.

In rabbinical Judaism, they made 'a fence around the Torah', attempting to prevent the misuse of the divine Name, and especially its misuse in false or superfluous oaths, according to the 3rd commandment, 'You shall not take the name of the Lord in vain, for the Lord will not hold him guiltless, who takes His Name in vain.' (Exodus 20:7). But Jesus goes further than the false or superfluous. He says, *'Swear not at all'* (Matthew 5:35 A.V.). Even 'harmless' oaths are included in the prohibition for they may be used deceitfully, to imply a constancy or rightness of conduct which is not realised, and to use the name of God to support that implication is desecration indeed.

In addition, oaths contradict the concept of human integrity. The person who speaks, speaks on the grounds that what he or she speaks is completely reliable and does not need to be confirmed by another authority. But there are those who would attempt to substantiate that authority by using the Name of God. The oath substantiates the expectation that what is said is truthful.

Jesus does not expect that we should need to tell the truth by a formula, that by attuning one's words to a formula guarantees its truthfulness. In fact, frequent swearing may include the listener to the conclusion that this person is untrustworthy. But there is a yet more important reason for not using oaths.

It assumes that God is at our disposal.

How can we even think this?

In swearing, we are not taking account of the will of God. There is an assumption of the Name and by extension the character of Almighty God, which could be totally antithetical to what we are proposing. Jesus is concerned with the sanctification of God's name, of His majesty, of His holiness. Caiaphas is tempting Him to swear by the life of the Living God. If anyone was more competent, or worthy of using God in this way, it would have been His Son who lived in constant fellowship with Him. But Jesus could only say in reply to Caiaphas, *'You have said so'* (verse 64) putting the responsibility back, in effect, on Caiaphas, σύ εἶπας, you have said, leaving the responsibility for Caiaphas' statement with him, without contesting the truth.

But, Jesus says to Caiaphas, you have missed a vital point here.

It is quite probable that none of the religious leaders had been present when Jesus had said to His disciples in Matthew 16:27, that, 'The Son of Man would come with His angels in the glory of the Father' or in Matthew 24:30 when He said that the sign of the Son of Man would appear in heaven, and that all the tribes of the earth will mourn as they see Him coming on the clouds of heaven with power and great glory.

Jesus was always consistent when speaking of that which was to come. Could something of what He had said been reported back to the Sanhedrin? Here and now, before Caiaphas, Jesus is reaffirming the future as He answered Caiaphas in these prophetic words, 'I tell you, hereafter you will see the Son of Man seated at the right hand of power, and coming on the clouds of heaven.' (Matthew 26:64).

This was indeed blasphemy according to Caiaphas. Caiaphas' familiarity with the Hebrew scriptures would compel him to recognise the reference by Jesus to Psalm 110:1 and Daniel 7:13,14., and to understand that Jesus was stating that He was indeed the Son of Man.

Psalm 110:1 declares, 'The Lord said unto my Lord, sit at My right hand till I make your enemies your footstool'. And Daniel 7:13, 'I saw in the night visions, and behold with the clouds of heaven there came One like a Son of Man, and He came to the Ancient of Days, and was presented before Him.'

Jesus' statement was indeed blasphemy if what He was claiming was not true. Caiaphas would know that Jesus was claiming to be the Son of God, the Messiah. He had said to Jesus, 'Are you the Christ? The Son of God?' (verse 63). Jesus, knowing that if He said 'No,' there could be no real change against Him, had yet given an emphatic 'Yes'. Yes, He was the Christ, the Messiah foretold in those scriptures and others. Yes, He will be seated at the right hand of God and coming in the clouds of heaven, and Caiaphas would see that. Yes, He was truly God and truly Man. He did not need to use an oath to express what was so authoritative.

Caiaphas had the immediate reaction common to all who heard such blasphemy. *He rent his clothes (verse 65)*. Not only in His claim to being the Messiah as foretold in scripture but also in His claim to deity, Caiaphas was convinced of His blasphemy. For though He used His favourite redemptive definition of Himself as Son of Man, it is obvious from Daniel 7:13 that the Son of Man is divine. And in any case, Caiaphas needed no further excuse or reason for his decision to convict Jesus of the guilt of blasphemy.

It is not made clear in the text whether Caiaphas was wearing his ordinary clothes, or whether, since this was a formal trial, he would be wearing his official high priestly robes. But it has been suggested that as this was an official trial, and he was performing his official function, he would have been appropriately dressed in his official robes; and that the tearing of them was a sign similar to that of the tearing of the curtain in the temple as Jesus died. This was a sign of the end of the temple cult and the old covenant, and that the future High Priest would be after the order of Melchizedek, as Psalm 110:4 had prophesied. 'The Lord has sworn and will not change His mind. You are a priest forever after the order of Melchizedek,' the High Priest who is without beginning of days or end of life, the eternal One (Hebrews 7:3; 6:20), who has become a Priest by the power of an indestructible life, (Hebrew 7:16). *JESUS,* the surety, the guarantor of the new and better covenant. (Hebrews 7:22).

Without realising it, Caiaphas had proclaimed that his priesthood was at an end. Under the new covenant, we have a new and different High Priest, who is able to save to the uttermost those who come unto God by Him, seeing He ever lives to make intercession for them. (Hebrews 7:25 A.V.).

Jesus quietly stands before Caiaphas seeking to win him over with His silence and with His love. Paradoxically, He is the Judge in this situation; the reversal of the situation is obvious. But His love for Caiphas is dangerous. It causes Caiaphas to make distinctions, to decide. Can this be He? The One foretold? To the end of his life, Caiaphas is going to wonder. Who was this man who stood before him? Yet, as the high priest, he had to give an immediate verdict. 'You have heard His blasphemy. What need have we of further witnesses? (verse 65). And the other members of the Sanhedrin were unanimous. They answered, 'He is worthy of death' (verse 66). He deserves death.

Matthew 26:67-68. The first mistreatment of Jesus

Then they spat in His face and struck Him, and some slapped Him, saying, 'Prophesy to us, you Christ! Who is it that struck you?'

Matthew describes a scene of absolute brutality. The whole issue in the trial had been the High Priest's question about the Son of God. It may be that the perpetrators of this abuse had regarded this as a purely political question, and since He had answered the question in the affirmative, 'You have said so,' as confirmation that He was indeed claiming to be the Son of God. It may be that that in itself constituted the understanding that He had to be turned over to the Roman authorities as a political insurgent. This may agree with Pilate's political question in Matthew 27:11, Mark 15:2. 'Are you the King of the Jews?' But not with the theological issue of His being convicted of blasphemy. In cases of blasphemy, the divine Name must be said clearly according to their law, and Jesus had carefully used the title, 'Power' to substitute for 'God'. 'You will see the Son of Man seated at the right hand of Power' (verse 64).

But there was going to be no favourable outcome for Jesus in this false trial. Jesus was to be taken immediately to the Roman governor.

But first, they spit in His face and hit Him with their fists, and some slapped Him, saying to Him, 'Prophesy to us, Christ, who is hitting you?' (verse 67, literal translation, Luz p. 447). Were they hoping that by joining in their brutish game, He would prophesy, and so prove to be the Messiah, or were they trying to convince themselves that He was a fraud, or that he was claiming to be someone He was not.

There is an echo here of one of the servant songs of Isaiah. 'I gave My back to the smiters, and My cheeks to those who pulled out the beard. I hid not My face from shame and spitting.For the Lord God helps Me, therefore I have not been confounded, therefore I have set My face as a flint, and I know I shall not be ashamed'. (Isaiah 50:6). Ironically, scornfully, His abusers say, 'Prophesy to us, O Christ! They are ridiculing His claim to be the Messiah with prophetic gifts. They do not refer to Him as Son of Man. This is a title He has always kept for Himself, and generally in His later ministry, only when speaking with His disciples.

To spit in someone's face is an expression of the deepest contempt. Perhaps they believed that subjecting Him to blows and indignities would prove the hollowness of His claim to be Messiah, and perhaps that the end justified the means (which it seldom does).

These are solemn, experienced, leaders of the people, with accompanying gravitas, representing God to His people. It is inconceivable that they should behave in this way, except that they see Jesus as being so radically opposed to everything they stood for, everything they believed, their whole life's purpose. 'Who is it that struck you?' they cry in childish contempt, (verse 68), as if playing a childhood game, reminding us of the question at the table of the Last Supper. 'Lord, is it I?' But in this case, the difference is obvious. They are all guilty. Guilty of rejecting Him who came to save them. They had become the assailants of One who would have gathered them in His bosom and gently led them like a shepherd. (Isaiah 40:11) They did not recognise the one whom they diligently worshipped day and night in His temple. To them He was an Unknown God.

Worship is the realistic awareness and reverence for who God is, someone whom we know to be altogether worthy, totally different from us, beautiful, good, excellent. We esteem Him for His great goodness. We bow ourselves down to Him and still feel we have not begun to worship. but we believe our effort to do so is precious to God.

They thought to challenge Jesus. But He was the One who challenged them.

Matthew 26:69-75. Peter's denial of Jesus

Now Peter was sitting outside in the courtyard. And a maid came up to him, and said, 'You also were with Jesus the Galilean.' But he denied it before them all, saying, 'I do not know what you mean.' And when he went out to the porch, another maid saw him and she said to the bystanders, 'This man was with Jesus of Nazareth.' And again he denied it with an oath. 'I do not know the man.' After a little while the bystanders came up and said to Peter, 'Certainly you are also one of them, for your accent betrays you.' Then he began to invoke a curse on himself and to swear, 'I do not know the man.' And immediately the cock crowed.

And Peter remembered the saying of Jesus, 'Before the cock crows, you will deny Me three times.' And he went out and wept bitterly.

This gentle but powerful narrative shows us three things: Peter was not the rock on which Jesus would build His church. The rock was the statement which Peter made at Caesarea Philippi, 'You are the Christ, the Son of the living God.' (Matthew 16:16).

Jesus is the Rock. (1 Corinthians 10:4). The Rock was Christ. (Ephesians 2:19, 20).

Secondly, that however destructively, inexcusably we have sinned, there is always an opportunity for repentance, and consequently, ultimately, for forgiveness, (John 21:15-19). Jesus recommisions Peter by the lakeside after His resurrection and gives him a second invitation to 'Follow Me.'

Thirdly, that there is, or should be, that about a follower of Jesus which betrays that he or she has been with Him. The A.V. translation has, 'Surely thou art also one of them, for your speech *betrayeth* thee'. (verse 73). They were unsure whether Peter had been with Jesus the Galilean (verse 69), or with Jesus of Nazareth (verse 7), unsure how to describe Him. But they knew he had been with Jesus. Surely your speech betrays you. You have been with Jesus.

The first time Peter was accused of having been with Jesus was by a maid as he sat outside the high priest's palace. Though it was springtime, a welcome fire was burning in the courtyard, according to Luke 22:55, and Peter sat among them. The light from the fire enabled the maid to see him clearly. 'You were with Him,' she said. And getting up and moving towards the gateway, or the porch, he said, 'I do not know what you mean'. (verse 30).

Perhaps here, in the gateway (Mark 14:68), or in the porch (Matthew 26:71), Peter could have a direct line of vision of the trial. But he couldn't get away from his accusers.

Another maid (verse 71) saw him standing in the porch and said 'to the bystanders', not to Peter directly, but with supreme confidence, 'This man was with Jesus of Nazareth.' She was the second witness, by which every word had to be established according to Deuteronomy 19:15. And again Peter denied it with an oath, 'I do not know the man!' (verse 72).

In a sense, that was true. His knowledge of Jesus was real, but imperfect. Who has known the mind of the Lord? Or who has been His counsellor? (Romans 11:34). But yet he knew Him sufficiently well to have declared that though all denied Him, he would not. (Matthew 26:35). He was not only denying Jesus, he was also denying his own ability to be constant to what he himself had declared. 'Even if I must die with you, I will not deny you.' This was self-revelation of a particularly fundamental kind. He was capable of making the grand gesture, but when the test came, when the moment of reality struck, he was unable to be true to what he had sincerely believed himself able to do.

After a little while, Matthew tells us, or after an interval of about an hour according to Luke 22:59, one of the bystanders came up to Peter and said, 'Certainly you are also one of them, for your accent, your speech betrays you'. (Matthew 26:75). He was recognised as being from Galilee, though it is by no means certain that simply being from Galilee equated with being a disciple of Jesus.

But there was something about Peter that suggested that he had been with Jesus, and this recognition, instead of causing Peter to retract all his former statements, drove him to an extremity. He began to invoke a curse on himself and to swear saying, 'I do not know the man' (verse 74).

And while he was speaking, the cock crowed.

Somehow, Luke tells us, Jesus was in Peter's direct line of vision.

And the Lord turned, and looked on Peter. (Luke 22:61).

How intense, how loving, that look must have been. The look of Jesus towards His loving companion, with whom He had shared so much, on the storm tossed sea, on the mountain where He had been transfigured, on long walks along dusty roads, as He healed many and fed many.

And Peter remembered the word of the Lord, how He had said to him, 'Before the cock crows, you will deny Me three times. And he went out and wept bitterly' (verse 75).

Peter had gone from being in the courtyard by the fire, to the porch, to being outside, the longest journey of his life.

From then on, with the bitter tears running down his face, we read nothing of him throughout the rest of Matthew's passion narrative. He felt himself to be 'out' indeed. He had denied his Lord, first by claiming ignorance of Him (verse 70), then by denying that he had been with Him (verse 72), and then for the third time, in front of all those standing by, he curses and swears, 'I do not know the man' (verse 74).

Judas had abandoned Jesus. The disciples had run away, and now Peter, who had become the representative disciple, the one whom Jesus had called first in Matthew 4:18, 20 and 10:2, the one who had at least 'followed' Jesus, to the courtyard, (verse 58) even though it was at a distance, had now denied Him.

The work of redemption which He was now to undertake, lay entirely in the hands, feet, side and Spirit of the Lord Jesus. He had no human companion with Him.

But tears may have a rehabilitating purpose. It was fear that caused Peter to deny his Lord. Suppose the authorities had discovered that he had been with Jesus, an accessory to the crime of blasphemy? The one who was even at this very moment being tried by the highest Jewish court in the land, the Sanhedrin? What would happen to Peter? Careless talk costs lives. The careless talk of these maidservants and the repetition of what they had said to the bystanders, amongst whom could certainly be servants of the high priest (John 18:26), or his officers, could be dangerous.

The accusation against Peter has become public. It was bad enough when he was accused privately by the first maidservant. Peter wanted at all costs to prevent it becoming public, but the exposure of him has gone too far. The people standing around say, 'Certainly, you are one of them' [verse 73). They know him by his speech.

He becomes completely distraught. He is beside himself. Perhaps he does not entirely know what he is saying. Does he still belong to Christ, or not? The conflict going on inside his breast is unsupportable.

Suddenly, the cock crows. And Peter remembers Jesus. He remembers the words that Jesus spoke to him that he would deny Him, but most of all he remembers *Him*. Jesus, whom he loved so much. Out he goes, into the dark, out into a place of utter darkness for him, full of remorse, weeping bitterly.

Matthew does not mention him again until 28:16-20, but he is there, on the mountain to which Jesus had directed them, there with the other 10 disciples. He was there for their commissioning by Jesus to go and make disciples of all nations, he was there to receive the promise, 'Lo I am with you always, even to the end of the world.'

Peter had left the courtyard, the place of temptation to sin, where he had been among the crowd of those waiting to hear, or perhaps see, the humiliation of Jesus, if it was only from a distance. He had gone out to be alone with his repentance, his grief. Peter cannot stay among people who care so little for truth and justice, but only for a sadistic enjoyment of another person's suffering, for surely, if Peter could look into the court where the trial of Jesus was taking place, even as Jesus could look out, these 'bystanders' could do the same.

Peter goes out, full of fear, and probably not even fully aware of what he was doing through his tears. But Peter had gone out with the remembrance of Jesus, of His grace, of His love.

In Luke, we have a record of the assurance that Jesus gave to Peter. 'I have prayed for you, that your faith fail not'. (Luke 22:32). The power of the grace of the Lord Jesus and His prayer for Peter is more powerful than the deepest failure.

Peter did not take that failure lightly, but he was forever a changed man. The story of Peter is a story of hope. It was Peter, standing up with the eleven on the Day of Pentecost who spoke publicly to the crowds about the purpose of the coming of the Holy Spirit to glorify Jesus, to testify that He had been exalted to the right hand of God after His resurrection, and that God had made Him both Lord and Christ, this One whom they had crucified. Because of Him, they could repent, be baptised and receive the forgiveness of sins, and receive the gift of the Holy Spirit.

Peter was an apostle, one sent out by His Lord in His service. (Matthew 10:2). He became a man of God. And above all, he became a shepherd. He writes as a 'fellow elder' in the church, as one who is 'tending the flock of God'. (1 Peter 5:1,2). He had learned the hard way how to be compassionate and caring for these sheep, to stand with them in their suffering, (1 Peter 4:12,19), fully aware that, 'after they have suffered a little while, the *God of all grace will Himself restore, establish and strengthen you*'. (1 Peter 5:10). For has he not experienced the same? He knows from personal experience how great and wonderful that restoration can be, and that even in this, God may be glorified (1 Peter 4:11).

Matthew Chapter 27

Matthew 27:1-27. Jesus brought before Pilate

When morning came, all the chief priests and the elders of the people took counsel against Jesus to put Him to death. And they bound Him and led Him away and delivered Him to Pilate the governor. (Matthew 27:1-2)

Was this a second meeting of the Sanhedrin, or a continuation of what had gone before? The cock had crowed, a new day had begun.

Whetherthis was a continuation of the trial under Caiaphas or a second session which began at daybreak is not immediately obvious. It is noteworthy however, that *all* the chief priests and elders of the people were assembled and *all* took counsel against Jesus to put Him to death.

The Sanhedrin has achieved its first goal, its first objective, the united decision to have Jesus put to death. What remains is the second objective, His death.

It appears that this goal, this aspiration was not at first a unanimous decision. These religious leaders 'took counsel'. Perhaps, even at that late stage, there were members of the Sanhedrin who needed to be convinced that this was indeed what was required, or a necessary outcome of what Caiaphas had apparently achieved by convicting Jesus of blasphemy. But eventually, after some discussion all the chief priests and elders of the people formally condemned Jesus to death, and led Him bound to Pilate the governor, the Roman procurator of the province of Judaea.

The usual residence of the governor when in Jerusalem was the Tower of Antonia, next to the temple. The Tower of Antonia housed a cohort of Roman soldiers, and was well protected against any incursion by disaffected Jews. But apparently, Pilate preferred the palace of Herod, the highest, most elevated residence in Jerusalem.

However, John 18:28 explains that Jesus was led from the house of Caiaphas to the Praetorium, and when Pilate gave judgement, it was at a place called 'The Pavement' or 'Gabbatha' (John 19:130), an official location which was more likely to be at Antonia.

It is difficult to determine from the gospels alone what Pilate was like as a man. John portrays him as incompetent and insensitive, even though he appeared to be a seeker after truth; and as hostile to Jesus. Like describes him as being careless, of not wanting to be bothered by these Jewish people and their law, but prepared to go along with them for the sake of law and order, and his reputation.

Matthew and Mark are more sympathetic to the character of Pilate, yet he is still needlessly cruel, and aware that he himself might not get a good report when the circumstances of this trial are referred back to the Emperor Tiberius.

Pilate is of course an historical figure, and according to the Jewish historian Josephus, Pilate was in office from 15 A.D. to 26 A.D. a relatively long time. (Josephus, The Jewish War 2. 169-177. Antiquities 18. 55-62, 85-89). If Jesus was born at about 4 or 6 B.C, this occasion would have been towards the end of Pilate's time as Procurator. He is described as constructing an aqueduct in Jerusalem, but by using money from the temple treasury, and for imprinting coins with heathen images, showing an insensitivity to the particular religious and cultural situation over which he was governor.

Was his an evil administration? Or merely a weak and incompetent one? Completely unaware of the nature and destiny of the accused Person before him, he was an instrument in the hand of God for the fulfilment of His purposes. All the minor disagreements about the character of Pilate are subsumed under this fact. And to Pilate Jesus was now led.

Matthew 27:3-10. The thirty pieces of silver

When Judas, His betrayer, saw that He was condemned, he repented, and brought back the thirty pieces of silver to the chief priests and the elders, saying 'I have sinned in betraying innocent blood.' They said, 'What is that to us? See to it yourself.' And throwing down the pieces of silver in the temple, he departed, and he went and hanged himself.

Here there is an interruption in the narrative, giving details about the money given by the chief priests to Judas. This episode is not recorded in the gospels of Mark, Luke or John, though Luke does describe another aspect of the story in the Acts of the Apostles 1:16-20.

Thirty shekels of silver was the price of a slave (Exodus 21:32). That was the price put upon Jesus' head by the chief priests and the elders, their estimation of His value, in effect of no more value than a despised slave, the dregs of their society, and a rebellious slave at that.

It is possible that Judas, though he had wanted to force Jesus' hand, and bring about the rising of the people against their oppressors, accelerating the end of the Roman tyranny, did not expect his obsession with the politics of his day to actually lead to the condemnation to death of Jesus, which was the objective of the chief priests and the elders of the people.

Was he naive? Was he just a tool in their hands? To bring about their desired result without dirtying their own hands?

It appears that not until Judas 'saw that Jesus was condemned' (Matthew 27:3), that he repented, and brought back the thirty pieces of silver to the chief priests 'I have sinned in betraying innocent blood,' he said. (Matthew 27:4). At last, he sees Jesus for who and what He is, but his repentance comes too late for restitution, though not too late for forgiveness. The chief priests will not accept back the money they have given him. It is blood money, the price of a man's life. They dare not touch it for fear of defilement. They throw the money into the temple treasury, where there is already money acquired by all sorts of means, both righteous and unrighteous. The proud Pharisee who declared, 'I give tithes of all that I possess.' (Luke 18:12) did not give as much as the poor widow who put in two mites, two copper coins, as a sacrifice to the Lord whom she loved, 'even all her living'. (Mark 12:41-44, Luke 21:1-4).

Money is neutral, but has within it the power, the capacity for both good and evil.

Thirty pieces of silver was enough to buy a field from a potter, the Potter's Field, in which they could bury strangers. It may have been that the Potter's Field already belonged to Judas, bought with the thirty pieces of silver, since their return had been rejected by the chief priests according to Acts 1:18, 19 and that the chief priests and elders requisitioned it after Judas' death.

There could also be some discrepancy in the version of events surrounding the death of Judas. Obviously, the Potter's Field was a location with which Judas was familiar. Matthew says that he went there to hang himself (verse 5) and Luke describes in Acts, how he fell and that in so doing 'he burst open in the middle and all his bowels gushed out'. One version appears to consider his death premeditated, and the other accidental, but a combination of both is possible.

This is surely an example of the oral tradition, passed on from person to person, from generation to generation, which will sometimes differ in detail (were there two blind men or one?) and on which so much of the gospel is based. It brings into focus the source of so much which may appear contradictory, yet has a sense of reality, of eyewitness events or remembered occasions when it is affirmed that Jesus did this, or said this, for anything that He said or did would surely be remembered compulsively and authoritatively. How grateful we are to the four evangelists for collating all the evidence and presenting it, primarily of course for those for whom they may have had spiritual responsibility, like the Syrian church for which Matthew was writing (Hill p. 52), but also for us, the inheritors of this vast wealth. Eye witness accounts become historical tradition which becomes food for the hungry believer, longing to know more of the Lord who has been revealed to them by the Holy Spirit given to them.

There are differences of opinion on the 'synoptic problem', when there is not always a coincidence of data. But there is only gratitude for the hungry believer who has all the richness of this table spread before him or her.

The potter's field would have been unsuitable for agriculture, for it would have retained many fragments of broken pottery over the years. It may also have been outside the gate of Jerusalem known as the Potsherd Gate in the time of Jeremiah (Jeremiah 19:4). This gate led out to the valley known as Topheth, or the valley of slaughter, the valley of the sons of Hinnom which in times past had been the site of the high place where the worship of their god Molech, including the burning of their sons as a burnt offering to Molech,had taken place, and where incense was burned to other gods. It was indeed the valley of slaughter (Jeremiah 19:1-6). Hinnom in Hebrew is ge-hinnom, which especially in post -exilic Palestine was designated the place of the fiery destruction of the wicked, or Gehenna.

How amazing that God has even the redemption not only of people but of places in view. The entrance to the valley of slaughter was about to be redeemed. The chief priests took counsel and bought the potter's field to bury strangers in. (Matthew 27:7). In contrast to the usual Jewish xenophobia, it was to be the place to bury strangers, aliens, in της ξένης, a place of burial for people far away from home, from those who loved them and would have wanted them to be buried with their own families. Here was a place for them.

Matthew quotes Zechariah 11:12-13 and alludes to Jeremiah 18:2,3 and 32:6-15. It remains the Field of Blood, Akeldama, Acts 1:19 as a reminder of what it had been, and as a reminder that there is nothing outside God's control. He had known and spoken of this happening through His servant Zechariah, (Zechariah 11:13), many years earlier 'Then I took the thirty pieces of silver and cast them into the treasury in the house of the Lord'.

There could also be an oblique reference in Jeremiah 18:4 when Jeremiah went down to the potter's house (verse 3) and saw a vessel which had been spoiled, marred in the potter's hand, but which the potter had reworked into another vessel. The Lord has His own way of redeeming from evil, from that which has been spoiled by His enemy, from that which had formerly refused His grace and turned against Him to other gods. Full of mercy are the ways and thoughts of God towards men and women, and sometimes it requires a tragedy, a failure, a time of absolute weakness and despair to recognise it. Let us return to the Lord, that He may have mercy on us, and to our God, for He will abundantly pardon. (Isaiah 55:7).

Matthew 27:11-26. The trial before Pilate continued

The narrative of Judas' repentance and subsequent death has interrupted the narrative of the trial of Jesus, but is now resumed.

Jesus has been bound and led away, and delivered to Pilate the governor (Matthew 27:2). But then Matthew had interposed a relatively long section on Judas, (verses 3-10), Judas who in the certain knowledge that Jesus is condemned to death, repents of betraying his Master, and takes back to the chief priests and elders in the temple the thirty pieces of silver.

The chief priests and the elders had now bound Jesus and gone to seek out Pilate in the Praetorium, to deliver Him to the Governor. As they surrounded Jesus, Pilate asked Jesus, 'Are you the King of the Jews?' (Matthew 27:11). Perhaps Pilate understood a little of their hypocrisy as men of some kind of religious faith, although he had no means of knowing of their hypocrisy in regard to the betrayal of Jesus by Judas.

We have noted how the chief priests and the elders had given him thirty pieces of silver so that he could betray Jesus, only to regard it as 'blood money' when Judas returned it to them. With Judas' repentance starkly portrayed before them, a situation which they had created, they could only say to Judas, 'What is that to us? See to it yourself'. (Matthew 27:4). Whether or not Pilate was aware of the means by which Jesus had been delivered to him, he was astute enough to recognise that these men were avaricious for power, and frustrated by the intervention of a higher power in the person of the governor. They are contemptuous of a person like Judas who does not view his own behaviour consistently, yet they are far from consistent themselves, except in their self-justification of what they have done by buying the potter's field.

They have set the stage for an illegal murder and must now face Pilate, although in a very different way from that in which Jesus faces him.

Irascible, unpredictable in his questions as he looks at Jesus, Pilate may yet have seen something of the kingly quality of Jesus, for the claim that He was the king of the Jews was not quite the charge brought against Him by the chief priests and elders gathered around. 'Are you the king of the Jews?' Pilate asks Jesus.

This second trial, although held under Roman jurisdiction, puts the deed of the chief priests and elders into the foreground. But even that was according to God's plan. Jesus had been sold cheaply to them by Judas, and in effect by their deal with Judas to the governor, yet His price was far above rubies. They had thought to get rid of Him, but for what were all their machinations worth when He rose again from the dead? It appears that Judas, though guilty, had repented of his sin. There is no indication of repentance on the part of these Jewish leaders, but only bitter malice against One whose purity of thought and deed exposed their hypocrisy for what it was.

Judas had declared Him to be innocent, saying, 'I have betrayed innocent blood' (verse 4). This testimony is the keynote to the trial before Pilate, and will be repeated by Pilate's wife (27:19) and Pilate himself (27:24), the testimony that even before the trial begins, there is an acknowledgement that Jesus is innocent. The grace of God had led Judas to repentance, but that same grace had been repudiated by the religious leaders of Jesus' day.

The gospel of justification on the grounds of *sola gratia,* grace alone, is valid for all, if only they will receive it. The hands of the Lord, His hands, are stretched out to all who will come to Him. But they also have the right to turn away from Him.

They do not however have the right to turn others away from Him, as the chief priests now sought to do. They persuade the people to ask for Barabbas and destroy Jesus (27:20).

Matthew 27:11-26. Jesus before Pilate

But now, Jesus stood before the governor (Matthew 27:11)

Until now, Matthew's gospel has had little to do with the prevailing political atmosphere of uncertainty, of dark things simmering away under the veneer of law and order instituted by the Roman authorities. Now Jesus has come face to face with Pilate, the representative of Rome, and its Emperor, and its pantheon of religious deities, and its iron control over the peoples in its empire who have been subjugated under its complete dominion.

Though only a procurator, Pilate has all this power and might behind him, and is no doubt aware of it. It is with a mocking smile on his face that he asks Jesus, 'Are you the king of the Jews?' (verse 11). Even if He were indeed what the chief priests had purported Him to be, who are the Jews when compared to the might of Rome? Who can claim to be a king when contrasted with the Emperor? The Emperor could squash Him like a fly on his dinner plate, and never notice.

Jesus' answer must have surprised him. 'Jesus said, you have said so.' (verse 11).

Jesus had given the same answer to Caiaphas when we had asked Him if He were the Christ, the Son of the living God (Matthew 26:64). Jesus was placing the responsibility of the actions of these two men, Caiaphas the Jew, and Pilate the Gentile, absolutely within their own jurisdiction. Caiaphas had used Jesus' apparently affirmative words as a clear indication that He was guilty of blasphemy. Pilate could have used Jesus' words as confirmation that He was guilty of sedition.

And yet he hesitated.

The chief priests and the elders continued to accuse Jesus before Pilate, so Pilate turned to Jesus and said, 'Do you not hear how many things they testify against you?' (verse 13), for Jesus had made no answer to their accusations. 'So that the governor wondered greatly, exceedingly.' (verse 14).

What is even more serious is that being unable to get a reply from Jesus, the chief priests and the elders should stir up the people, encourage their own people to reject Jesus. If Pilate was going to neglect to make the decision to have Jesus put to death, then another way must be found. 'Now at the feast, the governor was accustomed to release for the crowd any one prisoner whom they wanted'. (verse 15). Either they or Pilate, the chief priests desperately wanting Jesus' death, or Pilate not quite sure what he wanted, had remembered the custom which had arisen as a concession to the Jews from their Roman overlords. At their Passover feast, one man could be released from prison, even a prisoner like Barabbas who according to Luke 23:19 and Mark 15:11, had committed murder in a recent rebellion or insurrection against the Romans authority. In John's gospel Barabbas is called a robber, (John 18:39), In the A.V. of Matthew 27:16 Barabbas is called a *notable* prisoner. The R.S.V. calls him *notorious*. (Matthew 27:16). He was obviously well-known, even famous, for his notorious deeds, and though completely undesirable, could yet be regarded by the Jews not as an insurrectionist, but as a freedom fighter, the kind of person the Jews would want to be released for his patriotism.

'Whom do you want me to release to you, Barabbas or Jesus who is called Christ?' Pilate says to the crowd in verse 17, for he knew that it was for envy that they had delivered him up. (verse 18).

And while the chief priests and the elders are persuading the people to ask for Barabbas and destroy Jesus (verse 20), Pilate's wife sent word to him saying, 'Have nothing to do with that righteous, innocent man, for I have suffered many things in a dream today because of Him' (verse 19). Though she does not defend Jesus, her intervention is determinative of her husband's future behaviour.

In verse 21, the governor repeats his question to the people. 'Which of the two do you want me to release for you?' And they said 'Barabbas'. 'Then what shall I do with Jesus who is called Christ?' They all said, 'Let Him be crucified.' And he said, 'Why, what evil has he done? But they shouted all the more, 'Let Him be crucified'. (verses 21-23).

This time it was the crowd who answered him. The chief priests and the elders had done their work well. They had convinced the people that it was Barabbas whom they wanted to be released and Jesus whom they wanted to be crucified. But the responsibility for this decision rested with the religious leaders.

Did Pilate nevertheless feel some trepidation about allowing those Jewish people to have their way? Doubtless, the warning from his wife carried some weight with him. He wanted to be seen as a good, even merciful, governor. He wanted to be seen as acting in a way commensurate with his high position, maintaining at least a semblance of authority over these intractable people, and anyway, he could see that a riot was beginning. (verse 24). Though he was a Roman, he may have heard of the custom of the Jews to wash their hands publicly, as a witness that they themselves had not shed innocent blood, based on Deuteronomy 21:6. So, willing to exculpate himself, he calls for a bowl of water, and dramatically, extravagantly and publicly washes his hands in the sight of both the Jewish leaders and the crowd, saying, 'I am innocent of this man's blood. See to it yourselves.'(verse 24)

'Alright,' is the verdict of the crowd, 'you do not want His blood on your hands. Let His blood be on us and on our children!' (verse 25).

To use their response to justify anti-Semitism is a misuse of scripture, and has brought unending suffering to Jews. The people are so stirred up by the events unfolding before them that they can have little cognizance or appreciation of what these terrible words mean. They call down the responsibility for His death, for His blood being poured out upon them and their children, not knowing that that blood is the blood of redemption, the blood that atones even for this sin. It comes upon them as the Saviour's blood, (Matthew 1:21), the blood of Jesus, His Son, which cleanses and goes on cleansing from all sin. (1 John 1:7).

But they are rejecting their Messiah.

Pilate was sitting on the judgement seat, (verse 19), an elevated 'tribunal' raised above the level of the court, from which he could pronounce his verdict. This tribunal or platform, or dais-like structure would be at the front of the Praetorium and open to the public, so that all his words would be completely audible to the people. And in saying, 'I am innocent of the blood of this righteous Man,' he is passing the verdict of 'innocent' on the Prisoner before him. Yet we cannot help but perceive that the ones on trial were the chief priests and the elders, Pilate, and the people, rather than Jesus.

Was it from the fear of the consequences of a possible riot, fear for his own reputation, or cowardice, that Pilate 'released for them Barabbas, and having scourged Jesus, delivered Him to be crucified'? (verse 26).

Could there be any significance in the use of the deceptive word 'crowd' ὄχλος (*common people*) in verse 15, and a different word for people λαός in verse 20? Matthew's use of λαός usually refers to the *people of Israel*. There an indication here that the salvation history of the people of Israel is now at an end, that henceforth, the blood of Jesus, their promised Messiah, their promised king would seal for them and for all mankind 'the New Covenant in His blood'? The old covenant which God had had with His people is now suspended. It has been fulfilled, not cancelled but fulfilled in the New Covenant which has come about through the death of Jesus on the cross. (1 Corinthians 11:25).

The undisciplined crowd *'oxlos'*, had been replaced, in Mathew's terminology, not only theologically, but actually, by the chosen people of God, the people of Israel, *'laos'*, and by all those who have discovered to their great relief that the blood of Jesus cleanses from all sin. There is no barrier, no obstacle to the people of Israel, or any member of the human race, to entering into the New Covenant. The only barrier is their own repudiation of all that they have previously thought, erroneously, that He stands for, and for all the perceived hardship which could be theirs as a consequence of consecration to His way of righteous living, a strong possibility for Jews under Roman domination.

God never has, and never will, cast off His people whom He foreknew. (Romans 11:2). When they come to Him, God will grant them the faith to confess with their lips that Jesus is Lord, and to believe in their hearts that God raised Him from the dead, and they will be saved. (Romans 10:9). The cry goes out to all. 'Believe in the Lord Jesus Christ and you will be saved. (Acts 16:31). Those who put their hand into the hand of God, who trust Him to take control, who have heard the word of truth and believed in Him, (Ephesians 1:13) by His grace have been saved,

(Ephesians 2:5,8), through faith, and this not of themselves, it is the gift of God. The requirement is faith, but even that is given to the hungry heart by God.

Barabbas is released, and Jesus delivered by Pilate to be scourged and then crucified. (Matthew 27:26). Where did the crowd go? It is probable that many would have followed Jesus after He had again been maltreated and had set forth upon the road, carrying His cross.

Matthew 27:27-31. The second mistreatment of Jesus

Pilate does what the people wanted, believing himself to be exonerated by the symbolic washing of his hands from causing the death of Jesus.

It was customary for prisoners condemned to crucifixion to be beaten beforehand, in order to render them weaker, and to die more quickly once they were on a cross. Not infrequently, people would have died under the lashing of whips, which sometimes incorporated pieces of bone or lead (Luz p.503).

Jesus, weakened from His first beating, was taken to the Praetorium by the soldiers of the whole battalion (27:27) or cohort. In this scene of frenetic activity, Jesus is absolutely passive, and yet He remains the central figure. As an innocent, righteous Man, He has unjustly been condemned to death, even death on a cross. He has remained silent, not only before the accusations of His enemies, but now even before these soldiers of the governor. They sadistically mock Him, strip Him of His clothes and put a scarlet robe upon Him, and a reed in His right hand, and plaiting a crown of thorns they place it on His head. Kneeling before Him, they mock him saying, 'Hail, King of the Jews!' (verse 29) 'And they spat upon Him and took the reed and struck Him on the head.' (verse 30).

After a while, after they had tired of the cruel game, for they were playing with someone who did not rise to their insults, or show any aggression or belligerence towards them, they removed the scarlet robe and put His own clothes on Him, and 'led Him away to crucify Him'. (verse 31).

Even during this mockery and maltreatment of Him, the soldiers had recognised His kingly bearing, and had mocked Him with a crown, though it was of thorns, a scarlet robe, and a reed for a sceptre. The crown, the robe and the sceptre were the three insignia of kingship. But instead of a royal diadem or laurel wreath, this crown was of thorns, the scarlet robe was probably a soldier's parade cloak or cape, and the sceptre a weak and shaking reed. These were the emblems of royalty with which they mocked Him.

Mark 15:7 describes the robe as purple, emphasising the royalty of Jesus and possibly (but speculatively) usually worn by Pilate. A robe of purple would be a very expensive garment, using dye from the secretion of a type of snail found almost exclusively at sites along the Mediterranean coast. Scarlet was cheaper, being dyed from the juice of 'scarlet berries', the name given to certain insects who lived in the leaves of oak trees. Matthew has given us a cheaper imitation, a 'substitute royal robe' as part of the ridiculing of Him as king.

But ridicule becomes brutality as they spit on Him and strike Him with His own apparently weak instrument of authority, the reed which had become the sceptre, on the head, on the crown of thorns, causing extra pain and suffering, pain and suffering soon to be increased by what follows.

How little soldiers understood of the actual coronation of which they had made a mockery! *The head that once was crowned with thorns, Is crowned with glory now! A royal diadem adorns the mighty Victor's brow* (T. Kelly. Hymns Ancient and Modern 301).

Even the replacing of His own clothes on His flayed back must have been excruciating, and the weight of the wooden cross on His shoulders, weakened as He was, too heavy to bear. Perhaps He stumbled and fell, perhaps He could not walk as fast as the soldiers wanted, for they had a job to do, and did not want to take all day about it. They had already wasted too much time, having fun at His expense. They may even have been given a time slot in order to get a routine job finished by a certain time. Cruel as it was, it was all in a day's work for them. They found a man in the crowd who looked strong and healthy. His name was

Simon and he came from Cyrene. 'This man they compelled to carry His cross' (verse 32). Even so, it was a long walk for Him to the place of Golgotha, the place of a skull, or *Calvary* in the A.V. of Luke 23:33.

The details of His mistreatment could be read as unnecessarily graphic instances of a lurid account of the mockery and persecution of Jesus. Was it necessary for Matthew to include all this? They are also included in Mark's gospel, but not in Luke or John, suggesting that Matthew and Mark had access to some of the same source material which had not been available to Luke and John. Did Matthew's readers need to know all that Jesus went through on His way to the Cross, even before the terrible agony of the cross itself?

Because Matthew has so often used quotations from the Old Testament, and usually from the Septuagint, LXX, version of the Old Testament, we cannot but assume that in recounting these events as they occurred, he had in mind the prophecies of Psalm 22 and Isaiah 53 from both of which he could have quoted extensively of the suffering of 'the Man of sorrows and acquainted with grief, (isaiah 53:3) the One who was despised and rejected of men.' The terrible suffering of Jesus even before He reached the point of crucifixion was not some accidental happening, but had been prophesied by so many of the Lord's servants through the ages. Matthew is making absolutely certain that his readers know that Jesus was indeed the Son of God, the fulfilment of all the scriptures; the one on whom they could totally rely for salvation. Matthew is giving a faithful account of all that happened to Jesus. He passes no judgement on these soldiers of the governor, (verse 27), noting only that even in their rough game, they recognise the kingship of Jesus, kneeling before Him even though it was in mockery of worship. (verse 29).

Jesus had predicted that He would be mocked and scourged as well as crucified, in Matthew 20:19. But even in mockery, the soldiers were paying homage to Jesus. He was the Logos, the incarnated Son of God. His suffering was altogether human, but also altogether divine.

But perhaps it is legitimate to ask, where was God, His heavenly Father, when Jesus was put to such degradation, such brutality, such wickedness?

Orthodoxy requires us to believe that God is impassible, incapable of suffering. The first of the 39 Articles in the Book of Common Prayer states: *There is but one, living and true God, everlasting, without body parts or passions, of infinite power, wisdom and goodness.* But God is surely suffering in the person of Jesus. And as the Father looks upon the suffering of His only begotten Son, He must Himself suffer.

This is the mystery of Divine suffering. Where was God when Jesus suffered? The status of God's impassibility is expressed in classical theism, which teaches that God is omnipotent, omniscient, immutable, impassible and simple,that is, without complexity.

And yet we read that in all their affliction, the affliction of His people, the children of Israel, He was afflicted, and the angel of His presence saved them. (Isaiah 63:9). When the task of leading the children of Israel through the wilderness seemed to be too great. God said to Moses, 'My presence shall go with you and I will give you rest.' (Exodus 33:14). And to Joshua, 'The Lord your God is with you, wherever you go' (Joshua 1:9). The Psalmist's declaration of faith was of a God who is 'our refuge and strength, a very present help in time of trouble'. (Psalm 46:1). And David who gratefully exclaims, 'Even though I walk through the valley of the shadow of death, I will fear no evil, for You are with me'. (Psalm 23:4).

Of course, many other examples could be given.

Though God is great and highly to be praised, (Psalm 48:1) and reigns from the unapproachable height of His throne, it yet appears that He loved the men and women He had created so much that He wants to accompany them on their journey through life. God's self-definition of Himself to Moses was of 'a God merciful and gracious, slow to anger and abounding in steadfast love and faithfulness, keeping steadfast love, *hesed*, covenant love, for thousands.' (Exodus 34:6). Would not such a God be with them in their suffering as well as in their times of joy? As they lived in His presence?

God's impassibility according to classical theism understands that He does not suffer, for suffering brings about change, and He cannot change for He is immutable, always the same. He cannot change for He is God.

Can God suffer pain and not change? 'I the Lord change not, therefore you are not consumed,' we read in Malachi 3:6. Somehow, God absorbs all the misery, the pain, the suffering into Himself as He comes alongside His child who needs Him, and is not changed in His ultimate pristine Being. He is love, ever-flowing, inexhaustible, infinite love.

God is love (1 John 4:8). The sum of the whole world's suffering cannot change who He is, His essential nature. Suffering may change human beings. We cannot say God cannot allow Himself to suffer in case it caused Him to change. Anyone who has ever been with a loved one who is suffering knows that love hurts. God loves, and suffers, but does not change.

In God's manifold dealings with the human beings whom He loves, it may be that in their suffering, He may well draw them closer to Himself. But although God suffers with His people, He does not change. In their suffering, He suffers with them. They call to Him, and He answers them (Isaiah 65:24). Yoked together with Him they find that their yoke is easy and their burden light. (Matthew 11:28).

Is God then an interventionist God?

This does not mean that God is a passible God, a God who suffers, and that He will therefore immediately lift men and women out of their troubles, will immediately intervene to prevent sickness or war or famine or plague.

But it does mean that in the suffering He endures with His beloved sons and daughters there is redemption. Redemption, salvation is at the heart of our faith. God will save us. He is not defeated by our vulnerability.

To misquote Geoffrey Studdert Kennedy, 'There are tears on the heart of the Eternal, there is pain to pierce the soul of God,' and Jurgen Moltmann argues passionately in 'The Crucified God' that God suffers with Christ. These men, like Dietrich Bonhoeffer, in both the First and Second world wars had seen the devastation in the trenches, had been scarred by the Holocaust (C.T. 6.11.20).

Bonhoeffer wrote from prison:

> And when this cup you give is full to brimming
> With bitter suffering, hard to understand,
> We take it thankfully and without trembling
> Out of so good, and so beloved, a Hand.

God was in, and with Christ, reconciling the world to Himself. (2 Corinthians 5:19). It was not until the sin of the whole world was placed upon His spotless, sinless, shoulders that Jesus cried out, 'My God, My God, why have you forsaken Me?' (Matthew 27:46).

Jesus was the treasure in the heart of God, yet even we, as earthen vessels, may know that within us is a light, the light of the knowledge of the glory of God in the face of Jesus Christ, and that this light has been commanded by God, even as at the beginning, to shine out of the darkness, the darkness of adversity, of persecution, of despair, as Paul discovered according to 2 Corinthians 4:7. We have this treasure in our earthen vessels.

Conclusion: God is impassible in His nature, for nothing can change Him. But He allows Himself to be altered by human suffering, to suffer with those He came to save through His Son. In all their afflictions, He *is* afflicted and the Angel of His Presence, the Lord Jesus Himself, *does* save them. 'I am with you,' says Jesus, 'even unto the end of the age.' (Matthew 28:20).

And God was with Jesus even as He suffered mockery and brutality and the crown of thorns and the nails and the spear in His side. God was in Christ, while He was reconciling the world to be Himself. (2 Corinthians 5:19), for Jesus said, 'I and the Father are One'. (John 10:30).

And they led Him away, to crucify Him. (Matthew 27:31).

Matthew 27:32. Jesus is crucified

As they went out, they came upon a man of Cyrene, Simon by name. This man, they compelled to carry His cross. And when they came to a place called Golgotha (which means, the place of a skull), they offered Him wine to drink, mingled with gall, but when He tasted it, He would not drink it. And when they had crucified Him, they divided His garments among them by casting lots. Then they sat down and kept watch over Him there. And over His head they put the charge against Him, which read, 'This is Jesus the King of the Jews' (Matthew 27:32-37).

This most significant and precious event in the whole of human history, and beyond, even to eternity, is concluded in terms of such extreme brevity, in such simple terms.

Was this because both Matthew and his readers knew the end of the story? That although this was a cosmic battle over sin and death, victory was assured as God raised Him from the dead, and that He lives forever at God's right hand?

Yet all the details, such as they are, only seem to enhance the pivotal sense of Jesus, in spite of the cruelty, and the mockery, and the pain, Jesus is still absolutely the One who controls everything. He had spoken at His arrest in the Garden of the twelve legions of angels whom He could instantly call to His relief. (Matthew 26:53).But then how should the scriptures be fulfilled that this must be so? (Matthew 26:54). No doubt, even at this later stage, the angels were 'gazing down with sad and wondering eyes to see the approaching sacrifice.'(A.H.B. 167).

Matthew 27:32. Outside the city wall

The place of crucifixion was outside the city wall. *'And as they went out'* to Golgotha. (verse 32). The very frugality of the text causes us to reflect on the meaning behind it.

Execution by crucifixion normally took place outside the city, demonstrating the rejection and abhorrence felt by more law-abiding citizens for all the deeds done by these outcasts of society. "We do not want them in our city," was the general attitude to lawbreakers, traitors, sinners.

The author of Hebrews more specifically, alone of all the New Testament writers, has a comment on this. 'For the bodies of those animals whose blood is brought into the sanctuary by the high priest as a sacrifice for sin, are burned outside the camp'. In the Jewish sacrificial system, in the wilderness years, after the blood of the animal had been shed, its body was originally taken outside the camp, but latterly of course, outside the city, for burial. 'So Jesus also suffered outside the (city) gate *'extra portam'* in order to sanctify the people through His own blood. Therefore, let us go forth to Him outside the camp and bear the abuse He endured'. (Hebrews 13:11-13). This is not just a geographical location for the author of Hebrews, though it was that, but a symbolic reflection of all that is defined by 'the city'.

Jerusalem, Zion, the City of God has turned its back on the One sent by God to redeem it. God has always shown His mercy and loving kindness to His special city. Psalm 87:1,2 says 'The Lord loves the gates of Zion... glorious things are spoken of you, O city of God.' But now, to enter into and receive that relationship with God, sinners need to go out of the city, to go forth to Jesus outside the camp, outside the city gate, 'bearing His reproach', (Hebrew 13:13 A.V.), for that place, the place of His suffering, is the only place of sanctification, of holiness (verse 12), through His blood.

How privileged were those in the Old Testament who could say of Jerusalem, 'This one was born there' (Psalm 87:6). How much more privileged are those who are born, not of blood, nor of the will of the flesh, but of God, (John 1:12), and who have symbolically entered a new Zion, have been symbolically born there, a new city of Jerusalem to which also they can look forward at the end of time. The Lamb of God, who takes away the sin of the world, our precious Lord Jesus, is already standing on His spiritual Mount Zion, the mountain where Jerusalem is located, with one hundred and forty four thousand who have His Name and His Father's Name written on their foreheads (Revelation 14:1).

The time will come, when there will be a holy city, New Jerusalem, coming down out of heaven from God, the church prepared as a Bride adorned for her Husband, the church for which He gave His life. (Revelation 21:2; Ephesians 5:25). This is the mystery of Christ and the church. (Ephesians 5:32). Christ loved the church and gave Himself up for her. How blessed we are to be part of what He is doing in the world, building His church, increasing day by day the number of those who are being sanctified by faith in Him, that He might present the church to Himself *a glorious church,* a church in splendour, without spot or wrinkle or any such thing, (Ephesians 5:27), His bride, His Beloved One. The glorious city has been replaced by the glorious church. And in the New Jerusalem, they are one.

The Lord Jesus was crucified outside the old city of Jerusalem, for His intention was to have a new city, a new Jerusalem prepared in heaven as a Bride adorned for her Husband. (Revelation 21:2).

And when they came to a place called Golgotha, which means the place of a skull, they offered Him wine to drink mingled with gall, but when He had tasted it He would not drink it. (Matthew 27:33). So Jesus is crucified outside the city with the soldiers sitting on the ground beneath His cross, to watch Him. (Matthew 27:36). Did they suspect that even now His disciples would come and take Him away before He had died? They surely could not have imagined that He would come down from the cross as the passers-by mockingly appeared to do, saying, 'If you are the Son of God, come down from the cross'. (verse 40). 'Those who passed by derided Him, wagging their heads and saying, 'You who would destroy the temple and build it in three days, save yourself! If you are the Son of God, come down from the cross'.

So also the chief priests with the scribes and the elders, mocked Him, saying, 'He saved others; He cannot save Himself. He is the King of Israel; let Him come down from the cross and we will believe in Him. He trusted in God that He would deliver Him; let Him deliver Him if He delight in Him, for He said "I am the Son of God"'. (Mathew 27:42).

Matthew 27:34. The wine mingled with gall

Both Matthew and Mark record that before they crucified Him, they offered Him wine. Matthew says that the wine was mingled with gall (27:34) and Mark that it was mixed with myrrh. (Mark 15:23). Myrrh was often mixed with wine as a narcotic, probably to deaden pain. But it was very bitter, as gall is bitter, and Matthew may have used 'mingled with gall' (verse 34) metaphorically, for gall was poisonous. He may also have had a possible reminiscence of Psalm 69:21, 'They gave me also gall for my food, and in my thirst they gave me vinegar to drink.'

This bitter cup, the cup of His suffering, which took all the bitterness away from us, was not to be diluted with narcotics, whether the intention was philanthropic or a continuation of their mockery of Him. Jesus had said, 'The cup which the Father has given Me, shall I not drink it?' (John 18:11). But this was man's cup, not God's.

Matthew 27:35.They divided His garments

When they had crucified Him, they divided his garments among them by casting lots.

One of the perquisites of having taken part in an execution was that the soldiers were allowed to keep the clothes of the delinquent. In those days, when having even one change of clothes was fortunate indeed, the clothes of those crucified could be a small source of income when sold. And when they had crucified Him, they divided His garments among them by casting lots. (verse 38). For Matthew this is another reminder of Psalm 22:18, the Psalm of suffering. 'They divided my garments among them, and for my raiment, they cast lots.'

There are many prophetic traces of His suffering in Psalm 22:1,7,8,13-18. Psalm 22 is a psalm of David. David was not crucified. He died in his bed. (1 Kings 1:1-2:10), but God had prophetically allowed him a glimpse of what the cruel death of the Son of God would entail. The suffering of David of which he speaks so eloquently in the psalm was physical, psychological and even spiritual. It was real. But it was not a *salvific* sacrifice even though offered up to God.

Throughout the Christian era, there have been many who have suffered deeply and have offered up their suffering to God as a sacrifice. Paul writes, 'While we live, we are always being given up to death for Jesus' sake, so that the life of Jesus may also be manifested in our mortal flesh.' (2 Corinthians 4:11). Paul lived a sacrificial life.

In His great compassion and understanding of our human nature, God has allowed us to offer up our suffering to Him. Romans 5:2 explains for us a connection between our hope of having the glory of God, in which we rejoice, and rejoicing in our suffering, affirming an interdependence between the glory of God and our suffering for Him, totally reliant on His love being poured into our hearts by the Holy Spirit.

This interdependence is echoed in the words of Romans 8:16,17. The Spirit Himself bears witness with our spirit that we are children of God, and if children then heirs, heirs of God and fellow-heirs, joint-heirs, with Christ, provided we *suffer with Him* that we also may be *glorified with Him*.

Peter too knew about suffering. He says, 'Rejoice in so far as you share Christ's sufferings'. (1 Peter 4:18).

So, *therefore,* Paul says, 'Present your bodies as a *living sacrifice,* holy and acceptable unto God, which is your spiritual worship' (R.S.V.) your reasonable service (A.V.). The body and mind and spirit in relation to one another, together making up the living person whose only *raison d'etre,* only desire, is to be offered up in worship to the One who has shown mercy, who is rich in knowledge and wisdom. For from Him and through Him and to Him are all things.To Him be glory for ever. (Romans 11:31-36).

Even before the great gift has been given to us to offer up our sufferings as a sacrifice to God, the Psalmist says, 'The sacrifice acceptable to God is a broken spirit. A broken and a contrite heart, O God, Thou wilt not despise'. (Psalm 51:17).

That God allows the suffering of His children is a mystery. That through our suffering we can share in the suffering of Christ is a concomitant, co-existing, accompanying mystery, and we could not even express such a thought if the word of God had not given us permission to do so. Matthew's gospel describes the suffering of Christ objectively. These are the facts as he understands them, what has been given to him by oral transmission or other resource material, and inspired in him by the Holy Spirit.

Matthew's gospel is 'God-breathed', (2 Timothy 3:16) as is all scripture. Though written objectively, it allows us subjectively to live those scenes imaginatively for ourselves. As the reader visualises the horror of the cross, as he stands with his head bowed in its shadow, the magnitude of what Jesus has done for him overwhelms him. Even though he cannot fully understand. *'My God, My God, why have you forsaken Me?',* he can certainly understand, *'Father, forgive them, for they know not what they do',* and can include himself in that costly forgiveness.

And this is the king whom we want to serve for the rest of our lives, even if it means suffering. Indeed, to suffer for Him is a privilege, a gift. 'Unto you it is *given* in the behalf of Christ, not only to believe in Him, but to suffer for His sake'. (Philippians 1:29).

This is not to minimise His suffering but to see the triumph of the cross and all that it stands for in the life of believers; redeemed by His blood, the life-blood of the Son of God, poured out upon the cross, the power of the cross in the life of the believer. As Paul so carefully expresses it in Galatians 6:14, 'God forbid that I should glory save in the cross of our Lord Jesus Christ, by which the world has been crucified to me and I to the world'. There is a work of grace going on in the life of the believer, and it is being accomplished by the power of the cross, changing him or her from one degree of glory to another when they turn to the Lord. (2 Corinthians 3:18). For the cross, frugally and delicately narrated by Matthew, is the beginning and focus of something absolutely tremendous that God is doing in human lives and throughout time and eternity, 'for God so loved the world that He gave His only begotten Son, that whoever believes in Him should not perish but have everlasting life'. (John 3:16). According to His own word, we take up our cross, the cross of His persistent work in us, that deals with all that is self determined and out of harmony with the life of the crucified Christ within us, and follow Him.

Matthew 27:37. Jesus is the King

'And over His head they put the charge against Him, which read, "This is Jesus, the king of the Jews".' (verse 37).

Over the cross there was placed an inscription on a tablet pointing to His kingship. Even though quite probably politically motivated by Pilate, perhaps in mockery, it expressed a most profound truth. Jesus was crucified in weakness, but lives in the power of God. (2 Corinthians 13:4). This is an emphatic truth.

Matthew's text is a catalyst. From science we learn that a catalyst remains unchanged while allowing change to take place around it. The truth of the glorious gospel, the cross of the Lord Jesus remains unchanged while all around it swirl and fight for dominance all the treasures of meaning that the text encourages.

And this includes the kingship of Jesus. How do we understand His kingship?

The self-interested religious and political powers have made Him a victim. They have understood Him as a revolutionary because of what they see as His unauthorised understanding, not only of the scriptures, but the cultural realities of their period of history. And in a sense they were right. Though His authority came from God, His teaching certainly *was* revolutionary, but the revolution He envisaged was the life-changing experience offered to individuals who would follow the path of obedience and enjoy fellowship with His Father.

It was never offered to groups of people. Though He may have been speaking to crowds of people, to each one was given the responsibility to respond. This was true even when He was speaking to the religious leaders, Pharisees and Sadducees, scribes and elders of the people.

Pilate had said to Jesus, 'Are you a king then?' And Jesus had replied, 'My kingdom is not of this world. If my kingdom were of this world, then would My servants fight.' (John 18:36,37). Pilate's question has the implication, 'What kind of king are you?'

And over His broken body, hanging on a cross, Pilate had caused it to be written. 'This is Jesus, the king of the Jews', by this means implying the puny challenge of Jesus to Pilates' world, the Roman empire, and its powerful emperor, the emperor Tiberius; as if Jesus is challenging any kind of reality or expectation that the power and glory of Rome, could ever be eradicated, and especially that it could be eradicated for ever! In his ignorance and total misapprehension of the ways of God, Pilate would be able to say in self justification, 'What kind of king was that man Jesus whom I had crucified.'

How little did he know of the power of the cross. How inadequate his perception of the kingly authority of Him who hung upon it. 'Are you a king then'? he said. But could it be that behind the mockery was a wistfulness to know of another kind of jurisdiction than the one he served?

Throughout his gospel, Matthew has been telling us of the kind of king that Jesus was.

Though not always customary, when someone was sentenced to death by crucifixion, a tablet, 'titulus', title, the word used in John 19:19, containing a statement of the crime was sometimes hung around the neck, or carried in front of the condemned man. But in the case of Jesus, the tablet was nailed above His head. John states that the title was written in Hebrew (Aramaic), in Latin and in Greek. (John 19:20). These were the three languages in use in first century Palestine and symbolise the universality of the kingship of Jesus. Though Pilate may have intended to mock Jesus' claim to kingship, his intention made *actual* the intention of Jesus, declaring the reality of the purpose of God for mankind, for His sacrifice on the Cross was intended not for the Jews only, but for the whole world, for people of every race and language.

What had been a change against Him had become a title acknowledging Him as king, a Christological title. He was the true king whom God had chosen. The Magi paid homage to Him as king in Matthew 2:1-12. He entered Jerusalem as a humble king in Matthew 21:5, fulfilling the prophecy of Zechariah 9:9, 'Behold, your king is coming to you, humble and riding upon an ass, and on a colt, the foal of an ass.' He is the king who will one day judge all the nations, seated at the right hand of the Father. (Matthew 25:34,40).

And above all, from the very beginning of His ministry, Jesus spoke constantly of the Kingdom of Heaven. ``Repent,He said, for the kingdom of heaven is at hand'. (Matthew 4:17). It was never enough for His Father that He should be the king of ages, immortal, invisible (1 Timothy 1:17), He should also open the Kingdom of Heaven to all believers, that they should become 'a chosen race, a royal priesthood, a holy nation, God's own people, 'that you may declare the wonderful deeds of Him who called you out of darkness into His marvellous light. Once you were no people, but now you are God's people. Once you had not received mercy, but now you have received mercy'. (1 Peter 2:9,10).

In the Kingdom of Jesus, the Kingdom of Heaven, all the world has been given the opportunity of being blessed, of entering into the Kingdom of God, where Christ is, seated on His Father's throne in glorious majesty, always making intercession for His beloved ones. (Romans 8:14). We may enter that kingdom now, through repentance and faith, and enjoy forever the blessing of life lived in union with Him, while waiting for the coming, the revelation of our Lord Jesus Christ, (1 Corinthians 1:7) 'who will sustain you to the end, when the Son of Man will send out His angels with a loud trumpet call, and they will gather together His elect, His chosen ones. (Matthew 24:30,31).

We have a king who intercedes for us. When we consider the kingship of Jesus, all our previously held concepts of kingship are completely overturned. Many a good king holds his kingship lightly on behalf of his subjects, as indeed does our own beloved, faithful Queen. But a king who makes intercession, who intercedes for His subjects, who will not allow Himself to be separated from the love He has for them, and they for Him; this is kingship beyond all that we could ask or think. It lifts us up to His throne in worship and praise. It gives us a new understanding of who we are in Christ, beloved, understood, pardoned, protected, united with Him. Nothing in all creation can separate us from His love. (Romans 8:39). To be the subject of such a king is privilege and blessing untold. It was not to angels that this great grace was given, but to us, who were sinners, who had despised and mocked Him, who had strayed from His ways like lost sheep. He has raised us up and made us to sit with Him at His right hand in the heavenly places, in Christ. (Ephesians 1:20).

God did not create the world and then withdraw from it. He had a higher purpose in view, to bring many sons to glory, as was once said, from the guttermost to the uttermost, from the despair and guilt of sin to the throne on high. This is the mystery of love, the mystery of what God accomplished on the cross. Wonderful, amazing love.

Matthew 27:18. The two robbers

Then two robbers were crucified with Him, one on the right and one on the left.

We have a fuller account of the experiences of these two robbers, 'malefactors' (A.V.) in Luke 23:33-43. Matthew's laconic account tells us very little, yet is not without its importance.

Isaiah 53:12 says, 'He was numbered with the transgressors' and Mark 15:38 includes this verse as prophetic of the robbers on either side of Him. But are we not all transgressors? He was suffering not only on behalf of these men, but on behalf of us all, for which of us could claim not to have transgressed His holy law.

As we have seen, the soldiers had crucified Him, then parted His garments among them and were now keeping watch over Him. Matthew continues by commenting that there had been those who derided and mocked Him, wagging their heads and saying, "You who would destroy the temple and build it in three days, save yourself! If you are the Son of God, come down from the cross." (verses 39, 40).

We have also seen how it was not only 'those who passed by' who derided Him. 'So also the chief priests with the scribes and the elders mocked Him, saying, 'He saved others, He cannot save Himself. He is the king of Israel. Let Him come down now from the cross and we will believe Him. He trusts in God.

Let God deliver Him now if he desires Him, for He said, "I am the Son of God.'" (verses 41-44). And the robbers who were crucified with Him also reviled Him in the same way. (verse 44). Even as He hung on the cross, the robbers, the passers-by, the religious leaders still appeared to be concerned with who Jesus actually was. Could it possibly be that He was indeed the long-awaited Messiah? The Son of God? The King of Israel?

Their mockery of Him had only served to underline their basic perception that somehow they had missed the mark, that perhaps He was who He claimed to be. Their thought was, 'If only He performed the miracle of coming down from the cross, then we could believe in Him.' They could not appreciate that the miracle lay in the fact that He was on the cross at all. He had power to lay down His life, and He had power to take it again. This He had received from His Father. (John 10:15).

But He had given up His right to human life. He had allowed wicked men to condemn Him to death, wicked hands to take hold of His sacred Body and nail it to a cross. He was determined to do the will of His Father, to go the way of the cross so that men and women could receive forgiveness of sins, so that their sins could be blotted out, so that they could approach a Holy God and live in the light of His presence.

He gave His life as a sacrifice, (Hebrews 10:12). that we might be reconciled to God by the death of His Son. (Romans 5:10). While we were yet sinners, Christ died for us. (Romans 5:8). This is the whole meaning of what these people were looking for. Jesus, not only a worker of miracles, but the Son of God, the King of Israel. But they missed it. They wanted a sign, preferably a sign from heaven, and they missed the thing signified, Christ crucified, to the Jews a stumbling clock, to the Gentiles foolishness, but to us who are being saved, Christ the power of God and the wisdom of God (1 Corinthians 1:22).

What these people have seen however, has caused them inadvertently to become witnesses to the sonship of Jesus as the Son of God, to His kingship as King of Israel. *He is who He says He is.* He is both God and Man, and He will be king, not only of Israel, but of the whole inhabited earth, and in heaven.

In Matthew there is no mention of the robber's repentance. Jesus is alone, Son of God, Son of Man. And the robbers who were crucified with Him also reviled Him in the same way.

Matthew 27:45-50. The death of Jesus

The mockers have mocked, the blasphemers have blasphemed, but 'the Son of God is obedient unto death, even death on a cross'. (Philippians 2:8).

God is about to intervene, the turning point is about to happen. God will make clear that this is no ordinary crucifixion, but the focus of history. All that ever came before it, and all that follows has been planned from eternity. The scope of its absolute significance is so vast, so enormous. We stand on holy ground and must take the shoes from off our feet, for this is God. This is *our* God.

Now from the sixth hour there was darkness over all the land until the ninth hour (Matthew 27:45).

God had caused a curtain of darkness to fall over the suffering of His Son; from the sixth hour to the ninth hour, from noon to 3 p.m. Three hours of tremendous significance, for a cosmic battle was going on in Jesus. Jesus was about to tread all the powers of darkness and evil down. This was not a natural eclipse of the sun, but supernatural darkness, not a natural phenomenon, but God hiding the face of His Son as He took upon Himself the sins of the whole world.

Matthew does not spell this out in his account of the death of Jesus. We have to wait for the revelation given to other New Testament writers for the explanation of what was transpiring within that darkness, for Matthew gives no explanation.

All over the land of Palestine, people are unaccountably having to light candles in the middle of the day as the light of the world, Jesus, extinguishes all the darkness, overcoming the darkness of evil, the darkness of death. The cosmos holds its breath in silence, as in a vacuum, as the work of redemption goes on. Jesus was disarming the principalities and powers, and making a show of them openly, making a public example of them, revealing them for what they are, triumphing over them in the cross. (Colossians 2:15). Sin is condemned and its power broken. The demands of the law are cancelled. His people are set free. The 'bond', that which bound them to keep God's law and satisfy all its demands, all that persistent legality, has been nailed to the cross (Colossians 2:14), it no longer has dominion over God's redeemed people. We cannot pay the debt we owe to God, so God has cancelled the debt, for the blood of Christ paid the debt for us. Christ has redeemed us from the curse of the law, the law which we could not keep 'having become a curse for us', for it is written, 'Cursed be everyone who hangs on a tree'. (Galatians 3:13).

The description of sin as debt is commonplace in the New Testament. (Matthew 6:12, Luke 16:1-8). At Sinai, God had set forth His covenant with His people, (Exodus 19:5, 20:1-21), but the people did not obey His covenant. They dismissed their loyalty to God. They owed Him their very life, but they transgressed His word and His commandments. They became debtors, sinners, as a nation, but also as individuals.

We too are debtors. We owe our very life to God, but have disowned Him, disobeyed Him, sinned against Him. The debt we owe is not overlooked or ignored, but paid by Jesus. Nailed with Christ on His cross, our debts, our sins, went with him to His burial, and they are buried forever. Sin no longer has dominion over us, for we are no longer under law but under grace. (Romans 6:14).

Jesus has mastered and overcome all those principalities and powers which sought to control human beings, rendering them impotent, powerless (Colossians 2:15). The cross of His suffering has become the cross of our deliverance. Jesus *breaks the power of cancelled sin. He sets the prisoner free. His blood can make the foulest clean, His blood availed and keeps on availing for me.* Charles Wesley H.E.T. 22

There are principalities and powers in the unseen realm according to the scriptures, which would seek to take control over people's lives. In modern times, they may be given physical, psychological or economic labels, but they are nonetheless real. (Ephesians 6:12). The message of the cross is the antidote to despair, to frustration. The forces of the universe are subject to Christ. Their hostility has been conquered in the cross. There is a glorious liberty for the children of God, (Romans 8:21), and nothing, absolutely nothing in all creation, can separate them from Him, and from His love for them. ([Romans 8:38, 39).

But how terribly costly was the conflict with the powers of evil, with the sin of the whole world, which Jesus was taking upon Himself.

Matthew 27:46. The cry from the cross

And about the ninth hour, Jesus cried with a loud voice, 'Eli, Eli, lama sabachthani?' That is, 'My God, My God, why hast Thou forsaken Me?' (Matthew 27: 46)

Out of the darkness came His cry, and it brought to an end the darkness too. His work of redemption completed, the sin which drove men and women far from God taken upon His shoulders, He can turn again to His Father. But He turns to Him with a cry of desolation, 'Eli, Eli, lama sabachthani?' That is, 'My God, My God, why hast Thou forsaken Me?'

'Eli' is Hebrew for God. Mark uses the Aramaic, 'Eloi' for God, but both provide confusion for 'some of the bystanders' (verse 47), who think He is calling for Elijah, who did not die, but went up to heaven in a chariot of fire, (2 Kings 2:11), and was regarded superstitiously as one who would come to the rescue of someone in distress. Perhaps they thought Jesus was calling on Elijah to take Him to heaven in his chariot.

Important though Elijah was in the history of the Jewish people, making it perhaps inevitable that legends should have sprung up about his having a continuing ministry to those in distress, Jesus was not calling for Elijah, but for His God. 'My God, why?' The words of Psalm 22:1, spring unbidden to His lips. Familiar though He was with the Hebrew scriptures, David's psalm could by no means fully express what had happened, and was still about to happen in the cause of redemption, for David's suffering, though great, came nowhere near what was being accomplished by Jesus on the cross. But David had had this extreme sensation that God had forsaken him and Jesus' perception that God, His Heavenly Father, had forsaken Him was all too real.

WHY? said Jesus. Had God forsaken Him? And if He had, what purpose did it serve? He had lived His whole life in constant love and fellowship with His Father, and it appears that His Father has now abandoned Him. Has the darkness which He has fought and overcome caused the separation? Can He still be doing the will of His Father since His Father has left Him? Is this all part of the plan of salvation which They had purposed together? There is no-one else to whom He can turn, and certainly not to His beloved servant Elijah.

But He does not say, 'Why has God forsaken Me?' But, 'Why have *YOU* forsaken me?' His cry is still to His loving Father. And Jesus received no answer from God. But when He cries a second time, God receives the spirit which He yields up to Him (verse 50).

We turn again to those wonderful words of 2 Corinthians 5:19. 'God was in Christ, reconciling the world to Himself.' They were together in their joint endeavour of salvation. In the love which Jesus had for His Father, and for those whom God was calling out of the world and into His Kingdom; and in His obedience to His Father's will, Jesus had allowed the whole weight of the sin of the world to be laid upon Him. Peter put it so simply and yet so profoundly. 'He Himself bore our sins in His Body on the Tree' (1 Peter 2:24).

But God is of purer eyes than to behold evil (Habakkuk 1:!3).

The Father turned His face away from His beloved Son. He cannot look upon evil. For the once and only moment in time and eternity, God turns His face away from His Son. And this is absolute proof that Jesus has indeed taken upon Himself the sin of the whole world. The cry of desolation from the cross validated the fact that sin and death had been conquered, overcome, as Jesus hung there, a living sacrifice, opening the way to heaven for all believers.

But how can He bear it? The pain of the Cross is as nothing compared to this separation from His Father. And yet, He knows that it must be so. He knew the cross would be costly, perhaps even more than He could bear, but to bear separation from His Father, even for a moment, was the greatest cost of all.

Yet He was wounded for our transgressions. He was bruised for our iniquities, the chastisement of His God was upon Him, the chastisement that made us whole and gave us peace with God. (Isaiah 53:5 R.S.V., A.V.) *The suffering Father. The suffering Son.*

Matthew 27:51-53. The veil of the temple

And suddenly, the veil of the Temple was torn in two, from the top to the bottom, and there was such an earthquake that the earth shook and the rocks split, and the tombs were opened and many bodies of the saints who had fallen asleep were raised, and coming out of the tombs after His resurrection, went into the city and appeared to many.

Having intervened with a curtain of 'darkness over all the land' (verse 45). God now intervened by shattering the darkness in an area of the temple which no longer represented God's purpose for His people. This darkness had surrounded the Holiest of all, the Holy of Holies, a place or room containing the Ark of the Covenant, into which only the High Priest could go once a year on the Day of Atonement, for there was a veil, a curtain, between it and the Holy Place (Exodus 26:33). The Holy Place contained the seven-branched lampstand, the altar of incense and the Table of shewbread, the Bread of the Presence, but the Most Holy Place contained only the Ark of the Covenant. And there was a veil, a curtain between the Holy Place and the Holiest of All.

This was the darkness which was shattered and burst open. The curtain which prevented access to the Ark of the Covenant was split from the top, where God was, to the bottom, where men and women were.

Job's cry had come down through the ages, 'O that I knew where I might find Him, that I might come even to His seat!'

(Job 23:3). The tabernacle, the tent in the wilderness, had at least partly fulfilled that desire. It provided access to God.

We know that God overflows everywhere. As Solomon rightly said at the dedication of the first temple, 'Behold, heaven and the highest heaven cannot contain Thee. How much less this house which I have built!' (1 Kings 8:27)

But God had said to Moses, 'Let them build Me a sanctuary, that I may dwell in their midst.' (Exodus 25:8).

So, according to His commandment, Moses had constructed the tabernacle with the Ark of the Covenant within the Most Holy Place, behind the veil, thus providing a place for the expiation for sin. Above the Ark, was the Mercy Seat. This was the place where sins were dealt with. This was the place where men and women might find forgiveness of their sins, and also find God, for He had promised to dwell with them. This was the whole purpose of the tabernacle, the tent of Meeting. In the wilderness God was providing a place where He could be with His people, for He said, 'I will dwell with them and be their God' (Exodus 29:45) 'My dwelling place shall be with them and I will be their God and they shall be My people' (Ezekiel 37:27).

And when there is a new heaven and a new earth, God is still wanting to be with His people. 'The tabernacle, the tent, the dwelling of God is with men. He will dwell with them, and they shall be His people.' (Revelation 21:3).

In the wilderness, they lived in tents, so He also dwelt in a tent. In the time of King Solomon, the people lived in houses, so Solomon built Him a House, the Temple. Wherever His people were, there God wanted to be.

The Ark of the Covenant had been constructed as a chest, or box made of acacia wood, the common wood of the wilderness, but covered over with gold, 'overlaid within and without with gold' (Exodus 25:11), speaking of its preciousness. And over the Ark there was a cover, covering the Ark, otherwise known as the Mercy Seat. (Exodus 25:2). The Ark was the visible expression of the presence of the Lord with His people, the symbol of the Ark of His might. (Psalm 132:8,13).

But both in the tabernacle and later in the temple, this precious object had been hidden away behind the curtain, into which the High Priest, on behalf of the congregation of Israel, entered once a year, carrying the blood of the sacrificial animal. This animal had *involuntarily* given its blood, for without the shedding of blood there is no remission for sins. (Hebrews 9:22). And the atoning blood, the blood that made atonement for sins, was sprinkled on the mercy seat, (A.V.) or atonement cover. (N.I.V.).

All that the children of Israel were, was condemned, sentenced, and judged unworthy of the presence of the Lord by the contents of the Ark, the Ten Commandments. This was the moral law which they could not keep. But over the Ark, exactly fitting its dimensions was the Mercy Seat, sprinkled with the blood. The sacrifice was substitutionary, the life of the animal appropriated for the sins of the people, for the life was in the blood. 'It is the blood that makes an atonement for the soul.' (Leviticus 17:11 A.V.). The broken law was covered by the blood. Mercy was triumphing over judgement.

But the Ark was not there in the time of Jesus. After the destruction of the temple in 587 B.C. the Ark disappeared, and after the exile to Babylon under Nebuchadnezzar (2 Kings 25:9, 13-17; Jeremiah 52:12-16), was never recovered or replaced. Even so, even after the destruction, people still came to sacrifice there (Jeremiah 41:5).

There was however, still a place for forgiveness of sins at the altar of burnt offering outside, at the entrance to the Holy Place, according to all the demands of the Torah, for the character of the burnt offering was to sublimate the offered animal into a form which could be transported to God, into the smoke as it burned, and became what is described as a sweet savour to God as He looked down upon His penitent child. (Leviticus 1:9).

God tore away the veil of the temple when Jesus died, not to expose an empty room, but as a declaration of His intention to continue living with His people but on a different basis. The Old has gone. The New has come. The Old Covenant has been superseded by the New Covenant in the blood of Jesus, and it is now His blood that avails for sin, not the blood of bulls and goats as they were continually offered (Hebrews 10:4), but through the offering of the body of Jesus Christ once for all (Hebrews 10:10). His sacrifice has won access for us into His Holy presence. The veil which would separate us from Him has been done away with and we may freely enter in. His mercy has provided a way into the Holiest of all. His blood has opened for us a new and living way 'through the curtain, that is, His flesh'. (Hebrews 10:20).

Therefore, let us come boldly unto the throne of grace, that we may receive mercy, and find grace to help in time of need. (Hebrews 4:16). *The veil is rent in Christ alone,* the living way to heaven is seen. the middle wall is broken down, and all mankind may enter in. (C. Wesley)'

The veil was not partially destroyed, so that it could be mended again. It was irretrievably damaged, an unmistakable judgement on the part of God. Not just symbolically, but actually, God is saying that He wants His people to come to Him, come into His presence; that because of what His Son did on the cross, there is no longer a barrier, an obstacle, to His desire to be the 'alone' God with His beloved people, the one and only merciful, faithful God. The atonement, the at-one-ment, has been made not only possible but actual, as Jesus prayed to His Father 'That they might be one even as We are one. I in them and Thou in Me' (John 17:23). Could any prayer of Jesus even be denied Him? There is now nothing between, no veil between God and His beloved people. The blood of Jesus ratifies the purposes of God towards His children.

But how costly was the rending of that veil; opening up for us a new and living way into the holiest, by the blood of Jesus, a way consecrated for us through the veil, that is to say, His flesh. (Hebrews 10:20 A.V.).

Matthew 27:51. The earthquake

This was the third supernatural intervention. First, the darkness, then the veil of the Temple being torn in two, and now the earthquake, and each of these has a spiritual significance, a message from God, behind it.

God had covered the face of His Son with darkness as He poured out His life. He had torn the veil of the Temple in two to show that the work of redemption had been completed and now He causes 'the earth to shake and the rocks to split'. The tombs also were opened and many bodies of the saints who had fallen asleep were raised and coming out of the tombs after His resurrection they went into the holy city and appeared to many' (verse 51-53).

God did not stand by while His Son hung on the cross, but was displaying His absolute concurrence with Him as Jesus demonstrated once more His absolute obedience to Father's will, for the will of each was completely at one with the will of the other. And this demonstration was delivered through the physical world as an expression of what was happening in the spiritual dimension.

And these extraordinary events could only be through the activity and power of God Himself, for no human being could have caused them to take place. All creation was calling out, demonstrating that the most tremendous event through time and eternity was now taking place on a bare hillside outside Jerusalem, God and His Son combining and conspiring to raise fallen men and women to the throne on high, where they would reign with Them forever.

The very earth, upon which the cross stood, was shaken to its foundations. His Body was still there, though His spirit was now at home with His Father to whom He had yielded it. (verse 50).

So great is the power of life over death, the life of the Son of God over the sting of death, which is sin, (1 Corinthians 15:56), that the death of the saints of God could not hold them. As the earth rumbled around the tombs, they were raised up. The tombs cracked open. Even the rocks split. Nothing like it had ever been seen before. No wonder that when the centurion and those that were with him saw the earthquake, these men who were watching over Jesus, they 'saw the earthquake and what took place, and they were filled with awe and said, "Truly, this was the Son of God."' (verse 54).

The reaction of the centurion and those who were with him was entirely appropriate. The centurion was a Gentile, but he could see in this extraordinary crucifixion something he had never seen before, though it is quite possible that he had been involved or present at many crucifixions.

This crucifixion was unique. All the other crucifixions he had seen had been of sinners, but this man had been made sin for us who knew no sin, (2 Corinthians 5:21), although the centurion was almost certainly not aware of this. Nevertheless, he saw with his eyes, and felt with all his senses as the earthquake took hold and then subsided that this crucifixion was different. Even to his Gentile perception there could only be one explanation, 'This was the Son of God' (verse 54).

If he had but known it, the corollary of that statement was, 'And He is dying for me, for my sins,' for the power of that cross was not for Jews only, but for Gentiles too. Though with a burdened and heavy heart he may have gone about his duties as a soldier, all at once, he had an unexpected joy in his heart, a revelation from God as to who the Man on the cross was. He was the Son of God!

God was in Christ, reconciling not only the Jewish world but the Gentile world, to Himself.

How wonderful if this Roman soldier could have been with the other 119 people, waiting in Jerusalem after Jesus' resurrection and ascension, praying for the promised Holy Spirit (Acts 1:15). He may even have told Matthew about his experience, for Matthew was there too. (Acts 1:!3). We speculate of course, and have no scriptural authority for these speculations, but we do know that God does miracles, transforming miracles, in people's lives, and it is not unreasonable to hope that He did a miracle for the centurion.

The confession of the centurion, 'Truly, this was the Son of God,' (verse 54), is the confession too of the soldiers who were with him. 'They were filled with awe' (verse 54); they became exceedingly afraid, for they were in the presence of a great mystery. They were also Gentiles, brought into the presence of the Son of God. The saints who were unable to stay dead in the presence of the One who had overcome death were Jewish.

Here we have a further development of what Matthew has emphasised throughout his gospel, that both Gentiles and Jews are welcome in the Kingdom of Heaven; that this is the nucleus of the church which Jesus is building, and the gates of hell have no power at all to prevail against it. (Matthew 16:18).

Thus, these supernatural phenomena declare that God's purpose is to dwell with His people, and that His people are now no longer restricted to Jews only but to all, Jew or Gentile, who come to Him in faith, trusting in the shed blood of the Lord Jesus to prevent the sin which does so easily beset us (Hebrews 12:1), from causing any obstacle to fellowship with Him.

According to the witness of the Old Testament, God sometimes revealed Himself through earthquakes, for example, Exodus 19:18, Judges 5:5, 1 Kings 19:11,12, Psalm 18:8, and notably at Sinai when God made a covenant with His people and gave them the Ten Commandments, principles by which they could live. So important was the giving of the Law that God accompanied it with smoke, storm and earthquake (Exodus 19:18,19), manifesting His glory, power and holiness.

Even greater was the significance of the earthquake which surrounded the cross of His Son. No wonder the earth shook and trembled at what had happened as its Creator hung there. He is described in Colossians 1:15,16 as the firstborn of all creation, for whom all things were created. All things were created through Him and for Him (Colossians 1:16). And the world He had created responded by breaking open as He hung there, making peace though the blood of His Cross. (Colossians 1:20).

Now, 'many bodies of the saints arose' (verse 52). This was not a general resurrection. This was just a foretaste of what will happen when the Lord Jesus comes again, when He comes in glory to take His people to Himself. 'For the trumpet shall sound, and the dead will be raised incorruptible, and this mortal must put on immortality'. (1 Corinthians 15:52,53). 'The dead in Christ shall rise first, then we who are alive shall be caught up with them in the clouds to meet the Lord in the air, and so shall we ever be with the Lord'. (1 Thessalonians 4:16,17).

Already, God is looking forward to the Second Coming of His Son, the Parousia, when Jesus will be glorified, when the dead in Christ will rise, when all the tribes of the earth will see the Son of Man coming on the clouds of heaven with power and great glory. (Matthew 24:30). A limited expectation of what is to come is happening here, at the cross.

After Jesus is risen from the dead, He goes into Galilee (Matthew 28:16), where after forty days (Acts 1:3), He ascends to His Father. Matthew does not record for us the resurrection appearances to be found in Mark, Luke and John. But he does inform us of these resurrected saints who go into Jerusalem, there to testify that God is a God of resurrection as Jesus said at the grave of Lazarus. 'I am the resurrection and the life' (John 11:25).

His life was so powerful, His overcoming of death so immense that it overflowed to these saints of God, perhaps the prophets whom Jerusalem had killed and stoned. (Matthew 23:27). God had chosen these former servants of His to proclaim the message of the cross after His resurrection had taken place (verse 53), as they went into the holy city, proclaiming the completion, the fullness, the death *and* resurrection of His dear Son. His resurrection demonstrated without a doubt that Jesus was indeed the Son of God, and it is to this revelation that *both* the Jewish saints and the Roman soldiers had testified.

The earthquake at Sinai was the accompaniment of something tremendous which God was doing, instituting a covenant with His people, a covenant that ordained that as they walked with Him in obedience and faith, He would be all-in-all to them, their Protector, Guide, Companion, Friend, Redeemer, King, in other words, *GOD*.

But the earthquake at the cross was God's declaration that He was instituting a New Covenant. The Old Covenant was ratified in the blood of sacrificial animals. This was the New Covenant in the blood of His Son as Jesus Himself had said at the Last Supper, 'This is My blood of the New Covenant, which is poured out for many for the forgiveness of sins'. (Matthew 26:28).

This covenant was personal, as well as being universal. It was *personal* in the sense that every individual had to receive that covenant, and its conditional terms of repentance and faith, for themselves. It was *universal* in that it was available to all, unlike the previous covenant, The Old Covenant, with the people of Israel alone.

The Israelites did not continue in His covenant (Hebrews 8:9), so God promised that He would make a new covenant. 'This is the covenant that I will make with the house of Israel after those days,' says the Lord, 'for God still yearns after His people, though now He wants to include the whole human race' (Hebrews 8:10). 'This is the covenant that I will make in those days; says the Lord. I will put My laws into their minds and write them in their hearts, and I will be their God and they shall be My people. And they shall know Me, from the least to the greatest, and I will be merciful to their iniquities and I will remember their sins no more'. (Jeremiah 31:31-34; Hebrews 8:11,12).

A believer may truly say, God has made this covenant *with me; because of Jesus.* Again and again throughout scripture the cry of God's heart rings out. 'I will be their God and they will be My people.' God is still acting to bring people to Himself, for He loves them and wants to be their God. No wonder that there is joy in the presence of the angels of God over one sinner who repents (Luke 15:10). This is our merciful, loving God.

There may be a tendency to overload the text apocalyptically or eschatologically, but what Matthew has here portrayed in his gospel with such brevity, confining himself to the facts and not to the explanation or interpretation of the facts, we may legitimately, biblically understand in the light of both Old Testament and New Testaments insights. This is what other New Testament authors have enabled us to appreciate. The events surrounding the death and resurrection of Jesus Christ, the Son of Man, the Son of God, must, of necessity, be full of significance. This is the focal point of history. It follows that every detail carries with it something of what God is doing, and what He is saying through the death of His Son, and what that death has accomplished.

What God had promised, He was able also to perform. (Romans 4:21). Jesus was put to death for our trespasses, and raised for our justification (Romans 4:25). Therefore being justified by faith we have peace with God through our Lord Jesus Christ. Through Him we have obtained access to this grace in which we stand, and we rejoice in our hope of sharing the glory of God. (Romans 5:1,2). God is glorified in His Son, and chooses to share that glory with us. This is the gospel of our Lord Jesus Christ.

Matthew 27:55-56. The women at the cross

There were also many women there, looking on from afar, who had followed Jesus from Galilee, ministering to Him, among whom were Mary Magdalene, and Mary the mother of James and Joseph, and the mother of the sons of Zebedee.

How many women were there, at the cross, looking on while He suffered the most terrible agony, we do not know.

Only three women are mentioned in Matthew, two Marys, and possibly Salome (Mark 15:40), unnamed in Matthew but traditionally identified as the mother of James and John, the sons of Zebedee, in Matthew 27:56.

John's gospel further identifies Mary, the mother of James and Joseph as the wife of Clopas, who as the sister of Mary the mother of Jesus was also there, standing near to the disciple whom Jesus loved, and to whom in a last act of loving mercy, He committed her. (John 19:25-27).

What is remarkable about this group of women was not so much those individual women who were named, although it is of great value to understand their particular place in the ministry of Jesus, but that in a patriarchal, male dominated society, these women were still able to follow Him from Galilee. It is true that they looked on Him 'from afar', (Matthew 27:55), for the Roman soldiers could not allow members of the public to interfere with the work they had to do, but they were there for Him whom they had come to love as they ministered to Him.

These unnamed women had travelled to Jerusalem, perhaps from Capernaum, 90 miles away from Jerusalem, or perhaps from Nazareth, 70 miles away from Jerusalem, or other towns and cities in Galilee, on foot, following Jesus so that they could serve Him, leaving behind their homes and families and all that they held dear. They had ministered to Him in Galilee, (Mark 15:41), and saw no reason to stop their loving of Him because He had decided to go to Jerusalem. Did they know, as the disciples knew, that Jesus was going to be crucified? Could they have foreseen the danger of coming up against the ruling religious leaders? Perhaps all they knew was that their beloved master was suffering, and they wanted Him to know that humanly speaking, He was not alone as He died His cruel death. As far as was possible, they wanted to suffer with Him.

The house in Jerusalem of Acts 1:13, and 2:1, is going to be quite crowded as we imagine that many, or even all of these women, would be among those praying and waiting for the promised Holy Spirit, (Acts 1:15) after His resurrection and ascension to His Father.

Of the three women mentioned by Matthew, Mary Magdalene was perhaps the most conspicuous, for Luke tells us that Jesus had cast seven demons out of her, (Luke 8:2), but that she was now one of a group of women who had been healed of evil spirits and infirmities. Of this group also were Joanna, the wife of Chuza, Herod's steward, and Susanna, and many others 'who provided' for Jesus and His disciples 'out of their means'. (Luke 8:3).

The restored and beloved Mary of Magdala has been identified with the woman 'who was a sinner'. (Luke 7:37). This woman brought an alabaster flask of ointment to Jesus, in the house of Simon the Pharisee and weeping, began to wet His feet with her tears, and wipe them with the hair of her head, and kissed His feet and anointed them with the ointment. (Luke 7:38). And Jesus said to Simon, 'Her sins which are many, are forgiven, for she loved much'. (Luke 7:47). Then He said to the woman, 'Your sins are forgiven, go in peace'. (verses 48, 50). She was not saved by her love, but for her faith. (verse 50). 'Your faith has saved you.' He said. But how her love rejoiced His heart.

Was this woman of Luke 7 the Mary Magdalene of Luke 8? Luke does not tell us, but Matthew 26:6-12; Mark 14:3-9; and

John 12:1-8 tell a similar story but with significant discrepancies in the detail. Neither Matthew or Mark describe the woman as 'a sinner' which is probably a synonym in this case for 'prostitute'. Luke says the incident took place in the home of a Pharisee called Simon, while Matthew and Mark suggest it was in the house of 'Simon the Leper'. (Matthew 26:6; Mark 14:3). It is unlikely that as a leper, Simon could have been a Pharisee as part of the Sanhedrin but he may have shared the theological convictions of the Pharisees, or may have been born into a Pharisaical family.

Matthew and Mark place the event in Bethany, 2 miles outside Jerusalem, as also does John, but Luke times it earlier on in Jesus' Galilean ministry, while Mark and Matthew place it immediately before Judas' decision to betray Jesus.

John's account is the most consistent with that of Matthew and Mark, though it has its problems too. According to John, the anointing of Jesus took place in Bethany at the home of Mary, Martha and Lazarus and it was this Mary who anointed His feet and wiped His feet with her hair. (John 12:3), and the house was filled with the fragrance of worship and love. This was timed as Jesus came to Jerusalem *before* His triumphal entry as their King, receiving the acclamation of the crowds as they went out to meet Him with branches of palm trees crying, 'Hosanna!' Blessed is He who comes in the name of the Lord! (John 12:12-15).

In Mark and Matthew, it was the *head* of the Lord Jesus which was anointed, and the anointing took place *after* His triumphant entry into Jerusalem.

Do the chronology, or the identification of the worshipping, loving women really matter? Was it Mary Magdalene or Mary of Bethany – or even perhaps both – who ministered to Him in this way, so similar, and yet so different? Does it matter whether the ointment was poured upon the precious Head, so soon to receive a crown of thorns, according to Matthew and Mark, or on His feet, according to Luke and John. Those precious feet, as Jesus had walked so many miles, as He went about doing good and healing all that were oppressed by the devil, for God was with

Him. (Acts 10:38]). Dirty and dusty and sore and blistered as they were, soothed and comforted by the tears and ointment of the unknown woman.

It may be that there was more than one instance of this particular ministry being given to Jesus; a reminder of that wonderful love song (Psalm 45:7), as Jesus prophetically received the anointing of the oil of gladness above His fellows, the Bridegroom waiting for His Bride, the church, as she bows to Him and worships Him as Her Lord. (Psalm 45:13). Mary Magdalene, a woman among many waiting at His cross, may or may not have been the woman who anointed Him, but she was certainly there at His tomb very early in the day, to find His tomb empty and an angel sitting on it. Her ministry to Him was not incidental, but constant.

The second woman to be identified was Mary the mother of James and Joseph, or Joses (a diminutive of Joseph). Though Jesus had two brothers called James and Joseph, (Matthew 13:53), this Mary is not the mother of Jesus, otherwise she would have been called 'the mother of Jesus'. Mark calls her 'Mary the mother of James the less and of Joses'. James may have been of smaller stature, or even simply younger which was why he was called 'the less'. Is this Mary the wife of Alphaeus, the mother of 'James the son of Alphaeus' of Matthew 10:3? We do not know. According to John 19:25, she may have been the wife of Clopas, the sister of Mary, Jesus' mother, but it is unlikely that two sisters would both be Mary. Clopas may have been the Cleopas of Luke 24:18, who together with another disciple met Jesus on the road to Emmaus after His resurrection.

The third woman we know from Matthew 20:20, the mother of James and John the sons of Zebedee. Women were so often referenced in relation to their husbands or sons, but Mark gives us the additional information that her name was Salome, which together with Mary was a common name for women at that period.

The recording of this brief detail of the women at the cross has had enormous implication for women, for it enables the view that women too may be disciples, may 'follow' Jesus, a term

Matthew always uses for discipleship. Women's ministry may, and often does, revolve around the home and domestic duties; this was especially true at the time of Jesus. But there is also a place for them in Jerusalem as well as in Galilee, not only for providing for Him out of their means, as in Luke 8:3, but by ministering to Him the love and devotion of their hearts.

They stand in sorrow before His cross, weeping. They bow in worship at His empty Tomb. They do not replicate the ministry of the apostles, they complement it in a way the apostles cannot. They do not seek equality, but an opportunity to serve 'Him whom their soul loveth'. (Song of Solomon 1:7; 3:1)

The disciples forsook Him and fled. These 'many' women from Galilee are present at the cross, watching from a distance as His life blood ebbs away. Hidden in the darkness, unperturbed by the earthquake, they are the pioneers of what God is doing, beginning with the resurrection of His Son, and taking this hope and the glory that is to come into their homes, as their homes become the places where other disciples, coming to know Jesus as their Lord and Saviour, can meet together, 'break bread from house to house', have fellowship with one another and pray together (Acts 2:42), and share together memories of what He had done for them, and taught them while He was with them, as they were now inspired by the Holy Spirit who had now come upon them and filled them. (Acts 2:4)

In these two brief verses, Matthew has laid the foundations of what is to come. They followed Jesus from Galilee to the cross. They continue to follow Him after His resurrection and ascension in order to serve Him and to serve one another in His Name. They can truly claim to be His disciples and to say 'My beloved is mine and I am His'. (Song of Solomon 2:16).

Matthew 27:57-61. The burial of Jesus

When it was evening, there came a rich man from Aramathea, named Joseph, who also was a disciple of Jesus. He went to Pilate and asked for the body of Jesus. Then Pilate ordered it to be given to him. And Joseph took the body, and wrapped it in a clean linen shroud, and laid it in his own new tomb which he had hewn out of the rock. And he rolled a great stone to the door of the tomb and departed. Mary Magdalene and the other Mary were there, sitting opposite the sepulchre. (Matthew 27:57-61).

Jesus had died, but His dear body still hung upon the cross, and Friday was coming to an end. The next day, the Sabbath day was the day upon which no work could be done. His body had to be taken down from the cross before the Sabbath day.

People who had been crucified, and therefore regarded as criminals were usually buried without honour or ceremony in a public field. The Roman custom was to leave the bodies on the cross to decay, or to be attacked by birds such as ravens, but the Jews removed them in accordance with Deuteronomy 21:22-23.

Joseph foresaw that a problem was arising, so 'while it was yet evening', that is, before sunset, the time at which the Sabbath day would begin (for the Jewish day began at sunset, until the following sunset), Joseph made a decision.

Joseph was a rich man, from Aramathea, a town north west of Lydda and Joppa, and a disciple of Jesus. Mark and Luke present him as a respected member of the council, the Sanhedrin (Mark 15:43), who was also himself looking for the Kingdom of God, and in Luke 23:50 as a member of the Council, a good and righteous man who had not consented to their purpose and deed, and 'he was looking for the Kingdom of God'.

Whether he had become a fully committed disciple of Jesus, as in Matthew, or was nearly at the point of total commitment to Jesus, as in Mark and Luke, he was certainly a rich man, who had been able to purchase a site for a tomb to be hewn out of the rocky landscape surrounding Jerusalem. All the appurtenances of death, and the handing down to future generations, not only the wealth, but the wisdom that someone had accrued during their lifetime, was very important to Jews, though relatively few could hope to aspire to a tomb.

Joseph had one, a new one, which he had prepared against the time came for his death, and for his family too. It was a costly thing to do, to decide to give that tomb over to the body of Jesus. (verse 58). But he was a man of decision and purpose. He was able, probably because of his wealth and position, to gain access to Pilate, so he went to Pilate and asked for the body of Jesus.

With what care was that precious body taken down from the cross, and wrapped in a clean linen shroud, and laid in Joseph's own new rock-hewn tomb (verse 50), where no man had ever yet been laid. Joseph had managed to accomplish all this before the Sabbath day began. Rolling a great stone to the door of the tomb, he departed. (verse 60). His work was done. He had provided not only for Jesus, but for His followers, a safe place for His body to be laid.

He appeared not to have been there when the stone was rolled away from the tomb by the angel. This wonderful privilege was reserved for Mary Magdalene and the other Mary, but how he must have rejoiced that he had been allowed to participate in a small way in the wonderful transformation of Jesus' lifeless body, into the resurrected body of the Son of God. Any reservations which he may have had, according to Mark and Luke had were completely overruled, Luther, that great reformer, says that Joseph was emboldened by seeing Jesus on the cross, to come out of his obscurity and to confess openly that he was a disciple of Jesus. (Luz p582. Luther Passio).

During the mediaeval period, since the 12th Century, there was a portrayal in art, music and literature, in some detail, of Jesus being taken down from the cross by Joseph and Nicodemus, according to John 19:38-42, but then to rest at the foot of the cross in the arms of His mother, His head cradled in her lap as she caressed Him, with Mary Magdalene at His feet. In the light of so much human mortality, particularly in that era, these scenes of Mary's grief helped to meet the need of many to express sorrow, separation, and mourning for the death of loved ones.

These scenes may not have been biblical, but there are very human reasons for believing that His mother was there, as He was taken down from the cross. The gospels do not expressly confirm that she was, but piety, and the need for comfort, appear to have overtaken biblical texts; purporting to express a greater reality, that Jesus is with us in our suffering, even the suffering of losing our loved ones, as His mother Mary demonstrates.

Mary must indeed have been devastated at the death of her Son, but such an event is not recorded in any of the four gospels.

Matthew 27:61. The women keeping vigil

Mary Magdalene and the other Mary were there, sitting opposite the sepulchre. (Matthew 27:61).

Though Mary Magdalene and Mary the mother of James and Joseph (verse 56), may not have been involved in taking Jesus down from the cross, they were determined to stay by His tomb. They had seen where His body lay, and after Joseph of Aramathea had departed, they sat there, opposite the tomb. (verse 61). Having seen where He lay, they had prepared spices and ointments, and then returned to the tomb. (Luke 23:56).

It appears from the Matthean text that they sat there all through the long day of the Sabbath, watching over His tomb. Perhaps they had no knowledge as to why it was important for them to be there. Perhaps they just wanted to be near Him, even though it was only His broken body that was there, for His spirit had been yielded up to His Father. (verse 50). They waited and watched, all through that long day, until, after the Sabbath, toward the dawn of the first day of the week, they went to see the sepulchre. (Matthew 28:1).

Their constant watch had made it clear that there was no mistaking His burial place, and that no-one had come to remove Him from the tomb. Watching and waiting, close to Jesus, has been the experience of many of His lovers, from then until now, waiting for the revelation of Himself, and the next stage of the accomplishment of His will and purpose.

Matthew 27:62-66. The guard at the tomb

During that time of vigil, however, after the day of preparation, (verse 62), the chief priests and the Pharisees suddenly became alarmed. 'Did not that imposter say that after three days He would rise again from the dead?'

Hurriedly, they go to Pilate and say to him, 'Sir, we remember what that imposter said while He was still alive. After three days I will rise again, Therefore, order the sepulchre to be made secure until the third day, lest His disciples come and steal Him away, and tell the people, "He is risen from the dead," and the last fraud will be worse than the first.' (verse 64).

Pilate is not sympathetic to their request. His own soldiers have done their work. Why should he use them to do something founded exclusively on the fear and paranoia of these troublesome Jewish leaders? He dismisses them curtly. You have your own security people, your Temple guard. Get them to form a guard around His tomb if you are worried. I want nothing more to do with it.

With this limited permission, the chief priests and the Pharisees have to be content. They at least have the authorization to make the tomb secure by sealing the stone which formed the door to the tomb, and mounting a guard. (verse 66).

But when Jesus rose from the dead, the seal was broken, not to allow Jesus to come out, but for the disciples to go in.

Only Matthew records the incident with the guards, but in the light of the scepticism concerning the resurrection of Jesus which then arose, it was important to Matthew to include it. He is contrasting the vigil of the women who loved Jesus with the attitude of the guards, also watching and waiting, but waiting with trepidation in case a bruised and broken body should suddenly rise up before them, even though the tomb was sealed. The authority given to the chief priests and Pharisees is not going to save them from witnessing something horrendous.

They could accept that Jesus was a deceiver, an imposter. That would seem entirely logical. But supposing it was true, that He really meant what He said and could actually rise from the dead?

Though they had never seen such a thing, the fear of the unknown was certainly with them that day. They may even have thought that perhaps it was not Jesus who was the deceiver, deceiving them, but the chief priests and the Pharisees.

Matthew's inclusion of this episode, exclusive to him, surely underlies the conviction that even the Jewish authorities had no option but to believe the evidence of the witnesses whom they themselves had commissioned, that Jesus had risen from the dead as He had declared He would and that the grave was empty. Their only way of defending their position was to protest lamely that His disciples had come by night and stolen Him away while the guards slept. (Matthew 28:13).

Jesus always does what He says He will do. He *is* alive! We serve a *living* Saviour! He really died, and He really rose again from the dead, and He lives forevermore.

Meanwhile, the Sabbath day had come to an end. It was the next morning, the first day of the week, when the vigil of the women ended, and Mary Magdalene and the other Mary approached the sepulchre.

Matthew Chapter 28

Matthew 28:1-10. The resurrection of Jesus

Now, after the Sabbath, toward the dawn of the first day of the week, Mary Magdalene and the other Mary went to see the sepulchre. And behold, there was a great earthquake, for an angel of the Lord descended from heaven and came and rolled back the stone and sat upon it. His appearance was like lightning, and his raiment white as snow. And for fear of him, the guards trembled and became like dead men.

But the angel said to the women, 'Do not be afraid, for I know that you seek Jesus, who was crucified. He is not here, for He has risen, as He said. Come, see the place where He lay. Then go quickly and tell His disciples that He has risen from the dead, and behold, He is going before you to Galilee, there you will see Him. Lo I have told you.' (Matthew 28:1-7).

Now that the Sabbath day was over, the women could approach the tomb, and according to Mark and Luke, were bringing with them the ointment and spices they had prepared with which to anoint His dear body. (Mark 16:1, Luke 24:1). With what sorrow, with what halting feet they approached the tomb, lovingly prepared to do this last office for Him, but dreading it all the same.

As they went, the ground trembled again under their feet, for there was a great earthquake. Aware now that something unusual was happening, they were astonished to see that the stone had been rolled away from the tomb, and that an angel sat upon it! They knew that the stone was heavy, and had been wondering who they could ask to help them roll away the stone. Was it this angel who had rolled it away? Or had it happened during the earthquake?

They recognised him immediately as an angel. Their only way of describing him was that he was like lightning, light so fierce and bright that it hurt your eyes to look at it, and the whiteness of his clothes was like snow, white and bright and dazzling. But the angel's voice was calm and full of understanding. He knew that they were coming to anoint the body of Jesus, and he also knew that it was no longer necessary. 'He is not here,' he said. 'He is risen!' And he said it with a chuckle, for he and every angel in heaven had looked down with sad and wondering eyes to see Jesus as the sacrifice, as He approached the cross. And now He was risen! This angel had been given the wonderful privilege of announcing His resurrection to these faithful, loyal women. How surprised they were going to be!

To the guards he had nothing to say.

To the women he had said, 'Do not be afraid.' (verse 5).

The guards were very afraid, trembling with fear, becoming like dead men. But they had expected to see, if they were to see anything at all, a bruised and broken body coming out of the tomb if He were to rise again from the dead as He said He would. But now they were seeing an angel! They had not expected to see an angel, blazing with light, completely supernatural.

How was this possible? When they had somewhat recovered, all they could do was to go back to their masters, the chief priests, and tell them 'all that had taken place' (verse 11).

The angel now gave the women explicit instructions to go and tell His disciples that He had risen from the dead, and, 'Behold, He is going before you to Galilee. There you will see Him'. (verse 7). The women needed no second bidding. Full of joy, they departed quickly from the tomb and ran to tell His disciples. (verse 8). But they had not yet seen their risen Lord. They had seen with their own eyes the empty tomb. They had believed implicitly what the angel had told them, and were being obedient to the instructions he had given them.

Suddenly, whom should they confront but Jesus Himself, standing before them, their risen, loving Lord. Behold, Jesus met them and said, 'Hail!' It was enough. They fell at His feet and worshipped Him, for they knew Him in a way they had never experienced before, that He was indeed the Son of God (verse 9).

Yet mixed with their joy was their fear; their awe of who He was; and is. This One with whom they had spoken, ministered to, in the best way they knew how. They had left all to follow Him, just as certainly and surely as had His early disciples, Peter and Andrew, James and John. (Matthew 4:20,22). Here before then was One whom they knew and recognised, but different, glorious in His risen life, as He would be forever; Jesus, but a risen Jesus with all the marks of His crucifixion still upon Him; those marks which He would take into heaven with Him.

Of course they took hold of His feet and worshipped Him. (verse 9).

But, 'Do not be afraid,' said Jesus to them. (verse 10). He, more than anyone, much more even than the angel, was aware of all the complicated thoughts and feelings which were going through them. How could they take it all in? What did it mean for the future? Would it still be possible to love and worship this new and different Jesus as they had done before? Jesus gave them something to do for Him. 'Go and tell My brothers to go to Galilee, and there they will see Me'. (verse 10), so happily they went.

He could have gone straight to Galilee, but instead waited until He had comforted the hearts of these two women. Only He knew how to comfort, encourage, strengthen, the faith of those who trusted in Him.

It is perhaps surprising that Matthew gives no indication of the visit to the tomb of Peter and John, nor of His subsequent resurrection appearances during the forty days before He ascended into heaven. As Luke so happily writes, 'To them He presented Himself alive after His passion by many proofs, appearing to them during forty days, and speaking of the Kingdom of God'. (Acts 1:3). The gospels of Mark, Luke and John all have incidences of His resurrection appearances, but Matthew does not record them.

The angel had said to the women, 'Go quickly and tell His disciples that He has risen from the dead, and behold, He is going before you into Galilee; there you will see him' (verse 7). Jesus has the same message for the women to take to His disciples, but there is a difference. 'Then Jesus said to them, do not be afraid; go tell *My brothers* to go to Galilee, and there they will see Me'. (verse 10).

Jesus calls them "My brothers". There is no recrimination, no hint or expression of disappointment that these men had forsaken Him and fled. (Matthew 26:56). Jesus says, 'My brothers.' These men whom I love, My brothers, will be My messengers to take the gospel, the good news, to the ends of the earth. These men whom I chose, and who also chose Me, and have followed Me and heard My teaching and have seen Me die. These men, My brothers.

In Mark's gospel, we read, 'Go and tell His disciples, *and Peter,* that He is going before you into Galilee. There you will see Him' (Mark 16:7). This was the message from Mark's 'young man dressed in a white robe at the tomb', (Mark 16:5) identified by Matthew as an angel.This message was no doubt intended as a word of comfort to Peter after His denial of His Lord.

Matthew does not especially mention Peter as a recipient of the good news of the Risen Jesus. For Matthew, all the disciples were recipients. The good news for them all was that Jesus, now their risen Lord, still loved them and had a ministry for them. They were to go to Galilee. For us, as disciples, learners of Jesus, we too are recipients. No matter what we have done, He still loves us. And we all have the privilege of the proclamation of this wonderful truth, that He is alive for evermore, that He has conquered death, and that He is 'designated the Son of God in power, according to the Spirit of holiness by His resurrection from the dead, Jesus Christ our Lord.' (Romans 1:4).

Simon Peter is the representative disciples. He need not, according to Matthew, be mentioned separately, as if he is in some sense demoted because of His denial of Jesus, but is included as if such denial had never been. After all, they all forsook Him and fled. But he, with all of Jesus' brothers, needs to be told that the tomb is empty, as He, Jesus, had told them it would be, in Matthew 16:21; 17:22-23 and 20:18-19. They can absolutely trust His word, for He speaks with authority. The women run quickly, leaving the tomb, rejoicing in what they had seen and heard, and how they are going to share that joy with the disciples.

The four accounts of the resurrection of Jesus

Matthew 28:1-10; Mark 16:1-11; Luke 24:1-12; John 20:1-8

There is some degree of difference in the details of Jesus' resurrection reported by the four evangelists. Is it possible to harmonise the four gospel accounts?

In Matthew we have one angel, and the one resurrection appearance to two women and one to the disciples.

In Mark we have a 'young man' sitting on the right side of the tomb dressed in a white robe, and an appearance to Mary Magdalene only, unaccompanied by the other Mary. But there is also a reference to the two disciples on the road to Emmaus, and to the eleven disciples as they sat at table. (Mark 16:14).

In Luke, we have 'the women who had come with Him from Galilee' (Luke 23:55), without naming them, who went to the tomb and found two men in dazzling apparel (Luke 24:4). These women are later identified however as Mary Magdalene, and Joanna and Mary the mother of James and the other women with them who 'told all this to the eleven and to all the rest'. (Luke 24:8).

As in Mark, Luke also records the appearance of Jesus as the eleven had a meal together in Jerusalem. (Luke 24:33), and also to the two disciples on the road to Emmaus.

John perhaps gives the fullest account of all, writing so perceptively of the moment when Mary Magdalene (on her own) saw the Risen Lord, and of the experiences of Peter and John as they came to the tomb, and saw, not Him but His empty grave clothes, lying on a shelf within.

In John's account, Mary Magdalene saw two angels in white and spoke to them full of sorrow because she did not know what had happened to Him, until she turned at the sound of His voice calling her name, 'Mary!' (John 20:1). And she worshipped Him.

John goes on to record three other instances of His appearing to His disciples, and even suggests that there could have been others, as though Jesus was reluctant to leave them. His disciple John writes, 'Jesus did many other signs which are not written in this book, but these are written that you may believe that Jesus is the Christ, the Son of God, and that believing, you may have life in His Name'. (John 20:30).

These 'many other signs' may of course, refer to the many signs He did throughout His life, but we may assume, that as Luke says in Acts 1:3, He showed Himself alive by many proofs during the forty days before He ascended back to His Father.

We may ask, 'What then actually happened at the resurrection of Jesus?' In many circles, the answer would be: it all happened, and the only question is, in what order.

It could be something like this. There is an earthquake. The guards fall to the ground. (Matthew 28:3,4). Mary Magdalene goes to the tomb and reports to the disciples. (John 20:1,2). Peter and John enter the tomb. (John 20:6-10). Mary and the other women see an angel outside the tomb, and another angel in the tomb's vestibule but only one angel speaks to them. (Matthew 28:2,3; Mark 16:1-8). Inside the tomb they see two angels, where Jesus had been lying. (Luke 24:1-8; John 20:11-13). Jesus appears to Mary Magdalene outside the tomb. (John 20:14,18; Mark 16:9). Jesus appears to Mary Magdalene and the other Mary a second time as they are leaving the tomb. (Matthew 28:9-10). The women report to the disciples and are met with disbelief. (Luke 24:11).

This is the course of events as laid out by Augustine (Luz p598) as early as the fourth century. Calvin's explanation was that there may have been two angels, only one of whom spoke to the women and/or Mary Magdalene.

But is it necessary today to try to explain what appear to be contradictory accounts?

It is quite possible that each of the gospel writers was relying on a different oral tradition, or witnesses with divergent views on what actually took place, but who were all assured of this one thing; that Jesus was laid in the tomb a dead, broken, mutilated Body, and arose from the tomb a living glorified Saviour.

How it happened remains a sacred mystery. What the evangelists sought to do was to describe a visible, historical, concrete event. There are no histrionics, only a quiet dignity about each account. But the accounts are not only historical, they have an existential significance in the life of every believer, every true follower of Jesus. They mark the transition from sorrow to joy, from darkness to light, to new life in Christ.

His triumphant resurrection happened to Him, but to us too who believe, for we too have come by faith through His cross and resurrection from death to *Life*, the life abundant which He promised. (John 10:10).

Matthew had no doubts about the reality of Jesus' resurrection. For him, it was historical fact. God was at work, demonstrated by the earthquake, and by the angelic presence. But Matthew does not write about the resurrection itself. That remains holy, mysterious, invisible, something that the human mind may not discover or rationalise, summed up by the angel in the words, 'He is not here, He is risen!!'

That is all we need to know.

And yet, the angel meets the women with words of comfort and consolation, and gives them a task to do for their risen Saviour. Though they may not understand, they are involved. They are allowed to participate in this tremendous event, the most tremendous in the whole of history.

God opens tombs, breaks open tombs of imprisonment, and of darkness, and in the light of the resurrection of Jesus He says to us also, 'Rejoice! Hail! Joy! *Χαίρετε!*' For faith is a relationship to Him without fear, but with great joy.

Though the appearances of the Risen Lord in Matthew's gospel are limited, as their risen Saviour He is looking towards His decisive appearance in Galilee and wants His disciples to be present. There He will commission them to make disciples of all nations, Jew and Gentile alike, and conclude with His promise to be with them always even to the close of the age. (Matthew 28:19).

This is the important message, the message of the purpose of God towards men and women which He has purposed through His Son, and which has now become manifest and operable through His death and resurrection. This is the instruction delivered to the disciples, 'Go!' for the disciples needed to be told to go to Galilee and hear what their Risen Lord has to say to them for the last time before He returns to His Father. This is the significance of the message which the women need to deliver to 'His brothers'. 'Go and tell My brothers to go to Galilee. There they will see me.' (Matthew 28:11). And having delivered their message, the women disappear from Matthew's gospel, faithful to the end.

Ευλογητός ο Θεός
Praise God! Thanks be to God!

Matthew 28:11-15. The report of the guard

While they were going, behold, some of the guards went into the city and told the chief priests all that had taken place. And when they had assembled with the elders, and taken counsel, they gave a sum of money to the soldiers and said, 'Tell people, His disciples came by night and stole Him away while we were asleep. And if this comes to the governor's ears, we will satisfy him and keep you out of trouble.'

So they took the money, and did as they were directed; and this story has been spread among the Jews to this day.

Jesus has risen from the dead. The bewildered but rejoicing women have gone to tell the disciples the wonderful news. For them, all is accomplished. What Jesus had told them would happen has happened, and the disciples would follow the instructions given to them by the women and go to Galilee.

But for the guards who had been at the tomb and seen that it was empty, it was a different story. They had been given the task of keeping watch over the tomb, because the chief priests and elders and Pharisees (Matthew 27:62; 28:11), were terribly afraid that Jesus would do what He said He would do, and rise from the dead.

But their guarding of the tomb had been a complete failure. How could it have happened? Where *was* He? The appearance of the angel had caused them to fear and tremble and become like dead men, (verse 4), but they had not seen *Him*.

They decided to go back to the chief priests and tell them the whole story. They were not going to assume responsibility for these strange happenings, even if it reflected badly on their ability to guard the tomb of a dead Man.

These verses (Matthew 28:11-15), are peculiar to Matthew, narrated by him alone, and demonstrate once again the appalling behaviour of these religious leaders. It was not that they *could not* believe what Jesus had said while He was alive, but that they *would not*. They had an absolute determination to destroy any rumour of His resurrection among the people before it began. (verse 13).

Giving a sum of money to the guards, they said to them, 'Tell the people, His disciples came by night and stole Him away while you slept. And if this comes to the governor's ears (Pilate, of course) we will satisfy him and keep you out of trouble.' (verse 13, 14).

In any and every kind of administration, it is unusual to say the least to reward soldiers, security guards, for falling asleep while on duty, and especially to keep them out of trouble with the authorities if they had neglected their duties to such an extent. What could these men do? They took the bribe, the money which the chief priests gave them, thinking that they had probably earned it, considering all the trauma they had been through. But they could not prevent the story spreading that Jesus had not risen from the dead, but been stolen away from the tomb. 'And this story has been spread among the Jews to this day'. (verse 15). This is Matthew's editorial comment. There was no doubt of the truthfulness of the guard's account, or of its manipulation by the chief priests into quite a different story.

These chief priests were the representatives of all that had been so precious to the Jews as they contemplated their long history. They viewed their history in the light of their relationship to the one and only true God through His covenant with them. But they had now committed an unpardonable error, affecting their total belief system, for they were claiming that there was something an omnipotent God could not do: He could not raise someone from the dead.

But this affected not only their religious faith, but also their whole social and religious position as the leaders of God's people. In dismissing the story of Jesus' resurrection as a fraud, as a forgery, as having no basis in reality, they were condemning themselves, for Jesus had made it perfectly clear. 'He who is not with Me is against Me'. (Matthew 12:30), had been His warning to them.

They had achieved their purpose, in having Him put to death, but He had now brought about the complete reversal of all their plans against Him, for now He could never die again. He was alive forever! How impossible it was for them to believe this.

The women went to tell the disciples. The guards went to tell the chief priests. The disciples received the news with great joy, just as the women had done. (verse 8). The chief priests received the news with guilt and fear, because they had not believed it possible, and were afraid that though they had gathered together with the elders, and taken counsel together as what was best to be done, (verse 12), the news of His resurrection could still cause riotous behaviour among the people. They were right in that at least, as many incidents in the Acts of the Apostles show.

But having been given this account of the empty tomb by their own unprejudiced witnesses, the chief priests had no excuse for their unbelief. The guards had told them *all πᾶς* that had taken place. (verse 11). The bribery of the soldiers emphasised the lack of honesty on the part of the chief priests, but also the enormity of what the soldiers had told them. Perhaps we can appreciate the perceived, even actual threat to which the ministry of Jesus had exposed them during His lifetime leading to their desire to get rid of Him. This episode is the climax of all that Matthew had reported throughout his gospel of the attitude taken by the chief priests to the ministry of Jesus, and their deception of the people through their hypocrisy. This further deception is almost inevitable, and for Matthew, whose compassionate heart is affected by attempts to prevent people from coming to a knowledge of the relationship made possible with his friend and Saviour, it was necessary to report what had happened at that closely held conference of the chief priests and elders in Jerusalem. (verse 12).

The money given to the guards did not prevent the rumour from spreading among the Jewish people. It may even have encouraged people to find out the truth for themselves. God makes even the wrath of man to praise Him. (Psalm 76:10).

Matthew has contrasted the significance of what happened at the tomb to the women, with the humiliation of the guards as they reported on what they had seen. He now contrasts the malevolence of the chief priests and elders with the revelation given to the disciples, the contrast of the false report that the body of Jesus had been stolen away, with the truth of His appearance to the eleven disciples.

Matthew 28:16-20. The commissioning of the disciples

Now the eleven disciples went to Galilee, to the mountain to which He had directed them. And when they saw Him, they worshipped; but some doubted.

And Jesus came to them, and said, 'All authority in heaven and on earth has been given to Me. Go therefore, and make disciples of all nations, baptising them in the Name of the Father, and of the Son, and of the Holy Spirit, teaching them to observe all that I have commanded you.'

'And lo, I am with you always, even to the close of the age.' (Matthew 28:16-20).

Galilee was important in the ministry of Jesus. He had told His disciples that He anticipated returning there after He had risen from the dead as an encouragement to them. He said, 'But after I am raised up, I will go before you into Galilee' (Matthew 26:32), at a time when their hearts were full of sorrow.

Matthew gives no hint of what may have happened between that wonderful day of resurrection, and this equally wonderful day on the mountain in Galilee, listening to the closing words of Jesus 'Lo, I am with you, even to the close of the age' (verse 20). Some scholars suggest the possibility that He did not ascend at this time into heaven, but that after His commissioning of His disciple on this mountain in Galilee, He directed them to go to Jerusalem, where on a mountain top, 'from the mount called Olivet, which is near Jerusalem' (Acts 1:12), where a cloud took Him out of their sight. (Acts 1:9).

This interpretation would harmonise Matthew's and Luke's accounts, but both Mark (Mark 16:19), and Luke (Luke 24:51, Acts 1:9) make it very clear that the disciples saw Him being taken up into heaven. Matthew does not give us details of His ascension into heaven, but he does insist that the last act of Jesus was His commissioning of His disciples to witness for Him to the ends of the earth.

Like former mountain-top experiences, the confrontation that Jesus had with the devil, when He was tempted to worship him, claiming to give Him all the kingdoms of the world if He would do so; (Matthew 4:8); His seat on the mountain from which He preached the sermon on the mount; (Matthew 5:1); His transfiguration on the mountain-top before His disciples; (Matthew 17:1-9); and finally, on a mountain in Galilee, all these mountain-top experiences demonstrate and emphasise the authority of Jesus. He has authority over the devil, over the law and the prophets as He brings in a new covenant as Son of Man, not only in His earthly ministry but on all that had gone before in the history of the law and the prophecies of Israel; and His final declaration of authority as the foreordained, crucified and resurrected Lord at His transfiguration.

The mountain is significant, not as a geographical location, but as a symbol of authority, and as a complete fulfilment in this final appearance of all that He had done and taught during His years of ministry. The devil had offered Him his authority. He had refused it on the grounds that authority comes only from God, and is on the basis of the worship of God. 'Begone Satan, the adversary of God,' Jesus said, 'for it is written you shall worship the Lord your God, and Him only shall you serve.' (Matthew 4:10).

Now God had given Him 'all authority in heaven and upon earth', (Matthew 28:18), for what could have been a greater act of worship, of supreme worship, than recognising the authority of God; than to be utterly dedicated to the will of His Father, 'even unto death on a cross; wherefore God has highly exalted Him' (Philippians 2:8,9).

His sermon on the mount was also authoritative, for 'He taught as one with authority, and not as the scribes'. (Matthew 7:29). The crowds were astonished at His teaching, for they had heard it said, 'You shall not kill'; 'You shall not commit adultery'; 'You shall not swear falsely'; 'An eye for an eye and a tooth for a tooth', 'You shall love your neighbour and hate your enemy'. (Matthew 5:21-43)

But I say to you,' With these authoritative words, Jesus had gone *beyond* the teaching of Moses, on another mountain, Mount Sinai, to a place where as individuals they could enjoy fellowship with God as their Father, that loving relationship with Him as they prayed, 'Our Father in heaven' (Matthew 6:9), and as they lived with Him, becoming like HIm.

On the Mount of Transfiguration, He allowed His disciples to see Him as God saw Him, His face shining as the sun and His garments as light, (Matthew 17:2), and to hear the voice from heaven, 'This is My beloved Son with whom I am well-pleased. Hear Him'. (verse 5).

And on this final mountain-top, the disciples are permitted to hear Him for the last time in His bodily form. All their experience of Him is gathered up in these final verses of Matthew's gospel. They know absolutely and finally that He has defeated the devil through His death and resurrection. They know that His teaching changes peoples' hearts and consequently their lives. They have seen Him as He truly is, the transfigured One who has become the Resurrected One.

They are afraid to approach Him, this one whom they love, but who is so different. 'When they saw Him, they worshipped Him,' for they saw Him for what He was, the Son of God. (verse 17).

But Jesus came to them. (verse 18).

He came to them just as He had come to them on the Mount of Transfiguration. And 'when they lifted up their eyes, they saw no man, but *Jesus only*'. (Matthew 17:8) Jesus only; the Jesus whom they knew and loved, with whom they had shared their lives, listened to His teaching, watched His compassionate healing of those who were sick. Jesus only. They knew Him.

But from henceforth, they realise that their knowledge of Him is going to be different. He was commissioning them to do something for Him. As they lifted up their eyes to Him, He said, 'All authority in heaven and on earth has been given to Me. In the name of that authority I want you to go. Go therefore and make disciples of all nations, nations of the Gentiles, the nation of Israel, of the Jews. I want all the peoples of the world to know that there is peace for them, there is hope for them, as they trust in Me. And as they put their faith in Me, I want you to baptise them in water and that they should also be immersed in the Holy Spirit. (Matthew 3:11), in His Name, and in My Name, and in the Name of My Father, and all that Our Name represents in terms of our character and purpose. And also teach them as I have taught you, teach them to observe all that I have commanded you.' (verse 20).

And this different knowledge you have of Me, no longer as a man like yourselves (Hebrews 2:14,17) but as the Risen Son of God, will enable you to know Me as a constant presence, for, 'Lo, I AM with you, always, even to the close of the age.' (verse 20).

This saying of Jesus, His last words on earth to His disciples, is of inestimable importance. It is in three parts. The first is the word of authority. '*All* authority in heaven and earth is given to Me.' (verse 18). The second is an imperative. 'Go therefore and make disciples of *all* nations, teaching them to observe *all* that I have commanded you' (verse 19). The third is a promise, 'Lo, I am with you *all* the days, *always,* even unto the close of the age' (verse 20).

The little word 'all' πᾶς, provides a connecting, fundamental principle. All that Jesus began to do and to teach, until the day when He was taken up, (Acts 1:2) has now reached its fulfilment.

All is complete. We have before us the other 26 books of the New Testament, but in one sense, they are unnecessary. This gospel would be enough if the other writings ceased to exist, although how grateful we are to Paul and the other writers, especially of the epistles, for the light they shed on the gospel story.

But from Matthew's point of view, the appearance of the Risen Lord on the mountain in Galilee, and His words to His disciples represent both the present reality for the disciples, the coming reality as the gospel continued to be preached throughout the world, and the future reality, the coming again of the Lord Jesus in power and great glory, as He said He would, (Matthew 24:30), for that will be the close of the age.

Throughout all that time, as the I AM revealed to Moses in Exodus 3:14, and the I AM, the Alpha and Omega, the beginning and the end, of Revelation 21:6, *this I AM,* the Son of God, will be, and most certainly is, with His disciples and all who believe in Him *'always,* even unto the close of the age', for He is the anointed Son of God.

Those who have come to Christ are baptised 'in the Name of the Father, and of the Son, and of the Holy Spirit' (verse 19) and this phrase has become a liturgical formula as well as a Trinitarian declaration that all three Persons of the Trinity are at work in the wonderful, transformational process of redemption. There is evidence that the phrase was used liturgically in the early church (Ignatius, Odes of Solomon, Luz p 615). Together with the words of consecration at the Lord's Supper, it was perhaps inevitable that the recorded words of Jesus should be treated in this way. For those being baptised, it is certainly meaningful to have that immersive experience confirmed by all that is implied by that Name; the grace of the Lord Jesus, the love of God the Father, and the constant fellowship, and participation in, the Holy Spirit. (2 Corinthians 13:14).

We love the conciseness and the brevity of the words of Jesus to His disciples in John's gospel. 'As the Father has sent Me, *so send I you'* (John 20:21) καθὼς ἀπέσταλκέν με ὁ πατήρ, 'ἀπέσταλκέν', the sending word, the apostolic word. The risen Lord Jesus is conferring apostleship on His disciples as He said to them, 'Receive the Holy Spirit' (verse 22), the Empowerer of all that He was sending them to do.

But we also rejoice in the fuller implication of Matthew's recording of Jesus' words, not used as a liturgical instruction, but as the promise that in His Name, following His commandment, taking the knowledge of Him to the ends of the earth, baptising and teaching all who come to Him in faith, He would be with them, always, even to the close of the age.

The disciples had obeyed the word given to them by the women at the tomb. They had forsaken Him and fled, but now Jesus is reinstating them as His precious brothers (verse 10), and His forerunners, pioneers who would go from Galilee to the ends of the earth, preaching the good news of the Kingdom, all that He had taught them; all that His death and resurrection signified of redemption and new life in Him.

These were His concluding words to them, His extraordinary brief farewell and yet so appropriate to them The gospel begins with the names of the Baby who was to be born. 'You will call His Name Jesus, for He will save His people from their sins,' said the angel to Joseph [Matthew 1:21]. And His Name shall be called Immanuel, which means, 'God with us,' (Matthew 1:23) quoted by the angel from Isaiah 7:14.

'Go,' commands Jesus, 'Go, for Immanuel, God with us, is still My Name, and I will be with you. Go for My Name is Jesus and I will always be there for the sinner who calls upon My Name, and I will save him from his sin. From the beginning it was so, and it will be until the end of time.'

God, who had so loved the world, had given His only begotten Son, the gift of His Son not just as a Baby growing up to be an itinerant preacher and teacher in Palestine, but as the Son of Man, the Son of God, until, lifted up to die on that cruel cross, He could give the gift of eternal life to all who believed on Him, eternal life, both in quality and timelessness, life that begins now, and goes on forever, life beyond death, life of ultimate worship with all the redeemed before His throne, saying, 'Worthy is the Lamb who was slain' (Revelation 5:12). What a gift! What a Giver!

This final proclamation on the mountain is within the tradition of all God's dealings with His people. He always wanted a people near to Him, (Deuteronomy 4:7), a people who would be to Him a kingdom of priests, and a holy nation. (Exodus 19:6). But the Israelites of old, 'rebelled and grieved His Holy Spirit'. (Isaiah 63:10), they failed to be what He wanted them to be. So He sent His Son, to bring to birth (John 3:8), a people near to Him.

Now His Son has accomplished His purpose. Jesus has risen from the dead and now sits at the right hand of God interceding for those who have come unto God through Him, (Romans 8:34), their great High Priest. (Hebrews 2:17).

God has a body of believers which constitutes the church. Jesus has promised to build that church, and that the gates of hell shall not prevail against it. (Matthew 16:18). As the church obeys the commandments of Jesus, and as it is guided and in-filled by the Holy Spirit, men and women are still coming to Him, still finding that rest for their souls, given to all who come to Him. All the commandments, all that Jesus had taught His disciples is gathered up into that statement. Jesus said, 'come to Me, all who are weary and heavy laden, and I will give you rest. Take My yoke upon you and learn of Me, for I am meek and lowly of heart and you will find rest to your souls. For My yoke is easy and My burden is light'. (Matthew 11:28).

We need no other mountain-top experience.

It is from this place of rest that the disciples are 'therefore' (verse 19) able to go into all the world. Although they are under the authority of Jesus Himself, they go not to be served but to serve, not to be ministered to but to minister, and if necessary to lay down their lives, not as a ransom for many as Jesus did, but as martyrs, as witnesses to Him. (Matthew 20:25-28).

The very act of going, 'Go therefore' (verse 19), as Jesus commands them, involves leaving all that they had previously enjoyed of security, perhaps of family life, even maybe of going to another place, a different environment. 'Making disciples of all nations' (verse 18), is not a comfortable commandment to have been given, but a costly one, but they go in the name of the Lord, trusting Him to supply all their needs.

But 'go therefore' because all authority in heaven and earth has been given to Jesus. Nothing is outside His authority and nothing is outside His promise to His obedient, worshipping disciples, that He is with them, with us, always. His presence, His love and His grace, so freely given to us even unto the end of the world.

We see in the Acts of the Apostles how the command, and the promise were beginning to be fulfilled.

Select Bibliography

Gundry, Robert H, Matthew: A commentary on his handbook for a mixed Church under persecution (Wm. B Eerdmans Publishing Company, Michigan 1982)

Hill, David, The New century Bible Commentary: The Gospel of Matthew. (Marshall, Morgan and Scott, London, 1981)

Luz, Ulrich, *Matthew 1-7: A commentary*, tr. Linss, (T and T Clark Ltd., Edinburgh,1990)

Luz, Ulrich, *Matthew 8-20: A commentary*, tr. Crouch, (Augsburg Fortress, MN, 2001)

Luz, Ulrich, *Matthew 21-28: A commentary*, tr. Crouch, (Augsburg Fortress, MN, 2005)

Stanton, Graham, *A Gospel for a New People: Studies in Matthew* (T and T Clark Ltd., Edinburgh, 1992)

Stecker, Georg, *The Sermon on the Mount: An exegetical commentary*, tr Dean Jr. (T and T Clark, Edinburgh, 1988)

Milton Keynes UK
Ingram Content Group UK Ltd.
UKHW041821260923
429400UK00006B/257